LESBIANS KISSING

A 1996 Calendar proclaiming and celebrating our diversity

THE FIRST FULL COLOR LESBIAN CALENDAR

Twelve different photographers lend their talents to bring us a fascinating cross section of lesbian life. (Photos selected from the 1995 Lesbian Kissing National Photographic Competition.)

THE NAMES PROJECT
AIDS MEMORIAL

QUILT.

NOT ALL BATTLES
ARE FOUGHT WITH
A SWORD

OCTOBER 11-13
1996
WASHINGTON, D.C.

Once again we must unfold
the AIDS Memorial Quilt
in our nation's capital.
Why? Because until there is
an end to AIDS,
we are not going away.
Please join us.
Call The NAMES Project
Foundation at 415/882-5500.

THE NAMES PROJECT

AIDS Memorial Quilt

Curve

Formerly DENEUVE

Nation's Best-Selling lesbian magazine

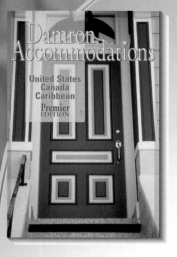

Women's Traveller T-Shirt
Damron Tank Top
100% heavyweight cotton

Names Project
T-Shirt
100% cotton
pre-shrunk

1996
West Coast
B&B Calendar & Travel Guide
7 3/4" x 9" - full color

OutLoud CD
A Benefit for the
International Gay & Lesbian Human
Rights Commission.
Features Indigo Girls, U2, Everything
But The Girl and many more

Mail Order

Women's Traveller....................................$11.95 ....

Women's Traveller T-Shirt   M-L-XL-XXL
                    (size_____).....$14.00 ....

(Women's Traveller & T-Shirt) Special Combo
                    (size _____).....$20.00 ....

Damron Tank Top   M-L-XL
                    (size_____)......$14.00 ....

Damron Accommodations......................$18.95 ....

Damron Address Book ....$14.95 ....

Damron Road Atlas ....$14.95 ....

Names T-Shirt M,L,XL
                    (size _____)....$15.00 ....

West Coast B&B 1996 Calendar ....$14.95 ....

OutLoud CD ....$12.95 ....

Best Guide To Amsterdam ....$18.95 ....

Damron Mail Order Catalog .... Free ....

                                     Subtotal ....

CA Residents add 8.25% sales tax   ....

postage & handling - add $4.00 + $1.00 per item   ....

overnight delivery add $15.00   ....

                                     Total   ....

Call: 1-800-462-6654 or 415-255-0404
Visa • Mastercard

Or Send Check or Money Order To:
Women's Traveller
P.O. Box 422458
San Francisco, CA 94142-2458

Orders processed as received.
Please allow 4-8 weeks for delivery.
Send no cash or postage stamp. No C.O.D. orders.

Hey writers!

Write up the local lesbian scene in your favorite city (150-500 words) and send it to us - if our editors like it, you'll be a finalist and we'll include it in the next edition of The Women's Traveller, with your name! Plus we'll send you free copies of The Women's Traveller and companion map guide The Damron Road Atlas (total value: $28)!

Contest Prizes:

One grand prize winner
wins 4 nights accommodation* in San Francisco at the Joie de Vivre Hotel, $200, a WT T-shirt and copies of the Women's Traveller, the Damron Road Atlas and Damron Accommodations.

Three runners-up
win $50 plus a T-shirt and copies of the Women's Traveller and the Damron Road Atlas.

All finalists
receive copies of the Women's Traveller and the Damron Road Atlas. Enter as many city essays as you like.

Deadline:
Must be received on or before August 31, 1996

(*Transportation not included.)

Contest Rules

Responsibility: Damron Company assumes no responsibility for any delay, loss or accident caused by fault or negligence of any hotel, transportation company or local operator rendering any part of tour services, nor for any damage or inconvenience caused by late air travel. Damron Company shall not be responsible for any expense caused by loss or damage of personal items including but not limited to luggage and its contents.

Deadline: Entries must be received by August 31, 1996.

Prize: 4 nights lodging at Le Joie de Vivre Hotel in San Francisco. Airfare/transportation not included.

Prize winners will be notified by mail and/or phone.

Eligibility: Open to anyone over 18 years of age, except employees of Damron Company, their affiliates and agencies or employees and agents for the resorts participating in these sweepstakes. Void where prohibited or restricted by law. All federal, state and local laws apply.

No purchase necessary.

Mail to: The Women's Traveller Overview Contest
PO Box 422458, San Francisco, CA 94142-2458

Email: WomenTravl@aol.com
Fax: (415) 703-9049

Entries become the property of The Damron Company, and may be edited.

Suggestions:

Keep it short! A few well-placed adjectives are preferable to long sentences describing the ambiance of each cafe or bar.

Emphasize the diversity your city offers. Include events and places for women of color, differently abled women, older women, young women, large women and women of different backgrounds (such as transgendered, bisexual, butch, femme, leather, separatist, etc).

Tell us about it! Don't just list places and events. Compose a witty, entertaining short essay that highlights popular lesbian gathering places as well as those that are unique-but-not-well-known.

Pretend you're just visiting. Think about your city in terms of a woman just coming through town for a few days - what would be most interesting or valuable? Where do you take friends who stay with you for a few days?

Editor's Letter

This is the seventh edition of the Women's Traveller...the seven year itch is something I relate to in a very personal way, so I bring that need for change to my guidebook.

This edition isn't a complete change for the Traveller, but it definitely is a variation of design and attitude for the late nineties and the ever-changing lesbian community. I have continued to analyze the readers' surveys to produce the type of guidebook that is needed for a community as diverse as the one to which we all belong.

You will notice in the photo on this page that there is quite a bit of diversity among my editor/ designer, art director and me. Missing from the photo is the other female WT staff member, but you can view her on the following pages—note the long-haired sassy model. Thank you all for your unquantifiable support, artistic influence and damn good work ethic.

I would also like to praise the other gender in my office. This group, too, has supported and helped me with the continued success of this non-traditional American company.

So, Mr. Philips, Mr. Howley, Mr. Shively & Mr. Gatta...I thank you.

Keep sending letters to let us know what we have missed and what you would like to see in the nation's leading guidebook for women.

Gina M. Gatta

Women's Traveller

PUBLISHER
Damron Company

PRESIDENT-EDITOR IN CHIEF
Gina M. Gatta

CHIEF FINANCIAL OFFICER
Edward Gatta

VICE PRESIDENT
Mikal Shively

MANAGING EDITOR
Ian Philips

ART DIRECTOR
Kathleen Pratt

EDITOR & DESIGNER
Beth Rabena Carr

ADVERTISING DIRECTOR
David Howley

COMPTROLLER
Louise Mock

PHOTOGRAPHY
Phyllis Christopher

EDITORIAL ASSISTANTS
Christine Hilliard
Anthony Robbins

DAMRON COMPANY
P.O. BOX 422458
SAN FRANCISCO, CA 94142-2458
(415) 255-0404 • (800) 462-6654
http://www.damron.com/ or
Damronco@aol.com

National Resources

AIDS/HIV

National AIDS/HIV Hotlines
[800] 342-2437
[800] 243-7889 (TTY)
[800] 344-7432 (en español)

Sexual Health Information Line (Canada)
[613] 563-2437

CANCER

Cancer Information Service
[800] 422-6237

Women's Cancer Resource Center
[510] 548-9272 (Berkeley, CA)

CHEMICAL DEPENDENCY

Pride Institute
[800] 547-7433

HATE CRIMES

National Hate Crimes Hotline
[800] 347-4283

YOUTH SERVICES

Hetrick-Martin Institute
[212] 674-2400 (TTY/New York City, NY)

LEGAL RIGHTS

Lambda Legal Defense Fund
[212] 995-8585 (New York City, NY)

National Gay/Lesbian Task Force
[202] 332-6483 (Washington, DC)
[202] 332-6219 (TTY)

TRAVEL

International Gay Travel Association
[800] 448-8550

Traveller Codes

▲ - This symbol precedes the listing of an establishment that has a display advertisement

Popular - So they say

Mostly Women - 80%-90% lesbian

Mostly Gay Men - Women are welcome

Lesbians/Gay Men - 60%/40% or 40%/60% mix

Mixed Gay & Straight - Says it all

Beer/Wine - Beer and/or wine. No hard liquor served.

Dancing - Usually has a DJ at least Fri & Sat

Live Shows - From piano bar to drag queens and dancers

Country/Western - Music and/or dancing

Neighborhood Bar - Regulars and local flavor, often has a pool table

Multi-racial Clientele - Our favorite category. We love a variety of colors.

Wheelchair Access - Including restrooms

IGTA - International Gay Travel Association (please support our industry)

Private Clubs - Mostly in the South where it's the only way to keep a liquor license. Call the bar before you go out and tell them you're visiting. They will advise you of their policy regarding membership. Private clubs usually have set-ups so you can BYOB.

Table of Contents

Table of Contents

Alabama

Auburn (334)

BOOKSTORES & RETAIL SHOPS
Etc. 125 N. College St. • 821-0080 • noon-6pm, clsd Sun • general

Birmingham (205)

INFO LINES & SERVICES
AA Gay/Lesbian • 933-8964 • 8pm Wed, 11am Sat, 6pm Sun • info

Lambda Resource Center 205 32nd St. S. • 326-8600 • info line 6pm-10pm, from 1pm wknds • info • library • drop-in coffeehouse

Lesbian Support Group • 798-3938 • 2pm 1st Sun at MCC • info

UAB Gay/Lesbian Student Union PO Box 34, Hill University Ctr., 1400 University Blvd., 35294 • info

BARS
22nd Street Jazz Cafe 710 22nd St. S. • 252-0407 • clsd Sun-Tue • gay-friendly • live shows • food served • alternative night Wed

Bill's Club 208 N. 23rd St. • 254-8634 • 6pm-4am, from 5pm Sun, clsd Mon • mostly women • dancing/DJ • live shows • wheelchair access

Buchanan's 414 21st St. S. • 328-4337 • 4pm-2am, til 4am Fri-Sat • popular • lesbians/gay men • neighborhood bar • dancing/DJ • wheelchair access

Club 21 117-1/2 21st St. N. • 322-0469 • 9pm-4am Th-Sat • gay-friendly • dancing/DJ • mostly African-American • live shows

Mikatam 3719 3rd Ave. S. • 592-0790 • 3pm-? • mostly gay men • hot tub • patio • wheelchair access

Pearl Productions PO Box 36691, 35236 • 940-7481 • call for events • mostly women • dancing/DJ

Quest 416 24th St. S. • 251-4313 • 24hrs • DJ Th-Sun • patio

RESTAURANTS & CAFES
Anthony's 2131 7th Ave. S. • 324-1215 • lunch & dinner, clsd Sun • lesbians/gay men • some veggie • full bar • $6-15

GYMS & HEALTH CLUBS
Casey's Gym 8 Office Park Cir., Hwy. 280 Mountain Brook • 870-1779 • 6am-9pm, noon-6pm Sun • lesbians/gay men • gay owned/run

BOOKSTORES & RETAIL SHOPS
Lodestar Books 2020 11th Ave. S. • 939-3356 • 10am-6pm, 1pm-5pm Sun • lesb gay/feminist • wheelchair access

TRAVEL & TOUR OPERATORS
Village Travel 1929 Cahaba Rd. • 870-4866/ (800) 999-2899 • IGTA member

SPIRITUAL GROUPS
BCC (Birmingham Community Church) PO Box 130221, 35233 • 520-9752 • also women's sports assoc. contact

Covenant MCC 5117 1st Ave. N. • 599-3363 • 11am & 7pm Sun

PUBLICATIONS
Alabama Forum 205 S. 32nd St. Ste. 216 • 328-9228 • monthly

EROTICA
Alabama Adult Books 901 5th Ave. N. • 322-7323 • 24hrs

Dothan (334)

BARS
Chuckie Bee's 134-A Foster St. • 794-0230 • 9pm-6am Th-Sun • lesbians/gay men • dancing/DJ • live shows

Gadsden (334)

BARS
Nitro 2461 E. Meighan Blvd. • 492-9724 • 8pm-2am, clsd Sun-Tue • lesbians/gay men • dancing/DJ • live shows

Huntsville (334)

INFO LINES & SERVICES
GALOP (Gay/Lesbian Org. of Professionals) PO Box 914, 35804 • 517-6127 • meets 4th Th

Pink Triangle Alliance • 539-4235 • 9am-9pm • resource & info line

BARS
Vieux Carre 1204 Posey • 534-5970 • 7pm-2am, from 4pm Sun • lesbians/gay men • neighborhood bar • dancing/DJ • live shows • karaoke Tue • country/western Wed • DJ Fri-Sat • shows Sun • patio

BOOKSTORES & RETAIL SHOPS

Rainbow's Ltd. 4321 University Dr. Ste. 400-B (rear) • 722-9220 • evenings weekly, all-day wknds • lesbigay

SPIRITUAL GROUPS

MCC 3015 Sparkman Dr. • 851-6914 • 11am & 6pm Sun, 7pm Wed

Jackson

INFO LINES & SERVICES

Southern Support Services PO Box 1053, 36784 • support group for Thomasville, Demopolis, Selma & Jackson

Mobile (334)

BARS

B-Bob's 6157 Airport Blvd. #201 • 341-0102 • 5pm til ? • lesbians/gay men • dancing/DJ • private club • wheelchair access

Gabriel's Downtown 55 S. Joachim St. • 432-4900 • 5pm - ? • mostly gay men • videos • private club

Golden Rod 219 Conti • 433-9175 • 9am-?, 24hrs wknds • lesbians/gay men • private club

Neimans 7 S. Joachim St. • 433-3262 • 9pm-? • lesbians/gay men • dancing/DJ • live shows • private club • food served

Society Lounge 51 S. Conception • 433-9141 • noon-? • popular • lesbians/gay men • dancing/DJ • live shows • private club • wheelchair access

Troopers 215 Conti St. • 433-7436 • 4pm-? • mostly gay men • neighborhood bar • private club

SPIRITUAL GROUPS

MCC 6345 Old Shell Rd. • 476-4621 • 7pm Sun

Montgomery (205)

INFO LINES & SERVICES

Montgomery Institute • 244-9623 • transgender info line • contact Christine

ACCOMMODATIONS

Lattice Inn 1414 S. Hull St. • 832-9931 • gay-friendly • full breakfast • swimming • nudity

BARS

Hojons 215 N. Court St. • 269-9672 • 8pm-?, til 2am Sat, clsd Sun-Mon • popular • lesbians/gay men • dancing/DJ • live shows • private club

Jimmy Mac's 211 Lee St. • 264-5933 • 7pm-? • lesbians/gay men • dancing/DJ • private club • wheelchair access

TRAVEL & TOUR OPERATORS

Alabama Bureau of Tourism & Travel PO Box 4309, 36103 • 242-4169/ (800) 252-2262

SPIRITUAL GROUPS

MCC 5290 Vaughn (Unitarian Church) • 279-7894 • 5:30pm Sun

Tuscaloosa (205)

INFO LINES & SERVICES

Gay/Lesbian/Bisexual Alliance UA Ferguson Student Center, 3rd flr. • 348-7210 • lesbians/gay men • social/support group • info • self-help/rap groups

Tuscaloosa Lesbian Coalition PO Box 6085, 35486-6085 • 333-8227 • meets 1st Fri • info • social/support group

BARS

Michael's 2201 6th St. • 758-9223 • 6:30pm-?, clsd Sun • lesbians/gay men • dancing/DJ • live shows

BOOKSTORES & RETAIL SHOPS

Illusions 519 College Park • 349-5725 • hours vary • progressive titles

Alaska

Anchorage   (907)

INFO LINES & SERVICES

AA Gay/Lesbian 1231 W. 27th Ave. • 272-2312 • 7pm Th • lesbians/gay men

Anchorage Gay/Lesbian Helpline • 258-4777 • irregular hours • leave message

IMRU • 258-5266 • 7:30pm Th • youth group

Women's Resource Center 111 W. 9th St. • 276-0528 • 9am-5pm Mon-Fri • one-on-one counseling & referrals

ACCOMMODATIONS

Arctic Feather B&B 211 W. Cook • 277-3862 • lesbians/gay men • 5 min. to downtown • nice view

Aurora Winds Resort B&B 7501 Upper O'Malley • 346-2533 • lesbians/gay men • situated on the hillside above Anchorage on nearly 2 acres

Cheney Lake B&B 6333 Colgate Dr. • 337-4391 • gay-friendly • lesbian-owned/run

The Lodge at Eagle River PO Box 90154, 99509 • 278-7575 • hot tub • self-catering 3-bdrm vacation home on 2 acres • deck • IGTA member

Northern Comfort B&B 2433 Glenwood St. • 278-2106 • seasonal • gay-friendly • sauna

▲ **The Pink Whale** 3627 Randolph St. • 563-2684 • gay-friendly • guesthouse • kids okay • kitchen • smoking outdoors • wheelchair access • women-owned/run

BARS

Blue Moon 530 E. 5th Ave. • 277-0441 • 1pm-2:30am • lesbians/gay men • dancing/DJ • live shows

O'Brady's Burgers & Brew 6901 E. Tudor Rd. • 338-1080 • 10am-midnight • food served • some veggie

Raven 618 Gambell • 276-9672 • 11am-2:30am • lesbians/gay men • neighborhood bar • wheelchair access

▲ **The Wave** 3103 Spenard Rd. • 561-9283 • 4pm-2am, from 7pm (summer), clsd Tue • gay-friendly • dancing/DJ • live shows • theme nights • videos • more gay Sat • also espresso bar upstairs • patio • wheelchair access

The Pink Whale

3627 Randolph Street
Anchorage, AK 99508
(907) 563-2684

A women-owned private accommodation.

Two bedrooms (one with two twins, other with one double)
Fully stocked kitchen with all manner of breakfast items
Private Patio • Cable TV • Stereo • Washer & Dryer

The Pink Whale has it all and it can be yours for an evening or a month, with rates available for all occasions. This fully furnished suite is just a few minutes from town.

Come Home to Midtown Anchorage

Relax and enjoy the summer sounds of birds and squirrels or the winter soft sounds of snow.

BOOKSTORES & RETAIL SHOPS

Bona Dea Women's Bookstore 2440 E. Tudor Rd. • 562-4716 • 11am-7pm, 10am-6pm Fri-Sat, clsd Sun • great community resource center

Cyrano's Bookstore & Cafe 413 'D' St. • 274-2599 • 10am-10pm • live shows • beer/wine • food served

TRAVEL & TOUR OPERATORS

Apollo 1207 West 47th Ave. • 561-0661/ (800) 770-0661

Triangle Tours 733 W. 4th Ave. Ste. 817 • 786-3707/ (800) 779-3701 • IGTA member

SPIRITUAL GROUPS

MCC 615 Hollywood Dr. Ste. 5 • 258-5266 • 11am & 7pm Sun

PUBLICATIONS

Identity Northview PO Box 200070, 99520 • 258-4777 • monthly • newsletter • also sponsors Fourth Fri Potluck

EROTICA

La Sex Shoppe 305 W. Diamond Blvd. • 522-1987 • 24hrs

Auke Bay

INFO LINES & SERVICES

Southeast Alaska Gay/Lesbian Alliance PO Box 211371, 99821 • also publishes monthly newsletter

Fairbanks   (907)

INFO LINES & SERVICES

Gay Info Line • 457-0246 • leave message on machine

ACCOMMODATIONS

Alta's B&B 5132 Haystack Mtn. Rd. • 389-2582/ 457-0246 • lesbians/gay men • log home in beautiful birch forest setting above Chatanika River on the outskirts of town

Billies B&B & Hostel 2895 Mack Rd. • 479-2034 • B&B & 6 campsites • also hostel

Fairbanks College Bunkhouse 1541 Westwood Wy. • 479-2627 • gay-friendly • B&B • also hostel

BARS

Palace Saloon Alaskaland • 456-5960 •
4pm-9pm, til 4am Fri-Sat (seasonal) •
gay-friendly • dancing/DJ • live shows •
mainly tourists • more gay after 11pm

TRAVEL & TOUR OPERATORS

Alaska Tourism Marketing Council PO
Box 110801, 99811 • 465-2010 • ask for
vacation planner

Homer (907)

ACCOMMODATIONS

Island Watch PO Box 1394, 99603 • 235-
2265 • gay-friendly • B&B • cabins •
kitchens • wheelchair access • women-
owned/run

Juneau (907)

INFO LINES & SERVICES

Women's Prerogative KTO 104.3 & 103.1
FM • 586-1670 • 9pm Wed • women's
music

RESTAURANTS & CAFES

Inn at the Summit Waterfront Cafe 455
S. Franklin St. • 586-2050 • 5pm-10pm •
American • full bar • $15-38

Arizona

Bisbee (520)

BARS

St. Elmo's 36 Brewery Gulch Ave. • 432-5578 • 10am-1am • gay-friendly • live bands Fri-Sat

TRAVEL & TOUR OPERATORS

One World Travel Agency 7 O.K. St. • 432-5359 • lesbian-owned/run

Bullhead City (520)

BARS

Lariat Saloon 1161 Hancock Rd. • 758-9741 • 9am-1am • gay-friendly • neighborhood bar • patio • wheelchair access

Cottonwood (520)

ACCOMMODATIONS

Mustang B&B 4257 Mustang Dr. • 646-5929 • lesbians/gay men • B&B • also 1 RV hookup

Flagstaff (520)

ACCOMMODATIONS

Charlie's 23 N. Leroux • 779-1919 • 11am-1am • gay-friendly • food served • some veggie • patio • wheelchair access • $7-14

▲ **Hotel Monte Vista** 100 N. San Francisco St. • 779-6971/ (800) 545-3068 • gay-friendly • hotel • food served • full bar • cafe • historic lodging circa 1927

BARS

The Depot 26 S. San Francisco St. • 773-9550 • 3pm-1am • gay-friendly • dancing/DJ • live shows • patio • wheelchair access

Monte Vista Lounge 100 N. San Francisco St. • 779-6971 • 10am-1am, cafe from 6am • gay-friendly • some veggie

BOOKSTORES & RETAIL SHOPS

Aradia Books 116 W. Cottage • 779-3817 • 10:30am-5:30pm, clsd Sun • lesbian/feminist • wheelchair access • women-owned/run

Kingman (520)

ACCOMMODATIONS

Kings Inn Best Western 2930 E. Andy Devine • 753-6101/ (800) 528-1234 • gay-friendly • swimming

Mesa (602)

TRAVEL & TOUR OPERATORS

Executive Tour Associates PO Box 42151, 85274-2151 • 898-0098/ (800) 382-1113 • IGTA member

EROTICA

Castle Boutique 8315 E. Apache Trail • 986-6114 • 24hrs

Phoenix (602)

INFO LINES & SERVICES

AA Lambda Club 2622 N. 16th St. • 264-1341 • noon, 6pm, 8pm

Camelback Business & Professional Assoc. PO Box 2097, 85001 • 225-8888

Lambda Club 2622 N. 16th St. • 264-1341 • noon, 6pm, 8pm

Lesbian Resource Project • 266-5542/ 266-5797 (TDD#) • many social/educational groups & events

Lesbian/Gay Community Switchboard PO Box 16423, 85011 • 234-2752/ 234-0873 (TDD#) • 10am-10pm (volunteers permitting)

Valley of the Sun Gay/Lesbian Center 3136 N. 3rd Ave. • 265-7283

Valley One In Ten • 264-5437 • youth group

WOMEN'S ACCOMMODATIONS

Avalon House • 276-5840 • seasonal • women only • guesthouse • kitchens • wheelchair access • $35

Be My Guest Bed & Breakfast • 893-6663 • women only • swimming • great location

Mom's 5903 W. Cortez, Glendale • 979-2869 • women only • B&B • swimming • private baths • cont'l breakfast • wheelchair access • women-owned/run • $45-75

ACCOMMODATIONS

Arizona Bed & Breakfast • 274-1474/ (800) 974-1474 • reservation service

Arrowzona 'Private' Casita PO Box 11253, Glendale, 85318 • 561-0335/ (800) 266-7829 • lesbians/gay men • hot tub • 2-rm B&B in private home

Larry's Bed & Breakfast 502 W. Claremont Ave. • 249-2974 • mostly gay men • full breakfast • hot tub • swimming • nudity

Stewart's B&B 1319 E. Hayward • 861-2500 • mostly gay men • full breakfast • near outdoor recreation • leather-friendly

Westways Resort PO Box 41624, 85080 • 488-1110 • lesbians/gay men • swimming • wheelchair access • IGTA member

Windsor Cottage 62 W. Windsor • 264-6309 • lesbians/gay men • swimming • nudity • 2 English Tudor-style cottages • poolside breakfast • patio

BARS

307 Lounge 222 E. Roosevelt • 252-0001 • 6am-1am, Sun brunch • mostly gay men • neighborhood bar • wheelchair access

Ain't Nobody's Bizness 3031 E. Indian School #7 • 224-9977 • 2pm-1am • mostly women • dancing/DJ • wheelchair access

Bananas/Metro 4102 E. Thomas Rd. • 224-9457 • 3pm-3am • mostly gay men • neighborhood bar • dancing/DJ • patio

Cash Inn 2140 E. McDowell Rd. • 244-9943 • 2pm-1am, clsd Mon-Tue • lesbians/gay men • dancing/DJ • country/western • wheelchair access

Country Club Bar & Grill 4428 N. 7th Ave. • 264-4553 • 11am-1am • mostly gay men • dancing/DJ • country/western • patio • wheelchair access

Desert Rose 4301 N. 7th St. • 248-0065 • 11am-1am • women only • country/western • food served • wheelchair access • women-owned/run

Foster's 4343 N. 7th Ave. • 263-8313 • 4pm-1am • lesbians/gay men • dancing/DJ • trash disco Sun • wheelchair access

Harley's 155 155 W. Camelback Rd. • 274-8505 • noon-1am • mostly gay men • dancing/DJ • also The Cell in back • mostly gay men • leather

Incognito Lounge 2424 E. Thomas Rd. • 955-9805 • 2pm-1am, til 3am Fri-Sat • popular • mostly women • dancing/DJ • live shows • wheelchair access

Phoenix (602)

LESBIGAY INFO: Valley of the Sun Gay/Lesbian Center: 265-7283, 3136 N. 3rd Ave. Lesbian/Gay Community Switchboard: 234-2752. 10am-10pm. Lesbian Resource Project: 266-5542

LESBIGAY PAPER: Echo Magazine: 602-266-0550. Western Express: 254-1324. Women's Central News: 898-4844 (Women's Central Inc.)

WHERE THE GIRLS ARE: Phoenix doesn't have one section of town where lesbians hang out, but the area between 5th Ave.-32nd St., and Camelback-Thomas streets does contain most of the women's bars.

LESBIGAY AA: AA Lambda Club: 264-1341. 2622 N. 16th St., noon, 6pm, 8pm.

LESBIGAY PRIDE: 352-7165. June

ANNUAL EVENTS: August - Dog Days of Summer: 266-5542. 3-day lesbian cultural extravaganza. September - Women's Music Festival: 266-5542. October - AIDS Walk: 265-3300

CITY INFO: Phoenix Visitors Bureau: 254-6500.

ATTRACTIONS: Castles & Coasters Park on Black Canyon Fwy & Peoria. Phoenix Zoo in Papago Park. Phoenix Desert Botanical Garden in Papago Park.

WEATHER: Beautifully mild (60°-80°) October through March or April, hot (90°-100°+) in summer. August brings the rainy season.

TRANSIT: Yellow Cab: 252-5252. Super Shuttle: 244-9000. Phoenix Transit: 253-5000

Phoenix

*C*an't stand another cloudy day? Sick of spending your summers in a fog bank and your winters in a snowdrift? Try this sunny get-away known as the Valley of the Sun.

Here the winters are warm and the summers sizzle. And each day ends with a dramatic desert sunset.

The people of Phoenix have perfected many ways to soak up the incredible sunshine. Some do it as they hike or horseback ride along the many trails along Squaw Peak (off Lincoln Dr.) or Camelback Mountain. Some do it by the pool or on the golf course or tennis court. Some do it as they hover over the valley in a hot air balloon.

Some do it between galleries as they enjoy the popular Thursday night **Art Walk** along Main St., Marshall Way and 5th Ave. in Scottsdale. Others do it dashing from the car to the Scottsdale Galleria or Fashion Square. Still others get sun in the car on the four hour trip north to **Rawhide** (563-1880 – admission is free!), Arizona's real live western town and Native American village.*

What do lesbians do in Phoenix? Pretty much the same things, but usually in couples. Couples will feel free to enjoy themselves at one of the three women-only B&Bs in town. The single lesbian traveller searching for another to share her journeys with should try one of the four friendly women's bars in town. We've heard **Livia's** Italian restaurant and bar is a good place to start. Phoenix also has a large sober women's community, and its own AA club house.

If you're in town in mid-August, call the **Lesbian Resource Project** to find out when this year's **Dog Days of Summer** (usually in August), will be – we're told it's a 3-day lesbian cultural extravaganza of films, performances, workshops and more! Mid-September brings Phoenix's own **Women's Music Festival**, while early December welcomes an annual women's concert.

*Driving in the Arizona desert during the summer can be dangerous. Always carry a few gallons of water in your vehicle, check all fluids in your car before you leave, and frequently during your trip.

J.C.'s Fun One Lounge 5542 N. 43rd Ave, Glendale • 939-0528 • 11am-1am • mostly gay men • dancing/DJ • live shows • wheelchair access

Marlys' 15615 N. Cave Creek Rd. • 867-2463 • 3pm-1am • lesbians/gay men • neighborhood bar

My Favorite Lounge & Grill 4809 N. 27th Ave. • 242-8102 • 11am-1am • lesbians/gay men • neighborhood bar • also a restaurant • some veggie • $3-10

Nasty Habits 3108 E. McDowell Rd. • 267-8707 • noon-1am • mostly women • dancing/DJ • karaoke • wheelchair access

Trax 1724 E. McDowell • 254-0231 • 6am-1am, til 3am Fri-Sat • popular • mostly gay men • dancing/DJ • alternative • leather • wheelchair access

Winks 5707 N. 7th St. • 265-9002 • 11am-1am • popular • mostly gay men • piano bar • lunch & Sun brunch served • wheelchair access • $5-9

RESTAURANTS & CAFES

AZ-88 7535 E. Scottsdale Mall • 994-5576 • 11am-11pm • upscale American • some veggie • $8-15

Eddie's Grill 4747 N. 7th St. • 241-1188 • lunch & dinner, clsd Sun • some veggie • full bar • patio • wheelchair access • $10-18

Evita's 1906 E. Camelback Rd. • 263-8482 • 5pm-10pm dinners only • live shows • Argentinian • full bar • wheelchair access • $10-15

Katz's Deli 5144 N. Central • 277-8814 • 7am-3pm, til 8pm Tue-Fri • some veggie • $5

Livia's 4221 N. 7th Ave. • 266-7144 • 5pm-10pm • Italian • full bar • wheelchair access • $7-15

Shorty'z 801 N. 1st St. • (207) 253-1985 • 7am-3pm • lesbians/gay men • some veggie

Top of Central 8525 N. Central • 861-2438 • 11am-1am, clsd Sun • live shows • cont'l • some veggie • full bar • patio • wheelchair access • $7-15

GYMS & HEALTH CLUBS

Beauvais Fitness Center 1301 E. University • 921-9551 • gay-friendly

BOOKSTORES & RETAIL SHOPS

The Short Skirt 33 W. Camelback Rd. • 235-9610 • 11am-7pm • wigs • leather • lingerie • shoes up to size 14

Tuff Stuff 1714 E. McDowell Rd. • 254-9651 • 10am-6pm, til 4pm Sat, clsd Sun-Mon • leather shop

TRAVEL & TOUR OPERATORS

All About Destinations Gallery Three Plaza, 3819 N. 3rd St. • 277-2703/ (800) 375-2703 • IGTA member

Arizona Office of Tourism • 542-8687

FirsTravel Ltd. 5150 N. 7th St. • 265-0666/ (800) 669-8885 • IGTA member

TGI Travel Agency 5540 W. Glendale Ave. #A-102, Glendale • 939-1445/ (800) 289-2172 • IGTA member

SPIRITUAL GROUPS

Casa de Cristo Evangelical Church 1029 E. Turney • 265-2831 • 10am & 6:30pm Sun

Dignity/Integrity PO Box 21091, 85036 • 258-2556 • call for info

Lutherans Concerned PO Box 7519, 85011 • 870-3611

MCC Gentle Shepherd 16th & Indian School • 274-6199 • 9am Sun

PUBLICATIONS

Echo Magazine PO Box 16630, 85011-6630 • 266-0550 • bi-monthly

The Other Book 5501 N. 7th Ave. #824 • 230-4127 • business directory for Phoenix

Western Express PO Box 5317, 85010-5317 • 254-1324

EROTICA

Book Cellar #2 2103 W. Camelback • 249-9788 • 24hrs

Castle Boutique 300 E. Camelback • 266-3348 • 24hrs

Castle Boutique 5501 E. Washington • 231-9837 • 24hrs

Castle Boutique 8802 N. Black Canyon Fwy. • 995-1641 • 24hrs

Scottsdale   (602)

BARS

B.S. West 7125 5th Ave. (pedestrian mall) • 945-9028 • 1pm-1am • mostly gay men • dancing/DJ • videos • Sun BBQ • wheelchair access

The Works 7223 E. 2nd St. • 946-4141 • 10pm-3am • popular • mostly gay men • dancing/DJ • alternative • videos • wheelchair access

RESTAURANTS & CAFES

Malee's 7131 E. Main • 947-6042 • Thai • $12-20

TRAVEL & TOUR OPERATORS

Dolphin Travel Services 10632-B N. Scottsdale Rd. • 998-9191/ (800) 847-2835 • IGTA member

Regency Travel 7744 E. Northland Dr. • 947-3377 • IGTA member

Sedona (520)

WOMEN'S ACCOMMODATIONS

Paradise Ranch 135 Kachina Dr. • 282-9769 • women only • guesthouse • full breakfast • private baths • kitchens • women-owned/run • $85-100

ACCOMMODATIONS

Anderson's Villas 125 Sugarloaf St. #5 • 284-9559/ (800) 350-2633 • gay-friendly • full service 2-bdrm villas • fireplace • private patios • non-smoking

Sacred Sedona • 204-2422 • available Dec/Jan • mostly women • guesthouse • near outdoor recreation • serene 2-room • deck • some work exchange • $50-70

Tempe (602)

BOOKSTORES & RETAIL SHOPS

Changing Hands 414 S. Mill • 966-0203 • 10am-9pm, til 10pm Fri-Sat, noon-5pm Sun • general • lesbigay section

Tucson (520)

INFO LINES & SERVICES

AA Gay/Lesbian • 624-4183 • call for info

Wingspan Community Center 422 N. 4th Ave. • 624-1779 • lesbigay & youth info • referrals • call for events

Womyn's Third Friday Coffeehouse 4831 E. 22nd (Unitarian Church) • 748-1551 • 8pm-midnight 3rd Fri

ACCOMMODATIONS

Casa Alegre B&B Inn 316 E. Speedway Blvd. • 628-1800/ (800) 628-5654 • gay-friendly • full breakfast • hot tub • swimming • 1915 craftsman-style bungalow w/ serene patio

Casa Tierra Adobe B&B Inn 11155 W. Calle Pima • 578-3058 • gay-friendly • full breakfast • hot tub • plenty veggie • 30 min. outside Tucson • patio

Catalina Park Inn 309 E. 1st St. • 792-4541/ (800) 792-4885 • gay-friendly • stylish environment of understated elegance & comfort

Elysian Grove Market 400 W. Simpson • 628-1522 • gay-friendly • renovated historic adobe building w/ an unusual & wonderful garden

Hampton Inn 6971 S. Tucson Blvd. • 889-5789 • mostly gay men

Montecito House PO Box 42352, 85733 • 795-7592 • mostly women

Natural B&B 3150 E. Presidio Rd. • 881-4582 • lesbians/gay men • full breakfast • massage available

Suncatcher B&B 105 N. Avenida Javelina • 885-0883/ (800) 835-8012 • lesbians/gay men • full breakfast • hot tub • swimming • nudity • on 4 acres

▲ **Tortuga Roja B&B** 2800 E. River Rd. • 577-6822/ (800) 467-6822 • lesbians/gay men • hot tub • swimming • nudity • 4 open acres of desert • IGTA member

BARS

Ain't Noboby's Bizness 2900 E. Broadway Ste. #118 • 318-4838 • mostly women • dancing/DJ • wheelchair access

Club 2520 Complex 2520 N. Oracle • 882-5799 • 3pm-1am, from noon wknds • mostly gay men • dancing/DJ • country/western • patio • wheelchair access

The Fineline 101 W. Drachman • 882-4953 • 6pm-1am, til 4pm Fri-Sat • gay-friendly • dancing/DJ • 18+

Hours 3455 E. Grant • 327-3390 • noon-1am • popular • lesbians/gay men • neighborhood bar • dancing/DJ • country/western • country/western Th • patio • wheelchair access

IBT's (It's About Time) 616 N. 4th Ave. • 882-3053 • noon-1am • mostly gay men • dancing/DJ • live shows • wheelchair access

Stonewall Eagle 2921 1st Ave. • 624-8805 • noon-1am • mostly gay men • dancing/DJ • leather • patio

BOOKSTORES & RETAIL SHOPS

Antigone Books 411 N. 4th Ave. • 792-3715 • 10am-6pm, til 5pm Sat, noon-5pm Sun • lesbigay/feminist • wheelchair access

TRAVEL & TOUR OPERATORS

Arizona Travel Center 2502 E. Grant Rd. • 323-3250/ (800) 553-5471 • IGTA member

SPIRITUAL GROUPS

Cornerstone Fellowship 2902 N. Geronimo • 622-4626 • 10:30am & 6pm Sun

MCC 3269 N. Mountain Ave. • 292-9151 • 9am, 10:45am, & 6:30pm Sun, 7pm Wed

PUBLICATIONS

The Observer PO Box 50733, 85703 • 622-7176 • weekly

EROTICA

The Bookstore Southwest 5754 E. Speedway Blvd. • 790-1550

Arkansas

Conway

INFO LINES & SERVICES

U of Central Arkansas Gay/Lesbian Student Union PO Box 7006, 72032 • info

Crosses   (501)

RESTAURANTS & CAFES

Pig Trail Cafe Rte. 16, east of Elkins • 643-3307 • 6am-9pm • popular • American/Mexican

Eureka Springs   (501)

WOMEN'S ACCOMMODATIONS

Golden Gate Cottage Rte. 5, Box 182, 72632 • 253-5291 • women only • B&B • hot tub • swimming • shared baths • private baths • kitchens • on the lake • women-owned/run

ACCOMMODATIONS

Arbour Glen B&B Victorian Inn 7 Lema • 253-9010/ (800) 515-4536 • lesbians/gay men • B&B • full breakfast • kids okay • historic Victorian home

Cedarberry Cottage B&B 3 Kings Hwy. • 253-6115/ (800) 590-2424 • gay-friendly • full breakfast • kids okay

Cliff Cottage B&B Inn 42 Armstrong St. • 253-7409/ (800) 799-7409 • gay-friendly • B&B • full breakfast • swimming • suites & guestrooms in 1892 'Painted Lady' • women-owned/run

Crescent Dragonwagon's Dairy Hollow House 516 Spring St. • 253-7444/ (800) 562-8650 • gay-friendly • B&B • also a restaurant • country fresh nouvelle • plenty veggie • upscale dining Th-Sun • BYOB • $25-36

Gardener's Cottage c/o 11 Singleton, 72632 • 253-9111/ (800) 833-3394 • seasonal • gay-friendly • full breakfast • private cottage on wooded site • women-owned/run

Greenwood Hollow Ridge Rte 4, Box 155, 72632 • 253-5283 • lesbians/gay men • B&B • RV • full breakfast • near outdoor recreation • shared baths • private baths • kitchens • exclusively gay • on 5 quiet acres • wheelchair access

Maple Leaf Inn 6 Kings Hwy. • 253-6876/ (800) 372-6542 • gay-friendly • full breakfast • hot tub • restored Victorian • gay-owned/run

Palace Hotel & Bath House 135 Spring St. • 253-7474 • gay-friendly

Pond Mountain Lodge & Resort Rte. 1, Box 50, 72632 • 253-5877/ (800) 583-8043 • gay-friendly • full breakfast • swimming • 159-acre mountain-top inn • lesbian-owned/run

Purple Iris Inn Rte. 2, Box 339 (Hwy. 62 W.), 72632 • 253-8748/ (800) 831-4747 • lesbians/gay men • seasonal • wheelchair access • women-owned/run

Rock Cottage Gardens 10 Eugenia St. • 253-8659/ (800) 624-6646 • lesbians/gay men • cottages • full breakfast • hot tub

Singleton House B&B 11 Singleton • 253-9111/ (800) 833-3394 • gay-friendly • B&B • full breakfast • restored 1890s country Victorian home • near shops • women-owned/run

The Woods 50 Wall St. • 253-8281 • lesbians/gay men • cottages • wheelchair access

BARS

Celebrity Club 75 Prospect (Crescent Hotel) • 253-9766 • 4pm-1am, clsd Sun-Mon (seasonal) • gay-friendly • live shows

Center Street Bar & Grille 10 Center St. • 253-8102 • 5pm-2am, clsd Sun • gay-friendly • live shows • also a restaurant • Mexican • plenty veggie • $4-12

Chelsea's Corner Cafe 10 Mountain St. • 253-6723 • 11am-2am, clsd Sun • gay-friendly • also a restaurant • plenty veggie • patio • women-owned/run

RESTAURANTS & CAFES

Ermilio's 26 White • 253-8806 • clsd Th • Italian • plenty veggie • $8-17

Plaza 55 S. Main • 253-8866 • lunch & dinner • French cuisine • $9-19

SPIRITUAL GROUPS

MCC of the Living Spring 17 Elk St. • 253-9337 • 7pm Sun

Fayetteville   (501)

INFO LINES & SERVICES

AA Live & Let Live Group • 756-8367 • 7pm Tue

Gay/Lesbian Student Association
University of Arkansas, AU517, 72701 •
info • referrals • social/support group •
hours vary

Spinsterhaven PO Box 718 , 72702 •
search committee planning women's
retirement community in NW Arkansas

Womyn's Library 17-1/2 N. Block • 442-
7164 • noon-2pm Sat, 3:30pm-6:30pm
Tue • lending library by appt. • call for
hours

BARS

Ron's Place 523 W. Poplar St. • 442-3052
• 9pm-2am, clsd Mon-Tue • mostly gay
men • dancing/DJ • private club

BOOKSTORES & RETAIL SHOPS

Passages 200 W. Dickson • 442-5845 •
10am-6pm, til 8pm Fri, 1pm-5pm Sun •
new age/metaphysical

SPIRITUAL GROUPS

MCC of the Ozarks 10571 N. Hwy. 265 •
443-4278 • 11am Sun

PUBLICATIONS

Ozark Feminist Review PO Box 1662 ,
72701

Fort Smith

INFO LINES & SERVICES

BGLAD PO Box 2897, 72702

**WAGLTF (Western Arkansas
Gay/Lesbian Task Force)** PO Box 5824 ,
72913

BARS

Court Garden 305 Garrison Ave. • 783-
9822 • 5pm-5am • lesbians/gay men •
dancing/DJ • live shows • private club •
courtyard • wheelchair access

Kinkead's 1004-1/2 Garrison • 783-9347
• 8am-1am, clsd Sun • lesbians/gay men
• dancing/DJ • country/western • live
shows • beer/wine • patio • wheelchair
access

BOOKSTORES & RETAIL SHOPS

Talisman 4119 Grand Ave. • 782-7522 •
11am-6pm, from 1pm Sun

Hot Springs   (501)

BARS

Our House Lounge & Restaurant 660 E.
Grand Ave. • 624-6868 • 7pm-3am •
popular • lesbians/gay men • dancing/DJ
• shows monthly • wheelchair access

Little Rock   (501)

INFO LINES & SERVICES

AA Gay/Lesbian 3rd & Pulaski (Capitol
View Methodist) • 664-7303 • 8pm Wed
• women's meeting 1pm at 218 W. Cherry
in Rodgers

**AGLTF (Arkansas Gay/Lesbian Task
Force)** PO Box 45053, 72214

Gay/Lesbian Switchboard PO Box
45053, 72214 • 375-5504/ (800) 448-8305
(in-state only) • 6:30pm-10:30pm •
statewide • crisis & referrals

Women's Project 2224 Main St. • 372-
5113 • 10am-5pm Mon-Fri • educational
group • lesbian support group 2nd & 4th
Tue 7pm • also library & bookstore

ACCOMMODATIONS

Little Rock Inn 601 Center St. • 376-8301
• gay-friendly • swimming • pets okay •
kids okay • full bar • wheelchair access

BARS

Backstreet 1021 Jessie Rd. #Q • 664-
2744 • 9pm-? • lesbians/gay men • danc-
ing/DJ • live shows • private club • also
The Annex • mostly women • open Fri-
Sat • wheelchair access

Discovery III 1021 Jessie Rd. • 664-4784
• from 9pm, clsd Sun-Wed • popular •
gay-friendly • dancing/DJ • live shows •
private club • wheelchair access

Michael's (at Little Rock Inn) • 376-8301
• 9pm-2am, 4pm-10pm Sun •
lesbians/gay men • dancing/DJ • live
shows • also Christopher Lounge • from
5pm, from 7pm Sat • wheelchair access

Silver Dollar 2710 Asher Ave. • 663-9886
• 4pm-1am, 3pm-midnight Sat, clsd Sun
• mostly women • dancing/DJ •
beer/wine • wheelchair access • women-
owned/run

RESTAURANTS & CAFES

Vino's Pizza 923 W. 7th St. • 375-8466 •
beer/wine • inquire about monthly
women's coffeehouse

BOOKSTORES & RETAIL SHOPS

Twisted Entertainment 7201 Asher Ave.
• 568-4262 • 11am-11pm, clsd Tue • gift
shop

Wild Card 400 N. Bowman • 223-9071 •
10am-8pm, 1pm-5pm Sun • novelties &
gifts

Little Rock

*I*f you want a city with a pace of life all its own, a city surrounded by natural beauty, you've made the right choice to visit Little Rock. And rumor has it that Bill Clinton's boyhood home is owned by a friendly lesbian couple.

At night, you can make an evening of it with dinner, a program at the Arkansas Arts Center and a visit to Little Rock's two lesbian bars, **Backstreet** and **Silver Dollar**. If you're in town at the right time of the month, cruise by the monthly women's coffeehouse at **Vino's Pizza** – call the **Women's Project** for dates.

Of course, if that isn't enough excitement, you can always head for the funky Ozark Mountain resort town of Eureka Springs. There are loads of gay-friendly B&B's in this quaint town of old-fashioned arts, as well as a popular Passion Play. We hear that **Crescent Dragonwagon's Dairy Hollow House** is a must for unique, quirky food and spectacle, **Golden Gate Cottage** is the women-only B&B, while **Center St. Bar** is the casual place to dance.

Little Rock (501)

LESBIGAY INFO: Gay/Lesbian Switchboard & AIDS Info: 375-5504/(800)448-8305 (in-state only). 6:30pm-10:30pm. Women's Project: 372-5113. 2224 Main St., 10am-5pm Mon-Fri.

LESBIGAY PAPER: Triangle Rising

WHERE THE GIRLS ARE: Scattered. Popular hangouts are the Women's Project, local bookstores, and Vino's Pizza - women's coffeehouse.

LESBIGAY AA: 664-7303. 3rd & Pulaski (Capitol View Methodist), 8pm Wed & Sun 6pm

LESBIGAY PRIDE: June

CITY INFO: Arkansas Dept. of Parks and Tourism: 682-7777

ATTRACTIONS: Hot Springs National Park

BEST VIEW: Quapaw Quarter (in the heart of the city)

WEATHER: When it comes to natural precipitation, Arkansas is far from being a dry state. Be prepared for the occasional severe thunderstorm or ice storm. Summers are hot and humid (mid 90°s). Winters can be cold (upper 30°s) with some snow and ice. Spring and fall are the best times to come and be awed by the colorful beauty of Mother Nature.

TRANSIT: Black & White Cab: 374-0333.

TRAVEL & TOUR OPERATORS

Arkansas Department of Tourism One Capitol Mall, 72201 • (800) 628-8725

Travel by Philip PO Box 250119, 72225-5119 • 227-7690 • specializes in gay motor coach tours • IGTA member

SPIRITUAL GROUPS

MCC of the Rock 2017 Chandler, North Little Rock • 753-7075 • 11am Sun

Unitarian Universalist Church 1818 Reservoir Rd. • 255-1503 • wheelchair access

PUBLICATIONS

The Lesbian/Gay News-Telegraph PO Box 14229-A, St. Louis, 63178 • (314) 664-6411 • covers AR,IL,KS,MO,TN

Triangle Journal News Box 11485, Memphis, 38111 • (901) 454-1411 • covers TN & sometimes AR

Triangle Rising PO Box 45053, 72214

Ponca   (501)

TRAVEL & TOUR OPERATORS

Walk In Beauty Womyn's Wilderness Trips HC 70 Box 17, 72670-9620 • 861-5506 • women only • eco-tours • also accommodations available

California

Alleghany (916)

ACCOMMODATIONS

Kenton Mine Lodge PO Box 942, 95910 • 287-3212 • gay-friendly • cabins • campsites • food served • in the Sierras

Anaheim (714)

INFO LINES & SERVICES

Gay/Lesbian Community Services Center 12832 Garden Grove Blvd. Ste. A • 534-0862 • 10am-10pm

ACCOMMODATIONS

Country Comfort B&B 5104 E. Valencia Dr. • 532-4010 • lesbians/gay men • full breakfast • hot tub • swimming • 7 mi. from Disneyland • wheelchair access • women-owned/run

PUBLICATIONS

Directory - Orange County 4102 E. 7th St. #621, Long Beach • (310) 434-7129 • semi-annual directory of gay & gay-supportive businesses

Bakersfield (805)

INFO LINES & SERVICES

Gay Valley Alliance PO Box 304, 93302 • 398-8663 • support groups & community outreach

BARS

Casablanca Club 1030 20th St. • 324-1384 • 7pm-2am • lesbians/gay men • neighborhood bar • dancing/DJ

The Mint 1207 19th St. • 325-4048 • 6am-2pm • gay-friendly • neighborhood bar

The Place 3500 Wilson Rd. • 835-0494 • 11am-2am, from 6pm wknds • lesbians/gay men • country/western

Town Casino Lounge 1813 'H' St. (Padre Hotel) • 324-2594 • 10am-2am • gay-friendly • live piano Fri-Sat

SPIRITUAL GROUPS

MCC of the Harvest 2421 Alta Vista Dr. • 327-3724 • 7pm Sun

EROTICA

Wildcat Books 2620 Chester • 324-4243

Benicia (707)

ACCOMMODATIONS

Captain Walsh House 235 E. 'L' St. • 747-5653 • full breakfast • gracious gothic charm • wheelchair access

BOOKSTORES & RETAIL SHOPS

Lielin West Jewelers PO Box 733, 94510 • 745-9000 • women's imagery in precious metals • studio hours by appt. • catalog

Big Bear Lake (909)

ACCOMMODATIONS

Eagles' Nest 41675 Big Bear Rd. • 866-6465 • gay-friendly • B&B • 7 cottages • spa • wheelchair access

Grey Squirrel Resort PO Box 1711-39372 Big Bear Blvd., 92315 • 866-4335 • cabins • hot tub • one room • one suite

Hillcrest Lodge 40241 Big Bear Blvd. • 866-6040/ (800) 843-4449 (primary) • gay-friendly • motel • cabins • hot tub • suites • wheelchair access

▲ **Smoke Tree Resort** 40210 Big Bear Blvd. • 866-2415/ (800) 352-8581 • gay-friendly • cabins • hot tub • B&B rooms

RESTAURANTS & CAFES

Ché Faccia 607 Pine Knot Ave. • 878-3222 • 11am-10pm • Italian • plenty veggie • full bar • $10-15

Maggie's Place 39904 Big Bear Blvd. • 866-9592 • 3pm-9pm • wheelchair access • $8-12

Bishop (619)

INFO LINES & SERVICES

Wild Iris Women's Services PO Box 57, 93515 • 873-6601/ 873-7384 (24hrs) • counseling • shelter

ACCOMMODATIONS

Starlite Motel 192 Short St. • 873-4912 • gay-friendly • swimming

BOOKSTORES & RETAIL SHOPS

Spellbinder Books 124 N. Main • 873-4511 • 9:30am-5:30pm, clsd Sun • small women's section • wheelchair access

Buena Park (714)

BARS

Ozz Supper Club 6231 Manchester Blvd. • 522-1542 • 6pm-2am • popular • lesbians/gay men • dancing/DJ • cabaret • also a restaurant • women's country/western dancing Sun

Cambria (805)

ACCOMMODATIONS

The J. Patrick House 2990 Burton Dr. • 927-3812/ (800) 341-5258 • gay-friendly • fireplaces • no smoking • authentic log cabin B&B

Carmel (408)

ACCOMMODATIONS

Happy Landing Inn PO Box 2619, 93921 • 624-7917 • gay-friendly • full breakfast • Hansel & Gretel 1925 Inn

Castroville (408)

BARS

Franco's Norma Jean Bar 10639 Merritt St. • 633-2090/ 633-6129 • call for hours • mostly gay men • dancing/DJ • mostly Latino-American • live shows • also a restaurant • some veggie • $10-15

Chico (916)

INFO LINES & SERVICES

Chico State Student Group • 898-4420

Gay Hotline • 891-5718 • hours vary

Stonewall Alliance Center 820 W. 7th St • 893-3338/ 893-3336 (office) • social 6pm-10pm Fri • Gay AA 7pm Tue

BARS

Rascal's 900 Cherry St. • 893-0900 • 6pm-2am • lesbians/gay men • dancing/DJ

Chula Vista (619)

EROTICA

▲ **F St. Bookstore** 1141 3rd Ave. • 585-3314 • 24hrs

Claremont   (909)

BOOKSTORES & RETAIL SHOPS

▲ **Wild Iris Bookstore** 143 Harvard Ave.
Ste. A • 626-8283 • 10am-5:30pm, noon-
4pm Sun • women's • books • music •
much more • women-owned/run

Clearlake   (707)

ACCOMMODATIONS

Blue Fish Cove Resort 10573 E. Hwy. 20,
Clearlake Oaks • 998-1769 • gay-friendly
• lakeside resort cottages • boat facilities

Lake Vacations Reservations 1855 S.
Main St. • 263-7188

SeaBreeze Resort 9595 Harbor Dr.,
Glenhaven • 998-3327 • gay-friendly •
cottages • swimming • RV hookups

Cloverdale   (707)

ACCOMMODATIONS

Vintage Towers B&B 302 N. Main St. •
894-4535 • gay-friendly • full breakfast •
Queen Anne Mansion

Corona del Mar   (714)

TRAVEL & TOUR OPERATORS

New Directions Travel Company 2435
E. Coast Hwy. • 675-5000/ (800) 222-5531
• IGTA member

Costa Mesa   (714)

BARS

Lion's Den 719 W. 19th St. • 645-3830 •
6pm-2am, from 8pm Sat • lesbians/gay
men • dancing • more women wknds

Metropolis 4255 Campus Dr., Irvine •
725-0300 • 7pm-2am • gay-friendly •
dancing/DJ • also a restaurant •
Californian & sushi • 18+ Fri & Sun • les-
bians/gay men Sun

Newport Station 1945 Placentia • 631-
0031 • 9pm-2am • popular •
lesbians/gay men • dancing/DJ • live
shows • more women Th • wheelchair
access

Tin Lizzie 752 St. Clair • 966-2029 •
noon-2am, from 2pm wknds • mostly gay
men • neighborhood bar • more women
Sun

Wild Iris Bookstore

and Women's Center

*... promoting the writing, art
and well-being of all women*

| Women's Music |
| Videos |
| Jewelry |
| Cards |
| Art |
| Posters |
| Teen's & Children's Books |
| Unique Gifts |
| **OPEN EVERY DAY** |

Sunday 12:00-4:00
Monday-Saturday 10:00-5:30

Friday open 'til 7:00

Special Events
Fridays 7:00-9:00

Genevieve

143A Harvard Avenue
Claremont, CA 91711
(909) 626-8283

SPIRITUAL GROUPS

MCC Ocean of Life 1259 Victoria St. (Unitarian Church) • 548-2955 • 6:45pm Sun

Cupertino (408)

BARS

Silver Fox 10095 Saich Wy. • 255-3673 • 2pm-2am • mostly gay men • neighborhood bar • live shows • wheelchair access

BOOKSTORES & RETAIL SHOPS

Women In The Moon 10203 Parkwood Dr. #7, 95014 • 253-3329 • women of color book publishing company • mail order • readings • 'The Spirit' newsletter • women-owned/run

Davis (916)

RESTAURANTS & CAFES

Cafe Roma 231 'E' St. • 756-1615 • 7:30am-midnight • popular • coffee & pastries • student hangout • wheelchair access

East Bay (510)

INFO LINES & SERVICES

Berkeley Women's Health Center 2908 Ellsworth St., Berkeley • 843-6194 • hours vary

Dyke TV Channel 8 • 7:30pm Wed • 'weekly half hour TV show produced by lesbians for lesbians'

Fruit Punch 94.1-FM (KPFA), Berkeley • 848-6767 • 7pm-7:30pm Wed • lesbigay radio

Gay Switchboard (at the Pacific Center), Berkeley • 841-6224 • 10am-10pm Mon-Fri, til 4pm Sat

Gay/Lesbian Alanon (at the Pacific Center), Berkeley • 548-8283 • 7pm Fri

Infoshop 3124 Shattuck Ave. (Long Haul Activist Space), Berkeley • 540-0751 • women's social night

La Peña 3105 Shattuck Ave., Berkeley • 849-2568/ 849-2572 • noon-5pm Mon-Fri • multicultural center • hosts meetings, events, dances & more • also cafe 6pm-10pm Wed • mostly Latino-American/African American

Pacific Center 2712 Telegraph Ave., Berkeley • 548-8283 • 10am-10pm, from noon Sat, 6pm-9pm Sun • support groups & counseling

What's Up! Events Hotline for Sistahs, Berkeley • 835-6126 • for lesbians of African descent

Womanlink 2124 Kittredge #257, Berkeley, 94704 • women's S/M penpals & contacts

Women's Cancer Resource Center 3023 Shattuck Ave., Berkeley • 548-9272 • support groups • networking & referral service

WOMEN'S ACCOMMODATIONS

La Grande Maison 1 Arlington Ct., Kensington • 526-0265 • women only • B&B • hot tub • French chateau in the Berkeley Hills • patio

ACCOMMODATIONS

Elmwood House 2609 College Ave., Berkeley • 540-5123 • gay-friendly • IGTA member

Western Exposure PO Box 2116, Berkeley, 94702 • 869-4395 • accommodations in private homes in Bay Area

BARS

Bella Napoli 2330 Telegraph Ave., Oakland • 893-5552 • 1pm-2am • gay-friendly • dancing/DJ • multi-racial • wheelchair access

Bench & Bar 120 11th St., Oakland • 444-2266 • 3pm-2am, from 5pm Sat • popular • mostly gay men • dancing/DJ

Cabel's Reef 2272 Telegraph Ave., Oakland • 451-3777 • noon-2am • mostly gay men • dancing/DJ • multi-racial • women's night Wed

Country Dance Nights 1650 Mountain Blvd. (Mountclair Women's Club), Oakland • 428-2144 • 9pm-11pm Fri • women only • lessons at 7pm • smoke/alcohol/scent-free

Town & Country 2022 Telegraph Ave., Oakland • 444-4978 • 11am-2am • mostly gay men • neighborhood bar • wheelchair access

White Horse 6551 Telegraph Ave., Oakland • 652-3820 • 1pm-2am, from 3pm Mon-Tue • lesbians/gay men • popular Fri night • wheelchair access

RESTAURANTS & CAFES

Betty's To Go 1807 4th St., Berkeley • 548-9494 • 6:30am-5pm, 8am-4pm Sun • sandwiches • some veggie • $5

Bison Brewery 2598 Telegraph at Parker, Berkeley • 841-7734 • 11am-1am • beer/wine • sandwiches • some veggie • live music • wheelchair access • $5-10

East Bay

So just what exactly is the East Bay? Mostly it's Berkeley and Oakland, San Francisco's neighbors across the Bay, with weather that's consistently sunnier and 10-20° warmer than the Fog City.

Berkeley, the city and the campus of the University of California, was immortalized in the '60s as a hotbed of student/counterculture activism. Today, most of the people taking to the streets are tourists or kids from the suburbs in search of anything tie-dyed, a good book, exotic food, or just a cup of coffee. As for Oakland, native Gertrude Stein once said, "There is no there there." But a lot has changed since Gertrude and her lover Alice — natives both — were last "there." The birthplace of the Black Panthers, this city has been influential in urban African-American music, fashion and politics.

And where are all the women? Well, many are in couples or covens. Start searching at **Mama Bear's** or one of the other women's bookstores – they're also great informal resource centers, and often host lectures and author signings. Try breakfast at the famous, cooperatively-run **Brick Hut**, and have tea for two at the **Tea Spot**.

For a plethora of groups and events, cruise by the **Pacific Center**, the Bay Area's only lesbian/gay center, located in Berkeley. Those interested in women's spirituality should check out local events on the **Reclaiming** pagan infoline.

If you're the outdoors type, consider an adventure in Northern California with **Mariah Wilderness Expedition** or **Wild Women Trips**. Or make a day of it at one of the nearby state parks: Pt. Reyes is a beautiful destination with a hostel, and Pt. Isabel is rumored to be a good meeting place for lesbians with dogs.

If you'd rather exercise indoors, make some moves on the dancefloor of the **White Horse** or at the **Montclair Women's Club** on Country Dance Night. For plays, performances and events, grab a **Bay Times** and check out the calendar section. Or pick up some entertainment of your own at the brand-new East Bay **Good Vibrations** or **Passionflower** – both are friendly, clean sex toy stores.

There are also lots of resources for women of color in the East Bay. Start with **La Peña Cultural Center**, an active center with many events for Latino-Americans and African-Americans. Then there's **What's Up!**, an events hotline for lesbian sistahs of African descent. For anarchists and radicals of any color, the **Infoshop** at Longhaul Activist Space has weekly women's social nights.

▲ **Brick Hut** 2512 San Pablo, Berkeley • 486-1124 • 7:30am-2pm, 8:30am-3pm wknds, dinner 5:30pm-10pm Wed-Sat • popular • lesbians/gay men • some veggie • popular for breakfast • $5-10

Cafe Sorrento 2510 Channing, Berkeley • 548-8220 • 7am-7pm, 9am-4pm wknds • multi-racial • Italian • vegetarian • $5-10

Cafe Strada corner of College & Bancroft, Berkeley • 843-5282 • popular • students • great patio & white bianca mochas

The Edible Complex 5600 College, Oakland • 658-2172 • 7am-midnight, til 1am Fri-Sat • some sandwiches & soups • cafe • mostly students

Mama's Royale 4012 Broadway, Oakland • 547-7600 • 7am-3pm, from 8am wknds • popular • come early for excellent weekend brunch

Mimosa Cafe 462 Santa Clara, Oakland • 465-2948 • 11am-9pm, clsd Mon • natural & healthy • plenty veggie • $7-12

Tea Spot Cafe 2072 San Pablo Ave., Berkeley • 848-7376 • 8am-9pm, til 2:30pm Sun, clsd Mon • beer/wine • eclectic American • plenty veggie • wheelchair access • lesbian-owned/run • $5-10

BOOKSTORES & RETAIL SHOPS

Ancient Ways 4075 Telegraph Ave., Oakland • 653-3244 • extensive occult supplies • classes • readings

Boadecia's Books 398 Colusa Ave., Kensington • 559-9184 • 11am-9pm, til 7pm Sun • women's • lesbigay section • wheelchair access • women-owned/run

Cody's 2454 Telegraph Ave., Berkeley • 845-7852 • 10am-9pm, til 10pm Fri-Sat • general • lesbigay section • frequent readings & lectures

Easy Going 1385 Shattuck (at Rose), Berkeley • 843-3533 • 10am-7pm, noon-6pm Sun • travel books & accessories • also 1617 Locust, Walnut Creek • 947-6660

East Bay (510)

LESBIGAY INFO: Pacific Center: 548-8283, lesbian/gay groups, & info, 10am-10pm, noon-10pm Sat, 6pm-9pm Sun. What's Up? Events Hotline for Sistahs: 835-6126. See also San Francisco.

LESBIGAY PAPER: Bay Times: (415) 626-8121. Out Now: (408) 895-7516

WHERE THE GIRLS ARE: Though there's no lesbian ghetto, you'll find more of us in north Oakland and north Berkeley, Lake Merritt, around Grand Lake & Piedmont, the Solano/Albany area, or at a cafe along 4th St. in Berkeley.

LESBIGAY AA: East Bay AA: 839-8900

LESBIGAY PRIDE: June in Berkeley

ANNUAL EVENTS: June: Gay Prom: 247-8200, $15 preregistered, for ages 16-25 only. October:

Halloween Spiral Dance: 893-3097, rite celebrating the crone.

CITY INFO: Oakland Visitors Bureau: 839-9000

ATTRACTIONS: Berkeley: Jack London Square, UC Berkeley. Telegraph Ave., The Claremont Hotel Restaurant. Oakland: Emeryville Marina Public Market, The Paramount Theater.

BEST VIEW: Claremont Hotel, or various locations in Berkeley and Oakland Hills.

WEATHER: Sunny and warm in summer. Some areas even get hot (90°s-100°s). As for the winter, the temperature drops along with rain (upper 30°s-40°s in the winter). In spring the brown hills explode with wildflowers.

TRANSIT: Yellow Cab: 848-3333 (Berkeley), 836-1234 (Oakland)

Gaia Bookstore & Catalogue Co. 1400 Shattuck Ave., Berkeley • 548-4172 • 10am-7pm • eco-spiritual/goddess • feminist • wheelchair access

Mama Bears Bookstore 6536 Telegraph Ave, Oakland • 428-9684 • 10am-7pm, til 9pm Th-Fri • mostly women • woman's books • also 'Mama Bears News & Notes' book review • wheelchair access • lesbian-owned/run

Shambhala Booksellers 2482 Telegraph Ave., Berkeley • 848-8443 • 10am-7pm, til 9pm Fri-Sat • metaphysical feminist/goddess section • wheelchair access

TRAVEL & TOUR OPERATORS

Mariah Wilderness Expeditions PO Box 248 , Point Richmond, 94807 • 233-2303 • white water rafting & other adventures for women • IGTA member • women-owned/run

New Venture Travel 404 22nd St., Oakland • 835-3800 • IGTA member • women-owned/run

Travel By Design 3832 Piedmont Ave., Oakland • 653-6668 • women-owned/run

SPIRITUAL GROUPS

Albany Unified Methodist Church 980 Stannage Ave., Albany • 526-7346 • 10am Sun

MCC New Life 1823 9th St., Berkeley • 843-9355 • 12:30pm Sun • wheelchair access

Reclaiming PO Box 14404, San Francisco, 94110 • 236-4645 • pagan info-line & network

Women's Circle Network 2124 Kittredge St. #11, Berkeley, 94704 • contact for women's spirituality circles

PUBLICATIONS

San Francisco Bay Times 288 7th St., San Francisco, 94103 • (415) 626-8121 • popular • a must for Bay Area resources & personals

EROTICA

▲ **Good Vibrations** 2504 San Pablo, Berkeley • 841-8986 • 11am-7pm • mostly women • clean, well-lighted sex toy store • also mail order

Passion Flower 4 Yosemite Ave., Oakland • 601-7750 • toys • lingerie • leather

The Brick Hut Cafe

2512 San Pablo Ave. (at Dwight Way)
Berkeley, CA • (510) 486-1124
Fax (510) 486-1120

OPEN 7 DAYS FROM 8 AM TO 3 PM

NOW SERVING DINNER WED THRU SAT,

5:30 PM TO 10 PM
Patio seating - private
Catering Available

A WOMEN OWNED & OPERATED BUSINESS SINCE 1975

PARTIES - ART - MUSIC - COMMUNITY EVENTS

El Cajon (619)

EROTICA

▲ F St. Bookstore 158 E. Main • 447-0381 • 24hrs

El Monte (818)

BARS

Infinities 2253 Tyler Ave. • 575-9164 • 3pm-2am • lesbians/gay men • dancing/DJ • wheelchair access

Sugar Shack 4101 N. Arden Dr. • 575-9534 • 3pm-2am • lesbians/gay men • dancing/DJ • live shows • beer only • wheelchair access • women-owned/run

Escondido (619)

EROTICA

▲ F St. Bookstore 237 E. Grand Ave. • 480-6031 • 24hrs

Eureka (707)

INFO LINES & SERVICES

Gay/Lesbian Alliance of Humboldt County PO Box 2368, 95502 • 444-1061

ACCOMMODATIONS

Carter House Victorians 301 'L' St. • 444-8062/ (800) 404-1390 • gay-friendly • B&B • full breakfast • enclave of 3 unique inns • wheelchair access

BARS

Club Triangle (Club West) 535 5th St. • 444-2582 • 9pm-2am • gay-friendly • dancing/DJ • alternative • 18+ • gay Tue & Sun • also Star's Hamburgers • 8pm-11pm • wheelchair access

Lost Coast Brewery Pub 617 4th St. • 445-4480 • 11am-2am • gay-friendly • beer/wine • food served • wheelchair access • women-owned/run

BOOKSTORES & RETAIL SHOPS

Booklegger 402 2nd St. • 445-1344 • lesbigay section • some lesbian titles • wheelchair access

PUBLICATIONS

The 'L' Word PO Box 272, Bayside, 95524 • lesbian newsletter for Humboldt County • available at Booklegger

Fairfield (707)

INFO LINES & SERVICES

Solano County Gay/Lesbian Info Line • 448-1010

Ferndale (707)

ACCOMMODATIONS

Gingerbread Mansion Inn 400 Berding St. • 786-4000/ (800) 952-4136 • popular • gay-friendly • a grand lady in the Victorian village of Ferndale w/ beautifully restored interior

Fort Bragg (707)

ACCOMMODATIONS

Aslan House 24600 N. Hwy. 1 • 964-2788 (800) 400-2189 (in-state) • gay-friendly • cottages • hot tub • ideal place for romance & privacy on the Mendocino Coast • partial ocean view

Cleone Lodge Inn 24600 N. Hwy. 1 • 964-2788/ (800) 400-2189 (in-state) • gay-friendly • cottages • hot tub • country garden retreat on 9-1/2 acres

Jug Handle Beach B&B 32980 Gibney Ln. • 964-1415 • gay-friendly • full breakfast

BOOKSTORES & RETAIL SHOPS

Windsong Books & Records 324 N. Main • 964-2050 • 10am-5:30pm, til 4pm Sun • general • large selection of women's titles

Fremont (510)

INFO LINES & SERVICES

East Bay Network of Fremont PO Box 1238, 94538-0123 • social/support group

EROTICA

L'Amour Shoppe 40555 Grimmer Blvd. • 659-8161 • 24hrs

Fresno (209)

INFO LINES & SERVICES

Bulletin Board at Valley Women's Books • popular resource for community info

Community Link PO Box 4959, 93744 • 266-5465/ 485-5333 • lesbigay support • also publishes Pink Pages directory

GUS Inc. (Gay United Service) 1999 Tuolumne Ste. 625 • 268-3541 • 8am-5pm Mon-Fri • counseling • referrals

Serenity Fellowship AA 925 N. Fulton • 221-6907 • various mtg. times

The Yosemite Chapter, Knights of Malta PO Box 4162, 93744 • 496-4144 • lesbigay leather group

BARS

The Express 708 N. Blackstone • 233-1791 • 5pm-2am, from 3pm Sun • popular • lesbians/gay men • dancing/DJ • 3 bars • patio • wheelchair access

Palace 4030 E. Belmont St. • 264-8283 • 3pm-2am • mostly women • neighborhood bar • dancing/DJ • live shows • wheelchair access

Red Lantern 4618 E. Belmont • 251-5898 • 2pm-2am • mostly gay men • neighborhood bar • country/western

RESTAURANTS & CAFES

Cafe Express 708 N. Blackstone • 233-1791 • 6pm-9pm, champagne brunch 10am-3pm Sun, clsd Mon • fine dining

Java Cafe 805 E. Olive • 237-5282 • 7am-10pm • popular • plenty veggie • bohemian • wheelchair access • women-owned/run • $8-12

BOOKSTORES & RETAIL SHOPS

Valley Women's Books 1118 N. Fulton St. • 233-3600 • 10am-6pm, til 9pm Th-Fri • lesbigay section • wheelchair access

TRAVEL & TOUR OPERATORS

The Travel Address 6465 N. Blackstone Ave. • 432-9095/ (800) 800-9095 • IGTA member

SPIRITUAL GROUPS

Morrigan Tower Coven of Wyrd PO Box 7137, 93744-7137 • 264-4074 • monthly • co-gender

EROTICA

Only For You 1468 N. Van Ness Ave. • 498-0284 • noon-9pm, til 10pm Th-Sat

Wildcat Book Store 1535 Fresno St. • 237-4525

Garberville   (707)

ACCOMMODATIONS

Giant Redwoods RV & Camp PO Box 222, Myers Flat, 95554 • 943-3198 • gay-friendly • campsites • RV • located off the Avenue of the Giants on the Eel River

Garden Grove   (714)

INFO LINES & SERVICES

AA Gay/Lesbian 9872 Chapman Ave. #15 (Ash Inc.) • 534-5820/ 537-9968 • 6pm-9:30pm

BARS

Frat House 8112 Garden Grove Blvd. • 897-3431 • 9am-2am • popular • mostly gay men • dancing/DJ • multi-racial • live shows • theme nights • piano bar • wheelchair access

Happy Hour 12081 Garden Grove Blvd. • 537-9079 • 2pm-2am, from noon wknds • mostly women • dancing/DJ • wheelchair access • women-owned/run

Nick's 8284 Garden Grove Blvd. • 537-1361 • 9pm-2am, 24hrs wknds • mostly gay men • dancing/DJ

Glendale   (818)

SPIRITUAL GROUPS

MCC Divine Redeemer 346 Riverdale Dr. • 500-7124 • 10:45am Sun, 7:30pm Wed & Fri (rosary)

Grass Valley   (916)

ACCOMMODATIONS

Murphy's Inn 318 Neal St. • 273-6873 • gay-friendly • B&B • full breakfast • no smoking or pets • wheelchair access

Half Moon Bay   (415)

ACCOMMODATIONS

Mill Rose Inn 615 Mill St. • 726-8750/ (800) 900-7673 • gay-friendly • classic European elegance by the sea

Hawthorne   (310)

BARS

El Capitan 13825 S. Hawthorne • 675-3436 • 4pm-2am, from noon Fri-Sun • lesbians/gay men • neighborhood bar • beer/wine • women's night Tue

Hayward   (510)

BARS

▲ **Driftwood Lounge** 22170 Mission Blvd. • 581-2050 • 2pm-2am • mostly women • dancing/DJ • wheelchair access • women-owned/run

I.J.'s Getaway 21859 Mission Blvd. • 582-8078 • noon-2am, til 4am Fri-Sat • lesbians/gay men • dancing/DJ • karaoke Th

Rumors 22554 Main St. • 733-2334 • 10am-2am, from 6am wknds • mostly gay men • neighborhood bar • wheelchair access

Turf Club 22517 Mission Blvd. • 881-9877 • 10am-2am • lesbians/gay men • dancing/DJ • country/western • live shows • patio bar in summer

Healdsburg (707)
ACCOMMODATIONS
Camellia Inn 211 North St. • 433-8182/(800) 727-8182 • gay-friendly • full breakfast • wheelchair access

Madrona Manor PO Box 818, 95448 • 433-4231 • gay-friendly • full breakfast • swimming • elegant Victorian country inn • wheelchair access

Twin Towers River Ranch 615 Bailhache • 433-4443 • gay-friendly • B&B • 1864 Victorian farmhouse located on 5 rolling acres

RESTAURANTS & CAFES
Tre Scalini 241 Healdsburg Ave. • 433-1772 • 5pm-10pm, clsd Sun • Italian • some veggie • $30-35

Idyllwild (909)
ACCOMMODATIONS
Inn at Pine Cove 23481 Hwy. 243 • 659-5033 • gay-friendly • B&B • on 3 wooded acres

Wilkum Inn B&B PO Box 1115, 92549 • 659-8087/ (800) 659-4086 • gay-friendly • 1938 shingle-style inn • cabin available • wheelchair access • women-owned/run

Inglewood (310)
BARS
Annex 835 S. La Brea • 671-7323 • noon-2am, from 10am wknds • mostly gay men • neighborhood bar

Caper Room 244 S. Market St. • 677-0403 • 11am-2am, from 4pm Sun • mostly gay men • dancing/DJ • mostly African-American

Lafayette   (510)

RESTAURANTS & CAFES

Java Jones 100 Lafayette Cir. #101 • 284-5282 • 9am-3pm, til 10pm Th-Sat, clsd Mon • lesbians/gay men • beer/wine • some veggie • brunch Sun • patio • wheelchair access • lesbian-owned/run • $6-13

Laguna Beach   (714)

INFO LINES & SERVICES

AA Gay/Lesbian 31872 Coast Hwy. (South Coast Medical Hospital) • 499-7150 • 8pm Mon & Tue • call for additional mtgs.

Laguna Outreach • 497-4237 • educational/social group for Orange County • call for details

ACCOMMODATIONS

California Riviera 800 1400 S. Coast Hwy. Ste. 104 • 376-0305/ (800) 621-0500 • extensive reservation & accommodation services • IGTA member

▲ **Casa Laguna B&B Inn** 2510 S. Coast Hwy. • 494-2996/ (800) 233-0449 • gay-friendly • swimming • romantic mission-style inn & cottages overlooking Pacific

Coast Inn 1401 S. Coast Hwy. • 494-7588/ (800) 653-2697 • lesbians/gay men • swimming • oceanside accommodations w/ 2 bars & restaurant

Hotel St. Maarten 696 S. Coast Hwy. • 494-1001 • gay-friendly • swimming

Inn By The Sea 475 N. Coast Hwy. • 497-6645/ (800) 297-0007 • gay-friendly • hot tub • swimming • wheelchair access

Laguna Brisas Spa & Hotel 1600 S. Coast Hwy. • 497-7272/ (800) 624-4442 • gay-friendly • swimming • sundeck • across from beach

BARS

Boom Boom Room (at the Coast Inn) •
10am-2am • popular • lesbians/gay men
• dancing/DJ • live shows • videos

Hunky's Video Bar (at the Coast Inn) •
10am-2am • lesbians/gay men • videos •
some veggie • also grill

Little Shrimp 1305 S. Coast Hwy. • 494-
4111 • opens 1pm, from 11am wknds,
brunch Sun • popular • lesbians/gay men
• piano bar • also a restaurant •
seafood • some veggie • patio • wheelchair access • $8-30

Main St. 1460 S. Coast Hwy. • 494-0056
• noon-2am • mostly gay men • piano
bar • women-owned/run

RESTAURANTS & CAFES

Cafe Zinc 350 Ocean Ave. • 494-6302 •
7am-5pm, til noon Mon, clsd Sun • vegetarian • also market • patio • $5-10

Cafe Zoolu 860 Glenneyre • 494-6825 •
dinner • Californian • some veggie •
wheelchair access • $10-20

Cottage 308 N. Coast Hwy. • 494-3023 •
7am-10pm • popular • homestyle cooking • some veggie • $10-12

Dizz's As Is 2794 S. Coast Hwy. • 494-
5250 • open 5:30pm, seating at 6pm,
clsd Mon • cont'l • full bar • patio •
$16-25

Leap of Faith 1440 Pacific Coast Hwy. •
494-8595 • 6am-11pm (seasonal) • les-
bians/gay men • live shows • beer/wine
• American/gourmet desserts • plenty
veggie • patio • $10-20

BOOKSTORES & RETAIL SHOPS

A Different Drummer 1027 N. Coast
Hwy. Ste. A • 497-6699 • 10am-7pm,
11am-5pm wknds • women's • lesbigay
section • wheelchair access • women-
owned/run

TRAVEL & TOUR OPERATORS

Festive Tours 1220 N. Coast Hwy. • 494-
9966 • IGTA member

PUBLICATIONS

Orange County Blade PO Box 1538,
92652 • 494-4898

EROTICA

Video Horizons 31674 Coast Hwy. • 499-
4519

Laguna Niguel (714)

SPIRITUAL GROUPS

S.D.A. Kinship PO Box 7320, 92677 •
248-1299

Lake Tahoe (916)

WOMEN'S ACCOMMODATIONS

▲ **Holly's Place** PO Box 13197, S. Lake
Tahoe, 96151 • 544-7040/ (800) 745-7041
• women only • cabins • near outdoor
recreation • kitchens • nudity • kids okay
• pets okay • 2 blks to the lake • 2 miles
to casinos • 3 miles to gay bar • IGTA
member

ACCOMMODATIONS

Bavarian House B&B PO Box 624507, S.
Lake Tahoe, 96154 • 544-4411/ (800) 431-
4411 • lesbians/gay men • B&B • full
breakfast • exclusively gay/lesbian • gay-
owned/run

Ridgewood Inn 1341 Emerald Bay Rd. •
541-8589/ (800) 800-4640 • gay-friendly •
hot tub • small country inn • quiet
wooded setting

Sierrawood Guest House PO Box 11194,
96155-0194 • 577-6073 • lesbians/gay
men • full breakfast • hot tub • romantic,
cozy chalet

Silver Shadows Lodge 1251 Emerald
Bay Rd. • 541-3575 • gay-friendly • hot
tub • swimming • 18 units

BARS

Faces 270 Kingsbury Grade, Stateline •
(702) 588-2333 • 3pm-4am •
lesbians/gay men • dancing/DJ

RESTAURANTS & CAFES

Driftwood Cafe 4119 Laurel Ave. • 544-
6545 • 7:30am-2pm • homecooking •
some veggie • non-smoking • wheelchair
access • $4-8

Lancaster (805)

INFO LINES & SERVICES

Antelope Valley Gay/Lesbian Alliance
PO Box 2013, 93539 • 942-2812

BARS

Back Door 1255 W. Ave. 'I' • 945-2566 •
6pm-2am • lesbians/gay men • danc-
ing/DJ

holly's

A SPECIAL PLACE FOR WOMEN

LAKE TAHOE

A wonderful place to meet new friends, Hike, Bike, Ski,
BBQ, Hot Tub, Relax by a fire or visit the casinos
Quiet, Private and Very Comfortable.

**Cozy cabins/guest rooms decorated
in rustic elegance.**

Fireplaces, Lofts, Kitchens, Tv/vcr, Videos, & more
Rates range from $85 to $185
Conference/Workshop room available

*Two blocks to Lake, two miles to casinos, close to all recreation
1 hour from Reno, 3 1/2 hours from San Francisco*

**Call about cabin and group specials
916-544-7040   or   800-745-7041**
(business)   *(reservations/brochures only)*

smoking outside only   a percentage of proceeds donated to breast cancer & A.I.D.S. research

SPIRITUAL GROUPS

Antelope Valley Unitarian Universalist Fellowship 43843 N. Division St. • 272-0530 • 11am Sun

MCC 45303 23rd St. W. • 942-7076 • 11am Sun

Long Beach   (310)

INFO LINES & SERVICES

AA Gay/Lesbian (Atlantic Alano Club) 441 E. 1st St. • 432-7476 • 11am-10pm

Lesbian/Gay Center & Switchboard 2017 E. 4th St. • 434-4455 • 10am-10pm, 9am-6pm Sat, clsd Sun

South Bay Center 2009 Artesia Blvd. Ste. A, Redondo Beach • 379-2850 • 7pm-10pm Wed & Fri • lesbigay support & education for El Segundo, Torrance, Palo Verdes, Manhattan, Redondo & Hermosa Bch

BARS

5211 5211 N. Atlantic St. • 428-5545 • 6am-2am • mostly gay men • neighborhood bar • karaoke Wed • wheelchair access

The Club 740 740 E. Broadway • 437-7705 • 6pm-2am • popular • mostly gay men • dancing/DJ • mostly Latino-American

Club Broadway 3348 E. Broadway • 438-7700 • 11am-2am • mostly women • neighborhood bar • wheelchair access • women-owned/run

De De's on the Queen Mary • 433-1470 • 3rd Sat of the month 7pm-1am • mostly women • dancing/DJ

Executive Suite 3428 E. Pacific Coast Hwy. • 597-3884 • 8pm-2am, clsd Tue • popular • lesbians/gay men • dancing/DJ • live shows • theme nights • more women wknds

Floyd's 2913 E. Anaheim St. (entrance on Gladys St.) • 433-9251 • 6pm-2am, from 2pm Sun • mostly gay men • dancing/DJ • country/western • wheelchair access

Que Sera Sera 1923 E. 7th St. • 599-6170 • 3pm-2am, from 2pm wknds • mostly women • dancing/DJ • live shows • wheelchair access • women-owned/run

Ripples 5101 E. Ocean • 433-0357 • noon-2am, buffet Sun • popular • mostly gay men • dancing/DJ • piano bar • patio

Long Beach

*T*hough it's often overshadowed by Los Angeles, Long Beach is a large harbor city with plenty of bars, shopping, and of course, lesbians.

According to local rumor, Long Beach is second only to San Francisco in lesbian/gay population, at approximately 45,000 – though many of these gay residents are "married," making this a bedroom community of professional couples.

The city itself is melded from overlapping suburbs and industrial areas. The cleaner air, mild weather, and reasonable traffic make it an obvious choice for those looking for a livable refuge from L.A. Of course the nightlife is milder as well, but nobody's complaining about the three fulltime women's bars – **Club Broadway** and **Sweet Water** for casual hanging out, and **Que Será Será** for dancing and shows. Though it's a mixed club, we hear the **Executive Suite** is packed with lesbians on weekends. For other events, check with **Pearl's Booksellers**, the women's bookstore, or the **Lesbian/Gay Center**.

Sweet Water 1201 E. Broadway • 432-7044 • 6am-2am • mostly gay men • neighborhood bar • popular days

Utopia 145 W. Broadway • 432-7202 • 6pm-2am, from 4pm Sun, clsd Mon • lesbians/gay men • dancing/DJ • also a restaurant • Californian/French • some veggie • more straight Tue-Wed • wheelchair access • $10-12

RESTAURANTS & CAFES

Birds of Paradise 1800 E. Broadway • 590-8773 • 10am-1am • lesbians/gay men • American • some veggie • Sun brunch • cocktails • live piano Wed-Sun • wheelchair access • $10

Cha Cha Cha 762 8th • 436-3900 • lunch & dinner • Caribbean • plenty veggie • wheelchair access • $20-30

Egg Heaven 4358 E. 4th St. • 433-9277 • 7am-3pm • American • some veggie • $4-7

Lori Lou's Coffeehouse 2040 E. 4th St. • 439-1964 • 11am-9pm, til midnight Sat, clsd Sun-Mon • gourmet coffee & desserts/sandwiches • wheelchair access • women-owned/run

Madame JoJo 2941 Broadway • 439-3672 • 5pm-close, clsd Sun-Mon • popular • beer/wine • Mediterranean • some veggie • wheelchair access • $12-20

Original Pack Pantry 2104 E. Broadway • 434-0451 • lunch & dinner, live shows Sat & Mon • Mexican/American/Asian • some veggie • $8-12

BOOKSTORES & RETAIL SHOPS

Chelsea Books 2501 E. Broadway • 434-2220 • 10am-10pm, til 6pm Sun • lesbi-gay section • wheelchair access

Dodd's Bookstore 4818 E. 2nd St. • 438-9948 • 10am-10pm, noon-6pm Sun • lesbigay section • wheelchair access

Hot Stuff 2121 E. Broadway • 433-0692 • 11am-7pm, til 5pm wknds • cards • gifts • toys • etc. • wheelchair access

Pearls Booksellers 224 Redondo Ave. • 438-8875 • 11am-7pm, noon-5pm wknds • women's • lesbigay section • wheelchair access • women-owned/run

TRAVEL & TOUR OPERATORS

Touch of Travel 3918 Atlantic Ave. • 427-2144/ (800) 833-3387 • IGTA member

Long Beach (310)

LESBIGAY INFO: Lesbian/Gay Center & Switchboard: 434-4455, 2017 E. 4th St. 9am-10pm, til 6pm Sat, clsd Sun. South Bay Center: 379-2850. 2009 Artesia Blvd. Ste. A, Redondo Beach, 7pm-10pm Wed & Fri.

WHERE THE GIRLS ARE: Schmoozing with the boys on Broadway between Atlantic and Cherry Avenues, or elsewhere between Pacific Coast Hwy. and the beach. Or at home snuggling.

LESBIGAY AA: Atlantic Alano Club: 432-7476. At 441 E. 1st St., 11am-10pm. South Bay Gay/Lesbian AA: 379-2850, at the South Bay Center, Thursdays at 7:30pm.

LESBIGAY PRIDE: May 18 & 19, 1996. 987-9191

ANNUAL EVENTS: September - Pride Picnic. August - The Pre-Gatsby ala Manhattan, AIDS benefit dinner, $25. November - The Gatsby at Sheraton

CITY INFO: Long Beach Visitor's Bureau: 436-3645

ATTRACTIONS: The Queen Mary

BEST VIEW: On the deck of the Queen Mary, docked overlooking most of Long Beach. Or Signal Hill, off 405 - take the Cherry exit.

WEATHER: Quite temperate: highs in the mid-80°s July through September, and cooling down at night. In the "winter," January to March, highs are in the upper 60°s, and lows in the upper 40°s.

TRANSIT: Long Beach Yellow Cab: 435-6111. Super Shuttle: 782-6600. Long Beach Transit & Runabout (free downtown shuttle): 591-2301

SPIRITUAL GROUPS

Christ Chapel 3935 E. 10th St. • 438-5303 • 10am Sun & 7pm Wed • non-denominational

Dignity PO Box 15037, 90815 • 984-8400

Universal Mind Science Church 3212 E. 8th St. • 434-3453 • 11:30am Sun & 8pm Th

PUBLICATIONS

Directory - Long Beach 4102 E. 7th St. #621 • 434-7129 • directory of gay & gay-supportive businesses • published Jan & July

EROTICA

The Crypt on Broadway 1712 E. Broadway • 983-6560 • leather • toys • piercings

Los Angeles

L.A. is listed under 7 areas:

Overview

INFO LINES & SERVICES

AA Gay/Lesbian • (213) 993-7400/ 936-4343 (AA#) • 12:30pm Tue/Th • meets at LA Lesbian/Gay Community Services Center Rm. 106C

Alcoholics Together Center 1773 Griffith Park Blvd. • (213) 663-8882 • call for mtg. times • open to groups on 12-step system

Asian/Pacific Lesbians/Gays West Hollywood PO Box 433 Ste. 109, 90096 • (213) 660-2131 • 1st Sun • Asian/Pacific Islanders & friends

Bi-Social (Pansocial) Center & Bi-Line 7136 Matilija Ave., Van Nuys • (213) 873-3700/ (818) 989-3700 • 24hr hotline for bi, transgendered & gay info & referrals

Black Gay/Lesbian Leadership Forum 1219 S. La Brea, 90019 • (213) 964-7820 • nat'l group that sponsors annual conference

The Celebration Theatre 7051-B Santa Monica Blvd. • (213) 957-1884 • lesbigay theater • call for more info

Dyke TV Century Channel 3 & Cont'l Channel 37 • 9:30pm Tue • 'weekly half hour TV show produced by lesbians for lesbians'

Gay/Lesbian Youth Phone Line • (213) 993-7475 • 7pm-10pm, clsd Sun • referrals & support for those 23 & under • women's night Mon

IMRU Gay Radio KPFK LA 90.7 FM • (818) 985-2711 • 10pm Sun • also 'This Way Out' 4:30pm Tue

International Gay/Lesbian Archives 626 N. Robertson • (310) 854-0271 • 3pm-7pm Mon & Th, 11am-2pm Sat

June Mazer Collection 626 N. Robertson • (310) 659-2478 • 6pm-9pm Wed, 11am-5pm Sun (by appt.) • lesbian archives

Los Angeles Gay/Lesbian Community Center 1625 N. Shrader Ave. • (213) 993-7400 • 9am-10pm, til 6pm Sun • wide variety of services

Southern CA Women for Understanding 7985 Santa Monica #207, 90046 • (213) 654-7298 • professional group working to challenge lesbian stereotypes

Women's Business Network • (818) 995-6646 • 9am-5pm • parent group of Women's Yellow Pages & Women's Referral Service

ACCOMMODATIONS

Bed & Breakfast of California 3924 E. 14th St., Long Beach • (310) 498-0552/ (800) 383-3513 • B&B reservation service of California

SPIRITUAL GROUPS

Beth Chayim Chadashim 6000 W. Pico Blvd. • (213) 931-7023 • 8pm Fri

PUBLICATIONS

Community Yellow Pages 2305 Canyon Dr. • (213) 469-4454/ (800) 745-5669 • annual survival guide to lesbigay southern CA

Female FYI 8033 Sunset Blvd. Ste. 2013, 90046 • (310) 657-5592 • monthly • lesbian lifestyle/entertainment magazine

Lesbian News 2 Lincoln Blvd., Santa Monica, 90405 • (310) 392-8224/ (800) 458-9888

Pink Pages 2101 S. Standard Ste. C • (714) 241-7465/ (800) 844-6574 • semi-annual directory for southern CA

LESBIGAY INFO: Los Angeles Gay/Lesbian Community Center: (213) 993-7400. 1625 N. Shrader Ave., 9am-10pm, til 6pm Sun. Women's Project at the Center: (213) 993-7443

LESBIGAY PAPER: Nightlife: (213) 656-2960. Yes!: (213) 848-2220, LA club scene. Female 411: (818) 244-9332, dyke scene. Lesbian News: (310) 392-8824, Southern California lesbian newspaper.

WHERE THE GIRLS ARE: Hip dykes hang out with the boys along Santa Monica Blvd, or in funky Venice Beach and Santa Monica. Glamourdykes pose in chichi clubs and posh eateries in West LA and Beverly Hills. And more suburban lesbians frequent the women's bars in Studio City and North Hollywood. If you're used to makeup-free lesbians, you may be surprised that coiffed and lipsticked lesbian style is the norm in LA.

ENTERTAINMENT: Celebration Theatre: (213) 957-1884. 7051-B Santa Monica Blvd. Highways: (310) 453-1755. 1651 18th Santa Monica. Theatre Geo: (213) 466-1767. 1229 N. Highland Ave.

LESBIGAY AA: AA Gay/Lesbian: (213) 936-4343, 8206 Santa Monica (at Crescent Heights), noon daily. Alcoholics Together Center: (213) 663-8882, 1773 Griffith Park Blvd.

LESBIGAY PRIDE: Christopher St. West: June. (213) 656-6553

ANNUAL EVENTS: July - Outfest: (213) 951-1247, L.A.'s lesbian & gay film and video festival. August - Sunset Junction Fair: (213) 661-7771, carnival, arts & information fair on Sunset Blvd. in Silverlake benefits Sunset Junction Youth Center. August - Labor Day L.A.: (800) 522-7329, AIDS fundraising celebration with many events. September - Gay Night at Knotts Berry Farm: (818) 893-2777. Gay Cruise Catalina: (818) 893-2777. November - Gay Night at Disneyland: (818) 893-2777. December - New Years Cruise in Long Beach Harbor: (818) 893-2777.

CITY INFO: LA Visitors Bureau: (213) 624-7300

ATTRACTIONS: Melrose Ave. in W. Hollywood, Universal Studios, Venice Beach, Sunset Blvd. in Hollywood, Westwood Village, Chinatown, Theme Parks: Disneyland, Knotts Berry Farm or Magic Mountain

BEST VIEW: Drive up Mulholland Drive, in the hills between Hollywood and the Valley, for a panoramic view of the city, and the Hollywood sign.

WEATHER: Summers are hot, dry and smoggy with temperatures in the 90°s -100°s. LA's weather is at its finest — sunny, blue skies and moderate temperatures (mid 70°s) — during the months of March, April and May.

TRANSIT: Yellow Cab: (213) 870-4664. LA Express: (800) 427-7483 ext.2. Metro Transit Authority: (213) 626-4455.

Los Angeles

*T*here is no city more truly American than LA. Here fantasy and reality have become inseparable. The mere mention of the 'City of Angels' conjures up images of palm-lined streets, sun-drenched beaches and wealth beyond imagination, along with smog, over-crowded freeways, searing poverty and urban violence.

Most travellers come only for the fantasy. They come to 'stargaze' at Mann's Chinese Theatre in Hollywood, at movie and television studios (Fox, Universal) in Burbank, at famous restaurants (Spago, The City, Chasen's, Citrus, Ivy's, Chaya Brasserie, Morton's, etc.) and, of course, all along Rodeo Drive. (Our favorite stargazing location is **Canter's Deli** after 2am.)

But if you take a moment to focus your gaze past the usual tourist traps, you'll see the unique – and often tense – diversity that L.A. offers. You'll find museums, centers and theatres celebrating the cultures of the many peoples who live in this valley. An excellent example is West Hollywood's **June L. Mazer Lesbian Collection**. Other cultural epicenters include Olvera Street, Korea Town, China Town and the historically Jewish Fairfax District. Call the L.A. Visitor's Bureau for directions and advice.

Kitsch fans should explore **La Luz de Jesus Gallery** (on Melrose above the famous neon "Wacko" sign, 213/651-4875), cult store **Archaic Idiot/Mondo Video** or video theater **EZTV** (on Melrose, 310/657-1532) while trash or kink fans should schedule time at **Trashy Lingerie** (on LaCienega, 310/652-4543) or the **Pleasure Chest** to get an outfit for the latest **E.S.P. Hotline** perverted happening.

As for lesbian nightlife in LA, there are 5 full-time women's bars (3 of them in the Valley), and 5 or 6 women's nights. LA is where the one-night-a-week women's dance bar revolution began, so make sure to double-check the papers before you go out.

But the big new deal for women in L.A. is the retro-chic supper-club – a perfect combo of dinner, schmooze and entertainment. Try the Women's Night at **Atlas** on Tuesday or call to find out about the latest **Klub Banshee** supperclub.

You'll really find out the buzz at **Little Frida's Café** or at **Sisterhood Bookstore**, both great spots to get caught up or checked out. Pick up a copy of **Female FYI** party guide or the more newsy, suburban **Lesbian News**. And there's the ever-popular lesbian **Girl Bar**.

The Women's Yellow Pages • (818) 995-6646/ (818) 995-6869 (fax) • annual

Yes! • (213) 848-2220/330 • covers LA club scene

Hollywood (213)

ACCOMMODATIONS

Hollywood Celebrity Hotel 1775 Orchid Ave. • 850-6464/ (800) 222-7017 • gay-friendly • 1930s Art Deco hotel • IGTA member

Hollywood Metropolitan Hotel 5825 Sunset Blvd. • 962-5800/ (800) 962-5800 • gay-friendly • also a restaurant • American • $10-15

BARS

Blacklite 1159 N. Western • 469-0211 • 6am-2am • lesbians/gay men • neighborhood bar

Tempo 5520 Santa Monica Blvd. • 466-1094 • from 8pm, from 6pm Sun, til 4am wknds • mostly gay men • dancing/DJ • mostly Latino-American • live shows

RESTAURANTS & CAFES

Hollywood Canteen 1006 Seward St. • 465-0961 • popular • classic

Il Piccolino Trattoria 641 N. Highland Ave. • 936-2996 • lunch, dinner til midnight, clsd Mon • Italian/cont'l • $10-20

La Poubelle 5909 Franklin Ave. • 465-0807 • 6pm-11pm • French/Italian • some veggie • wheelchair access • $20-25

Prado 244 N. Larchmont Blvd. • 467-3871 • lunch & dinner • Caribbean • some veggie • wheelchair access • $20-30

Quality 8030 W. 3rd St. (at Laurel) • 658-5959 • 8am-4pm • homestyle brkfst • some veggie • wheelchair access • $8-12

BOOKSTORES & RETAIL SHOPS

Archaic Idiot/Mondo Video 1724 N. Vermont • 953-8896 • noon-10pm • vintage clothes • cult & lesbigay videos

TRAVEL & TOUR OPERATORS

Jacqleen's Travel Service 6222 Fountain Ave. #314 • 463-7404 • IGTA member

SPIRITUAL GROUPS

Dignity-LA PO Box 42040, 90042 • 344-8064 • 5:30pm Sun

THE·PALMS

COCKTAIL LOUNGE

PARKING AVAILABLE — CALL FOR INFO
8572 SANTA MONICA BOULEVARD • (310) 652-6188

West Hollywood   (310)

ACCOMMODATIONS

Grove Guesthouse 1325 N. Orange Grove Ave. • (213) 876-7778 • lesbians/gay men • swimming • 1-bdrm guest cottage in a quiet & historic neighborhood

Holloway Motel 8465 Santa Monica Blvd. • (213) 654-2454 • mostly gay men • centrally located to the gay community • IGTA member

▲ **Le Montrose Suite Hotel** 900 Hammond St. • 855-1115/ (800) 776-0666 • popular • gay-friendly • hot tub • swimming • fireplaces • also a restaurant • IGTA member

Le Parc Hotel de Luxe 733 N. West Knoll Dr. • 855-8888 • gay-friendly • swimming • also a restaurant • tennis courts • wheelchair access • IGTA member

Le Reve 8822 Cynthia St. • 854-1114/ (800) 835-7997 • gay-friendly • swimming • wheelchair access • IGTA member

Ma Maison Sofitel 8555 Beverly Blvd. • 278-5444/ (800) 521-7772 • gay-friendly • hotel • swimming • food served • wheelchair access

Ramada West Hollywood 8585 Santa Monica Blvd. • 652-6400/ (800) 845-8585 • gay-friendly • swimming • food served • modern art deco hotel & suites • wheelchair access

San Vincente B&B Resort 845 San Vincente Blvd. • 854-6915 • mostly gay men • swimming

West Hollywood Suites 1000 Westmount Dr. • 652-9600/ (800) GAY-0069 • lesbians/gay men • hot tub • swimming • deluxe all-suite hotel

BARS

7969 7969 Santa Monica Blvd. • (213) 654-0280 • 9pm-2am • gay-friendly • live shows • theme nights

Axis 652 N. La Peer • 659-0471 • 9pm-2am Tue-Sun • mostly gay men • dancing/DJ • women only Fri

Checca Bar & Cafe 7323 Santa Monica Blvd. • (213) 850-7471 • 11:30am-2am • popular • lesbians/gay men • dancing/DJ • live shows • theme nights • also a restaurant • French/Italian (dinner only) • some veggie • patio

Comedy Store 8433 Sunset Blvd. • (213) 656-6225 • 8pm-1am • gay-friendly • stand-up club • lesbigay comedy Wed in Belly Room

E.S.P. • (213) 463-7868 • lesbians/gay men • dancing/DJ • annual Fetish Ball in July • call for events

▲ **Girl Bar at Axis** 652 N. La Peer • (213) 460-2531 • 9pm-2am Fri • popular • mostly women • dancing/DJ • call hotline for events

Klub Banshee Hotline • 288-1601 • popular • mostly women • dance parties in the LA area

Love Lounge 657 N. Robertson • 659-0471 • 9pm-2am • lesbians/gay men • dancing/DJ • alternative • live shows • women only Sat

Maverick Productions • (714) 854-4337 • mostly women • special events for women including Singlefest & County Fever

▲ **Palms** 8572 Santa Monica Blvd. • 652-6188 • noon-2am • popular • mostly women • neighborhood bar • dancing/DJ

Revolver 8851 Santa Monica Blvd. • 659-8851 • 4pm-2am, til 4am Fri-Sat, from 2pm Sun • popular • mostly gay men • alternative • videos

RESTAURANTS & CAFES

The 442 Restaurant 442 N. Fairfax • (213) 651-4421 • 6pm-10:30pm, clsd Sun • fresh healthy cuisine • plenty veggie • full bar • wheelchair access • $20-30

The Abbey 692 N. Robertson • 289-8410 • 7am-3am • lesbians/gay men • patio • wheelchair access

Butterfields 8426 Sunset Blvd. • (213) 656-3055 • upscale California dining • some veggie • mostly gay Sun brunch • patio • women-owned/run • $15-25

Caffe Luna 7463 Melrose Ave. • (213) 655-9177 • 8am-3am, til 5am wknds • Italian country food • some veggie • popular afterhours • $15-25

Canter's Deli 419 N. Fairfax • (213) 651-2030 • 24hrs • Jewish/American • some veggie • hip afterhours

Capone's 8277 Santa Monica Blvd. • (213) 654-7224 • dinner • popular • fine Euro-Californian cuisine • full bar • wheelchair access • $10-15

Figs 7929 Santa Monica • (213) 654-0780 • dinner, Sun brunch • Californian • some veggie • $8-15

Girl Bar
LOS ANGELES

The nation's largest
dance club for women located
in the heart of West Hollywood, CA

Co-Host of the largest
parties held in Palm Springs during
the Dinah Shore Weekend in March

Club Info & Mailing List (213) 460-2531

French Quarter Market Place 7985 Santa Monica Blvd. • (213) 654-0898 • 7am-2:30am, til 3:30am Fri-Sat • popular • lesbians/gay men • American/cont'l • some veggie • $5-12

The Greenery 8945 Santa Monica Blvd. • 275-9518 • 7am-4am • Californian • some veggie • $7-12

Hoy's Wok 8163 Santa Monica Blvd. • (213) 656-9002 • noon-11pm, from 4pm Sun • Mandarin • plenty veggie • wheelchair access • $8-12

La Fabula 7953 Santa Monica Blvd. • (213) 650-8517 • lunch & dinner • popular • Mexican • some veggie • wheelchair access • $10-15

Luna Park 655 N. Robertson • 652-0611 • dinner • eclectic European/Mediterranean • some veggie • cabaret Fri-Sun • wheelchair access • $10-15

Mani's Bakery 519 S. Fairfax Ave. • (213) 938-8800 • opens 6:30am, 7:30am wknds • coffee & dessert bar • wheelchair access

Marix 1108 N. Flores • (213) 656-8800 • 11am-midnight • lesbians/gay men • TexMex • some veggie • great margaritas • wheelchair access • $10-15

Mark's Restaurant 861 N. La Cienega Blvd. • 652-5252 • opens 6pm • popular • Italian/Southwestern • plenty veggie • upscale dining • $15-25

Melrose Place 650 N. La Cienega Blvd. • 657-2227 • 5pm-11pm • live shows • cont'l/Californian • some veggie • full bar • wheelchair access • $8-15

Nature Club Cafe 7174 Melrose Ave. (at Formosa) • (213) 931-4763 • noon-10pm • vegetarian • also elixir bar • yoga & massage • wheelchair access • $8-12

Paradise Grill 8745 Santa Monica Blvd. • 659-6785 • noon-10pm, til 11pm Fri-Sat • lesbians/gay men • beer/wine • Californian • plenty veggie • patio • wheelchair access • $10-15

Six Gallery Cafe 8861 Santa Monica Blvd. • 652-6040 • 8am-3am, from 10am wknds • popular • lesbians/gay men • live shows • coffeehouse

Tango Grill 8807 Santa Monica Blvd. • 659-3663 • noon-11pm • lesbians/gay men • beer/wine • some veggie • wheelchair access • $6-12

Tommy Tang's 7313 Melrose Ave. • (213) 937-5733 • noon-11pm • popular • beer/wine • popular Tue nights w/ Club Glenda

Who's On Third Cafe 8369 W. 3rd St. •
(213) 651-2928 • 8am-6pm, til 3pm Sun
• American • $8-12

Yukon Mining Co. 7328 Santa Monica
Blvd. • (213) 851-8833 • 24hrs •
beer/wine • champagne Sun brunch

GYMS & HEALTH CLUBS

Body Builders 2516 Hyperion Ave. •
(213) 668-0882 • popular • lesbians/gay
men

Powerhouse Gym 8053 Beverly Blvd. •
(213) 651-3636 • gay-friendly

BOOKSTORES & RETAIL SHOPS

A Different Light 8853 Santa Monica
Blvd. • 854-6601 • 10am-midnight •
popular • lesbigay

Camp WeHo 8350 Santa Monica Blvd.
#105 • (213) 656-6133 • campy T-shirts •
pride jewelry • much more

Don't Panic 802 N. San Vicente Blvd. •
652-3668 • 11am-11pm, til midnight Fri-
Sat • T-shirts • trinkets

Dorothy's Surrender 7985 Santa Monica
Blvd. #111 • (213) 650-4111 • cards •
periodicals • T-shirts • gifts

Eighth Muse 8713 Santa Monica Blvd. •
659-2545 • art gallery

Plutonian Books 638-1/8 N. Almont Dr. •
858-6638 • noon-6pm, clsd Mon • col-
lector's edition lesbigay titles

TRAVEL & TOUR OPERATORS

Embassy Travel 906 N. Harper Ave. Ste.
B • (213) 656-0743/ (800) 227-6668 • IGTA
member

▲ **Friends Travel** 322 Huntley Dr. Ste. 100 •
652-9600/ (800) GAY-0069

Gunderson Travel, Inc. 8543 Santa
Monica Blvd. #8 • 657-3944/ (800) 872-
8457 • IGTA member

Magnum Select Travel Service 8500
Wilshire Blvd. Ste. 900 • 652-7900/ (800)
782-9429 • IGTA member

SPIRITUAL GROUPS

West Hollywood Presbyterian Church
7350 Sunset Blvd. • (213) 874-6646 •
11am Sun • wheelchair access

EROTICA

Circus of Books 8230 Santa Monica
Blvd. • (213) 656-6533 • videos • erotica
• toys

Drake's 8932 Santa Monica Blvd. • 289-
8932 • gifts • toys • videos • also at 7566
Melrose Ave. • (213) 651-5600

Gauntlet 8720-1/2 Santa Monica Blvd. •
657-6677 • body piercings

Pleasure Chest 7733 Santa Monica Blvd.
• (213) 650-1022

Skin Graffiti 8722 Santa Monica Blvd.
(upstairs) • 358-0349 • noon-7pm, til
4pm Sun, clsd Mon

Midtown   (213)

BARS

Jewel's Catch One Disco 4067 W. Pico
Blvd. • 734-8849 • 3pm-2am, til 4am Fri-
Sat • popular • lesbians/gay men •
multi-racial • 2 bars • upstairs opens
9pm Th-Sun for dancing • wheelchair
access • women-owned/run

The Red Head 2218 E. 1st St. • 263-299?
• 2pm-2am • lesbians/gay men • neighborhood bar • beer only • women's night
Fri

RESTAURANTS & CAFES

Atlas 3760 Wilshire Blvd. • 380-8400 •
lunch & dinner except Sun • global cuisine • some veggie • also bar • 11am-
2am • $8-19

Silverlake   (213)

INFO LINES & SERVICES

Uptown Gay/Lesbian Alliance PO Box
65111, 90065 • 258-8842 • monthly
social 2pm-5pm 2nd Sun • also publishes newsletter

BARS

Drag Strip 66 2500 Riverside Dr.
(Rudolpho's) • 969-2596 • popular •
queer dance club • call for events

RESTAURANTS & CAFES

Casita Del Campo 1920 Hyperion Ave. •
662-4255 • 11am-10pm • Mexican •
also Plush Cabaret Wed • call 969-2596
for details • patio

Cha Cha Cha 656 N. Virgil (at Melrose) •
664-7723 • 11am-11pm • lesbians/gay
men • Caribbean • plenty veggie •
wheelchair access • $20-30

The Cobalt Cantina 4326 Sunset Blvd. •
953-9991 • 11am-11pm • popular • les-
bians/gay men • Calmex • some veggie
• full bar • patio • $10-15

The Crest Restaurant 3725 Sunset Blvd.
• 660-3645 • 6am-11pm • diner/Greek
• $5-10

Da Giannino 2630 Hyperion Ave. • 664-7979 • lunch (Tue-Fri) & dinner, clsd Mon

El Conquistador 3701 Sunset Blvd. • 666-5136 • 5pm-11pm, from 11am wknds • Mexican • $5-10

Rudolpho's 2500 Riverside Dr. • 669-1226 • lunch & dinner, clsd Mon • French • patio

GYMS & HEALTH CLUBS

Body Builders 2516 Hyperion Ave. • 668-0802 • gay-friendly

TRAVEL & TOUR OPERATORS

Burgan Travel 428 N. Azusa Ave., West Covina • (818) 915-8617 • IGTA member

SPIRITUAL GROUPS

Holy Trinity Community Church 4209 Santa Monica Blvd. • 662-9118 • 10am Sun

MCC Silverlake 3621 Brunswick Ave. • 665-8818 • 6pm Sun

EROTICA

Circus of Books 4001 Sunset Blvd. • 666-1304 • 24hrs Fri-Sat

Valley (818)

BARS

Apache Territory 11608 Ventura Blvd., Studio City • 506-0404 • 8pm-2am, til 4am Fri-Sat • popular • lesbians/gay men • dancing/DJ • live shows

Champions Restaurant & Bar 11935 Ventura Blvd. • 508-2585 • 11am-2am • mostly gay men • neighborhood bar • also a restaurant • some veggie • wheelchair access

Club 22 4882 Lankershim, North Hollywood • 760-9792 • 4pm-2am • mostly women • dancing/DJ • country/western Wed • patio • wheelchair access

Escapades 10437 Burbank Blvd., North Hollywood • 508-7008 • 1pm-2am • popular • lesbians/gay men • neighborhood bar • live shows • wheelchair access

Gold 9 13625 Moorpark St., Sherman Oaks • 986-0285 • 11am-2am • mostly gay men • neighborhood bar

Incognito Valley 7026 Reseda Blvd., Reseda • 996-2976 • noon-2am • popular • mostly gay men • dancing/DJ • wheelchair access

Mag Lounge 5248 N. Van Nuys Blvd., Van Nuys • 981-6693 • 11am-2am • popular • mostly gay men • wheelchair access

Oxwood Inn 13713 Oxnard, Van Nuys • 997-9666 (pay phone) • 3pm-2am, from noon Fri & Sun • mostly women • neighborhood bar • one of the oldest bars in the country • women-owned/run

Queen Mary 12449 Ventura Blvd., Studio City • 506-5619 • 11am-2am, clsd Mon-Tue • popular • gay-friendly • live shows

Rawhide 10937 Burbank Blvd., North Hollywood • 760-9798 • 7pm-2am, from 2pm Sun, clsd Mon-Tue • popular • mostly gay men • dancing/DJ • country/western

Rumors 10622 Magnolia Blvd. • 506-9651 • 6pm-2am, from 3pm Fri-Sun • mostly women • patio • women-owned/run

The Studio City Bar & Grill 11002 Ventura Blvd. • 763-7912 • 4pm-2am • gay-friendly • also a restaurant • American • wheelchair access • $8-15

RESTAURANTS & CAFES

Venture Inn 11938 Ventura Blvd., Studio City • 769-5400 • lunch & dinner, champagne brunch Sun • popular • lesbians/gay men • cont'l • full bar • wheelchair access • $10-15

Wellington's 4354 Lankershim, North Hollywood • 980-1430 • 11am-11pm • lesbians/gay men • live shows • cont'l • wheelchair access • $15-20

SPIRITUAL GROUPS

MCC in the Valley 5730 Cahuenga Blvd. • 762-1133 • 10am Sun

West L.A./South Bay (310)

(see also Redondo Beach)

INFO LINES & SERVICES

South Bay Lesbian/Gay Community Organization PO Box 2777, Redondo Beach, 90278 • 379-2850 • support/education for Manhattan, Hermosa & Redondo Beaches, Torrance, Palos Verdes, El Segundo

Women's Motorcycle Coalition • (213) 664-3964 • monthly Sun brunch • also publishes newsletter

ACCOMMODATIONS

The Malibu Beach Inn 22878 Pacific Coast Hwy. • 456-6444/ (800) 462-5428 • gay-friendly • on the ocean • wheelchair access

Rose Avenue Beach House 55 Rose Ave., Venice • 396-2803 • gay-friendly • B&B • 1 blk from Venice Beach

BARS

Connection 4363 Sepulveda Blvd., Culver City • 391-6817 • 2pm-2am, from noon wknds • popular • mostly women • dancing/DJ • women-owned/run

J.J.'s Pub 2692 S. La Cienega • 837-7443 • 10am-2am • wheelchair access

J.R. Bryan's 2105 Artesia Blvd., Redondo Beach • 371-7859 • 4pm-2am • mostly gay men • dancing/DJ • more women Fri-Sat

RESTAURANTS & CAFES

The Local Yolk 3414 Highlands Ave., Manhattan Beach • 546-4407 • brkfst & lunch

Siamese Princess 8048 W. 3rd St. • (213) 653-2643 • 5:30pm-11pm • beer/wine • Thai • lunch weekdays • $6-10

BOOKSTORES & RETAIL SHOPS

Her Body Books 8721 Beverly Blvd. • 553-5821 • 9am-6pm • women's health books • gifts & supplies • women-owned/run

NaNa 1228 3rd St., Santa Monica • 394-9690 • 11am-7pm, til 11pm Fri-Sat • hip shoes & clothes • also Nana outlet at 8727 W. 3rd St. • (213) 653-1252

▲ **Sisterhood Bookstore** 1351 Westwood Blvd. • 477-7300 • 10am-8pm • women' • periodicals • music & more • women-owned/run

TRAVEL & TOUR OPERATORS

Atlas Travel Service 8923 S. Sepulveda Blvd. • 670-3574/ (800) 952-0120 (not L.A.) • IGTA member

Firstworld Travel Express 1990 S. Bundy Dr. Ste. 175 • 820-6868/ (800) 366-0815 • IGTA member

SPIRITUAL GROUPS

MCC LA Pico Blvd. & Arlington • (213) 460-2911 • 9am & 11:15am Sun

Manhattan Beach   (310)

ACCOMMODATIONS

Sea View Inn at the Beach 3400 Highland Ave. • 545-1504 • gay-friendly • ocean views

Marina Del Rey   (310)

ACCOMMODATIONS

Mansion Inn 327 Washington Blvd. • 821-2557/ (800) 828-0688 • gay-friendly • B&B • 43 room European-style inn • wheelchair access

Mendocino   (707)

WOMEN'S ACCOMMODATIONS

Bellflower Box 867 , 95460 • 937-0783 • women only • lesbians only • secluded cabin with kitchen • 2-night min.

Sallie & Eileen's Place PO Box 409 , 95460 • 937-2028 • women only • cabins • kitchens • kids okay • pets okay • 2 night min.

Wildflower Ridge PO Box 2132 , San Ramon, 94583 • 735-2079 • women only • secluded cabin in Medocino • women-owned/run

ACCOMMODATIONS

Glendeven 8221 N. Hwy. 1, Little River • 937-0083 • gay-friendly • charming farm-house on the coast

McElroy's Inn 998 Main St. • 937-1734/ 937-3105 • gay-friendly • pleasant rooms & stes. • located in the Village

Mendocino Coastal Reservations PO Box 1143, 95460 • (800) 262-7801 • 9am-6pm • gay-friendly • call for available rentals

Seagull Inn 44594 Albion St. • 937-5204 • gay-friendly • 9 units in the heart of historic Mendocino

Stanford Inn By The Sea Coast Hwy. 1 & Comptche-Ukiah Rd. • 937-5615 • gay-friendly • full breakfast • wheelchair access

RESTAURANTS & CAFES

The Cafe Beaujolais 961 Ukiah • 937-5614 • dinner & wknd brunch • California country food • some veggie • wheelchair access • women-owned/run • $20-30

BOOKSTORES & RETAIL SHOPS

Book Loft 45050 Main • 937-0890 • 10am-6pm • wheelchair access

PUBLICATIONS

Visible Box 1494 , 95460 • 964-2756 • Mar, July, Nov, • women only • ageful lesbian (50+) publication • essays • letters • drawings • women-owned/run

Midway City (714)

BARS

The Huntress 8122 Belsa Ave. • 892-0048 • 2pm-2am, from noon Sat-Sun • mostly women • dancing/DJ • wheelchair access

Mission Viejo (714)

TRAVEL & TOUR OPERATORS

Sunrise Travel 23891 Via Fabricante #603 • 837-0620

Modesto (209)

INFO LINES & SERVICES

AA Gay/Lesbian 1203 Tully Rd. Ste. B • 531-2040 • 8pm daily, 7pm Sun • lesbians/gay men

BARS

The Mustang Club 413 N. 7th St. • 577-9694 • 4pm-2am, from 2pm Fri-Sun • lesbians/gay men • dancing/DJ • live shows • open 30 years! • wheelchair access • women-owned/run

RESTAURANTS & CAFES

Espresso Caffe 3025 Mettenig Ave. • 571-3337 • 10am-midnight, til 10pm Su • $4-7

BOOKSTORES & RETAIL SHOPS

Bookstore 2400 Coffee Rd. • 521-0535 • 10am-6pm, til 8pm Th, til 5pm Sat, noon 5pm Sun • wheelchair access

Monterey (408)

INFO LINES & SERVICES

AA Gay/Lesbian at the Little House in the Park, at Cental & Forest • 373-3713 8pm Th • lesbians/gay men • also 10:30am Sat at St. James Church at Franklin & High

WOMEN'S ACCOMMODATIONS

▲ **Misty Tiger** 9422 Acorn Circle, Salinas • 633-8808 • women only • hot tub • no smoking • video library

ACCOMMODATIONS

Gosby House Inn 643 Lighthouse Ave., Pacific Grove • 375-1287 • gay-friendly • full breakfast • wheelchair access

Monterey Fireside Lodge 1131 10th St. • 373-4172/ (800) 722-2624 (in-state) • gay-friendly • hot tub • fireplaces • cont'l breakfast

BARS

After Dark 214 Lighthouse Ave. • 373-7828 • 8pm-2am • lesbians/gay men • dancing/DJ • patio

RESTAURANTS & CAFES

The Clock Garden Restaurant 565 Abrego • 375-6100 • 11am-1am bar • American/cont'l • some veggie • patio • wheelchair access • $10-20

The Fishery 21 Soledad Dr. • 373-6200 • seafood • some veggie

Mountain View (415)

BARS

Daybreak 1711 W. El Camino Real • 940-9778 • 3pm-2am, from 4pm wknds • lesbians/gay men • dancing/DJ • wheelchair access

Mt. Shasta (916)

ACCOMMODATIONS

Evergreen Lodge 1312 S. Mt. Shasta Blvd. • 926-2143 • gay-friendly • hot tub • swimming • 20 unit motel

Myers Flat (707)

ACCOMMODATIONS

The Giant Redwoods RV & Camp 455 Boy Scout Rd., 95554 • 943-3198 • gay-friendly • swimming • full service campground on the Eel River

Napa (707)

ACCOMMODATIONS

Bed & Breakfast Inns of Napa 1310 Napa Town Center • 226-7459 • 9am-5pm • gay-friendly • call for extensive brochure

The Ink House B&B 1575 St. Helena Hwy., St. Helena • 963-3890/ (800) 553-4343• popular • gay-friendly • full breakfast • historic & grand 1884 Italianate Victorian among the vineyards

Willow Retreat 6517 Dry Creek Rd. • 944-8173 • gay-friendly • hot tub • swimming • day use available • wheelchair access • women-owned/run

BOOKSTORES & RETAIL SHOPS

Ariadne Books 3780 Bel Aire Plaza • 253-9402 • 9:30am-6pm, clsd Sun • spiritual • lesbigay section • also espresso bar • women-owned/run

Nevada City (916)

RESTAURANTS & CAFES

Friar Tucks 111 N. Pine St. • 265-9093 • dinner nightly • full bar • also full bar • wheelchair access • $15-20

BOOKSTORES & RETAIL SHOPS

Nevada City Postal Company 228 Commercial St. • 265-0576 • 9am-6pm, clsd Sun • community bulletin board available

Oceanside (619)

BARS

Capri Lounge 207 N. Tremont • 722-7284 • 10am-2am• popular • mostly gay men • neighborhood bar • wheelchair access

Palm Springs (619)

INFO LINES & SERVICES

AA Gay/Lesbian • 324-4880 • call for schedule of mtgs.

Desert Business Association PO Box 773, 92263 • 324-0178 • lesbigay business association • IGTA member

Desert Women's Association PO Box 718, Cathedral City, 92235 • 363-7565 • social/support group

Gay/Lesbian Alliance of the Desert PO Box 861, Cathedral City, 92235 • 322-8769 • 24hr helpline

WOMEN'S ACCOMMODATIONS

▲ **Bee Charmer Inn** 1600 E. Palm Canyon Dr. • 778-5883 • women only • swimming • wheelchair access • lesbian-owned/run

Delilah's Enclave 641 San Lorenzo • 325-5269/ (800) 621-6973 • women only • hot tub • swimming • nudity • private patios

ACCOMMODATIONS

The Abbey West 772 Prescott Cir. • 320-4333/ (800) 223-4073 • mostly gay men • B&B • hot tub • swimming • IGTA member

Anderson's Villas 680 W. Arena Rd. #1 • 323-5043 • gay-friendly • hot tub • swimming • kitchens • no smoking • luxury villas • private patios

Aruba Hotel Suites 671 S. Riverside Dr. • 325-8440/ (800) 842-7822• popular • lesbians/gay men • hot tub • swimming • nudity • gorgeous apartments on 2 levels

Desert Palms Inn 67-580 E. Palm Canyon Dr., Cathedral City • 324-3000/ (800) 483-6029 • mostly gay men • swimming • also a restaurant • American • some veggie • full bar • huge courtyard • wheelchair access • $8-12

El Mirasol Villas 525 Warm Sands Dr. • 327-5913/ (800) 327-2985• popular • lesbians/gay men • hot tub • swimming • nudity • private

Le Garbo Inn 287 W. Racquet Club • 325-6737 • mostly women • B&B • nudity • lesbian-owned/run

Smoke Tree Inn 1800 SmokeTree Ln. • 327-8355/ (800) 654-6935 • gay-friendly • hot tub • swimming • secluded on 4-1/2 acres

Stardust Hotel 1610 Via Entrada • 323-5043 • gay-friendly • swimming

The Villa Hotel 67-670 Carey Rd., Cathedral City • 328-7211/ (800) 845-5265• popular • lesbians/gay men • hot tub • swimming • individual bungalows

BARS

Backstreet Pub 72-695 Hwy. 111 #A-7, Palm Desert • 341-7966 • 3pm-2am, from noon wknds • lesbians/gay men • neighborhood bar • wheelchair access • women-owned/run

C.C. Construction Co. 68-449 Perez Rd. #10, Cathedral City • 324-4241 • 4pm-2am, from 2pm wknds• popular • dancing/DJ • leather • country/western Sun • wheelchair access

Choices 68-352 Perez Rd. • 321-1145 • 3pm-2am, from noon wknds • lesbians/gay men • dancing/DJ • live shows • patio • wheelchair access

Delilah's 68-657 Hwy. 111, Cathedral C. • 324-3268 • 4pm-2am, clsd Mon-Tue • mostly women • dancing/DJ • live shows • call for events

Richard's 68-599 E. Palm Canyon Dr., Cathedral City • 321-2841 • 10am-2am • lesbians/gay men • also a restaurant • wheelchair access

Spurs 367-37 Cathedral Canyon, Cathedral City • 321-1233 • 2pm-2am • lesbians/gay men • dancing/DJ • country/western • wheelchair access

Streetbar 224 E. Arenas • 320-1266 • 2pm-2am, from 10am wknds • lesbians/gay men • neighborhood bar • wheelchair access

Two Glorias 1117 N. Palm Canyon Dr. • 322-3224 • 10am-2am • popular • mostly gay men • piano bar • also a restaurant • wheelchair access • women-owned/run

RESTAURANTS & CAFES

Bangkok 5 69-930 Hwy. 111, Rancho Mirage • 770-9508 • lunch & dinner, seasonal • Thai • $8-15

Bar & Grill 36-815 Cathedral Canyon Dr., Cathedral City • 770-1290 • 7am-10pm • full bar

Bistro 111 70-065 Hwy. 111, Rancho Mirage • 328-5650 • clsd Sun-Tue • healthy American • some veggie

Buddy's Deli 401 E. Tahquitz Wy. • 325-6102 • beer/wine • kosher deli • wheelchair access

Flamingo Bar & Grill 233 E. Saturnino • 325-4948 • 4pm-1am, seasonal • live shows • piano bar • homecooking • some veggie • full bar • wheelchair access • $6-10

Hamburger Mary's 266 S. Palm Canyon Dr. • 320-5555 • 11am-2am, seasonal • lesbians/gay men • dancing/DJ • live shows • full bar • patio

Maria's Italian Cuisine 67-778 Hwy. 111, Cathedral City • 328-4378 • 5:30pm-9:30pm dinner only, clsd Mon • Italian • plenty veggie • $8-15

Miss Evie's 32-123 Cathedral Canyon • 324-1480 • lunch & dinner, seasonal • full bar

Mortimer's (at the Casablanca Hotel) • 320-4333 • lunch & dinner, clsd Mon • live shows • international • full bar • $15-30

Rainbow Cactus Cafe 212 S. Indian Canyon • 325-3868 • 11am-2am • Mexican • full bar

Palm Springs

Palm Springs has a well-deserved reputation as one of the top resort destinations for lesbian and gay travellers. However, it's a man's world – except during **Dinah Shore Weekend** in late March.

The same is true for this desert resort's bumper crop of gay inns. Most are men only, either in practice or policy. However, there are a few women-only inns. Wherever you're staying, make sure they have a misting machine to take the edge off dry desert summers.

For nightlife, you have **Choices** for dancing with the boys, or **Delilah's** for a drink with the girls. To find out about special events for women, call the **Desert Women's Association**.

The most popular event for women – a sort of informal Lesbian Festival, attracting thousands of lesbians from all over the western United States – is the **Nabisco Dinah Shore Golf Tournament** (call 619-324-4546 for details) in late March. The local lesbian and gay paper, **The Bottom Line**, and LA's **Lesbian News** publish special editions in March just to keep up with all the parties, contests and jubilation.

Palm Springs (619)

LESBIGAY INFO: Gay/Lesbian Alliance of the Desert: 322-8769. Desert Women's Association: 363-7565.

LESBIGAY PAPER: Bottom Line: 323-0552. Life Style Magazine: 321-2685, biweekly gay mag.

WHERE THE GIRLS ARE: Socializing with friends at private parties – you can meet them by getting in touch with a women's social organization like the Desert Women's Association. Vacationers will be staying on E. Palm Canyon near Sunrise Way. If they're not relaxing with the girls at Delilah's, women do hang out at the boys' bars too; try the popular disco C.C. Construction Co., the bar at The Desert Palms Inn, or just about anywhere on Perez Rd.

LESBIGAY AA: 324-4880.

LESBIGAY PRIDE: November. 322-8769

ANNUAL EVENTS: March 25-31, 1996 - Dinah Shore Golf Tournament: 324-4546, one of the biggest gatherings of lesbians on the continent. Easter - The White Party: (310) 659-3555/(213) 874-4007, gay boys. March - Lesbo Expo: 363-7565.

CITY INFO: Palm Springs Visitors Bureau: 778-8418

ATTRACTIONS: Palm Springs Aerial Tramway to the top of Mt. San Jacinto, on Tramway Rd.

TRANSIT: Airport Taxi: 321-4470. Desert City Shuttle: 329-3334. Sun Line Transit Agency: 343-3451.

Red Tomato 68-784 Grove St. at Hwy. 111, Cathedral City • 328-7518 • beer/wine • pizza & pasta • plenty veggie • wheelchair access • $10-15

Robí 78-085 Avenida La Fonda, La Quinta • 564-0544 • dinner only, clsd Mon (seasonal April-Oct) • beer/wine • cont'l • some veggie • wheelchair access • $45

Shame on the Moon 68-805 Hwy. 111, Cathedral City • 324-5515 • 6pm-10:30pm, clsd Mon (summer only) • cont'l • plenty veggie • full bar • wheelchair access • $10-20

Wild Goose 67-938 Hwy. 111, Cathedral City • 328-5775 • from 5:30pm • cont'l/wild game • plenty veggie • full bar • wheelchair access • $20-40

GYMS & HEALTH CLUBS

Athletic Club 543 S. Palm Canyon • 323-7722 • 6am-11pm, til midnight Fri-Sat, til 9pm Sun • gay-friendly

Gold's Gym 40-70 Airport Center Dr. • 322-4653 • 6am-10pm, 8am-8pm Sat, 9am-5pm Sun • gay-friendly

BOOKSTORES & RETAIL SHOPS

Between the Pages 214 E. Arenas Rd., Cathedral City • 320-7158 • 11am-9pm • lesbigay • also espresso bar

Moonlighting 614 E. Sunny Dunes Rd. • 323-8830 • 6pm-2am, til 6am Th-Sun

TRAVEL & TOUR OPERATORS

Journey's Travel 42462 Bob Hope Dr. at Hwy. 111, Rancho Mirage • 340-4545/ (800) 733-3646

Las Palmas Travel 403 N. Palm Canyon Dr. • 325-6311/ (800) 776-6888 • IGTA member

Rancho Mirage Travel 71-428 Hwy. 111, Rancho Mirage • 341-7888/ (800) 369-1073 • IGTA member

SPIRITUAL GROUPS

Christ Chapel of the Desert 4707 E. Sunny Dunes • 327-2795 • 10am Sun, 7:30pm Tue

Unity Church of Palm Springs 815 S. Camino Real • 325-7377 • 11am Sun

PUBLICATIONS

The Bottom Line 1243 Gene Autry Tr. Ste. 121 • 323-0552 • bi-weekly

Hijinx 255 N. El Cielo Rd. • 329-2421 • free lesbigay guide to Palm Springs & desert resorts

Lifestyle Magazine PO Box 2803, Rancho Mirage, 92270 • 321-2685

EROTICA

Black Moon Leather 68-449 Perez Rd. #7, Cathedral City • 770-2925/ (800) 945-3284 • 3pm-2am, from noon wknds

Palo Alto (415)

INFO LINES & SERVICES

Lesbian/Gay/Bisexual Community Center PO Box 8265, Stanford, 94309 • 723-1488 • recorded info

Palo Alto Lesbian Rap 4161 Alma (YMCA) • 583-1649 • 7:30pm Th • social discussion & support group

Peninsula Women's Group (at Two Sisters Bookstore) • 7:30pm Wed

BOOKSTORES & RETAIL SHOPS

Stacey's Bookstore 219 University Ave. • 326-0681 • 9am-9pm, til 10pm Fri-Sat, 11am-6pm Sun • lesbigay

▲ **Two Sisters** 605 Cambridge Ave. , Menlo Park • 323-4778 • 11am-9pm, 10am-5pm Sat, from noon Sun, clsd Mon • women's • wheelchair access • women-owned/run

Pasadena (818)

BARS

Boulevard 3199 E. Foothill Blvd. • 356-9304 • 1pm-2am• popular • mostly gay men • neighborhood bar • piano bar Sun

Club Three-Seven-Seven-Two 3772 E. Foothill Blvd. • 578-9359 • 4pm-2am, from noon Fri, 2pm-10pm Sun • popular • mostly women • dancing/DJ • live bands Fri-Sat • wheelchair access

Encounters 203 N. Sierra Madre Blvd. • 792-3735 • 2pm-2am • mostly gay men • dancing/DJ

Nardi's 665 E. Colorado Blvd. • 449-3152 • 1pm-2am • lesbians/gay men • neighborhood bar • wheelchair access

RESTAURANTS & CAFES

Catavino's Cafe 119 W. Green St. • 578-1764 • lunch & dinner • Mexican • plenty veggie • wheelchair access • $8-12

La Risata 60 N. Raymond (at Union) • 793-9000 • lunch & dinner • Northern Italian • patio • wheelchair access • $10-25

Little Richy's 39 S. Fair Oaks Ave. • 440-0306 • 11am-10pm, clsd Mon • Latin American • some veggie • wheelchair access

BOOKSTORES & RETAIL SHOPS

Page One Books 1200 E. Walnut • 796-8418 • 11am-6:30pm, noon-5pm Sun, clsd Mon • women's • women-owned/ru

Pescadero (415)

ACCOMMODATIONS

Oceanview Farms 515 Bean Hollow Rd. • 879-0698/ (800) 642-9438 • lesbians/ga men • B&B • full breakfast • located on working horse breeding farm

Petaluma (707)

TRAVEL & TOUR OPERATORS

Sunquest Travel Co. 789 Hudis St., Rohnert Park • 588-8747

Placerville (209)

ACCOMMODATIONS

Rancho Cicada Retreat PO Box 225, Plymouth, 95669 • 245-4841 • lesbians/gay men • swimming • nudity • secluded riverside retreat in the Sierra foothills w/ two-person tents & cabin

Pomona (909)

INFO LINES & SERVICES

Gay/Lesbian Community Center Hotlin • 884-5447 • 6:30pm-10pm • info • refe rals

Pomona/San Gabriel Valley Gay/Lesbian Coalition 281 S. Thomas Ste. 505 • 620-8987 • 9am-2pm, clsd Su • rap & support groups • newsletter

BARS

Alibi East 225 E. San Antonio Ave. • 623 9422 • 10am-2am, til 4am Fri-Sat• popu lar • mostly gay men • dancing/DJ • live shows

BVD's 732 W. Holt Ave. • 622-7502 • 10am-2am • mostly gay men • dancing/DJ • piano bar • wheelchair access

Mary's 1047 E. 2nd St. • 622-1971 • 2pm-2am • lesbians/gay men • dancing/DJ • also a restaurant • wheelchair access

Robbie's 390 E. 2nd St. (at College Plaza) • 620-4371 • 6pm-2am, clsd Tue-Wed • lesbians/gay men • dancing/DJ • live shows • men's night Mon • ladies night Th

RESTAURANTS & CAFES

Haven Coffeehouse & Gallery 296 W. 2nd St. • 623-0538 • 11am-midnight • live shows • sandwiches & salads

Redding (916)

BARS

Club 501 1244 California St. (enter rear) • 243-7869 • 6pm-2am • lesbians/gay men • dancing/DJ • food served

Redondo Beach (310)

(see also Los Angeles: West L.A.)

INFO LINES & SERVICES

South Bay Center 2009 Artesia Blvd. Ste. A • 379-2850 • 7pm-10pm Wed & Fri • social/support group

BARS

Dolphin 1995 Artesia Blvd. • 318-3339 • 1pm-2am • mostly gay men • neighborhood bar

J.R. Bryan's 2105 Artesia Blvd. • 371-7859 • 4pm-2am • popular • mostly gay men • dancing/DJ • patio • wheelchair access

Redwood City (415)

BARS

Shouts 2034 Broadway • 369-9651 • 11am-2am • lesbians/gay men • neighborhood bar • wheelchair access

SPIRITUAL GROUPS

MCC of the Peninsula 2124 Brewster Ave. (Unitarian Church) • 368-0188 • 5pm Sun

Riverside (909)

(see also San Bernardino)

BARS

Menagerie 3581 University Ave. • 788-8000 • 4pm-2am • mostly gay men • dancing/DJ • women's night Mon • wheelchair access • women-owned/run

VIP 3673 Merrill Ave. • 784-2370 • 4pm-2am • lesbians/gay men • dancing/DJ • food served • wheelchair access

SPIRITUAL GROUPS

St. Bride's PO Box 1132, 92501 • 369-0992 • 11am Sun • celtic catholic service

Russian River (707)

INFO LINES & SERVICES

Country Inns of the Russian River PO Box 2416, Guerneville, 95446 • (800) 927-4667 • info & referrals for 6 inns

GLBA (Gay/Lesbian Business Association), Guerneville • 869-9000

ACCOMMODATIONS

Applewood-An Estate Inn 13555 Hwy. 116, Guerneville • 869-9093 • gay-friendly • full breakfast • swimming • food served

Avalon 4th & Mill St., Guerneville • 869-9566 • gay-friendly • swimming

The Chalet c/o 48 Henry St., San Francisco, 94114 • (415) 864-5111 • rental home on 1/4 acre sleeps 6 • 4 min. to downtown Guerneville

Cottage at Russian River 6471 Old Trenton Rd., Guerneville • 575-1033 • lesbians/gay men • hot tub • nudity

Faerie Ring Campground 16747 Armstrong Woods Rd., Guerneville • 869-2746 • gay-friendly • campsites • RV • near outdoor recreation • on 14 acres

Fern Falls PO Box 228, Cazadero, 95421 • 632-6108 • lesbians/gay men • hot tub • main house w/deck overlooking creek • guest house • waterfall

Fern Grove Inn 16650 River Rd., Guerneville • 869-9083/ (800) 347-9083 • gay-friendly • swimming • California craftsman cottages circa 1926

Fife's Resort PO Box 45, Guerneville, 95446 • 869-0656/ (800) 734-3371 • popular • lesbians/gay men • cabins • campsites • swimming • also a restaurant • some veggie • full bar • IGTA member • $10-20

Golden Apple Ranch 17575 Fitzpatrick Ln., Occidental • 874-3756 • gay-friendly • also a restaurant • wheelchair access

▲ **Highland Dell Inn** 21050 River Blvd., Monte Rio • 865-1759/ (800) 767-1759 • gay-friendly • full breakfast • swimming • serene retreat on the river

Highlands Resort 14000 Woodland Dr., Guerneville • 869-0333 • popular • lesbians/gay men • hot tub • swimming • nudity • country retreat on 4 wooded acres

Russian River

*T*he Russian River resort area is in the redwood forests of northern California, an hour and a half north of San Francisco. The warm summer days and cool starlit nights have made it a favorite secret getaway for many of San Francisco's lesbians and gays. Despite torrential floods last year that destroyed much of the river town of Guerneville, this resort is making a quick comeback.

Life at 'the River' is laid back. You can take a canoe ride, hike under the redwoods or just lie on the river bank and soak up the sun. There's plenty of camping and RV parking, and even top 40 or country/western dancing for in-town evenings.

'The River' is in the heart of the famous California 'Wine Country'. Plan a tour to the many wineries — don't forget to designate a sober driver, so you can taste the world-class wines as you go. Or just cruise the breathtaking coastline along the Pacific Coast Highway!

And 'The River' becomes a jam-packed lesbian garden of earthly delights during **Women's Weekend** in May and late September.

Russian River   (707)

LESBIGAY INFO: Gay/Lesbian Business Association (GLBA): 869-9000 ext. 8 (24hr touch-tone)

LESBIGAY PAPER: We The People: 526-4910

WHERE THE GIRLS ARE: Guerneville is a small town, so you won't miss the scantily-clad, vacationing women walking toward the bars downtown or the beach.

LESBIGAY AA: Santa Rosa AA 544-1300

ANNUAL EVENTS: May & September - Women's Weekend: 869-9000 ext. 8, ext. 3.

CITY INFO: Russian River Visitors Info: (800) 253-8800

BEST VIEW: Anywhere in Armstrong Woods, the Napa Wine Country and on the ride along the coast on Highway 101.

WEATHER: Summer days are sunny and warm (80°s - 90°s) but usually begin with a dense fog. Winter days have the same pattern but are a lot cooler. Winter nights can be very damp and chilly (low 40°s).

House of A Thousand Flowers 11 Mosswood, Cazadero • 632-5571 • gay-friendly • full breakfast • country B&B overlooking the Russian River

Huckleberry Springs Country Inn PO Box 400, Monte Rio, 95462 • 865-2683/ (800) 822-2683 • gay-friendly • cottages • swimming • IGTA member • women-owned/run

Jim & Rodney's Guest Cottage PO Box 1946, Guerneville, 95446 • 869-1146 • lesbians/gay men • large deck

Mountain Lodge 16350 First St., Guerneville • 869-3722 • lesbians/gay men • hot tub • swimming • condo-style 1-bdrm apartments on the river

Paradise Cove 14711 Armstrong Woods Rd., Guerneville • 869-2706 • lesbians/gay men • hot tub • fireplaces • studio units • decks

Redwood Grove RV Park & Campground 16140 Neely Rd., Guerneville • 869-3670 • gay-friendly

Rio Villa Beach Resort 20292 Hwy. 116, Monte Rio • 865-1143 • gay-friendly • cabins • on the river

Riverbend Campground & RV Park 11820 River Rd., Forestville • 887-7662 • gay-friendly

Russian River Resort (Triple 'R') 16390 4th St., Guerneville • 869-0691/ (800) 417-3767 • lesbians/gay men • hot tub • swimming • also a restaurant • American • full bar • wheelchair access • $5-10

Schoolhouse Canyon Park 12600 River Rd., Guerneville • 869-2311 • open April-Oct • gay-friendly • campsites • RV • private beach

▲ **Villa Messina** 316 Burgundy Rd., Healdsburg • 433-6655 • lesbians/gay men • full breakfast • in-room hot tubs

Village Inn 20822 River Blvd., Monte Rio • 865-2304• popular • gay-friendly • also a restaurant • cont'l • some veggie • full bar • $12-15

Wildwood Resort Retreat Old Cazadero Rd., Guerneville • 632-5321 • gay-friendly • swimming • facilities are for groups of 20 or more

.**The Willows** 15905 River Rd., Guerneville • 869-2824/ (800) 953-2828 • lesbians/gay men • old-fashioned country lodge & campground

Woods Resort 16881 Armstrong Woods Rd., Guerneville • 869-0111/ (800) 479-6637 • lesbians/gay men • cabins • swimming • nudity • full bar • cafe

BARS

Jungle 16135 River Rd., Guerneville • 869-1400 • 4pm-2am, clsd Mon-Wed • popular • lesbians/gay men • dancing/DJ • call for events • wheelchair access

Rainbow Cattle Co. 16220 River Rd., Guerneville • 869-0206 • 6am-2am • popular • mostly gay men • neighborhood bar

RESTAURANTS & CAFES

Breeze-Inn Barb-Q 15640 River Rd., Guerneville • 869-9208/ 869-9209 • popular • take-out & delivery • some veggie • women-owned/run • $5-10

Burdon's 15405 River Rd., Guerneville • 869-2615 • call for hours • popular • lesbians/gay men • cont'l/pasta • plenty veggie • wheelchair access • $10-15

Coffee Bazaar 14045 Armstrong Woods Rd., Guerneville • 869-9706 • 7am-8pm • soups/salads/pastries • cafe

Flavors Unlimited 16450 Main St. (River Rd.), Guerneville • 869-0425 • hours var • custom-blended ice cream • women-owned/run

Hiding Place 9605 Old River Rd., Forestville • 887-9506 • 7am-9pm • homecooking • some veggie • wheelcha access • $5-12

Lalita's 16225 Main St., Guerneville • 869-3238 • 11am-10pm • mostly wome • live shows • Mexican • some veggie • full bar • $5-9

Little Bavaria Restaurant 15025 River Rd., Guerneville • 869-0121 • lunch & dinner, Sun brunch • German/American • some veggie • wheelchair access • $10-15

Mill St. Grill (at Triple 'R' Resort), Guerneville • 869-0691 • lesbians/gay men • full bar • patio • wheelchair access

River Inn Restaurant 16141 Main St., Guerneville • 869-0481 • seasonal • American • wheelchair access • $10-15

Sweet's River Grill 16251 Main St., Guerneville • 869-3383 • 9am-10pm • beer/wine

OOKSTORES & RETAIL SHOPS

Up the River 16212 Main St., Guerneville • 869-3167 • cards • gifts • T-shirts • much more

PIRITUAL GROUPS

Russian River MCC 14520 Armstrong Woods Rd. (Guerneville Community Church), Guerneville • 869-0552 • noon Sun

Sacramento   (916)

NFO LINES & SERVICES

Lambda Community Center 1931 'L' St. • 442-0185 • 10am-7pm, til midnight Fri, clsd wknds • youth groups plus many other groups

Northall Gay AA 2741 34th St. • 454-1100 • 8pm daily

Sacramento Area Career Women's Network 1616 29th St. Ste. 310 • 451-8034 • networking • monthly socials • newsletter

Sacramento Women's Center 1924 'T' St. • 736-6942 • 9am-5pm • employment services & resources

CCOMMODATIONS

Hartley House B&B Inn 700 22nd St. • 447-7829/ (800) 831-5806 • gay-friendly • full breakfast • turn-of-the-century mansion • conference facilities

ARS

Buffalo Club 1831 'S' St. • 442-1087 • 2pm-2am • mostly women • dancing/DJ • also dinner nightly • American • some veggie • wheelchair access • women-owned/run • $5-10

Faces 2000 'K' St. • 448-7798 • 3pm-2am, from 1pm wknds • popular • mostly gay men • dancing/DJ • country/western • wheelchair access

Jammin' Jo's 2721 Broadway • 457-7888 • 4pm-2am • lesbians/gay men • dancing/DJ • also brunch from 10am Sun

Joseph's Town & Country Bar 3514 Marconi • 489-8221 • 4pm-2am • lesbians/gay men • dancing/DJ • live shows • also a restaurant • Italian • some veggie • $7-12

The Mirage 601 15th St. • 444-3238 • 2pm-2am • lesbians/gay men • neighborhood bar • wheelchair access • women-owned/run

The Townhouse 1517 21st St. • 441-5122 • 3pm-2am, from 10am wknds • mostly gay men • neighborhood bar • also dinner Fri-Sat, Sun brunch • wheelchair access

RESTAURANTS & CAFES

Cafe Lambda (at the Lambda Center) • 442-0185 • 8pm-midnight Fri • lesbians/gay men • live shows

Constant Cravings 6494 Broadway • 457-2233 • 6am-8pm, clsd Sun

Ernesto's 1901 16th St. • 441-5850 • 11am-10pm, from 9am wknds • Mexican • full bar

Rick's Dessert Diner 2322 'K' St. • 444-0969 • 10am-11pm, from noon Sun-Mon • coffee & dessert • wheelchair access

GYMS & HEALTH CLUBS

Valentis 921 11th St. • 442-2874 • gay-friendly • also juice bar

BOOKSTORES & RETAIL SHOPS

Films for Days 2300 '0' St. • 448-3456 • lesbigay titles

Lioness Book Store 2224 'J' St. • 442-4657 • 11am-7pm, noon-6pm Sat, til 5pm Sun • women's • wheelchair access • women-owned/run

TRAVEL & TOUR OPERATORS

Aladdin Travel 818 'K' St. Mall • 446-0633/ (800) 655-0633 (in-state only) • IGTA member

Mad About Travel 930 Bell Ave. • 567-1958/ (800) 856-0441

The Sports Leisure Travel 9527-A Folsom Blvd. • 361-2051/ (800) 321-4758 • IGTA member

PUBLICATIONS

Capital Quarterly 3104 '0' St. #400, 95816 • 682-4939

MGW (Mom Guess What) 1725 'L' St. • 441-6397 • bi-monthly • women-owned/run

EROTICA

Goldies I 201 N. 12th St. • 447-5860 • 24hrs • also 2138 Del Paso Blvd. location • 922-0103

L'Amour Shoppe 2531 Broadway • 736-3467

San Bernardino　(909)

(see also Riverside)

INFO LINES & SERVICES

AA Gay/Lesbian • 825-4700 • numerous mgts. for Inland Empire • call for times

Gay/Lesbian Community Center 1580 N. 'D' St. Ste. 7 • 884-5447 • 6:30pm-10pm • raps • counseling • library

Great Outdoors Inland Empire Chapter PO Box 56586, 92517 • 792-2255 • 3rd Th • outdoor social group

Inland Empire Couples PO Box 3023, Rancho Cucamonga, 91729 • 793-5994 • call for mtg. times & location

Project Teen • 335-2005 • 7:30pm Wed • support group for lesbigay teens

BARS

Grand Central 345 W. 7th St. • 889-5204 • 7pm-2am, clsd Mon-Tue • lesbians/gay men • dancing/DJ

Skylark 917 Inland Center Dr. • 884-2404 • noon-2am • lesbians/gay men • dancing/DJ • country/western • patio

RESTAURANTS & CAFES

Green Carnation Coffeehouse 1580 N. 'D' St. Ste. 7 • 384-1940 • 6pm-midnight til 2am Fri-Sat • lesbians/gay men

SPIRITUAL GROUPS

St. Aelred's Parish 1580 N. 'D' St. Ste. 5 • 384-1940 • 11am Sun, 7pm Wed

San Diego　(619)

INFO LINES & SERVICES

AA Gay/Lesbian 1730 Monroe St. • 298-8008 • 10:30am-10pm • Live & Let Live Alano • also contact for Sober Sisters

Center for Women's Studies & Services 2467 'E' St. • 233-8984/ 233-3088 (24hrs) • crisis & workshop center • counseling shelter

Gay/Lesbian Asian Pacific Social Support PO Box 89174, 92138

Gay/Lesbian Association of North County PO Box 2866, Vista, 92085 • 945-2478 • social/support group

Gay/Lesbian Info Line • 294-4636 • 24hrs • touchtone

San Diego

*S*an Diego is a coastal paradise of beaches and foothills. If there is a drawback to San Diego, it's the constant conservative cold front blowing out of nearby Orange County.

Stay at one of the city's quaint lesbian-friendly inns. During the days, follow the tourist circuit: the world-famous **San Diego Zoo** and **Sea World**. Call the **Visitor's Center** for a brochure on all the sites.

Once the sun sets, you're ready to tour the lesbian circuit. Where to begin? Check out San Diego's two lesbian dance bars or two-step it at **Kicker's**. In the mood for theater? Look up **Labrys Productions** (297-0220 8am-5pm), the city's own lesbian theater group, or check out **Diversionary Theatre** (574-1060) for gay & lesbian theater.

In December, don't miss the annual **Lesbian Community Cultural Arts Fest**. Call 281-0406 or 464-3831 for info. In mid-August, there's the **Hillcrest Street Fair**, popular with the many lesbian and gay residents of Hillcrest. And anytime of year there's likely to be a **Shirttails** social for women only. To network, stop in at the **Community Center**.

Lesbian/Gay Men's Community Center 3916 Normal St. • 692-4297 • 9am-10pm • resource information line • center

Lesbians in North County • 439-5286 • Fri night • social group

SAGE of California • 282-1395 • social 1st Wed • seniors' social group

Womancare Clinic 2850 6th Ave. Ste. 311 • 298-9352 • 8:30pm-5pm • feminist healthcare clinic • also mental health referrals

ACCOMMODATIONS

Balboa Park Inn 3402 Park Blvd. • 298-0823/ (800) 938-8181• popular • gay-friendly • charming guest house in the heart of San Diego • wheelchair access

The Beach Place 2158 Sunset Cliffs Blvd. • 225-0746 • lesbians/gay men • hot tub • nudity • 4 blks from beach

Blom House B&B 1372 Minden Dr. • 467-0890 • gay-friendly • charming 1948 cottage style home w/ a magnificent view

Carole's B&B Inn 3227 Grim Ave. • 280-5258 • gay-friendly • hot tub • swimming • comfy early California bungalow

Dmitri's B&B 931 21st St. • 238-5547 • lesbians/gay men • hot tub • swimming • overlooks downtown

Eagle Crest Hotel 3942 8th Ave. • 298-9898 • gay-friendly • gay-owned/run

Elsbree House 5058 Narragansett Ave. • 226-4133 • gay-friendly • B&B

Heritage Park B&B 2470 Heritage Park Row • 239-4738 • gay-friendly • full breakfast • wheelchair access

▲ **Hillcrest Inn Hotel** 3754 5th Ave. • 293-7078/ (800) 258-2280 • lesbians/gay men • international hotel in the heart of Hillcrest • wheelchair access • IGTA member

Keating House 2331 2nd Ave. • 239-8585/ (800) 995-8644 • gay-friendly • full breakfast • graceful 150-yr-old Victorian B&B on Bankers Hill

Park Manor Suites 525 Spruce St. • 291-0999/ (800) 874-2649 • gay-friendly • 1926 hotel

Travelodge 2223 El Cajon Blvd. • 296-2101/ (800) 843-9988 • gay-friendly • swimming • also a restaurant • wheelchair access

San Diego (619)

LESBIGAY INFO: Lesbian/Gay Men's Community Center: 692-4297, 3916 Normal St., 9am-10pm. Gay/Lesbian Info Line: 294-4636. 24hrs. North County Gay/Lesbian Association: 945-2478

LESBIGAY PAPER: Gay/Lesbian Times: 299-6397

WHERE THE GIRLS ARE: Lesbians tend to live near Normal Heights, in the northwest part of the city. But for partying, women go to the bars near I-5, or to Hillcrest to hang out with the boys.

ENTERTAINMENT: Diversionary Theatre. 574-1060. gay & lesbian theater. Labrys Productions, lesbian theater company. 297-0220 (M-F, 8am-5pm). Aztec Bowl, 4356 30th St., North Park, 283-3135

LESBIGAY AA: Live & Let Live Alano Club: 298-8008. 1730 Monroe St., 10:30am-10pm, from 8:30am wknds.

LESBIGAY PRIDE: July. 297-7683

CITY INFO: San Diego Visitors Bureau: 232-3101

ATTRACTIONS: Sea World. San Diego Zoo.

BEST VIEW: Cabrillo National Monument on Point Loma or from a harbor cruise

TRANSIT: Yellow Cab: 234-6161 Radio Cab: 232-6566

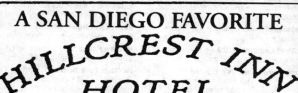

Welcome Inn 1550 E. Washington St. • 298-8251 • gay-friendly • wheelchair access

BARS

▲ **Club Bombay** 3175 India St. (enter from Spruce St.) • 296-6789 • 4pm-2am, from 2pm wknds • popular • mostly women • dancing/DJ • live shows • Sun BBQ • patio • wheelchair access • women-owned/run

Davids' Place 3766 5th Ave. • 294-8908 • 7am-midnight, til 4am wknds • lesbians/gay men • live shows • non-profit coffeehouse for positive people & their friends • patio • wheelchair access

Flame 3780 Park Blvd. • 295-4163 • 5pm-2am, from 4pm Fri • popular • mostly women • dancing/DJ • women-owned/run

Kickers 308 University Ave. • 491-0400 • 7pm-2am • mostly gay men • dancing/DJ • country/western • wheelchair access

The No. 1 Fifth Ave. (no sign) 3845 5th Ave. • 299-1911 • noon-2am • popular • mostly gay men • videos • patio

North Park Country Club 4046 30th St. • 563-9051 • noon-2am • lesbians/gay men • neighborhood bar • beer/wine • wheelchair access

Redwing Bar & Grill 4012 30th St. • 281-8700 • 10am-2am • popular • mostly gay men • neighborhood bar • food served • $5-10

West Coast Production Company 2028 Hancock • 295-3724 • open Wed, Fri-Sat • popular • mostly gay men • dancing/DJ • call for events • patio

RESTAURANTS & CAFES

Bayou Bar & Grill 329 Market St. • 696-8747 • lunch & dinner, Sun champagne brunch • Creole/Cajun • full bar • $12-16

Big Kitchen 3003 Grape St. • 234-5789 • 6am-2pm • American • some veggie • wheelchair access • women-owned/run • $5-10

Cafe Eleven 1440 University Ave. • 260-8023 • lunch & dinner, clsd Mon • country French • some veggie • wheelchair access • $15-20

Cafe Roma UCSD Price Carter #76, La Jolla • 450-2141 • 10am-8pm

California Cuisine 1027 University Ave. • 543-0790 • 11am-10pm, clsd Mon • French/Italian • some veggie • wheelchair access • $15-20

Calliope's Greek Cuisine 3958 5th Ave. • 291-5588 • noon-10pm

City Deli 535 University Ave. • 295-2747 • 7am-midnight, til 2am Fri-Sat • NY deli • plenty veggie • $5-10

Crest Cafe 425 Robinson • 295-2510 • 7am-midnight • American • some veggie • wheelchair access • $5-10

Hamburger Mary's 308 University Ave. • 491-0400 • 11am-10pm, from 8am wknds • American • some veggie • full bar • wheelchair access • $5-10

Liaison 2202 4th Ave. • 234-5540 • lunch & dinner • French country • wheelchair access • $18-24 (prix fixe)

Pasta Al Dente 420-A Robinson • 295-2727 • from 11:30am, from noon Fri-Sun • Italian • some veggie • wheelchair access • $8

Quel Fromage 523 University Ave. • 295-1600 • 6am-11pm

The Sally D's 1288 University Ave. • 291-1288 • 11am-11pm • lesbians/gay men • Italian • some veggie • full bar • patio • wheelchair access • $4-16

GYMS & HEALTH CLUBS

Hillcrest Gym 142 University Ave. • 299-7867 • lesbians/gay men

BOOKSTORES & RETAIL SHOPS

Auntie Helen's 4028 30th St. • 584-8438 • 10am-5pm, clsd Sun-Mon • thrift shop benefits PWAs

Blue Door Bookstore 3823 5th Ave. • 298-8610 • 9am-9pm • large lesbigay section

Eclectic Pleasures 3825 5th Ave. • 298-2260 • 11:30am-9pm, til 8pm Sun • gifts • candles • incense

Groundworks Books UCSD Student Center 0323, La Jolla • 452-9625 • 10am-8pm, til 6pm summer • lesbigay section • alternative • wheelchair access

Moose Leather 2923 Upas St. • 297-6935 • noon-10pm, clsd Sun-Mon

Obelisk the Bookstore 1029 University Ave. • 297-4171 • 11am-10pm, noon-8pm Sun • cafe • lesbigay

TRAVEL & TOUR OPERATORS

Draper World Travel 1551 4th Ave. Ste. 104 • 531-0070/ (800) 477-3888 • IGTA member

Firstworld Travel of Mission Gorge 7443 Mission Gorge Rd. • 265-1916 • contact Dennis

Hillcrest Travel 431 Robinson Ave. • 291-0758/ (800) 748-5502 • IGTA member

Lowe's World Travel 141 University Ste. 4 • 298-8595/ (800) 260-1011

Midas Travel 525 University Ave. • 298-1160 • IGTA member

Sports Travel International Ltd. 4869 Santa Monica Ave. Ste. B • 225-9555/ (800) 466-6004 • IGTA member

Undersea Expeditions PO Box 9455, Pacific Beach, 92169 • 270-2900/ (800) 669-0310 • scuba trips worldwide • IGTA member

SPIRITUAL GROUPS

Anchor Ministries 3441 University Ave. • 284-8654 • 10am Sun • non-denominational

Dignity 4190 Front St. • 645-8240 • 6pm Sun

First Unitarian Church 4190 Front St. • 298-9978 • 10am (summer); 9am & 11am (winter)

MCC 4333 30th St. • 280-4333 • 9am, 11am & 6pm Sun

MCC East County 2770 Glebe Rd., Lemon Grove • 447-4660 • 6pm Sun

Yachad PO Box 3457, 92163 • 492-8616 • Jewish lesbian/gay social group

PUBLICATIONS

Gay/Lesbian Times 3636 5th Ave. Ste. 101 • 299-6397 • weekly

San Diego Dyke/Dyke Review 1010 University Ave. #183, 92103

Update 2801 4th Ave. • 299-4104 • weekly

EROTICA

The Condoms Plus 1220 University Ave. • 291-7400 • 10am-2am, from noon Sun • safer sex gifts for women & men

Crypt 1515 Washington • 692-9499 • 10am-10pm, 2pm-10pm wknds • also 30th St. location • 284-4724

▲ **F St. Bookstore** 2004 University Ave. • 298-2644 • 24hrs

▲ **F St. Bookstore** 3112 Midway Dr. • 221-0075 • 24hrs

▲ **F St. Bookstore** 4626 Albuquerque • 581-0400 • 24hrs

▲ **F St. Bookstore** 751 4th Ave. • 236-0841 • 24hrs

▲ **F St. Bookstore** 7865 Balboa Ave., Kearney Mesa • 292-8083 • 24hrs

▲ **F St. Bookstore** 7998 Miramar Rd. • 549-8014 • 24hrs

San Francisco (415)

San Francisco is divided into 7 geographical areas:

OVERVIEW

CASTRO

SOUTH OF MARKET

HAIGHT, FILLMORE & WEST

MISSION DISTRICT

POLK STREET AREA

DOWNTOWN

Overview

INFO LINES & SERVICES

18th St. Services • 861-4898 • 9am-7pm • lesbigay AA mtgs. at 15th & Market • offices at 217 Church St.

AA Gay/Lesbian • 621-1326

APS (Asian Pacific Sisters) PO Box 170596, 94117-0596 • 227-0946 • social/support group for lesbian/bi women of Asian/Pacific Islander descent • special events • newsletter

BACW (Bay Area Career Women) 55 New Montgomery St. Ste. 606, 94105 • 495-5393 • 9am-5pm • lesbian professional group

The Bay Area Bisexual Network • 703-7977

Dyke TV Channel 53 • 6pm Sun • 'weekly half hour TV show produced by lesbians for lesbians'

Frameline 346 9th St. • 703-8650/ (800) 869-1996 (out-of-state only) • lesbigay media arts foundation that sponsors the annual SF Internat'l Lesbian/Gay Film Festival each June

Gay/Lesbian Sierrans • 281-5666 • outdoor group

GELAAM (Gente Latina de Ambiente) 995 Market St. #1114, 94131 • 243-9534 • lesbigay Latino group • events • newsletter

Lesbian/Gay Switchboard • (510) 841-6224 • 10am-10pm Mon-Fri • info • referrals • rap line

LGBA (Lesbian/Gay/Bisexual Alliance) SFSU Student Center #M-100-A, 1650 Holloway Ave. • (510) 338-1952 • hours vary

LINKS PO Box 420989, 94142 • 703-7159 • S/M play parties & calendar

Lyon-Martin Women's Health Services 1748 Market St. Ste. 201 • 565-7667 • sliding scale medical services for women • also support groups & other services

LYRIC (Lavender Youth Recreation/ Information Cntr) 3543 18th St. #31 • 703-6150/ (800) 246-7743 (out-of-state only) • support & social groups • also crisis counseling for lesbigay youth under 24 at 863-3636 (hotline #)

The National Leather Association 584 Castro St. Ste. 444 • 863-2444 • nat'l assoc. for leather, S/M, fetish community

Pervert Scouts 3288 21st St. #19 • 285-7985 • women only • casual social group for women interested in S/M • bi-weekly mtgs • call for location • newcomers welcome

San Francisco Gender Information PO Box 423602, 94142 • send $3 & SASE for listings of transgender resources in northern CA

WOMEN'S ACCOMMODATIONS

One In Ten Guesthouse • 664-0748 • women only • kitchen use • right on the beach in the sunset area • near Golden Gate Park

ACCOMMODATIONS

American Property Exchange 170 Page St. • 863-8484/ (800) 747-7784 • daily, weekly & monthly furnished rentals in San Francisco & New York • women-owned/run

Mi Casa Su Casa • (510) 268-8534/ (800) 215-2272 • international home exchange network

San Francisco

(415)

LESBIGAY INFO: Lesbian/Gay Switchboard: (510) 841-6224. 10am-10pm Mon-Fri.

LESBIGAY PAPER: Bay Times: 626-8121. Bay Area Reporter (BAR): 861-5019. Odyssey Magazine: 621-6514, party paper. Dykespeak/Icon: 282-0942.

WHERE THE GIRLS ARE: Younger, radical dykes call the Mission or the lower Haight home, while upwardly-mobile couples stake out Bernal Heights and Noe Valley. Hip, moneyed dykes live in the Castro. The East Bay is home to lots of lesbian feminists, older lesbians and lesbian moms (see East Bay listings).

ENTERTAINMENT: Luna Sea: 863-2989, 2940 16th St., women's performance space. Theatre Rhinoceros: 861-5079, 2926 16th St., live queer theater. Josie's Cabaret: 861-7933, 3583 16th St., live. Castro Theater: 621-6120, rep film. Roxie Theater: 957-1212, rep film.

LESBIGAY AA: 621-1326

LESBIGAY PRIDE: June. 864-3733, Dyke March: Sat. night before Pride March.

ANNUAL EVENTS: March - AIDS Dance-a-thon: (415) 392-9255, AIDS benefit dance at the Moscone Center. April 19-21, 1996 - Readers/Writers Conference: 431-0891. May - California AIDS Ride: (800) 474-3395, AIDS benefit bike ride from San Francisco to L.A. June - S.F. Int'l Lesbian/Gay Film Festival: (415) 703-8650, a slew of films about us. July - Up Your Alley Fair: 861-3247, local SM/leather street fair held in Dore Alley, South-of-Market. October - Castro St. Fair: (415) 467-3354, street fair co-founded by Harvey Milk. September - Folsom St. Fair, 861-3247. Huge SM/leather street fair, topping a week of kinky events. Festival of Babes: (510) 452-6252, lesbian soccer tournament.

CITY INFO: San Francisco Visitors Bureau: 391-2000

BEST VIEW: After a great Italian meal in North Beach, go to the top floor of the North Beach parking garage on Vallejo near Stockton, next to a police station. If you're in the Castro or the Mission, head for Dolores Park, at Dolores and 18th-20th St. Other good views: Kirby Cove (a park area to the left just past Golden Gate Bridge in Marin), Coit Tower, Twin Peaks, the beach at sunset.

WEATHER: It's called the Fog City for a reason; every afternoon at 4pm, the fog descends, bringing temperatures down drastically until 9 or 10pm when the fog dissipates. Rainy and 40-50s January through April, warm days & cold nights June-August, and a beautiful summer follows in September-October.

TRANSIT: Yellow Cab: 626-2345 Luxor Cab: 282-4141. Quake City Shuttle: 255-4899. Muni: 673-6864. Bay Area Rapid Transit (BART): 673-6864, subway.

San Francisco

San Francisco may be a top tourist destination because of its cable cars, beatniks, quaint beauty, and the Haight-Ashbury district, but we know what really makes it shine: its legendary population of queers. So unless kitsch is your thing, skip Fisherman's Wharf, Pier 39, and the cable cars, and head for the Mission, the Castro, Noe Valley, or South of Market (SoMa).

Any lesbian walking along Valencia between Market St. and 24th St. will spot hot women of all sizes and colors. This rapidly gentrifying neighborhood known as Valencia Corridor borders the gay-boy Castro area and the Mission, one of San Francisco's Latino neighborhoods. This intersection of cultures results in a truly San Franciscan mix of punk dykes, dykes of color, lesbian-feminists, working class straights and funky artists - and the yuppies who flock to see them, while sampling the exotic restaurants along Valencia.

Your first stop in the Mission should be either punk dyke hangout **Red Dora's Bearded Lady Café & Gallery** or resource center **The Women's Building**. After that, rush to **Good Vibrations** women's sex toy store before they close at 7pm. Pick up a famous "San Francisco Mission-Style Burrito" (as they're advertised in New York these days) at one of the many cheap and delicious taquerias. The Mission has lots of fun queer performance at places like **Build** and **Brava!** and **Luna Sea** – check the bi-weekly **Bay Times** calendar. If you're into artsy or radical video, get a calendar from **Artists' Television Access** (824-3890). Ready to relax? Stop in **Osento**, the women's bathhouse.

You'll also find lots of lesbians in nearby Noe Valley, though this area tends to be a 'couples heaven' for liberal professionals. If that's your dream, call Bay Area Career Women about their upcoming social events, or drop in on their TGIF social, downtown. And enjoy an afternoon in the many quirky shops and cafés along 24th St.

If you cruise the Castro, you'll be surprised how many sisters – ranging from executives to queer chicks – you'll see walking the streets of what was the 'Boys' Town' of the 1970s. Be sure to drop in at **Urban Womyn's Land** on 18th at Dolores, the only official dyke space in the Castro, or **The Café** for a game of pool or girl-watching from the balcony (Mondays especially). The Castro also hosts two great 24-hour diners – Bagdad Café and Sparky's – as well as **Josie's Cabaret & Juice Joint**, great for vegetarian brunch, comedy and shows. For lesbigay-centric films, don't miss **The Castro** (621-6120).

You might also want to check out the women's S/M scene in this kinky city: **Stormy Leather** is the only women-run fetish store we know, and has a great bulletin board papered with flyers of interest. Or call the **Pervert Scouts** hotline to find out when their next "Bowling for Dildoes" or other fun events will be. You might also want to finally get that piercing you've been thinking about at a queer-friendly piercing parlors – our favorite is **Body Manipulations**, right between the Mission and the Castro on 16th St. at Guerrero.

SoMa also contains lots of dancing, poetry and kink for the daring. For the less daring, there's the ever-popular, more mainstream **G-Spot** (Girl-Spot) danceclub on Saturday nights, **Diva** at The Transmission (11th & Folsom) on the 3rd Friday, the Top 40 **Club Q** on the 1st Friday of the month, or **The Box** on Thursday nights. Or try **Comme Nous**, a racially diverse women's speakeasy below **CoCo's** on Saturday and Tuesday nights. On Sunday nights, this location hosts **Sister Spit**, a poetry slam for dykes. For the more adventurous, **Faster Pussycat** hosts dyke bands on Wednesday nights, while the truly queer **Litterbox** mixes it up with dykes, fags, bis & straights on Friday nights at **Cat's Alley Bar** (Clementine & 8th).

As of this writing, the Mission is home to two hip Sunday night dyke danceclubs: **Red** for women of color, at **Blondie**'s, and **Muffdive** at **Casanova**, just across the street!

And for a truly hot dance party, call the **ABLUNT** hotline to find out when their latest dance for Asian, Black and Latina women (and their friends) will be. For other nightlife, check out the latest issue of **Odyssey**, the party paper with the scoop for the club-going "Jet Girl," or **ICON**, the city's only lesbian newspaper. And remember – all of these nightclubs are here one night, gone the next – so before you get all dressed up, call to make sure it's still there!

If you're a fan of Diane Di Prima, Anne Waldman, Allen Ginsberg or other beatniks, **City Lights Bookstore** in North Beach is a required pilgrimage. Afterward, have a drink or an espresso at beatnik hangout **Café Vesuvius**, just across Jack Kerouac Alley from City Lights.

Sounds like a lot? Well, this is just the tip of the areola.

You could still explore the many other women's events and groups throughout the rest of 'The City' and the East Bay. For instance, the critically acclaimed **Women's Philharmonic** (543-2297).

Western Exposure PO Box 2116, Berkeley, 94702 • (510) 869-4395 • arranges accommodations in private homes in Bay Area

DANCE CLUBS

ABLUNT Hotline (Asians, Blacks, & Latinas Uniting New Tribes) • 703-0862 • 1st & 3rd Wed • popular • multi-racial • roving dance parties

Club Q • 647-8258 • popular • women only • roving dance party DJ'd by mixtress Page Hodel

MT Productions • 337-4962 • women's dance parties including Girl Spot & Club Skirts

TRAVEL & TOUR OPERATORS

Kent's Convertible Tours PO Box 26566, 94126 • 561-9155 • 24hr recorded info • comfy unique Northern California tours

SPIRITUAL GROUPS

Bay Area Pagan Assemblies • (408) 559-4242

Dharma Sisters • 824-4142 • events & weekly meditations for lesbians & bi women interested in practicing Buddhism

Dignity PO Box 11280, 94110 • 681-2491 • lesbigay Catholic services

Evangelicals Concerned • 621-3297 • also in East Bay & San Jose • sponsors annual women's retreat

Lutherans Concerned 566 Vallejo St., 94133 • 956-2069

Reclaiming PO Box 14404, 94110 • 929-9249 • pagan info line & network

PUBLICATIONS

B.A.R. (Bay Area Reporter) 395 9th Ave., 94103 • 861-5019 • weekly

Cuir Underground 3288 21st St. #19, 94110 • 487-7622 • monthly • S/M newspaper w/ complete calendar of events • e-mail: cuirpaper@aol.com • $20/year

▲ **Curve (formerly Deneuve)** 2336 Market St #15, 94114 • 863-6538 • monthly • popular • lesbian magazine (see ad front color section)

Fat Girl 2215-R Market St. #193, 94114 • 550-7202 • fat dyke 'zine

FBN (Feminist Bookstore News) PO Box 882554, 94188 • 626-1556 • bi-monthly • nat'l journal about feminist bookstores & publications

▲ **Girlfriends** 3415 Cesar Chavez Ste. 101, 94110 • 648-9464 • bi-monthly • lesbian lifestyle magazine (see inside back cover)

GirlJock PO Box 882723, 94188-2723 • 282-6833 • pan-athletic magazine for lesbians (see ad in front color section)

▲ **ICON: The Thinking Lesbians Newspaper** 4104 24th St. #181 • 648-6251, formerly

Odyssey Magazine 584 Castro St. #302, 94114 • 621-6514 • all the dish on SF's club scene

San Francisco Bay Times 288 7th St., 94103 • 626-8121 • bi-weekly • a 'must read' for Bay Area resources & personals

Women's Sports Connection PO Box 31580 , 94131-0580 • general women's quaterly newsletter • provides game schedules & ticket info

Castro Area

INFO LINES & SERVICES

Gay/Lesbian Outreach to Elders 1853 Market St. • 626-7000 • 10am-2pm

Harvey Milk Public Library 3555 16th St. • 554-9445 • 1pm-6pm Mon, Th-Fri, from 10am Tue, 1pm-9pm Wed

WOMEN'S ACCOMMODATIONS

▲ **House O' Chicks Guesthouse** • 861-9849 • women only • women-owned/run

Nancy's Bed • 239-5692 • women only • kids okay • no smoking • private home

ACCOMMODATIONS

24 Henry 24 Henry St. • 864-5686/ (800) 900-5686 • mostly gay men • one-bdrm apt. also available 1 blk from guesthouse • IGTA member

▲ **Albion House Inn** 135 Gough St. • 621-0896/ (800) 625-2466 • gay-friendly

Anna's Three Bears 114 Divisadero St. • 255-3167/ (800) 428-8559 • gay-friendly • rental apt B&B • IGTA member

The Beck's Motor Lodge 2222 Market St. • 621-8212 • gay-friendly

Dolores Park Inn 3641 17th St. • 621-0482 • gay-friendly • full breakfast • historical two-story Italianate Victorian mansion

Haus Kleebauer 225 Clipper St. • 821-3866 • gay-friendly • full breakfast • no smoking • storybook-like Victorian home • IGTA member

Inn on Castro 321 Castro St. • 861-0321
• lesbians/gay men • full breakfast • B&B
known for its hospitality & friendly
atmosphere

Le Grenier 347 Noe St. • 864-4748 • les-
bians/gay men • B&B • women-
owned/run

▲ **Pension SF** 1668 Market St. • 864-1271 •
shared baths • also a restaurant

▲ **San Francisco Cottage** 224 Douglass St.
• 861-3220 • lesbians/gay men • self-
catering cottage & studio apt

Studio 285 285 Church St. • 487-0677/
(800) 261-8495 • gay-friendly • B&B

Travelodge Central 1707 Market St. •
621-6775 • gay-friendly

▲ **The Villa** 379 Collingwood St. • 282-1367/
(800) 358-0123 • lesbians/gay men •
swimming

Willows B&B Inn 710 14th St. • 431-4770
• mostly gay men • B&B in the true tradition of European country inns • IGTA
member

BARS

▲ **The Cafe** 2367 Market St. • 861-3846 •
noon-2am • popular • lesbians/gay men
• dancing/DJ • deck overlooking Castro &
Market Sts. • more women Fri night

Cafe du Nord 2170 Market St. • 861-
5016 • 4pm-2am • popular • gay-friendly
• supper club • some veggie • live jazz •
$5-10

Elephant Walk 18th & Castro Sts.• popular • mostly gay men • piano bar • food
served

Josie's Cabaret & Juice Joint 3583 16th
St. • 861-7933 • call for events • popular
• lesbians/gay men • live shows •
cabaret • food served • plenty veggie •
$8-12

The Metro 3600 16th St. • 703-9750 •
3pm-2am • popular • mostly gay men •
also a restaurant • Chinese • karaoke
Tue

The Mint 1942 Market St. • 626-4726 •
2pm-2am, 11am-2am wknds • popular •
lesbians/gay men • karaoke • videos •
also a restaurant

Moby Dick's 4049 18th St. • mostly gay
men • neighborhood bar • videos

Phoenix 482 Castro St. • 552-6827 • noon-2am• popular • mostly gay men • dancing/DJ • some Latinas

Uncle Bert's Place 4086 18th St. • 431-8616 • 6am-2am • mostly gay men • neighborhood bar • patio

RESTAURANTS & CAFES

Amazing Grace 216 Church St. • 626-6411 • 11am-10pm • lesbians/gay men • vegetarian • wheelchair access • $5-10

Anchor Oyster Bar 579 Castro St. • 431-3990 • lesbians/gay men • beer/wine • seafood • some veggie • women-owned/run • $10-20

Bad Man Jose's 4077 18th St. • 861-1706 • healthy Mexican • some veggie • $5-7

Bagdad Cafe 2295 Market St. • 621-4434 • 24hrs • lesbians/gay men • American • some veggie • $5-10

Cafe Flore 2298 Market St. • 621-8579 • 8am-11:30pm, til midnight Fri-Sat • popular • lesbians/gay men • food served • American • some veggie • patio • $5-8

Cafe Sanchez 3998 Army St., Noe Valley • 641-5683 • 8am-11pm, clsd Mon • women-owned/run

Caffe Luna Piena 558 Castro St. • 621-2566 • lesbians/gay men • Californian • patio

China Court 599 Castro • 626-5358 • 5pm-11pm • beer/wine • Chinese • some veggie • $5-10

Chloe's Cafe 1399 Church St., Noe Valley • 648-4116 • 8am-3:30pm, til 4pm wknds • popular • come early for the excellent weekend brunch

Counter Culture 2073 Market St. • 621-7488 • gourmet take-out • some veggie • $5-10

Cove Cafe 434 Castro St. • 626-0462 • 7am-10pm • lesbians/gay men • American • plenty veggie • wheelchair access • $8-12

Eric's Chinese Restaurant 1500 Church St., Noe Valley • 282-0919 • 11am-9pm • popular • some veggie • $7-12

Hot 'N Hunky 4039 18th St. • 621-6365 • 11am-11pm • popular • lesbians/gay men • hamburgers • some veggie • $5-10

It's Tops 1801 Market St. • 431-6395 • 7am-3pm • diner • $5-7

Jumpin' Java 139 Noe St. • 431-5282 • 7am-10pm

Just Desserts 248 Church St. • 626-5774 • 7am-11pm • popular • lesbians/gay men • cafe • great patio

La Paloma 4416 18th St. • 863-2237 • café bakery • dinner Wed-Sun

Little Italy 4109 24th St. • 821-1515 • dinner only • popular • beer/wine • plenty veggie • $15-20

M&L Market (May's) 691 14th St. • 431-7044 • popular • great huge sandwiches • some veggie

Ma Tante Sumi 4243 18th St. • 552-6663 • cont'l cuisine w/ a Japanese accent

Orbit Room Cafe 1900 Market St. • 252-9525 • til midnight, til 2am Fri-Sat • popular • beer/wine • great view of Market St. & trolley cars

Patio Cafe 531 Castro St. • 621-4140 • lesbians/gay men • American • outdoor dining • $10-20

Pozole 2337 Market St. • 626-2666 • Mexican specialties • some veggie • $5-10

Sausage Factory 517 Castro St. • 626-1250 • noon-1am • beer/wine • pizza & pasta • some veggie • $8-15

Sparky's 242 Church St. • 626-8666 • 24hrs • diner • some veggie • $8-12

Valentine's Cafe 1793 Church St., Noe Valley • 285-2257 • 6:30am-7pm, 8am-5pm wknds • brkfst, lunch, & take-out dinners • plenty veggie

Welcome Home 464 Castro St. • 626-3600 • 8am-11pm • lesbians/gay men • beer/wine • homestyle • some veggie • $7-12

Without Reservations 460 Castro St. • 861-9510 • 7am-2am • lesbians/gay men • some veggie • wheelchair access • $7-12

Zuni Cafe 1658 Market St. • 552-2522 • clsd Mon • popular • upscale cont'l/Mediterranean • full bar • $30-40

GYMS & HEALTH CLUBS

Market Street Gym 2301 Market St. • 626-4488 • popular • lesbians/gay men

Woman's Training Center 2164 Market St. • 864-6835 • popular • women only

BOOKSTORES & RETAIL SHOPS

A Different Light 489 Castro St. • 431-0891 • 10am-11pm, til midnight Fri-Sat • popular • bookstore & queer information clearinghouse

Books Etc. 538 Castro St. • 621-8631

Botanica 1478 Church St. at 27th, Noe Valley • 285-0612 • 11am-7pm • witches' supply store

Does Your Mother Know? 4079 18th St. • 864-3160 • 10am-8pm • popular • cards • T-shirts

The Gauntlet 2377 Market St. • 431-3133 • noon-7pm • piercing parlor • jewelry

Headlines 557 Castro • 626-8061 • clothes • cards • novelties

Headlines for Women 549 Castro St. • 252-1280 • 10am-9pm • clothing • jewelry

Image Leather 2199 Market St. • 621-7551 • 9am-10pm, 11am-7pm Sun • customized leather

Just for Fun 3982 24th St., Noe Valley • 285-4068 • 9am-9pm, til 7pm Sun • gift shop

Lodestar Books 313 Noe St. • 864-3746 • noon-10pm, til 11pm Fri-Sat • metaphysical & used • small lesbigay section

Rolo 2351 Market St. • 431-4545 • popular • designer labels • also 450 Castro location • 626-7171

Under One Roof 2362 Market St. • 252-9430 • 11am-7pm • 100% of sales are donated for AIDS relief

TRAVEL & TOUR OPERATORS

Adventure Walks 2226 15th St., 94114 • 252-9485 • custom tailored private walking tours w/ San Francisco resident • IGTA member

Cruisin' the Castro 375 Lexington St. • 550-8110 • guided walking tour of the Castro • IGTA member

Now, Voyager 4406 18th St. • 626-1169/(800) 255-6951 • IGTA member

▲ **Orion Travel** 563 Castro St. • 864-3233/(800) 552-3326 • IGTA member

Passport to Leisure 2265 Market St. • 621-8300 • IGTA member

Winship Travel 2321 Market St. • 863-2555/(800) 545-2557 • ask for Susan • IGTA member

SPIRITUAL GROUPS

Congregation Sha'ar Zahav 220 Danvers St. • 861-6932 • 8:15pm Fri & 10:30am 2nd Sat • lesbian/gay synagogue

MCC of San Francisco 150 Eureka St. • 863-4434 • 9am, 11am & 7pm Sun

SEX CLUBS

Ecstasy Lounge • 985-5252 • call for times & locations • lesbian sex club

South of Market

ACCOMMODATIONS

The Victorian Hotel 54 4th St. • 986-4400/ (800) 227-3804 • gay-friendly • 1913 landmark hotel

BARS

The Box 715 Harrison St. • Th only • popular • lesbians/gay men • dancing/DJ • multi-racial

Brain Wash 1122 Folsom St. • 431-9274 • 8am-11pm, til 1am Fri-Sat • popular • gay-friendly • beer/wine • laundromat & cafe

Club Universe 177 Townsend • 985-5241 • 9:30pm-7am Sat • lesbians/gay men • dancing/DJ • alternative

Coco's 139 8th St. (entrance on Minna) • 626-2337 • mostly women • multi-racial • live shows • call for events

Diva 314 11th St. • 487-6305 • monthly • lesbian dance parties • call for events

Endup 401 6th St. • 495-9550 • popular • mostly gay men • dancing/DJ • multi-racial • many different theme nights • esp. popular Sun mornings • patio

Girl Spot (G-Spot) 399 9th St. (at The Stud) • 337-4962 • 9pm Sat only • popular • mostly women • dancing/DJ • go-go dancers

Junk 399 9th St. (at The Stud) • 621-5877 • 9pm-2am Th • popular • mostly women • dancing/DJ • alternative • dancing & slamming

Pleasuredome 177 Townsend (at 3rd St.) • 255-6434x69 • Sun night dance club • popular • mostly gay men • dancing/DJ • call hotline for details

Rawhide II 280 7th St. • 621-1197 • noon-2am • popular • mostly gay men • dancing/DJ • country/western

Stud 399 9th St. • 863-6623 • 5pm-2am • popular • gay-friendly • dancing/DJ • theme nights • women's night Th & Sun • mostly men Wed

Twenty Tank Brewery 316 11th St. • 255-9455 • gay-friendly • food served • some veggie • microbrewery

RESTAURANTS & CAFES

Bistro Roti 155 Steuart • 495-6500 • lunch & dinner • country French • full bar • $15-20

Caribbean Zone 55 Natoma St. • 541-9465 • popular • some veggie • festive decor • cocktails • $7-15

Eichelberger's 2742 17th St. at Florida • 863-4177 • 5pm-11pm • neo-American • some veggie • cabaret Sat • $8-15

Fringale 570 4th St. • 543-0573 • lunch & dinner • Mediterranean • wheelchair access

Half Shell 64 Rausch St. • 552-7677 • lunch & dinner • lesbians/gay men • seafood • some veggie • full bar • $8-15

Hamburger Mary's 1582 Folsom St. • 626-5767 • 10am-2am, clsd Mon • popular • American • some veggie • full bar • $7-15

Line Up 398 7th St. • 861-2887 • 11am-10pm • Mexican • some veggie • $8-15

Lulu 816 Folsom St. • 495-5775 • lunch & dinner • popular • upscale Mediterranean • some veggie • full bar • wheelchair access • $12-20

Slow Club 2501 Mariposa • 241-9390 • 7am-2am, clsd Sun • full bar

Wa-Ha-Ka! 1489 Folsom • 861-1410 • beer/wine • Mexican • plenty veggie • $5-10

BOOKSTORES & RETAIL SHOPS

Leather Etc. 1201 Folsom St. • 864-7558 • 11am-7pm

TRAVEL & TOUR OPERATORS

Above & Beyond Travel 330 Townsend • 284-1666/ (800) 397-2681 • IGTA member

Castro Travel Company 435 Brannan Ste. 214 • 357-0957/ (800) 861-0957 • IGTA member

China Basin Travel Center 185 Berry St. • 777-4747

EROTICA

A Taste of Leather 317-A 10th St. • 252-9166/ (800) 367-0786 • noon-8pm

Mr. S Leather 310 7th St. • 863-7764 • 11am-7pm, noon-6pm Sun • erotic goods • leather • latex

Rob Gallery 22 Shotwell • 252-1198 • leather • latex • artwork

Stormy Leather 1158 Howard St. • 626-6783 • noon-6pm • leather • latex • toys • magazines • women-owned/run

Haight, Fillmore & West

WOMEN'S ACCOMMODATIONS

Sappho's Fulton at Fillmore St. • 775-3243 • women only • hostel & transitional housing • $15

ACCOMMODATIONS

Alamo Square Inn 719 Scott St. • 922-2055/ (800) 345-9888 • gay-friendly • full breakfast • 1895 Queen Anne & 1896 Tudor Revival Victorian mansions

Archbishops Mansion 1000 Fulton St. • 563-7872/ (800) 543-5820 • popular • gay-friendly • one of San Francisco's grandest homes

Bock's B&B 1448 Willard St. • 664-6842 • gay-friendly • restored 1906 Edwardian residence • IGTA member • women-owned/run

Carl St. Unicorn House 156 Carl St. • 753-5194 • gay-friendly • 1895 Victorian house • women-owned/run

▲ **The Chateau Tivoli** 1057 Steiner St. • 776-5462/ (800) 228-1647 • popular • gay-friendly • historic San Francisco B&B

Gough Hayes Hotel 417 Gough St. • 431-9131

Holiday Lodge 1901 Van Ness Ave. • 776-4469/ (800) 367-8504 • gay-friendly • swimming • tropical resort & pool oasis in the heart of San Francisco • IGTA member

Hotel Majestic 1500 Sutter St. • 441-1100/ (800) 869-8966 • gay-friendly • one of SF's earliest grand hotels • also a restaurant • Mediterranean • some veggie • full bar • $15-20

Inn at the Opera 333 Fulton St. • 863-8400/ (800) 325-2708 • gay-friendly • B&B • also a restaurant • Mediterranean

Lombard Plaza Motel 2026 Lombard St. • 921-2444 • gay-friendly

The Mansions 2220 Sacramento St. • 929-9444/ (800) 826-9398 • gay-friendly • full breakfast

Metro Hotel 319 Divisadero St. • 861-5364 • gay-friendly • food served

▲ **The Queen Anne Hotel** 1590 Sutter St. • 441-2828/ (800) 227-3970• popular • gay-friendly • beautifully restored 1890 landmark • IGTA member

BARS

Alta Plaza 2301 Fillmore • 922-1444 • 11am-2am • mostly gay men • professional • also a restaurant • cont'l • some veggie • $10-15

Hayes & Vine 377 Hayes St. • 626-5301 • 4pm-midnight, til 10pm Sun, clsd Mon • lesbians/gay men • wine bar

Chateau Tivoli

B&B

**San Francisco's
opulent landmark mansion
800-228-1647
415-776-5462**

The Lion Pub 2062 Divisadero St. • 567-6565 • noon-2am • mostly gay men • professional • theme nights

Marlena's 488 Hayes St. • 864-6672 • 11am-2am • lesbians/gay men • neighborhood bar • wheelchair access

Noc Noc 557 Haight St. • 861-5811 • 5pm-2am • gay-friendly • beer/wine

RESTAURANTS & CAFES

Blue Muse 409 Gough St. • 626-7505 • 7am-11pm • cont'l • some veggie • $10-15

Cha Cha Cha's 1805 Haight St. • 386-5758 • popular • Cuban/Cajun • excellent sangria • worth the long wait!

Charpe's Grill 131 Gough St. • 621-6766 • dinner nightly • American • some veggie • full bar • $10-15

Geva's Caribbean 482 Hayes St. • 863-1220 • dinner

Greens Fort Mason • 771-6222 • dinners, Sun brunch, clsd Mon • popular • gourmet prix fixe vegetarian • $20-40

Ivy's 398 Hayes St. • 626-3930 • lunch & dinner • vegetarian • $15-25

Kan Zaman 1793 Haight • 751-9656 • noon-1am, from 6pm Mon • beer/wine • Mediterranean • some veggie • hookahs & tobacco available

Mad Magda's Russian Tearoom & Cafe 579 Hayes St. • 864-7654 • popular • lesbians/gay men • eclectic crowd • magic garden • tarot & palm readers daily

Oppenheimer 2050 Divisadero St. • 563-0444 • dinner nightly, clsd Sun-Mon • popular

BOOKSTORES & RETAIL SHOPS

Body Manipulations 3234 16th St. • 621-0408 • noon-6pm • piercing (walk-in basis) • jewelry

La Riga 1391 Haight St. • 552-1525 • leather

Mainline Gifts 1928 Fillmore St. • 563-4438 • 10am-6pm, til 9pm Th-Fri

Nomad 1881 Hayes St. • 563-7771 • 11am-7pm • piercing (walk-in) • jewelry

EROTICA

▲ **Romantasy** 199 Moulton St. • 673-3137 • 11am-7pm • books • videos • toys • clothing • women-owned/run

Mission District

INFO LINES & SERVICES

21 Bernice St. Playhouse 21 Bernice St. • 863-5946 • queer arts & performance space

Brava! 2180 Bryant St. (at 20th) • 641-7657 • culturally diverse performances by women

Luna Sea 2940 16th St. Rm. 216-C • 863-2989 • lesbian performances

The Marsh 1062 Valencia (at 22nd St.) • 641-0235 • queer-positive theater

Theatre Rhinoceros 2926 16th St. (at Van Ness) • 861-5079 • popular • lesbi-gay theater

Urban Womyn's Land 3690 18th St. • 626-2161 • 7pm-10pm Wed & Fri, from 8pm Th, from noon wknds • chem-free dyke-space • site of many mtgs.

Women's Building 3543 18th St. • 431-1180 • 9am-7pm Mon-Fri, later for meetings • space for many women's organizations • social/support groups • housing & job listings • beautiful murals

ACCOMMODATIONS

▲ **Andora Inn** 2434 Mission • 282-0337/ (800) 967-9219 • lesbians/gay men • guesthouse • no smoking • also a restaurant • expanded cont'l breakfast • parking • room service • near Castro & public transportation • IGTA member

▲ **Inn San Francisco** 943 S. Van Ness Ave. 641-0188/ (800) 359-0913 • popular • gay friendly • hot tub • fireplaces • patio • IGTA member

BARS

El Rio 3158-A Mission St. • 282-3325 • gay-friendly • neighborhood bar • mostly Latino-American • live bands • popular Sun afternoons • patio

Esta Noche 3079 16th St. • 861-5757 • 2pm-2am • mostly gay men • dancing/DJ • mostly Latino-American • live shows • salsa & disco

Female Trouble 1233 17th St. (at Bottom of the Hill) • 626-4455 • monthly • women's dance parties

Muff Dive 917 Folsom (at the Covered Wagon) • 864-7386 • 9pm-2am Sun • women only • dancing/DJ

Bed AND Breakfast

Distinct San Franciscan hospitality.
Gracious 1872 Victorian Mansion.
Historic residential neighborhood.
Antiques, fresh flowers, beverages.
Spa tubs, hot tubs, fireplaces.
Sundeck, lovely English Garden.
Full Buffet Breakfast.

The Inn San Francisco

943 SOUTH VAN NESS AVENUE
SAN FRANCISCO, CA 94110
FACSIMILE (415) 641-1701

For Reservations
(415) 641-0188   (800) 359-0913

Phone Booth 1398 S. Van Ness Ave. • 648-4683 • 10am-2am • lesbians/gay men • neighborhood bar

Wilde Side West 424 Cortland • 647-3099 • 1pm-2am • mostly women • neighborhood bar • magic garden • patio

RESTAURANTS & CAFES

Cafe Commons 3161 Mission St. • 282-2928 • 7am-7pm • sandwiches • plenty veggie • patio • wheelchair access • women-owned/run • $4-7

Cafe Istanbul 525 Valencia St. • 863-8854 • 11am-midnight • popular • Mediterranean • some veggie • authentic Turkish coffee • bellydancers Sat

El Nuevo Fruitlandia 3077 24th St. • 648-2958 • lunch & dinner • Cuban/Puerto Rican • some veggie • women-owned/run • $5-10

Farleys 1315 18th St., Potrero Hill • 648-1545 • 7am-10pm, from 8am wknds • popular • coffeehouse

Just For You 1453 18th St., Potrero Hill • 647-3033 • 7am-3pm • popular • lesbians/gay men • American/Cajun • some veggie • women-owned/run • $4-7

Klein's Delicatessen 501 Connecticut St., Potrero Hill • 821-9149 • 7am-7pm • beer/wine • sandwiches & salads • some veggie • patio • women-owned/run • $4-10

New Dawn Cafe 3174 16th St. • 553-8888 • 8am-3pm • popular • hearty breakfasts • some veggie • $4-7

Pancho Villa 3071 16th St. • 864-8840 • 11am-10pm • popular • some veggie • best 'Mission-style' burritos in city • also El Toro at 18th & Valencia • $4-8

Pauline's Pizza Pie 260 Valencia St. • 552-2050 • dinner only, clsd Sun-Mon • popular • lesbians/gay men • beer/wine

Picaro 3120 16th St. • 431-4089 • Spanish tapas bar

Red Dora's Bearded Lady (Dyke Cafe & Gallery) 485 14th St. (at Guerrero) • 626-2805 • 7am-7pm • popular • mostly women • funky brunch & sandwiches • plenty veggie • performances Fri-Sat nights (call for events) • patio • women-owned/run • $4-7

Stimulus 3369 Mission • 641-5349 • 7:30am-8pm, til 9pm Th-Sat, 10am-6pm Sun • 'alternative to corporate cookie cutter coffee house' • also artspace

Ti-Couz 3108 16th St. • 252-7373 • 11am-11pm • beer/wine • dinner & dessert crepes • plenty veggie • $5-10

Val 21 995 Valencia St. • 821-6622 • dinner, Sun brunch • popular • eclectic Californian • some veggie • $7-15

GYMS & HEALTH CLUBS

Osento 955 Valencia St. • 282-6333 • 1pm-midnight • women only • baths • hot tub • massage

BOOKSTORES & RETAIL SHOPS

381 381 Guerrero St. • 621-3830 • 11am-6pm, til 7pm wknds • great kitsch & candles

Bernal Books 401 Cortland Ave., Bernal Hts. • 550-0293 • 10am-7pm, til 4pm Sun, clsd Mon • lesbigay section • community bookstore for Bernal Heights & beyond

Leather Tongue Video 714 Valencia St. • 552-2900 • great collection of camp, cult & obscure videos

Modern Times Bookstore 888 Valencia St. • 282-9246 • 11am-8pm, til 6pm Sun • alternative • lesbigay section • wheelchair access

EROTICA

▲ **Good Vibrations** 1210 Valencia St. • 550 7399/ 974-8980 • 11am-7pm • popular • mostly women • clean, well-lighted sex toy store • also mail order • women-owned/run

Polk Area

ACCOMMODATIONS

Atherton Hotel 685 Ellis St. • 474-5720/ (800) 474-5720 • gay-friendly • also a restaurant • brunch & lunch • full bar • affordable but classic hotel • IGTA member

▲ **Essex Hotel** 684 Ellis St. • 474-4664/ (800) 453-7739 • gay-friendly • boutique hotel known for its European-style hospitality

Hotel Richelieu 1050 Van Ness Ave. • 673-4711/ (800) 227-3608 • gay-friendly • gym • also full bar • wheelchair access

▲ **Leland Hotel** 1315 Polk St. • 441-5141/ (800) 258-4458 • mostly gay men • IGTA member

The Lombard Hotel 1015 Geary St. • 673-5232/ (800) 777-3210 • gay-friendly • swimming • wheelchair access

the *Essex* HOTEL

With a European charm and tradition, the Essex is only one block from Polk Street. Close to shopping, bars, restaurants, theatres, and the City's gay life!

415-474-4664

Rooms from $59

- Toll free for reservation -
1-800-453-7739 USA • 1-800-443-7739 CA
684 Ellis Street · S.F., CA · 94109

Pensione International Hotel 875 Post St. • 775-3344 • gay-friendly • Victorian-styled B&B hotel built in early 1900s

The Phoenix Hotel 601 Eddy St. • 776-1380/ (800) 248-9466 • popular • gay-friendly • swimming • also a restaurant • Caribbean • some veggie • full bar • 1950s style motor lodge for the artistic & creative • IGTA member • $10-20

RESTAURANTS & CAFES

Grubstake II 1525 Pine St. • 673-8268 • 5pm-4am, 10am-4am wknds • lesbians/gay men • beer/wine

Rendezvous Cafe 1760 Polk St. • 292-4033 • 7am-10pm • American • some veggie • $6-10

Spuntino 524 Van Ness Ave. • 861-7772 • opens 7am • popular • beer/wine • cont'l • also cafe & desserts • $8-12

Stars Cafe 500 Van Ness Ave. • 861-4344• popular • beer/wine • new American • $15-25

BOOKSTORES & RETAIL SHOPS

A Clean Well Lighted Place For Books 601 Van Ness Ave. • 441-6670 • general • lesbigay section

Headlines Chestnut (at Scott) • 441-5550 • 10am-9pm, til 11pm Fri-Sat • clothes • novelties

Hog On Ice 1630 Polk St. • 771-7909 • 10am-10pm, til 6pm Sat • novelties • books • CDs

TRAVEL & TOUR OPERATORS

Beyond the Bay 726 Polk St. • 441-3440/ (800) 542-1991 • IGTA member • women-owned/run

Jackson Travel 1829 Polk St. • 928-2500 • IGTA member

Downtown

ACCOMMODATIONS

The Abigail 246 McAllister St. • 861-9728/ (800) 243-6510 • popular • gay-friendly • also a restaurant • Euro-Mediterranean • some veggie • IGTA member

Amsterdam Hotel 749 Taylor St. • 673-3277/ (800) 637-3444 • gay-friendly • charming European-style hotel

Commodore Hotel 825 Sutter • 923-6800/ (800) 338-6848 • gay-friendly

Dakota Hotel 606 Post St. • 931-7475 • gay-friendly • near Union Square

Hotel Mark Twain 345 Taylor St. • 673-2332/ (800) 288-9246 • gay-friendly • full breakfast • wheelchair access

The Hotel Vintage Court 650 Bush St. • 392-4666/ (800) 654-1100 • popular • gay-friendly • also home of world-famous 5-star Masa's restaurant • wheelchair access

Howard Johnson Pickwick Hotel 85 5th St. • 421-7500/ (800) 227-3282 • gay-friendly

Hyde Park Suites 2655 Hyde St. • 771-0200/ (800) 227-3608 • gay-friendly • Mediterranean-inspired 1- & 2-bdrm suites • gym • sundeck • IGTA member

The King George Hotel 334 Mason St. • 781-5050/ (800) 288-6005 • gay-friendly • European-style boutique hotel • also The Bread & Honey Tearoom w/ morning & afternoon teas

Miyako Hotel 1625 Post St. • 922-3200 • gay-friendly • located in the heart of Japantown • wheelchair access

Nob Hill Lambourne 725 Pine St. • 433-2287/ (800) 274-8466 • gay-friendly • luxurious, private, tastefully appointed 'business accommodation'

▲ **Pacific Bay Inn** 520 Jones St. • 673-0234/ (800) 445-2631 • gay-friendly • cafe

Triton Hotel 342 Grant Ave. • 394-0500/ (800) 433-6611 • gay-friendly • wheelchair access • IGTA member

York Hotel 940 Sutter St. • 885-6800/ (800) 808-9675 • gay-friendly • boutique hotel • IGTA member

BARS

The Gate 1093 Pine St. • 885-9871 • 3pm-2am, 11am-2am wknds, Sun brunch • mostly gay men • neighborhood bar

Gilmore's Pub 1068 Hyde St. • 441-9494 • 10am-2am • lesbians/gay men • neighborhood bar

Sutter's Mill 10 Mark Ln. (off Bush St.) • 788-8377 • 10am-10pm • popular • mostly gay men • lunch weekdays • popular cocktail hour

RESTAURANTS & CAFES

Akimbo 116 Maiden Ln. • 433-2288 • lesbians/gay men

Basque Hotel & Restaurant uphill alley of Broadway between Columbus & Kearney • 788-9404 • beer/wine

Cafe Claude 7 Claude • 392-3505 • popular • live jazz • as close to Paris as you can get in SF

Campo Santo 240 Columbus Ave., North Beach • 433-9623 • beer/wine • Mexican • some veggie • hip decor • $8-15

China Moon Cafe 639 Post St. • 775-4789 • lunch & dinner • popular • unique California nouvelle w/ Chinese accent • some veggie • $15-25

US Restaurant 431 Columbus Ave., North Beach • 362-6251 • 6am-9pm, clsd Sun-Mon • beer/wine • Italian food just like home

BOOKSTORES & RETAIL SHOPS

City Lights Bookstore 261 Columbus Ave., North Beach • 362-8193 • 10am-midnight • historic beatnik bookstore • many progressive titles

TRAVEL & TOUR OPERATORS

Doing It Right Tours & Travel 1 St. Francis Pl. Ste. 2106 • 243-4157/ (800) 666-3646 • also Gay Travel Club meets 1st Wed • women-owned/run

San Jose (408)

INFO LINES & SERVICES

AA Gay/Lesbian • 297-3555

Billy DeFrank Lesbian/Gay Community Center 175 Stockton Ave. • 293-2429 • 6pm-9pm, from 3pm Wed, noon-6pm wknds

South Bay Leather/Uniform Group PO Box 2519, Santa Clara, 95055 • weekly socials • monthly potlucks • workshops • newsletter

BARS

641 Club 641 Stockton • 998-1144 • 2pm-2am, from 11am wknds • lesbians/gay men • dancing/DJ • multiracial • patio

Buck's 301 W. Stockton Ave. • 286-1176 • noon-2am, from noon Fri til 2am Sun • lesbians/gay men • neighborhood bar • dancing/DJ

FX 400 S. 1st St. • 298-9796 • clsd Sun • gay-friendly • dancing/DJ • alternative • call for events

Greg's Ballroom 551 W. Julian • 286-4388 • noon-2am • lesbians/gay men • dancing/DJ • live shows

Selections 1984 Oakland Rd. • 428-0329 • 4pm-2am, clsd Mon • mostly women • men's night Th

RESTAURANTS & CAFES

Cafe Leviticus 1445 The Alameda • 279-8877 • 7:30am-midnight • lesbians/gay men

El Faro 610 Coleman Ave. • 294-7468 • lunch & dinner, Sun champagne brunch 10am-3pm • Mexican • some veggie • $10-20

Hamburger Mary's 170 W. St. John St. • 947-1667 • from 11:30am, from 9am wknds • lesbians/gay men • dancing/DJ • live shows • American • some veggie • full bar • patio • $5-10

BOOKSTORES & RETAIL SHOPS

Sisterspirit 175 Stockton Ave. • 293-9372 • 6:30pm-9pm, noon-6pm Sat, 1pm-4pm Sun • women's • periodic coffeehouse • wheelchair access

TRAVEL & TOUR OPERATORS

Yankee Clipper Travel 260 Saratoga Ave., Los Gatos • 354-6400/ (800) 624-2664 • contact Jim • IGTA member

SPIRITUAL GROUPS

Hosanna Church of Praise 24 N. 5th St. • 293-0708 • 2pm Sun • charismatic pentecostal

MCC of San Jose 65 S. 7th St. • 279-2711 • 10:30am Sun

PUBLICATIONS

Entre Nous PO Box 412, Santa Clara, 95052 • 297-0666 • monthly • lesbian newsmagazine & calendar for South Bay

Our Paper PO Box 23387, 95153 • 226-0823 • women-owned/run

Out Now! 45 N. 1st St. #124 • 991-1873 • bi-weekly

EROTICA

Leather Masters 969 Park Ave. • 293-7660 • leather & fetish • clothes • toys • publications

San Leandro (510)

BARS

Bill's Eagle 14572 E. 14th • 357-7343 • noon-2am • lesbians/gay men • neighborhood bar • dancing/DJ • live shows • patio • women-owned/run

San Lorenzo (510)

SPIRITUAL GROUPS

Maranatha MCC 100 Hacienda (Christ Lutheran Church) • 481-9720 • 12:30pm Sun

San Luis Obispo (805)

INFO LINES & SERVICES

GALA (Gay/Lesbian Alliance of the Central Coast) PO Box 3558, 93403 • 541-4252

Lesbian Rap Groups, Santa Maria • 929-3197 • social/support groups • lesbians of color meet 3rd Sat • 534-0808

Women's Resource Center 1009 Morro St. #201 • 544-9313 • counseling • support • referrals

ACCOMMODATIONS

Adobe Inn 1473 Monterey St. • 549-0321 • gay-friendly • full breakfast • cozy, comfortable & congenial inn

Casa De Amigas B&B 1202 8th St., Los Osos • 528-3701 • lesbians/gay men • women-owned/run

BARS

▲ **Breezes Pub & Grill** 11560 Los Osos Valley Rd., Laguna Village #160 • 544-8010 • 11:30am-2am Wed-Sun • lesbians/gay men • dancing/DJ • beer/wine • also a restaurant • Caribbean • some veggie • $5-10

RESTAURANTS & CAFES

Linnea's Cafe 1110 Garden • 541-5888 • brkfst & lunch • healthy American • plenty veggie • $5

BOOKSTORES & RETAIL SHOPS

Coalesce Bookstore & Garden Wedding Chapel 845 Main St., Morro Bay • 772-2880 • 10am-5:30pm, 11am-4pm Sun • lesbigay section • women-owned/run

Earthling Bookshop 698 Higuera St. • 543-7951 • 10am-11pm • lesbigay section

Volumes of Pleasure 1016 Los Osos Valley Rd., Los Osos • 528-5565 • 10am-6pm, clsd Sun • general • lesbigay section • wheelchair access • lesbian-owned/run

HOURS
WED - TUE
8 PM - 2 AM
FRI & SAT
6 PM - 2 AM

GRILL HOURS
WED - SAT
5PM - 11 PM

• **NIGHTLY D.J.** •
• **MIXED MEN & WOMEN** •

11560 LOS OSOS VALLEY ROAD #160
SAN LUIS OBISPO, CA 93405

(805) 544-8010

SPIRITUAL GROUPS

MCC 2333 Meadow Ln. • 481-9376 • 10:30am Sun

San Mateo (415)

BARS

'B' Street 236 S. 'B' St. • 348-4045 • 4pm-2am Fri-Sat • popular • lesbians/gay men • dancing/DJ • live shows • theme nights • live bands • 3 flrs. • more women Fri • patio • wheelchair access

San Rafael (415)

BARS

Aunt Ruby's 815 W. Francisco Blvd. • 459-6079 • 4pm-midnight, 2pm-2am Fri-Sat, from noon Sun • lesbians/gay men • dancing/DJ • wheelchair access

San Ysidro (619)

EROTICA

▲ **F St. Bookstore** 4650 Border Village • 497-6042

Santa Ana (714)

SPIRITUAL GROUPS

Christ Chapel MCC 720 N. Spurgeon • 835-0722 • 10am Sun

Santa Barbara (805)

INFO LINES & SERVICES

Gay/Lesbian Resource Center 126 E. Haley St. Ste. A-17 • 963-3636 • 10am-5pm Mon-Fri • social/educational & support services

ACCOMMODATIONS

Glenborough Inn 1327 Bath St. • 966-0589/ (800) 962-0589 • lesbians/gay men • full breakfast • 3 different homes w/ 3 different personalities

Ivanhoe Inn 1406 Castillo St. • 963-8832/ (800) 428-1787 • gay-friendly • lovely old Victorian house

BARS

Club Oasis 224 Helena • 966-2464 • 4pm-2am, from 2pm wknds • popular • lesbians/gay men • dancing/DJ • piano bar • patio

Gold Coast 30 W. Cota • 965-6701 • 4pm-2am • popular • mostly gay men • dancing/DJ • wheelchair access

Zelo's 630 State • 966-5792 • Sun only • popular • gay-friendly • dancing/DJ • also a restaurant

RESTAURANTS & CAFES

Acacia 1212 Coast Village Rd. • 969-8500 • dinner, lunch wknds • modern American • full bar • wheelchair access • $15-20

Green Dragon 22 W. Mission • 667-1902

Hot Spot Espresso Bar & Reservation Service • 564-1637

Sojourner 134 E. Canon Perdido • 965-7922 • 11am-11pm • beer/wine • veggie • wheelchair access

BOOKSTORES & RETAIL SHOPS

Choices Books & Espresso Bar 901 De La Vina St. • 965-5477 • 7am-6pm, til 9pm Wed-Fri, 9am-5pm Sat, clsd Sun • lesbigay • wheelchair access • women-owned/run

Earthling Books & Cafe 1137 State St. • 965-0926 • 9am-11pm, til midnight Fri-Sat • lesbigay

Santa Clara (408)

BARS

▲ **Savoy** 3546 Flora Vista • 247-7109 • 3pm-2am • popular • mostly women • dancing/DJ • live shows • wheelchair access • women-owned/run

Tynker's Damn 46 N. Saratoga • 243-4595 • 3pm-2am, 1pm-2am wknds • popular • mostly gay men • dancing/DJ

EROTICA

Borderline 36 N. Saratoga Ave. • 241-2177 • toys • videos

Santa Cruz (408)

INFO LINES & SERVICES

AA Gay/Lesbian • 457-2559 • call for mtgs.

Lesbian/Gay/Bisexual Community Center 1328 Commerce Ln. • 425-5422 • call for hours

WOMEN'S ACCOMMODATIONS

El Mar Vista 5115 Ironwood, Soquel, 95073 • 476-5742 • women only • full breakfast • shared baths

The Grove 40 Lily Wy. • 724-3459 • mostly women • 2 cabins on a mini-farm near the beach

ACCOMMODATIONS

Chateau Victorian B&B Inn 118 1st St. • 458-9458 • gay-friendly • 1885 Victorian turned into an elegant B&B inn w/ a warm friendly atmosphere

BARS

Blue Lagoon 923 Pacific Ave. • 423-7117 • 4pm-2am • popular • lesbians/gay men • dancing/DJ • alternative • live shows • wheelchair access

RESTAURANTS & CAFES

Costa Brava Taco Stand 505 Seabright • 423-8190 • 11am-11pm • Mexican • some veggie • $4-8

Crêpe Place 1134 Soquel Ave. • 429-6994 • 11am-midnight, 9am-1am wknds • beer/wine • plenty veggie • garden patio • wheelchair access • $5-11

Herland Book Cafe 902 Center St. • 429-6636 • 8am-6pm, bookstore from 10am • vegetarian & vegan • wheelchair access • $3-6

Saturn Cafe 1230 Mission • 429-8505 • 11:30am-midnight • sandwiches/salads/soups • plenty veggie • $4-7

GYMS & HEALTH CLUBS

Heartwood Spa Hot Tub & Sauna Garden 3150-A Mission Dr. • 462-2192 • gay-friendly • call for women-only hours & days

BOOKSTORES & RETAIL SHOPS

Book Loft 1207 Soquel Ave. • 429-1812 • 10am-10pm, noon-6pm Sun, 10am-6pm Mon • lesbigay section • mostly used

Bookshop Santa Cruz 1520 Pacific Garden Mall • 423-0900 • 9am-10pm • cafe • general • lesbigay section • wheelchair access

Chimney Sweep Books 419 Cedar St. • 458-1044 • 11am-6pm, clsd Sun-Mon • lesbigay section • mostly used

TRAVEL & TOUR OPERATORS

Eco-Explorations PO Box 7944, 95061 • 335-7199 • lesbigay & women's scuba & seakayaking trips • IGTA member • women-owned/run

Pacific Harbor Travel 519 Seabright Ave. • 425-5020/ (800) 435-9463 • IGTA member • women-owned/run

Santa Maria (805)

Info Lines & Services

Gay/Lesbian Resource Center 2255 S. Broadway #4 • 349-9947

Restaurants & Cafes

Cafe Monet 1555 S. Broadway • 928-1912 • 7am-7pm, til 10pm Wed & Fri, 9am-5pm Sun • men's night Wed • wheelchair access

Santa Rosa (707)

Bars

Santa Rosa Inn 4302 Santa Rosa Ave. • 584-0345 • noon-2am • lesbians/gay men • dancing/DJ

Restaurants & Cafes

Aroma Roasters 95 5th St. (Railroad Square) • 576-7765 • 7am-midnight • lesbians/gay men • live bands • coffee/desserts • wheelchair access

Bookstores & Retail Shops

North Light Books 95 5th St. (Historic Railroad Square) • 579-9000 • 9am-9pm, til 7pm Fri-Sat, 10pm-8pm Sun • anti-establishment • strong lesbigay emphasis • also coffeehouse • lesbian-owned/run

Sawyer's News 733 4th St. • 542-1311 • 7am-9pm, til 10pm Fri-Sat • general news & bookstand

Travel & Tour Operators

Santa Rosa Travel 542 Farmers Ln. • 542-0943/ (800) 227-1445

Sun Quest 1208 4th St. • 573-8300/ (800) 444-8300 • IGTA member

Spiritual Groups

New Hope MCC 3632 Airway Dr. • 526-4673 • noon Sun

Publications

We the People PO Box 8218, 95407 • 573-8896 • monthly

Stockton (209)

Info Lines & Services

Gay/Lesbian Association San Joaquin County 820 N. Madison • 464-3550

Bars

Paradise 10100 N. Lower Sacramento Rd. • 477-4724 • 6pm-2am, from 4pm wknds • popular • lesbians/gay men • dancing/DJ • live shows

Tustin (714)

Bookstores & Retail Shops

A Different Drummer II 14131 Yorba St. Ste. 102 • 731-0224/3632 • 10am-9pm, til 4pm Fri, clsd for lunch • lesbigay • self-help titles in conjuction w/ Christopher St. Counseling Center

Ukiah (707)

Bars

Sunset Grill 228 E. Perkins St. • 463-0740 • clsd Tue • gay-friendly • dancing/DJ • also a restaurant • Californian • $10-15

Vacaville (707)

Info Lines & Services

Solano County Gay/Lesbian Info Line • 448-1010/ 449-0550

Bookstores & Retail Shops

Vacaville Book Co. & Coffeehouse 315 Main St. • 449-0550 • 10am-8pm, til 10pm Fri-Sat, clsd Sun • women-owned/run

Spiritual Groups

St. Paul's United Methodist Church 101 West St. • 448-5154 • 10:30am Sun • reconciling congregation

Vallejo (707)

Bars

Nobody's Place 437 Virginia St. • 645-7298 • 10am-2am • mostly gay men • dancing/DJ • patio • wheelchair access

The Q 412 Georgia St. • 644-4584 • 1pm-2am • mostly gay men • dancing/DJ • wheelchair access

Ventura (805)

Info Lines & Services

AA Gay/Lesbian 739 E. Main • 389-1444 • 8pm Fri

Gay/Lesbian Community Center 1995 E. Main • 653-1979 • 10am-4pm, 6:30pm-9pm, clsd Sat-Sun

Gay/Lesbian Resource Center of Ventura County 363 Mobile Ave., Camarillo • 389-1530 • taped info on mtgs. • resources & support groups • also publishes 'In the Light' newsletter

BARS

Charleston Club Cafe 2819 E. Main St. • 643-4849 • 5pm-2am, clsd Sun • lesbians/gay men • dancing/DJ • also a restaurant • cont'l • wheelchair access • $8-17

Club Alternative 1644 E. Thompson Blvd. • 653-6511 • 3pm-2am, from 1pm wknds • popular • lesbians/gay men • dancing/DJ • live shows • patio

Paddy McDermott's 577 E. Main St. • 652-1071 • 5pm-2am, from 4pm wknds, clsd Mon • lesbians/gay men • dancing/DJ • live shows • karaoke

SPIRITUAL GROUPS

MCC Ventura 1848 Poli (Church of Latter Day Saints) • 643-0502 • 6:30pm Sun

Victorville   (619)

BARS

West Side 15 16868 Stoddard Wells Rd. • 243-9600 • noon-2am • lesbians/gay men • beer/wine

Walnut Creek   (510)

INFO LINES & SERVICES

AA Gay/Lesbian 1924 Trinity Ave. (St. Paul's Episc. Church) • 939-4155 • 8:30pm Fri

BARS

D.J.'s 1535 Olympic Blvd. • 930-0300 • 4pm-2am• popular • lesbians/gay men • piano bar • also a restaurant • cont'l • some veggie • wheelchair access • $8-12

J.R.'s 2520 Camino Diablo • 256-1200 • 5pm-2am, til 4am Fri-Sat • lesbians/gay men • dancing/DJ • more women Sat • wheelchair access

Twelve Twenty 1220 Pine St. • 938-4550 • 4pm-2am • popular • mostly gay men • dancing/DJ

SPIRITUAL GROUPS

MCC Diablo Valley 1648 Geary • 945-6859 • 12:30pm Sun

Whittier (310)

ACCOMMODATIONS

Whittier House 12133 S. Colima Rd. • 941-7222 • mostly women • B&B • cottages • full breakfast • hot tub • IGTA member

SPIRITUAL GROUPS

MCC Good Samaritan 11931 E. Washington • 696-6213 • 10am Sun, 7:30pm Wed

Willits (707)

RESTAURANTS & CAFES

Tsunami 50 S. Main St. • 459-4750 • 9:30am-8pm • popular

BOOKSTORES & RETAIL SHOPS

Leaves of Grass 630 S. Main St. • 459-3744 • 10am-5:30pm, noon-5pm Sun • alternative

TRAVEL & TOUR OPERATORS

Skunk Train California Western 299 E. Commercial St. • 459-5248 • scenic train trips

Yosemite Nat'l Park (209)

ACCOMMODATIONS

The Ahwahnee Hotel Yosemite Valley Floor • 252-4848 • gay-friendly • swimming • food served • incredibly dramatic & expensive grand fortress

▲ **The Homestead** 41110 Rd. 600, Ahwahnee • 683-0495 • gay-friendly • cottages • full breakfast • kitchens • fireplaces • on 160 acres at the gateway to Yosemite

Colorado

Aspen (303)

INFO LINES & SERVICES

Aspen Gay/Lesbian Community PO Box 3143, 81612 • 925-9249 • info/resource • outdoor activities • monthly events

ACCOMMODATIONS

Aspen Bed & Breakfast Lodge 311 W. Main • 925-7650/ (800) 362-7736 • gay-friendly • hot tub • swimming

Hotel Aspen 110 W. Main St. • 925-3441/ (800) 527-7369 • gay-friendly • hot tub • swimming • mountain breakfast • wheelchair access

Hotel Lenado 200 S. Aspen St. • 925-6246/ (800) 321-3457 • gay-friendly • full breakfast • hot tub • full bar

Sardy House 128 E. Main St. • 920-2525/ (800) 321-3457 • gay-friendly • hot tub • swimming • also a restaurant

BARS

Double Diamond 450 S. Galena • 920-6905 • seasonal • gay-friendly • live shows

Silver Nugget Hyman Ave. Mall • 925-8154 • 10pm-2am • gay-friendly • dancing/DJ • country/western • live shows • also a restaurant • steak & seafood • wheelchair access

The Tippler 535 E. Dean • 925-4977 • 9pm-2am (seasonal) • lesbians/gay men • dancing/DJ

RESTAURANTS & CAFES

Syzygy 520 E. Hyman • 925-3700 • 5pm-10pm, bar til 2am • live shows • some veggie • wheelchair access

BOOKSTORES & RETAIL SHOPS

Explore Booksellers & Bistro 221 E. Main • 925-5336 • 10am-11pm • plenty veggie

Boulder (303)

INFO LINES & SERVICES

LBGT (Lesbian/Bisexual/Gay/ Transgendered) Alliance University Memorial Center Rm. 28, CU-Boulder, 80309 • 492-8567 • events schedule & resource info

TLC (The Lesbian Connection) 2525 Arapahoe Ave. • 443-1105 • social/cultural/business group • newsletter • good source for info & referrals

WOMEN'S ACCOMMODATIONS

Boulder Guesthouse 1331 Marshall St. • 938-8908 • mostly women • private home • kitchen privileges

ACCOMMODATIONS

Boulder Victorian Historic B&B 1305 Pine St. • 938-1300 • gay-friendly • patio • wheelchair access

The Briar Rose 2151 Arapahoe Ave. • 442-3007 • gay-friendly • B&B

BARS

Boulder Blue Steel Aspen Plaza • 786-8860 • 5pm-7am • gay-friendly • women's night Th

Marquee 1109 Walnut • 447-1803 • 7pm-2am • gay-friendly • dancing/DJ • live shows • call for events

The Yard 2690 28th St. #C • 443-1987 • 4pm-2am, from 2pm wknds • lesbians/gay men • dancing/DJ • wheelchair access

RESTAURANTS & CAFES

Walnut Cafe 3073 Walnut • 447-2315 • 7am-11pm, til 3pm Sun-Mon • some veggie • patio • wheelchair access • women-owned/run • $5-9

BOOKSTORES & RETAIL SHOPS

Aria 2043 Broadway • 442-5694 • 10am-6pm, noon-5pm Sun • cards • T-shirts • gifts • wheelchair access

Left Hand Books 1825 Pearl St., 2nd flr. • 443-8252 • noon-9pm, 1pm-4pm Sun

Word Is Out 1731 15th St. • 449-1415 • 10am-6pm, noon-5pm Sun, clsd Mon • women's • lesbigay section

TRAVEL & TOUR OPERATORS

Adventure Bound Expeditions 711 Walnut St. • 449-0990 • mountain tours & hiking excursions

SPIRITUAL GROUPS

Gay/Lesbian Concerned Catholics 904 14th St. • 443-8383 • monthly events • call for events

PUBLICATIONS

Colorado Community Directories PO Drawer 2270, 80306 • 443-7768 • extensive statewide resources

Breckenridge   (303)

ACCOMMODATIONS

Allaire Timbers Inn 9511 Hwy. 9, S. Main St. • 453-7530/ (800) 624-4904 • gay-friendly • hot tub • wheelchair access

Colorado Springs   (719)

INFO LINES & SERVICES

Pikes Peak Gay/Lesbian Community Center Helpline PO Box 574, 80901 • 471-4429 • call for events

ACCOMMODATIONS

Pikes Peak Paradise PO Box 5760, Woodland Park, 80866 • (800) 354-0989 • gay-friendly • full breakfast • Southern mansion w/ spectacular view of Pikes Peak

BARS

Hide & Seek Complex 512 W. Colorado • 634-9303 • 10:30am-2am, til 4am Fri-Sat • popular • mostly gay men • dancing/DJ • country/western • live shows • also a restaurant • some veggie • 4 bars & restaurant • wheelchair access • $5-12

Hour Glass Lounge 2748 Airport Rd. • 471-2104 • 10am-2am • mostly women • neighborhood bar • women-owned/run

The Penthouse 1715 N. Academy • 597-3314 • 3pm-2am, til 4am Fri-Sat • mostly gay men • neighborhood bar • dancing/DJ • wheelchair access

True Colors 1865 N. Academy Blvd. • 637-0773 • 3pm-2am, clsd Mon • mostly women • dancing/DJ • multi-racial • wheelchair access • women-owned/run

RESTAURANTS & CAFES

Art of Espresso 2021 W. Colorado Ave. • 632-9306 • 7am-10pm, til midnight Fri-Sat, til 6pm Sun

Dale Street Cafe 115 E. Dale • 578-9898 • 11am-9:30pm, clsd Sun • full bar

BOOKSTORES & RETAIL SHOPS

Abaton 2525 W. Pikes Peak, Unit C • 475-2508 • call for hours • lesbigay bookstore

SPIRITUAL GROUPS

Pikes Peak MCC 730 N. Tejon (Unitarian Church) • 634-3771 • 5pm Sun

PUBLICATIONS

New Phazes PO Box 6485, 80934 • 634-0236 • monthly • women's newsletter

EROTICA

First Amendment Adult Bookstore 220 E. Fillmore • 630-7676

Denver   (303)

INFO LINES & SERVICES

AA Gay/Lesbian • 322-4440 • many meetings

Dyke TV Channel 12 • 11pm Th • 'weekly half hour TV show produced by lesbians for lesbians'

Gay/Lesbian/Bisexual Community Center 1245 E. Colfax Ave. Ste. 125 • 831-6268/ 837-1598 (TDD) • 10am-6pm Mon-Fri • extensive resources & support groups • wheelchair access

Gender Idenity Center 3715 W. 32nd Ave. • 458-5378 • resources & statewide support group for transgendered people

Rocky Mountain Career Women PO Box 18156, 80218 • 889-1001 • 6:30pm 3rd Fr • social/networking group for professional women • newsletter

Sister II Sister • Black lesbian support group • contact Community Center

Women's Outdoor Club PO Box 300085, 80203

Young Alive Group • 860-1819 • social/support group for ages 18-29 • sponsored by MCC

ACCOMMODATIONS

Castle Marve 1572 Race St. • 331-0621/ (800) 926-2763 • gay-friendly • grand historic mansion

Elyria's Western Guest House 4700 Baldwin Ct. • 291-0915 • lesbians/gay men • Western ambience in historic Denver neighborhood

Mile Hi B&B • 329-7827/ (800) 513-7827 • lesbians/gay men

P.T. Barnum Estate 360 King St. • 830-6758/ (800) 778-8788 • popular • B&B • turn-of-the-century estate

Queen Anne Inn 2147 Tremont Pl. • 296-6666 • gay-friendly • full breakfast

Spectacular View B&B 1044 Downing St. Ste. 707 • 830-6758 • gay-friendly • swimming • high-rise apartment

Stapleton Plaza Hotel 3333 Quebec St. • 321-3500/ (800) 950-6070 • gay-friendly • swimming • also a restaurant • wheelchair access

Victoria Oaks Inn 1575 Race St. • 355-1818/ (800) 662-6257 • gay-friendly • B&B

BARS

Aqua Lounge/69 720 E. 17th Ave. • 832-3474 • clsd Mon • gay-friendly • hours vary • dancing/DJ • alternative • popular happy hour buffet • gay night Th • call for events • wheelchair access

B.J.'s Carousel 1380 S. Broadway • 777-9880 • 10am-2am • popular • mostly gay men • neighborhood bar • live shows • also a restaurant • American • volleyball court • patio • wheelchair access

Bandits 255 S. Broadway • 777-7100 • noon-2am • lesbians/gay men

The Bobcat 1700 Logan • 830-0535 • 4pm-2am • lesbians/gay men • dancing/DJ • live shows • wheelchair access

Colfax Mining Co. 3014 E. Colfax Ave. • 321-6627 • 10am-2am • lesbians/gay men • neighborhood bar • dancing/DJ

Den 5110 W. Colfax Ave. • 534-9526 • 11am-2am • lesbians/gay men • neighborhood bar • food served

Denver Detour 551 E. Colfax Ave. • 861-1497 • 11am-2am • lesbians/gay men • dancing/DJ • live shows • lunch & dinner daily • some veggie • wheelchair access • $5-9

The Elle 716 W. Colfax, Denver • 572-1710 • 4pm-2am, 2pm-midnight Sun, clsd Mon-Tue • mostly women • dancing/DJ • patio • wheelchair access

Flavors 1700 Logan • 830-0535 • 4pm-2am • lesbians/gay men • dancing/DJ • live shows • wheelchair access

The Grand Bar & Restaurant 538 E. 17th Ave. • 839-5390 • 11am-2am • lesbians/gay men • live shows • also a restaurant • plenty veggie • upscale piano bar • patio

Highland Bar 2532 15th St. • 455-9978 • 1pm-2am • mostly women • neighborhood bar • wheelchair access

Maximilian's 2151 Lawrence St. • 297-0015 • gay-friendly • hours vary • dancing/DJ • multi-racial • salsa

Metro Express 314 E. 13th St. • 894-0668 • 4pm-2am, from 2pm Sun • popular • lesbians/gay men • dancing/DJ • live shows • videos • patio • wheelchair access

Mike's 60 S. Broadway • 777-0193 • 11am-2am • lesbians/gay men • dancing/DJ • wheelchair access • women-owned/run

Denver (303)

LESBIGAY INFO:
Gay/Lesbian/Bisexual Community Center: 831-6268. 1245 E. Colfax Ave. Ste. 125, 10am-6pm Mon-Fri.

LESBIGAY PAPER: Out Front: 303-778-7900. Lesbians in Colorado: 355-9202.

WHERE THE GIRLS ARE: Many lesbians reside in the Capitol Hill area, near the gay and mixed bars, but hang out in cafes and women's bars scattered around the city.

LESBIGAY AA: 322-4440.

LESBIGAY PRIDE: July. 831-6268 ext. 26.

ENTERTAINMENT: Denver Women's Chorus: 274-4177.

CITY INFO: Denver Visitors Bureau: 892-1112

BEST VIEW: Lookout Mountain (at night especially) or the top of the Capitol rotunda.

WEATHER: Summer temperatures average about 90° and winter ones about 40°s. The sun shines an average of 300 days a year.

TRANSIT: Yellow Cab: 777-7777. Metro Taxi: 333-3333.

Ms C's 7900 E. Colfax Ave • 322-4436 • 5pm-midnight, til 2am Fri-Sat • mostly women • dancing/DJ • multi-racial • wheelchair access

Rock Island 1614 15th St. • 572-7625 • gay-friendly • dancing/DJ • call for events • wheelchair access

Three Sisters 3358 Mariposa St. • 458-8926 • 12:30pm-2am • popular • mostly women • neighborhood bar • dancing/DJ

Ye 'O Matchmaker Pub 1480 Humboldt • 839-9388 • 10am-2am • lesbians/gay men • dancing/DJ • multi-racial • live shows • also a restaurant • Mexican/American • $5-7

RESTAURANTS & CAFES

Alfresco's 100 E. 9th (at Lincoln) • 894-0600 • lunch & dinner, Sun brunch, bar from 11am • full bar • patio

Basil's Cafe 30 S. Broadway • 698-1413 • lunch & dinner, clsd Sun • beer/wine • nouvelle Italian • plenty veggie • wheelchair access • women-owned/run • $5-10

Blue Note Cafe 70 S. Broadway • 744-6774 • 8am-10pm, til midnight Fri-Sat, clsd Mon • lesbians/gay men • live shows

City Spirit 1434 Blake • 575-0022 • 11am-midnight • live shows • full bar • wheelchair access

Denver Sandwich Co. 1217 E. 9th Ave. • 861-9762 • 10:30am-9pm, noon-8pm Sun • wheelchair access

Devine Cafe 2033 E. Colfax Ave. • 333-8463 • lunch & dinner, Sun brunch, clsd Mon • some veggie • full bar • $7-14

Footloose Cafe 104 S. Broadway • 722-3430 • 9am-10pm, til 5pm Sun • lesbians/gay men • some veggie • full bar • wheelchair access • women-owned/run • $8-12

Java Creek 287 Columbine St. • 377-8902 • 7am-10pm, til 5pm Sun • live shows • sandwiches & desserts • coffee house • wheelchair access

Las Margaritas 1066 Old S. Gaylord St. • 777-0194 • from 11am, bar til 2am • Mexican • some veggie • wheelchair access • $6-14

News Stand Cafe 630 E. 6th Ave. • 777-6060 • 7am-10pm, til 5pm Sun • wheelchair access • women-owned/run

Denver

*F*or many of us, Denver evokes images of the Rocky Mountains and snow. But to those who live here, Denver is a big city with a friendly small town feel, where the sun always shines.

First off, hit the women's **Book Garden** or the **Gay/Lesbian/Bisexual Center**. Here you'll get the inside scoop on where to go and what to do in Denver. If you ask, you'll even pick up some hints on how to 'have a gay old time' in Cheesman Park or at touristy sites like the 16th St. Mall. Next, pick up a copy of **Lesbians in Colorado** (LIC), sip coffee at the **Blue Note Cafe**, and peruse the books at the lesbigay **Category Six**. For night-time fun, taste the local cuisine at the women-owned **Basil Cafe**, have a cocktail at **The Elle** women's bar, dance at the **Denver Detour**, a popular gay nightclub, or hoof it up at **Ms. C's** country/western bar.

Outside the 'Mile High City', be sure to take advantage of the Rocky Mountain snows with a ski trip to one of the many nearby resorts: Aspen, Telluride or Rocky Mountain National Park.

GYMS & HEALTH CLUBS

Broadway Bodyworks 160 S. Broadway • 722-4342 • 6am-9pm, 7am-6pm Sat, 10am-4pm Sun • gay-friendly • wheelchair access

BOOKSTORES & RETAIL SHOPS

Book Garden 2625 E. 12th Ave. • 399-2004/ (800) 279-2426 • 10am-6pm, noon-5pm Sun • women's • jewelry • posters • spiritual items • wheelchair access • women-owned/run

Category Six 1029 E. 11th Ave. • 832-6263 • 10am-6pm, 11am-5pm wknds • lesbigay

Isis Bookstore 5701 E. Colfax Ave. • 321-0867 • 10am-7pm, til 6pm Fri-Sat, noon-5pm Sun • new age • metaphysical • wheelchair access

Magazine City 200 E. 13th Ave. • 861-8249 • 8am-7pm, 10am-6pm wknds

Tattered Cover Book Store 2955 E. 1st Ave. • 322-7727/ (800) 833-9327 • 9:30am-9pm, 10am-6pm Sun • 4 flrs. • wheelchair access

Thomas Floral & Adult Gifts 1 Broadway Ste. 108 (at Ellsworth) • 744-6400 • 8:30am-6pm, til 5pm Sat, clsd Sun • wheelchair access

TRAVEL & TOUR OPERATORS

B.T.C. World Travel 2120 S. Holly Ste. 100 • 691-9200 • women-owned/run

ColoradoTourism Board PO Box 38700, 80238 • (800) 265-6723

Compass Travel 1001 16th St. Ste. A-150 • 534-1292/ (800) 747-1292 • IGTA member • women-owned/run

Executive Travel 907 17th St. • 292-3600/ (800) 972-2400 • IGTA member

Metro Travel 90 Madison Ste. 101 • 333-6777 • IGTA member • women-owned/run

Travel 16th St. 535 16th St. #250 • 595-0007/ (800) 222-9229 • IGTA member

Travel Junction 5455 W. 38th Ave. Ste. C • 420-4646/ (800) 444-8980 • IGTA member • women-owned/run

SPIRITUAL GROUPS

Congregation Tikvat Shalom Box 6694, 80206 • 331-2706 • lesbigay Jewish fellowship

Dignity-Denver 1100 Fillmore (Capitol Hts. Presb. Church) • 322-8485 • 5pm Sun

the Book Garden
a women's store
2625 east 12th avenue
denver, colorado
80206

phone and mail orders are welcome

00-279-2426 & 303-399-2004

Integrity 1280 Vine St. (St. Barnabas) • 388-6469 • 7pm Sun

MCC of the Rockies 980 Church St. • 860-1819 • 9am, 11am • wheelchair access

Pagan Rainbow Network PO Drawer E , 80218 • 377-6283 • 11am 3rd Sun • at Community Center • wheelchair access

St. Paul's Church (Methodist) 1615 Ogden • 832-4929 • 11am Sun • reconciling congregation

PUBLICATIONS

Colorado Woman News PO Box 22274, 80222 • 355-9229 • professional/feminist newspaper

Lesbians in Colorado PO Box 12259 , 80212 • 477-6421 • statewide • calendar w/ political, social & arts coverage

Out Front 244 Washington • 778-7900 • bi-weekly

Quest 430 S. Broadway • 722-5965 • monthly

EROTICA

The Crypt 131 Broadway • 733-3112 • 10am-10pm, noon-8pm Sun • erotica • leather

Durango   (303)

ACCOMMODATIONS

Dragonback Ranch HC 60 Box 58A-864 Pagosa Springs, 81147 • 731-4534 • April-Oct • lesbians/gay men • wilderness workshops • women-owned/run

Leland House 721 2nd Ave. • 385-1920/ (800) 664-1920 • popular • gay-friendly • full breakfast

Estes Park   (303)

ACCOMMODATIONS

Distinctive Inns of Colorado PO Box 2061, 80517 • 866-0621 • great brochure

Sundance Cottages PO Box 4830, 80517 • 856-3922 • gay-friendly • wheelchair access • women-owned/run

Fort Collins   (303)

INFO LINES & SERVICES

Gay/Lesbian/Bisexual Alliance Lory Student Ctr., LSU Box 206, 80523 • 491-7232 • call for info

ARS

Nightingales 1437 E. Mulberry St. • 493-0251 • 4pm-2am, clsd Mon • popular • lesbians/gay men • dancing/DJ • country/western Th • 18+ Fri • call for events • patio • wheelchair access

RAVEL & TOUR OPERATORS

Fort Collins Travel 333 W. Mountain Ave. • 482-5555/ (800) 288-7402

Never Summer Nordic PO Box 1983, 80522 • 482-9411 • lesbians/gay men • yurts (tipi-like shelters) sleep 8-12 in Colorado Rockies • mountain-biking & skiing

Grand Junction (303)

ARS

Quincy's 609 Main St. • 242-9633 • gay after 8pm • wheelchair access

Greeley (303)

NFO LINES & SERVICES

Greeley Gay/Lesbian Alliance at U. of Northern Colorado • 351-2065 • hours vary • call for events • leave message for referrals

ARS

C Double R Bar 1822 9th St. Plaza • 353-0900 • 4pm-2am, from noon Sun • lesbians/gay men • dancing/DJ • country/western • wheelchair access

daho Springs (303)

CCOMMODATIONS

Glacier House B&B 603 Lake Rd. • 567-0536 • lesbians/gay men • unique home-stay-style B&B in a modern mountain chalet

Keystone (303)

CCOMMODATIONS

Tanrydoon 463 Vail Circle • 468-1956 • lesbians/gay men • magnificent mountain home amidst the world-class resorts of Keystone, Breckenridge, Copper Mtn.

Moffat (719)

WOMEN'S ACCOMMODATIONS

Harmony Ranch Women's Retreat Center PO Box 398, 81143 • 256-4107 • women only • B&B • cottages • campsites • women-owned/run

Pueblo (719)

INFO LINES & SERVICES

Pueblo After 2 PO Box 1602, 81002 • 564-4004 • social/educational network • newsletter

BARS

Pirates Cove 409 N. Union • 542-9624 • 2pm-2am, from 4pm Sun, clsd Mon • lesbians/gay men • neighborhood bar • wheelchair access

SPIRITUAL GROUPS

MCC Pueblo Bonforte & Liberty (Christ Cong. Church) • 543-6460 • 12:30pm Sun

Steamboat Springs (303)

ACCOMMODATIONS

Elk River Estates PO Box 5032, 80477-5032 • 879-7556 • gay-friendly • full breakfast • suburban townhouse B&B near hiking, skiing & natural hot springs

Vail (303)

RESTAURANTS & CAFES

Sweet Basil 193 E. Gore Creek Dr. • 476-0125 • lunch & dinner • some veggie • full bar • wheelchair access

Winter Park (303)

ACCOMMODATIONS

Silverado II 490 Kings Crossing Rd. • 726-5753 • gay-friendly • condo ski resort

RESTAURANTS & CAFES

Silver Zephyr (at Silverado II) • 726-8732 • 5pm-10pm • full bar • wheelchair access

Woodland Park (719)

ACCOMMODATIONS

Hackman House 602 W. Midland Ave. • 687-9851 • gay-friendly • Victorian B&B • massage available • women-owned/run

Connecticut

Bridgeport (203)

RESTAURANTS & CAFES

Bloodroot Restaurant 85 Ferris St. • 576-9168 • clsd Mon • plenty veggie • women's night Wed • call for events • patio • wheelchair access • women-owned/run • $8-12

BOOKSTORES & RETAIL SHOPS

Bloodroot 85 Ferris St • 576-9168 • clsd Mon • feminist bookstore • wheelchair access

SPIRITUAL GROUPS

Church of the Celestial Ministries • 384-1660 • call for events

Danbury

INFO LINES & SERVICES

Lesbian Support Group at Women's Center • 7:30pm Wed

BARS

Triangles Cafe 66 Sugar Hollow Rd. Rte. 7 • 798-6996 • 5pm-2am, clsd Mon • popular • lesbians/gay men • dancing/DJ • live shows • patio

TRAVEL & TOUR OPERATORS

Aldis The Travel Planner 46 Mill Plain Rd. • 778-9399 • IGTA member

Women's Center of Danbury 256 Main St • 731-5200 • 9am-2:30pm Mon-Fri • extensive info & referrals • support groups

East Windsor (203)

RESTAURANTS & CAFES

The Eatery 297 S. Main St. • 627-7094 • lunch Mon-Fri, dinner nightly • full bar • wheelchair access • $6-12

Enfield (203)

EROTICA

Bookends 44 Enfield St. (Rte. 5) • 745-3988

Hamden (203)

TRAVEL & TOUR OPERATORS

Adler Travel 2323 Whitney Ave. • 288-8100/ (800) 598-2648 • IGTA member

Hartford (203)

INFO LINES & SERVICES

AA Gay/Lesbian (see listing in 'Metroline' magazine) • daily at Gay/Lesbian Community Center • call for info

Gay/Lesbian Community Center 1841 Broad St. • 724-5542 • noon-10pm, wkn hrs vary • also coffeehouse • wheelchair access

Gay/Lesbian Guide Line • 327-0767 • 7pm-10pm Tue, Th • statewide info, referals & support

Lesbian Rap Group 135 Broad St. (YWCA) • 525-1163 • 7:30pm Tue

XX Club PO Box 387, 06141-0387 • transexual support group

ACCOMMODATIONS

1895 House B&B 97 Girard Ave. • 232-0014 • gay-friendly • full breakfast • Victorian home designed by woman architect, Genevra Whittemore Buckland

BARS

Chez Est 458 Wethersfield Ave. • 525-3243 • 3pm-2am, from noon wknds • popular • mostly gay men • dancing/DJ

Nick's Cafe House 1943 Broad St. • 956-1573 • 4pm-1am, til 2am Fri-Sat • lesbians/gay men • dancing/DJ • quiet from cafe • disco in back

OUT • popular • women only • women's roving parties • also newsletter • see 'Metroline' for time & place

The Sanctuary 2880 Main St. • 724-127 • 8pm-2am, from 6pm Sun, clsd Mon-Tu • mostly gay men • dancing/DJ • videos wheelchair access

Starlight Playhouse & Cabaret 1022 Main St. • 289-0789 • 4:30pm-1am Th (club), Fri-Sat (shows) • lesbians/gay men • food served • deli menu

BOOKSTORES & RETAIL SHOPS

MetroStore 493 Farmington Ave. • 231-8845 • 8am-8pm Tue, Wed, Sat, clsd Sun • books • leather • more

Reader's Feast Bookstore Cafe 529 Farmington Ave. • 232-3710 • 10am-9pm, til 10pm Fri-Sat, til 2:30pm Sun • popular • live shows • feminist progressive bookstore cafe • some veggie

SPIRITUAL GROUPS

Congregation Am Segulah • (800) 734-8524 • Shabbat services for lesbigay Jew

Dignity-Hartford 144 S. Quaker Ln. (Quaker Mtg. House) • 296-9229 • 6pm Sun

MCC 50 Bloomfield Ave. (meeting house) • 724-4605 • 7pm Sun

PUBLICATIONS

MetroLine 1841 Broad St. • 278-6666 • regional newspaper/entertainment guide

Manchester (203)

INFO LINES & SERVICES

Women's Center at Manchester Community College 60 Bidwell • 647-6056 • 8:30am-4:30pm, til 7pm Tue & Th, clsd Sat-Sun

Middletown (203)

INFO LINES & SERVICES

Wesleyan Women's Resource Center 287 High St. • 347-9411 ext 2669 • library

New Britain (203)

TRAVEL & TOUR OPERATORS

Weber's Travel Services 24 Cedar St. • 229-4846 • IGTA member

New Haven (203)

INFO LINES & SERVICES

Yale Women's Services 198 Elm St. • 432-0388 • resources • support groups • library • wheelchair access

BARS

168 York St. Cafe 168 York St. • 789-1915 • 2pm-1am • lesbians/gay men • also a restaurant • some veggie • patio • wheelchair access • $6-14

The Bar 254 Crown St. • 495-8924 • 4pm-1am • gay-friendly • dancing/DJ • more gay Tue • wheelchair access

Cafe 1150 1150 Chapel St. • 789-8612 • 11:30am-1am, til 2am Fri-Sat, from 3pm Sun • lesbians/gay men • piano bar • also a restaurant • some veggie • wheelchair access • $8-14

DV8 148 York St. • 865-6206 • lesbians/gay men

BOOKSTORES & RETAIL SHOPS

Golden Thread Booksellers 915 State St. • 777-7807 • 11am-6pm, til 5pm Sat, 1pm-5pm Sun, clsd Mon • feminist bookstore w/ book readings • special events • wheelchair access • women-owned/run

TRAVEL & TOUR OPERATORS

Plaza Travel Center 49 College St. • 777-7334/ (800) 933-3782 • IGTA member

SPIRITUAL GROUPS

Dignity PO Box 9362 , 06533 • 6:30pm Sun

MCC 34 Harrison St. (United Church) • 389-6750 • 11:30am & 4pm Sun

PUBLICATIONS

MetroLine 1841 Broad St., Hartford, 06114 • 278-6666 • regional gay newspaper/entertainment guide

The Newsletter: A Lesbian Position PO Box 9205, 06533-0205 • monthly

New London (203)

INFO LINES & SERVICES

New London People's Forum Affirming Lesbian/Gay Identity 76 Federal (St. James) • 443-8855 • 7:30pm Wed • educational/support group

BARS

Frank's Place 9 Tilley St. • 443-8883 • 4pm-1am, til 2am Fri-Sat • lesbians/gay men • dancing/DJ • live shows • patio • wheelchair access

Heroes 33 Golden St. • 442-4376 • noon-1am • lesbians/gay men • neighborhood bar • dancing/DJ • more women Th

RESTAURANTS & CAFES

Natone's 27 Shaw St. • 442-6894 • 4pm-midnight • cafe • late night breakfast • wheelchair access

Norfolk (203)

ACCOMMODATIONS

Loon Meadow Farm 41 Loon Meadow Dr. • 542-1776 • gay-friendly • B&B • full breakfast • wheelchair access • women-owned/run • $65-95

Manor House B&B 69 Maple Ave., Norwalk • 542-5690 • gay-friendly • full breakfast • elegant & romantic 1898 Victorian Tudor estate w/ Tiffany windows

Norwalk (203)

INFO LINES & SERVICES

Triangle Community Center 25 Van Zant St. • 853-0600 • 7:30pm-9:30pm Mon-Fri • activities • newsletter

TRAVEL & TOUR OPERATORS

B.W. Travel 9 Mott Ave. • 852-0200 • IGTA member

Norwich (203)

INFO LINES & SERVICES

Info Line for Southeastern Connecticut 74 W. Main St. • 886-0516 • 8am-8pm Mon-Fri • info • referrals • crisis counseling

Portland (203)

TRAVEL & TOUR OPERATORS

Brownstone Travel Agency 278 Main St. • 342-3450/ (800) 888-4169

Rocky Hill (203)

BARS

Club Mirage 80 Townline Rd. (Townline Plaza) • 257-0233 • Th-Sat • gay-friendly • dancing/DJ • call for events

Stamford (203)

INFO LINES & SERVICES

Gay/Lesbian Guide Line PO Box 8185, 06905 • 327-0767 • 7pm-10pm Tue & Th • statewide referrals & crisis counseling

BARS

Art Bar 84 W. Park Pl. • 973-0300 • 9pm-1am • gay-friendly • dancing/DJ • alternative • gay night Sun from 8pm

Storrs (203)

INFO LINES & SERVICES

Bisexual/Gay/Lesbian Association Box U-8, 2110 Hillside Rd., Univ. of CT, 06268 • 486-3679 • 7:30pm Th

Women's Center 417 Whitney Rd. Box U-118 • 486-4738 • wheelchair access

Stratford (203)

BARS

Stephanie's Living Room • 377-2119 • popular • mostly women • multi-racial • 'quality social events for women' • dances • concerts • bus trips • discount for physically challenged • call for event • wheelchair access

Wallingford (203)

BARS

Choices 8 North Turnpike Rd. • 949-9380 • 7pm-1am • mostly gay men • dancing/DJ • 'Girl Twirl' Fri

Waterbury (203)

BARS

The Brownstone 29 Leavenworth St. • 597-1838 • 3pm-1am, clsd Mon • lesbians/gay men • wheelchair access

Maxie's Cafe 2627 Waterbury Rd. • 574-1629 • 6pm-1am, til 2am Fri-Sat, clsd Mon • lesbians/gay men • dancing/DJ • live shows • women-owned/run

Westport (203)

BARS

The Brook Cafe 919 Post Rd. E. • 222-2233 • 5pm-1am, til 2am Fri-Sat, 4pm-11pm Sun • popular • mostly gay men • dancing/DJ • downstairs is wheelchair accesible • patio

Williamantic (203)

EROTICA

Thread City Book & Novelty 503 Main St. • 456-8131

Delaware

Bethany Village   (302)

BARS

Nomad Village Rte. 1 (3 mi. N. in Tower Shores) • 539-7581 • 10am-1am (seasonal) • gay-friendly • also Oasis • lesbians/gay men • dancing/DJ

Dover   (302)

BARS

Rumors 2206 N. DuPont Hwy. • 678-8805 • 11am-2am, from 5pm Sun • popular • lesbians/gay men • dancing/DJ • live shows • also a restaurant • ladies night Wed • wheelchair access • $10-15

TRAVEL & TOUR OPERATORS

Delaware Tourism Office PO Box 1401, 19903 • (800) 441-8846/ (800) 282-8667 (in-state only) • info

Milton   (302)

WOMEN'S ACCOMMODATIONS

▲ **Honeysuckle** 330 Union • 684-3284 • women only • B&B • full breakfast • swimming • nudity • also rental house $125-150 • women-owned/run • $80-95

Rehoboth Beach   (302)

INFO LINES & SERVICES

Camp Rehoboth 39-B Baltimore Ave. • 227-5620 • 10am-5pm, clsd wknds • info service for lesbigay businesses • also newsletter

ACCOMMODATIONS

Anna B. House 8 Anna B. St • 276-1408 • lesbians/gay men • swimming

At Melissa's Bed & Breakfast 36 Delaware Ave • 227-7054/ (800) 396-8090 • clsd Jan • gay-friendly • women-owned/run

Beach House B&B 15 Hickman St. • 227-7074/ (800) 283-4667 • gay-friendly • swimming • women-owned/run

Guest Rooms at Rehoboth/Southside Suites 45 Baltimore Ave./44 Delaware Ave. • 227-8355 • lesbians/gay men

Honeysuckle

A Women's Victorian Inn & Adjoining Houses near the Delaware beaches

by day
- Inn guests will enjoy a great breakfast
- Go to the women's beach
- Swim nude in our pool
- Schedule a massage
- Use our hot tubs & sauna
- Enjoy our women-only space

by night
- Go out to a marvelous restaurant
— Well, use your imagination!

Reservations required • Mary Ann & Julie   (302) 684-3284

Mallard Guest House 67 Lake Ave. • 226-3448 • lesbians/gay men • also 60 Baltimore Ave.

Rehoboth Guest House 40 Maryland Ave. • 227-4117 • lesbians/gay men • Victorian beach house near boardwalk, beach & Atlantic Ocean

Renegade Restaurant & Lounge/Motel 4274 Hwy. 1 • 227-4713 • popular • lesbians/gay men • swimming • dancing/DJ • also a restaurant • dinner only • some veggie • full bar • 10-acre complete resort for every taste • wheelchair access • $7-14

Sand in My Shoes Canal & 6th St. • 226-2006/ (800) 231-5856 • lesbians/gay men • B&B • full breakfast • hot tub • pets okay • sundeck • some kitchenettes

The Shore Inn at Rehoboth 703 Rehoboth Ave. • 227-8487/ (800) 597-8899 • open seasonally • mostly gay men • B&B • hot tub

Silver Lake 133 Silver Lake Dr. • 226-2115/ (800) 842-2115 • lesbians/gay men • luxurious accommodations near Poodle Beach • lake & ocean views • IGTA member

BARS

Blue Moon 35 Baltimore Ave. • 227-6515 • 4pm-2am, clsd Dec-Jan • popular • gay-friendly • dinner & Sun brunch • plenty veggie • happy hour • popular T-dance • $12-26

The Strand 137 Rehoboth • 226-0888 • Fri-Sat only • popular • lesbians/gay men • dancing/DJ • 18+ • inquire locally

RESTAURANTS & CAFES

Back Porch Cafe 59 Rehoboth Ave. • 227-3674 • lunch & dinner, Sun brunch • some veggie • full bar • open seasonally • wheelchair access • $9-20

Celsius 50-C Wilmington Ave. • 227-5767 • 5:30pm-11pm • Italian/French • some veggie • wheelchair access • $15-20

Ground Zero 50 Wilmington Ave. • 227-8041 • 6pm-2am • lesbians/gay men • some veggie • full bar • wheelchair access • $14-18

Iguana Grill 52 Baltimore Ave. • 227-0948 • 11am-1am • Southwestern • full bar • patio • $7-12

Java Beach 59 Baltimore Ave. • 227-8418 • cafe • patio

La La Land 22 Wilmington Ave. • 227-3887 • 6pm-1am (seasonal) • full bar • patio • $18-24

Square One 37 Wilmington Ave. • 227-1994 • 5pm-1am (seasonal) • lesbians/gay men

Sydney's Side Street Restaurant & Blues Place 25 Christian St. • 227-1339 • 5pm-1am, from 11am Sun, clsd Mon-Tue • live shows • heart healthy entrees • full bar • patio • $12-20

Tijuana Taxi 207 Rehoboth Ave. • 227-1986 • full bar • wheelchair access • $5-11

The West Side Cafe 137 Rehoboth • 226-0888 • 6pm-1am, bar opens 5pm • lesbians/gay men • dancing/DJ • 18+ • wheelchair access • $7-11

GYMS & HEALTH CLUBS

Body Shop 401 N. Boardwalk • 226-0920 • 8am-7pm • lesbians/gay men

BOOKSTORES & RETAIL SHOPS

Lambda Rising 39 Baltimore Ave. • 227-6969 • 10am-midnight • lesbigay

Wilmington (302)

INFO LINES & SERVICES

Gay AA at the Gay/Lesbian Alliance • 8pm Tue & Th

Gay/Lesbian Alliance of Delaware 601 Delaware Ave. • 652-6776 • 10am-9pm, til 7pm Sat, clsd Sun

Women's Support Group call Gay/Lesbian Alliance

BARS

814 Club 814 Shipley St. • 657-5730 • 5pm-1am • lesbians/gay men • dancing/DJ • also a restaurant • American • $8-15

Renaissance 107 W. 6th St. • 652-9435 • 10am-2am • popular • lesbians/gay men • dancing/DJ • live shows • sandwiches served

Roam 913 Shipley St. (upstairs) • 658-7626 • 5pm-1am • popular • lesbians/gay men • dancing/DJ • multiracial

RESTAURANTS & CAFES

The Coyote Cafe 1801 Lancaster Ave. • 652-1377 • 5pm-10pm, from 11am Th-Fri • plenty veggie • full bar • patio • $7-14

The Shipley Grill 913 Shipley St. • 652-7797 • lunch & dinner • live shows • fine dining • full bar • $13-22

SPIRITUAL GROUPS

More Light Hanouver Presb. Church
(18th & Baynard) • 764-1594 • 1st & 3rd
Sun • dinner 5:30pm & worship 6:45pm

PUBLICATIONS

New Moon 3 Maple Ave., New Castle •
monthly lesbian newsletter

District of Columbia

Washington (202)

Info Lines & Services

AA Gay/Lesbian • 797-3580 • substance abuse info line • also see listings in the 'Washington Blade'

Adventuring PO Box 18118, 20036 • lesbigay outdoors group

BiCentrist Alliance PO Box 2254, 20013-2254 • 828-3065 • national bisexual organization w/ mtgs. & newsletter • taped info

Black Lesbian Support Group 1736 14th St. NW • 797-3593 • 3pm 2nd & 4th Sat • women only

Bon Vivant PO Box 576 , Derwood, 20855 • (301) 907-7920 • social club for lesbian professionals • call for details

Coalition of Gay Sisters • (301) 868-8225 • social group for DC area

Dyke TV Channel 25 • 9pm Wed • 'weekly half hour TV show produced by lesbians for lesbians'

Feminist Walking Tours of Capitol Hill PO Box 30563, Bethesda, 20824 • (301) 805-5611 • sponsored by Feminist Institute April-Oct

Gay/Lesbian Hotline (Whitman-Walker Clinic) • 833-3234 • 7pm-11pm • resources • crisis counseling

Gay/Lesbian Switchboard • 628-4667/ 628-4669 (TDD) • 7:30pm-10:30pm • peer counseling & referrals • also Lesbian Line • 628-4666

Hola Gay • 332-2192 • 7pm-11pm Th • hotline en español

Latino/a Lesbian/Gay Organization (LLEGO) 703 'G' St. SE • 544-0092 • 9am-6pm Mon-Fri • also produces bi-monthly newsletter 'Noticias de LLEGO'

Lesbian Resources & Counseling 1407 'S' St. NW (Whitman-Walker Clinic) • 332-5935 • 7pm-9pm Mon w/rap group 7:30pm-9pm

Lesbian/Gay Youth Helpline (at Sexual Minority Youth Assistance League) • 546-5911 • 7pm-10pm M-F • for youth under 21

Nubian Womyn Box 65274, 20035-5274 • group for Black lesbians over 35

OWLS (Older, Wiser Lesbians) 11212 Lombard Rd., Silver Spring, 20901 • 593-6371 • group for women 39+

Roadwork (Sisterfire) 1475 Harvard St. NW • 234-9308 • clsd Mon • women's events production company

S&Mazons PO Box 53394, 20009 • 722-0056 • women's S/M group

Transgender Education Association PO Box 16036, Arlington, 22215 • (301) 949-3822 • social/support group for transvestites & transsexuals

Triangle Club 2030 'P' St. NW • 659-864 • site for various 12-Step groups • see listings in 'The Washington Blade'

Women's Accommodations

Creekside B&B south of Annapolis, MD • (301) 261-9438 • women only • swimming • private home • 45 min. from DC

Accommodations

1836 California 1836 California St. NW • 462-6502 • lesbians/gay men • B&B • historic house (1900) w/ period furnishings & sundeck • patio

Alternative Accommodations • (800) 209-9408 • hotels • guesthouses • B&Bs • corporate apts/stes. • all in metro DC area

The Brenton 1708 16th St. NW • 332-5550/ (800) 673-9042 • mostly gay men • B&B • IGTA member

Capitol Hill Guest House 101 5th St. NE • 547-1050 • gay-friendly • turn-of-the-century Victorian rowhouse B&B in the historic Capitol Hill district • gay-owned/run

The Carlyle Suites 1731 New Hampshire Ave. NW • 234-3200/ (800) 964-5377 • gay-friendly • art deco hotel • Neon Cafe on premises

Embassy Inn 1627 16th St. NW • 234-7800/ (800) 423-9111 • gay-friendly • hotel • small hotel w/ a B&B atmosphere

▲ **Kalorama Guest House at Kalorama Park** 1854 Mintwood Pl. NW • 667-6369 • gay-friendly • B&B • IGTA member

▲ **Kalorama Guest House at Woodley Park** 2700 Cathedral Ave. NW • 328-0860 • gay-friendly • B&B • IGTA member

The Little White House 2909 Pennsylvania Ave. SE • 583-4074 • lesbians/gay men • B&B • colonial revival-style mansion • IGTA member

The River Inn 924 25th St. NW (at 'K' St.) • 337-7600/ (800) 424-2741 • gay-friendly • cafe • wheelchair access • $15-25

Savoy Suites Hotel 2505 Wisconsin Ave. NW, Georgetown • 337-9700/ (800) 944-5377 • gay-friendly • also a restaurant • Italian • wheelchair access

The William Lewis House 1309 'R' St. NW • 462-7574 • mostly gay men • restored turn-of-the-century B&B near Logan Circle & Dupont Circle

The Windsor Inn 1842 16th St. NW • 667-0300/ (800) 423-9111 • gay-friendly • small hotel w/ B&B atmosphere

BARS

Bachelors Mill (downstairs in Back Door Pub) • 544-1931 • 8pm-2am, til 5am Fri-Sat, clsd Mon • lesbians/gay men • dancing/DJ • multi-racial • live shows • more women Wed • wheelchair access

Back Door Pub 1104 8th St. SE • 546-5979 • 5pm-2am, til 3am Fri-Sat • mostly gay men • mostly African-American

The Blue Penguin 801 Pennsylvania Ave. SE • 547-4568 • 3pm-2am, from 11am Sun • lesbians/gay men • dancing/DJ • live shows • karaoke • T-dance Sun • also a restaurant • American • $7-14

Chief Ike's Mambo Room 1725 Columbia Rd. NW • 332-2211 • 4pm-2am • gay-friendly • dancing/DJ • gay night Sun

The Edge 56 'L' St. SE • 488-1200 • 7pm-2am, til 4am Fri-Sun • lesbians/gay men • dancing/DJ • wheelchair access

El Faro 2411 18th St. NW • 387-6554 • noon-2am • lesbians/gay men • mostly Latino-American • live shows • also a restaurant • Mexican/El Salvadorean • $9-14

Fireplace 2161 'P' St. NW • 293-1293 • 1pm-2am • mostly gay men • neighborhood bar • videos

Hung Jury 1819 'H' St. NW • 279-3212 • open Fri-Sat only • popular • mostly women • dancing/DJ • call for events • wheelchair access

Mr. Henry's Capitol Hill 601 Pennsylvania Ave. SE • 546-8412 • 11am-1am • popular • gay-friendly • also a restaurant • lunch & dinner

Phase One 525 8th St. SE • 544-6831 • 7pm-2am, til 3am Fri-Sat • mostly women • neighborhood bar • dancing/DJ • wheelchair access

Fashionable Inns In Fashionable Neighborhoods

o *Walk to Dupont Circle, fashionable clubs and restuarants, and the subway (Metro)*
o *Enjoy breakfast and evening aperitif*

THE KALORAMA GUEST HOUSES
Kalorama Park (202) 667-6369
Woodley Park (202) 328-0860

Washington D.C.

*E*ven though Washington D.C. is known worldwide as a showcase of American culture and a command center of global politics, many people overlook this international 'hot spot' when travelling in the United States. Instead, they're off to exciting cities like New York, LA or Miami. But D.C. is not all boring museums and egocentric bureaucrats.

For instance, begin your stay in D.C. at one of the quaint lesbian/gay B&Bs near the city. **Devonshire House** in Virginia is for women only, while **The Little White House** caters to lesbians and gay men.

Of course, you could tour the usual sites – starting with the heart of D.C., the 'Mall', a two-mile-long grass strip bordered by many museums and monuments: the Smithsonian, the National Air and Space Museum, the National Gallery of Art, the Museum of Natural History, the Museum of American History, the Washington Monument, the Lincoln Memorial and the Vietnam Veterans Memorial.

But for real fun and infotainment, check out these less touristy attractions: the outstanding **National Museum of Women in the Arts**, a **Feminist Walking Tour of Capitol Hill**, the hip shops and exotic eateries along Massachusetts Ave., and of course, DuPont Circle, the pulsing heart of lesbigay D.C.

Here you'll find **Lammas Books**, D.C.'s only women's bookstore – the perfect place to browse, network and get the dirt on what lesbians in D.C. and 'beyond the beltway' love to do after dark and where. The Circle is also home to the famous lesbigay bookstore **Lambda Rising** and the kinky **Pleasure Place**.

For nightlife, don't miss the **Hung Jury**, D.C.'s hippest dyke dancespot, or **Tribate** on Friday or Saturday nights. **Phase One** is a more casual bar for lesbians, and there are several women's nights at the mixed bars.

Still can't find your crowd? Try **HOLA GAY**, the lesbian/gay hotline in Spanish and English, or the **Black Lesbian Support Group**. For the more serious minded, D.C. is home to plenty of political and social women's groups – just call the **Lesbian/Gay Switchboard** or the **Lesbian Resources** line for info.

Scandal 2122 'P' St. • 822-8909 • 4pm-2am • lesbians/gay men • dancing/DJ • mostly Latino-American • also a restaurant • Tex-Mex • some veggie • women's night Th • $5-13

Tracks 1111 First St. SE • 488-3320 • 9pm-4am • popular • lesbians/gay men • dancing/DJ • live shows • food served • women's T-dance last Tue • call for events • wheelchair access

Tribate 2122 'P' St. NW (The Frat House) • 223-4917 • 10pm-2am Fri-Sat • popular • mostly women • dancing/DJ • alternative

Trumpets 1603 17th St. NW • 232-4141 • 4pm-2am, from 11am Sun (brunch) • popular • lesbians/gay men • also a restaurant • New American • some veggie • ladies night Wed • wheelchair access • $10-18

The Underground 1629 Connecticut Ave. NW (at The Circle bar) • 462-5575 • 9pm-2am • popular • lesbians/gay men • dancing/DJ • live shows • women's night Wed

Ziegfields 1345 Half St. SE • 554-5141 • 8pm-3am Th-Sun • lesbians/gay men • dancing/DJ • alternative • live shows • wheelchair access

Restaurants & Cafes

Annie's Paramount Steak House 1609 17th St. NW • 232-0395 • opens 11am, 24hrs Fri-Sat • full bar

Armand's Chicago Pizza 4231 Wisconsin Ave. NW • 686-9450 • 10am-11pm, til 1am Fri-Sat • full bar • also 226 Massachusetts Ave. NE, Capitol Hill • 547-6600

The Belmont Kitchen 2400 18th St. NW • 667-1200 • clsd Mon • plenty veggie • full bar • popular brunch • patio • wheelchair access • women-owned/run • $12-18

Cafe Berlin 322 Massachusetts Ave. NE • 543-7656 • lunch & dinner, dinner only Sun • German • some veggie • $7-20

Cafe Japoné 2032 'P' St. NW • 223-1573 • 5:30pm-2am • mostly Asian-American • live shows • karaoke • Japanese • full bar • $10-15

Washington DC (202)

LESBIGAY INFO: Gay/Lesbian Switchboard: 628-4667. 7:30pm-10:30pm. Gay/Lesbian Hotline: 833-3234. 7pm-11pm

LESBIGAY PAPER: Washington Blade: 797-7000.

WHERE THE GIRLS ARE: Strolling around DuPont Circle or cruising another bar in the lesbigay bar ghetto southeast of The Mall.

ENTERTAINMENT: Gay Men's Chorus: 338-3464.

LESBIGAY AA: 797-3580. Triangle Club: 659-8641. 2030 'P' St. NW.

LESBIGAY PRIDE: June. 298-0970.

ANNUAL EVENTS: October - Reel Affirmations Film Festival: 986-1119.

CITY INFO: D.C. Visitors Association: 789-7000.

BEST VIEW: From the top of the Washington Monument.

WEATHER: Summers are hot (90°s) and MUGGY (The city was built on marshes). In the winter, temperatures drop to the low 30°s and some rain. Spring is the time of cherry blossoms.

TRANSIT: Yellow Cab: 544-1212.

Cafe Luna 1633 'P' St. • 387-4005 • 11am-11pm • popular • lesbians/gay men • multi-racial • healthy • plenty veggie

Dining on the Avenue 1629 Connecticut Ave. NW (upstairs at The Circle) • 462-5575 • 11am-2am, til 3am Fri-Sat • deli • full bar

Ferrarra's Dupont Connecticut Ave. at 'Q' St. NW • 232-1107 • 7am-10pm, til 11pm Fri-Sat • coffee/desserts

Gabriel 2121 'P' St. NW • 956-6690 • 10:30am-midnight • live shows • Southwestern • some veggie • full bar • wheelchair access • $13-18

Guapo's 4515 Wisconsin Ave. NW • 686-3588 • lunch & dinner • Mexican • some veggie • full bar • wheelchair access • $5-11

HIV+ Coffeehouse 2111 Florida Ave. NW (Friends Meeting House) • 483-3310 • 7:30pm-10:30pm Sat • HIV+ & friends

Howard's Grill 613 Pennsylvania Ave. SE • 543-2850 • 11am-2am • lesbians/gay men • American • some veggie • full bar

The Islander 1762 Columbia Rd. NW • 234-4955 • noon-10pm, from 5pm Mon, clsd Sun • BYOB • Caribbean • some veggie

Lauriol Plaza 1801 18th St. NW • 387-0035 • noon-midnight • Latin American

Pepper's 1527 17th St. NW • 328-8193 • global American • full bar • wheelchair access • $7-14

Roxanne 2319 18th St. NW • 462-8330 • 5pm-11pm, bar til 2am wknds • American/Southwestern • some veggie • also Peyote Cafe • Tex/Mex • $8-18

Sala Thai 2016 'P' St. NW • 872-1144 • lunch & dinner

Skewers 1633 'P' St. NW • 387-7400 • noon-11pm • popular • Middle-Eastern • full bar • $7-13

Straits of Malaya 1836 18th St. NW • 483-1483 • lunch & dinner • Singaporean/Malaysian • full bar • rooftop patio

Trio 1537 17th St. NW • 232-6305 • 7:30am-midnight • some veggie • full bar • wheelchair access • $6-10

Trocadero Cafe 1914 Connecticut Ave. (Hotel Pullman) • 797-2000 • French • intimate restaurant • wheelchair access • $25-35

Two Quail 320 Massachusetts Ave. NE • 543-8030 • lunch Mon-Fri & dinner nightly • New American • some veggie • full bar • $10-18

BOOKSTORES & RETAIL SHOPS

Earth Star Connection 1218 31st St. NW • 965-2989 • 10am-7pm • rock shop • crystals • Native American handcrafts

Kramer Books & Afterwords 1517 Connecticut Ave. NW • 387-1400 • opens 7:30am, 24hrs wknds • cafe • general • wheelchair access

Lambda Rising 1625 Connecticut Ave. NW • 462-6969 • 10am-midnight • lesbigay • wheelchair access

▲ **Lammas Women's Books & More** 1426 21st St. NW • 775-8218 • 10am-10pm, 11am-8pm Sun • lesbian/feminist • readings • gifts • music • wheelchair access • women-owned/run

The Map Store, Inc. 1636 'I' St. NW • 628-2608/ (800) 544-2659 • extensive maps & travel guides

Serenity Works 1419 22nd St. NW • 296-1622 • 10am-8pm, clsd Mon • self-help • metaphysical • recovery

Vertigo Books 1337 Connecticut Ave. NW • 429-9272 • 10am-7pm, noon-5pm Sun • global politics • literature • African-American emphasis • wheelchair access

TRAVEL & TOUR OPERATORS

Kasper's Livery Service 201 'I' St. Ste. 512 • 554-2471/ (800) 455-2471 • limousine service serving DC, MD & VA • gay-owned/run

Passport Executive Travel 1025 Thomas Jefferson St. NW • 337-7718/ (800) 222-9800 • IGTA member

Travel Escape 1725 'K' St. NW • 223-9354/ (800) 223-4163 • IGTA member

Washington, DC Convention & Visitors Association 1212 New York Ave. NW • 789-7000

SPIRITUAL GROUPS

Affirmation 3133 Dumbarton NW (Dumbarton United Methodist) • 462-4897 • 6pm Sun

Bet Mishpachah 5 Thomas Cir. NW • 833-1638 • 8:30pm Fri • lesbigay synagogue

Dignity Washington 1820 Connecticut Ave. NW (St. Margaret's Church) • 387-4516 • 4:30pm & 7:30pm Sun

Faith Temple (Evangelical) 1313 New York Ave. NW • 232-4911 • 1pm Sun

Friends (Quaker) 2111 Florida Ave. NW (enter on Decatur) • 483-3310 • 9am, 10am, 11am Sun, 7pm Wed

Lambda Light-DC PO Box 7355, Silver Springs, 20907 • 961-1001 • new age meditational group

Lesbian/Gay Zen Meditation Box 21022, Kalorama Station, 20009-0522 • 6:30-8pm • mail-access only • include your phone number

MCC Washington 474 Ridge St. NW • 638-7373 • 9am, 11am & 7pm Sun

More Light Presbyterians 400 'I' St. SW (Westminister Church) • 484-7700 • 7pm, 11am Sun

PUBLICATIONS

LLEGO Informacion 300 'I' St NE (4th flr.) • 544-0092 • Latina newsletter

Off Our Backs 2337-B 18th St. NW • 234-8072 • international feminist newspaper • 11 times/year

Washington Blade 1408 'U' St. NW 2nd flr. • 797-7000 • weekly

Women's Monthly 1001 N. Highland St., Arlington, 22201 • (703) 527-4881 • covers DC & VA community events

EROTICA

▲ **Pleasure Place** 1063 Wisconsin Ave. NW, Georgetown • 333-8570 • leather • body jewelry

▲ **Pleasure Place** 1710 Connecticut Ave. NW • 483-3297

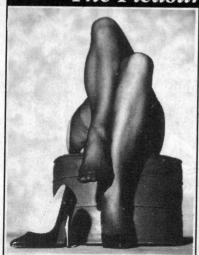

Florida

Amelia Island (904)

ACCOMMODATIONS

Amelia Island Williams House 103 S. 9th St. • 277-2328 • gay-friendly • magnificent 1856 antebellum mansion

Boca Grande (813)

TRAVEL & TOUR OPERATORS

Whelk Women PO Box 10067, 33921 • 964-2027 • boat tours for women • dolphin watching • Charlotte Harbor • outfitted camping offered • women-owned/run

Boca Raton (407)

INFO LINES & SERVICES

Boca Lesbian Rap Group PO Box 485, Deerfield Beach, 33443 • 368-6051 • 7:30pm Tue

ACCOMMODATIONS

Floresta Historic B&B 755 Alamanda St. • 391-1451 • lesbians/gay men • swimming

BARS

Choices 21073 Powerline Rd. 2nd flr. • 482-2195 • 3pm-2am, til 3am Fri-Sat • lesbians/gay men • dancing/DJ • live shows • videos • wheelchair access

SPIRITUAL GROUPS

Church of Our Savior MCC 4770 Boca Raton Blvd. Ste. C • 998-0454 • 10:30am & 7pm Sun • wheelchair access

Clearwater (813)

INFO LINES & SERVICES

Gay/Lesbian Referrral Service of Pinellas County • 586-4297 • 7pm-11pm • also touchtone service 24hrs

BARS

Lost & Found 5858 Roosevelt Blvd. (State Rd. 686) • 539-8903 • 4pm-2am, clsd Mon • mostly gay men • live shows • karaoke • patio • wheelchair access

Pro Shop Pub 840 Cleveland • 447-4259 • 11:30am-2am, from 1pm Sun • popular • mostly gay men • neighborhood bar

Rumors 16100 Fairchild Dr. • 531-8817 • 4pm-2am, from 8pm Mon • mostly women • dancing/DJ • wheelchair access

Cocoa Beach (407)

ACCOMMODATIONS

Triangle Palms Guest House 131 Sunny Ln. • 799-2221/ (800) 799-4297 • lesbians/gay men • swimming • luxurious accommodations on a secluded 1-acre compound w/ private sundeck

BARS

Blondies 5450 N. Atlantic Ave. • 783-5339 • 2pm-2am • lesbians/gay men • dancing/DJ • live shows • wheelchair access

RESTAURANTS & CAFES

Mango Tree 118 N. Atlantic Ave. • 799-0513 • opens 6pm, clsd Mon • beer/wine • fine dining • $12-17

SPIRITUAL GROUPS

Breaking the Silence MCC 1261 Range Rd., Cocoa • 631-4524

Crescent City (904)

ACCOMMODATIONS

Crescent City Campground Rte. 2 Box 25 • 698-2020/ (800) 634-3968 • gay-friendly • swimming • tenting sites & RV hook-ups • laundry & showers

Daytona Beach (904)

INFO LINES & SERVICES

Lambda Center 320 Harvey Ave. • 255-0280 • info & support groups

Live & Let Live AA 1130-B Ridgewood Ave. (Easy Does It Club) • 258-9407 • wheelchair access

RESPECT, Inc. PO Box 5218, 32118 • 257-7071 • gay youth educational group • also referrals

ACCOMMODATIONS

Buccaneer Motel 2301 N. Atlantic Ave. • 253-9678/ (800) 972-6056 • gay-friendly • swimming • IGTA member

Coquina Inn 544 S. Palmetto Ave. • 254-4969/ (800) 805-7533 • gay-friendly • B&B • swimming • fireplaces • wheelchair access • IGTA member

Villa 801 N. Peninsula Dr. • 248-2020 • lesbians/gay men • swimming • nudity • elegant accommodations in historic Spanish mansion • IGTA member

BARS

7-69 Restaurant & Lounge 769 Alabama • 253-4361 • 5pm-3am • lesbians/gay men • neighborhood bar • food served • $3-4

Barndoor 615 Main St. • 252-3776 • 11am-3am, restaurant 8am-midnight • lesbians/gay men • neighborhood bar • also a restaurant • also Hollywood Complex • mostly gay men • dancing/DJ • $3-7

Barracks & Officers' Club 952 Orange Ave. • 254-3464 • 3pm-3am, from noon wknds • mostly gay men • dancing/DJ • live shows • theme nights

Beach Side Club 415 Main St. • 252-5465 • 2pm-3am, from noon wknds • popular • mostly gay men • dancing/DJ • live shows

RESTAURANTS & CAFES

Cafe Frappes 174 Beach St. • 254-7999 • lunch & dinner • some veggie • patio

SPIRITUAL GROUPS

Hope MCC 56 N. Halifax (Unitarian Church) • 254-0993 • 7pm Sun

Dunedin　(813)

BARS

1470 West 325 Main St. • 736-5483 • 4pm-2am, from 3pm Sun, from 8pm Mon • lesbians/gay men • dancing/DJ • live shows • patio • wheelchair access

Fort Lauderdale　(954)

INFO LINES & SERVICES

Broward Women in Network PO Box 9744, 33310 • 537-0866 • professional women's organization

Gay/Lesbian Community Center 1164 E. Oakland Park Blvd. • 563-9500 • 10am-10pm

Lambda South 1231 E. Las Olas Blvd. • 761-9072 • 12-step clubhouse • wheelchair access

ACCOMMODATIONS

215 Guesthouse 215 SW 7th Ave. • 527-4900 • mostly gay men • B&B

Fort Lauderdale

*H*oneycombed by the Intercoastal Waterway of rivers, bays, canals and inlets, Fort Lauderdale is an American Venice – boats are used for transportation! Land-lubbers can see the Everglades, a jai alai game, or shop at Sawgrass Mills outlet mall.

For more breathtaking attractions, however, check out the lesbian community. First, you'll find a number of guesthouses, including the **Club Caribbean Resort**. Spend the day on a chartered **Rainbow Adventure** cruise. Then peruse **Outbooks**, the lesbigay bookstore.

As for bars, Fort Lauderdale has two: **Otherside** and **Partner's Cafe**. Of course, there're several lesbian-friendly bars like **The Copa**, a complete bar complex. Or check out **Gay Skate Night** on Tuesdays at Gold Coast Roller Rink.

Definitely avoid this partytown during Spring Break in late March/early April, when thousands of hormone-driven college-aged heterosexuals descend from points north to engage in drunken revelry and bacchanalia. Unless, of course, that's your thing.

Admiral's Court 21 Hendricks Isle • 462-5072/ (800) 248-6669 • lesbians/gay men • motel • swimming • IGTA member

Club Caribbean Resort 2851 N. Federal Hwy. • 565-0402 • lesbians/gay men • swimming • dancing/DJ • 51 units on 3 acres • also 2 bars & 1 restaurant • IGTA member • $6-11

King Henry Arms Motel 543 Breakers Ave. • 561-0039/ (800) 205-5464 • lesbians/gay men • swimming • small & friendly motel just steps to the ocean • IGTA member

La Casa del Mar 3003 Granada St. • 467-2037/ (800) 739-0009 • lesbians/gay men • swimming • exclusively lesbian & gay home providing a non-cruisy atmosphere • IGTA member

Robindale Suites 709 Breakers Ave. • 565-4123/ (800) 342-7109 • gay-friendly • motel • swimming • wheelchair access

BARS

Boot's 901 SW 27th Ave. • 792-9177 • noon-2am, til 3am Sat • mostly gay men • neighborhood bar • wheelchair access

Bushes 3038 N. Federal Hwy. • 561-1724 • 9pm-2am, til 3am Sat • popular • mostly gay men • neighborhood bar • piano bar • wheelchair access

Copa 624 SE 28th St. • 463-1507 • 9pm-4am • popular • lesbians/gay men • dancing/DJ • live shows • videos • 2 patio bars

Eagle 1951 Powerline Rd. (NW 9th Ave.) • 462-6380 • 2pm-2am • popular • mostly gay men • leather • also Chains leather store • opens 8pm, from 2pm wknds • wheelchair access

End Up 3521 W. Broward Blvd. • 584-9301 • 4pm-4am • mostly gay men • dancing/DJ • T-dance Sun

Everglades Bar 1931 S. Federal Hwy. • 462-9165 • 9am-2am, from noon Sun • mostly gay men • neighborhood bar • wheelchair access

Gold Coast Roller Rink 2604 S. Federal Hwy. (1blk N of the Copa) • 523-6783 • lesbians/gay men • gay skate night 8pm-midnight Tue only

Jungle 545 S. Federal Hwy. • 832-9550 • 9am-2am, from noon-2am Sun • mostly gay men • videos • patio

Otherside of Fort Lauderdale 2283 Wilton Dr. (NE 4th Ave.) • 565-5538 • 6pm-2am, til 3am Sat • popular • mostly women • dancing/DJ • wheelchair access

Fort Lauderdale (954)

LESBIGAY INFO: Gay/Lesbian Community Center: 563-9500. 1164 E. Oakland Park Blvd., 10am-10pm.

LESBIGAY PAPER: TWN (The Weekly News): 757-6333. *Hot Spots*: 928-1862, weekly bar guide. Scoop Magazine: 565-8924, bar guide.

WHERE THE GIRLS ARE: On the beach near the lesbigay accommodations, just south of Birch State Recreation Area. Or at one of the cafes or bars in Wilton Manors or Oakland Park.

LESBIGAY AA: Lambda South: 761-9072. 1231-A E. Las Olas Blvd. Also meetings at the Community Center.

LESBIGAY PRIDE: June. 771-1653.

CITY INFO: Ft. Lauderdale Visitors Bureau: 765-4466

WEATHER: The average year-round temperature in this sub-tropical climate is 75-90°.

TRANSIT: Yellow Cab: 565-5400. Super Shuttle: 764-1700. Broward County Transit: 357-8400

Partner's Cafe 625 E. Dania Beach Blvd., Dania • 921-9893 • noon-3am • mostly women • neighborhood bar

Side Street 1753 N. Andrews Ave. • 525-2007 • 2pm-2am • mostly gay men • videos • karaoke Th-Fri • patio

The Stud 1000 State Rd. 84 • 525-7883 • 4pm-2am, from 2pm Sun • mostly gay men • dancing/DJ • more women Sun

Tropic's Cabaret & Restaurant 2004 Wilton Dr. (NE 4th Ave.) • 537-6000 • 4pm-2am • mostly gay men • neighborhood bar • live shows • also a restaurant • New American • wheelchair access • $4-12

RESTAURANTS & CAFES

Chardee's 2209 Wilton Dr. • 563-1800 • 5pm-2am • lesbians/gay men • live shows • some veggie • full bar • wheelchair access • $12-30

Dalt's Grill 1245 N. Federal • 565-2315 • cont'l • $4-13

The Deck 401 N. Atlantic (Bahama Hotel) • 467-7315 • breakfast, lunch & dinner • cont'l • some veggie • also oceanfront cafe • $8-12

Galeria G'Vannis: The Boulevard Dining Gallery 625 E. Las Olas Blvd. • 524-5246 • live shows • Italian • some veggie • full bar • wheelchair access • $11-30

Legends Cafe 1560 NE 4th Ave. (Wilton Manors Dr.) • 467-2233 • 6pm-10pm, clsd Mon • lesbians/gay men • BYOB • multi-ethnic homecooking • some veggie • wheelchair access • $8-14

Lester's Diner 250 State Rd. 84 • 525-5641 • 24hrs • popular • more gay late nights • $5-10

Sukothai 1930 E. Sunrise Blvd. • 764-0148 • popular • Thai • some veggie

Victoria Park 900 NE 20th Ave. • 764-6868 • dinner only • beer/wine • nouveau • some veggie • call for reservations

BOOKSTORES & RETAIL SHOPS

Broward Video Alternative 710 W. Broward Blvd. • 463-6006 • 11am-11pm, noon-8pm Sun • lesbigay • pride products

▲ **Fallen Angel** 3045 N. Federal Hwy. • 563-5230 • opens 11am • leather • cards • toys

Outbooks 1239 E. Las Olas Blvd. • 764-4333 • 11am-9pm, noon-5pm Sun • lesbigay

TRAVEL & TOUR OPERATORS

Rainbow Adventures • (305) 568-5770/ (800) 881-4814 • lesbigay sailing charters • women-owned/run

Travel I 1619 SW 81st Ave., North Lauderdale • 721-4111

SPIRITUAL GROUPS

Sunshine Cathedral MCC 330 SW 27th St. • 462-2004 • 8:30am, 10am, 11:30am, 7pm Sun • wheelchair access

PUBLICATIONS

The Fountain 2221 Wilton Dr. • 565-7479 • statewide lesbian magazine

Hot Spots 5100 NE 12th Ave. • 928-1862 • weekly • bar guide

Scoop Florida 2219 Wilton Dr. • 561-9707

EROTICA

Fetish Factory 821 N. Federal Hwy. • 462-0032 • 11am-7pm, noon-6pm Sun

Fort Myers (813)

INFO LINES & SERVICES

SW Florida Support Inc. PO Box 546, 33902 • 332-2272 • 8am-11pm • gay switchboard • also publishes 'Support-line' newsletter

BARS

The Alternative 4650 Cleveland Ave. Unit 1-A • 277-7002 • 3pm-2am • lesbians/gay men • neighborhood bar • dancing/DJ • wheelchair access

Bottom Line 3090 Evans Ave. • 337-7292 • 2pm-2am • lesbians/gay men • dancing/DJ • live shows • wheelchair access

Office Pub 3704 Grove • 936-3212 • noon-2am • mostly gay men • neighborhood bar • beer/wine

RESTAURANTS & CAFES

The Oasis 2222 McGregor Blvd. • 334-1566 • 7am-3pm • beer/wine • American • wheelchair access • women-owned/run • $4-6

The Velvet Turtle 1404 Cape Coral Pkwy. • 549-9000 • 5am-9pm, clsd Sun • plenty veggie • full bar • wheelchair access • $8-16

TRAVEL & TOUR OPERATORS

Holiday Mansion Houseboats, Lake Whales • 676-1176

SPIRITUAL GROUPS

St. John the Apostle MCC 2209 Unity • 278-5181 • 10am & 7pm Sun, 7pm Wed

Fort Walton Beach (904)

BARS

Frankly Scarlett 223 Hwy. 98 E. • 664-2966 • 8pm-2am, til 4am wknds • lesbians/gay men • dancing/DJ • live shows • patio • wheelchair access

Gainesville (904)

INFO LINES & SERVICES

Gay Switchboard • 332-0700 • volunteers 6pm-11pm, 24hr touchtone service • extensive info on Gainesville area

Lesbian/Gay/Bisexual Student Union PO Box 118505, 32611-8505 • 392-1665 x310 • several weekly mtgs.

BARS

Melody Club 4130 NW 6th St. • 376-3772 • 8pm-2am Th-Sat • popular • lesbians/gay men • dancing/DJ • live shows • small side bar 'Ambush' open 4pm daily • wheelchair access

The University Club 18 E. University Ave. • 378-6814 • 5pm-2am, til 4am Fri-Sat, til 11pm Sun • lesbians/gay men • dancing/DJ • live shows • more women Fri • patio • wheelchair access

BOOKSTORES & RETAIL SHOPS

Iris Books 802 W. University Ave. • 375-7477 • 10:30am-6:30pm, 11am-4pm Sun • lesbigay • feminist bookstore

SPIRITUAL GROUPS

Trinity MCC 11604 SW Archer Rd. • 495-3378 • 10:15am Sun • wheelchair access

Hallandale (305)

ACCOMMODATIONS

Club Atlantic Resort 2080 S. Ocean Dr. • 458-6666/ (800) 645-8666 • gay-friendly • swimming • rooms & suites on the beach

Holiday (813)

SPIRITUAL GROUPS

Spirit of Life MCC 4810 Mile Stretch Dr. • 942-8616 • 10:30am Sun, 7:30pm Wed • wheelchair access

Hollywood (305)

ACCOMMODATIONS

Maison Harrison Guesthouse 1504 Harrison • 922-7319 • gay-friendly • B&B • spa

BARS

Zachary's 2217 N. Federal Hwy. • 920-5479 • 4pm-2am, from 11am wknds • mostly women • neighborhood bar • beer/wine • wheelchair access • women-owned/run

TRAVEL & TOUR OPERATORS

Post Haste Travel 4555 Sheridan St. • 966-7690/ (800) 881-7690

Jacksonville (904)

INFO LINES & SERVICES

Gay/Lesbian Information & Referral System • 396-8044 • touchtone database for NE Florida

BARS

In Touch Tavern 10957 Atlantic Blvd. • 642-7506 • noon-2am, from 3pm Sun • lesbians/gay men • neighborhood bar • beer/wine • wheelchair access

The Metro 2929 Plum St. • 388-8719 • 4pm-2am, clsd Mon • lesbians/gay men • neighborhood bar • dancing/DJ • patio

My Little Dude/Jo's Place 2952 Roosevelt Blvd. • 388-9503 • 4pm-2am • mostly women • dancing/DJ • live shows • wheelchair access

Park Place Lounge 2712 Park St. • 389-6616 • noon-2am • mostly gay men • neighborhood bar • more women Th nights • wheelchair access

Third Dimension 711 Edison Ave. • 353-6316 • 3pm-2am, from 1pm wknds • mostly gay men • dancing/DJ • alternative • live shows • wheelchair access

BOOKSTORES & RETAIL SHOPS

Otherside of the Rainbow 2709 Park St. • 389-5515 • 11am-7pm, clsd Sun • lesbigay • pride gift store • T-shirts • flags • cards

SPIRITUAL GROUPS

St. Luke's MCC 1140 S. McDuff Ave. • 358-6747 • 10am & 6pm Sun

PUBLICATIONS

The Last Word PO Box 60582, 32236 • 384-6514/ (800) 677-0772

Jacksonville Beach (904)

BARS

Bo's Coral Reef 201 5th Ave. N. • 246-9874 • 2pm-2am • lesbians/gay men • dancing/DJ • live shows

Jasper (904)

ACCOMMODATIONS

The Swan Lake B&B 238 Rte. 129 • 792-2771 • lesbians/gay men • full breakfast hot tub • swimming • nudity

Key West (305)

INFO LINES & SERVICES

Gay AA • 296-8654 • call for times & locations

Helpline • 296-4357 • gay-friendly referrals & assistance

Key West Business Guild PO Box 1208, 33041 • 294-4603/ (800) 535-7797 • IGTA member

WOMEN'S ACCOMMODATIONS

▲ **Rainbow House** 525 United St. • 292-1450/ (800) 749-6696 • popular • women only • guesthouse • hot tub • swimming • nudity • cont'l breakfast • herb teas • smoking outdoors • 1 suite wheelchair access • lesbian-owned/run • $69-169

ACCOMMODATIONS

Alexander Palms Court 715 South St. • 296-6413/ (800) 858-1943 • gay-friendly • swimming

Alexander's Guest House 1118 Fleming St. • 294-9919/ (800) 654-9919 • mostly gay men • B&B • swimming • nudity • IGTA member

▲ **Andrew's Inn** Zero Whalton Ln. • 294-7730 • popular • lesbians/gay men • swimming • elegantly restored rooms & garden cottages • wheelchair access

The Artist House 534 Eaton St. • 296-3977 • gay-friendly • hot tub • Victorian guesthouse

Atlantic Shores Resort 510 South St. • 296-2491/ (800) 526-3559 • gay-friendly • swimming • also a restaurant • also 3 bars • IGTA member

Authors of Key West 725 White St. • 294-7381 • popular • gay-friendly • swimming

Banana's Foster Bed 537 Caroline St. • 294-9061/ (800) 653-4888 • gay-friendly • swimming • historic Conch house B&B • wheelchair access

Big Ruby's Guesthouse 409 Appelrouth Ln. • 296-2323/ (800) 477-7829 • popular • mostly gay men • full breakfast • swimming • nudity • evening wine service • wheelchair access • IGTA member

Blue Parrot Inn 916 Elizabeth St. • 296-0033/ (800) 231-2473 • gay-friendly • swimming • nudity

The Brass Key Guesthouse 412 Frances St. • 296-4719/ (800) 932-9119 • mostly gay men • full breakfast • swimming • luxury guesthouse • spa • wheelchair access • IGTA member

The Captain Saunders House 322 Elizabeth St. • 296-0088 • lesbians/gay men • hot tub • luxury apts w/ weekly rental rates • IGTA member

▲ **Chelsea House** 707 Truman Ave. • 296-2211/ (800) 845-8859 • gay-friendly • swimming • nudity • wheelchair access • IGTA member

Coconut Grove Guesthouse 817 Fleming St. • 296-5107/ (800) 262-6055 (Resv. Only) • mostly gay men • swimming • nudity • 2 Victorian mansions set in lush tropical gardens • IGTA member

▲ **Colours - The Guest Mansion** 410 Fleming St. • 294-6977/ (800) 277-4825 • popular • lesbians/gay men • swimming • complimentary sunset cocktails • IGTA member

Cuban Club Suites 1102-A Duval St. • 296-0465/ (800) 432-4849 • gay-friendly • hotel • award-winning historic hotel overlooking Duval St. • IGTA member

Deja Vu 611 Truman Ave. • 292-1424 • gay-friendly • hot tub • swimming

Duval House 815 Duval St. • 294-1666/ (800) 223-8825 • gay-friendly • B&B • swimming • IGTA member

Duval Suites 724 Duval St. • 293-6600/ (800) 648-3780 • lesbians/gay men • nudity

Eaton Lodge 511 Eaton St. • 292-2170/ (800) 294-2170 • gay-friendly • hot tub • swimming • 1886 mansion & conch house adjacent to Duval St.

Incentra Carriage House Inn 729 Whitehead St. • 296-5565/ (800) 636-7432 • gay-friendly • swimming • 3 houses surrounding lush garden & pool • wheelchair access

Key Lodge Motel 1004 Duval St. • 296-9750/ (800) 458-1296 • popular • gay-friendly • swimming

Key West Realty Inc. 1109 Duval St. • 294-3064/ (800) 654-5131 • gay-friendly • vacation rental info

Key West Reservation Service 628 Fleming St. • 294-7713/ (800) 327-4831 • gay-friendly • hotels • guesthouses • rentals

The Knowles House 1004 Eaton St. • 296-8132/ (800) 352-4414 • lesbians/gay men • B&B • swimming • nudity • restored 1880s Conch house just 5 blocks from Duval Street

La Casa de Luces 422 Amelia St. • 296-3993/ (800) 432-4849 • gay-friendly • guesthouse • early 1900s Conch house • wheelchair access • IGTA member

La Terraza/ La Te Da 1125 Duval St. • 296-6706/ (800) 528-3320 • popular • lesbians/gay men • swimming • guesthouse in a tropical setting • gourmet restaurant • 2 bars • Sun T-dance • IGTA member

Marquesa Hotel 600 Fleming St. • 292-1919/ (800) 869-4631 • gay-friendly • swimming • also a restaurant • some veggie • full bar • wheelchair access • $17-26

Merlin Guesthouse 811 Simonton St. • 296-3336 • gay-friendly • full breakfast • swimming • wheelchair access

The Mermaid and the Alligator 729 Truman Ave. • 294-1894/ (800) 773-1894 • gay-friendly • full breakfast • swimming • nudity

Pegasus International 501 Southard • 294-9323/ (800) 397-8148 • hotel

Pier House Resort & Caribbean Spa 1 Duval St. • 296-4600/ (800) 327-8340 • gay-friendly • swimming • private beach • restaurants • bars • spa • fitness center • IGTA member

Pilot House Guest House 414 Simonton St. • 294-8719/ (800) 648-3780 • lesbians/gay men • hot tub • swimming • 19th century Victorian in Old Town

Sea Isle Resort 915 Windsor Ln. • 294-5188/ (800) 995-4786 • mostly gay men • hot tub • swimming • nudity large private courtyard • gym • sundeck IGTA member

Seascape Guest House 420 Olivia St. • 296-7776/ (800) 765-6438 • gay-friendly • swimming • recently restored inn circa 1889 • located in the heart of Old Town

▲ **Simonton Court Historic Inn & Cottages** 320 Simonton St. • 294-6386/ (800) 944-2687 • popular • lesbians/gay men • hot tub • swimming • 23 unit compound built in 1880s • 3 pools • IGTA member

Tropical Inn 812 Duval St. • 294-9977 • gay-friendly • guesthouse • apts • swimming • daily rentals

Watson House 525 Simonton St. • 294-6712/ (800) 621-9405 • gay-friendly • swimming

William Anthony House 613 Caroline St • 294-2887/ (800) 613-2276 • gay-friendly • swimming • wheelchair access

The William House 1317 Duval St. • 294-8233/ (800) 848-1317 • gay-friendly • turn-of-the-century guesthouse • spa

BARS

801 Bar 801 Duval St. • 294-4737 • 11am-4am • popular • mostly gay men • live shows • also Dan's Bar from 9pm • mostly gay men • country/western

Club International 900 Simonton St. • 296-9230 • 2pm-2am • lesbians/gay men • neighborhood bar • videos

Copa - Key West 623 Duval St. • 296-8522 • garden bar 3pm-4am, dance bar 10pm-4am Wed-Sun • popular • mostly gay men • dancing/DJ • live shows • videos • patio

One Saloon 524 Duval St. (enter on Appelrouth Ln.) • 296-8118 • 10pm-4am • popular • mostly gay men • dancing/DJ • 3 bars • patio • wheelchair access

RESTAURANTS & CAFES

Antonia's 615 Duval St. • 294-6565 • 6pm-11pm • popular • beer/wine • also a restaurant • Northern Italian • some veggie • $16-22

B.O.'s Fish Wagon corner of Duval & Fleming • 294-9272 • lunch • popular • seafood & eat it • $3-8

Cafe des Artistes 1007 Simonton St. • 294-7100 • 6pm-11pm • tropical French • full bar • $22-30

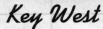

Key West

*T*his tiny 'Caribbean' island at the very tip of Florida, closer to Cuba than to Miami, is a lesbian and gay tropical paradise. The famous Old Town area is dotted with Victorian homes and mansions. Many of them are now fully renovated as accommodations, such as the women-only **Rainbow House**.

Perhaps because Key West life is so relaxed, there's only one mixed bar, **Club International**, and two boys' bars. You can also relax while sailing the emerald waters around Key West with **Women on the Water**. The ocean is home to the hemisphere's largest living coral reef, accessible by snorkeling and scuba vessels. Or rent a moped from one of the many bike rental shops to cruise the island.

Don't miss **Women in Paradise** in September, the annual women's week in Key West – the ideal time and place to experience women entertainers, sailing, a street fair, dances and more. **Fantasy Fest** in October is seven days of Halloween in tropical heaven: costumes, contests, parades, and parties galore.

Key West   (305)

LESBIGAY INFO: Key West Business Guild: 294-4603 / (800) 535-7797.

LESBIGAY PAPER: Southern Exposure: 294-6303.

WHERE THE GIRLS ARE: You can't miss 'em during Women In Paradise in September, but other times they're just off Duval St. somewhere between Eaton and South Streets. Or on the beach. Or in the water.

LESBIGAY AA: 296-8654. 1215 Petronia St.

ANNUAL EVENTS: June - International Gay Arts Fest: (800) 535-7797, cultural festival of film, theatre, art, concerts, seminars, parties and a parade.

September - Women in Paradise: 296-4238 / (800) 535-7797.
October - Fantasy Fest: (800) 535-7797, week-long Halloween celebration with parties, masquerade balls & parades.

CITY INFO: Key West Chamber of Commerce: 294-2587.

BEST VIEW: Old Town Trolley Tour (1/2 hour).

WEATHER: The average temperature year round is 78°, and the sun shines nearly everyday – any time is the right time for a visit.

TRANSIT: Yellow Cab: 294-2227.

Croissants de France 816 Duval St. • 294-2624 • 7:30am-4pm • lesbians/gay men • French pastries/crepes/gallettes • some veggie • patio • $5-7

Dim Sum 613-1/2 Duval St. • 294-6230 • clsd Tue • beer/wine • Pan-Asian • plenty veggie • sake cocktails • $13-17

Duffy's Steak & Lobster House 600 Truman Ave. • 296-4900 • 11am-11pm • full bar • $15-30

Dynasty 918 Duval St. • 294-2943 • 5:30pm-10pm • beer/wine • Chinese • $7-16

La Trattoria Venezia 524 Duval St. • 296-1075 • lesbians/gay men • Italian • full bar • $12-22

Louie's Backyard 700 Waddell Ave. • 294-1061 • lunch & dinner, bar 11:30am-2am • popular • cont'l • fine dining • $22-30

Mango's 700 Duval St. • 292-4606 • 11am-2am • internat'l • plenty veggie • full bar • wheelchair access • $10-22

Palm Grill 1029 Southard St. • 296-1744 • some veggie • $16-20

Pancho & Lefty's Southwestern Cafe 632 Olivia St. • 294-8212 • 5pm-10:30pm, clsd Tue • beer/wine • Mexican • $5-10

The Quay 10 Duval St. • 294-4446 • gourmet • some veggie • $13-18

Rooftop Cafe 310 Front St. • 294-2042 • live shows • American/Caribbean • some veggie • cocktails • $10-22

Savannah 915 Duval St. • 296-6700 • dinner nightly • popular • lesbians/gay men • Southern homecooking • garden bar • $11-16

South Beach Seafood & Raw Bar 1405 Duval St. • 294-2727 • 7am-10pm • around $15 for dinner

Square One 1075 Duval St. • 296-4300 • 6:30pm-10:30pm, Sun brunch • American • full bar • wheelchair access • $14-22

The Twisted Noodle 628 Duval St. • 296-6670 • 5pm-10:30pm • Italian • $7-15

Yo Sake 722 Duval St. • 294-2288 • 6pm-11pm • Japanese/sushi bar • $10-18

GYMS & HEALTH CLUBS

Duval Square Health & Fitness 1075 Duval St. • 292-9683 • 6am-11pm, 9am-10pm wknds • lesbians/gay men • full gym • sauna • massage therapy available

Pro Fitness 1112 12th St. • 294-1865 • 6pm-9pm, from 9am Sat & 11am Sun • women-owned/run

BOOKSTORES & RETAIL SHOPS

Blue Heron Books 538 Truman Ave. • 296-3508 • 10am-10pm, til 9pm Sun • lesbigay section • general

Caroline St. Books & Cafe 800 Caroline St. • 294-3931 • 10am-10pm • alternative • also coffee bar • wheelchair access

Fast Buck Freddie's 500 Duval St. • 294-2007 • 11am-7pm • clothing • gifts

Key West Island Books 513 Fleming St. • 294-2904 • 10am-6pm • new & used rare books

Lido 532 Duval St. • 294-5300 • 10am-7pm, til 10pm Th-Sat, 11am-7pm Sun • clothing • gifts • gay-owned/run

Star Gazers 425-A Front St. • 296-1186/ (800) 291-1186 • 10am-10pm • new age • metaphysical

TRAVEL & TOUR OPERATORS

Escape Cruises Key West Bight marina • 296-4608 • 3-hr reef trip & sunset cruise on 'SS Sunshine'

IGTA (International Gay Travel Association) PO Box 4974, 33041 • 296-6673/ (800) 448-8550 • active organization for lesbian/gay travel industry

Regency Travel 1075 Duval St. #19 • 294-0175/ (800) 374-2784 • IGTA member

Women on the Water PO Box 502, 33041 • 294-0662 • day & evening sails • snorkle trips • lesbian-owned/run

SPIRITUAL GROUPS

MCC Key West 1215 Petronia St. • 294-8912 • 9:30am & 11am Sun

PUBLICATIONS

Southern Exposure 819 Peacock Plaza Ste. 575, 33041 • 294-6303 • monthly

EROTICA

Leather Masters 418-A Appelrouth Ln. • 292-5051 • custom leather

Lake Worth (407)

BARS

Inn Exile 6 S. 'J' St. • 582-4144 • 3pm-2am, til midnight Sun • mostly gay men • live shows • videos • karaoke Tue

K & E's 29 S. Dixie Hwy. • 533-6020 • 11am-2am, from 2pm wknds • lesbians/gay men • food served

Lakeland (813)

INFO LINES & SERVICES

PGLA (Polk Gay/Lesbian Alliance) PO Box 8221, 33802-8221 • 644-0085

ACCOMMODATIONS

Sunset Motel & RV Resort 2301 New Tampa Hwy. • 683-6464 • gay-friendly • swimming • motel, apts, RV hookups & private home all sharing 3 acres • wheelchair access

BARS

Dockside 3770 Hwy. 92 E. • 665-2590 • 4pm-2am • lesbians/gay men • dancing/DJ • live shows • gay-owned/run

Roy's Green Parrot 1030 E. Main St. • 683-6021 • 4pm-2am, til midnight Sun • popular • mostly gay men • dancing/DJ • live shows • beer/wine

Madeira Beach (813)

BARS

Surf & Sand Lounge/ Back Room Bar 14601 Gulf Blvd. • 391-2680 • 8am-2am • mostly gay men • neighborhood bar • beach access • wheelchair access

Melbourne (407)

BARS

Loading Zone 4910 Stack Blvd. • 727-3383 • 8pm-2am • popular • lesbians/gay men • dancing/DJ • videos • wheelchair access

Saturday's Lounge 4060 W. New Haven Ave. • 724-1510 • 2pm-2am, clsd Mon • popular • lesbians/gay men • dancing/DJ • live shows

Miami (305)

(See also Miami Beach/
South Beach)

INFO LINES & SERVICES

**Gay/Lesbian/Bisexual Hotline of
Greater Miami** • 759-3661

Lambda Dade AA 410 NE 22nd St.
(Carriage House) • 573-9608 • 8:30pm
daily • call for other mtg. times • wheelchair access

South Florida Bisexual Network • 936-
5934 • 24hr message • meetings weekly
in Dade & Broward counties

Switchboard of Miami 75 SW 8th St. •
358-4357 • 24hrs • gay-friendly info &
referrals for Dade County

BARS

Cheers 2490 SW 17th Ave. , Coconut
Grove • 857-0041 • 9pm-3am, clsd Mon
• mostly women • dancing/DJ • live
shows

On the Waterfront 3615 NW South River
Dr. • 635-5500 • call for events • popular
• lesbians/gay men • dancing/DJ • multi-
racial • live shows • call for events

RESTAURANTS & CAFES

LB's 5813 Ponca de Leon Blvd. • 661-
7091 • 11am-4pm • homecooking •
some veggie • $5-10

Oak Feed 2911 Grand Ave. , Coconut
Grove • 446-9036 • 11am-10pm •
sushi/vegetarian

Something Special 7762 NW 14th Ct.
(private home) • 696-8826 • noon-9pm,
2pm-7pm Sun • women only • vegetarian • plenty veggie • also tent space

BOOKSTORES & RETAIL SHOPS

Lambda Passages Bookstore 7545
Biscayne Blvd. • 754-6900 • 11am-9pm,
noon-6pm Sun • gay/lesbian/feminist
bookstore

Ouch Boutique 3415 Mountain Hwy.,
Coconut Grove • 443-6824 • club clothes

TRAVEL & TOUR OPERATORS

Amazon Tours & Cruises 8700 W. Flagler
Ste. 190 • (800) 423-2791 • IGTA member

Professional Travel Management 195
SW 15th Rd. Ste. 403 • 858-5522/ (800)
568-4064 • IGTA member

Vision Travel: Carlson Travel Network
2222 Ponce de Leon Blvd. • 444-8484/
(800) 654-4544

SPIRITUAL GROUPS

Christ MCC 7701 SW 76th Ave. • 284-
1040 • 9:30am & 7pm Sun • wheelchair
access

Grace MCC 10390 NE 2nd Ave., Miami
Shores • 758-6822 • 11:30am Sun

PUBLICATIONS

The Fountain 2221 Wilton Dr. , Ft.
Lauderdale, 33305 • 565-7479 •
statewide lesbian magazine

TWN (The Weekly News) 901 NE 79th
St. • 757-6333

Miami Beach/
South Beach (305)

INFO LINES & SERVICES

**Lesbian/Gay/Bisexual Community
Center** 1335 Alton Rd. • 531-3666 •
2pm-9pm

South Beach Business Guild • 234-7224
• maps & info

ACCOMMODATIONS

Abbey Hotel 300 21st St. • 531-0031 •
gay-friendly • studios • kitchens

The Bayliss 504 14th St. • 534-0010 •
lesbians/gay men • art deco hotel

Bohemia Gardens 825 Michigan Ave. •
556-9997 • gay-friendly

Chelsea Hotel 944 Washington Ave. •
534-4069 • gay-friendly

Collins Plaza 318 20th St. • 532-0849 •
gay-friendly • hotel

Colours - The Mantell Guest Inn 255 W.
24th St. • 538-1821/ (800) 277-4825 • les-
bians/gay men • swimming • several art
deco hotels & apts available • IGTA
member

European Guesthouse 721 Michigan
Ave. • 673-6665 • lesbians/gay men •
B&B • full breakfast • hot tub • IGTA
member

Fountainbleu Hilton Resort & Spa 4441
Collins Ave. • 538-2000/ (800) 445-8667 •
gay-friendly • swimming • wheelchair
access

Hotel Impala 1228 Collins • 673-2021/
(800) 646-7252 • gay-friendly • luxury
hotel near beach • wheelchair access

Jefferson House 1018 Jefferson Ave. •
534-5247 • lesbians/gay men • newly renovated B&B • tropical garden • IGTA
member

Kenmore Hotel 1050 Washington Ave. •
531-4199 • gay-friendly • swimming

▲ **Lily Guesthouse** 835 Collins Ave. • 535-
9900 • popular • lesbians/gay men • studios • suites • sundeck • patio

Lord Balfour 350 Ocean Dr. • 673-0401/
(800) 501-0401 • gay-friendly

Marlin Hotel 1200 Collins Ave. • 673-
8770/ (800) 688-7678 • gay-friendly •
upscale • wheelchair access

Moline Garden Guesthouse 825
Michigan Ave. • 556-9997 • gay-friendly

Park Washington 1020 Washington •
532-1930 • gay-friendly • hotel • swimming

Penguin Hotel & Bar 1418 Ocean Dr. •
534-9334/ (800) 235-3296 • lesbians/gay
men • also a restaurant • plenty veggie •
full bar • cafe/juice bar

South Beach Central • (800) 538-3616 •
gay-friendly • hotel reservations • vacation rentals • IGTA member • gay-
owned/run

South Beach Destinations • 666-0163/
(800) 443-8224 • reservation service

South Beach Hotel 236 21st St. • 531-
3464 • gay-friendly • historic art deco
hotel w/ 24hr cafe • 1/2 block from
clothes optional beach

Villa Paradiso Guesthouse 1415 Collins
Ave. • 532-0616 • gay-friendly • studios

Winterhaven Hotel 1400 Ocean Dr. •
531-5571/ (800) 395-2322 • gay-friendly •
Italian • full bar • cafe • classic example
of deco architecture • IGTA member

Bars

821 821 Lincoln Rd • 534-0887 • 10am-
5pm • mostly gay men • neighborhood
bar • women's night Th from 6pm

Bash 655 Washington Ave. • 538-2274 •
10pm-5am, clsd Mon-Tue • gay-friendly •
dancing/DJ

Kremlin 727 Lincoln Rd. • 673-3150 •
10am-4am, clsd Sun-Wed • lesbians/gay
men • dancing/DJ • more women Sat

Lucky's 1969 71st St. • 868-0901 • 4pm-
5am • mostly gay men • neighborhood
bar

Paragon 245 22nd St. (at Collins Ave.) •
534-1235 • 9:30pm-5am Sat & Tue, clsd
Mon & Th • popular • mostly gay men •
dancing/DJ • live shows • wheelchair
access

Miami & South Beach

*A*s a key center of business and politics in the Americas, Miami has an incredibly multicultural look and feel. You'll discover a diversity of people, from a growing population of transplanted senior citizens to large communities of Cubans, Latin-Americans, and Americans of African descent.

Miami is also a tourists' 'winter wonderland' of sun, sand and sea. Make the most of it with trips to Miami Beach, Seaquarium, Key Biscayne or the nearby Everglades. As for Miami's 'women wonderland', check out **Cheers** or try one of the multi-racial, mixed lesbian/gay bars. For a more low-key evening, try the 3rd Friday Night Womyn's Group at the **Lesbian/Gay/Bisexual Community Center** or the **Women's Film Series** on the 4th Friday at the **New Alliance Theater** (600 Lincoln Rd. #219 at Penn Ave.).

Or make reservations to dine at **Something Special**, a women-only restaurant in a private home. Get the latest dirt from **Lips**, South Florida's "female newspaper," or **The Fountain** women's magazine, both available at **Lambda Passages**, the lesbigay bookstore.

But if you're really hungry for loads of lesbigay culture, head directly for South Beach. This section of Miami Beach has been given an incredible makeover by gays and lesbians, and is fast becoming the hot spot on the East Coast – even Madonna and Prince have staked out the area!

Much of the scene there is gay boys and drag queens, but svelte, hot-blooded women are in abundance too. During the day, 12th St. beach is the place to be seen. Hang out at **Gertrude's** coffeehouse or try the **Palace Grill** for a queer mid-afternoon munch and great people-watching across from the 12th St. gay beach. **821** attracts professional women on their women's nights hosted by Mary D, and on Saturdays Latina women exercise social graces at the **Miami Racquet & Fitness Club** on Bird Rd. at 93rd Ave. Saturday afternoons **The Penguin**'s ladies happy hour is the place for lesbian lounge lizards. Serious dance-aholics cruise the **Kremlin** on Saturday nights. Later, head to **Wolfie's** or the **News Cafe** for an after-dancing meal.

If you're dazzled by South Beach's historic Art Deco architecture, take the walking tour that leaves from the **Miami Welcome Center** at 1224 Ocean Dr. (672-2014) for under $10.

Miami

(305)

LESBIGAY INFO: Gay/Lesbian Community Center: 531-3666. 1335 Alton Rd., 6am-9pm.
Gay/Lesbian/Bisexual Hotline of Greater Miami: 759-3661.

LESBIGAY PAPER: TWN (The Weekly News): 757-6333. The Wire: 538-3111. She-Times: 573-6303. Lips: 534-4830. Contax: 757-6333. The Fountain: 565-7479.

WHERE THE GIRLS ARE: In Miami proper, Coral Gables and the University district, as well as Biscayne Blvd. along the coast, are the lesbian hangouts of choice. You'll see women everywhere in South Beach, but especially along Ocean Dr., Washington, Collins and Lincoln Roads.

ENTERTAINMENT: Bridge Theater Play Readings at the Community Center, Wednesdays.

LESBIGAY AA: Lambda Dade AA: 573-9608. 410 NE 22nd St. (Carriage House), 8:30pm daily.

LESBIGAY PRIDE: June. 771-1653.

ANNUAL EVENTS: March - Winter Party: (305) 593-6666, AIDS benefit dance on the beach. November - White Party Vizcaya: (305) 757-4444, AIDS benefit.

CITY INFO: Greater Miami Convention and Visitors Bureau: 539-3000.

BEST VIEW: If you've got money to burn, a helicopter flight over Miami Beach is a great way to see the city. Otherwise, hit the beach.

WEATHER: Warm all year. Temperatures stay in the 90ºs during the summer and drop into the mid 60ºs in the winter. Be prepared for sunshine!

TRANSIT: Yellow Cab: 444-4444. Metro Taxi: 888-8888..

Splash 5922 S. Dixie Hwy. • 662-8779 • 4pm-2am, clsd Mon • mostly gay men • dancing/DJ • live shows

Sugar's 17060 W. Dixie • 940-9887 • 3pm-6am • mostly gay men • neighborhood bar • dancing/DJ • videos • more women Sat • wheelchair access

Twist 1057 Washington Ave. • 538-9478 • 1pm-5am • popular • mostly gay men • dancing/DJ • wheelchair access

The Warsaw 1450 Collins Ave. • 531-4555 • 9:30pm-5am Wed-Sun, clsd Mon-Tue & Th • popular • mostly gay men • dancing/DJ • live shows • progressive music

Westend 942 Lincoln Rd. • 538-9378 • 8am-5am • mostly gay men • neighborhood bar

RESTAURANTS & CAFES

11th Street Diner 11th & Washington • 534-6373 • til midnight, 24hrs on wknds • some veggie • full bar • $6-14

A Fish Called Avalon 700 Ocean Dr. • 532-1727 • 6pm-11pm • popular • some veggie • full bar • patio • wheelchair access • $12-22

Bang 1516 Washington • 531-2361 • popular • internat'l • full bar

Beehive 630 Lincoln Rd. • 538-7484 • noon-midnight • pizza/pasta • patio

Cafe Atlantico 429 Espanola Wy. • 672-1168 • 6pm-midnight, bar til 3am • New World tapas • some veggie • wheelchair access • $15-25

El Rancho Grande 1626 Pennsylvania Ave. • 673-0480 • Mexican

The Front Porch 1420 Ocean Dr. • 531-8300 • 8am-midnight • healthy home-cooking • some veggie • full bar • $6-10

Gertrude's 826 Lincoln Rd. • 538-6929 • 11am-3pm, 6pm-11pm • lesbians/gay men • coffeehouse • women-owned/run

Jams Tavern & Grill 1331 Washington • 532-6700 • 11am-5am • beer/wine

Larios on the Beach 820 Ocean Dr. • 532-9577 • 11am-midnight, til 2am Fri-Sat • Cuban • $5-12

Lucky Cheng's 1412 Ocean Dr. • 672-1505 • 6pm-midnight • popular • live shows • full bar

Lulu's 1053 Washington • 532-6147 • 11am-2am • popular • Southern home-cooking • full bar • wheelchair access • $5-11

News Cafe 800 Ocean Dr. • 538-6397 • 24hrs • popular • healthy sandwiches • some veggie • $4-6

Norma's on the Beach 646 Lincoln Ave. • 532-2809 • opens 4pm, clsd Mon • popular • New World Caribbean • full bar • $11-19

Pacific Time 915 Lincoln Rd. • 534-5979 • lunch & dinner weekdays • Pan-Pacific • some veggie • $10-30

Palace Bar & Grill 1200 Ocean Dr. • 531-9077 • 8am-2am • American • full bar • $10-15

The Strand 671 Washington Ave. • 532-2340 • 6pm-2am • some veggie • full bar • wheelchair access • $7-12

Sushi Rock Cafe 1351 Collins Ave. • 532-2133 • sushi • full bar

Wolfie's Jewish Deli 2038 Collins Ave. (at 21st) • 538-6626 • 24hrs • gourmet deli • $6-8

WPA 685 Washington • 534-1684 • popular • gospel brunch Sun & cabaret Mon

BOOKSTORES & RETAIL SHOPS

The 9th Chakra 817 Lincoln Rd. • 538-0671 • clsd Mon • metaphysical books • supplies • gifts

GW's 720 Lincoln Rd. Mall • 534-4763 • 11am-10pm, til 8pm Sun • lesbigay emporium

Whittal & Schon 1319 Washington • 538-2606 • 11am-9pm, til midnight Fri-Sat • funky clothes

SPIRITUAL GROUPS

Congregation Etz Chaim 1921 Pembroke Rd. • 758-5991 • 8:30pm Fri • gay/lesbian synagogue

MCC 2100 Washington Ave. • 759-1015 • 11am Sun

PUBLICATIONS

Lips 2699 Collins Ave. #121 • 534-4830 • 'a female newspaper serving south Florida'

Wire 1638 Euclid Ave., 33139 • 538-3111 • weekly • guide to South Beach

Naples   (941)

INFO LINES & SERVICES

Lesbian/Gay AA • 262-6535 • several mtgs.

ACCOMMODATIONS

Festive Flamingo • 455-8833 • lesbians/gay men • swimming

BARS

The Galley 509 3rd St. S. • 262-2808 • 4pm-2am, from 1pm Sun • lesbians/gay men • neighborhood bar • more women Fri

RESTAURANTS & CAFES

Cafe Flamingo 947 3rd Ave. N. • 262-8181 • 8am-2pm, clsd Sat • some veggie • women-owned/run • $3-5

BOOKSTORES & RETAIL SHOPS

Book Nook 824 5th Ave. S. • 262-4740 • 8am-6pm • lesbigay

Lavender's 5600 Trail Blvd. #4 • 594-9499 • call for hours • lesbigay bookstore & pride shop

Orlando (407)

INFO LINES & SERVICES

Family Values WPRK 91.5 FM • 646-2398 • 7pm Wed • lesbigay radio

Gay/Lesbian Community Center 714 E. Colonial Dr. • 425-4527 • 11am-9pm, noon-5pm Sat, clsd Sun

Gay/Lesbian Community Services of Central Florida • 843-4297 • 24hr touch-tone helpline • extensive referrals

LCN (Loving Committed Network) PO Box 149512, 32814-9512 • 332-2311 • lesbian community social/support group • monthly events • 'LCN Express' newsletter

Metropolitan Business Association PO Box 568041, 32856 • 420-2182 • 6:30pm 1st Th • at the Radisson Hotel

WOMEN'S ACCOMMODATIONS

Leora's B&B PO Box 6094, 32853 • 649-0009 • women only • $45-75

ACCOMMODATIONS

A Veranda B&B 115 N. Summerlin Ave. • 849-0321/ (800) 420-6822 • gay-friendly • hot tub • conveniently located in downtown Orlando • wheelchair access

▲ **The Garden Cottage B&B** 1309 E. Washington Ave. • 894-5395 • lesbians/gay men • quaint & romantic 1920s private cottage in gay downtown area • women-owned/run

Orlando (407)

LESBIGAY INFO: Gay/Lesbian Community Center: 425-4527. 714 E. Colonial Dr., 11pm-9pm, noon-5pm Sat. Gay/Lesbian Community Services: 843-4297 (24hr touch-tone).

LESBIGAY PAPER: Triangle: 425-4527. The Fountain: (305) 565-7479, lesbian magazine. The Watermark: 481-2243, bi-weekly.

WHERE THE GIRLS ARE: Women who live here hang out at Three Women's Hotline (a bar & Italian restaurant) or Moorefield's restaurant. Tourists are - where else? - at the tourist attractions, including the Mannequins bar in Disney World.

ENTERTAINMENT: Orlando Gay Chorus: 645-5866.

LESBIGAY PRIDE: June.

ANNUAL EVENTS: June - Gay Day at Disneyworld: 857-5444. December - Red Ribbon Ball: 849-1452. September - Headdress Ball: 645-2577.

CITY INFO: Orlando Visitors' Bureau: 363-5871.

ATTRACTIONS: Walt Disney World: 824-4321. Universal Studios. Wet & Wild Waterpark. Sea World.

WEATHER: Mild winters, hot summers.

TRANSIT: Yellow Cab: 699-9999. Gray Line: 422-0744. Rabbit: 291-2424, public. Lynx: 841-8240, public.

Parliament House Motor Inn 410 N. Orange Blossom Tr. • 425-7571 • popular • mostly gay men • swimming • live shows • food served • 5 bars on premises

Rick's B&B PO Box 22318 , Lake Buena Vista, 32830 • 396-7751 • lesbians/gay men • full breakfast • swimming • patio

BARS

The Club/ The Firestone 578 N. Orange Ave. • 426-0005 • popular • lesbians/gay men • dancing/DJ • live shows • videos • call for events

The Complex 3400 S. Orange Blossom Tr. • 422-6826 • noon-2am • lesbians/gay men • dancing/DJ • live shows • various bars • gym • video store

The Edge 100 W. Livingston St. • 839-4331 • gay-friendly • dancing/DJ • live shows • gay night Th • call for events

Faces 4910 Edgewater Dr. • 291-7571 • 4pm-2am • popular • mostly women • dancing/DJ • live shows • wheelchair access

Mannequins Paradise Island at Disney World • popular • dancing/DJ • very straight except some gays on Employee Night Th

Phoenix 7124 Aloma Ave., Winter Park • 678-9220 • 4pm-2am • lesbians/gay men • live shows

Power House Disco (at Parliament House) • 425-7571 • 8pm-2am • popular • mostly gay men • dancing/DJ

Secrets 745 Bennett Rd. • 898-5603 • 9pm-2am, clsd Mon-Tue • lesbians/gay men • dancing/DJ • live shows

Southern Nights 375 S. Bumby Ave. • 898-0424 • 4pm-2am • lesbians/gay men • dancing/DJ • live shows • wheelchair access

Three Women's Hotline 801 State Rd. 436, Altamonte Springs • 788-7272 • 6pm-2am, clsd Tue-Wed • mostly women • dancing/DJ • live shows • also a restaurant • Italian • some veggie • wheelchair access • women-owned/run • $7-13

RESTAURANTS & CAFES

Dug Out Diner (at Parliament House) • 425-7571x711 • 24hrs • lesbians/gay men

Moorefields 123 S. Orange Ave. • 872-6960 • lunch & dinner, clsd Sun-Mon • popular • lesbians/gay men • beer/wine • healthy cont'l • some veggie • wheelchair access • $13-20

Orlando

*O*rlando is a city exploding with growth – just to keep up with the Walt Disney World amusement complex, home of the enormous Epcot Center, the Magic Kingdom, MGM Studios, shopping and much more. June – is when Disney World hosts an unofficial Gay/Lesbian day. Call **Disney World** for info; if they claim ignorance, try the **Gay/Lesbian Community Services** (GLCS) touchtone info line (press "o" to talk to a live person). While you're on the line, find out when the next Gay Day in the Busch (Gardens, that is) or at the State Fair will be.

Faces is the local lesbian bar, while **Southern Nights** and **The Club** (aka Firestone) are the places to dance. For education, stop by the local lesbigay store, **Out & About Books**, or the **Gay/Lesbian Community Center**, and pick up a copy of **The Triangle**. And for fun, go rollerskating at the bi-monthly **GaySkate** in nearby Castleberry, or watch a lesbian/gay-themed movie at The Club on Monday nights. Lesbian social group **LCN** sponsors plenty of other events, including picnics at Wekiva Falls, and a dance in mid-January.

Thorton Park Cafe 900 E. Washington • 425-0033 • 11am-10pm • beer/wine • seafood/Italian • some veggie • patio • wheelchair access • $9-17

White Wolf Cafe & Antique Shop 1829 N. Orange Ave. • 895-5590 • 10am-midnight, clsd Sun • live shows • beer/wine • salads/sandwiches • plenty veggie • wheelchair access • $5-12

BOOKSTORES & RETAIL SHOPS

Alobar 709 W. Smith St. • 841-3050 • 10am-9pm, noon-5pm Sun • books • music • wheelchair access

Blue Parrot Art Deco Shop (at Parliament House) • 425-7571 • 9pm-2am

Out & About Books 930 N. Mills Ave. • 896-0204 • 10am-8pm, noon-6pm Sun • lesbigay

TRAVEL & TOUR OPERATORS

Odyssey 334 E. Michigan St. • 841-8686/ (800) 327-4441 • IGTA member

SPIRITUAL GROUPS

Joy MCC 2351 S. Ferncreek Ave • 894-1081 • 10:30am & 7:15pm Sun, 7:15pm Wed

PUBLICATIONS

The Triangle PO Box 533446, 32853 • 425-4527 • monthly

EROTICA

Absolute Leather 3400 S. Orange Blossom Tr. • 843-8168/ (800) 447-4820 • noon-9pm, til midnight Th-Sat • wheelchair access

The Leather Closet 498 N. Orange Blossom Tr. • 649-2011 • noon-2am

Palm Beach   (407)

ACCOMMODATIONS

Palm Beach Polo B&B RPB Blvd. Box 384, Royal Palm Beach • 798-4072/ (800) 344-0335 • lesbians/gay men • swimming

Palm Beach Gardens (407)

TRAVEL & TOUR OPERATORS

Vagabond Travels 601 Northlake Blvd. • 848-0648/ (800) 226-3830 • IGTA member

Garden Cottage

Antiques
TV-Films
Stereo
Kitchen
Private
Garden
Courtyard
Close to
Disney
Hosts Lisa
& Sherry

in historic downtown orlando

4 0 7 8 9 4 5 3 9 5

Bed & BreakFast

Panama City   (904)

BARS

Fiesta Room 110 Harrison Ave. • 763-9476 • 8pm-3am • popular • lesbians/gay men • dancing/DJ • live shows • wheelchair access

La Royale Lounge & Liquor Store 100 Harrison • 763-9110 • 3pm-3am • popular • lesbians/gay men • neighborhood bar • courtyard • wheelchair access

Pembroke Pines   (305)

RESTAURANTS & CAFES

Blue Goose Cafe 1491 N. Palm Ave. • 436-8677 • from 5:30pm, clsd Mon • beer/wine • pasta/steak/seafood • some veggie • $7-15

Pensacola   (904)

INFO LINES & SERVICES

AA Gay/Lesbian 415 N. Alcaniz (MCC location) • 433-8528 • 8pm Fri

BARS

J.J.'s 810 Gregory • 436-2007 • 2pm-3am • mostly gay men • neighborhood bar • live shows

The Park 312 E. Government • 434-3441 • 11am-3am • lesbians/gay men • neighborhood bar • live shows • wheelchair access

Red Carpet 937 Warrington Rd. • 453-9918 • 3pm-3am • lesbians/gay men • dancing/DJ • live shows • patio

Round-up 706 E. Gregory • 433-8482 • 3pm-3am • popular • mostly gay men • dancing/DJ • videos • wheelchair access

BOOKSTORES & RETAIL SHOPS

Silver Chord Bookstore 10901 Lillian Hwy. • 453-6652 • 1pm-7pm, from 11am Sun • metaphysical • lesbigay section

SPIRITUAL GROUPS

Holy Cross MCC 415 N. Alcaniz • 433-8528 • 11am Sun, 7pm Wed

PUBLICATIONS

Christopher St. South PO Box 2752, 32513 • 433-0353 • quarterly

Pompano Beach   (305)

BARS

Adventures 303 SW 6th St. • 782-9577 • 2pm-2am • lesbians/gay men • neighborhood bar • wheelchair access

Port Richey   (813)

BARS

BT's 7737 Grand Blvd. • 841-7900 • 6pm-2am • lesbians/gay men • dancing/DJ • 18+ • live shows • wheelchair access

Port St. Lucie   (407)

BARS

Bourbon St. Cabaret & Cafe 2727 SE Morningside Blvd. • 335-8608 • 4pm-2am • popular • lesbians/gay men • live shows • food served • some veggie • more women Fri • wheelchair access

Sarasota   (941)

INFO LINES & SERVICES

Friends Group (Gay AA) 2080 Ringling Blvd. #302 • 951-6810 • 8pm Mon & Wed • also 8pm Fri at 538 Payne Pkwy.

BARS

Bumpers (Club X) 1927 Ringling Blvd. • 951-0335 • 9pm Th & Sat • gay-friendly • dancing/DJ

Club Chada 2941 N. Tamiami • 355-7210 • 3pm-2am • lesbians/gay men • live shows

Ricky J's 1330 Martin Luther King Jr. Wy. • 953-5945 • 4pm-2am • popular • mostly gay men • dancing/DJ • live shows • patio • wheelchair access

BOOKSTORES & RETAIL SHOPS

Charlie's 1341 Main St. • 953-4688 • 9am-10pm, til 5pm Sun • books • magazines • cards

TRAVEL & TOUR OPERATORS

Galaxsea Cruises 6584 Superior • 921-3456/ (800) 633-5159 • IGTA member

SPIRITUAL GROUPS

Church of the Trinity MCC 7225 N. Lockwood Ridge Rd. • 355-0847 • 10am Sun • wheelchair access

St. Augustine (904)

WOMEN'S ACCOMMODATIONS

Pagoda 2854 Costal Hwy. • 824-2970 • women only • guesthouse • swimming • 5 doubles • kitchen privileges • near beach • smoking outdoors • wheelchair access • women-owned/run • $15

St. Petersburg (813)

INFO LINES & SERVICES

Gay Information Line (The Line) • 586-4297 • volunteers 7pm-11pm • info & referrals • touchtone service 24hrs

WEB (Women's Energy Bank) • 823-5353 • many services & activities for lesbians

WOMEN'S ACCOMMODATIONS

Boca Ciega 3526 Boca Ciega Dr. N. • 381-2755 • women only • swimming • lesbian-owned/run

ACCOMMODATIONS

Garden Guest Houses 920 4th St. S. • 821-3665 • lesbians/gay men • near beach & Disney World

BARS

Bedrox 8000 W. Gulf Blvd., Treasure Island • 367-1724 • 10am-2am • popular • lesbians/gay men • dancing/DJ • live shows • also a restaurant • 4 bars • on the beach • wheelchair access • $5-15

The New Connection 3100 3rd Ave. N. • 321-2112 • 11am-2am • lesbians/gay men • neighborhood bar • live shows

Sharp A's 4918 22nd Ave. S., Gulfport • 327-4897 • 3pm-2am • popular • lesbians/gay men • dancing/DJ • wheelchair access

BOOKSTORES & RETAIL SHOPS

Brigit Books 3434 4th St. N. • 522-5775 • 10am-8pm, til 6pm Fri-Sat, 1pm-5pm Sun • women's/feminist bookstore

P.S. 111 2nd Ave. NE • 823-2937 • 10am-6pm • cards • gifts

SPIRITUAL GROUPS

King of Peace MCC 3150 5th Ave. N • 323-5857 • 10am & 7:30pm Sun • wheelchair access

PUBLICATIONS

Womyn's Words PO Box 15524, 33733 • 823-5353 • monthly

St. Petersburg Beach (813)

WOMEN'S ACCOMMODATIONS

Barge House PO Box 46526, 33741 • 360-0729 • women only • hot tub • 1/2 block to the beach • cabana & cottages available • women-owned/run

ACCOMMODATIONS

Pass-A-Grille Beach Motel 709 Gulfway Blvd. • 367-4726 • gay-friendly • swimming • apartment available

Tallahassee (904)

BARS

Brothers Bar 926 W. Tharpe St. • 386-2399 • 4pm-2am • lesbians/gay men

Club Park Ave. 115 E. Park Ave. • 599-9143 • 10pm-2am • popular • gay-friendly • dancing/DJ • live shows • more gay wknds • mostly African-American Sun

BOOKSTORES & RETAIL SHOPS

Rubyfruit Books 666-4 W. Tennessee St. • 222-2627 • 10:30am-6:30pm, til 8pm Th, clsd Sun • alternative bookstore • gay titles

TRAVEL & TOUR OPERATORS

Florida Division of Tourism • 487-1462

Tampa (813)

INFO LINES & SERVICES

Tampa Bay Business Guild 1222 S. Dale Mabry #656, 33629

University of South Florida Gay/Lesbian/Bisexual Coalition CTR 2466, 4202 E. Fowler Ave. • 974-4297 • active campus organization

Women's Center • 677-8136 • women's helpline • info & referrals

The Women's Show WMNF 88.5 - FM • 238-8001 • 10am-noon Sat

ACCOMMODATIONS

Gram's Place B&B & Artist Retreat 3109 N. Ola Ave. • 221-0596 • lesbians/gay men • nudity • BYOB • artists' retreat & music lovers paradise named in honor of Gram Parsons • patio

Ruskin House B&B 120 Dickman Dr. SW, Ruskin • 645-3842 • gay-friendly • full breakfast • 1910 multi-story home • 30 min. S. of Tampa & 30 min. N. of Sarasota

BARS

2606 2606 N. Armenia Ave. • 875-6993 • 3pm-3am • popular • mostly gay men • also leather shop opens after 9pm

The Bridge Club 5519 W. Hillsborough Ave. • opens 2am Th-Sun • lesbians/gay men • dancing/DJ • live shows • BYOB

Cherokee Club 1320 9th Ave. (2nd flr.), Ybor City • 247-9966 • 9pm-3am, clsd Tue-Wed • mostly women • dancing/DJ • live shows • call for events

City Side 3810 Neptune St. • 254-6466 • noon-3am • lesbians/gay men • neighborhood bar • patio

Paradise Cove 14802 N. Nebraska Ave. • 979-0919 • 3pm-3am • lesbians/gay men • dancing/DJ • volleyball • patio • wheelchair access

Rascal's 105 W. Martin Luther King Blvd. • 237-8883 • 3pm-3am • lesbians/gay men • neighborhood bar • also a restaurant • some veggie • wheelchair access • $4-13

Tracks Tampa 1430 E. 7th Ave. • 247-2711 • 8pm-3am, clsd Mon • popular • mostly gay men • dancing/DJ • live shows • videos • wheelchair access

RESTAURANTS & CAFES

De Milos 3316 S. Westshore • 837-1165 • 8am-9pm, til 10pm Th-Sat • BYOB • full bar

Moody's 4010 S. Dale Mabry Hwy. • 831-6537 • full bar

BOOKSTORES & RETAIL SHOPS

Tomes & Treasures 202 S. Howard Ave. • 251-9368 • 11am-8pm, 1pm-6pm Sun • lesbigay bookstore

SPIRITUAL GROUPS

MCC 408 Cayuga St. • 239-1951 • 10:30am Sun

PUBLICATIONS

Encounter 1222 S. Dale Mabry Hwy. #913 • 877-7913

Gazette PO Box 2650, Brandon, 33509-2650 • 689-7566

Stonewall 3225 S. Madill #220 • 832-2878 • monthly

West Palm Beach (407)

INFO LINES & SERVICES

The Whimsey • 686-1354 • also camping/RV space • resources & archives

ACCOMMODATIONS

Hibiscus House B&B 501 30th St. • 863-5633/ (800) 203-4927 • lesbians/gay men • full breakfast • swimming • complimentary sunset cocktails • IGTA member

West Palm Beach B&B 419 32nd St. • 848-4064/ (800) 736-4064 • mostly gay men • swimming • relaxing & fun place to kick off your sandals • IGTA member

BARS

5101 Bar 5101 S. Dixie Hwy. • 585-2379 • 7am-3am, til 4am Fri-Sat, noon-3am Sun • mostly gay men • neighborhood bar

Heartbreaker 2677 Forrest Hill Blvd. • 966-1590 • 10pm-5am Wed-Sun • popular • lesbians/gay men • dancing/DJ • live shows • more women Fri • Chatters lounge open 5pm daily

RESTAURANTS & CAFES

Antonio's South 3001 S. Congress Ave., Palm Springs • 965-0707 • dinner • popular • beer/wine • southern Italian • $9-18

Rhythm Cafe 3238 S. Dixie Hwy. • 833-3406 • from 6pm Tue-Sat (seasonal) • beer/wine • some veggie • $12-19

BOOKSTORES & RETAIL SHOPS

Changing Times Bookstore 911 Village Blvd. Ste. 806 • 640-0496 • 10am-7pm, noon-5pm Sun • lesbigay section • metaphysical • community bulletin board • wheelchair access

SPIRITUAL GROUPS

MCC 3500 W. 45th St. Ste. 2-A • 687-3943 • 11am Sun, 7pm Wed (signed for hearing impared)

PUBLICATIONS

Community Voice PO Box 17975 , 33416 • 471-1528 • monthly

ICE PO Box 16634, 33416 • weekly • gay-friendly entertainment guide

Georgia

Athens (706)

INFO LINES & SERVICES

Lesbian Support Group PO Box 7864, 30604 • 546-4611

LGBSU (Lesbian/Gay/Bisexual Student Union) Memorial Hall Rm. 213 • 549-9368 • 7pm Mon

BARS

Boneshakers 433 E. Hancock Ave. • 543-1555 • 7pm-2am, clsd Sun • lesbians/gay men • dancing/DJ • 18+ • country/western Th • wheelchair access

Forty Watt Club 285 W. Washington St. • 549-7871 • gay-friendly • call for events • alternative • theme nights • disco Mon very gay • wheelchair access

Georgia Bar 159 W. Clayton • 546-9884 • 4pm-2am, clsd Sun • gay-friendly • wheelchair access

The Globe 199 N. Lumpkin • 353-4721 • 4pm-2am, clsd Sun • gay-friendly • beer/wine

RESTAURANTS & CAFES

The Athens Coffeehouse 301 E. Clayton St. • 208-9711 • 9am-midnight, til 2am Th-Sat • gay-friendly • some veggie • full bar • wheelchair access • $6-11

The Bluebird 493 E. Clayton • 549-3663 • 8am-9pm • plenty veggie • popular Sun brunch • wheelchair access • $5-10

Espresso Royale Cafe 297 E. Broad St. • 613-7449 • 7am-midnight, from 8am wknds • best coffee in Athens

The Grit 199 Prince Ave. • 543-6592 • 10am-11pm • ethnic vegetarian • plenty veggie • great Sun brunch • wheelchair access • $5-10

BOOKSTORES & RETAIL SHOPS

Barnett's Newsstand 147 College Ave. • 353-0530 • 8am-10pm

Atlanta (404)

INFO LINES & SERVICES

AALGA (African-American Lesbian/Gay Alliance) PO Box 50374, 30302 • 239-8184 • 4pm 1st Sun • social/political group

Atlanta (404)

LESBIGAY INFO: Atlanta Gay Center: 876-5372, 71 12th St. NE.

LESBIGAY PAPER: ETC Magazine: 525-3821, bar & restaurant guide. Southern Voice: 876-1819, news.

WHERE THE GIRLS ARE: Many lesbians live in DeKalb county, in Decatur. For fun, women head for Midtown or Buckhead if they're professionals, Virginia-Highlands if they're funky or 3oish, and L'il 5 Points if they're young & wild.

ENTERTAINMENT: Atlanta Feminist Women's Chorus: (770) 438-5823. Lefont Screening Room: 231-1924.

LESBIGAY AA: Galano AA: 881-9188, 585 Dutch Valley.

LESBIGAY PRIDE: June. 662-4533.

ANNUAL EVENTS: April 11-14 - Lesbian/Gay Arts Fest: 874-8710. May 18 - Wigswood: 874-6782, 5th annual festival of peace, love and wigs. May 24-27 - Armory Sports Classic: 874-2710, softball & others. May - Southern Women's Music & Comedy Festival: (818) 893-4075. December - Women's Christmas Ball: 939-6527.

CITY INFO: 521-6600. Olympics Tickets: 744-1996.

ATTRACTIONS: Atlanta Botanical Gardens (near Piedmont Park): 876-5859. CNN Center: 827-2300. Coca-Cola Museum: 676-5151.

BEST VIEW: 7oth floor restaurant of the Peachtree Plaza.

WEATHER: Summers are warm and humid (upper 80°s to low 90°s). Winters are icy with occasional snows (50°s-30°s). Spring brings blossoming dogwoods, while fall delivers awesome fall foliage.

TRANSIT: 521-0200.

Atlanta

*I*f you're anywhere near Atlanta, you can't miss hearing about the **'96 Olympics** (July 19-August 4)! Southerners are proud to finally achieve international recognition for something other than the Old South - and they're working hard to present a modern, world-class city devoid of racism and heterosexism. Of course, Atlanta's large population of lesbians and gay is an integral part of that work.

But the South's prejudiced past is a valuable agent for future understanding. For example, Atlanta houses the must-see **Martin Luther King Jr. Center** and the **Carter Presidential Center** - both icons of peace and understanding - as well as the nationally known **Black Arts Festival** (730-7315) in late June this year.

Lesbian culture in Atlanta is spread out (a car is a must) - between **Charis** women's books in L'il Five Points (cruise their Thursday night readings), the **Atlanta Gay Center** in posh Midtown, and in between, along Piedmont and Cheshire Bridge roads. Midway between gay **Ansley Square** area (Piedmont at Monroe) and downtown, stop by **Outwrite**, Atlanta's lesbian/gay bookstore. Pick up a copy of **Southern Voice** to scope the political scene or **Etc.** to dish the bar scene.

For more shopping, **Brushstrokes** is Atlanta's only lesbigay goody store. While strolling around quaint/queer Virginia Highlands, stop to smell the flowers at **Maddix**, but don't miss brunch at **Murphy's Deli** in Virginia-Highlands - their melt-in-your-mouth biscuits are perfect!

Just a couple miles south on Highland, you'll run smack into funky shopping, dining and live music in the punk capital of Atlanta - L'il Five Points (not to be confused with "Five Points" downtown). Unless you're a serious mall-crawler, skip the overly commercial (but much hyped) Underground Atlanta, and head for **Lenox Mall** instead - you'll see more stylish queers, and fewer bratty hetero-tourists.

The two women's accommodations listed in Atlanta are actually about an hour north, in lush, wooded Dahlonega. So if you need to stay in the city, try one of the mixed hotels or B&Bs.

NOTE: Atlanta's area code will split into 404 inside the perimeter (the city is circled by I-285), and 770 outside the perimeter by 1996.

If you're a fan of R.E.M. or other Athens, Georgia bands, Athens is about an hour-an-a-half away, northeast on Hwys. 306 or 78. Avoid going on football season weekends, since traffic is hellish. Pick up a **Flagpole** magazine to find out what's going on, and stop by **Boneshakers**, Athens' lesbian/gay dancebar.

Atlanta Gay Center 71 12th St. NE • 876-5372 • 1pm-5pm Mon-Fri • social services center

Chrysalis Women's Center • 320-3355 • social, educational & informational programs

Dyke TV Channel 12 • 9:30pm Mon • 'weekly, half hour TV show produced by lesbians for lesbians'

Fourth Tuesday PO Box 7817, 30309 • 662-4353 • networking & social group for professional women

Friday Night Lesbian Support Group • 627-7387 • call for times & locations

Galano AA 585 Dutch Valley • 881-9188 • lesbigay club

Gay Graffiti WRFG 89.3 FM • 523-8989 • 7pm Th • lesbigay radio program

Gay Helpline • 892-0661 • 6pm-11pm • info & counseling

Greater Atlanta Business Coalition • 377-4258

WINK (Women in Kahoots) 1003 Hicksmil Ct. SW, Marrietta • 438-1421 • lesbian social group • monthly parties • newsletter (unconfirmed fall '95)

WOMEN'S ACCOMMODATIONS

Above the Clouds Rte. 4 Box 250 , Dahlonega • (706) 864-5211 • women only • full breakfast • mountainside B&B • 1 ste. w/ hot tub • 1 bdrm w/ private bath • lesbian-owned/run

Swiftwaters Rte. 3 Box 379, Dahlonega, 30533 • (706) 864-3229 • seasonal • women only • B&B • cabins • campsites • hot tub • deck • on scenic river • women-owned/run • $60-75 /$10-40 (campsites/cabins)

ACCOMMODATIONS

Alternative Accommodations • (800) 209-9408

Hello B&B • 892-8111 • mostly gay men • B&B in a private home

Magnolia Station B&B 1020 Edgewood Ave. NE • 523-2005 • mostly gay men • swimming

▲ **Midtown Manor** 811 Piedmont Ave. NE • 872-5846/ (800) 724-4381 • lesbians/gay men • charming Victorian guesthouse

Our Place, Dahlonega • 297-9825 • fully furnished cabin • lesbian-owned/run

Sheraton Colony Square Hotel 188 14th St. • 892-6000 • food served • full bar

Upper Echelons • 642-1313 • swimming • luxury penthouse in downtown Atlanta • women-owned/run

BARS

Armory 836 Juniper St. NE • 881-9280 • 4pm-4am • popular • mostly gay men • dancing/DJ • leather • 3 bars • wheelchair access

Backstreet 845 Peachtree St. NE • 873-1986 • 11am-7am, 24hrs on wknds • popular • mostly gay men • dancing/DJ • live shows

Burkhart's Pub 1492-F Piedmont Rd. (Ansley Sq. Shopping Center) • 872-4403 • 4pm-4am, from 2pm wknds • lesbians/gay men • neighborhood bar

Hoedowns 1890 Cheshire Bridge Rd. • 874-0980 • 3pm-3am • mostly gay men • dancing/DJ • country/western • live shows • wheelchair access

Loretta's 708 Spring St. NW • 874-8125 • 6pm-4am • gay-friendly • neighborhood bar • mostly African-American • wheelchair access

Model T 699 Ponce de Leon • 872-2209 • noon-4am • lesbians/gay men • neighborhood bar • wheelchair access

Moreland Tavern 1196 Moreland Ave. SE • 622-4650 • 6pm-4am • lesbians/gay men • neighborhood bar • food served • patio • wheelchair access

Opus I 1086 Alco St. NE • 634-6478 • 9pm-4am • mostly gay men • neighborhood bar • wheelchair access

The Otherside of Atlanta 1924 Piedmont Rd. • 875-5238 • 6pm-4am • popular • lesbians/gay men • dancing/DJ • live shows • food served • patio • women-owned/run

Revolution 293 Pharr Rd. • 816-5455 • 7pm-2am, from 5pm Wed-Fri & Sun, til 4am wknds • mostly women • dancing/DJ • country/western • deck • wheelchair access

Scandals 1510-G Piedmont Rd. NE (Ansley Sq. Shopping Ctr.) • 875-5957 • noon-4am • popular • mostly gay men • neighborhood bar • wheelchair access

Shahans Saloon 735 Ralph McGill • 523-1535 • 4pm-4am, from noon wknds • lesbians/gay men • neighborhood bar • wheelchair access

Spectrum 1492-B Piedmont Ave. (Ansley Sq. Shopping Ctr.) • 875-8980 • 11am-4am, restaurant til 7pm, til 4pm wknds • lesbians/gay men • dancing/DJ • live shows • also a restaurant • homecooking • wheelchair access • $3-9

Velvet 89 Park Pl. • 681-9936 • 10pm-4am, clsd Tue • popular • gay-friendly • dancing/DJ • theme nights • 'Venus Envy' on Fri • more gay men Mon & Sat • wheelchair access

RESTAURANTS & CAFES

Bridgetown Grill 689 Peachtree (across from Fox Theater) • 873-5361 • noon-11pm • popular • funky Caribbean • some veggie • also Lil' 5 Points location • 653-0110 • $5-10

Cafe Beausoleil 1365 Peachtree St. • 876-4570 • 11am-3pm, clsd wknds • mostly women • beer/wine • gourmet sandwiches/salads • some veggie • popular lesbian social Fri night • wheelchair access • women-owned/run • $5-10

Cafe Mythology 1140 Crescent Ave. • 873-0794 • 5pm-2am • more gay week days

Chow 1026-1/2 N. Highland Ave. • 872-0869 • lunch & dinner • popular • contemporary American • some veggie • popular Sun brunch • $8-15

Dunk N' Dine (aka Drunk N' Dyke) 2276 Cheshire Bridge Rd. • 636-0197 • 24hrs • lesbians/gay men • downscale diner • some veggie • $4-10

Eat Your Vegetables 438 Moreland Ave. • 523-2671 • lunch & dinner, Sun brunch • plenty veggie • $5-10

Einstein's 1077 Juniper • 876-7925 • noon-1am • American • some veggie • full bar • $8-12

The Flying Biscuit Cafe 1655 McLendon Ave. • (404) 687-8888 • 8:30am-10pm • healthy breakfast all day • plenty veggie • patio • wheelchair access • lesbian-owned/run • $6-12

Intermezzo 1845 Peachtree Rd. NE • 355-0411 • 8am-3am, 9am-3am Fri-Sat • plenty veggie • full bar • cafe • $7-10

Little 5 Points, Moreland & Euclid Ave. S. of Ponce de Leon Ave. • hip & funky area w/ too many restaurants & shops to list

Majestic Diner 1031 Ponce de Leon (near N. Highland) • 875-0276 • 24hrs • popular • some veggie • diner right from the '50s • cantankerous waitresses included • $3-8

Murphy's 997 Virginia Ave. • 872-0904 • 7am-10pm, til midnight Fri-Sat • popular • cont'l • plenty veggie • great brunch • $5-15

R. Thomas 1812 Peachtree Rd. NE • 872-2942 • 24hrs • popular • beer/wine • healthy Californian/juice bar • plenty veggie • $5-10

Veni Vidi Vici 41 14th St. • 875-8424 • lunch & dinner • upscale Italian • some veggie • wheelchair access • $14-25

GYMS & HEALTH CLUBS

Better Bodies 931 Monroe • 881-6875 • popular • full gym

Boot Camp 1544 Piedmont Ave. #105 • 876-8686 • full gym

Mid-City Fitness Center 2201 Faulkner Rd. • 321-6507 • lesbians/gay men

BOOKSTORES & RETAIL SHOPS

Brushstrokes 1510-J Piedmont Ave. NE • 876-6567 • 10am-10pm, noon-9pm Sun • lesbigay variety store

Charis Books & More 1189 Euclid St. • 524-0304 • 10:30am-6:30pm, til 8pm Wed, til 10pm Fri-Sat, noon-6pm Sun • lesbigay/feminist bookstore • wheelchair access

Condomart 632 N. Highland Ave. NE • 875-5665 • 11am-11pm, noon-7pm Sun • wheelchair access

Koolhipfunkystuff 1030 Monroe Dr. NE • 607-1095 • noon-6pm, clsd Sun-Mon • art gallery • all proceeds benefit HIV+ projects

Maddix 1034 N. Highland • 892-9337 • 11am-10pm, til 7pm Sun • flowers • chocolates • artful gifts • wheelchair access

▲ **Outwrite Books** 931 Monroe Dr. • 607-0082 • 11am-10pm, til midnight Fri-Sat • cafe • lesbigay

Oxford Books 2345 Peachtree • 364-2700 • 9am-midnight, til 2am Fri-Sat • many lesbigay books & magazines • also at 360 Pharr Rd. • 262-3333 • Cup & Chaucer cafe at both locations

TRAVEL & TOUR OPERATORS

Conventional Travel 1658 Lavista Rd. NE • 315-0107/ (800) 747-7107 • IGTA member

Midtown Travel Consultants 1830 Monroe Dr. Ste. F • 872-8308/ (800) 548-8904 • IGTA member

Real Travel 2459 Wawona Dr. • 872-8308/ (800) 551-4202 • IGTA member

Travel Affair 1205 Johnson Ferry Rd. #116, Marietta • 977-6824/ (800) 332-3417 • IGTA member

Trips Unlimited 1004 Virginia Ave. NE • 872-8747/ (800) 275-8747

SPIRITUAL GROUPS

All Saints MCC 575 Boulevard SE • 622-1154 • 7pm Sun • wheelchair access

Congregation Bet Haverim 701 W. Howard Ave. • 642-3467 • 8pm Fri • lesbian/gay synagogue • 2nd Fri veggie 7:30pm

First MCC of Atlanta 1379 Tullie Rd. NE • 325-4143 • 11am & 7:30pm Sun, 7:30pm Wed • wheelchair access

Integrity Atlanta 634 W. Peachtree (All Saints Church) • 642-3183 • 7:30pm 2nd & 4th Fri

Presbyterians for Lesbian/Gay Concerns PO Box 8362, 30306 • 373-5830 • social group

PUBLICATIONS

Atlanta Community Yellow Pages 1888 Emery St. Ste. 220, 30318 • 350-6720

ETC Magazine PO Box 8916, 30306 • 525-3821 • weekly • bar guide

The News 63 12th St. NE, 30309 • 876-5372 • bi-monthly

Southern Voice 1095 Zenolite Rd., 30306 • 876-1819 • weekly

EROTICA

The Poster Hut 2175 Cheshire Bridge Rd. • 633-7491 • 10am-9pm, til 6pm Sun

Starship 2275 Cheshire Bridge Rd. • 320-9101 • 10am-10pm • leather • novelties • 5 locations in Atlanta

Augusta   (706)

BARS

Walton Way Station 1632 Walton Wy. • 733-2603 • 9pm-3am, clsd Sun • lesbians/gay men • dancing/DJ • live shows • women's pool tournament Mon

SPIRITUAL GROUPS

MCC 609 Charton Dr. • 860-7131 • 7pm Sun • wheelchair access

Bowden   (404)

BARS

Rainbow Pub 1174 Hwy. 166 • 258-7766 • 8:30pm til ?, clsd Mon-Wed • lesbians/gay men • live shows

RESTAURANTS & CAFES

Scandals 110 City Hall Ave. • 258-7771 • 11am-10pm, from 5pm Fri-Sat, clsd Sun • pizza

Columbus   (706)

BARS

Fountain City Yacht Club 1214 1st Ave. • 322-8682 • 8pm-2am, clsd Sun • lesbians/gay men • dancing/DJ • military clientele

Macon   (912)

BARS

Topaz 695 Riverside Dr. • 750-7669 • 5pm-2am, clsd Sun • lesbians/gay men • dancing/DJ • live shows

Mountain City   (706)

ACCOMMODATIONS

The York House York House Rd • 746-2068 • gay-friendly • 1896 historic country inn

Savannah   (912)

INFO LINES & SERVICES

First City Network, Inc. 335 Tatnall St. • 236-2489 • complete info & events line • social group

ACCOMMODATIONS

912 Barnard Victorian B&B 912 Barnard • 234-9121 • lesbians/gay men • hot tub • shared baths • nudity • no smoking • in-room refrigerator • balcony

BARS

Club One 1 Jefferson St. • 232-0200 • 5pm-3am • lesbians/gay men • dancing/DJ • food served • live shows Wed, Fri-Sun

Faces II 17 Lincoln St. • 233-3520 • 11am-3am • mostly gay men • neighborhood bar • also a restaurant • American • patio • $8-10

Valdosta   (912)

BARS

Club Paradise 2100 W. Hill Ave. (exit 4 I-95) • 242-9609 • 9pm-2am, clsd Sun-Mon • popular • lesbians/gay men • dancing/DJ • live shows • patio

Hawaii

Hawaii (Big Island)

Captain Cook (808)

ACCOMMODATIONS

▲ **RBR Farms** PO Box 930, 96704 • 328-9212/ (800) 328-9212 • popular • lesbians/gay men • full breakfast • hot tub • swimming • nudity • renovated plantation home on a working macadamia nut & coffee plantation • IGTA member

Samurai House RR 1 Box 359 • 328-9210 • popular • gay-friendly • hot tub • traditional house brought from Japan • wheelchair access

Hawi (808)

ACCOMMODATIONS

Hale Anuenue (Rainbow House) PO Box 371, 96719 • 889-6187 • lesbians/gay men • B&B • cottages • full breakfast • hot tub • nudity

Honokaa (808)

ACCOMMODATIONS

Paauhau Plantation Inn PO Box 1375, 96727 • 775-7222/ (213) 542-2239 (Los Angeles) • gay-friendly • richly landscaped 5-acre B&B w/ cottages built on ocean point

Kailua-Kona (808)

ACCOMMODATIONS

Dolores Bed & Breakfast 77-6704 Kilohana • 329-8778 • lesbians/gay men • ocean views • full gourmet breakfast

Hale Kipa 'O Pele PO Box 5252, 96745 • 329-8676/ (800) 528-2456 • lesbians/gay men • hot tub • plantation-style B&B on a gated acre estate

▲ **Royal Kona Resort** 75-5852 Alii Dr. • 329-3111/ (800) 774-5662 • gay-friendly • swimming • set atop dramatic lava outcroppings, overlooking spectacular Kailua Bay • private beach • oceanside luau & revue

BARS

Mask Bar & Grill 75-5660 Kopiko St. •
329-8558 • 6pm-2am • lesbians/gay men
• neighborhood bar • dancing/DJ • only
gay & lesbian bar on the island

TRAVEL & TOUR OPERATORS

Ecoscapes 75-5626 Kuakini Hwy. Ste.1 •
329-7116/ (800) 949-3483 • IGTA member

Kurtistown　(808)

WOMEN'S ACCOMMODATIONS

The Butterfly Inn PO Box 6010, 96760 •
966-7936/ (800) 546-2442 • women only •
B&B • hot tub • kitchens • tropical
breakfast • women-owned/run • $55-60
($45-50 weekly)

PUBLICATIONS

The Jungle Vine PO Box 325, 96760 •
966-8584 • lesbian newsletter

Pahala　(808)

ACCOMMODATIONS

Wood Valley B&B Inn PO Box 37, 96777
• 928-8212 • mostly women • nudity •
plantation home B&B • veggie breakfast
• tent sites • sauna • women-owned/run

Pahoa　(808)

ACCOMMODATIONS

Anu'u Koa Niu RR 2 Box 4023, 96778 •
965-0830 • gay-friendly • swimming •
country retreat on 5 secluded acres •
near hiking • snorkeling • warm ponds

Huliaule'a B&B PO Box 1030, 96778 •
965-9175 • lesbians/gay men

Kalani Honua Retreat RR2 Box 4500,
Beach Rd., 96778 • 965-7828/ (800) 800-
6886 • gay-friendly • swimming • food
served • coastal retreat • conference center & campground w/in Hawaii's largest
conservation area • IGTA member

Lava Tree Guest Farm PO Box 881,
96778-0881 • 965-7325 • near outdoor
recreation • renovated plantation home
on working Macadamia farm

PUBLICATIONS

Outspoken PO Box 601, 96778 • 982-
7617 • newsletter printed 6 times a year

Volcano Village　(808)

ACCOMMODATIONS

Hale Ohia Cottages Hale Ohia Rd. •
967-7986/ (800) 455-3803 • gay-friendly •
B&B • wheelchair access • IGTA membe

Kauai

Anahola　(808)

ACCOMMODATIONS

Anahola Beach Club • 822-6966/ (800)
262-4652 • full breakfast • beachside
bunkhouse • IGTA member

Mahina Kai • 822-9451 • popular • les-
bians/gay men • hot tub • swimming •
Asian-Pacific country villa nestled in ter-
raced hillside gardens overlooking
Anahola Bay

Coconut Plantation　(808)

ACCOMMODATIONS

▲ **Kauai Coconut Beach Resort** PO Box
830, Kapaa, 96746 • 822-3455/ (800) 222-
5642 • gay-friendly • swimming • newly
redecorated oceanfront resort • tennis
facilities • nightly torchlighting ceremor
& luau

Hanalei　(808)

BARS

Tahiti Nui Kuhio Hwy. • 826-6277 •
noon-2am • gay-friendly • live shows •
luau Fri • live bands wknds •
country/western Mon • more gay Fri-Sat
• wheelchair access • $12-18

Kalaheo　(808)

ACCOMMODATIONS

Black Bamboo Guest House 3829 Wah
Rd. • 332-7518/ (800) 527-7789 • popula
• lesbians/gay men • swimming • planta
tion-style house • wheelchair access •
IGTA member

Garden Island B&B 4379 Panui St. •
332-7971/ (800) 558-5557 • gay-friendly •
modern, executive-style home overlooking Poipu • beautiful ocean & mountain
views • IGTA member

Kapaa (808)

ACCOMMODATIONS

Aloha Kauai B&B 156 Lihau St. • 822-6966/ (800) 262-4652 • lesbians/gay men • full breakfast • swimming • wheelchair access

Hale Kahawai 185 Kahawai Pl. • 822-1031 • lesbians/gay men • B&B • full breakfast • hot tub • mountain views

Mala Lani 5711 Lokelani Blvd. • 823-0422 • lesbians/gay men • hot tub • suites • lush gardens • mountain views • IGTA member

Mohala Ke B&B Retreat 5663 Ohelo Rd. • 823-6398 • gay-friendly • swimming

Ola Hou Guest Retreat 332 Aina Loli Pl. • 822-3052/ (800) 772-4567 • lesbians/gay men • swimming • vacation rental

Royal Drive Cottages 147 Royal Dr. • 822-2321 • lesbians/gay men • private garden cottages w/ kitchenettes

BARS

Sideout 4-1330 Kuhio Hwy. • 822-0082 • noon-1:30am • popular • gay-friendly • live shows • bands Tue, Th & wknds • wheelchair access

Kilauea (808)

ACCOMMODATIONS

Kai Mana PO Box 612, 96754 • 828-1280/ (800) 837-1782 • gay-friendly • B&B • cottages • kitchens • Shakti Gawain's paradise home • set on a cliff surrounded by ocean & mountains

Kalihiwai Jungle Home PO Box 717, 96754 • 828-1626 • lesbians/gay men • nudity • private clifftop rental home hideaway overlooking valley of jungle & waterfalls • near beaches

▲ **Pali Kai** • 828-6691 • lesbians/gay men • cottages • hot tub • hilltop B&B w/ oceanview • women-owned/run

Maui

Haiku (808)

ACCOMMODATIONS

Golden Bamboo Ranch 1205 Kaupakalua Rd. • 572-7824 • lesbians/gay men • cottages • 7-acre estate w/ panoramic ocean views • IGTA member

PALI KAI

Bed and breakfast hide-away on Kauai's spectacular North Shore

P. O. Box 450, Kilauea, HI 96754 • 808-828-6691

Halfway to Hana House • 572-1176 • mostly women • B&B • private studio w/ oceanview

Kailua Maui Gardens • 572-9726/ (800) 258-8588 • gay-friendly • cottages • hot tub • swimming • nudity • also suites

Hana　　　　　　　　　　(808)

ACCOMMODATIONS

Blair's Original Hana Plantation Houses • 248-7868/ (800) 228-4262 • mostly gay men • tropical cottages & houses in exotic gardens • IGTA member

Hana Alii Holidays • 248-7742/ (800) 548-0478 • accommodations reservations service

Napualani O'Hana • 248-8935 • gay-friendly • 2 full units • lanai • ocean & mountain views

Kihei　　　　　　　　　　(808)

WOMEN'S ACCOMMODATIONS

Hale Makaleka • 879-2971 • women only • B&B • full breakfast • women-owned/run • $60

Hale O'Wahine 2777 S. Kihei Rd. #B-105 • 874-5148 • women only • swimming • beach resort w/ singles & studios • women-owned/run • $75-95

▲ **Royal Hawaiian Accommodations** PO Box 424 Puunene, 96784/ (800) 659-1866 • deluxe oceanfront accommodations • tennis courts • beachfront • near gay nude beach • women-owned/run

ACCOMMODATIONS

▲ **Anfora's Dreams** PO Box 74030 Los Angeles, CA, 90004 • (213) 737-0731 • lesbians/gay men • hot tub • swimming • rental condo near ocean

Ko'a Kai Rentals 1993 S. Kihei Rd. #401 • 879-6058 • gay-friendly • swimming • inexpensive rentals

Koa Lagoon 800 S. Kihei Rd. • 879-3002/ (800) 367-8030 • gay-friendly • swimming • oceanfront suites • 5 night min. • wheelchair access

Triple Lei B&B PO Box 593, Kihei, 96753 • 874-8645/ (800) 871-8645 • mostly gay men • full breakfast • hot tub • swimming • nudity • near nude beach

Kula   (808)

ACCOMMODATIONS

Camp Kula - Maui B&B PO Box 111,
96790 • 878-2528 • popular •
lesbians/gay men • B&B • centrally located hideaway on the lush, rolling green
slopes of Mt. Haleakala • HIV+ welcome
• wheelchair access

Lahaina   (808)

INFO LINES & SERVICES

AA Gay/Lesbian • 244-9673 • 8pm Wed,
7:30am Sun

ACCOMMODATIONS

▲ **Kahana Beach Condominium Hotel**
4221 Lower Honoapiliani Rd. • 669-8611/
(800) 222-5642 • gay-friendly • oceanfront studios & one-bdrm suites • kitchenettes • private lanai

▲ **Royal Lahaina Resort** 2780 Kekaa Dr. •
661-3611/ (800) 447-6925 • gay-friendly •
swimming • full-service resort set along
27 tropical acres of Ka'anapali • world-
class tennis courts & golf courses

BARS

Blue Tropics 900 Front St. Bldg. 202-A •
667-5309 • 6pm-2am • gay-friendly •
dancing/DJ • food served • Euro-Pacific
• some veggie • more gay Sun • wheelchair access • $14-19

BOOKSTORES & RETAIL SHOPS

▲ **Skin Deep Tattoo** 626 Front St. • 661-
8531 • 9am-8pm • custom tattooing •
adult toys • Harley-Davidson T-shirts

TRAVEL & TOUR OPERATORS

▲ **Maui Magical Weddings** • (800) 779-
1320 • traditional/non-traditional com-
mittment ceremonies in secluded Maui
locations

▲ **Maui Surfing School** PO Box 424
Puunene, 96784 • 875-0625 • lessons for
beginners, cowards & non-swimmers •
'surf-aris' for advanced • women-
owned/run

▲ **Royal Hawaiian Weddings** PO Box 424
Puunene, 96784 • 875-0625/ (800) 659-
1866 • specializes in scenic gay weddings
• IGTA member • women-owned/run

H I L O

K I H E I

L A H A I N A

808 • 661 • TATU

Makawao (808)

TRAVEL & TOUR OPERATORS

Maui Network • 572-9555/ (800) 367-5221 • condo reservation service

Paia (808)

INFO LINES & SERVICES

Women's Event Hotline • 573-3077 • covers entire island

ACCOMMODATIONS

Huelo Point Flower Farm • 572-1850 • gay-friendly • swimming • 2-acre oceanfront estate & organic farm set on 300 ft cliff w/ dramatic views of Waipio Bay

PUBLICATIONS

Island Lesbian Connection Box 356 Ste. 171, 96779 • 575-2681 • newsletter

Wailuku (808)

BARS

Hamburger Mary's 2010 Main St. • 244-7776 • 10am-2am • popular • lesbians/gay men • dancing/DJ • American • plenty veggie • kitchen open til 10pm • $7-15

RESTAURANTS & CAFES

Cafe Kup A Kuppa 79 Church St. • 244-0500 • 7am-4pm, 8am-1pm Sat, clsd Su • some veggie

Molokai (808)

ACCOMMODATIONS

Molokai Beachfront Escapes, Hana • 248-7868/ (800) 228-4262 • gay-friendly • beachfront units on the exotic island of Molokai • IGTA member

Oahu

Honolulu (808)

INFO LINES & SERVICES

Gay/Lesbian AA 277 Ohua (Waikiki Health Ctr.) • 946-1438 • 8pm daily

Gay/Lesbian Bulletin Board 1820 University Ave., (2nd flr YWCA) • 926-1000 • 24hr touchtone info

Gay/Lesbian Community Center 1820 University Ave., 2nd flr. YMCA • 951-7000 • 9am-5pm Mon-Fri • info • referrals

Lesbian Support Group (at the Women's Center) • 942-7762 • 7pm Wed

Honolulu   (808)

Lesbigay Info: <u>Gay Community Center</u>: 951-7000, 1820 University Ave., 2nd flr. YMCA, 9am-5pm Mon-Fri.

Lesbigay Paper: <u>Island Lifestyle Magazine</u>: 737-6400. <u>Jungle Vine</u>: 966-8584, lesbian newsletter. <u>Island Lesbian Connection</u>: 575-2681. <u>Outspoken</u>: 982-7617.

Where the Girls Are: Where else? On the beach. Or cruising Kuhio Ave.

Lesbigay AA: 946-1438, 277 Oahu (Waikiki Health Ctr.), 8pm daily.

Lesbigay Pride: 951-7000, June.

Annual Events: February - <u>Hawaii Women's Festival</u>: (904) 826-0410.

City Info: <u>Hawaiian Visitors Bureau</u>: 923-1811.

Best View: From a helicopter tour over the islands.

Weather: Usually paradise perfect, but humid. It rarely gets hotter than the upper 80°s.

Transit: <u>Charley's</u>: 955-2211.

Women's Center 1820 University Ave. (Univ. of HI, Manoa) • 942-7762 • space for variety of groups • info & referrals

WOMEN'S ACCOMMODATIONS

▲ **The Mango House** 2087 Iholena St. • 595-6682/ (800) 776-2646 • popular • women only • B&B • kids okay • fax (808) 595-6682 • IGTA member • women-owned/run • $60-85

ACCOMMODATIONS

Bed & Breakfast Honolulu (Statewide) 3242 Kaohinani Dr. • 595-7533/ (800) 288-4666 • gay-friendly • represents 350 locations on all islands • clientele & ownership vary (most gay-friendly)

Bed & Breakfast in Manoa Valley 2651 Terrace Dr. • 988-6333 • gay-friendly • spectacular views • women-owned/run

The Coconut Plaza 450 Lewers St. • 923-8828/ (800) 882-9696 • gay-friendly • swimming • near beach • wheelchair access

Hotel Honolulu 376 Kaiolu St., Waikiki • 926-2766/ (800) 426-2766 • popular • mostly gay men • IGTA member

▲ **Pleasant Holiday Isle Hotel** 270 Lewers St. • 923-0777/ (800) 222-5642 • gay-friendly • swimming • private lanai • 1 blk from the world-famous Waikiki beach • also a full restaurant & lounge

Waikiki Vacation Condos 1860 Ala Moana Blvd. #108, Waikiki • 946-9371/ (800) 543-5663 • furnished one & two-bdrm units • reservation service

BARS

Club Bayside 444 Hobron Ln. #P-8 • 951-0008 • 4pm-2am • gay-friendly • dancing/DJ • karaoke • food served • women-owned/run

Fusion Waikiki 2260 Kuhio Ave., 3rd flr. • 924-2422 • 10pm-4am, from 8pm wknds • mostly gay men • dancing/DJ • live shows

Hula's Bar & Lei Stand 2103 Kuhio Ave. • 923-0669 • 10am-2am • popular • lesbians/gay men • dancing/DJ • live shows • videos • patio

Metropolis 611 Cooke St., Kakaako • 593-2717 • 8pm-2am, from 4pm Sun • lesbians/gay men • dancing/DJ • country/western Fri 7pm • more men Th • patio

Honolulu

*V*isions of volcanoes, sparkling beaches, lush tropical flowers, magnificent sunsets, grass skirts and an easy lifestyle draw people from around the world to the island Oahu and the city Honolulu.

If you forget your swimsuit, you'll have no problem finding one in the hundreds of beach shops. Or enjoy shopping at the outdoor stalls in the International Marketplace.

Where to stay? Honolulu has one B&B for women: **The Mango House**. **Bed & Breakfast Honolulu** is a reservation service for the islands that could help you find accommodations other than those in the touristy, expensive Waikiki area.*

What to do? Just head for Kuhio Ave. Here you'll find, along with several gay men's bars, **Banana's**, a mixed gay bar popular with lesbians. Browse at **Eighty Percent Straight**, the lesbigay boutique. Pick up an **Island Lifestyle**, or cruise the **Women's Center** at the University.

* Honolulu is very expensive by 'mainland' standards so bring plenty of cash and credit cards!

Windows 444 Hobrow Ln., Waikiki • 946-4442 • 11am-2am • lesbians/gay men • live shows

RESTAURANTS & CAFES

Banana's 2139 Kuhio Ave. #125, Waikiki • 922-6262 • 5pm-2am, clsd Mon • lesbians/gay men • neighborhood bar • Thai • full bar • wheelchair access

Cafe Sistina 1314 S. King St. • 596-0061 • lunch Mon-Fri, dinner nightly • northern Italian • some veggie • full bar • wheelchair access • $9-16

Caffe Guccinni 2139 Kuhio Ave., Waikiki • 922-5287 • 4pm-10:30pm • Italian • some veggie • full bar • women-owned/run

Keo's Thai 1200 Ala Moana Blvd. • 533-0533 • dinner • popular • also 1486 S. King St. • 947-9988

Malia's Cantina 311 Lewers St., Waikiki • 922-7808 • 11am-4am • dancing/DJ • live shows • Mexican/American • some veggie • full bar • wheelchair access • $6-17

Pieces of Eight 250 Lewers St., Waikiki • 923-6646 • 5pm-11pm • steak & seafood • full bar • wheelchair access • $8-15

Singha Thai 1910 Ala Moana • 941-2898 • 11am-11pm • live shows

BOOKSTORES & RETAIL SHOPS

Eighty Percent Straight 2139 Kuhio Ave., 2nd flr., Waikiki • 923-9996 • 10am-midnight • lesbigay clothing • books • cards

TRAVEL & TOUR OPERATORS

Bird of Paradise Travel PO Box 4157, 96812-4157 • 735-9103 • IGTA member

Hawaii Visitors Bureau 2270 Kalakaua Ave #801 • 923-1811

Island Pride Taxi & Tour 3151 Monsarrat Ave. #402 • 732-6518/ (800) 330-5598 • IGTA member

Pacific Ocean Holidays PO Box 88245, 96830 • 923-2400/ (800) 735-6600 • also publishes semi-annual 'Pocket Guide to Hawaii' • IGTA member

Tickets To Go 1910 Ala Moana Blvd. Ste. B • 942-7785 • IGTA member

Travel Travel 320 Ward Ave. Ste. 204 • 596-0336 • IGTA member

Vacations Hawaii 1314 S. King St. Ste. 1062 • 524-4711 • IGTA member

SPIRITUAL GROUPS

Dignity Honolulu 539 Kapahulu Ave. (St. Mark's Church) • 536-5536 • 7:30pm Sun • dancing/DJ

Ke Annenue O Ke Aloha MCC 1212 University Ave. (Church of the Crossroads) • 942-1027 • 7pm Sun • also 11am at Cafe Valentino 2139 Kuhio Ave.

Unitarian Universalists for Lesbian/Gay Concerns (Interweave) 2500 Pali Hwy. • 595-4047

Unity Church of Hawaii 3608 Diamond Head Cir. • 735-4436 • 7:30pm, 9am & 11am Sun

PUBLICATIONS

Island Lifestyle Magazine 2851-A Kihei Pl. • 737-6400 • monthly • inquire about resource/travel guide • women-owned/run

Kaneohe (808)

ACCOMMODATIONS

Windward Oahu B&B 46-251 Ikiiki St. • 235-1124/ (800) 235-1151 • lesbians/gay men • full breakfast • swimming • overlooks the bay

Idaho

Boise   (208)

Info Lines & Services

AA Gay/Lesbian 23rd & Woodlawn (First Cong. Church) • 344-6611 • 8pm Sun & Tue

Community Center PO Box 323, 83701 • 336-3870 • 7pm-10pm • info • referrals

WCP (Womyn's Company Production) PO Box 9232, 83707 • 345-7067

Bars

Emerald City Club 415 S. 9th • 342-5446 • 10am-2:30am • lesbians/gay men • dancing/DJ • wheelchair access • women-owned/run

The Oly 1108 Front St. • 342-1371 • 2pm-2am • mostly gay men • more women Sun • patio • wheelchair access

Partners 2210 Main St. • 331-3551 • 4pm-2am • lesbians/gay men • dancing/DJ • live shows

Restaurants & Cafes

The Flicks & Rick's Cafe American 646 Fulton St. • 342-4288 • opens at 4:30pm, from noon wknds • multi-racial • live shows • 2 movie theaters • patio • women-owned/run

Bookstores & Retail Shops

Blue Unicorn 1809 W. State St. • 345-9390 • 10am-9pm, 11am-5pm Sun • self-help w/ women's & gay/lesbian section • wheelchair access

Road Less Traveled Book & Gift Shop 3017 W. State St. • 384-5075/ (800) 816-7623 • 11am-6pm, from noon wknds • lesbigay

Travel & Tour Operators

Idaho Travel Council 700 W. State St. • (800) 635-7820

Spiritual Groups

MCC 408 N. Garden St. • 342-6764 • 5:45pm Sun

Publications

Diversity PO Box 323, 83701 • 323-0805 • monthly

Coeur D'Alene   (208)

Accommodations

The Clark House on Hayden Lake E. 4550 S. Hayden Lake Rd. • 772-3470/ (800) 765-4593 • popular • gay-friendly • B&B • full breakfast • mansion on wooded 12-acre estate • wheelchair access

Lava Hot Springs   (208)

Accommodations

Lava Hot Springs Inn 5 Portneuf Ave. • 776-5830 • gay-friendly • full breakfast • mineral pool • wheelchair access

Lewiston

Info Lines & Services

Lewiston Lesbian/Gay Society PO Box 2054, 83501 • meets 1st & 3rd Tue

Moscow   (208)

Info Lines & Services

Inland Northwest PO Box 8135, 83843 • 882-8034 • 1st Mon

University of Idaho Gay/Lesbian/Bisexual Group • 885-6331

Women's Center (Univ. of Idaho) corner of Idaho & Line Sts. • 885-6616 • library & resources • support • limited outreach • call first

Bookstores & Retail Shops

Bookpeople 512 S. Main • 882-7957 • 9am-8pm, til 5pm Sun • general

Pocatello   (208)

Bars

The Main Lander 305 N. Main • 232-9603 • 6pm-1am, clsd Sun-Mon • lesbians/gay men • dancing/DJ

Bookstores & Retail Shops

The Silver Fox 143 S. 2nd St. • 234-2477 • 11am-10pm, clsd Sun

Stanley   (208)

Accommodations

Las Tejanas B&B 3610 Rampart St., Boise, 83704 • 376-6077/ 774-3301 (B&B#) • May-Sept • lesbians/gay men • near outdoor recreation • full breakfast • natural hot tub • between 2 wilderness areas in the Sawtooth Mtns.

Illinois

Alton (618)

BARS

Alton Metro 602 Belle • 465-8687 • 4pm-1:30am • mostly gay men • dancing/DJ

Arlington Heights (708)

BOOKSTORES & RETAIL SHOPS

Prairie Moon 8 N. Dunton Ave. • 342-9608 • 11am-6pm, til 8pm Th, clsd Mon • feminist books • special events • wheelchair access • women-owned/run

Bloomingdale (708)

BOOKSTORES & RETAIL SHOPS

A Book for All Seasons 114 S. Bloomingdale Rd. • 893-9866 • 10am-8pm, 11am-5pm Sun • gay/lesbian section on 2nd flr.

Bloomington (309)

BARS

Bistro 316 N. Main St. • 829-2278 • 4pm-1am, from 8pm Sat, from 6pm Sun • lesbians/gay men • dancing/DJ • wheelchair access

BOOKSTORES & RETAIL SHOPS

Once Upon A Time 311 N. Main • 828-3998 • 2pm-8pm,10am-8pm Sat, noon-5pm Sun, clsd Tue & Th • alternative • wheelchair access

Blue Island (708)

BARS

Clubhouse Players 13126 S. Western • 389-6688 • 8pm-2am, til 3am Fri-Sat • lesbians/gay men • dancing/DJ • wheelchair access

Calumet City (708)

BARS

Are You Crazy 48 154th Pl. • 862-4605 • 7pm-2am • mostly gay men

Intrigue 582 State Line Rd. • 868-5240 • 6pm-2am, 7pm-3am Sat, 2pm-2am Sun • mostly women • dancing/DJ • wheelchair access • women-owned/run

Mr. B's 606 State Line Rd. • 862-1221 • 1pm-2am, til 3am Sat, Fri-Sat • popular • mostly gay men • dancing/DJ

Patch 201 155th St. • 891-9854 • 3pm-2am, til 3am Sat, 6pm-2am Sun, clsd Mon • mostly women • neighborhood bar • women-owned/run

Carbondale (618)

INFO LINES & SERVICES

The AA Lesbian/Gay • 549-4633

The Gay/Lesbian/Bisexuals & Friends at Southern Illinois University • 453-5151

Women's Services • 453-3655 • 8am-4:30pm • university support groups

Champaign/Urbana (217)

INFO LINES & SERVICES

Lesbian/Gay/Bisexual Switchboard • 384-8040 • 8pm-10pm, Mon-Fri

People for Lesbian/Gay/Bisexual Concerns of Illinois (at University of Illinois) • 333-1187 • 6pm Tue • student group

BARS

Chester Street 63 Chester St. • 356-5607 • 5pm-1am • gay-friendly • dancing/DJ • 'Trash Disco' Tue

BOOKSTORES & RETAIL SHOPS

Horizon Book Store 1115-1/2 W. Oregon • 328-2988 • 10am-6pm, clsd Sun

Jane Addams Book Shop 208 N. Neil • 356-2555 • 10am-5pm, noon-4pm Sun • full service antiquarian bookstore w/children's room • women's/gay/lesbian/ on 3rd flr.

Chicago (312)

Chicago is divided into 5 areas:

OVERVIEW
NEAR NORTH
NEW TOWN
NORTH SIDE
SOUTH SIDE

Overview

INFO LINES & SERVICES

AA Gay/Lesbian - Newtown Al-anon Club 4407 N. Clark • 271-6822 • site for many 12-step mtgs. • wheelchair access

Gay/Lesbian South Asians (SANGAT) PO Box 268463, 60626

Gerber/Hart Library & Archives 3352 N. Paulina St. • 883-3003 • 7pm-10pm Mon &Th, noon-4pm Sat • lesbigay resource center

Horizons Community Services 961 W. Montana • 472-6469 • 9am-10pm Mon-Th, til 5pm Fri

Kinheart Women's Center (see Evanston, IL)

Lesbian/Gay Helpline • 929-4357 • 6pm-10pm

BOOKSTORES & RETAIL SHOPS

Barbara's Bookstore 1350 N. Wells St. • 642-5044 • 9am-10pm, 10am-9pm Sun • women's/lesbigay • also 3130 N. Broadway • 477-0411 • 9am-11pm, 10am-9pm Sun • also Oak Park • (708) 848-9140 • wheelchair access • women-owned/run

TRAVEL & TOUR OPERATORS

Illinois Tourist Information Center 310 S. Michigan Ste. 108 • 822-0292

SPIRITUAL GROUPS

Congregation on Chadash 656 W. Barry (2nd Unitarian Church) • 248-9456 • Shabbat services & monthly activities

Dignity Chicago 3344 N. Broadway • 296-0780 • 7pm Sun

MCC Info Line • 262-0099 • info for all Chicago's MCC parishes

PUBLICATIONS

The Alternative Phone Book 425 W. Surf St. #114 • 472-6319 • directory of local businesses

Gay Chicago 3121 N. Broadway • 327-7271 • weekly

▲ **Outlines/Nightlines** 1115 W. Belmont Ave. #2-D • 871-7610 • monthly

Windy City Times 970 W. Montana St. • 935-1790 • weekly

Near North

ACCOMMODATIONS

Cass Hotel 640 N. Wabash Ave. • 787-4030 • gay-friendly • also a restaurant • full bar • in the heart of downtown

Hotel Lincoln 1816 N. Clark St. • 664-3040 • gay-friendly

Old Town Bed & Breakfast • 440-9268 • lesbians/gay men • patio

BARS

Artful Dodger 1734 W. Wabansia • 227-6859 • 5pm-2am, from 8pm Sat, clsd Sun • gay-friendly • dancing/DJ

Baton Show Lounge 436 N. Clark St. • 644-5269 • 8pm-4am Wed-Sun • lesbians/gay men • live shows • wheelchair access

Cairo 720 N. Wells • 266-6620 • 8pm-4am, 9am-5pm Sat, clsd Sun-Mon • gay-friendly • dancing/DJ • videos • more gay Sat • wheelchair access

The Crowbar 1543 N. Kingsbury • 243-4800 • 10pm-4am, clsd Mon-Tue • popular • gay-friendly • dancing/DJ • more gay Sun

The Generator 306 N. Halsted • 243-8889 • 9pm-4am, clsd Mon-Tue • lesbians/gay men • dancing/DJ • alternative • mostly African-American • wheelchair access

Ka-Boom 747 N. Green, River North • 243-4800 • from 9pm, clsd Sun-Wed • gay-friendly • dancing/DJ

RESTAURANTS & CAFES

Fireplace Inn 1448 N. Wells St. • 664-5264 • 4:30pm-midnight, from 11am wknds • lesbians/gay men • BBQ/American • full bar • wheelchair access • $10-20

Iggy's 700 N. Milwaukee, River North • 829-4449 • dinner nightly, til 4am Th-Sat • gay-friendly • Italian • some veggie • full bar • $8-12

Urbis Orbis Coffeehouse 1934 W. North Ave. • 252-4446 • 9am-midnight • lesbigay periodicals

GYMS & HEALTH CLUBS

Thousand Waves 1212 W. Belmont Ave. • 549-0700 • 5pm-10pm, 10am-3pm Sat, clsd Sun • women only • martial arts & self-defense for women & children • women's health spa • women-owned/run

TRAVEL & TOUR OPERATORS

C.R.C. Travel 2121 N. Clybourn • 525-3800/ (800) 874-7701 • IGTA member

Envoy Travel 740 N. Rush St. • 787-2400/ (800) 443-6869 • IGTA member

River North Travel 432 N. Clark St. • 527-2269 • IGTA member

Travel With Us, Ltd. 919 N. Michigan Ave. #3102 • 944-2244/ (800) 775-0919 • IGTA member

SPIRITUAL GROUPS

Presbyterians for Lesbian/Gay Concerns 600 W. Fullerton Pkwy. (Lincoln Park Preb.) • 784-2635 • 11am Sun (10am summers) • 'More Light' congregation

New Town

INFO LINES & SERVICES

Chicago 35 (at Ann Sather's Restaurant) • 262-6858 • 3:30pm-6pm, 3rd Sun of month • group for women over 35

ACCOMMODATIONS

City Suites Hotel 933 W. Belmont • 404-3400 • gay-friendly • accommodations w/ a touch of European style • IGTA member

Park Brompton Inn 528 W. Brompton Pl. • 404-3499 • gay-friendly • romantic 19th century atmosphere

Surf Hotel 555 W. Surf St. • 528-8400 • gay-friendly • 1920s hotel in the heart of Lincoln Park

Villa Toscana Guesthouse 3447 N. Halstead St. • 404-2643/ (800) 404-2643 • lesbians/gay men • full breakfast

BARS

Annex 3 3160 N. Clark St. • 327-5969 • noon-2am, til 3am Sat • lesbians/gay men • wheelchair access

Beat Kitchen 2100 W. Belmont • 281-4444 • noon-2am, clsd Sun • gay-friendly • live shows • food served • wheelchair access

Berlin 954 W. Belmont • 348-4975 • opening time varies, closes 4am • popular • lesbians/gay men • dancing/DJ • live shows • videos • women's night w/ dancers 1st & 3rd Wed • wheelchair access

Buddies 3301 N. Clark St. • 477-4066 • 7am-2am wknds • lesbians/gay men • also a restaurant • American • some veggie • $10-20

Closet 3325 N. Broadway St. • 477-8533 • 2pm-4am, from noon wknds • popular • lesbians/gay men • videos

Dandy's Piano Bar 3729 N. Halsted St. • 525-1200 • noon-2am • lesbians/gay men • neighborhood bar • piano bar • wheelchair access

Gentry 3320 N. Halsted • 348-1053 • 4pm-2am • lesbians/gay men • live shows

Chicago

Known for its frigid winters and legendary political corruption, Chicago is also home to strong communities of political radicals, African-Americans, artists and performers, and of course, lesbians and gays.

If you remember the Chicago 7, you might want to stop by the **Heartland Cafe** (465-8005) in Rogers Park for a drink, some food, or a T-shirt from their radical variety store! Or check in with the **Horizons Community Center** to find out about local lesbian/gay political (and social) groups.

The African-American communities in Chicage are large and influential – and make up about 40% of Chicago's population. In fact, Chicago was settled by an African-French man, whose name graces the **Du Sable Museum of African-American History** (947-0600). The South Side is the cultural center for Chicagoans of African descent, and houses the **South Side Community Art Center** (373-1026), and the **Olivet Baptist Church** (842-1081), a station on the Underground Railroad and site of Mahalia Jackson's 1928 debut. We've heard the home cooking at **Army & Lou's Restaurant** (483-3100) will put a smile in your stomach.

Many of Chicago's other immigrant neighborhoods are just as fascinating – call the **Chicago Office of Tourism** for details. However, if you love Indian food, don't miss the many delicious and cheap Indian buffets on Devon, just west of Sheridan.

What else is there to do? For starters, take a cruise on Lake Michigan. On land, you'll find superb shopping, real Chicago-style pizza, a great arts and theater scene and clubs where jazz and blues thrive, like the **Green Mill** (878-5552), known for originating "poetry slams," and its house big band.

And you'll never have a dull moment in Chicago's women's scene. For a good book or a good time, find **People Like Us**, the city's lesbigay bookstore, or **Women & Children First** bookstore. Pick up a copy of **Outlines** or **Nightlines** for the dish on what's hot. And while you're in New Town, cruise by **Berlin** for women's night Wednesday, and **Vortex** for one of their monthly women's parties.

On the Northside, treat yourself to the art at **Womanwild** women's gallery, grab a cup of java at the truly **Mountain Moving Coffeehouse** on Saturday, then boogie down at **Paris Dance** disco, or two-step Tuesdays at **Lost & Found**.

Launder Bar & Cafe 1344 W. Newport • 665-0555 • 8am-2am • gay-friendly • also a restaurant • American • some veggie • $5-12

Roscoe's 3354-3356 N. Halsted St. • 281-3355 • 2pm-2am, noon-3am Sat • popular • lesbians/gay men • neighborhood bar • dancing/DJ • patio

Smart Bar/Cabaret Metro 3730 N. Clark St. • 549-4140 • 9:30pm-4am • gay-friendly • dancing/DJ • live shows

Spin 3200 N. Halsted • 327-7711 • mostly gay men • dancing/DJ • videos

Vortex 3631 N. Halsted • 975-6622 • 9pm-4am, clsd Sun-Mon • mostly gay men • dancing/DJ • alternative • live shows • videos • monthly women's parties • call for details • wheelchair access

RESTAURANTS & CAFES

Angelina Ristorante 3561 Broadway • 935-5933 • Italian • $10-20

Ann Sather's 929 W. Belmont Ave. • 348-2378 • 7am-10pm, til midnight Fri-Sat • popular • some veggie • $5-10

Bentley's Coffee House 3322 N. Halsted • 549-9900 • 10am-2am, til 4am wknds • lesbians/gay men • 'Chicago's only gay coffee house' • wheelchair access

Cornelia's 750 Cornelia Ave. • 248-8333 • clsd Mon • some veggie • full bar • dinner nightly • wheelchair access • $10-20

The Mike's Broadway Cafe 3805 N. Broadway • 404-2205 • 7am-10pm, 24hrs Fri-Sat • lesbians/gay men • American • some veggie • wheelchair access • $5-10

The Pepper 3441 N. Sheffield • 665-7377 • 6pm-2am, clsd Mon • lesbians/gay men • live shows • supper club

The Raw Bar & Grill 3720 N. Clark St. • 348-7291 • 5pm-2am, from 1pm-2am • seafood • $8-12

The Scenes Coffee House & Dramatist Bookstore 3168 N. Clark St. • 525-1007 • 9:30am-midnight

Chicago (312)

LESBIGAY INFO: Horizons Community Services: 472-6469, 961 W. Montana, 9am-10pm Mon-Th, til 5pm Fri. Gay/Lesbian Helpline: 929-4357, 6pm-10pm.

WHERE THE GIRLS ARE: In the Belmont area – on Halstead or Clark streets – with the boys, or hanging out elsewhere in New Town. Upwardly-mobile lesbians live in Lincoln Park or Wrigleyville, while their working-class sisters live in Andersonville (way north).

LESBIGAY AA: Newtown Al-anon Club: 271-6822, 4407 N. Clark.

LESBIGAY PRIDE: June. 348-8243.

ANNUAL EVENTS: June 14 - Lambda Literary Awards: (202) 462-7924, the 'Lammies' are the Oscars of lesbigay publishing, coincides with the American Bookseller's Association Convention. November - Chicago Gay/Lesbian Film Festival: 384-5533.

CITY INFO: Chicago Office of Tourism: 744-2400/(800)487-2446.

BEST VIEW: Skydeck of the 110 story Sears Tower.

WEATHER: 'The Windy City' earned its name. Winter temperatures have been known to be as low as -46°. Summers are humid, normally in the 80°s.

TRANSIT: Yellow & Checker Cabs: 829-4222.

BOOKSTORES & RETAIL SHOPS

▲ **People Like Us** 1115 W. Belmont • 248-6363 • 10am-9pm • Chicago's only exclusively lesbigay bookstore

Unabridged Books 3251 N. Broadway St. • 883-9119 • 10am-10pm, til 8pm wknds • wheelchair access

We're Everywhere 3434 N. Halsted St. • 404-0590 • noon-7pm • also mail order catalog

SPIRITUAL GROUPS

MCC Good Shepherd 615 W. Wellington Ave. • 262-0099 • 9am & 7pm Sun

EROTICA

Male Hide Leathers 2816 N. Lincoln Ave. • 929-0069 • noon-8pm, til midnight Fri-Sat, clsd Mon

North Side   (312)

WOMEN'S ACCOMMODATIONS

Sister's Place 3712 N. Broadway #918, 60640 • 275-1319 • women only • women-owned/run • $20-45

ACCOMMODATIONS

Magnolia Place 5353 N. Magnolia • 334-6860 • lesbians/gay men • B&B

BARS

Big Chicks 5024 N. Sheridan • 728-5511 • noon-2am • lesbians/gay men • neighborhood bar • wheelchair access

Chicago Eagle 5015 N. Clark • 728-0050 • 8pm-4am • lesbians/gay men • leather • women's night Th • wheelchair access

Clark's on Clark 5001 N. Clark St. • 728-2373 • 4pm-4am • popular • mostly gay men • neighborhood bar

Different Strokes 4923 N. Clark St. • 989-1958 • noon-2am, til 3am Sat • mostly gay men • neighborhood bar

Lost & Found 3058 W. Irving Park Rd. • 463-9617 • 7pm-2am, from 4pm wknds, clsd Mon • mostly women • neighborhood bar • country/western Tue • women-owned/run

Madrigal's 5316 N. Clark St. • 334-3033 • 5pm-2am • lesbians/gay men • live shows

Off the Line 1829 W. Montrose • 528-3253 • 5pm-2am, from 3pm Sat, from noon Sun • mostly women • neighborhood bar • women-owned/run

Paris Dance 1122 W. Montrose • 769-0602 • 5pm-2am, 2pm-3am Sat, noon-2am Sun • popular • mostly women • dancing/DJ • food served • also cafe • clsd Mon-Tue • wheelchair access

Restaurants & Cafes

Fireside 5739 N. Ravenswood • 878-5942 • 11am-4am • plenty veggie • full bar • patio • wheelchair access • $6-15

Mountain Moving Coffeehouse 1545 W. Morse • 477-8362 • Sat only • women & girls only • live shows • non-alcoholic • collective run

Tendino's 5335 N. Sheridan • 275-8100 • 11am-11pm • pizzeria • full bar • wheelchair access

Bookstores & Retail Shops

Gay Mart 3457 N. Halsted St. • 929-4272 • 11am-8pm

KOPI: A Traveler's Cafe 5317 N. Clark St. • 989-5674 • 8am-11pm

WomanWild/Treasures by Women 5237 N. Clark St. • 878-0300 • 11am-7pm, til 8pm Fri, til 6pm wknds • art & gift gallery • commitment rings & gift registry • wheelchair access • lesbian-owned/run

Women & Children First 5233 N. Clark St. • 769-9299 • 11am-7pm, til 9pm Wed-Fri, 10am-7pm Sat, 11am-6pm Sun • women's bookstore • also videos & music • wheelchair access • women-owned/run

South Side

Bars

411 Club 411 E. 63rd St. • 684-0440 • noon-4am • lesbians/gay men • dancing/DJ • mostly African-American

Escapades 6301 S. Harlem • 229-0886 • 10pm-4am, til 5am Sat • mostly gay men • dancing/DJ • videos

Inn Exile 5758 W. 65th St. • 582-3510 • 6pm-2am, from noon Sun • mostly gay men • dancing/DJ • videos • wheelchair access

Jeffery Pub/Disco 7041 S. Jeffery • 363-8555 • 11am-4am • mostly gay men • dancing/DJ • multi-racial • wheelchair access

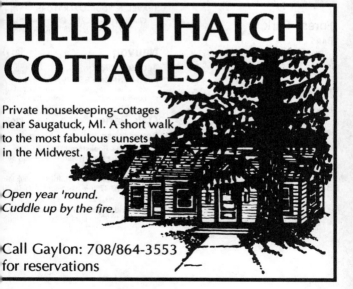

Martin's Den 5550 S. State St. • 363-9470 • noon-2am • mostly gay men • neighborhood bar • dancing/DJ • multi-racial

Elgin (708)

INFO LINES & SERVICES

Fox Valley Gay Association PO Box 393, 60120 • 392-6882 • 7pm-10pm Mon-Fri • info • referrals

Elk Grove Village (708)

BARS

Hunters 1932 E. Higgins • 439-8840 • 4pm-4am • popular • mostly gay men • dancing/DJ • videos

Evanston (708)

INFO LINES & SERVICES

Kinheart Women's Center 2214 Ridge Ave. • 491-1103 • lesbian only programs 8pm 2nd, 3rd & 4th Fri • counseling • referrals • educational programs

ACCOMMODATIONS

▲ **Hilby Thatch Cottages** 1720 Seward • 864-3553 • lesbians/gay men • kitchens • fireplaces • close to Saugatuck, MI

Forest Park (708)

BARS

Nut Bush 7201 Franklin • 366-5117 • 3pm-2am Mon, til 3am Fri-Sat • mostly gay men • dancing/DJ

Franklin Park (708)

BARS

Temptations 10235 W. Grand Ave. • 455-0008 • 4pm-4am, 3pm-2am Sun • popular • mostly women • dancing/DJ • videos

Granite City (618)

BARS

Club Zips 3145 W. Chain of Rocks Rd. • 797-0700 • 6pm-2am, til 3am Sat, 4pm-midnight Sun • lesbians/gay men • dancing/DJ • live shows • videos • volleyball • horseshoes • patio • wheelchair access

Hinsdale (708)

SPIRITUAL GROUPS

MCC Holy Covenant 17 W. Maple (Unitarian Church) • 325-8488 • 6pm Sun

Joliet (815)

BARS

Maneuvers 118 E. Jefferson, Joliet • 727-7069 • 8pm-2am, til 3am Fri-Sat • lesbians/gay men • dancing/DJ

Lansing (708)

RESTAURANTS & CAFES

Outriggers 2352 172nd St. • 418-0202 • seafood • some veggie • full bar • also comedy club • wheelchair access • $8-20

Lincolnwood (708)

TRAVEL & TOUR OPERATORS

Edward's Travel Advisors 7301 N. Lincoln Ave. #215 • 677-4420/ (800) 541-5158

Naperville (708)

TRAVEL & TOUR OPERATORS

Classic Travel 1271 E. Ogden Ave. #123 • 963-3030/ (800) 932-5789 • IGTA member

Nauvoo (217)

ACCOMMODATIONS

Ed-Harri-Mere B&B 290 N. Page St. • 453-2796 • gay-friendly • quiet Victorian bungalow • close to historic sites

Oak Park (708)

BOOKSTORES & RETAIL SHOPS

Barbara's Bookstore 1110 Lake St. • 848-9140 • 10am-10pm, 11am-8pm Sun • wheelchair access

The Left Bank Bookstall 104 S. Oak Park Ave. • 383-4700 • 10am-8pm Mon-Th, til 9pm Fri-Sat, 1pm-5pm Sun

The Pride Agenda 1109 Westgate • 524-8429 • 10:30am-6pm, til 8pm Th, 11am-5pm wknds • lesbigay

Peoria (309)

BARS

D.J.'s Timeout 703 SW Adams • 674-5902 • 1pm-1am, Sun brunch • lesbians/gay men • dancing/DJ

Quench Room 631 W. Main • 676-1079 • 5pm-1am, from 1pm wknds • lesbians/gay men • neighborhood bar • wheelchair access

Red Fox Den 800 N. Knoxville Ave. • 674-8013 • 9pm-4am • lesbians/gay men • dancing/DJ

PUBLICATIONS

The Alternative Times PO Box 5661, 61601 • 688-1930

Quincy (217)

BARS

Irene's Cabaret 124 N. 5th St. • 222-6292 • 7pm-1am, clsd Mon • lesbians/gay men • dancing/DJ • live shows

SPIRITUAL GROUPS

MCC 124-1/2 N. 5th • 224-2800 • 6pm Sun

Rock Island (309)

BARS

Augie's 313 20th St. • 788-7389 • 6am-3am, from 10am Sun • mostly women • neighborhood bar

J.R.'s 325 20th St. • 786-9411 • 3pm-3am, from noon Sun • dancing/DJ • wheelchair access

Madison Square 319 20th St. • 786-9400 • 4pm-3am • lesbians/gay men • dancing/DJ • live shows • wheelchair access

BOOKSTORES & RETAIL SHOPS

All Kinds of People 1806 2nd Ave. • 788-2567 • 10am-11pm • food served • progressive • wheelchair access

Rockford (815)

BARS

Office 513 E. State St. • 965-0344 • 5pm-2am, noon-midnight Sun • popular • lesbians/gay men • dancing/DJ • videos • beer only

RESTAURANTS & CAFES

Cafe Esperanto 107 N. Main • 968-0123 • noon-1am, 7pm-midnight Sun • full bar • gallery

Maria's 828 Cunningham • 968-6781 • 5pm-9pm, clsd Sun-Mon • Italian • full bar • $6-12

Springfield (217)

BARS

New Dimensions 3036 Peoria Rd. • 753-9268 • 8pm-3am Th-Sat • mostly gay men • dancing/DJ • beer only

The Smokey's Den 411 E. Washington • 522-0301 • 6pm-1am, til 3am Fri-Sat • lesbians/gay men • dancing/DJ • wheelchair access

The Station House 306 E. Washington • 525-0438 • 7am-1am, from noon Sun • gay-friendly • neighborhood bar • wheelchair access

SPIRITUAL GROUPS

MCC Faith Eternal 514 N. Walnut • 525-9597 • 5:45pm Sun

Sterling

INFO LINES & SERVICES

IAWIA (I Am What I Am) PO Box 1314, 61081 • support group for northwest IL • meetings & newsletter

Waukegan (708)

TRAVEL & TOUR OPERATORS

Carlson Travel Network/Cray's Travel 410 S. Greenbay Rd. • 623-4722 • IGTA member

Indiana

Bloomington (812)

INFO LINES & SERVICES

Bloomington Gay/Lesbian/Bisexual Switchboard • 855-5688 • irregular volunteer hours, recorded info 24hrs

The Indiana Youth Group • (800) 347-8336

Lesbian Discussion Group • 331-8598 • 8pm 1st & 3rd Mon • lesbian social group

Outreach • 855-3849 • 5:45pm Tue • support/discussion groups • call switchboard for hours & locations

BARS

The Bullwinkle's 201 S. College St. • 334-3232 • 7pm-3am, clsd Sun • lesbians/gay men • dancing/DJ • live shows • more women Th

The Other Bar 414 S. Walnut • 332-0033 • 4pm-3am, clsd Sun • lesbians/gay men • neighborhood bar • more women Tue & Th • patio • wheelchair access

RESTAURANTS & CAFES

Kansas City Burger Company 116 W. Washington St. • 829-4244 • 10am-3pm, clsd Sun • lesbians/gay men • some veggie • patio • wheelchair access

Village Deli 409 E. Kirkwood • 336-2303 • 7am-9pm, til 7pm wknds • some veggie • wheelchair access

BOOKSTORES & RETAIL SHOPS

Athena Gallery 108 E. Kirkwood • 339-0734 • 11am-6pm, til 8:30pm Fri-Sat, til 4pm Sun

SPIRITUAL GROUPS

Integrity Bloomington 400 E. Kirkwood Ave. (Trinity Episcopal Church) • 336-4466 • 7:30pm 2nd Wed • wheelchair access

Elkhart (219)

INFO LINES & SERVICES

Switchboard Concern • 293-8671 (crisis only) • 24hrs

SPIRITUAL GROUPS

Unitarian Universalist Fellowship 1732 Garden • 264-6525 • 10:30am Sun • wheelchair access

Evansville (812)

INFO LINES & SERVICES

Tri-State Alliance PO Box 2901, 47728 • 474-4853 • info • monthly social group • newsletter

BARS

The ShoBar 750 E. Franklin St. • 428-5970 • 9pm-3am Wed-Sat • gay-friendly • dancing/DJ • live shows

Someplace Else 930 Main St. • 424-3202 • 4pm-3am • lesbians/gay men • dancing/DJ • wheelchair access

BOOKSTORES & RETAIL SHOPS

A.A. Michael Books 1541 S. Green River Rd. • 479-8979 • noon-6pm, til 8pm Fri, 10am-5pm Sat • spiritual

Fort Wayne (219)

INFO LINES & SERVICES

Fort Wayne Feminists PO Box 10267, 46851 • 424-1700 • monthly mtgs • sponsors women's events

Gay/Lesbian AA (at Up the Stairs Community Center) • 744-1199 • 7:30pm Tue & Sat • call for schedule

Up the Stairs Community Center 3426 Broadway • 744-1199 • helpline 7pm-10pm, til midnight Fri-Sat, 6:30pm-9pm Sun • space for various groups

BARS

After Dark 231 Pearl St. • 424-6130 • 6pm-3:30am, clsd Sun • lesbians/gay men • dancing/DJ • live shows • wheelchair access

Riff Raff's 2809 W. Main St. • 436-4166 3pm-3am, clsd Sun • mostly gay men • neighborhood bar • wheelchair access

SPIRITUAL GROUPS

New World Church & Outreach Center 222 E. Leigh • 456-6570 • 11am Sun • wheelchair access

Open Door Chapel (at Up the Stairs Community Center) • 744-1199 • 7pm Sun

Indianapolis (317)

INFO LINES & SERVICES

AA Gay/Lesbian • 632-7864

Coming Out Positively (at Dreams & Swords) • 7:30pm 1st and 3rd Tue • lesbian coming out group

Diversity Center PO Box 441473, 46202 • 624-2089 • community center

Fellowship Indianapolis PO Box 2331, 46206-2331 • 326-4614 • social & support groups for lesbians/gay men

Gay/Lesbian Hotline PO Box 2152, 46206 • 253-4297 • 7pm-11pm daily

Gay/Lesbian Switchboard 630-4297

Lesbians Over 40 Group (at Dreams & Swords) • 7:30pm 1st & 3rd Th

Sweet Misery PO Box 11690, 46201-0690 • S/M support group primarily for lesbians

Thursday Night Lesbian Discussion Group (at Dreams & Swords) • 7:30pm 2nd & 4th Th

BARS

501 Tavern 501 N. College Ave. • 632-2100 • 3pm-3am, clsd Sun • popular • mostly gay men • country/western Tue • dancing/DJ Fri-Sat • also leather shop

Betty Boop's Lounge 637 Massachusetts Ave. • 637-2310 • noon-midnight • gay-friendly • neighborhood bar • food served

Brothers Bar & Grill Inc. 822 N. Illinois St. • 636-1020 • 11am-midnight, from 4pm wknds • lesbians/gay men • live shows • also a restaurant • American • some veggie • wheelchair access • $7-14

Club 151 151 E. 14th St. • 767-1707 • 8pm-3am, clsd Sun • lesbians/gay men • dancing/DJ • live shows • patio • wheelchair access

Illusions 1456 E. Washington • 266-0535 • 7am-3am, clsd Sun • lesbians/gay men • dancing/DJ • live shows • women's night Th

The Metro 707 Massachusetts • 639-6022 • 4pm-3am, noon-12:30am Sun • lesbians/gay men • dancing/DJ • also a restaurant • American • some veggie • patio • wheelchair access • $5-11

The Ten 1218 N. Pennsylvania St. (entrance in rear) • 638-5802 • 6pm-3am, clsd Sun • popular • mostly women • dancing/DJ • live shows • country/western Mon • wheelchair access

Tomorrow's 2301 N. Meridian • 925-1710 • 5pm-3am, til 12:30am Sun • lesbians/gay men • dancing/DJ • live show • more women Tue & Th • also a restaurant • Chinese/American • $7-10 • wheelchair access

Indianapolis

*I*ndianapolis, the capital of the 'Hoosier' state, looks like your typical midwestern industrial city. But you'll find a few surprises under the surface.

You probably won't find lesbians dancing in the streets (unless it's Pride Day). But they're there. Start at the women's bookstore, **Dreams & Swords**. While you're in the neighborhood, check out some of the fun boutiques and restaurants in the Broad Ripple district. Later fuel up on caffeine at **Coffee Zon** and dance with the girls at **The Ten**.

If you're into women's music, or plan on being in Indiana during the first weekend in June, drive down to Bloomington for the **National Women's Music Festival** (call Dreams & Swords for info). If fast cars are more your style, be in Indianapolis for the **Indy 500** on Memorial Day weekend.

Indianapolis   (317)

LESBIGAY INFO: Gay/Lesbian Switchboard: 630-4297, 7pm-11pm daily.

LESBIGAY PAPER: Indiana Word: 579-3075. Out & About Indiana: 574-0615.

WHERE THE GIRLS ARE: Spread throughout the city, but Broad Ripple serves as a friendly meeting point.

ENTERTAINMENT: Women's Chorus: 638-9039. Men's Chorus at the Crossroads Performing Arts: 931-9464. The Irving: 357-3792, film.

LESBIGAY AA: 632-7864

LESBIGAY PRIDE: June. Justice Inc.: 634-9212.

ANNUAL EVENTS: June 1-4 - National Women's Music Festival: (317) 927-9355/ 253-9966 in Bloomington.

CITY INFO: Indianapolis Visitor's Bureau: 639-4282.

ATTRACTIONS: Union Station, Indianapolis Speedway 500.

WEATHER: The spring weather is moderate (50°s - 60°s) with occasional storms. The summers are typically midwestern: hot (mid 90°s) and humid. The autumns are mild and colorful in southeastern Indiana. As for winter, it's the wind chill that'll get to you.

TRANSIT: Yellow Cab: 487-7777. Metro Transit: 635-3344.

The Vogue 6259 N. College Ave. • 259-7029 • 9pm-1am • gay-friendly • dancing/DJ • alternative • live shows • more gay Sun

RESTAURANTS & CAFES

Aesop's Tables 600 N. Massachusetts Ave. • 631-0055 • 11am-9pm, til 10pm Fri-Sat • beer/wine • authentic Mediterranean • some veggie • wheelchair access • $9-12

Coffee Zon 137 E. Ohio St. • 684-0432 • 6:30am-6pm, clsd wknds • lesbians/gay men • some veggie • cafe • $4-6

BOOKSTORES & RETAIL SHOPS

Awakening 6358 N. Guilford Ave. • 255-9907 • noon-6pm, clsd Sun • progressive

Borders Book Shop 5612 Castleton Corner Ln. • 849-8660 • 9am-10pm, 11am-6pm Sun

▲ **Dreams & Swords** 6503 Ferguson St. • 253-9966/ (800) 937-2706 • 10am-6pm, 10:30am-5pm Sat, noon-5pm Sun • lesbian-feminist bookstore

Indiana News 14 W. Maryland • 636-7680 • 6am-7pm, til 6pm wknds

Just Cards 145 E. Ohio St. • 638-1170 • 9am-5:30pm, clsd Sun • wheelchair access

Southside News 8063 Madison Ave. • 887-1020 • 6am-8pm, til 6pm Sun

TRAVEL & TOUR OPERATORS

Ross & Babcock Travel 832 Broad Ripple Ave. • 259-4194/ (800) 229-4194 • IGTA member

UniWorld Travel 1010 E. 86th St. #65E • 573-4919/ (800) 573-4919

SPIRITUAL GROUPS

Affirmation/Dignity & Integrity • 639-5937 • call switchboard for details

Jesus MCC 3620 N. Franklin Rd. (church) • 895-4934 • 6pm Sun • wheelchair access

PUBLICATIONS

The Indiana Word 225 E. North St. Tower 1 Ste. 2800 • 579-3075 • monthly

Out & About Indiana 133 W. Market St. #105 • 574-0615

Swagger & Sway PO Box 11690, 46201-0690 • quarterly • nat'l newsletter for butch/femme

Lafayette (317)

Bars

The Sportsman 644 Main St. • 742-6321
• 9am-3am, from 5pm Sat, clsd Sun •
lesbians/gay men • neighborhood bar •
dancing/DJ

Spiritual Groups

Dignity-Lafayette PO Box 4665, 47903 •
742-1926 • 7:30pm Wed • at Morton
Community Center

Monroe City (812)

Travel & Tour Operators

The Travel Club City Centre, Box 128,
47557 • 743-2919 • international mem-
bership-only non-profit travel club

Muncie (317)

Info Lines & Services

Live & Let Live AA 300 S. Madison (at
Grace Church) • 284-3331 • 7:30pm Mon

Bars

Carriage House 1100 Kilgore • 282-7411
• 4pm-2am • gay-friendly • neighborhood bar • also a restaurant •
steak/seafood • 3 flrs. • wheelchair
access • $7-10

Mark III Tap Room 107 E. Main St. •
282-8273 • 11am-3am, clsd Sun • les-
bians/gay men • dancing/DJ

Richmond (317)

Info Lines & Services

**Earlham Lesbian/Bisexual/Gay Peoples
Union** Box E-565 Earlham College, 47373
• active campus group

Bars

Coachman 911 E. Main St. • 966-2835 •
6pm-3am, clsd Sun • lesbians/gay men •
dancing/DJ • alternative • more women
Sat

South Bend (219)

Info Lines & Services

Community Resource Center Helpline •
232-2522 • 8am-5pm • limited gay/les-
bian info • also 24hr crisis hotline

IUSB Women's Resource Center
Northside IUSB Rm. #203 • 237-4494/
237-4491 • 8am-5pm Mon-Fri

Accommodations

Kamm's Island Inn 700 Lincoln Wy. W.,
Mishawaka • 256-1501/ (800) 955-5266 •
gay-friendly • swimming • wheelchair
access

Bars

Sea Horse II Cabaret 1902 W. Western
Ave. • 237-9139 • 8pm-3am • gay-friendly • dancing/DJ • live shows

Starz Bar & Restaurant 1505 S. Kendall
St. • 288-7827 • 8pm-3am, clsd Sun •
lesbians/gay men • dancing/DJ • live
shows • food served • burgers & snacks
• wheelchair access

Truman's The 100 Center, Mishawaka •
259-2282 • 5pm-3am, til midnight Sun •
popular • lesbians/gay men • dancing/DJ
• piano bar Fri-Sat • also cafe • plenty
veggie • large outdoor area • swimming

Bookstores & Retail Shops

Little Professor Book Center Martins
Ironwood Plaza North • 277-4488 • 9am-
9pm, 10am-5pm wknds

Terre Haute (812)

Info Lines & Services

**Gay/Lesbian/Bisexual Terre Haute Info
Line** • 237-6916 • extensive touchtone
directory of resources, bars & more

IYG-Terre Haute • 231-6829 • local
chapter of statewide youth group • 21
years & under

Bars

Hightowers 13th at Chestnut • 232-3443
• 8pm-3am • gay-friendly • dancing/DJ •
alternative • multi-racial • more popular
Th-Sat

Our Place 684 Lafayette Ave. • 232-9119
• 8pm-3am, clsd Sun-Mon • lesbians/gay
men • dancing/DJ • live shows • 2 flrs.

Iowa

Ames (515)

INFO LINES & SERVICES

Gay/Lesbian Alliance Iowa State University, 39 Memorial Union, 50011 • 294-2104 • 10am-4pm • meets 7:30pm Wed in Rm. 245

Help Central • 232-0000 • 9am-5pm • community info service • some lesbigay referrals

Margaret Sloss Women's Center Sloss House (ISU) • 294-4154 • call for programs

RESTAURANTS & CAFES

Lucallen's 400 Main St. • 232-8484 • 11am-11pm • Italian • some veggie • full bar • $6-12

Pizza Kitchen 120 Hayward • 292-1710 • 11am-10pm • lesbians/gay men • beer/wine

Burlington (319)

BARS

Steve's Place 852 Washington • 752-9109 • 9am-2am • gay-friendly • neighborhood bar • wheelchair access

Cedar Rapids (319)

INFO LINES & SERVICES

Gay/Lesbian Resource Center PO Box 1643, 52406 • 366-2055 • 6pm-9pm Mon • support group 1st & 3rd Wed

BARS

Side Saddle Saloon 525 'H' St. SW • 362-2226 • 5pm-2am • lesbians/gay men • dancing/DJ • country/western • live shows • 2 bars (one smoke- free) • dance lessons Mon & Th 8:30pm • wheelchair access

Council Bluffs (712)

BOOKSTORES & RETAIL SHOPS

Dream Riders Universe 2221 W. Broadway • 325-1257 • by appt. • custom clothes • accessories • fantasy role-playing drag • leather

Davenport (319)

BOOKSTORES & RETAIL SHOPS

Crystal Rainbow 1025 W. 4th St. • 323-1050 • 10am-5:30pm, clsd Sun • feminist bookstore • will order gay titles

SPIRITUAL GROUPS

MCC Quad Cities 3707 Eastern Ave. • 2:30pm Sun

Des Moines (515)

INFO LINES & SERVICES

GLRC (Gay/Lesbian Resource Center) 522 11th St. • 281-0634 • youth groups • many other mtgs.

Out-Reach PO Box 70044, 50311 • social/support group

Women's Cultural Collective PO Box 22063, 50322 • newsletter • monthly coffeehouses • social events • support groups

Women's Rap Group • 7pm 1st & 3rd Th • contact GLRC for info

Young Women's Resource Center 554 28th St. • 244-4901 • 8:30am-5pm Mon-Fri

ACCOMMODATIONS

Kingman House 2920 Kingman Blvd. • 279-7312 • lesbians/gay men • full breakfast • turn-of-the-century B&B • wheelchair access

Racoon River Resort • 279-7312 • lesbians/gay men • full breakfast • hot tub • nudity • food served • on the river • available for large groups • wheelchair access

BARS

Blazing Saddles 416 E. 5th St. • 246-1299 • 2pm-2am, from noon wknds • popular • mostly gay men • leather

Garden 112 SE 4th St. • 243-3965 • 6pm-2am • popular • lesbians/gay men • dancing/DJ • live shows • patio

Our Place Lounge 424 E. Locust • 243-9626 • 5pm-2am • lesbians/gay men • dancing/DJ • live shows • wheelchair access

Shooters Lounge 515 E. 6th • 245-9126 • noon-2am • lesbians/gay men • neighborhood bar • wheelchair access

RESTAURANTS & CAFES

Chat Noir Cafe 644 18th St. • 244-1353 • 10am-11pm, clsd Sun-Mon • beer/wine • cont'l • some veggie • $6-12

Side Saddle Cafe 418 E. 5th St. • 282-7041 • 6am-11pm, til 4am wknds • lesbians/gay men • $3-8

BOOKSTORES & RETAIL SHOPS

Borders Book Shop 1821 22nd St., W. Des Moines • 223-1620 • 9am-9pm, 11am-6pm Sun • wheelchair access

TRAVEL & TOUR OPERATORS

Iowa Division of Tourism 200 E. Grand Ave. • (800) 345-4692

PUBLICATIONS

Outword PO Box 7008, 50309 • 281-0634

Pen PO Box 1693, 50306 • 265-3214

EROTICA

Axiom 412-1/2 E. 5th St. • 246-0414 • tatoos • piercings

Grinnell   (515)

INFO LINES & SERVICES

Stonewall Resource Center Grinnell College Box U-5, 50112 • 269-3327 • also produces quarterly newsletter

Iowa City   (319)

INFO LINES & SERVICES

AA Gay/Lesbian • 338-9111

Gay/Lesbian/Bisexual People's Union c/o SAC/IMU University of Iowa, 52242 • 335-3251 • also publishes 'Gay Hawkeye' newsletter

Women's Resource/Action Center 130 N. Madison • 335-1486 • community center & lesbian support group

BARS

6:20 Club 620 S. Madison St. • 354-2494 • 9pm-2am, clsd Sun-Tue • popular • lesbians/gay men • dancing/DJ • wheelchair access

BOOKSTORES & RETAIL SHOPS

Prairie Lights Bookstore 15 S. Dubuque St. • 337-2681 • 9am-9pm, til 5pm wknds

Mason City

INFO LINES & SERVICES

GLNCI (Gays/Lesbians of North Central Iowa) Box 51, 50401

Newton   (515)

ACCOMMODATIONS

La Corsette Maison Inn 629 1st Ave. E. • 792-6833 • gay-friendly • upscale B&B w/ 4-star restaurant • 3 course breakfast • antique jacuzzi

Sioux City   (712)

BARS

3 Cheers 414 20th St. • 255-8005 • 9am-2am • lesbians/gay men • neighborhood bar • dancing/DJ • live shows • wheelchair access

Kings & Queens 417 Nebraska St. • 252-4167 • 7pm-2am • dancing/DJ

Waterloo   (319)

INFO LINES & SERVICES

Access PO Box 1682, 50704 • 232-6805 • weekly info & support • monthly newsletter

Lesbian/Bisexual Support Group PO Box 2241, 50704 • 233-7519 • 7:30pm 4th Mon

BARS

The Bar Ltd. 903 Sycamore • 232-0543 • 7pm-2am • lesbians/gay men • dancing/DJ • live shows • wheelchair access

Stilettos 1125 W. Donald • 234-6752 • 7pm-2am • lesbians/gay men • dancing/DJ • patio • wheelchair access

RESTAURANTS & CAFES

Joe's Country Grill 4117 University, Cedar Falls • 277-8785 • 11am-11pm, 24hrs wknds

EROTICA

Danish Book World III 1507 Laporte Rd. • 234-9340 • 24hrs

Kansas

Lawrence (913)

INFO LINES & SERVICES

Decca Center AA Support • 841-4138 • 8pm Th (Trinity Episcopal Church 1011 Vermont) • also 11am Sun & 7pm Tue at 714 Vermont

GLOSK (Gay/Lesbian Services of Kansas) University of Kansas Box 13 KS Union, 66045 • 864-3091

BARS

Jazz House 926-1/2 Massachusetts • 749-3320 • 4pm-2am • gay-friendly • live shows

Teller's Restaurant & Bar 746 Massachusetts Ave. • 843-4111 • 11am-2am • gay-friendly • live shows • also a restaurant • southern Italian/pizza • some veggie • 'Gay Family Night' Tue • wheelchair access • $9-15

BOOKSTORES & RETAIL SHOPS

Terra Nova Books 920 Massachusetts St. • 832-8300 • 10am-9pm, noon-6pm Sun • progressive • wheelchair access

Matfield Green (316)

WOMEN'S ACCOMMODATIONS

Prairie Women Retreat PO Box 2, 66862 • 753-3465 • women only • working cattle ranch • full breakfast & dinner available • wheelchair access • women-owned/run

Topeka (913)

INFO LINES & SERVICES

AA Gay/Lesbian (at MCC) • 8pm Tue & Fri

Gay Rap Phone Line • 233-6558 • 9pm-midnight Wed-Sun

LIFT (Lesbians in Fellowship Together) (at MCC) • 232-6196 • 6pm 3rd Th • call for details

BARS

Classics 601 SW 8th • 233-5153 • 4pm-2am • lesbians/gay men • live shows • wheelchair access

Expressions 110 SE 8th St • 233-3622 • 5pm-2am • popular • dancing/DJ • private club • wheelchair access

BOOKSTORES & RETAIL SHOPS

Town Crier Books 1301 SW Gage Blvd. Ste. 120 • 272-5060 • 9am-9pm, noon-6pm Sun

TRAVEL & TOUR OPERATORS

Kansas Travel & Tourism Department • (800) 252-6727

SPIRITUAL GROUPS

MCC Topeka 2425 SE Indiana Ave. • 232-6196 • Sun 10am & 6pm

Wichita (316)

INFO LINES & SERVICES

Gay/Lesbian Outreach • 267-1852

Wichita Gay Info Line • 269-0913 • 6pm-10pm

Wichita Gay/Lesbian Center 111 N. Spruce • 262-3991 • call for hours

ACCOMMODATIONS

Apartments by Appointments 1257 N. Broadway • 265-4323 • gay-friendly • unique apt. rentals • day, week or month

BARS

B.S.A. 2835 S. George Washington Blvd. • 688-1992 • 4pm-2am • lesbians/gay men • dancing/DJ • karaoke • more women Tue & Fri • wheelchair access

Dreamers 3210 E. Osie • 682-4461 • 4pm-2am, from 11am Sun • mostly women • karaoke • patio

Our Fantasy 3201 S. Hillside • 682-5494 • 8pm-2am Wed-Sun • lesbians/gay men • swimming • dancing/DJ • live shows • also South Forty • from 4pm • country/western • patio

R&R Brass Rail 2828 E. 31st St. S. • 685-9890 • noon-2am • lesbians/gay men • dancing/DJ • country/western • live shows • wheelchair access

Sidestreet Saloon 1106 S. Battie • 267-0324 • 2pm-2am • lesbians/gay men • neighborhood bar • patio

The T-Room 1507 E. Pawnee • 262-9327 • noon-2am • lesbians/gay men • neighborhood bar

RESTAURANTS & CAFES

Freedom Cafe 2819 E. Central • 686-3553 • 11am-10pm, til midnight wknds, noon-6pm Sun • clsd Mon • lesbians/gay men • homecooking • some veggie • patio • wheelchair access • lesbian-owned/run • $6-8

The Harbor (at Our Fantasy bar) • 682-5494 • 8pm-4am, clsd Mon-Tue • lesbians/gay men • full bar • wheelchair access • $4-7

The Lassen 155 N. Market St. • 263-2777 • lunch & dinner, clsd Sun • American • some veggie • $9-12

The Upper Crust 7038 E. Lincoln • 638-8088 • lunch only, clsd wknds • homestyle • some veggie • wheelchair access • $4-7

BOOKSTORES & RETAIL SHOPS

Visions & Dreams 2819 E. Central • 942-6333 • 10am-8pm, noon-6pm Sun • lesbigay bookstore • wheelchair access

SPIRITUAL GROUPS

1st Metropolitan Community Church 156 S. Kansas Ave. • 267-1852 • 10:30am & 7pm Sun

A Pentecostal Church 754 S. Pattie • 267-6270 • 11am Sun

PUBLICATIONS

▲ **Liberty Press** PO Box 16315, 67216 • 685-5002

Kentucky

Covington   (606)

BARS

Rosie's Tavern 643 Bakewell St. • 291-9707 • 3pm-1am, from1pm wknds • gay-friendly • live shows • gay-owned/run

Lexington   (606)

BARS

The Bar Complex 224 E. Main St. • 255-1551 • 4pm-1am, til 3:30am Fri-Sat, clsd Sun • popular • lesbians/gay men • dancing/DJ • live shows • wheelchair access

Joe's Bar & Cafe 120 S. Upper St. • 252-7946 • 5pm-1am, lunch & dinner wknds • lesbians/gay men • neighborhood bar • also a restaurant • French ecletic menu • wheelchair access • $5-10

The Timesquare 141 W. Vine • 253-7777 • 9pm-1am, clsd Sun-Mon • lesbians/gay men • dancing/DJ

RESTAURANTS & CAFES

Alfalfa 557 S. Limestone • 253-0014 • live shows • healthy multi-ethnic • plenty veggie • folk music Fri-Sat • wheelchair access • $6-12

BOOKSTORES & RETAIL SHOPS

Hypnotic Eye 504-1/2 Euclid Ave. • 255-8987 • 11am-9pm

Joseph-Beth 3199 Nicholasville Rd. • 271-5330 • 9am-10pm, 11am-6pm Sun • wheelchair access

Imperial Flowers 393 Waller Ave. (Shopping Ctr.) • 233-7486/ (800) 888-7486 • women-owned/run

TRAVEL & TOUR OPERATORS

Pegasus Travel Inc. 2040 Idle Hour Center, Richmond Rd. • 268-4337/ (800) 228-4337 • women-owned/run

SPIRITUAL GROUPS

Lexington MCC Green Leaf Hotel (conference room) 2280 Nicholasville Rd. • 271-1407 • 6pm Sun • wheelchair access

Pagan Forum PO Box 24203, 40524 • 268-1640 • 7:30pm every other Fri

PUBLICATIONS

GLSO (Gay/Lesbian) News PO Box 11471, 40575 • monthly • calendar

EROTICA

The New Bookstore 942 Winchester Rd • 252-2093 • 24hrs

Louisville   (502)

INFO LINES & SERVICES

Gay/Lesbian Hotline PO Box 2796, 4020 • 897-2475 • 6pm-10pm, til 1am Fri-Sat

Louisville Gender Society PO Box 5458 40255-0458 • 966-8701 • transsexual/ transvestite group

Louisville Youth Group • (800) 347-8336 • 24hrs recorded info • live 7pm-10pm Th-Sun

The Williams-Nichols Institute PO Box 4264, 40204 • 636-0935 • 6pm-9pm • lesbigay archives • library • referrals

BARS

Connection Complex 120 S. Floyd St. • 585-5752 • 5pm-4am • popular • lesbians/gay men • dancing/DJ • live shows • also a restaurant • some veggie • 7 bars • wheelchair access • $5-15

Magnolia's 1398 S. 2nd St. • 637-9052 • 11am-4am • gay-friendly • neighborhood bar • live shows

Murphy's Place 306 E. Main St. • 587-8717 • 11am-4am • mostly gay men • neighborhood bar • wheelchair access

Sparks 104 W. Main St. • 587-8566 • 10pm-4am • lesbians/gay men • dancing/DJ • alternative • live shows • wheelchair access

Tynkers 657 W. Shipp St. • 636-9271 • 5pm-4am, from 7pm Sat • mostly women • dancing/DJ wknds • wheelchair access • women-owned/run

The Upstairs 306 E. Main St. (Murphy's Place) • 587-1432 • 9pm-4am, clsd Mon • lesbians/gay men • dancing/DJ

BOOKSTORES & RETAIL SHOPS

Carmichael's 1295 Bardstown Rd. • 456-6950 • 10am-10pm, 11am-6pm Sun • lesbigay section • women-owned/run

Hawley Cooke Books 3042 Bardstown Rd. • 456-6660 • 9am-9:30pm, 11am-6pm Sun • also 27 Shelbyville Rd. Plaza • 893-0133

The TRI's Gallery & Coffeeshop 310 E. Main St. • 583-6788 • 8pm-3am, clsd Mon

Louisville

*B*eautiful Louisville sits on the banks of the Ohio River and is home to the world famous **Kentucky Derby**. This spectacular race occurs during the first week of May at Churchill Downs.

Louisville is also home to many whiskey distilleries. If neither watching horses run in circles, nor swilling home-grown booze excites you, you'll enjoy this city's slower pace of life and Southern charm – Louisville is known as the 'northern border for southern hospitality'.

Before you leave, check out the whiskey and the hospitality at the popular mixed bar **Connection Complex,** or at the women's bar, **Tynkers**. Then catch up on your culture and caffeine at **TRI's Gallery & Coffeeshop**.

And only a few hours to the east, stop by for a spell in Lexington, Kentucky.

Louisville   (502)

LESBIGAY INFO:
Gay/Lesbian/Bisexual Hotline, 897-2475, touchtone info, live info: 454-7613, 6pm-10pm. Williams-Nichols Institute: 636-0935, 6pm-9pm, lesbigay archives, referrals. Community Health Trust of Kentucky: 574-5496.

LESBIGAY PAPER: The Letter: 772-7570. Kentucky Word: 579-3075.

WHERE THE GIRLS ARE: On Main or Market Streets near 1st, and generally in the north-central part of town, just west of I-65.

ENTERTAINMENT: Bowling League: 456-5780, Monday nights. Community Chorus: 584-1627. The Vogue: 893-3646.

LESBIGAY AA: 582-1849.

LESBIGAY PRIDE: June.

ANNUAL EVENTS: Halloween Cruise on the Ohio River.

CITY INFO: Louisville Tourist Commission: (800) 626-5646.

ATTRACTIONS: May - Kentucky Derby. The Waterfront.

BEST VIEW: The Spire Restaurant and Cocktail Lounge on the 19th floor of the Hyatt Regency Louisville.

WEATHER: Mild winters and long, hot summers!

SPIRITUAL GROUPS

Dignity 1432 Highland Ave. (Trinity Church) • 473-1408 • 7pm 2nd & 4th Sun

MCC Louisville 4222 Bank St. • 775-6636 • 11am & 6:30pm Sun

Phoenix Rising 1434 S. 9th St., 40259 • 635-2013 • monthly • lesbigay pagans

PUBLICATIONS

The Kentucky Word 225 E. N. St. Tower I Ste. 2800, Indianapolis, 46204 • (317) 579-3075 • monthly

The Letter PO Box 3882, 40201 • 772-7570 • monthly

Owensboro   (502)

INFO LINES & SERVICES

Owensboro Gay Alliance • 685-5246

Paducah   (502)

BARS

Club DV8 1200 N. 8th St. • 443-2545 • 8pm-3am, clsd Sun • lesbians/gay men • dancing/DJ • live shows • beer/wine • beer garden • gift shop • wheelchair access

Moby Dick 500 Broadway • 442-9076 • 5pm-3am, from 7pm Sat, clsd Sun • lesbians/gay men • dancing/DJ • live shows • wheelchair access

Somerset   (606)

INFO LINES & SERVICES

Cumberland Cares • 678-5814 • 1st Sat 6pm • lesbigay social & support for southcentral & southeastern KY

Louisiana

Alexandria (318)

BARS

Unique Bar 3117 Masonic Dr. • 448-0555 • 7pm-2am, clsd Sun-Mon • popular • mostly gay men • dancing/DJ • cruisy • patio

Baton Rouge (504)

INFO LINES & SERVICES

AA Gay/Lesbian • 924-0030 • 7pm Mon, 8pm Th, 9pm Sat

Church of Mercavah PO Box 66703, 70896 • 665-7815 • 'safe house' for gay/lesbians, transexuals, activists & others • also publishes magazine • call for info

ACCOMMODATIONS

Brentwood House PO Box 40872, 70835-0872 • 924-4989 • lesbians/gay men • hot tub • 100+ yr old B&B on beautifully landscaped acre of land

BARS

Argon 2160 Highland Rd. • 336-4900 • 9pm-2am Wed-Sat • popular • lesbians/gay men • dancing/DJ • alternative

George's Place 860 St. Louis • 387-9798 • 3pm-2am, clsd Sun • popular • mostly gay men • neighborhood bar • patio • wheelchair access

Hideaway 7367 Exchange Pl. • 923-3632 • 8pm-2am Wed-Sat • mostly women • neighborhood bar • dancing/DJ • wheelchair access • women-owned/run

Mirror Lounge 111 3rd St. • 387-9797 • 2pm-2am, from 6pm Sat, clsd Sun • mostly gay men • dancing/DJ • live shows

RESTAURANTS & CAFES

Third Street Tavern & Deli 140 N. 3rd St. • 336-4281 • 11am-2am, 5pm-midnight, til 7am Fri-Sat, clsd Mon • lesbians/gay men • American • full bar • wheelchair access • $5-15

BOOKSTORES & RETAIL SHOPS

Hibiscus Book Store 635 Main St. • 387-4264 • 10am-6pm, from noon wknds • lesbigay

TRAVEL & TOUR OPERATORS

Out & About Travel 11528 Old Hammond Hwy. Ste. 610 • 272-7448 • IGTA member

SPIRITUAL GROUPS

Joie de Vivre MCC 333 E. Chimes St. • 383-0450 • 11am Sun

PUBLICATIONS

Voices Magazine Licorice Unicorn Press, PO Box 66703, 70896 • 665-7815 • offbeat articles on everything

Houma (504)

BARS

Kixx 112 N. Hollywood • 876-9587 • 6pm-2am, clsd Sun-Mon • lesbians/gay men • dancing/DJ • live shows • patio • wheelchair access

Lafayette (318)

INFO LINES & SERVICES

AA Gay/Lesbian • 234-7814 • call for locations

BARS

C'est La Guerre 607 N. University • 235-9233 • 7pm-2am • lesbians/gay men • neighborhood bar • live shows

Club Majestic 408 Maurice St. • 234-7054 • 8pm-2am, clsd Mon-Tue • lesbians/gay men • dancing/DJ • live shows

Frank's Bar 1807 Jefferson • 235-9217 • 2pm-2am, 11am-midnight Sun • mostly gay men • neighborhood bar • wheelchair access

Images 524 W. Jefferson • 233-0070 • 9pm-2am, clsd Mon-Tue • lesbians/gay men • dancing/DJ • live shows • wheelchair access

Lake Charles (318)

BARS

Billy B's 704 Ryan St. • 433-0263 • 6pm-2am, clsd Sun • lesbians/gay men • neighborhood bar • wheelchair access

Crystal's 112 W. Broad St. • 433-5457 • 9pm-2am, clsd Sun-Tue • lesbians/gay men • dancing/DJ • live shows • food served • wheelchair access

SPIRITUAL GROUPS

MCC Lake Charles 510 Broad St. • 436-0921 • 11am Sun

New Orleans

*Y*ou haven't been to New Orleans for Mardi Gras?! There's still time to plan next year's visit to the French Quarter's blowout of a block party with elaborate balls, parades and dancing in the streets. It all starts the day before Ash Wednesday.

Of course, there is more to New Orleans than Mardi Gras, especially if you like life hot, humid and spiced with steamy jazz and hot pepper. Venture into the **French Quarter**, where you'll find the infamous Bourbon Street, open 24-7. Kitsch-lovers won't want to miss **Pat O'Brien's**, home of the Hurricane – a campy photo in front of the fountain is a must. Jazz lovers, don't forget **Preservation Hall**.

Don't leave New Orleans without a trip through the Garden District to see the incredible antebellum and revival homes – a trip best made on the St. Charles Trolley.

Gourmands must try real Cajun & Creole food in its natural environment – though if you're vegetarian, the **Old Dog New Trick Cafe** is your best bet. For melt-in-your-mouth, hot, sugar-powdered beignets, **Cafe du Monde** (525-4544) is the place.

New Orleans is a town that knows how to party, and the lesbians are no different. Try **Charlene's** for drinks and tall tales, or get wild in the French Quarter with the boys (try **Rubyfruit Jungle**) – Gay Central in New Orleans is also party central for everyone. And during **Southern Decadence**, the gay mardi gras on Labor Day weekend, the quarter becomes a little queerer.

To find out the current women's nights at the guys' bars, stop by **Faubourg Marigny Bookstore** – the lesbian/gay bookstore – and pick up an **Impact** or an **AMbush** newspaper. Or drop by the **Lesbian/Gay Community Center** on North Rampart.

Of course, the morbidly inclined among us will see shadows of vampires and other creatures of the night in this town of mysticism and the occult. With residents like Anne Rice, Poppy Z. Brite, and the deceased Marie LaVeau stirring up the spirits, perhaps a protective amulet from **Marie LaVeau's House of Voodoo** (581-3751; 739 Bourbon St.) would be a good idea. For a peek at traditional voodoo – the creative spirituality, not the spooky movie gore – take the swamp tour that ends at a cottage in the bayou, with gumbo dinner and a performance by the **Mask Dance Voodoo Theater** (522-2904) for $75. Or sate that urge for blood with a body piercing at **Rings of Desire** or some fresh fetish wear from **Second Skin Leather**.

Monroe   (318)

BARS

Hot Shotz 110 Catalpa St. • 388-3262 • from 9pm, clsd Sun-Mon • mostly gay men • dancing/DJ

New Orleans   (504)

INFO LINES & SERVICES

AA Lambda Center 2106 Decatur • 947-0548 • noon daily • call for other mtgs & general info

Gay/Lesbian Business Association 940 Royal #350 • 271-0631 • mtg. 2nd Tue • call for further details

Gulf Area Gender Alliance PO Box 870213, 70187 • 943-6612 • 2nd Sat

Just for the Road Channel 49 • 943-3067 • 6:30pm Tue, 9pm Fri, 9:30pm Sun • gay/lesbian broadcast

Lesbian/Gay Community Center 816 N. Rampart • 522-1103 • noon-6pm Mon-Fri • movie night 6pm Sun

United Gender Support Group 601 Aberville • 524-1622 • info • counseling

ACCOMMODATIONS

424 Notre Dame 424 Notre Dame • 561-8400 • gay-friendly • IGTA member

A Private Garden 1718 Philip St. • 523-1776 • lesbians/gay men • hot tub • 2 private apts • enclosed garden

Alternative Accomodations 828 Royal St. #233 • 529-2915/ (800) 209-9408

Another Country Guest House 2026 Burgundy St. • 949-5384 • gay-friendly • 2 rm apt. in 1890s home

Big D's Bed & Breakfast 704 Franklin Ave. • 944-0216 • lesbians/gay men • women-owned/run

The Big Easy Guest House 2633 Dauphine St. • 943-3717 • gay-friendly • B&B • 8 blocks from French Quarter

The Biscuit Palace 730 Dumaine • 525-9949 • gay-friendly • B&B • apts • in the French Quarter

Bon Maison Guest House 835 Bourbon St. • 561-8498 • popular • gay-friendly • 3 studio apts • 2 suites

New Orleans   (504)

LESBIGAY INFO: Lesbian/Gay Community Center: 522-1103, 816 N. Rampart, noon-6pm Mon-Fri.

LESBIGAY PAPER: Ambush: 522-8049. Impact: 944-6722.

WHERE THE GIRLS ARE: Wandering the Quarter, or in the small artsy area known as mid-city, north of the Quarter up Esplanade St., and elsewhere.

LESBIGAY AA: AA Lambda Center: 947-0548, 2106 Decatur

LESBIGAY PRIDE: June. 897-3939.

ANNUAL EVENTS: February 10-20 - Mardi Gras: 566-5011, North America's rowdiest block party. April 4-7 - Gulf Coast Womyn's Festival at Camp SisterSpirit: (601) 344-1411, they won their lawsuit against the homophobes, now go support a celebration of womyn's land in the South! September - Southern Decadence: 529-2860, gay mini-Mardi Gras.

CITY INFO: 522-3500

ATTRACTIONS: Bourbon St. in the French Quarter. Cafe du Monde for beignets. Pat O'Brien's for a hurricane. Preservation Hall.

BEST VIEW: Top of the Mart Lounge (522-9795) in the World Trade Center of New Orleans.

WEATHER: Summer temperatures hover in the 90ºs with subtropical humidity. Winters can be rainy and chilly. The average temperature in February (Mardi Gras month) is 58º while the average precipitation is 5.23".

TRANSIT: United Cab: 522-9771. Airport Shuttle: 522-3500. Regional Transit: 569-2700.

Bourgoyne Guest House 839 Bourbon St. • 524-3621/ 525-3983 • popular • lesbians/gay men • 1830s Creole mansion • courtyard

Bywater B&B • 944-8438 • mostly women • kitchens • close to French Quarter & Faubourg Marigny

Casa de Marigny Creole Guest Cottages 818 Frenchman St. • 948-3875 • lesbians/gay men • swimming

Chartres St. B&B 2517 Chartres St. • 945-2339 • lesbians/gay men • swimming • handsome 1850s home • patio

The Chimes B&B Constantinople at Coliseum, Box 52257, 70152-2257 • 488-4640/ (800) 729-4640 • gay-friendly • 5 quaint guest suites & rooms in an 1876 home

Dauzat House 337 Burgundy St. • 524-2075/ (800) 272-2075 • popular • gay-friendly • swimming • homemade amaretto • fireplaces • kitchenettes

Desmond Place Vendome Pl. at Fontainbleu, Box 52257, 70152-2257 • 488-4640/ (800) 749-4640 • gay-friendly • also reservation service

Faubourg Guest House 1703 2nd St. • 895-2004 • lesbians/gay men • 1860s Greek Revival

Fourteen Twelve Thalia - A B&B 1412 Thalia • 522-0453 • gay-friendly • one-bdrm apt in the Lower Garden District

French Quarter B&B 1132 Ursuline St. • 525-3390 • lesbians/gay men • full breakfast • swimming

French Quarter Reservation Service 940 Royal St. Ste. 263 • 523-1246/ (800) 523-9091 • IGTA member

The Frenchmen Hotel 417 Frenchmen St. • 948-2166/ (800) 831-1781 • popular • lesbians/gay men • swimming • 1860s Creole townhouses • spa • wheelchair access

The Greenhouse 1212 Magazine St. • 561-8400/ (800) 966-1303 • lesbians/gay men • swimming

Guest House Deja Vu 1835 N. Rampart St. • 945-5912/ (800) 867-7316 • mostly gay men • individual Creole cottages

Hotel de la Monnaie 405 Esplanade Ave. • 947-0009 • gay-friendly • built 10 yrs ago to duplicate Victorian all-suite hotel (time share) • wheelchair access • IGTA member

Lafitte Guest House 1003 Bourbon St. • 581-2678/ (800) 331-7971 • popular • gay-friendly • full bar • elegant French manor house

Macarty Park Guesthouse 3820 Burgundy St. • 943-4994/ (800) 521-2790 • lesbians/gay men • swimming • beautiful bunkhouse, rooms & cottages • 5 minutes from the French Quarter • IGTA member

Mazant St. Guesthouse 906 Mazant St. • 944-2662 • gay-friendly

Mentone B&B 1437 Pauger St. • 943-3019 • gay-friendly • suite in a Victorian home in the Faubourg Marigny district • patio

New Orleans Guest House 1118 Ursulines St. • 566-1177/ (800) 562-1177 • gay-friendly • Creole cottage dated back to 1848 • courtyard

Parkview Guest House 726 Frenchmen St. • 945-7875 • lesbians/gay men

Rainbow House 2311-15 N. Rampart St. • 943-5805 • lesbians/gay men • walking distance to French Quarter • also apts • lesbian/gay-owned

Rathbone Inn 1227 Esplanade Ave. • 947-2100/ (800) 947-2101 • 1850s Greek Revival mansion • 2 blks from the French Quarter

Renaissance Realty • (800) 867-7316 • fully equipped rental properties

Rober House Condos 822 Ursulines St. • 529-4663 • lesbians/gay men • swimming • courtyard • wheelchair access • IGTA member

Royal Barracks Guest House 717 Barracks St. • 529-7269 • lesbians/gay men • hot tub • guest house • private patios • patio

Rue Royal Inn 1006 Royal St. • 524-3900/ (800) 776-3901 • historic inn in 1830s Creole townhouse in the heart of the French Quarter

St. Charles Guest House 1748 Prytania St. • 523-6556 • gay-friendly • swimming • little pensione-style guest house • patio

Sun Oak B&B 2020 Burgundy St. • 945-0322 • lesbians/gay men • Greek Revival Creole cottage circa 1836 • gardens

A tropical paradise.

Go for a splash in our refreshing heated pool. Beautiful, comfortable rooms and cottages. Private baths, cable TV, telephone, continental breakfast. A romantic 5-minute getaway from the French Quarter in a historic neighborhood. Reasonable rates.

RELAX

SWIM

PARTY

PLAY

EXPLORE

MACARTY PARK GUEST HOUSE

3820 Burgundy St. New Orleans 70117
800-521-2790 • 504-943-4994

▲ **Ursuline Guest House** 708 Ursulines St. • 525-8509/ (800) 654-2351 • popular • mostly gay men • hot tub • evening socials w/ wine • IGTA member

Vieux Carre Rentals 841 Bourbon • 525-3983 • gay-friendly • 1 & 2-bdrm apts

BARS

A Different Corner 706 Franklin Ave. • 948-2300 • 4pm-? • lesbians/gay men • Cajun & country/western • wheelchair access

Angles 2301 N. Causeway, Metairie • 834-7979 • 3pm-4am, 5pm-? wknds • lesbians/gay men • neighborhood bar • dancing/DJ • wheelchair access

Big Daddy's 2513 Royal • 948-6288 • 24hrs • lesbians/gay men • neighborhood bar • wheelchair access

Bourbon Pub 801 Bourbon St. • 529-2107 • 24hrs • popular • lesbians/gay men • videos • also The Parade • dancing/DJ

Cafe Lafitte in Exile 901 Bourbon St. • 522-8397 • 24hrs • popular • mostly gay men • videos • cruise bar upstairs

Charlene's 940 Elysian Fields • 945-932 • 5pm-?, from 2pm Fri-Sun, clsd Mon • mostly women • neighborhood bar • dancing/DJ • B&B accommodations avail able • wheelchair access

Check Point Charlie 501 Esplanade • 947-0979 • 24hrs • gay-friendly • food served • laundromat too • wheelchair access

Country Club 634 Lousia St. • 945-0742 • 10am-6pm • lesbians/gay men • dancing/DJ • swimming

Crash & Burn 1924 4th St. Harvey • 367-1803 • 4pm-? • lesbians/gay men • neighborhood bar

Footloose 700 N. Rampart • 524-7654 • 24hrs • lesbians/gay men • dancing/DJ • shows on wknds • transvestites/transsexuals welcome

The Friendly Bar 2801 Chartres St. • 943-8929 • 11am-? • lesbians/gay men • neighborhood bar • wheelchair access • women-owned/run

Good Friends Bar 740 Dauphine • 566-7191 • 24hrs • popular • gay-friendly • professional • good cocktails • also Queens Head Pub • 6pm-3am Wed-Sun • mostly gay men • neighborhood bar • wheelchair access

M.R.B./ Mr. B's on the Patio 515 St. Philip • 586-0644 • 24hrs • lesbians/gay men • neighborhood bar • live shows • patio

The Mint 504 Esplanade • 525-2000 • noon-3am • popular • lesbians/gay men • live shows • wheelchair access

Rawhide 740 Burgundy • 525-8106 • 24hrs • popular • mostly gay men • country/western

▲ **Rubyfruit Jungle** 640 Frenchman • 947-4000 • 4pm-?, from 1pm wknds • lesbians/gay men • dancing/DJ • alternative • live shows • wheelchair access • women-owned/run

The Sterling's 700 Burgundy • 522-1962 • 24hrs • mostly gay men • food served • English Pub

Xis 1302 Allo St., Marerro • 340-0049 • 5pm-? • lesbians/gay men • dancing/DJ • wheelchair access

RESTAURANTS & CAFES

Cafe Istanbul 534 Frenchmen (upstairs) • 944-4180 • clsd Tue • live shows • Turkish

Cafe Sbisa 1011 Decatur • 522-5565 • dinner & Sun brunch • French Creole • patio

Clover Grill 900 Bourbon St. • 523-0904 • 24hrs • popular • diner fare • $5-10

Feelings Cafe 2600 Chartres St. • 945-2222 • dinner nightly, Fri lunch, Sun brunch • Creole • piano bar wknds • $10-20

Fiorella's Cafe 45 French Market Pl. • 528-9566 • dinner, Sun brunch • home-cooking

Heartbreak Cafe 625 St. Philip St. • 568-1631 • Mexican • full bar • wheelchair access • $5-10

Jack Sprat 3240 S. Carrollton • 486-2200 • 11am-10pm, noon-5pm Sun • healthy vegetarian • $6-12

La Peniche 1940 Dauphine St. • 943-1460 • 24hrs • American diner • some veggie • $5-10

Mama Rosa 616 N. Rampart • 523-5546 • 11am-10pm, clsd Mon • Italian • $5-10

Mona Lisa 1212 Royal St. • 522-6746 • 11am-11pm • Italian • some veggie • $8-15

Old Dog New Trick Cafe 307 Exchange Alley • 522-4569 • 11am-9pm • vegetarian • wheelchair access • $5-10

Olivier's 911 Decatur St. • 525-7734 • 10am-10pm • Creole • wheelchair access • $10-15

Petunia's 817 St. Louis • 522-6440 • 8am-midnight • popular • Cajun/Creole • $10-20

PJ's 634 Frenchman St. • 949-2292 • 7pm-midnight • popular • wheelchair access • women-owned/run

Poppy's Grill 717 St. Peter • 524-3287 • 24hrs • diner

Quarter Scene 900 Dumaine • 522-6533 • 24hrs, clsd Tue • homecooking • some veggie • $8-15

Rienzi 533 Toulouse • 524-1479 • lunch & dinner • Creole/Cajun • some veggie

Sammy's Seafood 627 Bourbon St. • 525-8442 • 11am-midnight • Creole/Cajun • $9-28

Sebastian's 538 St. Philip • 524-2041

St. Ann's Cafe & Deli 800 Dauphine • 529-4421 • 24hrs • popular • American • some veggie • wheelchair access • $5-10

Vera Cruz 1141 Decatur St. • 561-8081 • noon-11pm, clsd Mon-Tue • Mexican • wheelchair access • $8-20

Whole Foods 3135 Esplanade Ave. • 943-1626 • 9am-9pm • healthy deli • plenty veggie • $5-10

BOOKSTORES & RETAIL SHOPS

Faubourg Marigny Bookstore 600 Frenchmen St. • 943-9875 • 10am-8pm, 10am-6pm wknds • lesbigay

Rings of Desire 1128 Decatur St. 2nd flr. • 524-6147 • 11am-7pm • piercing studio

Sidney's News Stand 917 Decatur • 524-6872 • 8am-9pm • general magazine store w/ lesbigay titles

TRAVEL & TOUR OPERATORS

Alternative Tours & Travel 3003 Chartres • 949-5917/ (800) 576-0238 • IGTA member

Avalon Travel Advisors 1206 Magazine, 70151 • 561-8400/ (800) 966-1303 • IGTA member

Gartrell Travel Service, Inc. 433 Gravier St. • 525-4040/ (800) 624-7619 • IGTA member

Louisiana Office of Tourism • (800) 334-8626

DARE TO...

be who you are...be proud ...be black... be white...be red...be gay ...be straight ...just love... ...have fun... ...live free... smile...laugh ...celebrate!

FRUITFRUIT JUNGLE

640 Frenchmen St
New Orleans, LA 70116
504-947-4000

SPIRITUAL GROUPS

Diginity 2048 Camp St. (Casa Maria) • 522-6059 • 4pm Sun

Vieux Carre MCC 1128 St. Roch • 945-5390 • 11am Sun

PUBLICATIONS

Ambush PO Box 71291, 70171-1291 • 522-8049 • bi-weekly

Impact PO Box 52079, 70152 • 944-6722 • bi-monthly

New Orleans Gay/Lesbian Yellow Pages 210 Baronne St. Ste. 1014 • 528-3070 • comprehensive lesbigay business directory

The Second Stone PO Box 8340, 70182 • nat'l paper for lesbigay Christians

EROTICA

Gargoyle's 1205 Decatur St. • 529-4387 • 11am-7pm, til10pm Fri-Sat • leather/fetish store

Second Skin Leather 521 St. Philip St. • 561-8167 • noon-10pm, til 6pm Sun • also Above & Below piercing studio upstairs

Shreveport (318)

BARS

Central Station 1025 Marshall • 222-2216 • 3pm-2am, from 5pm Sun • lesbians/gay men • dancing/DJ • country/western

Club 624 624 Commerce • 227-2197 • noon-2am, clsd Sun • lesbians/gay men • live shows

Florentine 728 Austin Pl. • 221-0360 • 9pm-2am Th-Sat • gay-friendly • dancing/DJ • call for events

EROTICA

Fun Shop 1601 Marshall • 226-1308 • also 9434 Mansfield • 688-2482

Maine

Augusta (207)

BARS

P.J.'s 80 Water St. • 623-4041 • 7pm-1am Tue-Sat • popular • lesbians/gay men • dancing/DJ • country/western

Bangor (207)

INFO LINES & SERVICES

AA Gay/Lesbian 126 Union (Unitarian Church) • 941-8326 • 7:30 Th

SPIRITUAL GROUPS

Dignity Bangor 300 Union St. • 2nd & 4th Sun 6pm

Bar Harbor (207)

ACCOMMODATIONS

Manor House Inn 106 West St. • 288-3759 • May-Nov • gay-friendly • B&B • full breakfast

Bath (207)

ACCOMMODATIONS

The Galen C. Moses House 1009 Washington St. • 442-8771 • gay-friendly • full breakfast • 1874 Victorian • gay-owned/run

Belfast (207)

ACCOMMODATIONS

Northport House B&B 197 Northport Ave. • 338-1422/ (800) 338-1422 • gay-friendly • full breakfast

Bethel (207)

ACCOMMODATIONS

Speckled Mountain Ranch RR 2 Box 717, 04217 • 836-2908 • gay-friendly • B&B • full breakfast • on a horse farm • lesbian-owned/run

Biddeford

INFO LINES & SERVICES

Out for Good PO Box 727 , 04005 • social/support group

Brunswick (207)

INFO LINES & SERVICES

College Gay/Lesbian/Straight Alliance Hubbard Hall 2nd flr., Bowdoin College, 04011 • 725-3620 • 9pm Wed

ACCOMMODATIONS

The Vicarage Rte. 1 Box 368-B, S. Harpswell, 04079 • 833-5480 • gay-friendly • full breakfast • wheelchair access • women-owned/run

BOOKSTORES & RETAIL SHOPS

Gulf of Maine Books 134 Maine St. • 729-5083 • 9:30am-5pm, clsd Sun • alternative

Camden (207)

ACCOMMODATIONS

The Old Massachusetts Homestead Campground PO Box 5 Rte. 1, Lincolnville Beach, 04849 • 789-5135 • May-Nov • gay-friendly • swimming • 5 cabins • 68 campsites • 38 RV hookups (separate campground for tenters)

Caribou (207)

INFO LINES & SERVICES

Gay/Lesbian Phoneline 398 S. Main St. • 498-2088 • 7pm-9pm Wed

Northern Lambda Nord PO Box 990, 04736 • social & networking for northern ME and western Brunswick

ACCOMMODATIONS

The Westman House PO Box 1231, 04736 • 896-5726 • popular • lesbians/gay men • B&B • great view

Corea Harbor (207)

ACCOMMODATIONS

The Black Duck PO Box 39, 04624 • 963-2689 • gay-friendly • B&B • cottages • full breakfast • restored farmhouse overlooking harbor

Dester (207)

ACCOMMODATIONS

Brewster Inn 37 Zions Hill • 924-3130 • gay-friendly • B&B in 19 room historic mansion • women-owned/run

Kennebunk (207)

ACCOMMODATIONS

Arundel Meadows Inn PO Box 1129, 04043 • 985-3770 • gay-friendly • full breakfast • 19th century farmhouse located on 3-1/2 acres next to Kennebunk River

Kennebunkport (207)

ACCOMMODATIONS

The Colony Hotel Ocean Ave. & Kings Hwy. • 967-3331/ (800) 552-2363 • gay-friendly • swimming • food served • 1914 grand oceanfront property

RESTAURANTS & CAFES

Bartley's Dockside by the bridge • 967-5050 • 11am-10pm • seafood • some veggie • full bar • wheelchair access

Lewiston (207)

INFO LINES & SERVICES

Bates Gay/Lesbian/Straight Alliance Hirasawa Lounge, Chase Hall, Bates College • 786-6255 • 8:30pm Sun • social group

Bars

The Sportsman's Club 2 Bates St. • 784-2251 • 8pm-1am, from 4pm Sun • popular • lesbians/gay men • dancing/DJ

Lincolnville Beach (207)

ACCOMMODATIONS

Sign of the Owl B&B RR 2 Box 85, 04849 • 338-4669 • lesbians/gay men • full breakfast

Lovell (207)

ACCOMMODATIONS

The Stone Wall B&B RR1, Box 26, 04051 • 925-1080/ (800) 413-1080 • lesbians/gay men • full breakfast • New England B&B on 5 scenic acres w/ views of the western Maine mtns. • IGTA member

Naples (207)

WOMEN'S ACCOMMODATIONS

▲ **Lambs Mill Inn** RR1 Box 676 Lamb's Mill Rd., 04055 • 693-6253 • full breakfast • hot tub • swimming • small country inn in the foothills of the White Mtns. & lakes • IGTA member • $75-85

Ewe Hike • Ewe Bike • Ewe Ski • Ewe zzzzz

Small country inn nestled in the heart of Maine's western lakes and mountains

- Hot Tub
- Full Country Breakfast
- Private Baths

Lamb's Mill Inn

Box 676, Lamb's Mill Rd.
Naples, Me. 04055
207-693-6253

Innkeepers
Laurie Tinkham • Sandy Long
Reservations suggested

Ogunquit (207)

WOMEN'S ACCOMMODATIONS

▲ **Heritage** 14 Marginal Ave., 03907-1295 • 646-7787 • mostly women • B&B • hot tub • lesbian-owned/run

ACCOMMODATIONS

Admiral's Inn 70 S. Main St. • 646-7093 • gay-friendly • swimming

The Clipper Ship Box 236, 03907 • 646-9735/ 646-9292 • gay-friendly • B&B

The Gazebo Rte 1, 03907 • 646-3733 • gay-friendly • full breakfast • swimming • 165 yr old Greek Revival farmhouse • wheelchair access

Grenadier Motor Inn 89 S. Main St. • 646-3432 • May-Oct only • gay-friendly

The Inn at Tall Chimney 94 Main St. • 646-8974 • April-Nov • lesbians/gay men

The Inn at Two Village Square 2 Village Square • 646-5779 • seasonal • lesbians/gay men • oceanview Victorian B&B perched on 5 acres of wooded hillside

Leisure Inn 6 School St. • 646-2737 • seasonal • gay-friendly • B&B guestrooms & apts w/ the quiet charm of old New England

Moon Over Maine Berwick Rd. • 646-6666/ (800) 851-6837

Ogunquit House 7 Kings Hwy., 03907 • 646-2967 • lesbians/gay men • cottages • Victorian B&B w/ beautiful gardens

Old Village Inn 30 Main St. • 646-7088 • gay-friendly • food served

Rockmere Lodge 40 Stearns Rd. • 646-2985 • gay-friendly • B&B

The Seasons Hotel 178 US Rte. 1 • 646-6041/ (800) 639-8508 • seasonal • gay-friendly

Yellow Monkey Guest Houses/Hotel 168 Main St. • 646-9056 • seasonal • lesbians/gay men • jacuzzi

BARS

The Club 13 Main St. • 646-6655 • open April-Oct, 9pm-1am, from 4pm Sun • popular • mostly gay men • dancing/DJ

RESTAURANTS & CAFES

Arrows Berrick Rd. (1.8 mi. W. of Center) • 361-1100 • 6pm-9pm Tue-Sun, clsd Dec-May • some veggie • $20-27

Clay Hill Farm Agamenticus Rd. (2 mile W. of Rte. 1) • 646-2272 • some veggie • also piano bar • wheelchair access • $13-24

Front Porch Cafe Ogunquit Square • 646-3976 • live shows • Mexican/American • some veggie • full bar • $6-12

Grey Gull Inn 321 Webhannet Dr., Wells • 646-7501 • dinner • New England fine dining • plenty veggie • full bar • $10-22

Johnathan's Bourne Ln. • 646-4777 • 5pm-9pm • cont'l • full bar

Poor Richard's Tavern Perkins Cove at Shore Rd. & Pine Hill • 646-4722 • 5:30pm-9:30pm • live shows • some veggie • full bar • seasonal • $9-15

Yvonne's La Trattoria 139 Main St. • 646-4234 • 5pm-11pm • northern Italian • beer/wine • also piano bar • $9-20

Orono (207)

INFO LINES & SERVICES

Wilde-Stein Club, Univ. of Maine Sutton Lounge, Memorial Union • 581-1731 • 6pm Th (Sept-May) • social/support group

ACCOMMODATIONS

Maine Wilderness Lake Island • 866-4547 • lesbians/gay men • rental cabins in the forest

Pembroke (207)

ACCOMMODATIONS

Yellow Birch Farm • 726-5807 • mostly women • B&B on working farm • daily & weekly rates • also cottage • lesbian-owned/run

Portland (207)

INFO LINES & SERVICES

Gays in Sobriety 32 Thomas St. (Williston W. Church) • 774-4060 • 6:30pm Sun, 8pm Th

Outright PO Box 5077, 04101 • 774-4357 • meets Fri 7:30pm • youth support group

Queer Alliance Univ. of Maine, The Power's House • 874-6596 • various mtgs. & groups

ACCOMMODATIONS

Guesthouse 378 Commercial St. • 236-3854 • lesbians/gay men • kitchens • lesbian-owned/run

The Inn at St. John 939 Congress St. • 773-6481 • gay-friendly • cont'l breakfast • unique historic inn

BARS

The Blackstones 6 Pine St. • 775-2885 • 4pm-1am • mostly gay men • neighborhood bar • wheelchair access

The Chart Room 117 Spring St. • 774-9262 • 5pm-1am, from 1pm wknds, clsd Mon • mostly gay men • neighborhood bar • wheelchair access

Raoul's Roadside Attraction 865 Forest Ave. • 773-6886 • 11:30am-1am • gay-friendly • live shows • also a restaurant • Mexican/American • $5-7

Sisters 45 Danforth St. • 774-1505 • 4pm-1am, clsd Mon-Tue • mostly women • dancing/DJ

Underground 3 Spring St. • 773-3315 • 4pm-1am • popular • lesbians/gay men • dancing/DJ • live shows

Zootz 31 Forest Ave. • 773-8187 • 9pm-1am • gay-friendly • dancing/DJ • alternative • more gay Th

RESTAURANTS & CAFES

Cafe Always 47 Middle St. • 774-9399 • dinner Tue-Sat • some veggie • full bar • $10-20

Cafe Brix 343 Gorham Rd. • 773-2262 • dinner only, clsd Sun • New American • plenty veggie • full bar • wheelchair access • $14-19

Katahdin 106 Spring St. • 774-1740 • 5pm-10pm, clsd Sun • full bar

Walter's Cafe 15 Exchange St. • 871-9258 • 11am-9pm • some veggie • $10-14

Westside 58 Pine St. • 773-8223 • lunch & dinner, clsd Mon • some veggie • beer/wine • $8-14

Woodford's Cafe 129 Spring St. • 772-1374 • 11am-10pm, til 1pm Fri-Sat, clsd Mon • full bar • $5-9

BOOKSTORES & RETAIL SHOPS

Central Beat 519 Congress • 780-8627 • books & more

Communiques 3 Moulton St. • 773-5181 • 10am-6pm, til 9pm during summer • cards • gifts • clothing

Drop Me A Line 615-A Congress St. • 773-5547 • 11am-6pm, til 8pm Th, clsd Sun

TRAVEL & TOUR OPERATORS

Adventure Travel 2 Elsie Wy., Scarborough • 885-5060/ (800) 234-6252 • IGTA member

SPIRITUAL GROUPS

Congregaton Bet Ha'am • 879-0028 • gay-friendly synagogue

Feminist Spiritual Community • 797-9217 • 7pm Mon • call for further info

PUBLICATIONS

▲ **Community Pride Reporter** 142 High St. Ste. 623 • 879-1342

Saco Bay   (207)

WOMEN'S ACCOMMODATIONS

Sea Forest • 282-1352 • women only • full breakfast • private house • $50-up

Sebago Lake   (207)

ACCOMMODATIONS

Maine-ly For You RR 2 Box 745, Harrison, 04040 • 583-6980 • gay-friendly • cottages • campsites

Stovington   (207)

WOMEN'S ACCOMMODATIONS

Sea Gnomes Home PO Box 33, 04681 • 367-5076 • clsd Oct-May • women only • guesthouse • lesbian-owned/run • $40

Tennants Harbor   (207)

ACCOMMODATIONS

Eastwind Inn Mechanic St. • 372-6366 • gay-friendly • full breakfast

Waterville   (207)

INFO LINES & SERVICES

Colby College Bi/Lesbian/Gay Community Bridge Room • 872-4149 • 7:30pm Mon

EROTICA

Priscilla's Book Store 18 Water St. • 873-2774 • clsd Sun

York Harbor   (207)

ACCOMMODATIONS

Canterbury House 432 York St. • 363-3505 • gay-friendly • spacious Victorian home

Maryland

Annapolis (410)

ACCOMMODATIONS

Bed & Breakfast of Maryland • 269-6232/ (800) 736-4667 • gay-friendly • accommodations service

William Page Inn 8 Martin St. • 626-1506/ (800) 364-4160 • full breakfast • elegantly renovated 1908 home

Baltimore (410)

INFO LINES & SERVICES

AA Gay/Lesbian • 433-4843

FIST (Females Investigating Sexual Terrain) PO Box 41032, 21203-6032 • 675-0856

Gay/Lesbian Community Center 241 W. Chase St. • 837-5445 • 10am-4pm • many programs • info & referrals • inquire about Womanspace

Gay/Lesbian Switchboard • 837-8888/ 837-8529 (TDD) • 7pm-10pm

Transgender Support Group at the Center

ACCOMMODATIONS

Biltmore Suites 205 W. Madison St. • 728-6550/ (800) 868-5064 • gay-friendly • B&B

Chez Claire B&B 17 W. Chase St. • 685-4666 • lesbians/gay men • 4-story townhouse in historical area

Mr. Mole Bed & Breakfast 1601 Bolton St. • 728-1179 • popular • gay-friendly • splendid suites on historic Bolton Hill

BARS

Allegro 1101 Cathedral St. • 837-3906 • 6pm-2am, from 4pm Sun • mostly gay men • dancing/DJ • theme nights • women's night Th

Baltimore Eagle 2022 N. Charles St. (enter on 21st) • 823-2453 • 6pm-2am • popular • mostly gay men • wheelchair access

Central Station 1001 N. Charles St. • 752-7133 • 11am-2am • popular • lesbians/gay men • neighborhood bar • videos • also a restaurant • American • some veggie • $7-15

Club Bunns 608 W. Lexington St. • 234-2866 • 5pm-2am • lesbians/gay men • dancing/DJ • mostly African-American • women's night Tue

Club Seventeen Twenty-Two 1722 N. Charles St. • 727-7431 • midnight til dawn Fri-Sat • lesbians/gay men • dancing/DJ • BYOB

The Drinkery 203 W. Read St. • 669-9820 • 11am-2am • lesbians/gay men • neighborhood bar

The Gallery 1735 Maryland Ave. • 539-6965 • 1pm-2am • lesbians/gay men • dancing/DJ • also a restaurant • more women Th & Sun

Hippo 1 W. Eager St. • 547-0069 • 3pm-2am • popular • lesbians/gay men • dancing/DJ • karaoke • videos • 3 bars • more women on Fri & Sun T-dance • wheelchair access

Lynn's of Baltimore 774 Washington Blvd. • 727-8924 • 6pm-1am, from 11am Sat, clsd Sun • mostly gay men • neighborhood bar • wheelchair access

Orpheus 1001 E. Pratt St. • 276-5599 • 9pm-2am, 7pm-11:30pm Sun, clsd Mon-Tue • gay-friendly • dancing/DJ • 18+

Port in a Storm 4330 E. Lombard St. • 732-5608 • 10am-2am • mostly women • neighborhood bar • dancing/DJ • wheelchair access • women-owned/run

Stagecoach 1003 N. Charles St. • 547-0107 • 4pm-2am • lesbians/gay men • dancing/DJ • country/western • piano bar • also a restaurant • Tex/Mex • some veggie • rooftop cafe • wheelchair access • $5-18

RESTAURANTS & CAFES

Cafe Diana 3215 N. Charles St. • 889-1319 • 8am-11pm • popular • BYOB • American • some veggie • women-owned/run • $3-8

Cafe Hon 1009 W. 36th St. • 243-1230 • 8am-10pm, clsd Sun • American • some veggie • $6-11

Donna's Coffee Bar 2 W. Madison • 385-0180 • beer/wine

Great American Melting Pot (GAMPY's) 904 N. Charles St. • 837-9797 • 11:30am-2am, til 3am Fri-Sat • lesbians/gay men • plenty veggie • wheelchair access • $5-12

Louie's The Bookstore Cafe 518 N. Charles • 962-1224 • live shows • plenty veggie • full bar • wheelchair access • $4-12

Mencken's Cultured Pearl Cafe 1114 Hollins St • 837-1947 • Mexican • full bar • wheelchair access • $6-12

Michael's Rivera Grill 120 E. Lombard St. (The Brookshire Hotel) • 547-8986 • 5pm-10pm, til 11pm Fri-Sat • popular • upscale cont'l • some veggie • rooftop dining • wheelchair access • $19-25

Mount Vernon Stable & Saloon 909 N. Charles St. • 685-7427 • lunch & dinner • some veggie • bar 11:30am-2am • $8-12

Spike & Charlie's Restaurant & Wine Bar 1225 Cathedral St. • 752-8144 • lunch, dinner & Sun brunch, clsd Mon • wheelchair access

BOOKSTORES & RETAIL SHOPS

Adrian's Book Cafe 714 S. Broadway, Fells Point • 732-1048 • 8am-8pm, til 11pm Fri-Sat, from 11am wknds • new & used • some gay titles

Lambda Rising 241 W. Chase St. • 234-0069 • 10am-10pm • lesbigay • wheelchair access

Lammas Women's Books & More 1001 Cathedral St. • 752-1001/ (800) 955-2662 • 11am-8pm, til 10pm Th-Sat • feminist • wheelchair access

TRAVEL & TOUR OPERATORS

Maryland Office of Tourism • (800) 543-1036

Mt. Royal Travel Inc. 1303 N. Charles St. • 685-6633/ (800) 767-6925

Safe Harbors Travel 25 South St. • 547-6565/ (800) 344-5656 • IGTA member

SPIRITUAL GROUPS

Integrity Baltimore Emmanuel Episcopal Church (Cathedral & Read St.) • 732-0718 • 7:30pm 3rd Fri

MCC 3401 Old York Rd. • 889-6363 • 10:30am Sun

PUBLICATIONS

The Baltimore Alternative PO Box 2351, 21203 • 235-3401 • monthly

The Baltimore Gay Paper PO Box 22575, 21203 • 837-7748

Gay Community Yellow Pages-Baltimore 1858 Emery St. NW Ste. 220, Atlanta, 30318 • 547-0380 • directory/resource guide

EROTICA

Leather Underground 136 W. Read St. • 528-0991 • 11am-7pm, til 8pm Fri, 10am-6am Sat, clsd Sun

Beltsville (301)

TRAVEL & TOUR OPERATORS

Your Travel Agent in Beltsville 10440 Baltimore Blvd. • 937-0966/ (800) 872-8537 • IGTA member

Columbia

INFO LINES & SERVICES

Gay/Lesbian Community of Howard County PO Box 2115, 21045 • mail access only • multi-interest social group

Cumberland (301)

ACCOMMODATIONS

Red Lamp Post 849 Braddock Rd. • 777-3262 • lesbians/gay men • B&B • hot tub • dinner optional

Frederick (301)

BARS

Talon's 5854 Urbana Pike (Rte. 355) • 698-1990 • 6pm-2am, til 3am Sat, clsd Sun-Tue • lesbians/gay men • dancing/D • videos • food served • wheelchair access

RESTAURANTS & CAFES

The Frederick Coffee Co. & Cafe 100 East St • 698-0039 • 8am-7pm, til 9pm Fri-Sat, 9am-6pm Sun • plenty veggie • patio • wheelchair access • lesbian-owned/run

Laurel

INFO LINES & SERVICES

Gay People Of Laurel PO Box 25, 2072

Parkton (410)

ACCOMMODATIONS

Hidden Valley Farm B&B 1419 Mt. Carmel Rd. (30 min. N. of Baltimore) • 329-8084 • lesbians/gay men • hot tub

Rockville (301)

INFO LINES & SERVICES

MCC of Rockville PO Box 10269, 20849 601-9112 • 7pm Sun

Silver Spring (301)

INFO LINES & SERVICES

GLASS (Gay/Lesbian Assoc. of Silver Spring) PO Box 8518, 20907 • 588-7330

TRAVEL & TOUR OPERATORS

Central Travel of Silver Spring 8767 Georgia Ave. • 589-9440 • IGTA member

Travel Central 8209 Fenton St. • 587-4000/ (800) 777-9922 • IGTA member

EROTICA

Max Wonder 9421 Georgia Ave. • 942-4196

Smith Island (410)

ACCOMMODATIONS

Smith Island Get-A-Way PO Box 187, Westport, 06881 • 425-4110/ (203) 579-9400 • gay-friendly • 2-bdrm apt. w/ kitchen •1 bath • in secluded community accessible only by boat

St. Michaels (410)

ACCOMMODATIONS

The Rainbow House • 745-3422 • mostly women • full breakfast • swimming

The Names Project Chapters in the U.S.

CALIFORNIA		NORTH CAROLINA	
Inland Empire	909/784-2437	Charlotte	704/376-2637
Long Beach	310/493-2305	**NEW JERSEY**	
Los Angeles	213/653-6263	New Jersey	908/739-4863
Orange County	714/490-3880	**NEW MEXICO**	
Sacramento	916/484-5646	Santa Fe	505/466-2211
San Diego	619/492-8452	**NEVADA**	
Ventura County	805/650-9546	Southern Nevada	702/226-2701
DISTRICT OF COLUMBIA		**NEW YORK**	
Capital Area	202/296-2637	Long Island	516/477-2447
DELAWARE		New York City	212/226-2292
Delaware	215/476-4010	**OKLAHOMA**	
GEORGIA		Tulsa Area	918/748-3111
Atlanta	404/605-7386	**OREGON**	
HAWAII		Portland	503/650-7032
Honolulu	808/735-1481	**PENNSYLVANIA**	
IOWA		Philadelphia	215/735-6263
Cedar Valley	319/266-7903	Susquahanna Valley	717/234-0629
ILLINOIS		**RHODE ISLAND**	
Chicago	312/472-4460	Rhode Island	401/847-7637
INDIANA		**TEXAS**	
Indianapolis	317/920-1200	Austin	512/480-8015
MASSACHUSETTS		Dallas	214/520-7397
Boston	617/262-6263	Fort Worth	817/336-2637
MAINE		Houston	713/526-2637
Portland, ME	207/774-2198	Waco	817/741-1428
MICHIGAN		**UTAH**	
Detroit	810/371-9599	Salt Lake City	801/581-1832
MINNESOTA		**VIRGINIA**	
Twin Cities	612/373-2468	Central Virginia	804/346-8047
MISSOURI		**WASHINGTON**	
Metro St. Louis	314/997-9897 #43	Seattle	206/285-2880

Massachusetts

Amherst (413)

INFO LINES & SERVICES

Everywomen's Center Wilder Hall, U of MA • 545-0883 • call for office hours

Women's Media Project WMUA 91.1 FM • 545-2876/ 545-3691 • radio shows: 'Girl Talk' 6pm-9pm Tue, 'Now's Time' 6pm-9pm Wed, 'Oblivion Express' 6am-9am Tue

ACCOMMODATIONS

Ivy House B&B 1 Sunset Ct. • 549-7554 • gay-friendly • full breakfast • handsomely restored Colonial Cape (portions circa 1740) • patio

BOOKSTORES & RETAIL SHOPS

Food For Thought 106 N. Pleasant St. • 253-5432 • 10am-6pm, til 8pm Wed-Fri, noon-5pm Sun • lesbigay section • progressive bookstore collectively run • wheelchair access

Oasis 63 Main St. • 256-4995 • 10am-6pm, til 9pm wknds

TRAVEL & TOUR OPERATORS

Adventura Travel 233 N. Pleasant St. • 549-1256

PUBLICATIONS

Valley Women's Voice U of MA • 545-2436

Ashby (508)

INFO LINES & SERVICES

LINC (Lesbians Inviting New Connections) PO Box 11 , 01431 • 386-7737 • network for women in rural areas

Barre (508)

ACCOMMODATIONS

Jenkins House B&B Inn Scenic Rte. 122 at Barre Common, 01005 • 355-6444/ (800) 378-7373 • gay-friendly • full breakfast • built circa 1834 w/ wrap-around poarch & English garden

Boston (617)

INFO LINES & SERVICES

BAGLY (Boston Alliance of Gay/Lesbian Youth) PO Box 814, 02103 • (800) 422-2459/ (800) 399-7337 • extensive support services for lesbigay youth 22 & under • women's mtg 6:45 Wed night

Black Lesbians/Gays 566 Columbus Ave (Harriet Tubman House) • 536-8610

Boston Bisexual Women's Network • 338-9595 • call for info • wheelchair access

Cambridge Women's Center 46 Pleasant St., Cambridge • 354-8807 • info • referrals • support & discussion groups • wheelchair access

Common Bond PO Box 390313, Cambridge, 02139 • 625-0103 • S&M support group for lesbian & bisexual women

Daughters of Bilitis 1151 Massachusetts Ave. (Harvard Sq.), Cambridge • 661-363 • women's social & support networks • call for schedule of many mtgs.

Dyke TV Cambridge Channel 19, Cambridge • 10pm Tue • 'weekly, half hour TV show produced by lesbians for lesbians'

Entre Nous, Inc. PO Box 984, 02103 • men's & women's leather group

Gay/ Lesbian Helpline • 267-9001 • 4:30pm-11pm, 6pm-11pm wknds

Lesbian Al-Anon (at the Women's Center) • 354-8807 • 6:30pm Wed

Moving Violations Motorcycle Club PO Box 217, New Town Branch, 02258 • riding & social events

Musically Speaking Women's Radio WMBR 88.1 FM • 253-8810/ 253-4000 • 6:30pm Mon • also 'Say It Sister' 7:30pm Wed • women-owned/run

OLE (Older Lesbian Energy) PO Box 1214, E. Arlington, 02174 • social group for lesbians over 40

Women's Health Group 720 Harrison Ave. #404 • 638-7428 • general practice medical & mental health services • wheelchair access

WOMEN'S ACCOMMODATIONS

Iris Bed & Breakfast PO Box 4188, Dedham, 02026 • 329-3514 • women onl • shared baths • private home • $60

Katie's Place, Cambridge • 876-1501 • women only • full breakfast • $50-60

Boston

*H*ome to 65 colleges and universities, Boston has been an intellectual center for the continent. Since that famed tea party, it's also been home to some of New England's most rebellious radicals. The result is a city whose character is both traditonal and free-thinking, high-brow and free-wheeling, stuffy and energetic.

Not only is this city complex, it's cluttered – with plenty of historic and mind-sparking sites to visit. Start with **Globe Corner Bookstore** for tourists maps and info – but if you're easily bored, check out the high/low culture in Harvard Square, the shopping along Newbury Street in the Back Bay, and the touristy vendors in Faneuil Hall.

Boston's women's community is, not surprisingly, strong and politically diverse. To find out what the latest hotspots are, pick up a copy of **Bay Windows** or **IN** at the well-stocked women's bookstores **Crones' Harvest** or **New Words Books**. Tired of reading? Restore your body with some boogy at one of the Sunday night dance clubs. Like San Francisco, Boston has no fulltime women's bar, so you'll have to seek out the latest women's night at the mixed bars.

Boston   (617)

LESBIGAY INFO: Gay/ Lesbian Helpline: 267-9001, 4pm-11pm, 6pm-11pm wknds. Women's Center: 354-8807.

LESBIGAY PAPER: Bay Windows: 266-6670. IN Newsweekly: 426-1279.

WHERE THE GIRLS ARE: Sipping coffee and reading somewhere in Cambridge or Harvard Square, strolling the South End near Columbus & Mass. Avenues, or hanging out in the Fenway or Jamaica Plain.

ENTERTAINMENT: Gay Men's Chorus: 247-2462. Triangle Theatre Co.: 426-3550. United Fruit Company & The Theatre Offensive: 547-7728.

LESBIGAY AA: 426-9444 (AA#)

LESBIGAY PRIDE: June. 1-976-PRIDE, $1.50 per call.

ANNUAL EVENTS: February 23-25 - Outwrite: (617) 426-4469, annual national lesbian/gay writers & publishers conference at the Boston Park Plaza Hotel.

CITY INFO: Boston Visitor's Bureau: (800) 374-7400 (touch-tone).

WEATHER: Extreme. From freezing winters to boiling summers with a beautiful spring and fall.

TRANSIT: Boston Cab: 536-5010. MBTA: (800) 392-6100. From the Airport: (800) 235-6486.

Victorian B&B • 536-3285 • women only • full breakfast • no smoking • parking • women-owned/run • $65

ACCOMMODATIONS

463 Beacon St. Guest House 463 Beacon St. • 536-1302 • popular • gay-friendly • accommodations in quiet residential setting minutes from Boston's heart • IGTA member

Amsterdammerje PO Box 865, 02103 • 471-8454 • lesbians/gay men • full breakfast

▲ **Chandler Inn** 26 Chandler St. • 482-3450/ (800) 842-3450 • popular • gay-friendly • call for events • small hotel in the center of the city

Citywide Reservation Services Inc. 25 Huntington Ave. Ste. 607 • 267-7424/ (800) 468-3593 • covers most of New England

Holworthy Place, Cambridge • 864-7042 • gay-friendly • full breakfast • near Havard Square

▲ **Oasis Guest House** 22 Edgerly Rd. • 267-2262 • popular • gay-friendly • attractive & affordable accommodations in a prime Back Bay location • IGTA member

Thoreau's Walden B&B 2 Concord Rd., Lincoln • 259-1899 • gay-friendly • full breakfast • across the road & w/in sight of historic Walden Pond

BARS

The Avalon 15 Lansdowne St. • 262-242 • 9pm-2am Sun only • popular • mostly gay men • dancing/DJ • wheelchair access

The Bar 99 St. Botolph St. • 266-3030 • 11am-1am • lesbians/gay men • neighborhood bar • food served

Campus 21 Brookline, Cambridge • 864-0400 • 9pm-1am, clsd Mon-Tue • gay-friendly • dancing/DJ • alternative • gay night Th • more women Sun

Chaps 27 Huntington Ave. • 266-7778 • noon-2am • popular • mostly gay men • dancing/DJ • videos • wheelchair access

Club Cafe 209 Columbus • 536-0966 • 2pm-2am, from 11:30am Sun • popular • lesbians/gay men • live shows • videos • 3 bars • more women Wed • also a restaurant • some veggie • $10-20 • wheelchair access

Coco's 965 Massachusetts Ave. • 427-7807 • 9pm-2am Fri-Sat only • popular • mostly women • dancing/DJ

BOSTON

On the edge of historic Back Bay and the wonderfully eclectic South End, Boston's most exciting small hotel offers visitors a myriad of fringe benefits.

$79
ONE PERSON

$89
TWO PEOPLE

Complimentary continental breakfast served daily in Fritz, one of Boston's most frequented gay bars.

1-800-842-3450

CHANDLER INN
HOTEL

28 Chandler at Berkeley, Boston, MA 02116 (617) 482-3458

Esmé 3 Boylston Pl. (Mercury Bar) • 482-7799 • 7pm-2am Sun only • mostly women • dancing/DJ

Fusion 212 Hampshire St. (Ryles Jazz Club), Cambridge • 876-9330 • 9pm Sat & T-dance Sun • mostly women • dancing/DJ

Luxor 69 Church • 423-6969 • 4pm-1am • popular • mostly gay men • videos • also a restaurant • Italian • also Jox • sports bar

Quest 1270 Boylston St. • 424-7747 • 9pm-2am, clsd Sun • popular • lesbians/gay men • dancing/DJ • videos • roof deck

The Venus de Milo 7 Lansdowne St. • 421-9595 • 10pm-2am Wed only • lesbians/gay men • dancing/DJ • wheelchair access

RESTAURANTS & CAFES

Art Zone Cafe 150 Kneeland St. • 695-0087 • 11am-4pm, til 4am Th, 24hrs Fri-Sat • lesbians/gay men • Southern BBQ • plenty veggie • full bar • wheelchair access • $7-15

The Blue Wave 142 Berkeley St. • 424-6711/ 424-6664 • noon-11pm, til 5pm Sun • lesbians/gay men • American • some veggie • full bar • $7-10

Casa Romero 30 Gloucester St. • 536-4341 • 5pm-10pm dinner only, til 11pm wknds • Mexican • some veggie • patio • $10-20

Icarus 3 Appleton St. • 426-1790 • dinner & Sun brunch, clsd Sun (summers) • New American • $30-40

Mario's 69 Church St. • 542-3776 • 5:30pm-10:30pm • Italian • some veggie • wheelchair access • $7-15

GYMS & HEALTH CLUBS

Metropolitan Health Club 209 Columbus • 536-3006 • 6pm-11pm, 9am-9pm wknds • gay-friendly

BOOKSTORES & RETAIL SHOPS

▲ **Crones Harvest** 761 Centre St., Jamaica Plain • 983-9530 • 10am-9pm, til 7pm Mon, noon-6pm Sun • live shows • women's bookstore & gallery • wheelchair access • women-owned/run

Designs for Living 52 Greensburg St. • 536-6150 • 7am-9pm • cafe

Glad Day Books 673 Boylston St. • 267-3010 • 9:30am-10pm, til 11pm Fri-Sat, noon-9pm Sun • lesbigay • wheelchair access

Globe Corner 1 School St. • (800) 358-6013 • also 49 Palmer St., Cambridge

New Words Bookstore 186 Hampshire St., Cambridge • 876-5310 • 10am-8pm, til 6pm Sat, noon-6pm Sun • women's bookstore w/ lesbian titles

Trident Booksellers & Cafe 338 Newbury St. • 267-8688 • beer/wine • wheelchair access

Unicorn Books 1210 Massachusetts Ave., Arlington • 646-3680 • 10am-9pm, til 5pm wknds • spiritual titles • women-owned/run

Waterstone's Booksellers 26 Exeter • 859-7300 • 9am-11pm • huge general bookstore • wheelchair access

We Think The World Of You 540 Tremont St. • 423-1965 • open daily • lesbigay

Wordsworth 30 Brattle St., Cambridge • 354-5201 • 9am-11pm, 10am-10pm Sun • general books • lesbigay titles

TRAVEL & TOUR OPERATORS

5 Star Travel 164 Newbury St. • 536-1999/ (800) 359-1999 • IGTA member

Friend in Travel 5230 Washington St., W Roxbury • 327-8600/ (800) 597-8267 • IGTA member • women-owned/run

Gibb Travel 673 Boylston St. • 353-0595 (800) 541-9949 • IGTA member

Massachusettes Office of Travel & Tourism 100 Cambridge St. 13th flr • (800) 447-6277

Omega International Travel 99 Summe St. • 737-8511/ (800) 727-0599 • IGTA member

Travel Management 160 Commonwealth Ave. • 424-1908/ (800) 532-0055

SPIRITUAL GROUPS

Am Tikva PO Box 11, Cambridge, 02238 926-2536 • lesbigay Jews

Dignity 35 Bowdoin St. (St. John's Episcopal Church) • 423-9558 • 5:30pm Sun

MCC 131 Cambridge St. (Old West Church) • 288-8029 • 7pm Sun

Western Orthodox Chruch 1151 Massachusetts Ave. (Old Cambridge Baptist), Cambridge • 227-5794 • 4pm Sun liturgy • unconventional-yet-traditional ceremonies

PUBLICATIONS

Bad Attitude, Inc. PO Box 390110, Cambridge, 02139 • (508) 372-6247 • magazine of lesbian erotica • women-owned/run

Bay Windows 1523 Washington St. • 266-6670

Boston's Gay Community Yellow Pages 398 Columbus Ave. Ste. 305 • 789-5570 • resource directory for Boston

Dykes, Disability & Stuff PO Box 6194, 02114 • quarterly in print form & braille

Gay Community News 29 Stanhope St • 262-6969

The Guide PO Box 593, 02199 • 266-8557 • monthly

In 398 Columbus Ave. Ste. 283 • 426-8246 • weekly • news magazine

Let's Go Harvard Student Agencies, Cambridge • provides info for travelling lesbian/gay youths

Sojourner-The Women's Forum 42 Seaverns Ave. • 524-0415 • monthly

EROTICA

Innovations in Leather 1254 Boylston St. (at Ramrod Bar) • 536-1546 • 10pm-1am • leather • piercings • body jewelry

Charlemont (413)

ACCOMMODATIONS

The Inn at Charlemont Rte. 2, Mohawk Trail • 339-5796 • gay-friendly • also a restaurant • American • some veggie • full bar • women-owned/run • $10-20

Chelsea (617)

BARS

Club 9-11 9-11 Williams St. • 884-9533 • 4pm-1am • lesbians/gay men • dancing/DJ • live shows

Chicopee (413)

BARS

Eclipse 13 View St. • 534-3065 • 7pm-2am, clsd Mon-Tue • lesbians/gay men • dancing/DJ • patio

Our Hide-away 16 Bolduc Ln. • 534-6426 • 6pm-2am, clsd Mon • mostly women • neighborhood bar • dancing/DJ • outdoor volleyball • wheelchair access • women-owned/run

Cochituate

PUBLICATIONS

Women's Investment Newsletter PO Box 5015, 01778 • 'advice on stocks, bonds, etc. without macho mystification'

Dartmouth

BARS

Fiddlesticks 460 Old Falls River Rd. • noon-2am • lesbians/gay men • dancing/DJ • piano bar • unconfirmed fall '95

Fitchburg (508)

BARS

The Country Lounge 860 Ashby State Rd. • 345-6703 • 7pm-1am • lesbians/gay men • dancing/DJ

Gloucester (508)

BOOKSTORES & RETAIL SHOPS

The Bookstore 61 Main St. • 281-1548 • 9am-6pm • women-owned/run

Great Barrington

PUBLICATIONS

Hikane: The Capable Woman PO Box 841, 01230-0841 • 'disabled wimmin's magazine for lesbians & our wimmin friends'

Greenfield (413)

BOOKSTORES & RETAIL SHOPS

World Eye Bookshop 60 Federal St. • 772-2186 • open 9am, from noon Sun • general bookstore • community bulletin board • wheelchair access • women-owned/run

Harwich (508)

TRAVEL & TOUR OPERATORS

Cape Escapes 166 Queen Anne Rd. • 430-0843/ (800) 540-0808 • IGTA member

Havenhill (508)

BOOKSTORES & RETAIL SHOPS

Radzukina's 714 N. Broadway • 521-1333 • call for hours • womyn-made fine arts & crafts • books • jewelry • music • women-owned/run

Hyannis (508)

INFO LINES & SERVICES

Gay/Lesbian AA • 775-7060 • call for mtgs.

ACCOMMODATIONS

Gull Cottage 10 Old Church St., Yarmouth Port • 362-8747 • lesbians/gay men • guest house near beach • wheelchair access

BARS

Duval Street Station 477 Yarmouth Rd. • 775-9835 • 4pm-1am • popular • lesbians/gay men • dancing/DJ • live shows • food served • Cape Cod's largest gay complex • wheelchair access

Lenox (413)

ACCOMMODATIONS

Summer Hill Farm 830 East St. • 442-2057 • gay-friendly • full breakfast • colonial guesthouse & cottage • wheelchair access

Walker House 64 Walker St. • 637-1271/ (800) 235-3098 • gay-friendly • B&B • wheelchair access

Lowell (508)

INFO LINES & SERVICES

Shared Times PO Box 8822, 01853-8822 • 441-9081 • social/support group for women • sponsors dances & quarterly newsletter

Lynn (617)

BARS

Fran's Place 776 Washington • 598-5618 • 1pm-2am • lesbians/gay men • dancing/DJ • wheelchair access

Joseph's 191 Oxford St. • 599-9483 • 5pm-2am • lesbians/gay men • dancing/DJ • videos • wheelchair access

Marblehead (508)

INFO LINES & SERVICES

North Shore Gay/Lesbian Alliance Box 806, 01945 • 745-3848 • event line

TRAVEL & TOUR OPERATORS

Around the World Travel Townhouse Square • 631-8620/ (800) 733-4337 • IGTA member

Martha's Vineyard (508)

ACCOMMODATIONS

Captain Dexter House 35 Pease's Point Way, Box 2798, Edgartown, 02539 • 627-7289 • gay-friendly • charming country inn circa 1840

Captain Dexter House of Vineyard Haven 100 Main St., Box 2457, Vineyard Haven, 02568 • 693-6564 • gay-friendly • 1843 home of sea captain • meticulously restored & exquisitely furnished

Webb's Camping Area RFD 3, Box 100, 02568 • 693-0233 • May-Sept • lesbians/gay men • women-owned/run

TRAVEL & TOUR OPERATORS

Martha's Vineyard Steamship Authority • 540-2022 • call for info & schedules of ferries from Boston

Methuen (508)

BARS

Xposure 280 Merrimack St. • 685-9911 • 9pm-2am Fri, til 1am Sat only • gay-friendly • dancing/DJ

Nantucket (508)

ACCOMMODATIONS

House of Orange 25 Orange St. • 228-9287 • May-Oct • gay-friendly • old captain's home located in historic Nantucket

New Bedford (508)

BARS

Le Place 20 Kenyon St. • 992-8156 • 2pm-2am, from noon-1am Sat • popular • lesbians/gay men • dancing/DJ • women-owned/run

Puzzles 428 N. Front St. • 991-2306 • 4pm-2am • lesbians/gay men • dancing/DJ • live shows • local fish menu & Sun brunch from 11am

Newton

INFO LINES & SERVICES

Dyke TV Channel 13 • 10pm Tue • 'weekly half hour TV show produced by lesbians, for lesbians'

Northampton (413)

INFO LINES & SERVICES

Bound & Determined PO Box 602, Hadley, 01035 • lesbian S/M group

Community Pride Line • 585-8839 • recorded info

Lesbian/Gay Business Guild PO Box 593, 01061 • 585-8839 • listing of lesbi-gay-owned & friendly businesses

New Alexandria Lesbian Library PO Box 402, 01060 • 584-7616 • archives • library • call for appointment

Out & About Cable TV Channel 2 • 9pm Mon

Shelix PO Box 416, Florence Station, 01060 • 584-7616 • New England S/M support group for lesbian/bi & transgender women • write for info

WOMEN'S ACCOMMODATIONS

Little River Farm 967 Huntington Rd. Rte 112, Worthington • 238-4261 • women only • full breakfast • women-owned/run

ACCOMMODATIONS

Corner Porches Baptist Corner Rd. (30 min. outside Northampton), Ashfield • 628-4592 • gay-friendly • full breakfast

Innamorata B&B 47 Main St., Goshen • 268-0300 • mostly women • full breakfast • near outdoor recreation • extensive grounds • women-owned/run

Old Red Schoolhouse 67 Park St., 01060 • 584-1228 • mostly women • apts • studios • also Lesbian Towers in East Hampton • gay-friendly • $65-200

Tin Roof B&B PO Box 296, Hadley, 01035 • 586-8665 • mostly women • 1909 farmhouse w/ spectacular view of the Berkshires • women-owned/run

BARS

Iron Horse 20 Center St. • 584-0610 • 8:30pm-? • gay-friendly • live shows • food served • Fresh American • some veggie • wheelchair access • $5-15

Northampton (413)

LESBIGAY INFO: Community Pride Line: 584-4848.

LESBIGAY PAPER: The Calendar: PO Box 5000, Ste. 132, 01060, lesbian events. Gayzette: PO Box 181, 01061.

WHERE THE GIRLS ARE: Just off Main St., browsing in the small shops, strolling down an avenue, or sipping a beverage at one of the cafés.

ANNUAL EVENTS: June - Golden Threads: PO Box 60475, Northampton, MA 01060-0475, gathering for lesbians over 50 & their admirers, at the Provincetown Inn. Fat Women's Gathering: (212) 721-8259. July - Northampton Lesbian Festival: 586-8251, 2nd-largest women's music festival.

BEST VIEW: At the top of Skinner Mountain, up Route 47 by bus, car or bike.

WEATHER: Late summer/early fall is the best season, with warm, sunny days. Mid-summer gets to the low 90°s, while winter brings snow from November to March, with temperatures in the 20°s and 30°s.

TRANSIT: Mystery Taxi: 584-0055. Peter Pan Shuttle: 586-1030. Pioneer Valley Transit Authority (PVTA): 586-5806.

Northstar 25 West St. • 586-9409 • dinner 5pm-10pm, dancing 10pm-1am, Sun brunch • gay-friendly • live shows • also a restaurant • seafood/cont'l • some veggie • patio • women-owned/run • $10-20

Pearl Street Cafe 10 Pearl St. • 584-7810 • 9pm-1am Wed only • lesbians/gay men • dancing/DJ • wheelchair access • women-owned/run

RESTAURANTS & CAFES

Bela 68 Masonic St. • 586-8011 • noon-8pm Mon-Wed, til 10pm Th-Sat, clsd Sun-Mon • vegetarian • wheelchair access • women-owned/run • $5-10

Curtis & Schwartz 116 Main St. • 586-3278 • 7:30am-3pm • neo-Eurpoean • some veggie • $8-15

Green Street Cafe 64 Green St. • 586-5650 • lunch & dinner • beer/wine • New American • plenty veggie • patio • $11-17

Haymarket Cafe 15 Amber Ln. • 586-9969 • 9am-midnight, clsd Mon • fresh pastries

Paul & Elizabeth's 150 Main St. • 584-4832 • seafood • plenty veggie • beer/wine • wheelchair access • $7-12

Squire's Smoke & Game Club Rte. 9, Williamsburg • 268-7222 • from 5pm Wed-Sun • popular • live shows • wood burning American cuisine • some veggie • full bar • wheelchair access • $12-17

BOOKSTORES & RETAIL SHOPS

Pride & Joy 20 Crafts Ave. • 585-0683 • 11am-6pm, til 8pm Th, from noon-5pm Sun • lesbigay • books & gifts

Third Wave Feminist Booksellers 90 King St. • 586-7851 • 10am-6pm, til 8pm Th, til 5pm Sun, clsd Mon • wheelchair access • lesbian-owned/run

PUBLICATIONS

Metroline 1841 Broad St., Hartford, CT 06114 • (203) 278-6666/ (800) 678-7944 • regional newspaper/ entertainment guide

Northampton

espite the hype about the fabled 10,000 lesbians living in Northampton, this small city is a quaint and quiet New England town. Sure, you'll be free to make out with your honey just about anywhere, but don't expect to see throngs of sapphic sisters.

There are two lesbian-friendly inns, and two restaurants popular with local girls: **Green St. Centre** and **Northstar**, which is also the club of choice (check out their calendar of events). For women's reading material – a popular pastime in Northampton – try the **New Alexandria Lesbian Library**. Or take the tour of **Emily Dickinson's House** in nearby Amherst. For diverse fun, pick up the **Lesbian Calendar**, a comprehensive monthly listing of events. It's available at **Pride & Joy** lesbian/gay bookstore, the informal community center. Ask about the group **De Colores**. Or call the **Community Pride Line**. For other events, pick up **Off Campus**, a paper for all five colleges here. In late July look for the **Northampton Lesbian Festival**, which usually happens in the Berkshires – for lack of enough public space in Northampton!

The NAMES Project
AIDS Memorial

QUILT.

NOT ALL BATTLES ARE FOUGHT WITH A SWORD

OCTOBER 11-13
1996

WASHINGTON, D.C.

Once again we must unfold
the AIDS Memorial Quilt
in our nation's capital.
Why? Because until there is
an end to AIDS,
we are not going away.
Please join us.
Call The NAMES Project
Foundation at 415/882-5500.

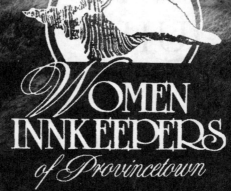

WOMEN INNKEEPERS
of Provincetown

Bradford Gardens Inn
Checker Inn • Dusty Miller Inn
Halle's • Hargood House at Bayshore
Heritage House • Lady Jane's Inn
Ravenwood • Rose Acre
Seventy Bradford St
The Fairbanks Inn • The Tucker Inn
Windamar House

We are a group of women-owned &
operated inns working together to provide
a unique, year-round, quality vacation for you.
Experience Cape Cod in a way that only we can
provide. We present such annual events as
Womens Week in October & Spring Fling
in May. Hope to see you soon.

Provincetown (508)

INFO LINES & SERVICES

Dyke TV Channel 19 • 10:30pm Mon • 'weekly half hour TV show produced by lesbians, for lesbians'

▲ **Provincetown Business Guild** 115 Bradford St., 02657 • 487-2313/ (800) 637-8696 • IGTA member

WOMEN'S ACCOMMODATIONS

▲ **Bradford Gardens Inn** 178 Bradford St. • 487-1616/ (800) 432-2334 • mostly women • full breakfast • 1820s colonial inn surrounded by gardens • women-owned/run • $65-225

Check'er Inn 25 Winthrop St. • 487-9029/ (800) 894-9029 • women only • guesthouse • apts • hot tub • women-owned/run • $60-125

▲ **Dexter's Inn** 6 Conwell St. • 487-1911 • mostly women • B&B • no smoking • parking • women-owned/run • $50-85

▲ **Dusty Miller Inn** 82 Bradford St. • 487-2213 • mostly women • women-owned/run • $50-110

▲ **Gabriel's Guestrooms & Apartments** 104 Bradford St. • 487-3232/ (800) 969-2643 • popular • mostly women • hot tub • beautiful old home & new workshop center • IGTA member • $50-150

Gull Walk Inn 300-A Commercial St. • 487-9027 • women only • cont'l breakfast • sundeck • women-owned/run • $40-90

▲ **Halle's** 14 W. Vine St. • 487-6310 • mostly women • cottages • apts • private baths • in quiet west end • women-owned/run • $65-95

▲ **Heritage House** 7 Center St. • 487-3692 • popular • lesbians/gay men • guesthouse • lesbian-owned/run • $49-85

▲ **Lady Jane's Inn** 7 Central St. • 487-3387 • mostly women • B&B • cont'l breakfast • IGTA member • women-owned/run • $80

The Little Inn 31 Pearl St. • 487-2407 • women only • B&B • women-owned/run • $45-75

▲ **Marigolds B&B** PO Box 39, 02652 • 487-9160/ (214) 824-7203 (off season #) • May-Oct • women only • full breakfast • women-owned/run • $40-85

Provincetown

*T*he country's largest lesbian and gay resort – with 15 women's guesthouses, and more than 60 gay-friendly B&B's – is a quintessential New England whaling village on the very tip of Cape Cod.

Provincetown has been popular for summers ever since Native American tribes came here to fish. The Vikings also stopped in for quick repairs, and the Pilgrims even made their first landing here. Over the centuries, Provincetown has shifted from a whaling village to a haven for whale-watching. Before you leave, treat yourself to the excitement of a whale-watching cruise. There are several cruise lines, and **Portuguese Princess Whale Watch** is women-owned.

Provincetown is also a haven for lesbians - the majority of the guest inns are lesbian-run. According to one regular, the typical lesbian itinerary goes as follows:

ARRIVAL: Rent a bike and explore the town's lesbigay shops and bookstores. Nobody drives in Provincetown. Pick up lunch at a deli on the way to Herring Cove. At the beach, head left to find the women.

AT THE BEACH: Go ahead, take off your top. Nudity is desirable here, but watch for the cops – they'll give you a ticket for bare breasts. Tip: if you're heading toward the sand dunes for a tryst (like everyone else), don't forget your socks. The hot, white sand can burn your feet.

3PM: Bike back to your room for a shower, then head to the afternoon T-dance at **Boatslip Beach Club** on Commercial St. Drink and dance til dinnertime, then take a relaxing few hours for dinner.

AFTER DINNER: Check out the bars; **The Pied** is the pick for women. If your energy's too low for the bar scene, most stores are open til 11pm during the summer. When the bars close, grab a slice of pizza and an espresso milkshake at **Spiritus**, and cruise the streets until they're empty – sometimes not til 4 or 5 a.m.

If you like your women packed together like sardines, pencil in **Provincetown Women's Weekend**, the third weekend in October. **The Womens Innkeepers of Provincetown** will be sponsoring games, barbecues, live shows, dances, cruises and more. Don't forget to call your favorite guesthouse early to make your reservations!

Just one last bit of advice: you may have heard others refer to Provincetown as 'P-town' but nothing rankles a native faster.

▲ **Pilgrim House** 336 Commercial St. • 487-6424 • mostly women • also a restaurant • full bar

▲ **Plums Bed & Breakfast** 160 Bradford St. • 487-2283 • March-Nov • women only • full breakfast • also condos & apts • $70-95

▲ **Ravenwood Guest House** 462 Commercial St. • 487-3203 • mostly women • 1830 Greek Revival home offering guest rooms • also apts & cottages • women-owned/run • $75-145

▲ **Rose Acre** Center St. • 487-2347 • women only • shuttle to beach for the car-less • women-owned/run • $65-145

▲ **Seventy Bradford Street** 70 Bradford St. • 487-4966 • women only • women-owned/run • $68-80

▲ **Windamar House** 568 Commercial St. • 487-0599 • mostly women • 1840s sea captain's home • women-owned/run • $60-125

ACCOMMODATIONS

A Tall Ship 452 Commercial St. • 487-2247 • gay-friendly • beach house

Admiral's Landing Guest House 158 Bradford St. • 487-9665 • seasonal • mostly gay men • spacious & comfortable 1840s captain's home & cottages

Ampersand Guesthouse 6 Cottage St. • 487-0959 • lesbians/gay men • mid-19th century Greek Revival architecture

▲ **Anchor Inn Guest House** 175 Commercial St. • 487-0432/ (800) 858-2657 • popular • lesbians/gay men • central location • private beach • spectacular view of harbor

Angel's Landing 353-355 Commercial St. • 487-1600 • seasonal • mostly women • efficiency units on waterfront

Asheton House 3 Cook St. • 487-9966 • gay-friendly • fully restored whaling captain's house built around 1840

Beachfront Realty 145 Commercial St. • 487-1397 • vacation rentals & housing/condo sales

Provincetown (508)

LESBIGAY INFO: Provincetown Business Guild: 487-2313/ (800) 637-8696.

WHERE THE GIRLS ARE: In this small resort town, you can't miss 'em!

LESBIGAY PRIDE: June, 521-0811.

ANNUAL EVENTS: August 14-21 - Provincetown Carnival: (800) 637-8696. October - Women's Week: (800) 637-8696, very popular - make your reservations early!

CITY INFO: Chamber of Commerce: 487-3424.

ATTRACTIONS: The beach.

BEST VIEW: Girl-watching at an outdoor cafe or on the beach.

WEATHER: New England's weather is unpredictable. Be prepared for rain, snow or extreme heat! Otherwise, the weather during the season consists of warm days and cooler nights.

Bradford Gardens Inn

Bradford Gardens Inn, woman-owned and featured in most national and international B & B guides, offers you charming, spacious rooms with fireplaces, private baths, cable TV and ceiling fans.

Included are full gourmet breakfasts, such as shirred eggs with tarragon mornay sauce, Portuguese flippers, homemade cinnamon-walnut pancakes with blueberry maple syrup...You can also choose fire-placed cottages situated in our beautiful gardens surrounding the inn.

Just park your car in our lot, and you are 5 minutes from the center of town for fine dining, nightclubs, whalewatching, beaches, galleries and shopping.

Built in 1820, this historic inn offers you New England charm combined with a natural informality. Rates: $69-$145. One block from the beach.

Bradford Gardens Inn
178 Bradford St.
Provincetown, MA 02657
(508) 487-1616

(800) 432-2334

GABRIEL'S

Come close to heaven

APARTMENTS & GUEST ROOMS

SIRENS WORKSHOP CENTER

Conference Center & Holistic Workshops
Sauna & Hot Tubs
Exercise Room & Steam Room
Gardens & Sundecks & Barbeque
Fireplaces & Breakfast
Color Cable TV & Phones
Internet Access & Computer Facilities
Always Open & In the Heart of Town

Find us on the World Wide Web:
http://www.provincetown.com
Under "Places to Stay"
Or call for our workshop catalogue

(800) 9MY-ANGEL

104 Bradford Street   (508) 487•3232
Provincetown, MA   FAX (508) 487•1605
02657-1440   gabriels@provincetown.com

Plums
Bed & Breakfast Inn

Drive past the tumble of Cape Cod houses to Plums Bed & Breakfast, an 1860s Dutch Gambrel. Inside the white picket fence, a garden of lilies, irises and dahlias beckon you across the wisteria-draped porch. Your key unlocks the quiet elegance of the Victorian whaling captain's house.

Inside, wide pine floors shine beneath Eastlake and Renaissance Revival antiques that grace Plums' large rooms. Fresh flowers add to the romance! And white lace curtains adorn windows that reach to high ceilings. Sit at a table of women for breakfast amid sterling silver, brass and period curios. Under a crystal chandelier, enjoy conversation, fresh fruit, baked goods, and gourmet entrees like cheese souffle or French toast stuffed with cream cheese and strawberries. Innkeepers to pamper you, parking and private baths for your comfort.

Come, experience the magic of Plums!
160 Bradford Street • Provincetown, MA 02657
(508) 487-2283 • Brochure available

WINDAMAR HOUSE
Guests

This stately, historic home is located in the quiet, residential East End of town directly across from picturesque Cape Cod Bay. We offer guest rooms and apartments distinctively decorated with antiques and original artwork. The front rooms have water views while rooms on the side and back of the house offer views of English flower gardens and manicured lawns. The common room, a central mingling space, is equipped with sink, refrigerator and cable TV with VCR. Homebaked continental breakfast is provided complimentary every morning for our guest rooms. Guests are encouraged to barbeque, picnic or sunbathe on our beautiful, spacious grounds. Ample on-site parking is provided for all our accommodations.

568 Commercial Street
Provincetown, Massachusetts 02657

508-487-0599

"It's all you'd imagine a grand ole Cape Cod home to be."

Bette Adams, Jan Doerler Innkeepers

Beaconlite Inn 12 Winthrop St. • 487-9603 • lesbians/gay men • 'home away from home' comfort & service

The Blue Beacon 8 Bradford St. • 487-0516/ (800) 287-0059 • gay-friendly • parking

Boatslip Beach Club 161 Commercial St. • 487-1669/ (800) 451-7547 • seasonal • popular • lesbians/gay men • swimming • also a restaurant • cont'l/seafood • some veggie • beachfront resort • several bars • popular T-dance • $10-25

Bradford House & Motel 41 Bradford St. • 487-0173 • lesbians/gay men

The Brass Key Guesthouse 9 Court St. • 487-9005/ (800) 842-9858 • seasonal • popular • mostly gay men • meticulously restored accommodations • heated spa • wheelchair access

The Buoy 97 Bradford St. • 487-3082 • lesbians/gay men • guesthouse

Burch House 116 Bradford St. • 487-9170 • seasonal • popular • mostly gay men • studios

Captain & His Ship 164 Commercial St. • 487-1850/ (800) 400-2278 • seasonal • popular • mostly gay men • 19th century sea captain's home

Captain Lysander's Inn 96 Commercial St. • 487-2253 • gay-friendly • elegant captain's guesthouse

▲ **Captain's House** 350-A Commercial St. • 487-9353/ (800) 457-8885 • seasonal • mostly gay men • B&B

Chancellor Inn 17 Center St. • 487-9423 • mostly gay men

Chicago House 6 Winslow St. • 487-0537 • popular • mostly gay men • B&B

The Claredon House 118 Bradford St. • 487-1645 • gay-friendly

Coat of Arms 7 Johnson St. • 487-0816 • seasonal • popular • mostly gay men • mid-Victorian house • located in the heart of Provincetown

Commons Guesthouse & Bistro 386 Commercial St. • 487-7800/ (800) 487-0784 • gay-friendly • room service

Crown & Anchor 247 Commercial St. • 487-1430 • popular • mostly gay men • swimming • also a restaurant • full bar • cafe • $10-20

Dunes Motel & Apartments 125 Bradford St. W. • 487-1956 • seasonal • lesbians/gay men • motel rooms • apartment suites • cottages

▲ **Elephant Walk Inn** 156 Bradford St. • 487-2543/ (800) 889-9255 • seasonal • popular • lesbians/gay men • inn • in the heart of Provincetown

Elliot House 6 Gosnold St. • 487-4029 • lesbians/gay men • full breakfast • central location • private gardens

▲ **Fairbanks Inn** 90 Bradford St. • 487-0386/ (800) 324-7265 • popular • lesbians/gay men • IGTA member

Flamingo Bay 27 Conwell St. • 487-0068/ (800) 352-6229 • lesbians/gay men

Four Bays 166 Commercial St. • 487-0859/ (800) 414-2297 • lesbians/gay men • Victorian home across the street from Cape Cod Bay & the Boatslip Beach Club

Hargood House at Bayshore 493 Commercial St. • 487-9133 • gay-friendly • apts • private beach • women-owned/run • $72-142

Haven House 12 Carver St. • 487-3031 • popular • mostly gay men • swimming

Holiday Inn of Provincetown Rte. 6-A Box 392, 02657 • 487-1711/ (800) 422-4224 • gay-friendly • swimming • also a restaurant • full bar • wheelchair access • IGTA member

The Inn at the Egg 1944 Rte. 6-A, Brewster • 896-3123/ (800) 259-8235 • gay-friendly • 20 min. from Provincetown • women-owned/run

Ireland House 18 Pearl St. • 487-7132/ (800) 474-7434 • lesbians/gay men • in the heart of Provincetown

John Randall House 140 Bradford St. • 487-3533 • lesbians/gay men

Lamplighter Inn 26 Bradford St. • 487-2529 • lesbians/gay men • B&B • wonderful views of the town, ocean & cape

Land's End Inn 22 Commercial St. • 487-0706 • lesbians/gay men

Lotus Guest House 296 Commercial St. • 487-4644 • April-Nov • lesbians/gay men • decks • gardens

Mayflower Apartments 6 Bangs St. • 487-1916 • gay-friendly • kitchens • off-street parking

▲ **Monument House** 129 Bradford St. • 487-9664 • seasonal • lesbians/gay men • banker's home dating from the 1840s • IGTA member

Normandy House 184 Bradford St. • 487-1197 • popular • lesbians/gay men • hot tub • intimate guest house at the very tip of Cape Cod • women-owned/run

Ocean's Inn 386 Commercial St. • 487-0358 • gay-friendly • live shows • also a restaurant • American • full bar • $10-30

Provincetown Inn 1 Commercial St. • 487-9500 • gay-friendly • swimming • some veggie • harbor view restaurant • wheelchair access • $13

▲ **Provincetown Reservations System** 293 Commercial St. #5 • 487-2400/ (800) 648-0364 • IGTA member

Red Inn 15 Commercial St. • 487-0050 • lesbians/gay men • elegant waterfront dinner & lodging

Renaissance Apartments 48 Commercial St. • 487-4600 • seasonal • lesbians/gay men • kitchens • decks

Revere Guesthouse 14 Court St. • 487-2292 • lesbians/gay men • restored captain's home of the Federal period circa 1820

Richmond Inn 4 Conant St. • 487-9193 • mostly gay men

Roomers 8 Carver St. • 487-3532 • seasonal • mostly gay men

Rose & Crown Guest House 158 Commercial St. • 487-3332 • lesbians/gay men • Victorian antiques & appealing artwork

▲ **Sandbars** PO Box 533, 02657 • 487-1290 • lesbians/gay men • motel • kitchens • all oceanfront rooms • private beach • women-owned/run

Sandpiper Beach House 165 Commercial St. • 487-1928/ (800) 354-8628 • popular • lesbians/gay men • Victorian guesthouse • in the heart of everything • IGTA member • gay-owned/run

Shamrock Motel, Cottages & Apartments 49 Bradford St. • 487-1133 • seasonal • gay-friendly • swimming

Shiremax Inn 5 Tremont St. • 487-1233 • mostly gay men • also 2 apts

▲ **Six Webster Place** 6 Webster Pl. • 487-2266/ (800) 693-2783 • popular • lesbians/gay men • 1750s B&B • patio • wheelchair access

Somerset House 378 Commercial St. • 487-0383 • seasonal • gay-friendly • B&B

South Hollow Vineyards Rte. 6-A, North Truro • 487-6200 • gay-friendly • women-owned/run

Sunset Inn 142 Bradford St. • 487-9810 • seasonal • lesbians/gay men

Swanberry Inn 8 Johnson St. • 487-4242/ (800) 847-7926 • lesbians/gay men

Three Peaks 210 Bradford St. • 487-1717/ (800) 286-1715 • lesbians/gay men • 1870s Victorian house transformed into an inn • IGTA member

Trade Winds 12 Johnson St. • 487-0138 • mostly gay men

▲ **Tucker Inn** 12 Center St. • 487-0381 • seasonal • gay-friendly • patio • women-owned/run

Victoria House 5 Standish St. • 487-4455 • lesbians/gay men

Watermark Inn Guest House 603 Commercial St. • 487-2506 • gay-friendly • kitchens • beachside

Watership Inn 7 Winthrop St. • 487-0094/ (800) 330-9413 • popular • lesbians/gay men

Westwinds Guest House 28 Commercial St. • 487-1841 • seasonal • lesbians/gay men • swimming

▲ **White Wind Inn** 174 Commercial St. • 487-1526 • lesbians/gay men • beautiful Victorian inn built during the mid-1800s • stay 2 nights & get 3rd free except holidays (Nov-Mar) • women-owned/run

The Willows Guest Complex 25 Tremont St. • 487-0520 • lesbians/gay men • guest complex on an acre of lovely landscaped grounds

Windsor Court 15 Cottage St. • 487-2620 • lesbians/gay men • hot tub • swimming • parking

BARS

Back Room (at Crown & Anchor accommodations) • 487-1430 • 10:30pm-1am, seasonal • popular • lesbians/gay men • dancing/DJ • live shows • check locally for women's night • patio

Boatslip Beach Club (at Boatslip Beach Club accommodations) • 487-1669 • popular • lesbians/gay men • dancing/DJ • also a restaurant • cont'l/seafood • some veggie • T-dance every day during season • wheelchair access • $10-25

Kitty's 67 Shank Painter Rd. • 487-8320 • 6pm-1am • mostly women • dancing/DJ • wheelchair access

▲ **Pied Piper** 193-A Commercial St. • 487-1527 • noon-1am • mostly women • wheelchair access • women-owned/run

Rooster Bar (at the Crown & Anchor accommodations) • 487-1430 • 6pm-1am • popular • lesbians/gay men • neighborhood bar • videos • food served • more women off season

Town House 291 Commercial St. • 487-0292 • 11am-1am • popular • lesbians/gay men • live shows • food served

Vixen 336 Commercial St. • 487-6424 • 11am-1am • mostly women • dancing/DJ • live shows • also a restaurant

RESTAURANTS & CAFES

Cafe Express 214 Commercial St. • 487-3382 • 9am-2am • lesbians/gay men • vegetarian • wheelchair access • $5-10

Dodie's Diner 401-1/2 Commercial St. • 487-3868 • 8am-10pm • American • some veggie • women-owned/run • $5-10

Dodie's Pizza 333 Commercial St. • 487-3388 • 9am-2am • popular • women-owned/run

The Flagship 463 Commercial St. • 487-4200 • live shows • women-owned/run

Franco's 133 Bradford St. • 487-3178 • lunch & dinner • popular • lesbians/gay men • American • some veggie • Luigi's upstairs • Italian • $15-35

Front Street Restaurant 230 Commercial St. • 487-9715 • 6pm-10:30pm, til 1am bar, April-Oct • lesbians/gay men • cont'l • full bar • $15-25

Gallerani's 133 Commercial St. • 487-4433 • 8am-2pm, 6am-10:30pm Th-Mon • popular • lesbians/gay men • cont'l • some veggie • beer/wine • $20-30

Landmark Inn Restaurant 404 Commercial St. • 487-9319 • dinner nightly 5:30pm-10pm April-Oct • lesbians/gay men • New England • $15-25

Lobster Pot 321 Commercial St. • 487-0842 • noon-10pm • seafood • some veggie • wheelchair access • $15-20

Mews 429 Commercial St. • 487-1500 • lunch & dinner, seasonal • popular • cont'l/cafe • some veggie • wheelchair access • $15-30

Napi's 7 Freeman St. • 487-1145 • internat'l/seafood • plenty veggie • wheelchair access • $15-25

Post Office Cafe Cabaret 303 Commercial St. (upstairs) • 487-3892 • 8am-midnight (breakfast til 3pm) • lesbians/gay men • live shows • American • some veggie • $8-15

Pucci's Harborside 539 Commercial St. • 487-1964 • seasonal • popular • American • some veggie • full bar • wheelchair access • $10-20

Sal's Place 99 Commercial St. • 487-1279 • popular • publisher's choice: cheese & butter pasta

Sebastian's Long & Narrow 177 Commercial St. • 487-3286 • 11am-10pm • American • wheelchair access • $10-15

Spiritus 190 Commercial St. • 487-2808 • 11am-2am • popular • great espresso shakes & late night hangout for a slice

GYMS & HEALTH CLUBS

The Provincetown Gym Inc. 170 Commercial St. • 487-2776 • lesbians/gay men

BOOKSTORES & RETAIL SHOPS

Don't Panic 192 Commercial St. • 487-1280 • lesbigay gifts • t-shirts

Far Side of the Wind 389 Commercial St. • 487-3963 • 11am-11pm, til 5pm off-season • healing-focused New Age books & gifts • Native American artifacts • wheelchair access

Now, Voyager 357 Commercial St. • 487-0848 • 11am-11pm, til 5pm off season • lesbigay bookstore • also mystery titles

Pride's 182 Commercial St. • 487-1127 • 10am-11pm (in-season) • lesbigay gifts • T shirts • books

Provincetown Bookshop 246 Commercial St. • 487-0964 • 10am-11pm, til 5pm off-season

Recovering Hearts 2-4 Standish St. • 487-4875 • 10am-11pm (in-season) • recovery • lesbigay & New Age books • wheelchair access

▲ **Womencrafts** 376 Commercial St. at Pearl St. • 487-2501 • 10am-11pm • women's crafts • gifts

TRAVEL & TOUR OPERATORS

Cape Air Barnstable Municipal Airport • 771-6944/ (800) 352-0714 • IGTA member

Portuguese Princess Whale Watch Shank Painter Rd., McMillan Wharf • 487-2651 • whale watching • day & evening cruises • special women's events cruises • wheelchair access • women-owned/run

▲ **RSVP-Town Reservations** PO Box 614, 02657 • 487-1883/ (800) 677-8696 • IGTA member

Sand Faces (at The Little Inn) • 487-2407 • April-Nov • women's oceanside & dune hikes • learn about flora & fauna

Your Way Travel 145 Commercial St. • 487-2992 • IGTA member

SPIRITUAL GROUPS

Dignity 1 Commercial St. (Provincetown Inn) • 487-9500 • 10:30am mass Sun (May-Oct.)

PUBLICATIONS

In 398 Columbus Ave., Boston, 02238 • (617) 426-8246

Provincetown Banner PO Box 1978, 02657 • 487-7400

Provincetown Magazine 14 Center St., 02657 • 487-1000 • weekly

Randolph (508)

BARS

Randolph Country Club 44 Mazeo Dr. (Rte. 139) • 961-2414 • 2pm-2am, (10am summer) • popular • lesbians/gay men • dancing/DJ • live shows • private club • volleyball court • swimming • wheelchair access

Salem (508)

BARS

Carmelina's 98 Wharf St. • 744-0472 • noon-1am • lesbians/gay men • also a restaurant • Italian • wheelchair access

Springfield (413)

INFO LINES & SERVICES

Gay/Lesbian Info Service PO Box 80891, 01138 • 731-5403

BARS

David's 397 Dwight St. • 734-0566 • 8pm-2am Wed-Sun • lesbians/gay men • dancing/DJ

Just Friends 23 Hampden St. • 781-5878 • 11am-2am • lesbians/gay men • dancing/DJ • videos • 3 flrs. • wheelchair access

Pub 382 Dwight • 734-8123 • 11am-2am, dinner Fri-Sun & Sun brunch • lesbians/gay men • neighborhood bar • dancing/DJ • live shows • 3 bars • wheelchair access

Sisters (at the Pub) • 9pm-2am Th-Sun • popular • mostly women • dancing/DJ

PUBLICATIONS

Metroline 1841 Broad St., Hartford • (203) 278-6666/ (800) 678-7944 • regional newspaper/entertainment guide

Ware (413)

ACCOMMODATIONS

The Wildwood Inn 121 Church St. • 967-7798 • gay-friendly • full breakfast • wheelchair access

West Springfield (413)

TRAVEL & TOUR OPERATORS

A&D Travel 30 Main St. • 737-5706/ (800) 737-5712 • IGTA member

Williamstown (413)

ACCOMMODATIONS

River Bend Farm B&B 643 Simonds Rd. • 458-3121 • gay-friendly

Worcester (508)

INFO LINES & SERVICES

AA Gay/Lesbian • 752-9000

Floating Dance Floor • 791-1327 • produces women's dances • call for info

Gay/Lesbian Youth Group PO Box 592, Westside Stn., 01602 • 755-0005 • 24hrs

WOBBLES (West of Boston Lesbians) • 386-7737 • 3rd Sun • social group • covers eastern MA

BARS

Club 241 241 Southbridge • 755-9311 • 6pm-2am, from 2pm wknds • popular • lesbians/gay men • dancing/DJ • rooftop deck • wheelchair access

GYMS & HEALTH CLUBS

Midtown Athletic Club 22 Front St. 2nd flr. • 798-9703 • 8am-8pm • gay-friendly

SPIRITUAL GROUPS

Morning Star MCC 231 Main St. • 892-4320 • 11:15am Sun • wheelchair access

Michigan

Ann Arbor   (313)

INFO LINES & SERVICES

Gay/Lesbian Open House 518 E. Washington St. • 665-0606 • 8:45pm Mon • social group

Lesbian/Gay AA • 482-5700

Lesbian/Gay Male/Bisexual Programs Office 3116 Michigan Union, 530 S. State St. • 763-4186 • 9am-5pm • info & referral service

Ozone House 608 N. Main St. • 662-2222 • lesbigay youth support group for ages 12-20

ACCOMMODATIONS

Judy's Place 906 Edgewood Pl. • 662-4812 • gay-friendly • full breakfast • shared baths • lesbian-owned/run

BARS

Ark 637-1/2 S. Main St. • 761-1451 • gay-friendly • concert house • women's music various times throughout year

\'aut\ Bar 315 Braun Ct. • 994-3677 • call for hours • lesbians/gay men • neighborhood bar • cafe • patio • wheelchair access

Blind Pig 208 S. 1st St. • 996-8555 • 3pm-2am • gay-friendly • live bands

Club Fabulous • 763-4186 • monthly chem-free dances during school year • call Lesbian/Gay/Bi office for details

Flame Bar 115 W. Washington St. • 662-9680 • 7:30pm-2am • popular • mostly gay men • neighborhood bar

LesBiGay Happy Hour/Social At Dominick's 812 Monroe St. (at Tappan Ave.) • 7pm-9pm Fri • seasonal

Nectarine 516 E. Liberty • 994-5835 • 9pm-2am Tue & Fri only • lesbians/gay men • dancing/DJ • videos

RESTAURANTS & CAFES

Earle 121 W. Washington • 994-0211 • 6pm-10pm, til midnight Fri-Sat, clsd summer Sun • French/Italian • some veggie • beer/wine • $15-25

BOOKSTORES & RETAIL SHOPS

Borders Book Shop 303 S. State St. • 668-7652 • 9am-9pm, 11am-6pm Sun • general

Common Language 215 S. 4th Ave. • 663-0036 • noon-8pm, til 4pm Sun, clsd Mon • lesbigay books • wheelchair access

Community News Center 330 E. Liberty • 663-6168 • 8:30am-11pm

Crazy Wisdom Books 206 N. 4th Ave. • 665-2757 • 10am-6pm, from noon Sun • holistic metaphysical bookstore

Webster's 2607 Plymouth Rd. • 662-6150 • 8am-11pm • lesbigay section • wheelchair access

TRAVEL & TOUR OPERATORS

Horizons Travel 475 Market Pl. • 663-3434/ (800) 878-7477 • IGTA member

SPIRITUAL GROUPS

Huron Valley MCC 1001 Green Rd. • 434-1452 • 2pm Sun

Lutherans Concerned-Ann Arbor PO Box 8417 Liberty Stn., 48107-8417 • 475-3684

Atwood   (616)

ACCOMMODATIONS

Stelle Wunderschönes 12410 Entrim Dr. • 599-2847 • lesbians/gay men • full breakfast • red cedar log home w/ panoramic views of Grand Traverse Bay & Lake Michigan

Battle Creek   (616)

BARS

Rascals 910 North Ave. • 964-7276 • 6pm-2am, clsd Mon (summers) • lesbians/gay men • dancing/DJ • more women Fri

Belleville   (313)

BARS

Granny's Place 9800 Haggerty Rd. • 699-8862 • 4pm-2am, from 10pm Fri • lesbians/gay men • live shows • wheelchair access

Detroit   (313/810)

INFO LINES & SERVICES

Affirmations Lesbian/Gay Community Center 195 W. 9-Mile Rd. Ste. 106, Ferndale • (810) 398-7105 • 1pm-6pm, 9am-2pm Sat • social/support groups • counseling

Lesbian/Gay Switchboard • (810) 398-4297 • 4:30pm-11pm, clsd Sat

Motor City Business Forum • (810) 546-9347 • business/social group • mtg. 2nd Tue • call for info

BARS

The Body Shop 22061 Woodward Ave., Ferndale • (810) 398-1940 • 4pm-2am • mostly gay men • dancing/DJ • also a restaurant • American • wheelchair access • $5-10

Gigi's 16920 W. Warren (rear entrance) • (313) 584-6525 • noon-2am, from 2pm wknds • mostly gay men • dancing/DJ • live shows

Off Broadway East 12215 Harper St. • (313) 521-0920 • 9pm-2am • mostly gay men • dancing/DJ • more women Sat • wheelchair access

Railroad Crossing 6640 E. 8 Mile Rd. • (313) 891-1020 • 7pm-2am, clsd Mon-Wed • mostly women • patio

Silent Legacy 1641 Middlebelt Rd. • (313) 729-8980 • 7pm-2am, clsd Mon • lesbians/gay men • dancing/DJ • live shows

Stingers Lounge 19404 Sherwood • (313) 892-1765 • 4pm-2am • lesbians/gay men • grill menu

Sugarbakers 3800 E. 8-Mile Rd. • 892-5203 • 6pm-2am • mostly women • sports bar & grill • wheelchair access • women-owned/run

Uptown Georgie 1880 E. 9 Mile Rd., Ferndale • (810) 547-4010 • 11am-2am, from 7pm wknds • lesbians/gay men • dancing/DJ • ladies night Wed • wheelchair access

Zippers 6221 E. Davison • (313) 892-8120 • opens 9pm, from 8pm Sun • lesbians/gay men • dancing/DJ • mostly African-American • live shows • wheelchair access

RESTAURANTS & CAFES

Backstage/Footlights 212 W. 6th St. • (810) 546-0526 • 11am-2am, til 4am Fri-Sat • live shows • full bar

Como's 22812 Woodward, Ferndale • (810) 548-5005 • 11am-2am, til 4am Fri-Sat, from 2pm wknds • American/Italian • some veggie • full bar • wheelchair access • $5-15

Detroit

*K*nown for its cars and stars, 'Motown' is the home of General Motors and living legends like Aretha Franklin, Diana Ross & the Supremes, the Temptations, Michael Jackson, Stevie Wonder, Anita Baker and Madonna. It's also rich in African-American culture. Be sure to check out the Museum of African-American History, multicultural gallery Your Heritage House, the Motown Museum, and lesbian/gay bar **Zippers**. And just under the river – via the Detroit/Windsor Tunnel – is the North American Black Historical Museum in Windsor, Canada.

Downtown, discover the impressive Renaissance Center. Before moving on to explore the districts of Greektown, Bricktown or Rivertown, take a spin around the Civic Center district on the Detroit People Mover, an elevated transit system.

You might want to start your stay with a visit to the **Affirmation Lesbian/Gay Community Center** or **A Women's Prerogative**, the women's bookstore. As for women's bars, **Railroad Crossing** has room for slow-dancing to Motown tunes, while **Sugarbakers** is a sports bar.

Harlequin Cafe 8047 Agnes St. • (313) 331-0922 • dinner nightly, Sun brunch, clsd Mon • French cont'l • wheelchair access • $15-20

La Dolce Vita 17546 Woodward Ave. • 865-0331 • 4pm-2am, from 10pm Tue, clsd Sun • lesbians/gay men • Italian • full bar • 'Hot Box' Tue • dancing/DJ

Rhinoceros 265 Riopelle • (313) 259-2208 • 11:30am-2am • American • some veggie • jazz club • $15-25

BOOKSTORES & RETAIL SHOPS

A Woman's Prerogative Bookstore 175 W. 9 Mile Rd. • (810) 545-5703 • noon-7pm, til 9pm Th, til 5pm Sun, clsd Mon • feminist • wheelchair access • women-owned/run

Chosen Books 120 W. 4th St., Royal Oak • (810) 543-5758 • noon-10pm • lesbigay • wheelchair access

TRAVEL & TOUR OPERATORS

Royal International Travel Services, Inc. 31455 South Field Rd., Birmingham • (810) 644-1600/ (800) 521-1600 • IGTA member

SPIRITUAL GROUPS

Dignity-Detroit 6th & Porter St. (Most Holy Trinity Church) • (313) 961-4818 • 6pm Sun

Divine Peace MCC 23839 John R, Hazel Park • (810) 544-8335 • 10am & 7pm Sun • wheelchair access

MCC of Detroit Pinecrest & Dreyton Ave. (Presbytarian Church), Ferndale • (810) 399-7741 • 10am & 7pm Sun

PUBLICATIONS

Between the Lines 1632 Church St., 48216 • (810) 615-7003 • covers southeastern MI

Cruise Magazine 660 Livernois Ave., Ferndale • (810) 545-9040

Metra PO Box 71844, Madison Heights, 48071 • (810) 543-3500 • covers IN, IL, MI, OH, PA, WI & Ontario, Canada

EROTICA

Noir Leather 415 S. Main, Royal Oak • (810) 541-3979 • 11am-8pm, 1pm-5pm Sun • leather • toys • erotica • piercing • wheelchair access

Detroit (810)

LESBIGAY INFO: Affirmations Lesbian/Gay Community Center: 398-7105, 195 W. 9-Mile Rd. Ste. 106, Ferndale, 1pm-6pm, 9am-2pm Sat. Lesbian/Gay Switchboard: 398-4297, 6pm-11pm.

LESBIGAY PAPER: Between The Lines: 615-7003.

WHERE THE GIRLS ARE: At the bars on 8-Mile Road between I-75 and Van Dyke Ave., with the boys in Highland Park or Dearborn, or shopping in Royal Oak.

LESBIGAY AA: 541-6565

LESBIGAY PRIDE: May, 825-6651.

ANNUAL EVENTS: May 3-5 - Geared for Life: 358-9849, 3rd annual AIDS fundraising art auction & parties in Motor City, topped off by Gear Party Saturday. August - Michigan Womyn's Music Festival: (616) 757-4766, one of the biggest annual gatherings of lesbians in the continent, in Walhalla.

CITY INFO: Detroit Visitor's Bureau: (313) 259-2680. Directory of Events Hotline: (313) 567-1170 (touchtone).

BEST VIEW: From the top of the 73-story Westin Hotel at the Renaissance Center.

TRANSIT: Checker Cab: (313) 963-7000.

Uptown Book Store 16541 Woodward Ave. • (313) 869-9477

Escanaba (906)

BARS

Club Xpress 904 Ludington St. • 789-0140 • 8pm-2am, clsd Mon • lesbians/gay men • dancing/DJ

Flint (810)

BARS

Club Triangle 2101 S. Dort 767-7552 • 4pm-2am • lesbians/gay men • dancing/DJ • wheelchair access

Copa Niteclub 565 S. Saginaw St. • 235-2500 • 9:30pm-2am • gay-friendly • dancing/DJ • 18+ • gay Wed only

Merry Inn 2402 N. Franklin St. • 234-9481 • 1pm-2am • lesbians/gay men • neighborhood bar

State Bar 2512 S. Dort Hwy. • 767-7050 • 4pm-2am, from 1pm wknds • popular • lesbians/gay men • dancing/DJ • live shows • wheelchair access

Studio 910 910 S. Dort • 234-2631 • 11am-2am, from 3pm wknds • lesbians/gay men • dancing/DJ

SPIRITUAL GROUPS

Redeemer MCC of Flint 1665 N. Chevrolet Ave. • 238-6700 • 6pm Sun

Gaylord (517)

ACCOMMODATIONS

Heritage House B&B 521 E. Main St. • 732-1199 • gay-friendly • full breakfast • country decor & homespun hospitality • women-owned/run

Glen Arbor (616)

WOMEN'S ACCOMMODATIONS

Duneswood Retreat (at Sleeping Bear Dunes Nat'l Lakeshore) • 334-3346 • women only • also Marge & Joanne's B&B • $45-85

Grand Rapids (616)

INFO LINES & SERVICES

Lesbian/Gay Network 909 Cherry SE • 458-3511 • 6pm-10pm, clsd wknds • info & referrals • AA meetings • lounge & library

BARS

Apartment 33 Sheldon • 451-0815 • 11am-2am, from 2pm Sun • mostly gay men • neighborhood bar • sandwiches served • wheelchair access

The Club 67 67 S. Division Ave. • 454-8003 • 4pm-2am • popular • mostly gay men • dancing/DJ • live shows • wheelchair access

Diversions 10 Fountain St. NW • 451-3800 • 11am-2am, from 8pm wknds • lesbians/gay men • dancing/DJ • live shows • American • plenty veggie • wheelchair access • $5-10

Taylors 8 Ionia SW • 454-4422 • 11am-2am, til 4am Fri-Sat, from 4pm Sun • lesbians/gay men • piano bar • also deli • $4-7

RESTAURANTS & CAFES

Cherie Inn 969 Cherry St. • 458-0588 • 8am-3pm, clsd Mon

BOOKSTORES & RETAIL SHOPS

Earth & Sky 6 Jefferson SE • 458-3520 • 11am-7pm, clsd Sun • wheelchair access

Sons & Daughters 962 Cherry SE • 459-8877 • noon-midnight, from 10am wknds • lesbigay bookstore • also coffeehouse • wheelchair access

TRAVEL & TOUR OPERATORS

Vacation Depot 973 Cherry SE • 454-4339 • ask for Karen • IGTA member

SPIRITUAL GROUPS

Dignity • 454-9779 • 8pm Wed • call for location

Reconciliation MCC 300 Graceland NE • 364-7633 • worship 10am Sun

Honor (616)

WOMEN'S ACCOMMODATIONS

Labrys Wilderness Resort 4115 Scenic Hwy. • 882-5994 • women only • cabins • $35-65

Kalamazoo (616)

INFO LINES & SERVICES

AA Gay/Lesbian 247 W. Level St. • 343-2711 • 8pm Tue

Alliance for Lesbian/Gay Support PO Box 226, Student Service Bldg., 49008 • 387-2134 • 2pm Sun (Kiba Room)

Kalamazoo Lesbian/Gay Resource Line • 345-7878 • 7pm-10pm • info & referrals

Lavender Morning PO Box 729, 49005 • 388-5656 • sponsors women's dances & concerts • also produces monthly newsletter

BARS

Brother's Bar 209 Stockbridge • 345-1960 • 4pm-2am • lesbians/gay men • dancing/DJ • live shows • private club • more women Sat • wheelchair access

Zoo 906 Portage St. • 342-8888 • 4pm-2am • dancing/DJ • 18+ Sun-Tue • wheelchair access • patio

BOOKSTORES & RETAIL SHOPS

Pandora's Books for Open Minds 226 W. Lovell St. • 388-5656 • 11am-6pm,1pm-5pm Sun, clsd Mon • feminist/lesbigay • wheelchair access

Triangle World 551 Portage St. • 373-4005 • noon-10pm, clsd Mon • lesbigay books • gifts • leather • wheelchair access

SPIRITUAL GROUPS

Phoenix Community Church 1758 N. 10th St. (Peoples Church) • 381-3222 • 6pm Sun

Lansing (517)

INFO LINES & SERVICES

AA Gay/Lesbian 1118 S. Harrison St. (United Ministries), E. Lansing • 321-8781 • 7:30pm Mon, 6:30pm Fri

Lansing Lesbian/Gay Hotline, E. Lansing • 332-3200 • 7pm-10pm Mon-Fri, 2pm-5pm Sun • info & referrals

Lesbian Alliance PO Box 6423, E. Lansing, 48826 • 372-2882 • lesbian community-based group • also publishes newsletter

Lesbian Center PO Box 811, 48826 • 371-5257 • sponsors lesbian programs, dances & events • lending library

Our Living Room Concert Series 303 S. Holmes • 487-6495 • 7:30pm 1st Sat • women's music • women only • boys up to 6

BARS

Club 505 505 Shiawassee • 374-6312 • 11am-2am • mostly women • neighborhood bar

Paradise 224 S. Washington Square • 484-2399 • 9pm-2am • popular • lesbians/gay men • dancing/DJ

BOOKSTORES & RETAIL SHOPS

Community News Center 418 Frandor Shopping Center • 351-7562 • 9am-9pm, til 7pm Sun • wheelchair access

Real World Emporium 1214-16 Turner St. • 485-2665 • noon-8pm, clsd Mon • lesbigay • also cafe • wheelchair access

SPIRITUAL GROUPS

Dignity PO Box 1265, E. Lansing, 48826

Ecclesia PO Box 6311, 48826 • 7:30pm Sun

PUBLICATIONS

Lesbian Connection PO Box 811, E. Lansing, 48826 • 371-5257 • bi-monthly • free nationwide grassroots forum for all lesbians

Marquette (906)

BOOKSTORES & RETAIL SHOPS

Sweet Violets 413 N. 3rd St. • 228-3307 • 10am-6pm, clsd Sun • feminist bookstore • wheelchair access

Midland (517)

ACCOMMODATIONS

Jay's B&B 4429 Bay City Rd. • 496-2498 • lesbians/gay men • nudity • deck

Mount Clemens (810)

BARS

Mirage 27 N. Walnut • 954-1919 • 4pm-2am, from 2pm wknds • lesbians/gay men • dancing/DJ • live shows • wheelchair access

Muskegon (616)

SPIRITUAL GROUPS

Muskegon MCC PO Box 132, Spring Lake, 49443 • 861-5275 • 6pm Sun at Christ Community Church

New Buffalo (708)

WOMEN'S ACCOMMODATIONS

A Women's Place 17 W. Mechanic St. • 446-7638 • women only • swimming • food served • B&B • also retreat w/ workshops & seminars

Niles

INFO LINES & SERVICES

LSG PO Box 1281, 49120 • lesbian
social/support group • write to inquire
about newsletter & events

Owendale   (517)

WOMEN'S ACCOMMODATIONS

Windover Resort 3596 Blakely Rd. •
375-2586 • seasonal • women only •
campsites • swimming • $20

Pontiac   (810)

BARS

Club Flamingo 352 Oakland Ave. • 253-
0430 • 2pm-2am • lesbians/gay men •
dancing/DJ • wheelchair access

Port Huron   (810)

BARS

Seekers 3301 24th St. • 985-9349 •
4pm-2am, from 2pm Th-Sun •
lesbians/gay men • dancing/DJ • patio

Saginaw   (517)

BARS

Bambi's 1742 E. Genessee • 752-9179 •
7pm-2am • lesbians/gay men • danc-
ing/DJ • live shows • wheelchair access

Heidelberg 411 S. Franklin • 771-9508 •
4pm-2am, from noon wknds • mostly gay
men • neighborhood bar • wheelchair
access

Saugatuck   (616)

WOMEN'S ACCOMMODATIONS

Deerpath Lodge PO Box 849, 49453 •
857-3337 • women only • full breakfast •
on 45 secluded acres • near beach • $80-
90

Drift-Woods 2731 Lakeshore Dr.,
Fennville • 857-2586 • mostly women •
swimming • kitchens • year round retreat
w/ 1 & 2-bdrm cottages • $65

ACCOMMODATIONS

Alpen Haus B&B 41 Spring St. • 857-
1119 • gay-friendly • full breakfast • hot
tub

Camp It Rte. 6635 118th Ave. , Fennville
• 543-4335 • seasonal • lesbians/gay
men • campsites

Campit Campground 6635 118th Ave., Fennville • 543-4335 • 30 campsites & 45 RV hookups

Douglas Dunes 333 Blue Star Hwy. • 857-1401 • popular • mostly gay men • swimming • motel/down-style rooms • cottages • women's wknds: 1st wk in April & 1st wk in Oct • wheelchair access • IGTA member

Grandma's House B&B 2135 Blue Star Hwy. • 543-4706 • lesbians/gay men • full breakfast • secluded Victorian country estate on 4 wooded acres

▲ **Hillby Thatch Cottages** 1438 & 1440 71st, Glenn • (708) 864-3553 • gay-friendly • cottages • kitchens • fireplaces • 15 min. from Saugatuck • women-owned/run

Kirby House 294 W. Center • 857-2904 • lesbians/gay men • full breakfast • swimming • Queen Anne Victorian manor w/ antiques

▲ **Lighthouse Motel** 130th Ave. & Blue Star Hwy., Douglas • 857-2271 • seasonal • gay-friendly • swimming • wheelchair access

Moore's Creek Inn 820 Holland St. • 857-2411/ (800) 838-5864 • gay-friendly • full breakfast • old-fashioned farmhouse

Newnham SunCatcher Inn 131 Griffith • 857-4249 • gay-friendly • full breakfast • hot tub • swimming • women-owned/run

Volare Inn 6492 Blue Star Hwy. • 857-4269 • lesbians/gay men • cottages • hot tub • wheelchair access

BARS

Douglas Disco (at Douglas Dunes resort) • 857-1401 • mostly gay men • dancing/DJ • live shows • cabaret • 2 bars • patio

RESTAURANTS & CAFES

Cafe Sir Douglas (at Douglas Dunes resort) • 857-1401 • 5pm-10pm, til 11pm Fri-Sat, clsd Mon-Wed • lesbians/gay men • cont'l • some veggie • $10-20

Loaf & Mug 236 Culver St. • 857-2974 • 8am-4pm, til 8pm Fri-Sat • American • some veggie • patio • wheelchair access • $5-10

Pumpernickel's 202 Butler St. • 857-1196 • 8am-5pm, clsd Wed • sandwiches/fresh breads • some veggie • wheelchair access • $5-10

Restaurant Toulouse 248 Culver St. • 857-1561 • lunch & dinner • country French • some veggie • full bar • wheelchair access • $10-20

BOOKSTORES & RETAIL SHOPS

Hoopdee Scootee 133 Mason • 857-4141 • 10am-9pm, til 6pm Sun, til 5pm winter • clothing • gifts

St. Clair (810)

ACCOMMODATIONS

William Hopkins 613 N. Riverside Ave. • 329-0188 • gay-friendly • full breakfast

Traverse City (616)

INFO LINES & SERVICES

Friends North PO Box 562, 49685 • 946-1804 • general networking & social group • newsletter

ACCOMMODATIONS

Interlochen 2275 M-137, PO Box 194, Interlochen, 49643 • 276-9291 • gay-friendly • near skiing, beaches & arts center • coffee house 5pm-1am • wheelchair access

Neahtawanta Inn 1308 Neath • 223-7315 • gay-friendly • swimming • sauna

BARS

The Side Traxx Nite Club 520 Franklin • 935-1666 • 6pm-2am, from 2pm wknds • lesbians/gay men • dancing/DJ

BOOKSTORES & RETAIL SHOPS

Bookie Joint 120 S. Union St. • 946-8862 • 10am-6pm, clsd Sun • lesbigay section • used books • wheelchair access

Ypsilanti (313)

BARS

Flick's 1435 E. Michigan Ave. • 483-2840 • 6pm-2:30am • lesbians/gay men • dancing/DJ

SPIRITUAL GROUPS

Tree of Life MCC 218 N. Adams St. (1st Congregational Church) • 485-3922 • 6pm Sun

Minnesota

Bemidji (218)

ACCOMMODATIONS

Meadowgrove Inn 13661 Powerdam Rd. NE • 751-9654 • gay-friendly • full breakfast • rural hideaway on 130 acres of rolling meadows, woods & wetlands • lunch & dinner available

Dorset (218)

ACCOMMODATIONS

Heartland Trail B&B Rte 3 Box 39, Park Rapids, 56470 • 732-5305 • gay-friendly • full breakfast

Duluth (218)

INFO LINES & SERVICES

Aurora: A Northern Lesbian Center 8 N. 2nd Ave E. Ste. 210 • 722-4903 • discussion groups & socials • music festival every Sept • 'Northern Lights Women's Music' 2nd Sat after Labor Day Festival

ACCOMMODATIONS

Stanford Inn Bed & Breakfast 1415 E. Superior St. • 724-3044 • gay-friendly • full breakfast • romantic 1886 B&B located in one of Duluth's historical districts

BOOKSTORES & RETAIL SHOPS

At Sara's Table 728 E. Superior St. • 723-8569 • 8am-7pm • cafe • wheelchair access • women-owned/run

Ely (218)

TRAVEL & TOUR OPERATORS

The Northern Alternative 36 N. 2nd Ave. W. • 365-2894 • canoe outfitting & trips • also B&B available • mostly women • $35-40

Hastings (612)

ACCOMMODATIONS

Thorwood & Rosewood Inns 315 Pine St. • 437-3297 • gay-friendly • full breakfast • circa 1880 mansion w/ amenities

Hill City (218)

ACCOMMODATIONS

Northwoods Retreat 5749 Mt. Ash Dr. • 697-8119 • lesbians/gay men • 2 cabins on 40 acres with 700 ft. of lakeshore • al meals included • wheelchair access • women-owned/run

Hinckley (612)

ACCOMMODATIONS

Dakota Lodge B&B Rte. 3, Box 178, 55037 • 384-6052 • gay-friendly • full breakfast • hot tub • lodge with rustic exterior & gracious interior set on 9 beautiful acres

Kenyon (507)

WOMEN'S ACCOMMODATIONS

Dancing Winds Farm 6863 Country 12 Blvd. • 789-6606 • mostly women • full breakfast • B&B & working dairy farm • tentsites • work exchange • women-owned/run

Mankato (507)

INFO LINES & SERVICES

Mankato State University Gay Advisor 389-1455 • 8am-5pm Mon-Fri during school year

RESTAURANTS & CAFES

Coffee Hag 329 N. Riverfront • 387-5533 • 9am-11pm, 11am-6pm Sun, clsd Mon live shows • veggie menu • wheelchair access • women-owned/run • $3-7

Minneapolis/St. Paul (612)

INFO LINES & SERVICES

Chrysalis Women's Center 2650 Nicollet Ave. • 871-0118 • 8:30am-8pm Mon-Th, til 5pm Fri • houses many women's groups • wheelchair access

District 202 2524 Nicollet Ave. S. • 871-5559 • 3pm-11pm, 3pm-1am Fri, from noon Sat, clsd Sun & Tue • resource center for lesbigay youth

Dyke TV Channel 32, Minneapolis • 8:30pm Mon • 'weekly half hour TV show produced by lesbians, for lesbians'

Dyke TV Channel 33, St. Paul • 10pm Wed • 'weekly half hour TV show produced by lesbians, for lesbians'

Fresh Fruit KFAI 90.3 FM • 341-0980 • 7pm-8pm Th • gay radio program

Gay/Lesbian Community Action Council 310 E. 38th St. • 822-0127/ (800) 800-0350 • 9am-5pm Mon-Fri • support groups

Gay/Lesbian Helpline • 822-8661/ (800) 800-0907 (in-state) • noon-midnight, from 4pm Sat, clsd Sun & holidays • counseling • info & referrals • covers IA, MN, NE, ND, SD, WI

GLEAM (Gay/Lesbian Elders Active in MN) 1505 Park Ave. • 721-8913 • 1pm 2nd Sun

Green & Yellow TV Cable Channel 6 • 11pm Th • gay news hour

Lambda AA • 874-7430

Lesbian/Gay/Bi Group University of MN • 626-2344 • 4:30pm Wed

Quatrefoil Library 1619 Dayton Ave., St. Paul • 641-0969 • 7pm-9pm Mon-Th, 1pm-4pm wknds • lesbigay library & resource center

WomenWorks PO Box 300106, 55403 • 377-9114 • social & professional women's events

Womyn's Braille Press PO Box 8475, Minneapolis, 55408 • 872-4352 • quarterly newsletter • resource & info exchange

ACCOMMODATIONS

Abbotts Como Villa B&B 1371 W. Nebraska Ave., St. Paul • 647-0471 • gay-friendly • centrally located • full breakfast wknds • gay-owned/run

Eagle Cove B&B Box 65, Maiden Rock, 54750 • 448-4302/ (800) 967-0279 • lesbians/gay men • hot tub • wheelchair access

The Garden Gate B&B 925 Goodrich Ave., St. Paul • 227-8430/ (800) 967-2703 • gay-friendly • massage available • IGTA member

Hotel Amsterdam 828 Hennepin Ave., Minneapolis • 288-0459/ (800) 649-9500 • lesbians/gay men • European-style lodging • gay-owned/run

Nan's B&B 2304 Fremont Ave. S., Minneapolis • 377-5118/ (800) 214-5118 • gay-friendly • full breakfast • 1895 Victorian family home w/ guest rooms

Minneapolis (612)

LESBIGAY INFO: Chrysalis Women's Center: 871-0118/ 2603. Gay/Lesbian Helpline: noon-midnight Mon-Fri 822-8661/ (800)800-0907. Gay/Lesbian Community Action Council: 822-0127/ (800)800-0350.

LESBIGAY PAPER: Q Monthly: 321-7300.

LESBIGAY AA: Lambda AA: 874-7430.

LESBIGAY PRIDE: July, 339-8203.

ANNUAL EVENTS: August- National Gay Softball World Series: (412) 362-1247.

CITY INFO: Minneapolis Visitors' Association: 348-4313. St. Paul Visitors' Bureau: 297-6985

BEST VIEW: Observation deck of the 32nd story of Foshay Tower (closed in winter).

WEATHER: Winters are harsh. If driving, carry extra blankets and supplies. The average temperature is 19°, and it can easily drop well below 0°, and then there's the wind chill! Summer temperatures are usually in the upper 80°s to mid 90°s.

TRANSIT: Town Taxi - Minn : 331-8294. Yellow Cab - St. Paul: 222-4433.

BARS

19 Bar 19 W. 15th St., Minneapolis • 871-5553 • 3pm-1am, from 1pm wknds • mostly gay men • neighborhood bar • beer/wine • wheelchair access

Bryant Lake Bowl 1810 W. Lake Bowl, Minneapolis • 825-3737 • 8am-2am • gay-friendly • live shows • bar, theatre, restaurant & bowling alley • wheelchair access

Club Metro 733 Pierce Butler Rte., St. Paul • 489-0002 • 3pm-1am, from 2pm wknds • mostly women • dancing/DJ • live shows • food served • American • wheelchair access • women-owned/run • $5-15

Gay 90s 408 Hennepin Ave., Minneapolis • 333-7755 • 8am-1am (dinner nightly 5pm-9pm) • lesbians/gay men • dancing/DJ • live shows • food served • 5 bar complex • erotica store • wheelchair access

Innuendo 510 N. Robert St., St. Paul • 224-8996 • 4pm-1am, clsd Sun • lesbians/gay men • neighborhood bar • grill menu (Th-Sat) • wheelchair access • $3-6

Rogue 105 5th • 371-0706 • 4pm-3am, from 7pm Sun, clsd Mon • gay-friendly • dancing/DJ • alternative • live shows • theme nights • some veggie • Queer Night Sun • also bistro • $10-20

Rumours 490 N. Robert St. (at 9th), St. Paul • 224-0703 • popular • lesbians/gay men • dancing/DJ • also a restaurant • wheelchair access

Saloon 830 Hennepin Ave., Minneapolis • 332-0835 • 11am-1am, til 3am Fri-Sun • popular • mostly gay men • dancing/DJ • grill menu • patio • wheelchair access • $3-6

Town House 1415 University Ave., St. Paul • 646-7087 • 2pm-1am, from noon wknds • popular • mostly gay men • dancing/DJ • country/western

RESTAURANTS & CAFES

Bar X Espresso 1008 Marquette Ave., Minneapolis • 371-9882 • 6am-midnight, 7am-2am Sat • lesbians/gay men • smoke-free espresso bar • wheelchair access

Cafe Wyrd 1600 W. Lake St., Minneapolis • 827-5710 • 7am-1am • lesbians/gay men • plenty veggie • women-owned/run • $3-6

Minneapolis & St. Paul

*I*f you're searching for a liberal oasis in the heartland of America, if you love Siberian winters or crave a diverse, active lesbian community, you'll fit right into the 'Twin Cities' of Minneapolis & St. Paul.

For the latest on local dyke poetry readings, plays, or concerts your first stop is **Amazon Bookstore** in Minneapolis. To find social groups for women of color, call the **Gay/Lesbian Community Action Council**. Or stop by **Minnesota Women's Press** bookstore, library and newspaper in St. Paul. Then go cafe-hopping in Minneapolis at the women-owned **Cafe Wyrd** or **Ruby's Cafe**. For a night on the town, you won't find any women's bars, but **Club Metro** is popular on weekends. **Rogue** attracts the young alternative crowd.

Whatever you do, don't stay indoors the whole time. In the summer, boating, water-skiing and bicycling are popular. With winter, you can enjoy snowmobiling, skiing or snuggling by a fire. For women's outdoor adventures, try **Women in the Wilderness** in St. Paul or **Woodswomen** in Minneapolis.

La Covina 1570 Selby Ave., St. Paul • 645-5288 • Mexican • $6-10

Ruby's Cafe 1614 Harmon Pl., Minneapolis • 338-2089 • 7am-2pm • popular • American • outdoor seating • women-owned/run • $5

Susan's Coffeehouse & Deli 2399 University Ave. • 644-7906 • 7am-7pm, 9am-5pm Sat, clsd Sun

GYMS & HEALTH CLUBS

Body Quest 245 N. Aldrich Ave. N., Minneapolis • 377-7222 • gay-friendly

BOOKSTORES & RETAIL SHOPS

A Brother's Touch 2327 Hennepin Ave., Minneapolis • 377-6279 • 11am-9pm, til 5pm wknds, til 7pm Mon-Tue • lesbigay bookstore • wheelchair access

▲ Amazon Bookstore 1612 Harmon Pl., Minneapolis • 338-6560 • 10am-9pm, til 7pm Fri, 6pm Sat, 5pm Sun • women's bookstore • wheelchair access • women-owned/run

Borders Bookshop 3001 Hennepin S. (Calhoun Square), Minneapolis • 825-0336 • general • wheelchair access

TRAVEL & TOUR OPERATORS

Partners In Travel, Ltd 825 On The Mall, Minneapolis • 338-0004/ (800) 333-3177 • IGTA member

Time Out Travel 1515 W. Lake St., Minneapolis • 823-7244/ (800) 373-7244 • women-owned/run

Travel Company 2800 University Ave. SE, Minneapolis • 379-9000/ (800) 328-9131 • IGTA member

Women in the Wilderness 566 Ottawa Ave., St. Paul • 227-2284 • outdoor adventure trips: canoeing, rafting, dogsledding, skiing etc. • women-owned/run

Woodswomen 25 W. Diamond Lake Rd. , Minneapolis • 822-3801/ (800) 279-0555 • outdoor adventures • one day to 3 wks • domestic & international • women-owned/run

SPIRITUAL GROUPS

Dignity Twin Cities Prospect Park Unitarian Methodist (Malcom & Orwin), Minneapolis • 827-3103 • 7:30pm 2nd & 4th Fri

Episcopal Outreach to Gay/Lesbian Community 5349 Park Ave. S. , Minneapolis • 822-6846

Lutherans Concerned 100 N. Oxford, Minneapolis • 224-3371 • 7:30pm Fri

MCC - All Gods Children 3100 Park Ave., Minneapolis • 824-2673 • 10:30am & 7pm Sun, 7pm Wed

Shir Tikvah, Minneapolis • 822-1440 • lesbigay Jews

PUBLICATIONS

Lavender Lifestyles 2344 Nicollet Ave. Ste. 50, Minneapolis • 871-5971

Maize PO Box 8742, Minneapolis, 55408 • lesbian country magazine

Matrices Women Studies Dept. U of MN, Minneapolis, 55455 • newsletter • also lesbian feminist resource network

Minnesota Women's Press 771 Raymond Ave., St. Paul • 646-3968 • bi-weekly • newspaper for women • also bookshop & library

Q Monthly 10 S. 5th St. #200 • 321-7300

Two Eagles PO Box 10229, Minneapolis, 55458 • newsletter for Native American lesbian/gays

Woodswomen News 25 W. Diamond Lake Rd., Minneapolis, 55419 • (800) 279-0555

EROTICA

Broadway Bookstore 901 Hennepin Ave., Minneapolis • 338-7303 • 24hrs

Rochester (507)

INFO LINES & SERVICES

Gay/Lesbian Community Service PO Box 454, 55903 • 281-3265 • 5pm-7pm Mon & Wed

Rushford (507)

ACCOMMODATIONS

Windswept Inn 207 N. Mill St. • 864-2545 • gay-friendly • wheelchair access

St. Peter (507)

ACCOMMODATIONS

Park Row B&B 525 W. Park Row • 931-2495 • gay-friendly • full breakfast

Two Harbors (218)

ACCOMMODATIONS

Star Harbor Resort 1098 Hwy. 61 E. • 834-3796 • gay-friendly • log cabins on N. Shore of Lake Superior • ask for wheelchair ramps

Wolverton (218)

RESTAURANTS & CAFES

District 31 Victoria's • 995-2000 • 5:30pm-9:30pm, clsd Sun • beer/wine • cont'l • reservations required • $15-25

Mississippi

Biloxi (601)

INFO LINES & SERVICES

Gay/Lesbian Community Center 308 Caillavet St. • 435-2398 • 1am-9pm, from 5pm Sun-Wed

BARS

Joey's 1708 Beach Blvd. (Hwy. 90) • 435-5639 • 9pm-2am, til 5am Fri-Sat, clsd Mon • lesbians/gay men • dancing/DJ • live shows • wheelchair access

Gulfport (601)

BARS

Mongoose 18272 28th St. • 868-1212 • 7pm-1am, from 11am Sun • mostly women • neighborhood bar • patio

Hattiesburg (601)

BARS

Courtyard 107 E. Front St. • 545-2714 • 11am-2pm, from 8pm Wed-Sat • lesbians/gay men • dancing/DJ • live shows • patio

Holly Springs (601)

ACCOMMODATIONS

Somerset Cottage 310 S. Cedar Hills Rd. • 252-4513 • gay-friendly • cottages

Jackson (601)

INFO LINES & SERVICES

Gay/Lesbian Community Switchboard PO Box 7737, 39284 • 373-8610 • 6pm-11pm • switchboard for many organizations • monthly publication

Lambda AA 4872 N. State St. (Unitarian Church) • 373-8610 • 6:30pm Mon & Wed, 8pm Th & Sat

BARS

Club Colours 200 N. Mill St. • 353-2041 • 10pm-? Wed, Fri-Sun • lesbians/gay men • dancing/DJ • mostly African-American • beer/wine • BYOB

Jack's Construction Site (JC's) 425 N. Mart Plaza • 362-3108 • 5pm-?, from 2pm Sun • mostly gay men • neighborhood bar • BYOB • more women Wed & Fri

Jaded 2460 Terry Rd (Jackson Sq. Shopping Ctr.) • 371-0478 • 5pm-2am, from 8pm wknds, clsd Mon-Tue • lesbians/gay men • dancing/DJ • live shows • beer/wine • BYOB • DJ Wed, Fri-Sat • wheelchair access

Sugarbakers 208 W. Capitol (back entrance) • 352-0022 • 10pm-1am, clsd Mon-Tue & Th • lesbians/gay men • dancing/DJ • BYOB

SPIRITUAL GROUPS

Integrity Mississippi PO Box 68314, 39286 • 853-4362

MCC Jackson 964 Horning • 366-1815 • 7pm Sun

St. Stephen's United Community Church 4872 N. State St. • 939-7181 • 5pm Sun

PUBLICATIONS

Mississippi Voice PO Box 7737, 39284 • 373-8610

Meridian (601)

BARS

Crossroads Rte. 1, Box 170, Enterprise, 39330 • 655-8415 • 9pm-? Fri-Sat • gay-friendly • dancing/DJ • live shows • call for directions • cabins available • wheelchair access

Olie Mae's at Crossroads • 655-8415 • 6pm-1am • gay-friendly

Ovett (601)

WOMEN'S ACCOMMODATIONS

Camp Sister Spirit PO Box 12, 39462 • 344-2005 • women only

Starkville (601)

INFO LINES & SERVICES

Lesbigay Student Group PO Box 6220, MS State University, 39406 • 325-1321

Missouri

Cape Girardeau (314)

BARS

Independence Place 5 S. Henderson St. • 334-2939 • 9pm-1am, from 7pm Fri-Sat, clsd Sun • lesbians/gay men • dancing/DJ • live shows Sat

Columbia (314)

INFO LINES & SERVICES

Gay/Lesbian Helpline • 449-4477 • 7pm-11pm Wed, Fri-Sun

Triangle Coalition A022 Brady Commons UMC, 65211 • 882-4427 • meets 7pm Th

Women's Center 229 Brady Commons UMC • 882-6621 • 8:30am-5pm, clsd wknds • social/support group • info • referrals • wheelchair access

World Women KOPN 89.50 FM • 874-5676 • 10am-noon Tue

BARS

Contacts 514 E. Broadway • 443-0281 • 5pm-1:30am, from 8pm Sat, clsd Sun • lesbians/gay men • neighborhood bar • live shows

Styx Inc. 3111 Old 63 South • 499-1828 • 3pm-1:30am, clsd Sun • lesbians/gay men • dancing/DJ • country/western Tue • patio

RESTAURANTS & CAFES

Ernie's Cafe 1005 E. Walnut • 874-7804 • 6am-8pm • American • some veggie • breakfast anytime

SPIRITUAL GROUPS

United Covenant Church PO Box 7152, 65205 • 449-7194 • 10am Sun • non-denominational

EROTICA

Eclectics 1122-A Wilkes Blvd. • 443-0873

Jefferson City (314)

ACCOMMODATIONS

Jefferson Victorian B&B 801 W. High St. • 635-7196 • gay-friendly

Joplin (417)

BARS

Partners 720 Main St. • 781-6453 • 3pm-1:30am, clsd Sun • lesbians/gay men • neighborhood bar • dancing/DJ • country/western • 2 bars

Kansas City (816)

INFO LINES & SERVICES

Gay Talk Crisis Line • 931-4470 • 6pm-midnight

Live & Let Live AA 4243 Walnut St. • 531-9668 • many mtgs

Unicorn Theatre 3820 Main • 531-3033 contemporary American theater

ACCOMMODATIONS

B&B in KC 9215 Slater, Overland Park • (913) 648-5457 • mostly women

Doanleigh Wallagh Inn 217 E. 37th St. • 753-2667 • gay-friendly • full breakfast

Inn the Park 3610 Gillham Rd. • 931-0797 • gay-friendly • full breakfast • swimming • German Victorian home overlooking Hyde Park

BARS

Dixie Bell Saloon 1922 Main St. • 471-2424 • 11am-3am • popular • mostly gay men • dancing/DJ • cafe • also leather shop • patio • wheelchair access

Edge 323 W. 8th (in the Lucas Bldg.) • 221-8900 • 8pm-3am, clsd Sun • lesbians/gay men • dancing/DJ • alternative • live shows

Fox 7520 Shawnee Mission Pkwy., Overland Park • (913) 384-0369 • noon-2am, from 6pm wknds • gay-friendly • neighborhood bar • more gay in evening

Jamie's 528 Walnut • 471-2080 • 10am-3am • mostly women • neighborhood bar • grill food • wheelchair access

Mari's Saloon & Grill 1809 Grand Blvd. 283-0511 • 5pm-11:30am, from 11am Sun • lesbians/gay men • American • plenty veggie • wheelchair access • $5-12

Other Side 3611 Broadway • 931-0501 • 4pm-1:30am, clsd Sun • mostly gay men • neighborhood bar

Sidekicks 3707 Main St. • 931-1430 • 2pm-3am, clsd Sun • mostly gay men • dancing/DJ • country/western

Ted's Bar & Grill 529 Walnut • 472-0569 • 8am-1:30am, 11am-midnight Sun • gay-friendly • neighborhood bar • country/western • lunch daily

Tools 518 E. 31st St. • 753-0263 • 6am-1:30am • mostly gay men • neighborhood bar

Tootsie's 3601 Broadway • 756-3585 • 11:30am-1am • popular • mostly women • dancing/DJ • grill food • some veggie • wheelchair access • $3-6

View on the Hill 204 Orchard, Kansas City, KS • (913) 371-9370 • 4pm-2am, from noon wknds • mostly gay men • neighborhood bar

Whistle Stop 1321 Grand Blvd. • 221-8008 • 11:30am-1:30am, from 5pm Mon, from 3pm Sat, clsd Sun • mostly women • dancing/DJ • wheelchair access

Restaurants & Cafes

City Seen 1111 Main St. • 472-8833 • 11am-8pm, til 10pm Fri-Sat • New American • some veggie • full bar • wheelchair access • $9-13

Classic Cup 301 W. 47th St. • 753-1840 • 7am-10pm • cont'l • some veggie • full bar • wheelchair access • $9-17

Corner Restaurant 4059 Broadway • 931-6630 • 7am-9pm, til 2am wknds • beer/wine • American • some veggie • wheelchair access • $5-7

Metropolis 303 Westport Rd. • 753-1550 • clsd Sun • New American • some veggie • full bar • lunch & dinner • wheelchair access • $9-17

Bookstores & Retail Shops

Larry's Gifts & Cards 205 Westport Rd. • 753-4757 • 10am-7pm, til 5pm Sun • lesbigay books

Travel & Tour Operators

Cruzin' 7948 Wornall Rd. Ste. 1203 • 363-2787 • IGTA member

Spiritual Groups

MCC Kansas City 3801 Wyandotte • 931-0750 • 9am & 11:15am Sun, 7:15pm Wed

MCC of Johnson County 12510 W. 62nd Terrace #106, Shawnee, KS 66216 • (913) 631-1184 • 10:30am Sun & 7:30pm Wed

Publications

Current News 809 W. 39th St. Ste. 1 • 561-2679 • weekly

Springfield (417)

Info Lines & Services

AA Gay/Lesbian SWM University (National off Cherry) • 862-9264 • 6pm Sat

Bars

Club 1105 1105 E. Commercial • 869-5451 • 9pm-1:30am, clsd Sun • popular • lesbians/gay men • dancing/DJ • country/western

Coliseum 2100 E. Pythain St. • 869-5451 • 4pm-1:30am • lesbians/gay men • dancing/DJ • patio • wheelchair access

Martha's Vineyard 219 W. Olive St. • 864-4572 • 4pm-1:30am, from 2pm Sat, clsd Sun • lesbians/gay men • neighborhood bar • patio

Peanut Gallery 424 N. Boonville • 865-1266 • 2pm-1:30am, clsd Sun • lesbians/gay men

Restaurants & Cafes

Black Forest Inn 2185 S. Campbell • 882-6767 • 3pm-11pm, clsd Sun • lesbians/gay men • live shows • American • full bar • wheelchair access • $5-16

Derby Fox 620 W. College • 865-4500 • American • some veggie • full bar • wheelchair access • $5-12

Bookstores & Retail Shops

Renaissance Books & Gifts 1337 E. Montclair • 883-5161 • 9am-7pm, noon-5pm Sun • women's/progressive • wheelchair access

St. Joseph (816)

Bars

Avis' Lounge 705 Esmond St. • 364-9748 • 4pm-1:30am, clsd Sun • lesbians/gay men • dancing/DJ • wheelchair access

St. Louis (314)

Info Lines & Services

Gay/Lesbian Hotline PO Box 23227, 63156 • 367-0084 • 6pm-10pm

Lambda Reports KRJY FM 96.3 • 781-9600 • 6am-6:30am Sun

St. Louis Gender Foundation • 997-9897 • cross gender info

Steps Alano Club 1935-A Park Ave. • 436-1858 • call for schedule

WOMEN'S ACCOMMODATIONS

River Spirit Retreat B&B 187 W. 19th St., Alton, IL 62002 • 569-5795/ (618) 462-4051 • women's reservation service

ACCOMMODATIONS

Brewers House 1829 Lami St. • 771-1542 • lesbians/gay men • Civil War vintage B&B in South St. Louis

Napoleon's Retreat B&B 1815 Lafayette Ave. • 772-6979 • lesbians/gay men • full breakfast • restored 1880s townhouse

St. Louis Guesthouse 1032-38 Allen Ave. • 773-1016 • lesbians/gay men • located in the historic Soulard district

BARS

Alton Metro 602 Belle St., Alton • (618) 465-8687 • 2pm-1am • mostly gay men • dancing/DJ • live shows

Attitudes 4100 Manchester • 534-3858 • 6pm-3am, clsd Sun-Mon • popular • mostly women • dancing/DJ • wheelchair access

Buster's 1449 Vandeventer • 535-1755 • 11am-1:30am • mostly gay men • live shows

Char Pei Lounge 400 Mascoutah Ave. , Bellville • (618) 236-0810 • 6pm-2am, from noon Sun • lesbians/gay men • dancing/DJ • wheelchair access

Clementine's 2001 Menard • 664-7869 • 10am-1:30am, clsd Sun • popular • mostly gay men • leather • also a restaurant • American • dinners & wknd brunch • $4-10

The Complex 3511 Chouteau Ave. • 772-2645 • 11am-3am, from 3pm Mon • mostly gay men • dancing/DJ • live shows • multiple bars • also a restaurant • American • some veggie • $3-15 • patio • wheelchair access

Drake Bar 3502 Papin St. • 865-1400 • 5pm-1:30am, clsd Sun • lesbians/gay men • live shows • patio • wheelchair access

Ernie's Class Act Restaurant & Lounge 3756 S. Broadway • 664-6221 • 3pm-1:30am, from 11am Fri-Sat, clsd Sun • mostly women • dancing/DJ • American • $5-7

Faces Complex 130 4th, E. St. Louis • (618) 271-7410 • 9pm-6am Wed-Sun • mostly gay men • dancing/DJ • live shows • 3 flrs. • beer garden

St. Louis

*M*ost visitors come to see the famous Gateway Arch, the US' tallest monument at 630ft, designed by architect Eero Saarinen. After you've ridden the elevators in the Arch and seen the view, come down to earth and take a trip to the historic Soulard, the "French Quarter of St. Louis." Established in 1779 by Madame and Monsieur Soulard as an open air market, today you'll find great food and jazz here.

Laclede's Landing is also a popular attraction. While you're down by the Gateway Arch, treat yourself to riverfront dining aboard any of the several riverboat restaurants on the Mississippi. For accommodations, try **River Spirit Reservation Service**, a women's B&B reservations service in nearby Alton, Illinois. Dining and shopping is most fun on Euclid St. between Delmar and Forest Park Blvds.

St. Louis has two lesbian/gay bookstores – **Left Bank Books** and **Our World Too** – and two women's bars: dance bar **Attitudes** and lounge bar **Ernie's Class Act**.

Fallout 1224 Washington Ave. • 421-0003 • popular • lesbians/gay men • dancing/DJ • alternative • 18+ • call for events

Gabriel's Club 6901 S. Broadway • 832-0656 • noon-1:30am • lesbians/gay men • live shows

Loading Zone 16 S. Euclid • 361-4119 • 2pm-1:30am, clsd Sun • popular • lesbians/gay men • videos

Magnolia's 5 S. Vandeventer • 652-6500 • 5pm-3am • popular • mostly gay men • live shows • American • some veggie • dinner nightly • wheelchair access • $7-11

Merlie's Bar 2917 S. Jefferson • 664-1066 • 6am-1:30am, clsd Sun • lesbians/gay men • country/western • wheelchair access

RESTAURANTS & CAFES

Cafe Balaban's 405 N. Euclid Ave. • 361-8085 • popular • fine dining • some veggie • full bar • $10-16

Duff's 392 N. Euclid Ave. • 361-0522 • clsd Mon • American • some veggie • full bar • wheelchair access • $12-16

Majestic Bar & Restaurant 4900 Laclede • 361-2011 • 6am-1am • diner fare • $4-7

On Broadway Bistro 5300 N. Broadway • 421-0087 • 11am-3am • American • full bar • wheelchair access • $4-12

Redel's 310 Debaliviere • 367-7005 • American • some veggie • full bar • wheelchair access • $4-16

Sunshine Inn 8-1/2 S. Euclid Ave. • 367-1413 • clsd Mon • vegetarian • plenty veggie • $5-8

West End Cafe 2 N. Euclid Ave. • 361-2020 • lunch & dinner • American • $6-8

BOOKSTORES & RETAIL SHOPS

Cheap Trx 3211 S. Grand • 664-4011 • noon-8pm, clsd Mon • body piercing • cards • gifts

Daily Planet News 243 N. Euclid Ave. • 367-1333 • 7am-8pm

Friends & Luvers 3550 Gravois • 771-9405 • 10am-10pm, noon-7pm Sun • novelties

St. Louis (314)

LESBIGAY INFO: Gay/Lesbian Hotline: 367-0084, 6pm-10pm, clsd Sun.

LESBIGAY PAPER: News-Telegraph: 664-6411.

WHERE THE GIRLS ARE: Spread out, but somewhat concentrated in the Central West End near Forest Park. Younger, funkier crowds hang out in the Delmar Loop, west of the city limits, packed with ethnic restaurants.

LESBIGAY AA: 436-1858, 1935-A Park Ave., Lafayette Square.

LESBIGAY PRIDE: October, 772-8888/533-5322.

CITY INFO: 421-1023.

BEST VIEW: Where else? Top of the Gateway Arch in the Observation Room.

WEATHER: 100% midwestern. Cold winters with little snow where temperatures can drop into the teens; hot summers that can go up into the 100°s. Spring and fall bring out the best in Mother Nature.

TRANSIT: County Cab: 991-5300.

Left Bank Books 399 N. Euclid Ave. •
367-6731 • 10am-10pm, til 5pm Sun •
lesbian, feminist & gay titles

Our World Too 11 S. Vanderventer • 533-
5322 • 10am-9:30pm, noon-8pm Sun •
lesbigay bookstore

Pages, Video & More 10 N. Euclid Ave.
• 361-3420 • 9am-9pm, til 5pm Sun

TRAVEL & TOUR OPERATORS

Dynamic Travel 7750 Clayton Rd.
Ste.105 • 781-8400/ (800) 237-4083 •
IGTA member

Lafayette Square Travel Co. 1801
Lafayette Ave. • 776-8747/ (800) 727-1480
• IGTA member

Patrik Travel 22 N. Euclid Ave. Ste. 101 •
367-1468/ (800) 678-8747 • IGTA member

SPIRITUAL GROUPS

Agape Church 2026 Lafayette • 664-3588
• 10:45am Sun

Dignity St. Louis 6400 Minnesota Ave. •
863-6002 • 7:30pm Sun

MCC 1120 Dolman • 231-9100 • 8:30am,
11am & 6pm Sun

PUBLICATIONS

Lesbian/Gay News Telegraph PO Box
14229-A, 63108 • 664-6411 • monthly

TWISL (This Week In St. Louis) PO Box
8068, Alton, IL 62002 • (618) 465-9370

Montana

Billings (406)

INFO LINES & SERVICES

AA Gay/Lesbian (at MCC location) • 245-7066

RESTAURANTS & CAFES

Stella's Kitchen & Bakery 110 N. 29th St. • 248-3060 • 6am-4pm, clsd Sun • some veggie • wheelchair access

BOOKSTORES & RETAIL SHOPS

Barjon's 2718 3rd Ave. N. • 252-4398 • 9:30am-5:30pm, clsd Sun • alternative • wheelchair access • women-owned/run

SPIRITUAL GROUPS

MCC Family of God 645 Howard St. • 245-7066 • 11am Sun & 7pm Wed • also 'Gospel Sing' 7pm 4th Sat

Boulder (406)

ACCOMMODATIONS

Boulder Hot Springs Hotel & Retreat PO Box 930, 59632 • 225-4339 • popular • gay-friendly • food served • spirituality/recovery retreat • hot springs • camping available • irregular hours • call for more info • wheelchair access

Bozeman (406)

INFO LINES & SERVICES

Lambda Alliance of Gay Men/Lesbians PO Box 51, Strand Union Bldg., MSU, 59717 • 994-4551 • local & campus social/political group

Women's Center Hamilton Hall, MSU • 994-3836 • some lesbian referrals

ACCOMMODATIONS

Gallatin Gateway Inn 76405 Gallatin Rd. • 763-4672/ (800) 676-3522 • gay-friendly • hot tub • swimming • historic inn • dinner nightly • Sun brunch • wheelchair access

RESTAURANTS & CAFES

Spanish Peaks Brewery 120 N. 19th St. • 585-2296 • 11am-2am • Italian • some veggie • patio • wheelchair access • $8-15

Butte (406)

BARS

M&M Bar & Cafe 9 N. Main St. • 723-7612 • 24hrs, bar til 2am • gay-friendly • American • some veggie • wheelchair access • $4-7

RESTAURANTS & CAFES

Matt's Place Montana & Rowe Rds. • 782-8049 • noon-7pm, clsd Sun-Mon • classic soda fountain diner

Pekin Noodle Parlor 117 S. Main, 2nd flr. • 782-2217 • 5pm-9pm, clsd Tue • Chinese • some veggie • $3-7

Pork Chop John's 8 W. Mercury • 782-0812 • 11am-10pm, clsd Sun • American • $3-5

Uptown Cafe 47 E. Broadway • 723-4735 • lunch & dinner, clsd Sun • beer/wine • bistro • wheelchair access • $15-20

Corwin Springs (406)

RESTAURANTS & CAFES

Ranch Kitchen Hwy. 89 • 848-7891 • seasonal • American • some veggie • wheelchair access • $3-15

Great Falls (406)

SPIRITUAL GROUPS

MCC Shepherd of the Plains 1505 17th Ave. SW • 771-1070 • 11am Sun, 7pm Wed

EROTICA

Studio 209 209 4th St. S. • 771-7266

Helena

TRAVEL & TOUR OPERATORS

Travel Montana Dept. of Commerce • (800) 541-1447

Missoula (416)

INFO LINES & SERVICES

AA Gay/Lesbian KC Hall 312 E. Pine • 523-7799 • 9:30pm Wed

Lambda Alliance (U of MT) PO Box 7611, 59807

Women's Resource Center Campus Dr. University Ctr. #119 • 243-4153/ 243-4198 • 2pm-5pm Mon, Wed-Fri (clsd summers)

Bars

Amvets Club 225 Ryman • 728-3137 • noon-2am, more gay after 8pm • gay-friendly • dancing/DJ

Restaurants & Cafes

Black Dog Cafe 138 W. Broadway • 542-1138 • lunch & dinner, dinner only Sat, clsd Sun • BYOB • vegetarian • wheelchair access

Heidelhaus/Red Baron Casino 2620 Brooks • 543-3200 • 6am-midnight, casino 24hrs • full bar

Bookstores & Retail Shops

Freddy's Feed & Read 1221 Helen Ave. • 549-2127 • 8am-8pm, til 7pm Sun • alternative books & deli

Second Thought 529 S. Higgins • 549-2790 • 6:30am-10pm • bookstore • also cafe & bakery • wheelchair access

University Center Bookstore Campus Drive (U of MT) • 243-4921 • 8am-6pm, from 10am Sat, clsd Sun • gender studies section • wheelchair access

Erotica

Fantasy for Adults Only 210 E. Main St. • 543-7760 • also 2611 Brooks Ave. • 543-7510

Ovando (406)

Accommodations

Lake Upsata Guest Ranch PO Box 6, 59854 • 793-5890 • gay-friendly • cabins • wildlife programs & outings • outdoor recreation • all meals

Ronan (406)

Accommodations

North Crow Vacation Ranch 2360 N. Crow Rd., Missoula, 59864 • 676-5169 • May 15-Oct 15 • lesbians/gay men • hot tub • nudity • 35-acre campground w/ cabins • tipis • 80 mi. S. of Glacier Park • women-owned/run

Your ADMIT ONE to the latest Lesbian Travel Info:

http://www.damron.com/

Any questions? WT@damron.com

Nebraska

Lincoln (402)

INFO LINES & SERVICES

AA Gay/Lesbian 63rd & A (Unitarian Church) • 438-5214 • 7:30pm Th

Crisis Center • 476-2110

INFORMATION (Information for Older Gay People) PO Box 22043, 68542-2043 • support groups for lesbians over 40

UNL Gay & Lesbian Student Assn. Nebraska Student Union Rm. 234 • 472-5644 • noon-6pm • support groups • info & referrals • library

Wimmin's Radio Show KZUM 89.3 FM • 474-5086 • 12:30pm-3pm Sun

Women's Resource Center Nebraska Union Rm. 340, UNL • 472-2597 • inquire for lesbian support services

Youth Talkline • 473-7932 • 7pm-midnight Fri-Sat • lesbigay info & referrals for age 23 & under

BARS

Panic 200 S. 18th St. • 435-8764 • 4pm-1am, from 1pm wknds • lesbians/gay men • neighborhood bar • live shows • videos • wheelchair access

The Q 226 N. 9th • 475-2269 • 8pm-1am, from 5pm Fri, clsd Mon-Tue • lesbians/gay men • dancing/DJ • women's night Wed

BOOKSTORES & RETAIL SHOPS

Avant Card 1323 'O' St. • 476-1918 • 10am-7pm

Under the Rainbow 1231 'F' St. • 477-5644 • noon-7pm, clsd Mon-Tue • lesbigay

TRAVEL & TOUR OPERATORS

Nebraska Travel & Tourism PO Box 94666, 68509 • (800) 228-4307

Omaha (402)

INFO LINES & SERVICES

AA Gay/Lesbian 819 S. 22nd (Omaha MCC) • 345-9916/ 345-2563 (MCC#)

Gay/Lesbian Information & Referral Line • 558-5303

OPC (Omaha Players Club) PO Box 34463, 68134 • 451-7987 • S/M education & play group • pansexual mtgs. 2nd Sat 2pm

BARS

Chesterfield 1901 Leavenworth St. • 345-6889 • 3pm-1am • mostly women • dancing/DJ • wheelchair access • women-owned/run

D.C.'s 610 S. 14th St. • 344-3103 • 3pm-1am, 11am-4am Sat • mostly gay men • neighborhood bar • country/western • leather • live shows • wheelchair access

Diamond Bar 712 S. 16th St. • 342-9595 • 9am-1am, from noon Sun • mostly gay men • neighborhood bar • wheelchair access

Gilligan's Bar 1823 Leavenworth St. • 449-9147 • 2pm-1am • lesbians/gay men • neighborhood bar • karaoke

Infield 1401 Jackson • 346-3030 • 4pm-1am • lesbians/gay men • neighborhood bar • women-owned/run

Max 1417 Jackson • 346-4110 • 4pm-1am • popular • lesbians/gay men • dancing/DJ • live shows • 4 bars • also Stosha's Saloon • mostly gay men • country/western • patio • wheelchair access

New Run 1715 Leavenworth St. • 449-8703 • 2pm-1am, til 4am Fri-Sat • mostly gay men • dancing/DJ • volleyball court • wheelchair access

RESTAURANTS & CAFES

French Cafe 1017 Howard St. • 341-3547 • lunch & dinner, brunch Sun • cont'l • $11-22

Neon Goose Cafe/Bar 1012 S. 10th • 341-2063 • lunch & dinner, clsd Mon • cont'l • some veggie • wheelchair access • $7-14

Old Market South Cafe 1017 S. 10th • 344-4221 • 11am-2pm, 6pm-2am • popular • lesbians/gay men • full bar

BOOKSTORES & RETAIL SHOPS

New Realities 1026 Howard St. • 342-1863 • 11am-10pm, til 6pm Sun • progressive • wheelchair access • women-owned/run

TRAVEL & TOUR OPERATORS

Regency Travel 10730 Pacific St. • 393-0585/ (800) 393-5482

PUBLICATIONS

New Voice PO Box 3512, 68103 • 556-9907 • monthly

Nevada

Lake Tahoe   (702)

(see also Lake Tahoe, CA)

ACCOMMODATIONS

Haus Bavaria PO Box 3308, Incline Village, 89450 • 831-6122/ (800) 731-6222 • gay-friendly • full breakfast • European-style B&B • offering views of surrounding mountains

Lakeside B&B Box 1756, Crystal Bay, 89402 • 831-8281 • mostly gay men • full breakfast • hot tub • sauna • views • near the best in skiing & gambling

Las Vegas   (702)

INFO LINES & SERVICES

Gay/Lesbian Community Ctr. 912 E. Sahara Ln. • 733-9800 • 1pm-8pm, til 5pm wknds

Lambda Alamo 953 E. Sahara Ste. 233 (entrance on State St.) • 737-0035 • 12:15pm & 8pm • lesbigay club for 12-step recovery programs

ACCOMMODATIONS

Las Vegas Private B&B • 384-1129 • mostly gay men

Secret Garden B&B 3670 Happy Ln. • 451-3231 • lesbians/gay men • full breakfast • swimming • nudity

BARS

Angles 4633 Paradise Rd. • 791-0100 • 24hrs • mostly gay men • neighborhood bar

Backdoor 1415 E. Charleston • 385-2018 • 24hrs • mostly gay men • neighborhood bar • karaoke Sat • wheelchair access

Backstreet 5012 S. Arville St., Mosco Park • 876-1844 • 24hrs, DJ 9pm-3am • lesbians/gay men • dancing/DJ • country/western • slots • cloggin' Wed • lessons Th • wheelchair access

Choices 1729 E. Charleston • 382-4791 • 24hrs • mostly gay men • neighborhood bar • live shows • slots • wheelchair access

Faces 701 E. Stewart • 386-7971 • 24hrs • mostly gay men • wheelchair access

Gipsy 4605 Paradise Rd. • 731-1919 • mostly gay men • dancing/DJ • call for women's nights

Goodtimes 1775 E. Tropicana (Liberace Plaza) • 736-9494 • 24hrs • mostly gay men • neighborhood bar • piano bar

Lace 4633 Paradise Rd. (enter behind Angles) • 791-1947 • 6pm-2am, til 5am Fri-Sun • popular • mostly women • dancing/DJ

The Las Vegas Eagle 3430 E. Tropicana • 458-8662 • 24hrs • mostly gay men • leather • slots • DJ Wed & Fri

RESTAURANTS & CAFES

Coyote Cafe (at MGM Grand) • 891-7349 • 9am-11pm • southwestern • plenty veggie • full bar • the original Santa Fe chef • wheelchair access • $8-13

Vicious Rumours 6370 Windy St. • 896-1993 • 5pm-midnight • lesbians/gay men • live shows • wheelchair access

BOOKSTORES & RETAIL SHOPS

Get Booked 4643 Paradise • 737-7780 • 10am-midnight, from noon Sun • lesbigay/feminist bookstore

Paper Moon 2841 Green Valley Pkwy., Green Valley • 454-1492 • 10am-7pm, clsd Sun • cards • gifts

TRAVEL & TOUR OPERATORS

A to Z Bargain Travel 3133 S. Industrial Rd. • 369-8671 • IGTA member

Cruise One 5030 Paradise Dr. Ste. B-101 • 256-8082 • IGTA member

Good Times Travel 624 N. Rainbow • 878-8900/ (800) 638-1066 • IGTA member

SPIRITUAL GROUPS

Dignity 2000 S. Maryland Pkwy. (side chapel) • 369-8127x344 • 6pm Sat

PUBLICATIONS

Las Vegas Bugle/Bugle Nightbeat PO Box 14580, 89114 • 369-6260 • monthly • news & classifieds

Reno   (702)

BARS

1099 Club 1099 S. Virginia • 329-1099 • 24hrs • popular • lesbians/gay men • neighborhood bar • live shows • slots • patio

Alley Club 100 N. Sierra (alley btwn. Virginia & Sierra) • 333-2808 • 24hrs • mostly gay men • wheelchair access

Bad Dolly's 535 E. 4th • 348-1983 • 3pm-3am, 24hrs Fri-Sun • mostly women • dancing/DJ

Bar West 210 Commercial Row • 786-0878 • 4pm-4am • mostly gay men • neighborhood bar • live shows

Five Star Saloon 132 West St. • 329-2878 • 24hrs • popular • mostly gay men • neighborhood bar • dancing/DJ • food served • slots

Shouts 145 Hillcrest St. • 829-7667 • 11am-3am • gay-friendly • neighborhood bar • wheelchair access

Visions Bar 340 Kietzke Ln. • 786-5455 • noon-4am, 24hrs Fri-Sun • popular • dancing/DJ • theme nights • also Glitter Palace gift shop wknds • patio

RESTAURANTS & CAFES

Cafe 47 1300 S. Virginia • 329-6969 • 24hrs wknds, 7am-3pm Mon-Th • diner

BOOKSTORES & RETAIL SHOPS

Grapevine Books 1450 S. Wells Ave. • 786-4869 • 10am-8pm, noon-6pm Sat, clsd Sun • lesbigay/feminist

TRAVEL & TOUR OPERATORS

Reno Gay Travel at 1099 Club • 329-1099

SPIRITUAL GROUPS

MCC of the Sierras 3405 Gulling Rd. (Temple Sinai) • 829-8602 • 7pm Sun

PUBLICATIONS

Las Vegas/Reno Bugle • 369-6260

EROTICA

The Chocolate Walrus 2490 Wrondel Wy. • 825-2267 • 10:30am-6:30pm, til 4:30pm Sat, clsd Sun • videos • novelties

Fantasy Faire 1298 S. Virginia • 323-6969 • 11am-7pm,til 4pm Sun • fetish • leather

New Hampshire

Ashland (603)

WOMEN'S ACCOMMODATIONS

▲ **Country Options** 27-29 N. Main St. • 968-7958 • gay-friendly • B&B • full breakfast • lesbian following • $35-54

Bethlehem (603)

WOMEN'S ACCOMMODATIONS

▲ **Highlands Inn** Rte. 302, Valley View Ln. • 869-3978 • a lesbian paradise • full breakfast • hot tub • swimming • 20 doubles • 14 private & 3 shared baths • 15 miles of walking/ski trails • 20% off for 7 nights (except holidays) • wheelchair access • IGTA member • $55-110

Bridgewater (603)

ACCOMMODATIONS

Inn on Newfound Lake 1030 Mayhew Trpk. Rte. 3-A • 744-9111 • gay-friendly • swimming • also restaurant • classic American • 11am-9pm • also full bar

Centre Harbor (603)

ACCOMMODATIONS

Red Hill Inn RFD # 1, Box 99-M, 03226 • 279-7001/ (800) 573-3445 • gay-friendly • swimming • restored country inn & restaurant on 60 acres overlooking Squam Lake & the White Mtns. • wheelchair access • IGTA member

Chocorua (603)

ACCOMMODATIONS

Mount Chocorua View House Rte. 16 • 323-8350 • gay-friendly • 10 mi. S. of N. Conway

COUNTRY OPTIONS

A SMALL BED & BREAKFAST CONVENIENTLY LOCATED IN CENTRAL NEW HAMPSHIRE'S LAKES REGION AT THE FOOTHILLS OF THE WHITE MOUNTAINS

Four light airy rooms, comfortably furnished with antiques. Share two Baths. Full Country breakfast included. Reasonable Rates year round. No smoking.
INNKEEPERS:
Sandra Ray
& Nancy Puglisi

27-29 N. MAIN ST., ASHLAND, NEW HAMPSHIRE 03217 • (603) 968-7958

Concord   (603)

INFO LINES & SERVICES

Gay Info Line • 224-1686 • 6pm-8pm, 24hr recorded info • also ask about Citizens Alliance for Gay/Lesbian Rights • active social/educational group

New Hampshire Lambda PO Box 1043, 03302 • 627-8675 • 3rd Sat • statewide social group for lesbians

TRAVEL & TOUR OPERATORS

Travel & Tourism Office PO Box 1856, 03302-1856 • 271-2666

SPIRITUAL GROUPS

Spirit of the Mountain 177 N. Main (1st Congregational Church) • 225-5491 • 5pm 2nd & 4th Sun

PUBLICATIONS

Breathing Space PO Box 816, 03302

WomenWise 38 S. Main St. • 225-2739 • quarterly • published by NH Federation of Feminist Health Centers • also many support groups

Dover   (603)

ACCOMMODATIONS

Payne's Hill B&B 141 Henry Law Ave. • 742-4139 • mostly women

Durham   (603)

INFO LINES & SERVICES

UNH Alliance UNH, M.U.B., 03824 • 862-4522

Franconia   (603)

ACCOMMODATIONS

Blanche's B&B 351 Easton Valley Rd. • 823-7061 • gay-friendly • full breakfast • non-smoking

▲ **Bungay Jar B&B** PO Box 15, Easton Valley Rd., 03580 • 823-7775 • gay-friendly • full breakfast • fireplaces • balconies • saunas • women-owned/run

Horse & Hound Inn 205 Wells Rd. • 823-5501 • clsd April & Nov • gay-friendly • full breakfast • restaurant open for dinner except Tue

Raynor's Motor Lodge Main St. (Rtes. 142 & 18) • 823-9586 • gay-friendly • swimming

Glen   (603)

ACCOMMODATIONS

Will's Inn Rte. 302 • 383-6757 • gay-friendly • swimming • great skiing

Jackson   (603)

ACCOMMODATIONS

Wildcat Inn & Tavern Rte. 16-A Main St. • 383-4245 • gay-friendly • full breakfast • restaurant 6pm-9pm • tavern 3pm-midnight wknds • landscaped gardens

Keene

INFO LINES & SERVICES

Monadnock Womyn's Group PO Box 332, 03431

BOOKSTORES & RETAIL SHOPS

Oasis 45 Central Square • 352-5355 • 10am-9pm, 11am-6pm Sun • alternative spiritual books & supplies

Manchester   (603)

ACCOMMODATIONS

Manchester House B&B 305 Taylor St. • 644-2303 • mostly gay men • cont'l breakfast

BARS

Front Runner/Manchester Civic Club 22 Fir St. • 623-6477 • 3pm-1:30am • popular • lesbians/gay men • dancing/DJ • private club

Merri-Mac Club 201 Merrimack • 623-9362 • 2pm-1am • popular • lesbians/gay men • dancing/DJ • private club

Sporters 361 Pine St. • 668-9014 • 5pm-1am, from 3pm Sun • mostly gay men • dancing/DJ

Northampton

INFO LINES & SERVICES

PMS Hunting Club PO Box 1267, 03862 • $19.95 membership • newsletter • bumper sticker • also '101 Reasons to Be A Lesbian' $5.95

Bungay Jar Bed & Breakfast

Peaceful Privacy in Franconia New Hampshire

Splendid VIEWS of the White Mountains

$65.-130. suites for 2

(603) 823-7775
fax: 603·444·0100

Janet, Kate & Julie welcome you!

smoke-free environment

Portsmouth (603)

BARS

Desert Hearts 948 Rte. 1 Bypass • 431-5400 • from 7pm Fri-Sat, from 6pm Sun • mostly women • dancing/DJ • private club • wheelchair access

Members 53 Green St. • 436-9451 • 8pm-1:30am, from 6pm Fri-Sun • popular • mostly gay men • dancing/DJ • live shows • videos • private club • piano lounge wknds

TRAVEL & TOUR OPERATORS

Worldwise Travel Co. Inc. 477 State St. • 430-9060/ (800) 874-9473

Webster (603)

TRAVEL & TOUR OPERATORS

Another Way RFD5 Box 290-B1, 03303 • 648-2751 • comfortable lesbian camping tours in New England

New Jersey

Ashbury Park/Ocean Grove (908)

INFO LINES & SERVICES

Gay/Lesbian Community Center 515 Cookman Ave. • 774-1809 • 2pm-7pm Sat & various evenings • call for events

ACCOMMODATIONS

The Talking Bird Hotel 224 Cookman • 775-9708 • lesbians/gay men

BARS

Bond Street Bar 208 Bond St. • 776-9766 • 4pm-midnight, til 2am Fri-Sat • mostly women • neighborhood bar

Down the Street 230 Cookman Ave. • 988-2163 • seasonal hours: approx 2pm-2am • popular • mostly gay men • dancing/DJ • live shows • food served • beach crowd • volleyball • wheelchair access

Key West 611 Heck St. • 988-7979 • 4pm-2am • mostly gay men • dancing/DJ • backyard • wheelchair access

Teddy's Pub 402 Emory St. • 774-9871 • 2pm-2am • lesbians/gay men • neighborhood bar • wheelchair access

RESTAURANTS & CAFES

Raspberry Cafe 16 Main Ave. • 988-0833 • breakfast & lunch

The Talking Bird (at the Talking Bird Hotel) • 775-9708 • lunch & dinner, til 4am Fri-Sat • American • $4-9

Atlantic City (609)

ACCOMMODATIONS

The Rose Cottage 161 S. Westminster Ave. • 345-8196 • lesbians/gay men • near bars & casinos

Surfside Guest House 18 S. Mt. Vernon Ave. • 347-0808 • small, upscale, straight-friendly hotel/guesthouse • sundeck • also restaurant in summer

BARS

Brass Rail Bar & Grill 12 S. Mt. Vernon Ave. • 348-0192 • 24hrs • popular • lesbians/gay men • neighborhood bar • live shows • women's night Fri • also Studio Six Video Dance Club • 348-3310 • 10pm-8am • dancing/DJ • live shows • wheelchair access

Ladies for the 80's PO Box 1, Oaklyn, 08107 • 784-8341 • scheduled parties for women by women • call for times & locations

Reflections 181 S. South Carolina Ave. • 348-1115 • lounge open 24hrs, dance bar 11pm • popular • lesbians/gay men • live shows • also a restaurant • wheelchair access

TRAVEL & TOUR OPERATORS

New Jersey Division of Travel & Tourism CN 826, Trenton, 08625-0826 • (800) 537-7397

Schreve Lazar Travel Boardwalk & Park Place • 348-1189/ (800) 322-8280 • at Bally's Park Place Casino Hotel • IGTA member

Bloomington (201)

INFO LINES & SERVICES

Gal-a-vanting Box 268, Bloomingdale, 07403 • 838-5318 • sponsors women's parties • call for details

Cherry Hill (609)

BARS

Gatsby's 760 Cuthbert Blvd. (off Rte. 70) • 663-8744 • 8:30pm-3am • popular • lesbians/gay men • dancing/DJ • live shows • women's night Tue & Th • T-dance 4pm Sun • wheelchair access

Harrison

PUBLICATIONS

Lavender Express PO Box 514, 07029 • monthly • journal of news • social calendar • poetry • fiction

Hazlet (908)

TRAVEL & TOUR OPERATORS

Galaxy Travel 3048 Rte. 35 (K-Mart Shopping Center), 07737 • 219-9600/ (800) 331-7245 • IGTA member

Highland Park (908)

BOOKSTORES & RETAIL SHOPS

All About Books 409 Raritan Ave. • 247-8744 • 9:30am-9pm, 11am-5pm Sun

Hoboken (201)

Bars

Excalibur 1000 Jefferson St. • 795-1023 • 9pm-2am, clsd Mon-Wed • popular • lesbians/gay men • dancing/DJ • live shows • wheelchair access

Restaurants & Cafes

Maxwell's 1039 Washington St. • 656-9632 • 5pm-2am, til 3am Fri-Sat • Italian/American • also dancing/DJ • live shows • wheelchair access • $7-12

Madison (201)

Bookstores & Retail Shops

Pandora Book Peddlers 9 Waverly Pl. • 822-8388 • 10am-6pm, til 7:30pm Th, til 5pm Sat, clsd Sun-Mon • feminist bookstore & book club

Maplewood (201)

Spiritual Groups

Dignity Metro New Jersey 550 Ridgewood Rd. (St. George's Episcopal Church) • 857-4040 • 8pm 1st & 3rd Tue

Montclair (201)

Info Lines & Services

Crossroads Real Estate Referral Network PO Box 1708, 07042 • (800) 442-9735 • non-profit lesbigay realtor referrals

Bookstores & Retail Shops

Cohen's 635 Bloomfield Ave. • 744-2399 • 6am-8pm, til 2pm Sun • magazines • cafe

Dressing for Pleasure 590 Valley Rd. • 746-5466 • noon-6pm, clsd Sun-Mon • lingerie • latex • leather • also mail order

Morris Plains (201)

Travel & Tour Operators

Frankel Travel 60 E. Hanover Ave. • 455-1111/ (800) 445-6433 • IGTA member

Morristown (201)

Info Lines & Services

Gay Activist Alliance in Morris County • 285-1595 • live 7pm-10pm • meets 8:30pm Mon at 21 Normandy Hts. Rd. • also Women's Network

New Brunswick (908)

Info Lines & Services

Lesbian/Gay Men of New Brunswick 109 Nichol Ave. (Quaker Meeting House) • 247-0515 • 8pm 2nd & 4th Tue • social group

Pride Center of New Jersey 211 Livingston Ave. • 846-2232 • 7pm-10pm • info & referrals • community center

Rutgers Univ. Lesbian/Gay/Bisexual Peer-Counseling • 932-7886 • 7pm-11pm Tue & Fri, call for details

Restaurants & Cafes

Frog and the Peach 29 Dennis St. • 846-3216 • 11:30am-11pm, til 1am Th-Sat • upscale American • full bar • wheelchair access • $40-60

J. August Cafe 100 Jersey Ave. • 545-4646 • lesbians/gay men

Stage Left 5 Livingston Ave. • 828-4444 • 5:30pm-2am, from 4:30pm Sun • popular • lesbians/gay men • some veggie • full bar • wheelchair access • $10-12

Spiritual Groups

MCC Christ the Liberator 40 Davidson Rd. (St. Michael's Chapel) • 846-8227 • 6:30pm Sun

Publications

Network, For the 10% Plus PO Box 10372, 08906 • 249-2926 • monthly

Newark (201)

Bars

First Choice 533 Ferry St. • 465-1944 • 8pm-2am, til 3am Th-Sat • lesbians/gay men • dancing/DJ • multi-racial • ladies night Th • more women Sat

Murphy's Tavern 59 Edison Pl. • 622-9176 • noon-2am, lunch daily • lesbians/gay men • dancing/DJ • mostly African-American • wheelchair access

Oak Ridge (201)

Bars

Yacht Club 5190 Berkshire Valley Rd. (5 mi. off of Rte. 15) • 697-9780 • 7pm-3am from 2pm Sun • popular • lesbians/gay men • dancing/DJ • videos • also Sun BBQ

Oakland (201)

INFO LINES & SERVICES

Feminine Connection • 337-6943 • social group for women over 25 • meets every other month • call for info

Orange (908)

INFO LINES & SERVICES

Intergroup AA • 668-1882 • 24hrs info & referrals

Perth Amboy (908)

BARS

Other Half Convery Blvd. (Rte. 35) & Kennedy • 826-8877 • 9pm-2am, til 3am Fri-Sat • popular • mostly gay men • dancing/DJ

Plainfield (908)

ACCOMMODATIONS

▲ **Pillars** 922 Central Ave. • 753-0922/ (800) 372-7378 • gay-friendly • B&B • Georgian/Victorian mansion on an acre of trees & wildflowers

BARS

Gin Mill 308 Watchung Ave. • 755-4000 • 10am-1am, til 2am Fri-Sat, 1pm-1am Sun • mostly gay men • neighborhood bar • videos

TRAVEL & TOUR OPERATORS

Vacation Design PO Box 1261, 07061 • 882-1742 • European vacation rentals • unverified for '96 • IGTA member

Princeton (609)

TRAVEL & TOUR OPERATORS

Edwards Travel Service 8 S. Tulane St. • 924-4443/ (800) 669-9692

Red Bank (908)

BOOKSTORES & RETAIL SHOPS

Earth Spirit 16 W. Front St. • 842-3855 • 10am-6pm, til 8pm Fri, noon-5pm Sun • new age center/bookstore w/ lesbigay sections

Ringwood (201)

WOMEN'S ACCOMMODATIONS

Ensanmar 2 Ellen St. • 831-0898/ 835-0546 • women only • B&B • women's community & retreat • support groups • $37-60

River Ridge (201)

BARS

Feather's Disco 77 Kinderkamack Rd. • 342-6410 • 9pm-2am, til 3am Sat • popular • mostly gay men • dancing/DJ • live shows • theme nights • wheelchair access

Rocky Hill (609)

TRAVEL & TOUR OPERATORS

Travel Registry, Inc. 127 Washington St. • 921-6900/ (800) 346-6901 • IGTA member

Rosemont (609)

RESTAURANTS & CAFES

Cafe 88 Kingwood - Stockton Rd. • 397-4097 • 8am-3pm, til 9pm Th-Sun, clsd Mon • BYOB • healthy American

Sandy Hook (908)

ACCOMMODATIONS

Seabird Inn B&B 60 Bay Ave., Highlands • 872-0123 • mostly women • full gourmet breakfast

Sayreville (908)

BARS

Colosseum Rte. 9 & Rte. 35 N. • 316-0670 • 9pm-3am, from 4pm Sun • lesbians/gay men • dancing/DJ • live shows • ladies night Wed

Sauvage 1 Victory Cir. • 727-6619 • 7pm-3am, from 4pm Sun • popular • mostly women • neighborhood bar • dancing/DJ • food served

Somerset (908)

BARS

Den 700 Hamilton St. • 545-7329 • 8pm-2am, from 5pm Sun • popular • lesbians/gay men • dancing/DJ • live shows • videos • 4 bars on property • wheelchair access

Teaneck (201)

INFO LINES & SERVICES

Lesbian Awareness 61 Church St. (St. Paul's Lutheran Church) • 779-1434 • 7:30pm 1st Tue • social group

Trenton (609)

BARS

Buddies Pub 677 S. Broad St. • 989-8566 • 5pm-2am, from 1pm Sun • lesbians/gay men • patio

Center House Pub 499 Center St. • 599-9558 • 4pm-2am, from 7pm wknds • lesbians/gay men • neighborhood bar • quiet conversation bar • garden patio

Union City (201)

BARS

Nite Lite 509 22nd St. • 863-9515 • 8pm-3am Wed-Sun • lesbians/gay men • dancing/DJ • live shows

Woodbury (609)

INFO LINES & SERVICES

Rainbow Place 1103 N. Broad • 848-2455 • info line & community center • call for hours

New Mexico

Albuquerque (505)

INFO LINES & SERVICES

Alternative Erotic Lifestyles • 345-6484 • pansexual S/M group

Common Bond Community Center 4013 Silver St. SE • 266-8041 • 7pm-10pm • many groups & resources

New Mexico Outdoors PO Box 26836, 87125 • 822-1093 • active lesbigay outdoors group

UNM Women's Center 1160 Mesa Vista Hall • 277-3716 • 8am-5pm Mon-Fri • offers many resources & some lesbian outreach • wheelchair access

Women in Movement • 255-7274 • production company • Memorial Day festival • monthly activities

ACCOMMODATIONS

Dave's B&B PO Box 27214, 87125-7214 • 247-8312 • mostly gay men • hot tub • Southwestern home located close to river • wheelchair access

Hacienda Antigua Retreat 6708 Tierra Dr. NW • 345-5399 • gay-friendly • full breakfast • hot tub • swimming

▲ **Hateful Missy & Granny Butch's Boudoir** 728 Lulac NW • 243-7063 • lesbians/gay men • cozy & private • centrally located

Mountain View PO Box 30123, 87190 • 296-7277 • gay-friendly • B&B • wheelchair access • lesbian-owned/run

▲ **Nuevo Dia** 11110 San Rafael Ave. • 856-7910 • lesbians/gay men • food served

Rainbow Lodge 115 Frost Rd., Sandia Park • 281-7100 • lesbians/gay men • mountain retreat nestled on 5 wooded acres w/ panoramic views of Sandia & Ortiz Mtns.

Rio Grande House 3100 Rio Grande Blvd. NW • 345-0120 • gay-friendly • full breakfast • fireplaces • landmark white adobe residence close to historic Old Town

Tara Cotta 3118 Rio Grande Blvd. NW • 344-9443 • gay-friendly

W.E. Mauger Estate 701 Roma Ave. NW • 242-8755 • gay-friendly • full breakfast • intimate Queen Anne residence

BARS

Albuquerque Social Club 4021 Central Ave. NE (rear alley) • 255-0887 • noon-2am, til midnight Sun • popular • lesbians/gay men • dancing/DJ • country/western • private club • wheelchair access

Club on Central 10030 Central SE • 291-1550 • 11am-2am • lesbians/gay men • dancing/DJ • food served • American • patio • wheelchair access • $3-7

Corky's 2428 San Mateo Pl. NE • 884-6800 • 5pm-2am, clsd Mon • women only • private club

Foxes Lounge 8521 Central Ave. NE • 255-3060 • 10am-2am • mostly gay men • dancing/DJ • wheelchair access

▲ **Legends West** 6132 4th St. NW • 343-9793 • 4pm-2am, from 6pm Sat, noon-midnight Sun, clsd Mon • lesbians/gay men • dancing/DJ

RESTAURANTS & CAFES

Chef du Jour 119 San Pasquale SW • 247-8998 • 11am-2pm, clsd wknds • New American • plenty veggie • wheelchair access • $4-9

Chianti's 5210 San Mateo NE • 881-1967 • 11am-10pm • Italian • some veggie • beer/wine • wheelchair access • $5-11

Double Rainbow 3416 Central SE • 255-6633 • 6:30am-midnight • plenty veggie • wheelchair access • $4-8

Now That's Italian 3718 Central NE • 764-8259 • 11am-9pm • some veggie • patio • $5-8

BOOKSTORES & RETAIL SHOPS

Full Circle Books 2205 Silver SE • 266-0022 • 10am-6pm, til 5pm wknds • feminist/lesbian bookstore

In Crowd 3106 Central SE • 268-3750 • 10am-6pm, noon-4pm Sun • lesbigay art • clothing • accesories

Page One 11018 Montgomery NE • 294-2026

Salt of the Earth Books 2128 Central SE • 842-1220 • 9am-9pm, til 5pm Sun

Sisters and Brothers Bookstore 4011 Silver Ave. SE • 266-7317 • 10am-10pm • lesbigay • wheelchair access

TRAVEL & TOUR OPERATORS

All World Travel 1930 Juan Tabo NE Ste. D • 294-5031/ (800) 725-0695

IT'S A NEW DAY IN
ALBUQUERQUE, NEW MEXICO

Gay & Lesbian
Guest Accommodations
in the Sandia Mountains

(505) 856-7910

Nuevo Dia

Nuevo Dia is a one of a kind, circular, adobe guesthouse. You'll be captivated by the breathtaking view of the Sandias and the city at night. A sauna and outdoor hot tub add to the ambience of Nuevo Dia, making your stay a complete experience.

Rates
$70-130 per night

North & South Travel & Tours 215 Central Ave. NW • 246-9100/ (800) 585-8016 • IGTA member

Travel Scene 2424 Juan Tabo Blvd. NE • 292-4343/ (800) 658-5779

SPIRITUAL GROUPS

Dignity New Mexico 1815 Los Lomas • 880-9031 • 7pm 1st Sun

Emmanuel MCC 201 Dallas NE • 268-0599 • 10am Sun

MCC 2404 San Mateo Pl. NE • 881-9088 • 10am

PUBLICATIONS

Hembra PO Box 40572, 87196 • 268-8623 • monthly women's newspaper

Out! Magazine PO Box 27237, 87125 • 243-2540 • monthly

Clovis   (505)

INFO LINES & SERVICES

Common Bond PO Box 663, 88101 • 356-2656 • lesbigay social/support group for Clovis & Portales

Galisteo   (505)

ACCOMMODATIONS

Galisteo Inn PO Box 4, 87540 • 466-4000 • clsd Jan • gay-friendly • swimming • also a restaurant • nouvelle Southwestern (Wed-Sun) • plenty veggie • 23 mi. SE of Santa Fe • wheelchair access • $12-18

Las Cruces   (505)

INFO LINES & SERVICES

Matrix PO Box 992, Mesilla, 88046 • newsletter • local inquiries

BOOKSTORES & RETAIL SHOPS

Spirit Winds Gifts 2260 Locust St. • 521-0222 • 7:30am-11pm, til 2pm Sun • cafe • gifts & more • wheelchair access

TRAVEL & TOUR OPERATORS

Uniglobe Above & Beyond Travel 2225 E. Lohman Ste. A • 527-0200/ (800) 578-5888 • IGTA member

Pecos   (505)

ACCOMMODATIONS

Wilderness Inn PO Box 1177, 87552 •
757-6694 • gay-friendly • nudity • adobe
inn 20 mi E. of Santa Fe • wheelchair
access

Ruidoso   (505)

ACCOMMODATIONS

Sierra Mesa Lodge PO Box 463, Alto ,
88312 • 336-4515 • gay-friendly • full
breakfast • hot tub

Santa Fe   (505)

INFO LINES & SERVICES

AA Gay/Lesbian 1915 Rosina St.
(Friendship Circle) • 982-8932

ACCOMMODATIONS

Casa Serena PO Box 8534, 87504 • 988-
4157 • summer rental

Casa Torreon 1631 Calle Torreon • 982-
6815 • gay-friendly • adobe guesthouse
w/ kitchen & great mtn. views

Four Kachinas Inn 512 Webber St. • 982-
2550/ (800) 397-2564 • gay-friendly •
wheelchair access

Hummingbird Ranch Rte. 10, Box 111,
87501 • 471-2921 • gay-friendly • 2-1/2
acre ranchette nestled amongst pinon
hills • women-owned/run

Marriott Residence Inn 1698 Galisteo
St. • 988-7300/ (800) 331-3131 • gay-
friendly • swimming • wheelchair access

Open Sky B&B Rte. 2 Box 918, Turquoise
Trail, 80575 • 471-3475/ (800) 244-3475 •
gay-friendly • wheelchair access

▲ **Triangle Inn** PO Box 3235, 87501-0235 •
455-3375 • lesbians/gay men • hot tub •
secluded rustic adobe compound providing 6 casitas & gym • IGTA member

RESTAURANTS & CAFES

Cafe Pasqual's 121 Don Gaspar • 983-
9340 • 7am-10pm • popular • beer/wine
• Southwestern • some veggie • $12-18

Dave's Not Here 1115 Hickock St., Santa
Fe • 983-7060 • 11am-9pm, clsd Sun •
mostly women • beer/wine • New
Mexican • some veggie • women-
owned/run

Maria's 555 W. Cordova Rd. • 983-7929 • lunch & dinner • Southwestern • some veggie • full bar • wheelchair access • $7-15

Paul's 72 Marcy St. • 982-8738 • modern/international • some veggie • beer/wine • wheelchair access • $11-18

SantaCafe 231 Washington Ave. • 984-1788 • lunch & dinner • Southwestern/Asian • some veggie • full bar • wheelchair access • $19-24

Tecolote Cafe 1203 Cerrillos Rd. • 988-1362 • 7am-2pm, clsd Mon • popular • some veggie • great breakfasts • wheelchair access • $5-8

Willy's 802 Canyon Rd. • 986-3833 • 9am-4pm • popular • white-trash home cooking

BOOKSTORES & RETAIL SHOPS

Ark 133 Romero St. • 988-3709 • 10am-8pm, til 5pm wknds • spiritual

Downtown Subscription 376 Garcia St. • 983-3085 • 8am-7pm • newsstand & coffee shop

Galisteo News 201 Galisteo St. • 984-1316 • 7am-7pm • gay periodicals & coffee shop

TRAVEL & TOUR OPERATORS

Earth Walks • 988-4157 • guided tour of American Southwest & Mexico

Hawk, I'm Your Sister PO Box 9109-WT, 87504 • 984-2268 • variety of women's wilderness trips & writers' retreats

Taos (505)

ACCOMMODATIONS

Michael & Annie's PO Box 1600, 87557 • 751-1358 • lesbians/gay men • fully furnished adobe home

▲ **Ruby Slipper** PO Box 2069, 87571 • 758-0613 • lesbians/gay men • guesthouse • no smoking • ideally situated a short walk from Taos Plaza • wheelchair access • women-owned/run

Stone House PO Box DD, Valdez, 87580 • 776-2146 • comfortable haven in the old New Mexican tradition of hospitality

RESTAURANTS & CAFES

Wild & Natural Cafe 812-B Paseo del Pueblo Norte • 751-0480 • clsd Sun • vegetarian • wheelchair access • women-owned/run • $2-9

Travel & Tour Operators

Artemis Wilderness Tours PO Box 1178, 87571 • 758-2203 • women's outdoor rafting trip May-Sept • cross-country skiing other months

Thoreau (505)

Accommodations

Zuni Mountain Lodge at Blue Water Lake HC62 Box 5114, 87323-9515 • 862-7769 • gay-friendly • full breakfast & dinner • wheelchair access

New York

Adirondack Mtns. (518)

INFO LINES & SERVICES

Adirondack GABLE PO Box 990, Saranac Lake, 12983 • 359-7358 • monthly social group

ACCOMMODATIONS

Amethyst B&B PO Box 522 , Cranberry Lake, 12927 • 848-3529/ (410) 252-5990 (winter) • summer only • women only • full breakfast • swimming

The Doctor's Inn Trudeau Rd., RR1, Box 375, Saranac Lake, 12983 • 891-3464/ (800) 552-2627 • gay-friendly • B&B • IGTA member

Stony Water B&B RR1 Box 69, Elizabethtown, 12932 • 873-9125 • gay-friendly • full breakfast • swimming • wheelchair access • lesbian-owned/run

Albany (518)

INFO LINES & SERVICES

Face the Music WRPI 91.5 FM • 276-6248 • 4pm-6pm Sun • feminist radio

Gay AA (at Community Center) • 7:30pm Sun • lesbian AA meets 7:30pm Tue

Homo Radio WRPI 91.5 FM • 276-6248 • noon-2:30pm Sun

KAT Productions Box 44, 12201 • 432-0818 • wknd multimedia events & dances for women

Lesbian/Gay Community Center 332 Hudson Ave. • 462-6138 • 7pm-10pm, til 11pm Fri-Sat, from 1pm Sun • 24hr touchtone directory info for referrals, nightclubs, library, cafe, AA meetings

Lesbian/Gay/Bisexual Young People's Meeting (at the Community Center) • 7:30pm Th

TGIC (Transgenderists Independence Club) PO Box 13604, 12212-3604 • 436-4513 • volunteers 8pm Th • social group meets weekly

Two Rivers Outdoor Club • 449-0758 • lesbigay

Women's Bulding 79 Central Ave. • 465-1597 • community center • wheelchair access

ACCOMMODATIONS

Turn Around Spa 201 Washington St. , Sharon Springs • 284-2271 • gay-friendly • kitchens • massage • mineral & steam baths • 45 min. from Albany

BARS

Longhorns 90 Central Ave. • 462-4862 • 4pm-4am • mostly gay men • country/western • patio

Oh Bar 304 Lark St. • 463-9004 • 2pm-2am • mostly gay men • neighborhood bar • videos

Power Company 238 Washington Ave. • 465-2556 • 2pm-2am, til 4am wknds • mostly gay men • dancing/DJ

Waterworks Pub 76 Central Ave. • 465-9079 • 2pm-4am • popular • mostly gay men • dancing Wed-Sun • garden bar

RESTAURANTS & CAFES

Cafe Hollywood 275 Lark St. • 472-9043 • lunch, dinner, Sun brunch • American • full bar • $6-18

Cafe Lulu 288 Lark St. • 436-5660 • 11am-midnight, til 1am Fri-Sat • plenty veggie • beer/wine • patio • $5-9

Debbie's Kitchen 290 Lark St. • 463-3829 • 10am-9pm, 11am-6pm Sat, clsd Sun • sandwiches & salads • plenty veggie • also take out • $3-5

Donnie's Cafe 75 75 Central Ave • 436-0378 • 7am-3pm, from 3am wknds • American • $4-7

El Loco Mexican Cafe 465 Madison Ave. • 436-1855 • clsd Mon • some veggie • full bar

Mother Earth 217 Western Ave. • 434-0944 • 11am-11pm • gay-friendly • vegetarian • Gay/Bi/Lesbian Club Night 4th Mon • wheelchair access • $3-6

Yono's 289 Hamilton St. • 436-7747 • 4:30pm-10pm, clsd Sun • Indonesian/cont'l • some veggie • full bar • patio

BOOKSTORES & RETAIL SHOPS

Romeo's 299 Lark St. • 434-4014 • 11am-9pm, noon-5pm Sun • gifts & books

Video Central 37 Central Ave. • 463-4153 • 10am-10pm • lesbigay books & magazines • wheelchair access

TRAVEL & TOUR OPERATORS

Atlas Travel Center Inc. 1545 Central Ave. • 464-0271 • IGTA member

Travel Company 41 State St. Ste. 110 • 433-9000 • gay-owned/run

SPIRITUAL GROUPS

Integrity 498 Clinton Ave. at Robbins St. (Grace & Holy Innocents Church) • 465-1112 • 6pm Sun

MCC of the Hudson Valley 275 State St. (Emmanuel Baptist Church) • 785-7941 • 1pm Sun • wheelchair access

PUBLICATIONS

Community PO Box 131, 12201 • 462-6138

EROTICA

Savage Leather & Gifts 88 Central Ave. • 434-2324 • 11am-9pm, til midnight Fri-Sat, clsd Sun-Mon

Annadale on Hudson (914)

INFO LINES & SERVICES

Bard Bisexual/Lesbian/Gay Alliance Bard College, 12504 • 758-6822 (general switchboard) • active during school year

Binghamton (607)

INFO LINES & SERVICES

AA Gay/Lesbian 183 Riverside Dr. (Unitarian Church) • 722-5983 • 7pm Wed & Sat

Gay/Lesbian/Bi Resource Line • 729-1921 • 7:30pm-9:30pm Wed • info & referrals

Lesbian/Gay/Bisexual Union • 777-2202 • info & referrals • mtgs 8pm Tue

Women's Center & Event Line PO Box 354, 13902 • 724-3462

BARS

Risky Business 201 State St. • 723-1507 • 9pm-1am, from 5pm Th-Fri, til 3am Fri-Sat • popular • mostly gay men • dancing/DJ • videos • gift shop on premises

Squiggy's 34 Chenango St. • 722-2299 • 5pm-1am, til 3am Fri-Sat, from 8pm Sun-Mon • lesbians/gay men • dancing/DJ

RESTAURANTS & CAFES

Kara's Kafe 585 Main St., Johnson City • 797-8567 • clsd Sun • live shows • California • plenty veggie • full bar • patio • wheelchair access • $10-15

Lost Dog Cafe 60 Main St. • 771-6063 • 11am-11pm, til 4am Fri-Sat • popular • lesbians/gay men • live shows

PUBLICATIONS

Amethyst PO Box 728 Westview Stn., 13905-0728 • 723-5790 • monthly

Hera c/o Women's Center PO Box 354, 13902 • local feminist newspaper

Lavender Life PO Box 898, 13902 • 771-1986

Buffalo (716)

INFO LINES & SERVICES

Buffalo Fetish Leather Organization PO Box 3, 14201 • 881-3428

Dyke TV Channel 18 • 10:30pm Tue • 'weekly half hour TV show produced by lesbians, for lesbians'

Gay/Lesbian Community Network 239 Lexington Ave. • 883-4750 • 7pm-10pm Fri

Gay/Lesbian Youth Services 190 Franklin St., 14202 • 855-0221 • 6pm-9pm Mon-Tue, Th-Fri

Lesbian/Gay/Bisexual Alliance 362 Student Union SUNY-Buffalo, Amherst, 14260 • 645-3063

BARS

Buddies 31 Johnson Park • 855-1313 • 1pm-4am • lesbians/gay men • dancing/DJ • mostly African-American • live shows • wheelchair access

Cathode Ray 26 Allen St. • 884-3615 • 1pm-4am • mostly gay men • neighborhood bar • wheelchair access

Club Marcella 150 Theatre Pl. • 847-6850 • 10pm-4am, from 4pm Fri, clsd Mon • lesbians/gay men • dancing/DJ • live shows • patio • wheelchair access

Compton's After Dark 1239 Niagara St. • 885-3275 • 4pm-4am • mostly women • dancing/DJ • live shows • also a restaurant • sandwiches • some veggie • $4-7

Lavender Door 32 Tonawanda St. • 874-1220 • 6pm-4am, from 4pm Fri, clsd Mon • mostly women • neighborhood bar • wheelchair access

Metroplex 729 Main St. • 856-5630 • 10pm-4am, clsd Mon • lesbians/gay men • dancing/DJ • alternative • 18+

Mickey's 44 Allen St. • 886-9367 • 9am-4am • gay-friendly • neighborhood bar

Tiffany's 490 Pearl St. • 854-4840 • 11am-2am, til 4am Fri-Sat • mostly gay men • piano bar • also a restaurant

Underground 274 Delaware Ave. • 855-1040 • 4pm-4am, from noon wknds • mostly gay men • dancing/DJ • more women Tue & Sun

BOOKSTORES & RETAIL SHOPS

Talking Leaves 3158 Main St. • 837-8554 • 10am-6pm, til 8pm Wed-Th, clsd Sun

Village Green Bookstore 765-A Elmwood Ave. • 884-1200 • 9am-11pm, til midnight Fri-Sat • wheelchair access

TRAVEL & TOUR OPERATORS

Destinations Unlimited 130 Theater Pl. • 855-1955/ (800) 528-8877 • IGTA member

Earth Travelers, Inc. 683 Dick Rd. • 685-2900/ (800) 321-2901 • IGTA member

SPIRITUAL GROUPS

Dignity PO Box 75, 14205 • 833-8995

Integrity 16 Linwood Ave. (Church of the Ascension) • 884-6362 (church #)

PUBLICATIONS

Volumé PO Box 106 Westside Stn., 14213 • 885-4580 • monthly • covers Buffalo, Rochester, & Southern Ontario, Canada

Catskill Mtns.

ACCOMMODATIONS

Bradstan Country Hotel Rte. 17-B, White Lake • (914) 583-4114 • gay-friendly • B&B • cottages • swimming • also piano bar & cabaret • 9pm-1am Fri-Sun • gay-owned/run

Palenville House B&B PO Box 465, 12463-0465 • (518) 678-5649 • gay-friendly • full breakfast • turn-of-the-century Victorian home located in a quaint hamlet

Point Lookout Mountain Inn Rte. 23 Box 33, East Windham, 12439 • (518) 734-3381 • also a restaurant • Mediterranean/classic American • spectacular views of 5 states • close to Ski Windham & Hunter Mountain • gay-owned

River Run B&B Main St., Box D-4, Fleischmanns, 12430 • (914) 254-4884 • gay-friendly • full breakfast • Queen Anne Victorian (c. 1887) at the edge of the Catskill Forest • IGTA member

Stonewall Acres Box 556, Rock Hill, 12775 • (914) 791-9474/ (800) 336-4208 (in-state only) • gay-friendly • full breakfast • hot tub • swimming • 100-year-old country guest & farmhouse & 2 one-bdrm cottages

BARS

Norm's Place at the Day's inn, Rte. 23-B • (518) 943-5800 • noon-4am • gay-friendly • also a restaurant • Italian

RESTAURANTS & CAFES

Catskill Rose Rte. 212, Mt. Tremper • (914) 688-7100 • from 5pm Wed-Sun • cont'l • some veggie • full bar • patio • $13-19

Cooperstown (607)

ACCOMMODATIONS

Toad Hall B&B RD1 Box 120, Fly Creek, 13337 • 547-5774 • gay-friendly • full breakfast

Tryon Inn 124 Main St., Cherry Valley • 264-3790 • gay-friendly • also a restaurant • French/American • some veggie • $12-16

Cuba (716)

ACCOMMODATIONS

Rocking Duck Inn 28 Genesee Pkwy. • 968-3335 • gay-friendly • full breakfast • 1852 Italianate brick Victorian on 4 landscaped acres • also Aunt Minnie's Tavern

Elmira (607)

ACCOMMODATIONS

Rufus Tanner House B&B 60 Sagetown Rd., Pine City • 732-0213 • gay-friendly • full breakfast • hot tub • 1864 Victorianized Greek Revival farmhouse on a small knoll

BARS

David 511 Railroad Ave. • 733-2592 • 4pm-1am, from 7pm wknds • popular • lesbians/gay men • dancing/DJ • karaoke

Fire Island (516)

INFO LINES & SERVICES

AA Gay/Lesbian (at the Fire House), Cherry Grove • 654-1150/ (816) 669-1124

ACCOMMODATIONS

Boatel Fire Island Pines • 597-6500 • seasonal • lesbians/gay men • swimming

Cherry Grove Beach Hotel Main & Ocean, Cherry Grove • 597-6600 • lesbians/gay men • swimming • 4 bars on premises

Dune Point, Cherry Grove • 597-6261 • year round • lesbians/gay men • wheelchair access

Fire Island Pines 9-B Ocean Walk, Fire Island Pines • 597-6767 • seasonal • mostly gay men • hot tub

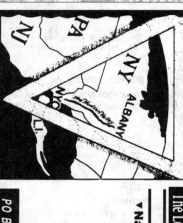

Holly House Holly Walk near Bayview Walk, Cherry Grove • 597-6911 • seasonal • lesbians/gay men

Island Properties 37 Fire Island Blvd., 11782 • 597-6900 • weekly, monthly, & seasonal rentals • also properties for sale

Pines Place PO Box 5309, Fire Island Pines, 11782 • 597-6162 • mostly gay men • B&B • cottages • hot tub • several locations available

Sea Crest Lewis Walk at Main Walk, Cherry Grove • 597-6849 • seasonal • lesbians/gay men

BARS

Cherry's Cherry Grove • 597-6820 • noon-4am (seasonal) • popular • lesbians/gay men • piano bar • wheelchair access

Ice Palace (at Cherry Grove Beach Hotel) • 597-6600 • hours vary • popular • lesbians/gay men • dancing/DJ • live shows • 4 bars • wheelchair access

Monster Ocean Walk near Dock Walk, Cherry Grove • 597-6888 • seasonal • popular • lesbians/gay men • dancing/DJ • live shows • daily brunch & dinner

Pines Pavillion Fire Island Blvd. • 597-6131 • 4pm-6am • popular • lesbians/gay men • dancing/DJ • popular T-dance

Top of the Bay Dock Walk at Bay Walk, Cherry Grove • 597-6699 • 7pm-midnight, seasonal • popular • lesbians/gay men • also a restaurant • cont'l • $18-23

Glen Falls (518)

BARS

Martini's 70 South St. • 798-9809 • 4pm-4am • lesbians/gay men • dancing/DJ • wheelchair access

Highland (914)

BARS

Prime Time Rte. 9 W. • 691-8550 • 9pm-4am, clsd Mon-Tue • mostly gay men • dancing/DJ • unconfirmed '96

Hudson Valley (914)

(see also Kingston, New Paltz, Poughkeepsie and Stone Ridge)

PUBLICATIONS

▲ **In The Life** PO Box 921, Wappingers Falls, 12590-0921 • 227-7456 • monthly

Ithaca (607)

INFO LINES & SERVICES

AA Gay/Lesbian (downtown) • 273-1541

Ithaca Gay/Lesbian Activities Board (IGLAB) PO Box 6634, 14851 • 273-1505 • 3rd Tue • ph# is for Common Ground bar • sponsors events including 'Finger Lake Gay/Lesbian Picnic'

LesBiGay Info Line (Cornell University) • 255-6482 • noon-4pm Mon-Fri • touch-tone info & referrals

Women's Community Building 100 W. Seneca • 272-1247 • 9am-5pm • evenings & wknds by appt.

WOMEN'S ACCOMMODATIONS

Cricket & Liz's Log Home • 277-6220 • open June-Dec • women only • B&B • full breakfast • hot tub • swimming • lesbian-owned/run • $60-75

ACCOMMODATIONS

Pleasant Grove B&B 1779 Trumansburg Rd., Jacksonville • 387-5420/ (800) 398-3963 • gay-friendly • full breakfast • comfortable country home from the 1930s on 86 acres above Cayuga Lake • sundeck

BARS

Common Ground 1230 Danby Rd. • 273-1505 • 4pm-1:30am, clsd Mon • popular • lesbians/gay men • dancing/DJ • also a restaurant • some veggie • wheelchair access • $5-8

RESTAURANTS & CAFES

ABC Cafe 308 Stewart Ave. • 277-4770 • lunch & dinner, wknd brunch, clsd Mon • beer/wine • vegetarian • $6-8

BOOKSTORES & RETAIL SHOPS

Borealis Bookstore, Inc. 111 N. Aurora St. • 272-7752 • 10am-9pm, noon-5pm Sun • independent alternative w/ lesbigay sections

Jamestown (716)

INFO LINES & SERVICES

10% Network 1255 Pendergast Ave. (Unitarian Church) • 484-7285/ 664-5556 • 7pm 3rd Sat • lesbigay social group

BARS

Nite Spot 201 Windsor • 7pm-2am • lesbians/gay men • dancing/DJ • live shows • no phone • dancing/DJ Th-Sun

Sneakers 100 Harrison • 484-8816 • 2pm-2am • lesbians/gay men • dancing/DJ • wheelchair access

Kingston (914)

INFO LINES & SERVICES

Ulster County Gay/Lesbian Alliance PO Box 3785, 12401 • 626-3203 • info & events line

BOOKSTORES & RETAIL SHOPS

Author, Author 89 Broadway • 339-1883 • 11:30am-6:30pm, til 9pm Fri-Sat • general • lesbigay section • also T-shirts • pride gifts

Lake George (518)

ACCOMMODATIONS

King Hendrick Motel Lake George Rd. (Rte. 9) • 792-0418 • gay-friendly • swimming • also cabin available

Lake Placid (518)

RESTAURANTS & CAFES

Artists' Cafe 1 Main St. • 523-9493 • 8am-10pm • some veggie • full bar • discreetly frequented by gays • $9-15

Nanuet (914)

TRAVEL & TOUR OPERATORS

Edlen Travel Inc. 161 S. Middletown Rd. • 624-2100 • IGTA member

Naples (716)

ACCOMMODATIONS

Landmark Retreat 6006 Rte. 21 • 396-2383 • gay-friendly • full breakfast • view of Lake Canandaigua • wheelchair access

New Paltz (914)

INFO LINES & SERVICES

Soujourner's Wimmin's Gathering Space PO Box 398, 12561 • sponsors variety of social/political events • write for calendar of events • wheelchair access

WOMEN'S ACCOMMODATIONS

▲ **Churchill Farm** 39 Canaan Rd. • 255-7291 (evenings)/ 687-7157 (days) • women only • full breakfast • hot tub • small country farmhouse in the mountains • women-owned/run • $75-95

ACCOMMODATIONS

Ujjala's B&B 2 Forest Glen • 255-6360 • gay-friendly • full breakfast • 1910 Victorian house nestled among apple trees • stress management • body therapy • sweat lodges

TRAVEL & TOUR OPERATORS

New Paltz Travel Center, Inc. 7 Cherry Hill Center • 255-7706 • IGTA member

New York City

New York City is divided into 10 areas:

OVERVIEW	(212)
THE VILLAGE / CHELSEA	(212)
MIDTOWN	(212)
UPTOWN	(212)
BRONX	(212)
BROOKLYN	(718)
QUEENS	(718)
LONG ISLAND/NASSAU	(516)
LONG ISLAND/SUFFOLK	(516)
STATEN ISLAND	(718)

Overview (212)

INFO LINES & SERVICES

AA Gay/Lesbian Intergroup • 647-1680 • many mtgs. at Lesbian/Gay Community Center

African Ancestral Lesbians United for Societal Change (at Lesbian/Gay Community Center) • 8pm Th

Asians & Friends of NY (at Lesbian/Gay Community Center) • 8pm 3rd Sat

Bisexual Gay/Lesbian Youth of NY (at Lesbian/Gay Community Center) • 3pm Sat

Bisexual Network • 459-4784 • recorded info on variety of social & political groups

Bisexual Women of Color (at Lesbian/Gay Community Center) • 6:30pm 1st & 3rd Fri

Bisexual Women's Group (at Lesbian/Gay Community Center) • 6:30pm 2nd & 4th Wed

Butch/Femme Society (at Lesbian/Gay Community Center) • 6:30pm 3rd Wed

Dyke TV PO Box 55, Prince St. Stn., 10012-0001 • 8pm 1st Wed Channel 32 • 'weekly half hour TV show produced by lesbians, for lesbians'

EDGE (Education in a Disabled Gay Environment) • 929-7178/ 749-9438 (TTY) • wheelchair access

Eulenspiegel Society 24 Bond St. • 388-7022 • 7:30pm Tue & Wed • S/M group • also newsletter

Fat is a Lesbian Issue (at Lesbian/Gay Community Center) • 5pm 2nd Sun • 'fat-positive anti-diet discussion group for fat women & their allies'

Gay Women's Alternative 160 Central Park W. (Unitarian Universalist Church) • 865-3979/ 595-8410 (church #) • 8pm 1st Th (Oct-June) • speakers • events

Gay/Lesbian Switchboard • 777-1800 • noon-midnight

Hetrick-Martin Institute 2 Astor Pl. • 674-2400 • extensive services for lesbigay youth • also publishes 'You Are Not Alone' resource directory

Just Couples (at Lesbian/Gay Community Center) • 3:30pm 1st Sun • 'discussion of topics relevant to couples' • also weekly activities

Kambal Sa Lusog (at Lesbian/Gay Community Center) • Pilipinas lesbians/gays/bisexuals • call Center for date

Las Buenas Amigas (at Lesbian/Gay Community Center) • 2pm 1st & 3rd Sun • Latina lesbian group

Legal Clinic (at Lesbian/Gay Community Center) • 6:30pm Tue • drop-in • free legal consultation

Lesbian Avengers (at Lesbian/Gay Community Center) • 967-7711x3204 • 8pm Mon

New York City

*I*n the film *Mondo New York*, club maven Joey Arias put it best: "New York is the clit of the world!"

Get ready for the most stimulating trip of your life! You've come to *the* city of world-famous tourist attractions from tall buildings, to the power centers of the hemisphere, to the theater and art pinnacles of the world. In fact, do your homework before you come, and call the huge **Lesbian/Gay Community Center** (meeting spaces for every conceivable group of lesbigaytrans+ people).

Whether you pride yourself on your cultural sophistication, or lack thereof, you're going to find endless entertainments. For starters, there are plays, musicals, operas, museums and gallery shows, performance art, street theater and street life.

New York's performance art is a must-see for any student of modern culture. The best bets for intelligent, cutting edge shows by women and queers are **W.O.W. (Women's One World) Cafe** (460-8067, at 59 E. 4th St.), and P.S. 122 on 1st Ave. at 9th St in St. Marks Place. Lesbian artist Holly Hughes got her start here, as have many other thorns in Jesse Helms' side.

For half-price tickets to Broadway and off-Broadway shows available the day of the show, stop by the **TKTS** booth on 47th St. at Broadway. For the latest reviews and hot off-off-Broadway theaters, check out **Manhattan Pride** or the **Village Voice** (extremely queer-friendly).

Of course, you can stimulate a lot more than your cultural sensibilities in New York. With endless time or credit, your palate could experience oral orgasms ranging from a delicate quiver to a blinding throb every day. And that's just your taste buds. For instance, before that Broadway show, head to one of the many restaurants along 46th St. at 9th Ave. When in Brooklyn, brunch along 7th Ave.; you'll find plenty of lesbigay company on a Sunday morning.

Shopping, too, affords shivers of delight. Check out the fabulous thrift shops and the designer boutiques. Cruise Midtown on Madison Ave., E. 57th St., or 5th Ave. in the 50's, at Trump Tower or another major shopping mall, and touch – actually *touch* – clothing more expensive than your last car.

Other recommended districts for blowing cash on the coolest/ funnest/ neatest stuff include St. Mark's Place in the Village (8th St.

at 1st and 2nd Avenues); Broadway from 8th to Canal St., and any major intersection in Soho and the East Village.

For a respite from overwhelming consumerism, peruse the shelves at the lesbigay **Oscar Wilde Memorial Bookshop,** or **Eve's Garden,** New York's women's erotic boutique — men must be escorted in by a woman! Or make an appointment to visit the **Lesbian Herstory Archives** in Brooklyn.

You could spend days at the big art museums in Uptown near Central Park, but budget some time for the galleries in SoHo (south of Houston, between Broadway and 6th Ave.). Pick up a gallery map in the area.

For musical entertainment, make your pilgrimage to **The Kitchen,** legendary site of experimental and freestyle jazz, or **CBGB's,** legendary home of noisy music for the next decade (the Ramones started punk here in 1974).

Nightlife... yeah, you've been holding your breath. Wait no more, go directly to the **Clit Club,** do not pass go. Friday nights on W. 14th St. are the sexiest, hottest dyke nights in, oh, the Northeast. **Crazy Nanny's** *happens* seven days a week, and several other women's bars are nearby. **Shescape** produces women's club nights at various locations, so call for their latest events. Kinky dykes should also check out **Buster's,** an S/M bar in Midtown, and get the latest schedule for **The Vault** partyspace in the Village.

Pick up a copy of **Homo Xtra** for up-to-the-minute club happenings – even though it's boy-heavy, it's got the skinny on *hip.* If hip's not your thing, try **Sappho's Isle,** a monthly for lesbians in the tri-state area.

Although it's the *hot* and humid season, June is when New York hosts a gazillion Lesbian/Gay Pride-related cultural events, from their week-long Film Festival to the Pride March itself. Immerse yourself in queer culture in the San Francisco of the East Coast.

In Brooklyn, call **SAL** (Social Activities for Lesbians) to find out the scoop. Nassau Countyites should stop by the **Women's Alternative Community Center** or **Bedrock** women's bar. On the other side of Long Island, **Forever Green** or **St. Marks Place** are the bars of choice, while **Womankind** bookstore is the only one of its kind.

Your Home Away From Home

The Lesbian and Gay Community Services Center New York

▼ *400 lesbian and gay organizations hold their meetings at the Center.*

▼ *5,000 people visit the Center each week.*

Come and enjoy our Lesbian Movie Night, our women's dances, our lesbian sexuality and health workshops, lesbian-sensitive 12-step meetings, our readings, exhibits, library and lectures, our gay and lesbian garden to rest your feet after a day of sightseeing, and much more!

LESBIAN AND GAY COMMUNITY SERVICES CENTER
208 West 13th Street, Greenwich Village
(14th Street stop on the ❶, ❷ and ❸ subway lines)
212 620-7310

Please add my name to the center mailing list!

Name

Address

Telephone

Lesbian Breast Cancer Support Group (at Lesbian/Gay Community Center) • 6pm 2nd & 4th Tue

Lesbian Herstory Archives PO Box 1258, 10116 • (718) 768-3953 • exists to gather & preserve records of lesbian lives & activities • located in Park Slope • wheelchair access

Lesbian Switchboard • 741-2610 • 6pm-10pm Mon-Fri

Lesbian/Gay Community Services Center 208 W. 13th St. • 620-7310 • 9am-11pm • meeting location for various groups • newsletter • wheelchair access

LSM (Lesbian Sex Mafia) PO Box 993, Murray Hill Stn., 10156 • women's S/M support group

NY CyberQueers (at Lesbian/Gay Community Center) • 7pm 3rd Th • lesbigay & transgender 'computer pros'

Party Talk Manhattan Cable Ch. 35 • 9pm Th & 11pm Sun • club reviews

SAGE (Senior Action in a Gay Environment) (at Lesbian/Gay Community Center) • 741-2247 • offers variety of social services

SAL (Social Activities for Lesbians) PO Box 150118, 11215 • 630-9505 • sponsors variety of activities • monthly calendar

SALGA (South Asian Lesbian/Gay Association) (at Lesbian/Gay Community Center) • 3:30pm 2nd Sat • or write PO Box 902, 10009-0902

Sirens Motorcycle Club (at Lesbian/Gay Community Center) • 8pm 3rd Tue

Support Group for Single Lesbians (at Lesbian/Gay Community Center) • 6:30pm Tue & Fri

Twenty Something (at Lesbian/Gay Community Center) • 8pm 1st & 3rd Tue • social alternative to bars/clubs for lesbigays in late teens, 20s & early 30s

Women About: The Adventure Social Club for Lesbians PO Box 280 JAF Stn., 10116 • 947-7439 • fun indoor/outdoor activities for women in tri-state area • quarterly calendar • write for info

Women Playwrights Collective (at Lesbian/Gay Community Center) • 6pm 1st, 3rd & 5th Wed

New York City (212)

LESBIGAY INFO: Lesbian & Gay Community Services Center: 620-7310, 208 W. 13th St., 9am-11pm. Gay Switchboard: 777-1800, noon-midnight.

LESBIGAY PAPER: Manhattan Pride: 268-0454. Homo Xtra: 627-0247. Sappho's Isle: (516) 747-5417.

WHERE THE GIRLS ARE: Upwardly mobile literary types hang in the West Village, hipster dykes cruise the East Village, upper-crusty Lesbians have cocktails in Midtown, and working class dykes live in Brooklyn.

LESBIGAY AA: Intergroup: 647-1680.

LESBIGAY PRIDE: June, 626-6925.

ANNUAL EVENTS: June - New York Int'l Gay/Lesbian Film Festival: 343-2707, week-long fest. September 1 - Wigstock: 620-7310, outrageous wig/drag/performance festival in Tompkins Square Park in the East Village. November - AIDS Dance-a-thon: 807-9255, AIDS benefit. November - Mix '96: New York Lesbian/Gay Experimental Film/Video Fest: 501-2309, film, videos, installations & media performances.

CITY INFO: 397-8222.

BEST VIEW: Coming over any of the bridges into New York, the Empire State Building or the World Trade Center.

WEATHER: A spectrum of extremes with pleasant moments thrown in.

TRANSIT: Taxi: An experience you'll always remember.

ACCOMMODATIONS

Aaah! Bed & Breakfast PO Box 2093, 10108 • 246-4000 • gay-friendly • reservations agency

New York Reservation Center PO Box 2646, 11969 • 977-3512 • lesbians/gay men • IGTA member

SPIRITUAL GROUPS

Axios (at Lesbian/Gay Community Center) • (718) 805-1952 • 8pm 2nd Fri • Eastern & Orthodox Christians

Buddhist Lesbians/Gays: Maitri Dorje (at Lesbian/Gay Community Center) • 6pm 2nd Tue

Congregation Beth Simchat Torah 57 Bethune St. • 929-9498 • 8:30pm Fri (8pm summers) • lesbian/gay synagogue • wheelchair access

Dignity-Big Apple 110 Christopher St. • 627-6488

Evangelicals Concerned c/o Dr. Ralph Blair 311 E. 72nd St. #1G, 10021 • 517-3171

Gay/Lesbian Yeshiva Day School Alumni (at Lesbian/Gay Community Center) • 8:30pm 4th Th • social/support to integrate Jewish & lesbian/gay identities

Integrity NYC 487 Hudson St. (St. Luke's) • 720-3054 • 7:30pm Th

MCC of New York 446 W. 36th St. • 629-7440 • 10am & 7pm Sun

Meditation for Gays/Lesbians/Bisexuals (at Lesbian/Gay Community Center) • 8pm 1st & 3rd Wed

National Conference for Catholic Lesbians PO Box 436 Planetarium Stn., 10024 • (718) 680-6107 • national group • biannual conference • quarterly newsletter • for local NY chapter call (212) 663-2963

Society of Friends (Quakers) 15 Rutherford Pl. (Meeting House) • 777-8866 • 9:30am & 11am Sun

PUBLICATIONS

Colorlife 301 Cathedral Park Wy. Box 287, 10026 • 222-9794 • focuses on lesbians/gays of color

Feminist Caucus of NAAFA PO Box 1154, 10023 • 721-8259 • fat women's newsletter

Gayellow Pages Box 533 Village Stn., 10014-0533 • 674-0120 • annual guidebook • national & regional editions

Homo Xtra 19 W. 21st Ste. 703 • 627-0747 • weekly complete party paper

Lesbian & Gay New York 225 Lafayette St. #1103, 10012 • 343-7200

▲ **Manhattan Pride** 242 W. 30th St. 5th flr. • 268-0454 • monthly

Network PO Box 10372, New Brunswick, NJ 08906 • (908) 249-2926 • regional newsmagazine • covers central East Coast

New York Native/Stonewall News PO Box 1475 Church St. Stn., 10008 • 627-2120 • weekly

Sappho's Isle 960 Willis Ave., Albertson, 11507 • (516) 747-5417 • monthly • lesbian paper for NYC area & tri-state region

The Village/Chelsea

INFO LINES & SERVICES

St. Mark's Women's Health Collective 9 2nd Ave. • 228-7482 • 6pm-10pm (appt. only) • 'serving the lesbian community since 1974 w/ low cost medical care'

WOW Cafe Cabaret 59 E. 4th St. • 460-8067 • Th-Sat • women's theater • call for events

WOMEN'S ACCOMMODATIONS

East Village B&B • 260-1865 • mostly women • second flr. apt. located in an urban, multi-ethnic neighborhood

ACCOMMODATIONS

A Village B&B • 387-9117 • lesbians/gay men • studio apts.

Abingdon B&B 13 8th Ave. (at W. 12th) • 243-5384 • lesbians/gay men • smoke-free

Chelsea Inn 46 W. 17th St. • 645-8989 • gay-friendly

Chelsea Mews Guest House 344 W. 15th St. • 255-9174 • mostly gay men

Chelsea Pines Inn 317 W. 14th St. • 929-1023 • popular • lesbians/gay men • IGTA member

▲ **Colonial House Inn** 318 W. 22nd St. • 243-9669/ (800) 689-3779 • lesbians/gay men • 20 rooms • sundeck • IGTA member

Holiday Inn 138 Lafayette St. • 966-8898 • gay-friendly • IGTA member

Incentra Village House 32 8th Ave. • 206-0007 • popular • lesbians/gay men • two red brick buildings built in 1841

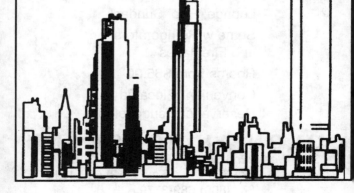

BARS

Bar 68 2nd Ave. (4th St.) • 674-9714 • 4pm-4am • mostly gay men • neighborhood bar • wheelchair access

The Boiler Room 86 E. 4th St. • 254-7536 • 4pm-4am • mostly gay men • neighborhood bar • dyke night 10pm Sun

Boots & Saddle 76 Christopher St. • 929-9684 • 8am-4am, noon-4pm Sun • mostly gay men • neighborhood bar

Clit Club 432 W. 14th St. (Bar Room) • 366-5680 • 10pm Fri • popular • mostly women • dancing/DJ • multi-racial • live shows • wheelchair access

▲ **Crazy Nanny's** 21 7th Ave. S. • 929-8356 • 4pm-4am • popular • mostly women • live shows • dancing/DJ after 10pm Th-Sat

Crow Bar 339 E. 10th St. • 420-0670 • 9pm-4am • lesbians/gay men • live shows

Cubbyhole 281 W. 12th St. • 243-9041 • opens 4pm • popular • mostly women • neighborhood bar • piano bar wknds

Dick's Bar 192 2nd Ave. (12th St.) • 475-2071 • 2pm-4am • mostly gay men • videos

Dugout 185 Christopher St. • 242-9113 • 4pm-2am, from noon Fri-Sun • mostly gay men • neighborhood bar • sports bar • wheelchair access

Eighty Eights 228 W. 10th St. • 924-0088 • 4pm-4am • gay-friendly • piano bar & cabaret • Sun brunch • wheelchair access

Five Oaks 49 Grove St. • 243-8885 • 5pm-4am • gay-friendly • piano bar • also a restaurant • dinner (except Mon) • piano bar • $15-20

Henrietta Hudson 438 Hudson (at Morton) • 243-9079 • 3pm-4am • popular • mostly women • neighborhood bar • wheelchair access

Marie's Crisis 59 Grove St. • 243-9323 • 5pm-3am • popular • lesbians/gay men • piano bar from 9:30pm

Mike's Club Cafe 400 W. 14th St. (at 9th) • 691-6606 • 2pm-4am • mostly gay men • neighborhood bar

Monster 80 Grove St. • 924-3557 • 4pm-4am, from 2pm wknds • popular • mostly gay men • dancing/DJ • piano bar

Nells 246 W. 14th St. (at 8th Ave.) • 675-1567 • gay-friendly • dancing/DJ

Events (212) 366-6312
Bar (212) 929-8356
Fax (212) 807-9195

Crazy Nanny's

A Place for Gay Women
Biological or Otherwise

2 Bars, Pool Table, Dancing, Cabaret, Outdoor Cafe

21 7th Avenue South   New York, NY 10014

One Potato 518 Hudson St. • 691-6260 • 4pm-2am, from noon wknds, til 4am Fri-Sat • lesbians/gay men • also a restaurant • American homestyle • $7-11

Roxy 515 W. 18th St. • 645-5156 • 11pm Tue & Sat • mostly gay men • rollerskating 8pm-2am Tue • dancing/DJ Sat

Ruby Fruit Bar & Grill 531 Hudson St. • 929-3343 • 3pm-4am, from noon Sun • mostly women • also a restaurant

S.O.S. 20 W. 20th St. (at 5th Ave.) • 631-1102 • 10pm Sat • mostly women • dancing/DJ

Shescape • 645-6479 • mostly women • dance parties held at various locations throughout NYC area • call for current schedule

Sneakers 392 West St. • 242-9830 • noon-4am • mostly gay men • neighborhood bar • multi-racial • wheelchair access

Stonewall Inn 53 Christopher St. • 463-0950 • 4pm-4am • mostly gay men • wheelchair access

Tunnel Bar 116 1st Ave. (7th St.) • 777-9232 • 2pm-4am • popular • mostly gay men • neighborhood bar • videos

Two Potato 143 Christopher St. • 255-0286 • noon-4am • mostly gay men • neighborhood bar • multi-racial

Wonder Bar 505 E. 6th St. (Ave. A) • 777-9105 • 8pm-4am • lesbians/gay men • neighborhood bar

WOW Bar 229 W. 28th St. • 631-1102 • 9:30pm Fri • mostly women • dancing/DJ • live shows

RESTAURANTS & CAFES

Black Sheep 344 W. 11th St. • 242-1010 • popular • fine dining w/ nostalgic country cooking • $16-25

Brunetta's 190 1st Ave. (11th) • 228-4030 • popular • lesbians/gay men • Italian • some veggie • $8-10

C.J. Blanda's 209 7th Ave. (22nd St.) • 206-7880 • lunch & dinner • popular • Italian • some veggie • full bar • $10-15

Cafe Tabac 232 E. 9th St. • 674-7072 • 6pm-3am • popular • full bar • women's party Sun night

Chelsea Clinton Cafe 184 8th Ave. (19th St.) • 989-5289 • noon-11pm • upscale French/Italian • full bar

Circa 103 2nd Ave. (E. 6th St.) • 777-4120 • open late • popular • new American menu • wheelchair access

Claire 156 7th Ave. (19th St.) • 255-1955

Cola's 148 8th Ave. • 633-8020 • popular • Italian • some veggie • inexpensive • $8-12

Empire Diner 210 10th Ave. (22nd St.) • 243-2736 • 24hrs • upscale diner

Florent 69 Gansevoort St. • 989-5779 • 24hrs • popular • French diner • $10-15

Food Bar 149 8th Ave. (17th St.) • 243-2020 • popular

Lucky Cheng's 24 1st Ave. (2nd St.) • 473-0516

Orbit Cafe 46 Bedford St. (7th) • 463-8717 • lunch & dinner, gospel brunch noon-5pm Sun, bar noon-2am, til 4am Fri-Sat • midscale American w/Latin accent • plenty veggie • full bar • wheelchair access • $9-20

Sazerac House Bar & Grill 533 Hudson • 989-0313 • noon-midnight • Cajun • full bar • $8-20

Sugar Reef 93 2nd Ave. (5th) • 477-8427 • 5pm-midnight • Caribbean • full bar • call for location of roving club Sugar Babies • $8-15

Sung Tieng 343 Bleeker St. (10th) • 929-7800 • popular • delivery

Universal Grill 44 Bedford St. • 989-5621 • lunch, dinner & Sun brunch • popular • lesbians/gay men

Viceroy 160 8th Ave. (18th St.) • 633-8484 • popular • full bar

GYMS & HEALTH CLUBS

Archives Gym 666 Greenwich Ave. • 366-3725 • lesbian-run

Better Bodies 22 W. 19th St. • 929-6789 • 6:30am-10:30pm, 9:30am-8pm wknds • lesbians/gay men

BOOKSTORES & RETAIL SHOPS

A Different Light 151 W. 19th St. • 989-4850/ (800) 343-4002 • 11am-10pm • lesbigay bookstore

Alternate Card & Gift Shop 85 Christopher St. • 645-8966 • noon-11pm

Don't Panic 98 Christopher St. • 989-7888 • outrageous T-shirts & more

Greetings 45 Christopher St. • 242-0424 • 11am-10pm

▲ **Oscar Wilde Memorial Bookshop** 15 Christopher St. • 255-8097 • 11:30am-9pm • lesbigay

The Rainbows & Triangles 192 8th Ave. • 627-2166 • 11am-9pm • lesbigay

Wendell's Books 302 W. 12th St. • 675-0877 • 7am-11pm • magazines at 22 8th Ave. 645-1197 • 10am-10pm, 11am-8pm Sun

TRAVEL & TOUR OPERATORS

Bon Adventure Travel 1173-A 2nd Ave. #135 • 759-2206 • IGTA member

Islander's Kennedy Travel 183 W. 10th St. • 242-3222/ (800) 988-1185 • also Queens location: 267-10 Hillside Ave., Floral Park • (800)237-7433 • IGTA member

Midtown   (212)

ACCOMMODATIONS

Central Park South B&B • 586-0652 • lesbians/gay men

Park Central Hotel 870 7th Ave. at 56th St. • 247-8000/ (800) 346-1359 • gay-friendly • also a restaurant • wheelchair access

BARS

Buster's 129 Lexington Ave. (at 29th) • 684-8832 • noon-4am • lesbians/gay men • neighborhood bar

Cat's Bar 232 W. 48th • 245-5245 • 8am-4am • mostly gay men • neighborhood bar • live shows

Cleo's Saloon 656 9th Ave. (46 St.) • 307 1503 • 8am-4am, from noon Sun • mostly gay men • neighborhood bar

Club 58 40 E. 58th St. • 308-1546 • 4pm 2am, til 4am Mon & Sat • mostly gay men • dancing/DJ • mostly Asian-American

Don't Tell Mama 343 W. 46th St. • 757-0788 • 4pm-4am • popular • gay-friendly • piano bar • cabaret

Edelweiss 580 11th Ave. (at 43rd St.) • 629-1021 • 2pm-4am • gay-friendly • dancing/DJ • fun mix of drag, transgende & everything else

Her/She Bar 229 W. 28th St. (7th & 8th Aves.) • 330-9172 • Fri only • mostly women • dancing/DJ • call for events

Julie's 204 E. 58th St. (3rd flr.) • 688-1294 • 5pm-4am • mostly women • professional • live shows

Sound Factory 530 W. 27th St. • 643-0728 • gay-friendly • dancing/DJ • live shows • juice bar • popular after hours • call for events

South Dakota 405 3rd Ave. (29 St.) •
684-8376 • 3pm-4am • mostly gay men •
neighborhood bar • country/western •
wheelchair access

Restaurants & Cafes

Cafe Un Deux Trois 123 W. 44th St. •
354-4148 • noon-midnight • bistro •
$12-24

Good Diner 554 42nd St. (at 11th Ave.) •
967-2661 • 24hrs • diner food, slightly
upscale • $8-10

Townhouse Restaurant 206 E. 58th (at
3rd) • 826-6241 • lunch & dinner, Sun
brunch, late on wknds • lesbians/gay
men • live shows • eclectic & elegant •
plenty veggie • $10-23

Travel & Tour Operators

Our Family Abroad • 459-1800 • all-
inclusive package & guided tours to
Europe, Asia, Africa & S. America

Pied Piper Travel 330 W. 42nd St. Ste.
1601 • 239-2412/ (800) 874-7312 • IGTA
member

Stevens Travel Management 432 Park
Ave. S., 9th flr. • 696-4300/ (800) 275-7400
• IGTA member

Erotica

Eve's Garden 119 W. 57th St. Ste. 420 •
757-8651 • noon-7pm, clsd Sun •
women's sexuality boutique & healing
arts center • no un-escorted men allowed

Uptown (212)

Accommodations

Malibu Studios Hotel 2688 Broadway •
222-2954/ (800) 647-2227 • gay-friendly

New York B&B 134 W. 119th St. • 666-
0559 • gay-friendly • also inexpensive
dorm rooms

Bars

Brandy's Piano Bar 235 E. 84th St. •
650-1944 • 4pm-4am • gay-friendly • live
shows • wheelchair access

Candle Bar 309 Amsterdam (at 74th St.)
• 874-9155 • 2pm-4am • popular •
mostly gay men • neighborhood bar

Erotica

Come Again 353 E. 53rd St. • 308-9394 •
clsd Sun

Bronx (212)

Info Lines & Services

**BLUES (Bronx Lesbians United in
Sisterhood)** PO Box 1738, 10451 • 330-
9196

Dyke TV Channel 70 • 9pm Th • 'weekly
half-hour TV show produced by lesbians,
for lesbians'

Brooklyn (718)

Info Lines & Services

Dyke TV Channel 34/67 • 10:30pm Tue •
'weekly half-hour TV show produced by
lesbians, for lesbians'

**GGALA (Greek Gay/Lesbian Associa-
tion)** (at Lesbian/Gay Community Center)
• 8pm 2nd & 4th Th

SAL (Social Activities for Lesbians) PO
Box 150118, 11215 • 630-9505 • sponsors
variety of activities • monthly calendar

Bars

One Hot Spot 1 Front St. • 852-0139 •
5pm-3am, clsd Mon • mostly gay men •
dancing/DJ • multi-racial • live shows

Roost 309 7th Ave. • 788-9793 • noon-
2am • gay-friendly • neighborhood bar

Spectrum 802 64th St. • 238-8213 •
9pm-4am Wed-Sun • popular • les-
bians/gay men • dancing/DJ • live shows

Bookstores & Retail Shops

A Room of Our Own 444 9th St. • 499-
2223 • 1pm-9pm, from 11am wknds •
lesbigay

Community Book Store 143 7th Ave. •
783-3075 • 10am-9pm

Travel & Tour Operators

Avalon Travel 9421 3rd Ave. • 833-5500 •
IGTA member

Deville Travel Service 7818 3rd Ave. •
680-2700 • IGTA member

J. Bette Travel 4809 Ave. 'N' #279 • 241-
3872

Queens (718)

BARS

Club Reflexions 69-45 51st Ave., Woodside • 429-8834 • 8pm-4am • mostly women • dancing/DJ • live shows

Krash 34-48 Steinway St., Astoria • 366-2934 • clsd Sun-Tue • lesbians/gay men • dancing/DJ • multi-racial • more women Sat

Love Boat 77-02 Broadway, Elmhurst • 429-8670 • mostly gay men • mostly Latino-American

Montana 40-08 74th St. • 429-9356 • noon-4am • mostly gay men • country/western

Long Island/Nassau (516)

INFO LINES & SERVICES

Middle Earth Hotline 2740 Martin Ave., Bellmore • 679-1111 • 24hrs • crisis & referral counseling • especially for youth

Pride for Youth Coffeehouse 170 Fulton St., Farmingdale • 679-9000 • 7:30pm-11:30pm Fri

Women's Alternative Community Center 699 Woodfield Rd., W. Hempstead, 11552 • 483-2050 • many events & activities • call for info

ACCOMMODATIONS

Summit Motor Inn 501 E. Main St., Bay Shore • 666-6000/ (800) 869-6363 • gay-friendly • wheelchair access

BARS

Bedrock 121 Woodfield Rd., West Hempstead • 486-9516 • 8pm-3am, from 1pm Sun, clsd Mon • mostly women • dancing/DJ • live shows • wheelchair access

Chameleon 40-20 Long Beach Rd., Long Beach • 889-4083 • 9pm-4am, clsd Mon-Wed • popular • lesbians/gay men • dancing/DJ • women's night Fri • T-dance Sun

Libations 3547 Merrick Rd., Seaford • 679-8820 • 3pm-4am • lesbians/gay men • neighborhood bar

Silver Lining 175 Cherry Ln., Floral Park • 354-9641 • 9pm-4am Wed-Sun • lesbians/gay men • dancing/DJ • live shows • videos • wheelchair access

TRAVEL & TOUR OPERATORS

All Continent Tours Inc. 250 Hempstead Ave., Malverne • (800) 553-0009

SPIRITUAL GROUPS

Dignity-Nassau County PO Box 48, East Meadow, 11554 • 781-6225 • 2nd & 4th Sat

PUBLICATIONS

Sappho's Isle 960 Willis Ave., Albertson, 11507 • 747-5417 • monthly • lesbian paper for tri-state region

Long Island/Suffolk (516)

INFO LINES & SERVICES

AA • 669-1124

EEGO (East End Gay Organization) PO Box 87, Southampton, 11968 • 324-3699 • events calendar & info

GLIB (Gay Men & Lesbians in Brookhaven) PO Box 203, Brookhaven, 11719-0203 • 286-6867 • women's support 8pm 1st & 3rd Th

ACCOMMODATIONS

132 North Main Guesthouse 132 N. Main, East Hampton • 324-2246 • seasonal • mostly gay men • swimming • mini-resort on 2 wooded acres • 5 min. from town & beaches

Centennial House 13 Woods Ln., East Hampton • 324-9414 • gay-friendly • full breakfast • swimming • weathered single house built in 1876

Cozy Cabins Motel Box 848, Montauk Hwy., East Hampton, 11975 • 537-1160 • seasonal • lesbians/gay men

Econo Lodge - MacArthur Airport 3055 Veterans Memorial Hwy., Ronkonkoma • 588-6800/ (800) 553-2666 • gay-friendly

EconoLodge - Smithtown/Hauppauge 755 Rte. 347, Smithtown • 724-9000/ (800) 553-2666 • gay-friendly

Sag Harbor B&B 125 Mt. Misery Dr., Sag Harbor • 725-5945 • lesbians/gay men • full breakfast • spacious cedar house nestled in the woods near the very private village of Sag Harbor • wheelchair access

Shady Pines Resort 380 Montauk Hwy., Wainscott • 537-1037 • lesbians/gay men • swimming

BARS

Club Swamp Montauk Hwy. at E. Gate Rd., Wainscott • 537-3332 • 6pm-4am, daily during summer, clsd Tue-Wed • mostly gay men • dancing/DJ • also a restaurant • cont'l/seafood (clsd Sun) • $16-20

Forever Green 841 N. Broome Ave., Lindenhurst • 226-9357 • 8pm-4am, from 7pm Sun • mostly women • neighborhood bar

St. Mark's Place 65-50 Jericho Pkwy., Commack • 499-2244 • 4pm-4am • lesbians/gay men • dancing/DJ • also a restaurant • American • some veggie • wheelchair access • lesbian-owned/run • $4-14

Thunders 1017 E. Jericho Trnpk., Huntington Station • 423-5241 • clsd Mon • lesbians/gay men • piano bar

RESTAURANTS & CAFES

Bayman's Katch 220 Montauk Hwy., Sayville • 589-9744 • 4pm-2am, clsd Tue • American • full bar • $9-17

BOOKSTORES & RETAIL SHOPS

▲ **Womankind Books** 5 Kivy St., Huntington Stn., 11746 • 427-1289 • extensive women's mail order company • large selection of lesbian titles, music & jewelry • free catalog

SPIRITUAL GROUPS

Dignity-Suffolk County Box 621-P, Bay Shore, 11706 • 654-5367

Unitarian Universalist Fellowship 109 Brown Rd., Huntington • 427-9547 • 10:30am Sun • many groups & social events

Staten Island (718)

INFO LINES & SERVICES

Lambda Associates of Staten Island PO Box 665, 10305 • 876-8786

BARS

Sand Castle 86 Mills Ave. • 447-9365 • 9am-4am • popular • lesbians/gay men • dancing/DJ • live shows • wheelchair access

Niagara Falls (716)

INFO LINES & SERVICES

GALS (Gay/Lesbian Support) PO Box 1464, 14302 • meets 2nd Sat

ACCOMMODATIONS

Olde Niagara House B&B 610 4th St. • 285-9408 • gay-friendly • full breakfast

BARS

Club Alternate 492 19th St. (Ferry) • mostly gay men • dancing/DJ • inquire locally

Nyack (914)

BARS

Barz 327 Rte. 9 W. • 353-4444 • 5pm-4am, from 3pm Sat, from noon Sun, clsd Mon • lesbians/gay men • dancing/DJ • wheelchair access

Coven Cafe 162 Main St. • 358-9829 • noon-midnight, til 2am Fri-Sat, Sun brunch, clsd Mon • gay-friendly • live shows • Wed men's night • also a restaurant • plenty veggie • $9-15 • wheelchair access

BOOKSTORES & RETAIL SHOPS

New Spirit Books & Beyond 128 Main St. • 353-2126 • noon-7pm, clsd Mon

Orange County (914)

INFO LINES & SERVICES

Orange County Gay/Lesbian Alliance PO Box 1557, Greenwood Lake, 10925 • 782-1525 • 7:30pm Tue • support groups

RESTAURANTS & CAFES

Folderol II Rte. 284, Westtown • 726-3822 • 5pm-11pm, from 11am Sun • French/farmhouse • some veggie • dancing/DJ after 11pm Sat • patio • wheelchair access • gay-owned/run • $13-20

Oswego (315)

INFO LINES & SERVICES

SUNY Oswego Women's Center 243 Hewitt Union, 2nd flr. • 341-2967

Owego (607)

TRAVEL & TOUR OPERATORS

Tioga Travel 189 Main St. • 687-4144

Plattsburg (518)

BARS

Blair's Tavern 30 Marion St. • 561-9071 • 4pm-2am • lesbians/gay men • dancing/DJ

Port Chester (914)

BARS

Sandy's Old Homested 325 N. Main St. • 939-0758 • 8am-4am • gay-friendly • also a restaurant • American • wheelchair access

Poughkeepsie (914)

INFO LINES & SERVICES

Poughkeepsie GALA (Gay/Lesbian Association) PO Box 289, Hughsonville, 12537 • 431-6756 • 7:30pm Tue

Vassar Gay People's Alliance Box 271, 12601 • 437-7203

BARS

Congress 411 Main St. • 486-9068 • 3pm-4am, from 8pm Sun • lesbians/gay men • neighborhood bar • wheelchair access

Rochester (716)

INFO LINES & SERVICES

AA Gay/Lesbian • 232-6720

Dyke TV Channel 15 • 8:30pm Mon • 'weekly half hour TV show produced by lesbians, for lesbians'

Finger Lakes Gay/Lesbian Social Group Box 941, Geneva, 14456 • 536-7753 • 1st Fri & 3rd Tue • ask for Sam Edwards

Gay Alliance 179 Atlantic Ave. • 244-8640 • 1pm-9pm, til 6pm Fri

BARS

Anthony's 522 Main St. E. • 325-1350 • noon-2am • lesbians/gay men • neighborhood bar

Atlantis 10-12 S. Washington St. • 255-8551 • mostly gay men • dancing/DJ • call for events

Avenue Pub 522 Monroe Ave. • 244-4960 • 4pm-2am • popular • mostly gay men • neighborhood bar • dancing/DJ • more women at happy hour • patio

Chena's 145 E. Main St. • 232-7240 • 11am-2am • mostly women • neighborhood bar • food served • wheelchair access

Club Marcella 123 Liberty Pole Wy. • 454-5963 • clsd Mon-Tue • lesbians/gay men • dancing/DJ • live shows

Common Grounds 139 State St. • 232-9303 • noon-2am • lesbians/gay men • neighborhood bar

Freakazoid 169 N. Chestnut St. • 987-0000 • gay-friendly • dancing/DJ • alternative • call for events

Muther's 40 Union • 325-6216 • 3pm-2am, from 11am wknds • lesbians/gay men • live shows • also a restaurant • American • some veggie • women's night 2nd & 3rd Th • $5-18

Stages/Vortex 88 Liberty Pole Wy. • 232-5070 • lesbians/gay men • dancing/DJ • 18+ • 2 flrs. • women's night Sat • call for events

Tara 153 Liberty Pole Wy. • 232-4719 • noon-2am • popular • lesbians/gay men • piano bar • cabaret & dancing/DJ upstairs

Zei 171 St. Paul St. • 232-1600 • popular • mostly gay men • dancing/DJ • live shows • call for events

RESTAURANTS & CAFES

City Grill 75 Marshall St. • 423-2233 • lunch & dinner, Sun brunch • upscale American • some veggie • full bar • $14-22

Little Theatre Cafe 240 East Ave. • 258-0412 • 6pm-10pm, from noon wknds, til midnight Fri-Sat • popular • live shows • plenty veggie • wheelchair access

BOOKSTORES & RETAIL SHOPS

Pride Connection 728 South Ave. • 242-7840 • 10am-9pm, noon-6pm Sun • lesbigay

Rochester Custom Leathers 274 N. Goodman St. • 442-2323/ (800) 836-9047 • 11am-9pm • popular • large selection of lesbian/gay mags & videos

Silkwood Books 633 Monroe Ave. • 473-8110 • 11am-6pm, til 9pm Th-Fri, noon-5pm Sun, clsd Mon • women's/new age • wheelchair access

Village Green Books 766 Monroe Ave. • 461-5380 • 6am-11pm • also 1954 West Ridge Rd. location • 723-1600 • open 9am

TRAVEL & TOUR OPERATORS

DePrez Travel 145 Rue De Ville • 442-8900/ 234-3615 • ask for Ray Breslin • IGTA member

Great Expectations 1649 Monroe Ave. • 244-8430

Park Ave. Travel 25 Buckingham St. • 256-3080 • IGTA member

SPIRITUAL GROUPS

Nayim PO Box 18053, 14618 • 473-6459 • lesbian/gays Jews

Open Arms MCC 875 E. Main St. • 271-8478 • 10:30am Sun • wheelchair access

PUBLICATIONS

Empty Closet 127 Atlantic Ave. • 244-9030 • monthly

Schenectady (518)

ACCOMMODATIONS

Widow Kendall B&B 10 N. Ferry St. • (800) 244-0925 • year-round • gay-friendly • hot tub • fireplaces • gourmet breakfast • located in historic 18th century tavern

BARS

Blythewood 50 N. Jay St. • 382-9755 • 10pm-4am • mostly gay men • neighborhood bar • wheelchair access

Clinton St. Pub 159 Clinton St. • 382-9173 • noon-4am • lesbians/gay men • neighborhood bar

Seneca Falls (315)

ACCOMMODATIONS

Guion House 32 Cayuga St. • 568-8129 • gay-friendly • full breakfast

Spring Valley (914)

BARS

Hideaway 105 S. Pascack Rd. • 425-0025 • 9pm-4am, from 4pm Fri & Sun • lesbians/gay men • dancing/DJ • live shows • Sun BBQ • patio

Stone Ridge (914)

ACCOMMODATIONS

Inn at Stone Ridge Rte. 209 • 687-0736 • gay-friendly • near outdoor recreation • swimming • also a restaurant • regional American • full bar • historic home on 40 acres

Syracuse (315)

INFO LINES & SERVICES

AA Gay/Lesbian • 463-5011 • many mtgs

Gay/Lesbian Conference Line • 422-5732

Lesbian Social Group 601 Allen St. (Women's Center) • 6:30pm 1st & 3rd Fri

Syracuse Peace Council 924 Burnet Ave. • 472-5478 • also houses the Front Room Bookstore • lesbigay • call for hours

Women's Information Center 601 Allen St. • 478-4636 • office 10am-4pm Mon-Fri • wheelchair access

ACCOMMODATIONS

John Milton Inn Carrier Circle - Exit 35 • 463-8555/ (800) 352-1061 • gay-friendly • motel

BARS

Barney's 425 N. Salina St. • 478-2922 • 11am-2am Tue • gay-friendly • wheelchair access

Claudia's U.B.U. 1203 Milton Ave. • 468-9830 • 4pm-2am, from 7pm Sat, from noon Sun, clsd Mon-Tue • mostly women • dancing/DJ

My Bar 205 N. West St. • 471-9279 • noon-2am, til 4am Wed-Sat • lesbians/gay men • live shows • also a restaurant • patio

Ryan's Someplace Else 408-410 Pearl St. • 471-9499 • 8pm-2am, from noon Sun, clsd Mon-Wed • popular • mostly gay men • dancing/DJ • videos • wheelchair access

Trexx 319 N. Clinton St. • 474-6408 • 8pm-2am, til 4am Fri-Sat, clsd Mon-Wed • mostly gay men • dancing/DJ • live shows

RESTAURANTS & CAFES

Happy Endings 317 S. Clinton St. • 475-1853 • 8am-11pm, 10am-2am Fri-Sat, 6pm-11pm Sun • vegetarian • also live shows • wheelchair access

Tu Tu Venue 731 Jay St. • 475-8888 • 4pm-1am, clsd Sun • full bar • $12-15

BOOKSTORES & RETAIL SHOPS

My Sister's Words 304 N. McBride St. • 428-0227 • 10am-6pm, til 8pm Th-Fri, clsd Sun (except Dec) • women's bookstore & community bulletin board

PUBLICATIONS

Pink Paper PO Box 6462, 13217 • 476-5186 • published 6 times year

Utica (315)

INFO LINES & SERVICES

Greater Utica Lambda Fellowship PO Box 122, 13505

BARS

Carmen D's 812 Charlotte St. • 735-3964 • 4pm-2am, from 8pm Sat, clsd Sun • lesbians/gay men • neighborhood bar

Options 1724 W. Oriskany • 724-9231 • 5pm-2am, clsd Mon-Tue • lesbians/gay men • patio

That Place 216 Bleecker St. • 724-1446 • 8pm-2am, from 4pm Fri • popular • mostly gay men • dancing/DJ • wheelchair access

White Plains (914)

INFO LINES & SERVICES

Lesbian Line • 949-3203 • 6pm-10pm

Loft 255 Grove St. • 948-4922 • switchboard 7pm-10pm • lesbigay center

BARS

Stutz 202 Westchester Ave. • 761-3100 • 5pm-4am, from 8pm wknds • popular • mostly gay men • dancing/DJ • live shows • patio

Woodstock (914)

INFO LINES & SERVICES

Wise Women Center PO Box 64, 12498 • 246-8081 • women's retreat center • healing & herbal medicines • self-healing instruction

ACCOMMODATIONS

Woodstock Inn 38 Tannery Brook Rd. • 679-8211 • year-round • gay-friendly • swimming hole • wheelchair access

BOOKSTORES & RETAIL SHOPS

Golden Notebook 29 Tinker St. • 679-8000 • 10:30am-7pm, til 9pm (summers) • general • lesbigay section • wheelchair access

Yonkers (914)

BARS

Harlee's 590 Nepperham Ave. • 965-6900 • 10pm-4am • lesbians/gay men • dancing/DJ

North Carolina

Asheville (704)

INFO LINES & SERVICES

CLOSER (Community Liason for Support, Education & Reform) PO Box 2911, 28802 • 277-7815 • 7:30pm Tue (at All Souls Episcopal Church) • social support group

WOMEN'S ACCOMMODATIONS

Camp Pleiades • 241-3050 • women only • cabins • swimming • food served • mountain retreat

Gate House 420 Sunset Dr. • 669-0507 • women only • rental bungalows • women-owned/run

ACCOMMODATIONS

Apple Wood Manor B&B 62 Cumberland Cir. • 254-2244 • gay-friendly • full breakfast

Bird's Nest 41 Oak Park Rd. • 252-2381 • lesbians/gay men • comfortable, secluded & quiet B&B • located on the second flr. of a turn-of-the-century home

Inn on Montford 296 Montford Ave. • 254-9569/ (800) 254-9569 • gay-friendly • full breakfast • English cottage designed by the supervising architect of the Biltmore House

Mountain Laurel B&B 139 Lee Dotson Rd., Fairview • 628-9903 • lesbians/gay men • full breakfast • contemporary house located in a totally secluded 13-acre mountain cove 25 miles from Asheville

Stillwell House B&B 1300 Pinecrest Dr., Hendersonville • 693-6475/ (800) 270-2902 • gay-friendly • 1925 two-story home reminiscent of an English Manor or country French home

BARS

Hairspray Cafe 38 N. French Broad Ave. • 258-2027 • 7pm-2am, from 1pm Sun • lesbians/gay men • dancing/DJ • live shows • private club

O'Henry's 59 Haywood St. • 254-1891 • 1pm-2am, from 11am Sat • lesbians/gay men • neighborhood bar • dancing/DJ • private club

Scandals 11 Grove St. • 252-2838 • 10pm-3am, clsd Sun-Wed • lesbians/gay men • dancing/DJ • live shows • also Getaways bar • country/western

RESTAURANTS & CAFES

Grove Street Cafe 12 Grove St. • 255-0010 • 5pm-10pm, til 11pm Fri-Sat, Sun brunch, clsd Mon-Tue • full bar

Laughing Seed Cafe 40 Wall St. • 252-3445 • 11:30am-9pm, til 10pm Th-Sat, clsd Sun • vegetarian/vegan • beer/wine • patio • wheelchair access • $4-9

Laurey's 60 Biltmore Ave. • 252-1500 • 10am-6pm, til 4pm Sat, clsd Sun • popular • bright cafe w/ delicious salads & cookies • also full service catering • wheelchair access • women-owned/run

BOOKSTORES & RETAIL SHOPS

Downtown Books & News 67 N. Lexington Ave. • 253-8654 • 8am-6pm, from 6am Sun • used books & new magazines

Malaprop's Bookstore & Cafe 61 Haywood Ave. • 254-6734 • 9am-8pm, til 10pm Fri-Sat, noon-6pm Sun • readings & performances

Phoenix Rising 70 Wall St. • 232-0092 • 11am-8pm, til 6pm Sun • lesbigay bookstore • T-shirts • cards • jewelry • music • wheelchair access

TRAVEL & TOUR OPERATORS

Kaleidoscope Travel 120 Merrimon Ave. • 253-7777/ (800) 964-2001

PUBLICATIONS

Community Connections PO Box 18088, 28814 • 258-8861

EROTICA

Octopus' Garden 102 N. Lexington Ave. • 254-4980 • 11am-11pm

Bat Cave (704)

ACCOMMODATIONS

Old Mill B&B Hwy. 74, Box 252, 28716 • 625-4256 • gay-friendly • full breakfast

Blowing Rock (704)

ACCOMMODATIONS

Stone Pillar B&B 144 Pine St. • 295-4141 • gay-friendly • full breakfast • historic 1920s house • wheelchair access

Cashiers (704)

WOMEN'S ACCOMMODATIONS

Jane's Aerie PO Box 1811, 28717 • 743-9002 • popular • mostly women • cottage in great mountain location

Chapel Hill   (919)

INFO LINES & SERVICES

Lambda AA 304 Franklin St. (Chapel of the Cross) • 967-5193 • 8pm Mon & Th

Orange County Women's Center 210 Henderson • 968-4610 • general info & referrals

WOMEN'S ACCOMMODATIONS

Joan's Place 1443 Poinsett Dr., 27514 • 942-5621 • women only • shared baths • B&B in the country • $45-48

RESTAURANTS & CAFES

Crooks Corner 610 Franklin St. • 929-7643 • 6pm-10:30pm, Sun brunch • Southern • some veggie • full bar • wheelchair access • $20-25

Weathervane Cafe Eastgate Shopping Center • 929-9466 • lunch & dinner, Sun brunch • New American • some veggie • full bar • patio • wheelchair access • $10-20

BOOKSTORES & RETAIL SHOPS

Internationalist Books 408 W. Rosemary St. • 942-1740 • noon-6pm, from 10am Sat

Charlotte   (704)

INFO LINES & SERVICES

AA Gay/Lesbian • 332-4387

Gay/Lesbian Switchboard • 535-6277 • 6:30pm-10:30pm • info • referrals • crisis counseling

W.O.W. PO Box 12072, 28220 • lesbian social/educational/political group

BARS

Brass Rail 3707 Wilkinson Blvd • 399-8413 • 5pm-2:30am, from 3pm Sun • mostly gay men • neighborhood bar • country/western • leather • wheelchair access

Chaser's 3217 The Plaza • 339-0500 • 5pm-2am, clsd Sun • mostly gay men • dancing/DJ • wheelchair access

Liaisons 316 Rensselaer Ave. • 376-1617 • 4pm-1am • popular • lesbians/gay men • neighborhood bar • wheelchair access • women-owned/run

Oleen's Lounge 1831 S. Blvd • 373-9604 • 8pm-2am, from 3pm Sun • popular • lesbians/gay men • dancing/DJ • live shows

Scorpio's Lounge 2301 Freedom Dr. • 373-9124 • 9pm-3:30am, clsd Mon • popular • lesbians/gay men • dancing/DJ • live shows • private club

Ye Olde Wishing Gate 1501 Elizabeth Ave. • 339-0350 • 4pm-2am, til midnight Tue-Th, 2pm-10pm Sun • mostly women • neighborhood bar • live shows • English pub • wheelchair access

RESTAURANTS & CAFES

300 East 300 East Blvd. • 332-6507 • 11am-11pm • new American • full bar • wheelchair access • $8-15

521 Cafe 521 N. College • 377-9100 • lunch Tue-Fri, dinner nightly • Italian • some veggie • wheelchair access • $8-15

Brenner's Coffee & Wine Garden 516 N. Graham St. • 334-0818 • 7am-11pm, 9am-1am Sat, 11am-10pm Sun • full bar • cafe • patio • wheelchair access • $3-6

County Boardwalk 1000 South Blvd. • 342-4004 • 7am-3pm, clsd Sun • deli • some veggie • $3-8

Dikadees Front Porch 4329 E. Independence Blvd. • 537-3873 • 11am-10pm, til 11pm Fri-Sat • American • some veggie • full bar • wheelchair access • $20-25

Lupie's Cafe 2718 Monroe Rd. • 374-1232 • homestyle • some veggie • wheelchair access • $5-10

BOOKSTORES & RETAIL SHOPS

Paper Skyscraper 330 East Blvd. • 333-7130 • 10am-6pm, til 9pm Fri, noon-5pm Sun • books on art, architecture, contemporary fiction • also t-shirts, cards & gifts • wheelchair access

Rising Moon Books & Beyond 316 East Blvd. • 332-7473 • 10am-7pm, til 6pm Fri-Sun • lesbigay & multicultural books • also 3100 N. Davidson St. • 347-4732 • 7pm-11pm Fri-Sat, 1pm-6pm Sun • wheelchair access

White Rabbit Books 834 Central Ave. • 377-4067 • 11am-11pm, til midnight Th-Sun, from 1pm Sun • lesbigay

TRAVEL & TOUR OPERATORS

Argo World Travel 8307 University Executive Park Ste. 263 • 547-1454/ (800) 467-2929 • IGTA member

Atlantis Travel 4801 E. Independence Blvd. #711 • 566-9779/ (800) 566-9779 • IGTA member

Pink Fairy Travels • 542-0244 • IGTA member

SPIRITUAL GROUPS

Lutherans Concerned 1900 The Plaza (Holy Trinity Church) • 651-4328 • 1st Sun

MCC Charlotte 4037 E. Independence Blvd. #726 • 563-5810 • 9am, 11am & 7:30pm Sun

New Life MCC 234 N. Sharon Amity Rd. (Unitarian Church) • 343-9070 • 7pm Sun

PUBLICATIONS

In Unison PO Box 8024, Columbia, SC 29202 • (803) 771-0804

Q Notes PO Box 221841, 28222 • 531-9988

Durham   (919)

INFO LINES & SERVICES

Lesbian/Gay Health Project PO Box 3203, 27715 • 286-4107 • 6pm-9pm • community referrals

Outright - Triangle Lesbian/Gay Youth PO Box 3203, 27715 • 286-2396/ (800) 879-2300 (in-state only) • 6pm-9pm info & referrals, 2pm Sat mtg.

Steps, Traditions & Promises AA 2109 N. Duke (Christ Lutheran) • 286-9499 • 7:30pm Tue

BARS

Competition 711 Rigsbee Ave. • 688-3002 • 7pm-? Wed, from 8pm Fri-Sat, from 5pm Sun • mostly women • dancing/DJ • private club

Power Company 315 W. Main St. • 683-1151 • 9pm-? Wed-Sun • lesbians/gay men • dancing/DJ • live shows • private club

BOOKSTORES & RETAIL SHOPS

Lady Slipper, Inc. 3205 Hillsboro Rd., 27705 • 683-1570 • distributor of women's music & videos • also newsletter

Regulator Bookshop 720 9th St. • 286-2700 • 9am-8pm Mon-Sat, til 5pm Sun

SPIRITUAL GROUPS

Dignity-Triangle 1852 Liberty St. (St. Andrew's) • 489-2560 • 7pm Sun • call for locations

PUBLICATIONS

Newsletter PO Box 2272, 27702 • monthly • lesbian newsletter

Triangle Area Directory of Women-Owned Businesses PO Box 15657, 27704 • 220-8177 • annual • directory for Raleigh, Durham, Chapel Hill areas

EROTICA

Venus 1720 New Raleigh Rd. • 598-3264

Elizabethtown (910)

TRAVEL & TOUR OPERATORS

North & South Travel 118 W. Broad St. • 862-8557/ (800) 585-8016 • IGTA member

Fayetteville (910)

BARS

Club Oz 2540 Gillespie St. • 485-2037 • 9pm-? , clsd Mon • mostly gay men • dancing/DJ • live shows Sun

Etc. 2540-B Gillespie St. • 485-0334 • 9pm-2:30am Fri-Sun • mostly women • dancing/DJ • unverified for '96

Franklin (704)

WOMEN'S ACCOMMODATIONS

Honey's Rainbow Acres PO Box 1367, 28734-1367 • 369-5162 • women only • guesthouse • hot tub • kitchen privileges • also cabin • $60-75

Gastonia (704)

TRAVEL & TOUR OPERATORS

All Travel Inc. 1708-A E. Garrison Blvd. • 853-1111 • IGTA member

Travel By Design 3302 S. New Hope • 861-0580 • IGTA member

Greensboro (910)

INFO LINES & SERVICES

Gay/Lesbian Hotline PO Box 4442, 27404 • 274-2100 • 7pm-10pm Sun, Tue-Th

Live & Let Live AA 2200 N. Elm (St. Pious Catholic Church) • 854-4278 • 8pm Tue

BARS

Babylon 221 S. Elm St. • 275-1006 • popular • lesbians/gay men • dancing/DJ • alternative • call for events

Palms 413 N. Eugene St. • 272-6307 • 9pm-2:30am • mostly gay men • dancing/DJ • live shows • private club

Warehouse 29 1011 Arnold St. • 333-9333 • 9pm-3am, clsd Mon-Tue • mostly gay men • dancing/DJ • live shows • private club • patio

BOOKSTORES & RETAIL SHOPS

White Rabbit Books 1833 Spring Garden St. • 272-7604 • 10am-7pm, 1pm-6pm Sun • lesbigay • wheelchair access

TRAVEL & TOUR OPERATORS

Carolina Travel 2054 Carolina Circle Mall • 621-9000/ (800) 289-9009 • IGTA member

SPIRITUAL GROUPS

St. Mary's MCC 3010 Monterey St. • 272-1606 • 7pm Sun

Greenville (919)

BARS

Paddock Club 1008-B Dickinson • 758-0990 • 8pm-2:30am Wed-Sun • lesbians/gay men • dancing/DJ • alternative • live shows • private club • wheelchair access

Hendersonvile (704)

ACCOMMODATIONS

Stillwell House 1300 Pinecrest Dr. • 693-6475/ (800) 270-2902 • lesbians/gay men • B&B • swimming • no smoking, pets, or children

Hickory (704)

BARS

Club Cabaret 101 N. Center St. • 322-8103 • 9pm-3am Th-Sun • lesbians/gay men • dancing/DJ • live shows • private club

SPIRITUAL GROUPS

MCC Hickory 109 11th Ave. NW (Unitarian Church) • 324-1960 • 7pm Sun

Hot Springs (704)

ACCOMMODATIONS

Deer Park Cabins PO Box 617, 28743 • 622-3516 • gay-friendly • hot tub • gay-owned/run

Duckett House Inn Hwy. 209 S. • 622-7621/ (800) 306-5038 • lesbians/gay men • Victorian farmhouse B&B w/ camping on Appalachian Trail • also a restaurant • vegetarian (reservations required)

Jacksonville (910)

BARS

Friends 1551 Lejeune Blvd. (rear entrance) • 353-9710 • 9pm-2am • popular • lesbians/gay men • dancing/DJ • live shows • private club • wheelchair access

Raleigh (919)

INFO LINES & SERVICES

AA Gay/Lesbian (The Light Group) • 783-6144

Gay/Lesbian Helpline of Wake County • 821-0055 • 7pm-10pm • info • referrals • crisis counseling

ACCOMMODATIONS

Oakwood Inn 411 N. Bloodworth St. • 832-9712 • gay-friendly • full breakfast

BARS

1622 Club 1622 Glenwood Ave. at Five Points • 832-9082 • 8pm-2am, from 5pm Sun, clsd Mon • lesbians/gay men • dancing/DJ • live shows • private club

CC 313 W. Hargett • 755-9599 • 8pm-?, from 4pm Sun • mostly gay men • dancing/DJ • live shows • wheelchair access

Legends 330 W. Hargett St. • 831-8888 • 9pm-?, from 4pm Sun (summers) • mostly gay men • dancing/DJ • private club • deck • more mixed crowd on wknds • wheelchair access

RESTAURANTS & CAFES

Black Dog Cafe 208 E. Martin • 828-1994 • lunch & dinner • full bar

Est • Est • Est Trattoria 19 W. Hargett St. • 832-8899 • 11am-10pm, clsd Sun • pasta • plenty veggie • full bar • wheelchair access • $8-20

Irregardless Cafe 901 W. Morgan St. • 833-8898 • lunch & dinner, Sun brunch • plenty veggie • full bar • wheelchair access • $9-15

Rathskeller 2412 Hillsborough St. • 821-5342 • 11am-11pm • cont'l • some veggie • full bar • wheelchair access • $10-20

BOOKSTORES & RETAIL SHOPS

Innovations 517 Hillsborough St. • 833-4833 • 11am-7pm, from 1pm Sun, clsd Mon-Tue • leather gear & clothing • fetish wear

Reader's Corner 3201 Hillsborough St. • 828-7024 • 10am-9pm, til 6pm Sat, 1pm-6pm Sun • used bookstore

White Rabbit Books 309 W. Martin St. • 856-1429 • 11am-9pm, til 7pm Sat, 1pm-6pm Sun • lesbigay

TRAVEL & TOUR OPERATORS

Rainbow Travel 2801 Blue Ridge Rd. • 571-9054/ (800) 633-9350 • IGTA member

SPIRITUAL GROUPS

Raleigh Religious Network for Gays/Lesbians • 783-7968 • discussion group

St. John's MCC 805 Glenwood Ave. • 834-2611 • 7:15pm Sun

Unitarian Universalist Fellowship 3313 Wade Ave. • 781-9635 • 9:30am & 11:15am Sun

PUBLICATIONS

Front Page PO Box 27928, 27611 • 829-0181 • bi-weekly

In Unison PO Box 8024, Columbia, SC 29202 • (803) 771-0804

Spruce Pine (704)

ACCOMMODATIONS

▲ **The Lemon Tree** 912 Greenwood Rd. • 765-6161 • gay-friendly • full breakfast • pets okay • kids okay • also Lemon Tree Restaurant on premises

Spruce Ridge (704)

WOMEN'S ACCOMMODATIONS

Shepherd's Ridge • 765-7809 • mostly women • cottage in the woods • sleeps 2-4 • open Mar-Nov

Wilmington (910)

INFO LINES & SERVICES

GROW Switchboard 3441 S. College Rd. Ste. 182, 28403 • 675-9222 • 6pm-10pm • info • counseling • AIDS resource

ACCOMMODATIONS

Inn on Orange 410 Orange St. • 815-0035/ (800) 381-4666 • gay-friendly • full breakfast • swimming • IGTA member

Ocean Princess Inn 824 Ft. Fischer Blvd., South Kure Beach • 458-6712/ (800) 762-4863 • gay-friendly • swimming • wheelchair access

Southern Heritage 614 S. 2nd St. • 341-7550 • lesbians/gay men • 10 min. from beach

Taylor House Inn 14 N. 7th St. • 763-7581/ (800) 382-9982 • gay-friendly • full breakfast • romantic turn-of-the-century house built in 1908 by a local merchant

BARS

Manor 208 Market St. • 251-9220 • 4pm-2am • mostly women • neighborhood bar • dancing/DJ

Mickey Ratz 115-117 S. Front St. • 251-1289 • 5pm-2:30am • lesbians/gay men • dancing/DJ • live shows • private club • wheelchair access

BOOKSTORES & RETAIL SHOPS

Rising Moon Books & Beyond 215-A Princess St. • 763-6500 • 10am-7pm, til 6pm Fri-Sat, 1pm-6pm Sun • lesbigay • wheelchair access • lesbian-owned/run

PUBLICATIONS

Between Ourselves Newsletter 2148 Harrison St., 28401

Winston-Salem (910)

INFO LINES & SERVICES

Gay/Lesbian Hotline PO Box 4442, 27404 • 274-2100 • 7pm-10pm

BARS

Bourbon Street 916 Burke St. • 724-4644 • 9pm-3am • lesbians/gay men • dancing/DJ • live shows • private club • patio • wheelchair access

Trade Street Market 701 N. Trade • 722-9388 • 5pm-2:30am, from noon Sun • mostly gay men • dancing/DJ • live shows • private club • more women Th • wheelchair access

BOOKSTORES & RETAIL SHOPS

Rainbow News & Cafe 712 Brookstown Ave. • 723-0858 • 9am-9pm, til 6pm Sun • alternative • cafe w/ lots of veggie • $6-9

North Dakota

Fargo (218)

INFO LINES & SERVICES

10% Society PO Box 266, MSU, Moorhead, MN 56563 • (218) 236-2200/236-5859 • confidential support group for lesbian/gay/bisexual students

Hotline PO Box 447, 58107 • 235-7335 • 24hrs • general info hotline (some lesbi-gay resources)

RESTAURANTS & CAFES

Fargo's Fryn Pan 300 Main St. • 293-9952 • 24hrs • popular • American • wheelchair access

Grand Forks (701)

INFO LINES & SERVICES

The UGLC (University Gay/Lesbian Community) Box 8136 University Stn., 58202 • 777-4321 • educational/social group

EROTICA

Plain Brown Wrapper 102 S. 3rd St. • 772-9021 • 24hrs

Ohio

Akron (216)

Bars

358 Club 358 S. Main • 434-7788 • 5pm-2:30am • mostly gay men • wheelchair access

Dr. Dan's 1225 Sweitzer • 773-0008 • 8pm-2:30am, clsd Sun-Mon • lesbians/gay men • dancing/DJ • live shows • patio

Interbelt 70 N. Howard St. • 253-5700 • 9pm-2:30am, clsd Tue & Th • mostly gay men • dancing/DJ • live shows

Roseto's 627 S. Arlington • 724-4228 • 6pm-1am • mostly women • dancing/DJ • country/western

Restaurants & Cafes

Cheryl's Daily Grind 1662 Merriman Rd. • 869-9980 • 7am-9pm, til 11pm Fri-Sat, 8am-3pm Sun • patio • lesbian-owned/run

Travel & Tour Operators

Parkside Travel 3310 Kent Rd., Stow • 688-3334 • IGTA member

Spiritual Groups

Akron Metropolitan Christian Church 1215 Kenmore Blvd. • 745-5757 • 10am & 7pm Sun

Cascade Community Church 1196 Inman St. • 773-5298 • 2pm Sun

Athens (614)

Info Lines & Services

Open Doors (Gay/Lesbian/Bisexual Assoc.) 18 N. College St. OU • 594-2385 • mostly students

Canton (216)

Bars

Dar's Bar 1120 W. Tuscarawas • 454-9128 • 9pm-2:30am • lesbians/gay men • dancing/DJ

La Casa Lounge 508 Cleveland Ave. NW • 453-7432 • 10am-2:30am • mostly gay men • neighborhood bar • wheelchair access

Side Street Cafe 2360 Mahoney St. NE • 453-8055 • 1pm-1am, clsd Sun • mostly women • neighborhood bar • wheelchair access

Publications

Gay People's Chronicle PO Box 5426, Cleveland, 44101 • 631-8646

Cincinnati (513)

Info Lines & Services

AA Lesbian/Gay • 861-9966

Alternating Currents WAIF FM 88.3 • 961-8900 • 3pm Sat • lesbigay public affairs radio program • also 'Everywomon' • 1pm Sat

Cincinnati Youth Group PO Box 19852, 45219 • 684-8405/ (800) 347-8336 • 24hr • info • referrals

Gay/Lesbian Community Switchboard • 651-0070 • 7pm-11pm Mon-Fri

Ohio Lesbian Archives 4039 Hamilton Ave., 3rd flr. • 541-1917 • call for hours

Women Helping Women 216 E. 9th St. • 381-5610 • 24hrs (hotline) • crisis center • support groups • lesbian referrals

Accommodations

Prospect Hill B&B 408 Boal St. • 421-4408 • lesbians/gay men • full breakfast • elegantly restored 1867 Italianate townhouse w/ spectacular views • IGTA member

Bars

Chasers 2640 Glendora • 861-3966 • 7pm-2:30am • lesbians/gay men • dancing/DJ • live shows

Dock 603 W. Pete Rose Wy. • 241-5623 • 8pm-2:30am, til 4am Fri-Sat • popular • lesbians/gay men • dancing/DJ • live shows • volleyball court • patio • wheelchair access

Plum St. Pipeline 241 W.Court • 241-5678 • 4pm-2:30am • popular • mostly gay men • neighborhood bar • live shows • videos

Shirley's 2401 Vine St. • 721-8483 • 8pm-2:30am, from 4pm Sun, clsd Mon • mostly women • dancing/DJ • wheelchair access

Shooters 927 Race St. • 381-9900 • 4pm-2:30am • mostly gay men • dancing/DJ • country/western • lessons 8:30pm Tue &Th

Simon Says 428 Walnut • 381-7577 • 11am-2:30am, from 1pm Sun • popular • mostly gay men • neighborhood bar

Subway's 609 Walnut • 421-1294 • 6am-2:30am, from noon Sun • mostly gay men • neighborhood bar • live shows

RESTAURANTS & CAFES

Carol's Corner Cafe 825 Main St. • 651-2667 • 11:30am-1am (bar til 2:30am), from 4pm Sat, from 10am Sun • popular • American • some veggie • full bar • wheelchair access • $4-8

Firehouse on Vine 2701 Vine St. • 961-1223 • 11:30am-9:30pm, til 11pm Fri-Sat, clsd Sun • bistro • plenty veggie • full bar • wheelchair access • $9-17

G.J.'s Gaslight Restaurant 354 Ludlow Ave. • 221-2020 • 8am-10pm, 10am-11pm Fri-Sat, til 9pm Sun • popular • beer/wine • American/Italian • some veggie • wheelchair access • $5-15

Jimmy's 1005 Walnut St. • 621-9828 • 11am-2:30am, from 2pm wknds

Kaldi's Cafe & Books 1204 Main St. • 241-3070 • 8am-1am, from 10am wknds • live shows • full bar • wheelchair access

Mullane's 723 Race St. • 381-1331 • 11:30am-11pm, clsd Sun • beer/wine • American • plenty veggie • $5-12

BOOKSTORES & RETAIL SHOPS

Crazy Ladies Bookstore 4039 Hamilton Ave. • 541-4198 • 10am-8pm, til 5:30pm Sat, noon-4pm Sun • women's bookstore

Fountain Square News 101 E. 5th St. • 421-4049 • 7:30am-6:30pm • magazines

LeftHanded Moon 48 E. Court St. • 784-1166 • 11:30am-7pm, clsd Sun • T-shirts • jewelry • cards

Pink Pyramid 36-A W. Court • 621-7465 • 11am-10:30pm, til midnight Fri-Sat, clsd Sun • lesbigay bookstore & gifts

TRAVEL & TOUR OPERATORS

Apache Travel 5017 Cooper Rd. • 793-5522 • ask for Laura

Victoria Travel 3330 Erie Ave. • 871-1100/ (800) 626-4932 • ask for Dan • IGTA member

SPIRITUAL GROUPS

Dignity PO Box 983, 45201 • 481-4760 • 7:30pm 1st & 3rd Sat

MCC New Spirit 65 E. Hollister Ave. (Church of Our Saviour) • 241-8216 • 7pm Sun

PUBLICATIONS

Dinah PO Box 1485, 45201 • women's publication

Gay People's Chronicle PO Box 12235, Columbus, 43212 • (614) 253-4038

EROTICA

Kinks 1118 Race St. • 651-2668 • 2pm-8pm, clsd Sun-Mon • leather

Pumps (at Plum St. Pipeline) • 10pm-1am, til 2am Fri-Sat • leather • cards

Cleveland (216)

INFO LINES & SERVICES

AA Gay/Lesbian • 241-7387 • call 9am-5pm Mon-Fri

Blue Fish Production Company • 371-9714 • producers/consultants for women's events

Buckeye Rainbow Society for the Deaf PO Box 6253, 44101

Cleveland Lesbian/Gay Community Center 1418 W. 29th St. • 522-1999 • 9am-5pm Mon-Fri • call for events • wheelchair access

Cleveland Lesbian/Gay Hotline • 781-6736 • recorded info 24hrs

GLOWS (Gay/Lesbian Older Wiser Seniors) • 331-6302 • 7:30pm 2nd Tue

Hard Hatted Women • 961-4449 • non-profit group to support women in skill trades

Oven Productions PO Box 18175, Cleveland Hts., 44118 • 321-7799 • 'produces events to promote feminist culture'

West Side Women's Center 4209 Lorain Ave. • 651-1450 • 9am-5pm Mon-Fri • houses a few lesbian groups

BARS

Five Cent Decision 4365 State Rd. • 661-1314 • 4pm-2:30am • mostly women • neighborhood bar

Grid 1281 W. 9th • 623-0113 • 4pm-2:30am • popular • lesbians/gay men • neighborhood bar • dancing/DJ • more women Sun

Legends 11719 Detroit, Lakewood • 226-1199 • 11am-2:30am, from 7pm Sun • popular • mostly gay men • dancing/DJ • karaoke

Metronome 1946 St. Clair Ave. • 241-4663 • 8:30pm-2:30am, 5pm-11pm Sun, clsd Mon-Tue & Th • mostly women • dancing/DJ • live shows • wheelchair access

Muggs 11633 Lorain • 252-6172 • 10am-2:30am • lesbians/gay men • neighborhood bar • food served

Ohio City Oasis 2903 W. 29th St. • 574-2203 • 8am-2:30am, from noon Sun • mostly gay men • leather • country/western Sun

Over the Rainbow 9506 Detroit Ave. • 651-9399 • 4pm-2:30am • popular • lesbians/gay men • neighborhood bar • also Beauregard's restaurant • 6pm Wed-Sun • American • some veggie • $6-16

Paradise Inn 4488 State Rd. • 741-9819 • 11am-2:30am • lesbians/gay men • neighborhood bar

Rec Room 15320 Brookpark Rd. • 433-1669 • 6pm-1am • mostly women • dancing/DJ • food served • wheelchair access • women-owned/run

Scarlet Rose's 2071 Broadview Rd. • 351-7511 • 5pm-2am, noon-8pm Sun • mostly women • neighborhood bar

U4ia 10630 Berea Rd. • 631-7111 • 9:30pm-2:30am Fri & Sun, til 4am Sat • popular • lesbians/gay men • dancing/DJ • live shows

RESTAURANTS & CAFES

Billy's on Clifton 11100 Clifton Blvd. • 281-7722 • 11am-9pm, clsd Mon • American • $5-12

Club Isabella 2025 University Hospital Rd. • 229-1177 • lunch & dinner, dinner only Sat, clsd Sun • Italian • full bar • live jazz • $15-25

Fulton Ave. Cafe 1835 Fulton Ave. • 522-1835 • 4pm-2:30am, from 8pm wknds • full bar

Harlows 11215 Detroit • 221-2111 • 6pm-10pm, til 11pm Fri-Sat, clsd Mon-Tue • lesbians/gay men • live shows • full bar

Inn on Coventry 2785 Euclid Heights Blvd., Cleveland Hts. • 371-1811 • 7am-9pm, 9am-3pm Sun • homestyle • some veggie • full bar • women-owned • $5-20

Lonesome Dove Cafe 3093 Mayfield Rd. • 397-9100 • 8am-6pm • some veggie • patio • $5-7

Patisserie Baroque 1112 Kenilworth Ave. • 861-1881 • 8am-5pm, from 10am Sat, clsd Sun-Mon • European-style pastry shop

Red Star Cafe 11604 Detroit Ave. • 521-7827 • 7am-11pm, til 1am Fri-Sat • lesbians/gay men • wheelchair access

Snickers 1261 W. 76th St. • 631-7555 • noon-10pm, 4pm-11pm Sat • American • some veggie • full bar • patio • $7-16

Cleveland

*C*leveland is making a comeback, after the recession and several economic facelifts. Actually, only some districts like 'the Flats' have had a beauty makeover. Other districts never lost the funky charm of this city that's home to the **Rock 'N Roll Hall of Fame**. Speaking of funky, University Circle is rumored to be another hangout of the avant garde, as is Murray Hill, known for its many galleries. While you're at it, make time for some serious art appreciation in the galleries of the world-famous **Cleveland Museum of Art**.

For the lesbian community, begin at **Gifts of Athena**, Cleveland's feminist bookstore. Here you can find out more about the ever-changing bar/coffeehouse scene in **The Gay People's Chronicle**, the local paper . Be sure to contact **Oven Productions** about any events they're putting on for feminists.

For a wholesome meal, try the women-run **Snickers** then head out to **Metronome**, a women's dance bar that also has live shows.

BOOKSTORES & RETAIL SHOPS

Bank News 4025 Clark • 281-8777 • 10:30am-8:30pm, clsd Sun • magazines & more

Bookstore on W. 25th St. 1921 W. 25th St. • 566-8897 • 10am-6pm, noon-5pm Sun • general w/ gay sensitivities

Borders Bookshop & Espresso Bar 2101 Richmond Rd., Beachwood • 292-2660 • 9am-10pm, til 11pm Fri-Sat, 11am-6pm Sun • lesbigay

Clifton Web 11512 Clifton Rd. • 961-1120 • 10am-9pm, noon-5pm Sun • cards • gifts • T-shirts

Condom Nation 401 Euclid #47 • 781-8533 • 11am-6pm, clsd Sun

Gifts of Athena 2199 Lee Rd., Cleveland Hts. • 371-1937 • 10am-7pm, til 6pm Sat, noon-5pm Sun, clsd Tue • women's bookstore

TRAVEL & TOUR OPERATORS

Flite II 23611 Chagrin Blvd., Beachwood • 464-1762/ (800) 544-3881

Green Road Travel 2111 S. Green Rd., South Euclid • 381-8060

Playhouse Square Travel 1160 Henna Bldg./1422 Euclid Ave. • 575-0823/ (800) 575-0813 • IGTA member

Sun Lovers' Cruises & Travel 3860 Rocky River Rd. • 252-0900/ (800) 323-1362 • IGTA member

University Circle Travel 11322 Euclid Ave. • 721-9500/ (800) 925-2339

SPIRITUAL GROUPS

Chevrei Tikva PO Box 18120, Cleveland Hts., 44118 • 932-5551 • 8:30pm 1st & 3rd Fri • lesbian/gay synagogue

Emmanuel MCC 10034 Lorain Ave. • 651-0129

Presbyterians for Lesbian/Gay Concerns • 932-1458 • 5:30pm 1st Sun • potluck & meeting

PUBLICATIONS

Gay People's Chronicle PO Box 5426, 44101 • 631-8646

EROTICA

Body Language 3291 W. 115th St. • 251-3330 • leather • toys

Cleveland (216)

LESBIGAY INFO: Cleveland Lesbian/Gay Community Center: 522-1999, 1418 W. 29th St., 9am-5pm Mon-Fri. Lesbian/Gay Hotline: 781-6736.

LESBIGAY PAPER: Gay People's Chronicle: 631-8646.

WHERE THE GIRLS ARE: Dancing downtown near Public Square, hanging out on State Rd. below the intersection of Pearl and Broadview/Memphis.

LESBIGAY AA: 241-7387: call 9am-5pm Mon-Fri.

CITY INFO: 621-4110

TRANSIT: Yellow-Zone Cab: 623-1500.

Columbus   (614)

INFO LINES & SERVICES

AA Gay/Lesbian • 253-8501

Briar Rose PO Box 16235, 43216 • support group for leather-oriented women

Sisters of Lavender 93 W. Weisheimer (Unitarian Church) • 235-1718 • 7:30pm Wed • lesbian support group

Stonewall Union Hotline/Community Ctr. 1160 N. High St. • 299-7764 • 10am-7pm, til 5pm Fri, clsd Sun • info • referrals • wheelchair access

WOW (Women's Outreach to Women) 1950-H N. 4th St. • 291-3639 • 9am-5pm (meetings 5pm-8pm) • women's recovery center • wheelchair access

ACCOMMODATIONS

Columbus Bed & Breakfast • 444-8888 • gay-friendly • referral service for German Village district

Five Forty-Two B&B 542 Mohawk St. • 621-1741 • gay-friendly • B&B

BARS

Downtown Connection 1126 N. High St. • 299-4880 • 3pm-2:30am • mostly gay men • sports bar

Garage Disco (at Trends Bar) • 9pm-2:30am • popular • lesbians/gay men • dancing/DJ • alternative

Herby's Tavern 349 Marconi Blvd. • 464-2270 • 1pm-2:30am • mostly gay men • neighborhood bar • food served

Imagination Too 283 E. Spring St. • 224-2407 • gay-friendly • dancing/DJ

Red Dog 196-1/2 E. Gay St. (rear) • 224-7779 • 4pm-2:30am • mostly gay men • live shows • wheelchair access

Slammers Pizza Pub 202 E. Long St. • 221-8880 • 11am-2:30am, from 3pm wknds • lesbians/gay men • live shows • wheelchair access

Summit Station 2210 Summit St. • 261-9634 • 4pm-2:30am • mostly women • neighborhood bar • dancing/DJ

Trends 40 E. Long St. • 461-0076 • 5pm-2:30am • popular • mostly gay men

Wall Street 144 N. Wall St. • 464-2800 • 8pm-2:30am, clsd Mon • popular • mostly women • dancing/DJ • live shows • more men Wed • wheelchair access

Columbus

*C*olumbus is an exciting university-town — full of districts with their own funky flavor, like German Village. In addition to quaint houses, good restaurants, and a strong arts scene, you'll find an energetic lesbian/gay scene in Columbus.

Just like everybody else, Columbusites do caffeine; the **King Ave. Coffeehouse** is popular, as is **Cafe Ashtray**, an avant-garde performance cafe at the **Acme Art Co.** If you like art, don't miss the monthly **Gallery Hop**, every 1st Sat from about 6pm-10pm. Many small galleries in the Short North area of Columbus (just north of downtown on High St.) stay open late. Bars and restaurants in the area also host special events for the evening — try **Wall Street**. Or if art's not your thing, escape to **Summit Station**, north of downtown on Summit.

RESTAURANTS & CAFES

Bermuda Onion 660 N. High • 221-6296 • call for hours • lesbians/gay men • full bar

Clubhouse Cafe 124 E. Main • 228-5090 • 4pm-1am, clsd Mon • lesbians/gay men

Grapevine Cafe 73 E. Gay St. • 221-8463 • 5pm-1am, clsd Mon • lesbians/gay men • live shows • some veggie • full bar • wheelchair access • $7-15

King Ave. Coffeehouse 247 King Ave. • 294-8287 • 11am-10pm, clsd Mon • popular • vegetarian • funky bohemians • no alcohol • $3-7

L'Antibes 772 N. High St. (at Warren) • 291-1666 • dinner from 5pm, clsd Sun-Mon • French (vegetarian on request) • full bar • wheelchair access • from $16

BOOKSTORES & RETAIL SHOPS

ACME Art Company 737 N. High St. • 299-4003 • 1pm-7pm Wed-Sat • alternative art space • call for hours • also Cafe Ashtray Fri

An Open Book 749 N. High St. • 291-0080 • 11am-10pm, til 6pm Sun • lesbigay • wheelchair access

Fan The Flames 3387 N. High St. • 447-0565 • 11am-7pm, noon-6pm wknds, clsd Mon • feminist bookstore • wheelchair access

Hausfrau Haven 769 S. 3rd St. • 443-3680 • greetings cards • wine & gifts

Kukala's Tanning & Tees 636 N. High St. • 228-8337 • 11am-8pm, 10am-6pm Sat, from noon Sun • lesbigay novelties & gifts • women-owned/run

M.J. Originals 745 N. High St. • 291-2787 • 11am-7pm, 1pm-5pm Sun • jewelry • posters • gifts

TRAVEL & TOUR OPERATORS

Just Travel, Inc. 82 S. High St., Dublin • 791-9500/ (800) 622-8660 • ask for Paul • IGTA member

Ohio Division of Travel & Tourism • (800) BUCKEYE

Travelplex East 555 OffiCenter Pl. Ste. 100 • 337-3155/ (800) 837-9909 • IGTA member

Columbus (614)

LESBIGAY INFO: Stonewall Union Hotline/Community Center: 299-7764, 47-49 W. 5th Ave., 9am-5pm, clsd wknds.

LESBIGAY PAPER: Gay People's Chronicle: (216) 631-8646. Stonewall Union Journal: 299-7764.

WHERE THE GIRLS ARE: Downtown with the boys, north near the University area, or somewhere in-between.

LESBIGAY AA: 253-8501.

LESBIGAY PRIDE: June: 299-7764.

ANNUAL EVENTS: September 9- Ohio Lesbian Festival: 267-3953. September 29- Red Party, (614) 294-8309, 19th annual.

CITY INFO: 221-2489.

WEATHER: Truly midwestern. Winters are cold, summers are hot.

TRANSIT: Yellow Cab: 444-4444.

SPIRITUAL GROUPS

New Creation MCC 1253 N. High St. • 294-3026 • 10:30am & 8pm Sun

PUBLICATIONS

Gay People's Chronicle PO Box 12235, 43212 • 253-4038

The Stonewall Union Journal PO Box 10814, 43201 • 299-7764

Dayton   (513)

INFO LINES & SERVICES

AA Gay/Lesbian • 222-2211 • 9am-4pm

Dayton Lesbian/Gay Center & Hotline 1424 W. Dorothy Ln. • 274-1776 • 7pm-11pm (hotline) • center 6:30pm Wed • coffeehouse 8pm Fri

Youth Quest PO Box 9343, 45409 • 275-8336

BARS

1470 West 1470 W. Dorothy Ln., Kettering • 293-0066 • 8:30pm-2:30am, til 5am Fri-Sat, clsd Mon-Tue • popular • lesbians/gay men • dancing/DJ • live shows • wheelchair access

Down Under 131 N. Ludlow St. • 228-1050 • 11:30am-2:30pm for lunch, from 7pm, clsd Sun-Mon • mostly women • dancing/DJ • wheelchair access

Dugout 619 Salem Ave. • 274-2394 • 7am-2:30am • lesbians/gay men • neighborhood bar • dancing/DJ • food served

Edge 1227 Wilmington • 294-0713 • 5pm-2:30am, clsd Sun • mostly gay men • dancing/DJ • country/western Tue • HiNRG Fri-Sat • wheelchair access

Foundry 34 N. Jefferson St. • 461-5200 • 9pm-2:30am, from 4pm Fri, til 4am Fri-Sat, 7pm-2:30am Sun • mostly gay men • dancing/DJ • alternative • wheelchair access

Jessie's City Cafe 121 N. Ludlow • 223-2582 • 3pm-2:30am • popular • mostly gay men • dancing/DJ • karaoke • patio • wheelchair access

Outback Saloon 131 N. Ludlow (lower level) • 228-2520 • 7pm-2:30am • mostly gay men • neighborhood bar • dancing/DJ • wheelchair access

Right Corner 105 E. 3rd St. • 228-1285 • noon-2:30am • mostly gay men • neighborhood bar • wheelchair access

BOOKSTORES & RETAIL SHOPS

Books & Co. 350 E. Stroop Rd. • 298-6540 • 9am-9pm

Q Giftshop 121 N. Ludlow St. • 223-4438 • 10pm-1am, til 2:30am Fri-Sat, clsd Mon-Tue • lesbigay

SPIRITUAL GROUPS

Community Gospel Church 546 Xenia Ave. • 252-8855 • 10am Sun, 7:30pm Wed

MCC 1630 E. 5th St. (at McClure) • 228-4031 • 10:30am & 6:30pm Sun

PUBLICATIONS

Gay People's Chronicle PO Box 12235, Columbus, 43212 • (614) 253-4038

Rightfully Proud PO Box 3032, 45401-3032 • 274-1616 • newspaper

Fremont   (419)

BARS

Saloon Bar 531 W. State • 334-9340 • 1pm-2:30am, from 4pm wknds, clsd Mon • mostly gay men • neighborhood bar

Glenford   (614)

ACCOMMODATIONS

Springhill Farm 5704 Highpoint Rd. • 659-2364 • mostly women • hot tub • swimming • cabins & restored barn on 30 acres

Guysville

WOMEN'S ACCOMMODATIONS

Moon Ridge Rte. 1 Box 240, 45735 • mostly women • campground

Kent   (216)

INFO LINES & SERVICES

Kent Lesbian/Gay/Bisexual Union KSU • 672-2068

RESTAURANTS & CAFES

Zephyr 106 W. Main St. • 678-4848 • 8am-10pm, from 9am wknds, clsd Mon • live shows • vegetarian • wheelchair access • women-owned • $3-7

Lima   (419)

BARS

Alternatives 138 W. 3rd St., Mansfield • 552-0044 • gay-friendly • dancing/DJ

Somewhere In Time 804 W. North St. •
227-7288 • 7pm-2:30am, from 8pm Fri-
Sat • lesbians/gay men • dancing/DJ Fri-
Sat

Logan (614)

ACCOMMODATIONS

Spring Wood Hocking Hills Cabins 15
miles NW of Logan • 385-2042 • les-
bians/gay men • hot tub • wheelchair
access • $85-90

Lorain (216)

INFO LINES & SERVICES

Gay/Lesbian Info Center 150 Foster Park
Rd. (Deca Realty Bldg. lower level),
Amherst • 988-5326/ (800) 447-7163 •
drop-in 6pm-9pm Wed • info • referrals

BARS

Nite Club 2223 Broadway • 245-6319 •
8pm-2:30am, from 3pm Sun • mostly gay
men • neighborhood bar • dancing/DJ •
patio • wheelchair access

Mentor (216)

INFO LINES & SERVICES

Hugs East PO Box 253, 44061 • 974-8909
• 7pm-9pm Wed, phone 24hrs • lesbigay
info, referrals & social group for
Ashtabula, Geauga & Lake counties

Newark (614)

BARS

Lavender Rose 380 Seroco Ave. • 349-
7023 • 7pm-2:30am, clsd Sun • mostly
women • neighborhood bar • wheelchair
access

Oberlin (216)

INFO LINES & SERVICES

Oberlin Lesbian/Gay/Bisexual Union
Wilder Rm. 202 (Box 88), 44074 • 775-
8179

Oxford (513)

INFO LINES & SERVICES

**Miami University Gay/Lesbian/Bisexual
Alliance** • 529-3823

Portsmouth (614)

ACCOMMODATIONS

1835 House B&B • 353-1856 • gay-
friendly • swimming • on the Ohio River

Sandusky (419)

BARS

X-Centricities 306 W. Water St. • 624-
8118 • 4pm-2:30pm, from 1pm wknds
(winter) • lesbians/gay men • dancing/DJ
• patio

Springfield (513)

BARS

Chances 1912 Edwards Ave. • 324-0383 •
gay-friendly

Stowe (216)

TRAVEL & TOUR OPERATORS

Parkside Travel 3310 Kent Rd. Ste. 6 •
688-3334/ (800) 552-1647 • IGTA member

Toledo (419)

INFO LINES & SERVICES

AA Gay/Lesbian • 472-8242

Pro Toledo Info Line • 472-2364 • 4pm-
11pm • info • referrals

BARS

Blu Jean Cafe 3606 Sylvania Ave. • 474-
0690 • 4pm-2:30am • popular • les-
bians/gay men • live shows • karaoke •
food served • more women Th

Bretz 2012 Adams St. • 243-1900 • 4pm-
2:30am, til 4:30am Fri-Sat, clsd Mon-Tue
• popular • mostly gay men • dancing/DJ

Caesar's Show Bar 133 N. Erie St. • 241-
5140 • 8pm-2:30am Th-Sun •
lesbians/gay men • dancing/DJ • live
shows

Hooterville Station 119 N. Erie St. • 241-
9050 • 5:30am-2:30am • mostly gay men
• dancing/DJ • leather • wheelchair
access

Scenic Bar 702 Monroe St. • 241-5997 •
1pm-2:30am • mostly women • danc-
ing/DJ

RESTAURANTS & CAFES

Sufficient Grounds 3160 Markway
(Cricket West Mall) • 537-1988 • 7am-
11pm, til 1am Fri-Sat, from 10am Sun •
also 420 Madison • 243-5282

BOOKSTORES & RETAIL SHOPS

Tallulah's 6725 W. Central • 843-7707 • 11am-6pm, til 8pm Tue-Th • feminist giftshop • wheelchair access

Thackeray's 3301 W. Central Ave. • 537-9259 • 9am-9pm, 10am-6pm Sun

TRAVEL & TOUR OPERATORS

Great Ways Travel 4625 W. Bancroft • 536-8000/ (800) 729-9297 • IGTA member

Toledo Travel Club 4612 Talmadge Rd. • 471-2820/ (800) 860-2820 • IGTA member

SPIRITUAL GROUPS

MCC Good Samaritan 720 W. Delaware • 244-0908 • 11am Sun

Tremont   (216)

BARS

Hi & Dry In 2207 W. 11th St. • 621-6166 • 4pm-2am • lesbians/gay men • neighborhood bar • food served • American • plenty veggie • patio • $5-10

Warren   (216)

BARS

Alley 441 E. Market St. • 394-9483 • 2pm-2:30am • lesbians/gay men • dancing/DJ

Crazy Duck 121 Pine St. SE • 394-3825 • 4pm-2:30am • popular • lesbians/gay men • dancing/DJ • 18+ • wheelchair access

Purple Onion 136 Pine St. • 399-2097 • noon-2:30am • lesbians/gay men • neighborhood bar • dancing/DJ • patio

Wooster

INFO LINES & SERVICES

Lambda Wooster Box C-3166, College of Wooster, 44691

WOMEN'S ACCOMMODATIONS

Kimbilio Farm Big Prairie • 378-2481 • women only • B&B • swimming • also cabin • wheelchair access (cabin only) • $50

Yellow Springs   (513)

INFO LINES & SERVICES

Gay/Lesbian Center Antioch College • 767-7331x601

RESTAURANTS & CAFES

Winds Cafe & Bakery 215 Xenia Ave. • 767-1444 • call for hours • vegetarian (organic) • full bar • women-owned/run • $13-17

BOOKSTORES & RETAIL SHOPS

Epic Bookshop 232 Xenia Ave. • 767-7997 • 10am-6pm, til 9pm Fri, noon-6pm Sun

Youngstown   (216)

BARS

Numbers II 114 Javit Ct., Austintown Township off Mahoning Ave. • 792-6279 • 9pm-2:30am, clsd Mon-Tue • lesbians/gay men • dancing/DJ • live shows • wheelchair access

Sophies 10 E. LaClede • 782-8080 • 4pm-2:30am • lesbians/gay men • neighborhood bar

Troubadour 2622 Market St. (main entrance via back parking lot) • 788-4379 • 9pm-2:30am • lesbians/gay men • dancing/DJ • live shows • wheelchair access

Oklahoma

Claremore (918)

TRAVEL & TOUR OPERATORS

International Tours of Claremore 608 W. Will Rogers Blvd. • 341-6866 • IGTA member

El Reno (405)

ACCOMMODATIONS

Good Life RV Resort Exit 108 I-40 1/4 mile S. • 884-2994 • gay-friendly • swimming • 31 acres of wooded countryside w/ 100 campsites & 100 RV hookups

Lawton (405)

BARS

Downtowner 116 SW 1st • 357-1430 • 7pm-2am, clsd Mon • lesbians/gay men • neighborhood bar • dancing/DJ • live shows • wheelchair access

Oklahoma City (405)

INFO LINES & SERVICES

AA Live & Let Live 3405 N. Villa • 947-3834 • noon, 5:30pm & 8pm

Gay/Lesbian Outreach 4400 N. Lincoln • 425-0399 • counseling for HIV affected • also substance abuse outreach • support groups for 14-20yrs, 21-29+

Herland Sister Resources Inc. 2312 NW 39th St. • 521-9696 • 10am-5pm Sat, from 1pm Sun • women's resource center • wheelchair access

Oasis Resource Center 2135 NW 39th St. • 525-2437 • 7pm-10pm, til midnight Fri-Sat

ACCOMMODATIONS

Habana Inn 2200 NW 39th Expressway • 528-2221 • lesbians/gay men • swimming • also bars & restaurant on premises • wheelchair access

BARS

Angles 2117 NW 39th St. • 528-0050 • 9pm-2am, clsd Mon-Tue • popular • lesbians/gay men • dancing/DJ • wheelchair access

Bunk House 2800 NW 39th St. • 943-0843 • 1pm-2am (restaurant 5pm-10pm, til 4am Fri-Sat) • popular • mostly gay men • dancing/DJ • country/western • leather • live shows • also a restaurant • southern homecooking • wheelchair access • $3-7

Coyote Club 2120 NW 39th St. • 521-9533 • 5pm-2am, from 3pm Sun, clsd Mon-Tue • mostly women • dancing/DJ • wheelchair access

▲ **Finish Line** (at Habana Inn) • 525-2900 • noon-2am • lesbians/gay men • dancing/DJ • country/western • wheelchair access

▲ **Gusher's Restaurant & Cabaret** (at Habana Inn) • 525-0703 • restaurant from 7am, club 9pm-2am • lesbians/gay men • dancing/DJ • live shows • wheelchair access

Hi-Lo Club 1221 NW 50th St. • 843-1722 • noon-2am • lesbians/gay men • neighborhood bar • live shows

K.A.'s 2024 NW 11th • 525-3734 • 2pm-2am • mostly women • neighborhood bar • beer bar • Sun brunch

Neon Moon 2805 NW 36th St. • 947-3422 • 7pm-2am, from 3pm Sun, clsd Mon-Tue • mostly women • dancing/DJ • live shows • volleyball court • patio

Park 2125 NW 39th St. • 528-4690 • 4pm-2am • popular • mostly gay men • patio

Tramps 2201 NW 39th St. • 521-9888 • noon-2am, from 10am wknds • popular • mostly gay men • dancing/DJ • wheelchair access

Tropical Heat 2805 NW 36th • 948-0572 • 5pm-2am, from 3pm wknds • mostly women • Sun brunch

Wreck Room 2127 NW 39th St. • 525-7610 • 9pm-? Fri-Sat • popular • lesbians/gay men • dancing/DJ • 18+ • juice bar

RESTAURANTS & CAFES

Grateful Bean Cafe 1039 Walker • 236-3503 • 8am-5pm, til midnight Fri, 10am-2am Sun • live shows

Kitchen 2124 NW 39th St. • 528-5133 • 5pm-3am, clsd Mon • popular • lesbians/gay men • family style • some veggie • wheelchair access • $5-7

Patio Cafe 5100 N. Classen • 842-7273 • 7am-2pm

TRAVEL & TOUR OPERATORS

Oklahoma Traveler Information • (800) 652-6552

SPIRITUAL GROUPS

Dignity & Integrity NW 19th & Portland (Lighthouse MCC) • 636-4388 • 7:30pm 2nd & 4th Tue

Lighthouse MCC 3629 NW 19th • 942-2822 • 10:30am Sun, 7:30pm Wed

Oklahoma City Religious Society of Friends (Quakers) 312 SE 25th St. • 632-7574 • 10am Sun

PUBLICATIONS

Gayly Oklahoman PO Box 60930, 73146 • 528-0800

Herland Voice 2312 NW 39th St., 73112 • 521-9696 • monthly • women's newsletter

Perspective PO Box 60938, 73146 • 236-4646

EROTICA

Jungle Red (at Habana Inn) • 524-5733 • novelties • leather • erotica

Stillwater   (405)

RESTAURANTS & CAFES

Snuffy's 2106 S. Main St. • 743-3659 • 6pm-2am, clsd Sun-Wed • mostly gay men • dancing/DJ

Tulsa   (918)

INFO LINES & SERVICES

Gay Info Line/TOHR PO Box 52729, 74152 • 743-4297 • 8pm-10pm • inquire about Women's Supper Club on Wednesdays

LesBiGay Alliance (at Tulsa University) • 583-9780

Rainbow Business Guild • 254-2100 • call for events

T.U.L.S.A. (Tulsa Uniform/Leather Seekers Assoc.) • 838-1222

BARS

Concessions 3340 S. Peoria • 744-0896 • 9pm-2am, clsd Mon-Wed • popular • lesbians/gay men • dancing/DJ • live shows • wheelchair access

Lola's 2630 E. 15th • 749-1563 • 4pm-2am, from 2pm wknds • lesbians/gay men • neighborhood bar • live shows

Renegade 1649 S. Main St. • 585-3405 • 2pm-2am • mostly gay men • neighborhood bar • live shows • wheelchair access

Silver Star Saloon 1565 S. Sheridan • 834-4234 • 7pm-2am, clsd Mon-Tue • mostly gay men • dancing/DJ • country/western • more women Sat • wheelchair access

T.N.T. 2114 S. Memorial • 660-0856 • 6pm-2am • popular • mostly women • dancing/DJ

Time n' Time Again 1515 S. Memorial • 664-8299 • 2pm-2am • lesbians/gay men • neighborhood bar • wheelchair access

Wild Nights 2405 E. Admiral • 582-4340 • 2pm-2am • mostly women • neighborhood bar • dancing/DJ

RESTAURANTS & CAFES

Java Dave's 1326 E. 15th St. (Lincoln Plaza) • 592-3317 • 7am-11pm • cafe

Whittier Cafe 416 S. Lewis • 582-2400 • 7am-2:30am

BOOKSTORES & RETAIL SHOPS

Tomfoolery 5451-E S. Mingo (Family of Faith MCC) • 583-1248 • noon-6pm wknds • gay gift store: T-shirts, cards, pride gifts

SPIRITUAL GROUPS

Family of Faith MCC 5451-E S. Mingo • 622-1441

MCC of Greater Tulsa 1623 N. Maplewood • 838-1715 • 10:45am Sun, 7pm Wed

PUBLICATIONS

Tulsa Family News PO Box 4140, 74159 • 583-1248

Oregon

Ashland (503)

Info Lines & Services

Womansource PO Box 335, 97520 • 482-2026 • feminist group sponsors cultural activities like 1st Fri Coffeehouse • also publishes 'Community News'

Women's Accommodations

Dandelion Garden Cottage • 488-4463 • women only • retreat

Willow-Witt Ranch Country Guesthouse 658 Shale City Rd. • 776-1728 • May-Oct • mostly women • full breakfast • hot tub • wheelchair access upon request • $60-120

Accommodations

Country Willows B&B Inn 1313 Clay St. • 488-1590/ (800) 945-5697 • gay-friendly • full breakfast • swimming • country inn snuggled against a rolling hillside

The Rose Cottage 272 N. 1st St. • 482-1645 • lesbians/gay men • secluded garden cottage • monthly only • full kitchen • sleeps up to 6 people

Royal Carter House 514 Siskiyou Blvd. • 482-5623 • gay-friendly • full breakfast • swimming

Will's Reste 298 Hargadine St. • 482-4394 • lesbians/gay men • travelers' accommodations • spa

Bars

Cook's Playbill Club 66 E. Main St. • 488-4626 • 5pm-2am • gay-friendly • dancing/DJ • live shows • more gay Th • wheelchair access

Restaurants & Cafes

Ashland Bakery/Cafe 38 East Main • 482-2117 • 7am-8pm • plenty veggie • wheelchair access • $5-8

Bookstores & Retail Shops

Bloomsbury Books 290 E. Main St. • 488-0029 • 9am-10pm

Astoria (503)

Accommodations

Rosebriar Hotel 636 14th St. • 325-7427/ (800) 487-0224 • gay-friendly • full breakfast • upscale classic hotel • some stes. w/ fireplaces & hot tub

Baker City

Info Lines & Services

Lambda Eastern Oregon Connection Box 382, 97814 • monthly mtgs.

Bend (503)

Bars

Other Side • 388-2395 • 9pm-1am Sat • lesbians/gay men • dancing/DJ • videos • BYOB • call for location • also info line for area

Corvallis (503)

Info Lines & Services

After 8 Club 101 NW 23rd • 752-8157 • mtgs. 7pm 2nd Tue • lesbigay educational & support group

Lesbian/Gay/Bisexual Alliance-OSU 24 Snell, Memorial Union East • 737-6363 • 7pm Mon at Women's Center

Bookstores & Retail Shops

Grass Roots Bookstore 227 SW 2nd St. 754-7668 • 9am-7pm, til 9pm Fri, til 5:30pm Sat, 11am-5pm Sun • wheelchair access

Monroe Ave. Book Bin 2305 NW Monroe • 753-8398 • 9am-6pm, from noon Sat, clsd Sun

Days Creek (503)

Women's Accommodations

Owl Farm PO Box 133, 97429 • 679-465 • women only • open women's land for retreat or residence • camping sites available • write for info • call for directions

Eugene (503)

Info Lines & Services

Gay/Lesbian AA 1262 Lawrence Ste. 7 • 342-4113

Lesbian/Gay/Bisexual Alliance-UO 346-3360

TLC (The Lesbian Connection) 2360 Fillmore, 97405 • 683-2793 • active lesbian social group • meets 3 times monthly

Women's Center University of Oregon • 346-3327 • umbrella organization for women's groups & referrals • some lesbian outreach

ACCOMMODATIONS

Campus Cottage B&B 1136 E. 19th Ave. • 342-5346 • gay-friendly • full breakfast • central location• women-owned

BARS

Club Arena 959 Pearl St. • 683-2360 • 7pm-2:30am • popular • lesbians/gay men • dancing/DJ • live shows

RESTAURANTS & CAFES

Keystone Cafe 395 W. 5th • 342-2075 • 7am-3pm • plenty veggie • popular breakfast

Perry's 959 Pearl St. • 683-2360 • 7am-9pm, clsd Sun • full bar • wheelchair access • $8-16

BOOKSTORES & RETAIL SHOPS

Hungry Head Bookstore 1212 Willamette • 485-0888 • 10am-6pm, clsd Sun • progressive alternative titles

Mother Kali's Bookstore 720 E. 13th Ave. • 343-4864 • 9am-6pm, from 10am Sat • lesbian/feminist & multi-racial sections

Peralandra Books & Music 199 E. 5th Ave., Station Square • 485-4848 • 10am-6pm, clsd Sun • metaphysical titles

Ruby Chasm 152 W. 5th #4 • 344-4074 • 10am-6pm, noon-5pm Sun • goddess gifts & books • wheelchair access

TRAVEL & TOUR OPERATORS

Global Affair 285 E. 5th Ave. • 343-8595/ (800) 755-2753 • IGTA member • women-owned/run

SPIRITUAL GROUPS

MCC • 345-5963 • 4pm Sun

PUBLICATIONS

View Magazine PO Box 11067, 97447 • 302-6523 • 'chronicle of gay & lesbian life'

Womyn's Press PO Box 562, 97440 • 689-3974 • feminist newspaper since 1970

EROTICA

Exclusively Adult 1166 S. 'A' St., Springfield • 726-6969 • 24hrs

Grants Pass   (503)

WOMEN'S ACCOMMODATIONS

Womanshare PO Box 681, 97526 • 862-2807 • women only • hot tub • cabin & campground • meals included • $10-30

Mother Kali's Books
"Celebrating Women's Lives in All Our Diversities"

women of color
Jewish women
lesbians

women's music
cards
recovery

(541) 343-4864
Mon-Sat. 10-6

2001 FranklinBlvd.
Eugene, OR 97401

Klamath Falls (503)

INFO LINES & SERVICES

KALA (Klamath Area Lambda Association) LesBiGay Hotline 1112 Pine St., 97601 • 882-7929 • social/support group

La Grande

INFO LINES & SERVICES

GALA of Eastern Oregon State College Student Activities Office, Hoke College Center EOS, 97850 • 7pm 2nd & 4th Mon (Loso Hall #232)

Lincoln City (503)

ACCOMMODATIONS

▲ **Ocean Gardens Inn** 2735 NW Inlet • 994-5007/ (800) 866-9925 • gay-friendly • hot tub • spacious units w/ spectacular views of the Pacific Ocean • 7.5 miles of walking beach

RESTAURANTS & CAFES

Over the Waves 2945 NW Jetty Ave. • 994-3877 • 8am-10pm, lounge open til 2am • live shows • $12-18

Medford (503)

INFO LINES & SERVICES

AA Gay/Lesbian • 773-4848

BOOKSTORES & RETAIL SHOPS

Hands On Books 211 W. Main • 779-6990 • 10am-5:30pm, clsd Sun • general • some lesbian/gay titles

Newport (503)

WOMEN'S ACCOMMODATIONS

Green Gables B&B (at Green Gables Bookstore) • 265-9141 • women only • 1 rm • full breakfast • shared bath • ocean view

BOOKSTORES & RETAIL SHOPS

Green Gables Bookstore 156 SW Coast St. • 265-9141 • 10am-5pm • women's • also used/children's books & music

O'Brien (503)

WOMEN'S ACCOMMODATIONS

Mountain River Inn PO Box 34, 97534 • 596-2392 • women only • full breakfast • also camping & RV sites • unconfirmed fall '95

Pacific City (503)

RESTAURANTS & CAFES

White Moon Cow Cafe 35490 Brooten Rd. • 965-5101 • 9am-6pm • coffee/teas/desserts/soups • also bookstore • wheelchair access• lesbian-owned • $3-4

BOOKSTORES & RETAIL SHOPS

Amazon Earthworks PO Box 248, 97135 • 392-3900 • matriarchal pottery images & sacred art • catalog available

Portland (503)

INFO LINES & SERVICES

Asian/Pacific Islander Lesbians & Gays PO Box 1615, 97207 • 232-6408 • educational/social/support group

Bad Girls c/o NLA PO Box 5161, 97008

Lesbian Community Project • 223-0071 • multi-cultural political & social events

Live & Let Live Club 2082 SE Ankeny St. • 231-3760 • various 12-step meetings

Northwest Gender Alliance PO Box 4928, 97208-4928 • 646-2802 • 3rd Tue & 2nd Sat • info & support for transsexuals & crossdressers

Phoenix Rising 620 SW 5th Ste. 710 • 223-8299 • info & referrals • counseling, youth group (for-profit counseling center)

Reed College Lesbian/Gay & Bisexual Union 3203 SE Woodstock Blvd., 97202

ACCOMMODATIONS

Holladay House B&B 1735 NE Wasco St. • 282-3172 • gay-friendly • full breakfast

Hotel Vintage Plaza 422 SW Broadway • 228-1212/ (800) 243-0555 • gay-friendly • upscale

MacMaster House 1041 SW Vista Ave. • 223-7362 • gay-friendly • historic mansion on prestigious King's hill near the Rose Gardens

Sullivan's Gulch B&B 1744 NE Clackamas St. • 331-1104 • lesbians/gay men • 1904 Portland home that offers Western comfort

BARS

Candlelight Room 2032 SW 5th • 222-3378 • 7am-2:30am • gay-friendly • live shows • food served

Choices Pub 2845 SE Stark St. • 236-4321 • 4pm-1am, til 2:30am wknds • mostly women • dancing/DJ • wheelchair access

City Nightclub 13 NW 13th Ave. • 224-2489 • 10pm-2am, til 4am Fri-Sat, clsd Mon-Tue • popular • lesbians/gay men • dancing/DJ • 18+ • live shows • no alcohol

Code Blue (various locations) • 282-6979 • mostly women • dancing/DJ • call for events

Crow Nightclub 4801 SE Hawthorne • 232-2037 • 4pm-2:30am • mostly gay men • beer/wine • patio • wheelchair access

Darcelle XV 208 NW 3rd Ave. • 222-5338 • 5pm-2:30am, clsd Sun • gay-friendly • live shows • food served • wheelchair access

Eagle PDX 1300 W. Burnside • 241-0105 • 5pm-2:30am • mostly gay men • leather

Egyptian Club 3701 SE Division • 236-8689 • mostly women • dancing/DJ • live shows • also a restaurant • pasta & more • some veggie • $5-10

Embers Nightclub 110 NW Broadway • 222-3082 • 11am-2:30am, til 4am Fri-Sat • popular • gay-friendly • dancing/DJ • live shows • wheelchair access

Hobo's 120 NW 3rd Ave. • 224-3285 • 4pm-2am • popular • gay-friendly • also a restaurant • American • some veggie • wheelchair access • $12-45

Panorama 341 SW 10th • 221-7262 • 9pm-4am Fri-Sat, til 2:30am Sun • gay-friendly • dancing/DJ • beer/wine • wheelchair access

Three Sisters Tavern 1125 SW Stark St. • 228-0486 • 12:30pm-2:30am, clsd Sun • mostly gay men • neighborhood bar • dancing/DJ

RESTAURANTS & CAFES

Adobe Rose 1634 SE Bybee Blvd. • 235-9114 • 4pm-9pm, clsd Sun • New Mexican • some veggie • beer/wine • $5-7

B.J.'s Brazilian Restaurant 7019 SE Milwaukie Ave. • 236-9629 • lunch & dinner, clsd Sun

Bastas Trattoria 410 NW 21st • 274-1571 • lunch & dinner • northern Italian • some veggie • full bar • $7-12

Bijou Cafe 132 SW 3rd Ave. • 222-3187 • 7am-3pm • natural breakfast & lunch • plenty veggie • $4-7

Cafe des Amis 1987 NW Kearney St. • 295-6487 • 5:30pm-10pm, clsd Sun • French • full bar • wheelchair access • $12-24

Caffe Fresco 2387 NW Thurman • 243-3247 • 7am-4pm, til 2pm Sun • Italian

Caribou Cafe & Bar 503 W. Burnside • 227-0245 • noon-1am, from 5pm Sat, from 3pm Sun • diner • some veggie • full bar • $4-9

Coffee Cow 5204 NE Sacramento • 282-9910 • 7am-7pm, til 10pm Sat, 9am-5pm Sun • open later in summer

Cup & Saucer Cafe 3566 SE Hawthorne • 236-6001 • 7am-8pm • full menu • smoke-free

Elephant Walk Sandwich Shop 4611 SE Hawthorne • 239-0869 • 10am-5pm • some veggie

Espress It! 1026 SW Stark • 227-2551 • 5pm-2:30am • lesbians/gay men • coffeehouse/sandwiches • also gallery

Fish Grotto (at Boxx's) • 226-4171 • 11:30am-10:30pm, from 4:30pm wknds • popular • some veggie • full bar • $8-24

Genoa 2832 SE Belmont • 238-1464 • clsd Sun • 7-course Italian dinner • beer/wine • $48 (wine & gratuity not included)

Hamburger Mary's 840 SW Park Ave. • 223-0900 • 7am-2am • popular • full bar • $7-11

Majas Tacqueria 1000 SW Morrison • 226-1946 • 11am-10pm

Old Wives Tales 1300 E. Burnside St. • 238-0470 • 8am-10pm, til 11pm Fri-Sat • beer/wine • wheelchair access • $7-14

Shakers Cafe 1212 NW Glisan • 221-0011 • 6:30am-4pm, from 7:30am Sat, clsd Sun • homecooking • beer/wine

Starky's 2913 SE Stark St. • 230-7980 • lunch & dinner (bar til 2:30am) • popular • lesbians/gay men • some veggie • full bar • $10-20

Zefiro 500 NW 21st • 226-3394 • lunch & dinner, clsd Sun • Mediterranean • $13-20

Portland

Despite on-going harassment from the Oregon Citizen's Alliance, Oregon is still a haven for lesbians – check out Portlandia, atop the Portland Building, both city landmark and powerful Amazon icon.

At the foot of Mt. Hood, sprawling along the Columbia River, you'll find this city that's home to rainy days, roses and the Riot Grrrls of 'zine & grunge fame – young activist punkgirls. Though you might expect blocks of women's bookstores and bars, lesbian life here focuses more on the outdoors and cocooning at home with small groups of friends. To get in touch, pick up a recent copy of **Just Out**, or call the **Lesbian Community Project**.

Still, if your scene is the bars, Portland has two for women: **Choices Pub** and **Egyptian Club** For a nourishing meal, hit **Old Wives Tales**, then pep up with java and art at **Espress It!** or the smoke-free **Cup & Saucer Cafe**. As for bookstores, **Powell's** is a huge new/used bookstore, and we've heard that the lesbian/gay section is a good meeting place on weekend nights – and Powell's even has a little cafe.

YMS & HEALTH CLUBS

Inner City Hot Springs 2927 NE Everett St. • 238-4010 • 10am-11pm, 1pm-10pm Sun • gay-friendly • wellness center • reservations required

Princeton Athletic Club 614 SW 11th Ave. • 222-2639 • 5am-10pm, 7am-7pm wknds • gay-friendly

OOKSTORES & RETAIL SHOPS

Crone Magic 3240-B SE Hawthorne • 231-9230 • 11am-6pm, noon-5pm Sun, clsd Mon • crystal & goddess crafts

In Her Image Gallery 3208 SE Hawthorne • 231-3726 • 10am-6pm • wheelchair access

In Other Words 3734 SE Hawthorne Blvd. • 232-6003 • 10am-9pm, til 10pm Fri-Sat, til 5pm Sun • women's books • music • gallery

Jellybean 721 SW 10th Ave. • 222-5888 • 10am-6pm, clsd Sun • cards • T-shirts • gifts • wheelchair access

Laughing Horse Bookstore 3652 SE Division • 236-2893 • 11am-7pm, clsd Sun • wheelchair access

Looking Glass Bookstore 318 SW Taylor • 227-4760 • 9am-6pm, from 10am Sat, clsd Sun

Powell's Books 1005 W. Burnside St. • 228-4651 • 9am-11pm, til 9pm Sun • new & used books • wheelchair access

Rocky Road Comics 916 W. Burnside (near 10th) • 274-0651 • noon-8pm, til 6pm Sun-Tue • lesbigay comics section • wheelchair access

Twenty-Third Ave. Books 1015 NW 23rd Ave. • 224-5097 • 9:30am-8pm

Widdershins PO Box 42395, 97242 • 232-2129 • mail order • out-of-print women's books

TRAVEL & TOUR OPERATORS

Advantage Travel Service 812 SW Washington St. Ste. 200 • 225-0186/ (800) 688-6690 • IGTA member

Gulliver's Travels & Voyages 514 NW 9th Ave. • 221-0013/ (800) 875-8009 • IGTA member

Hawthorne Travel Company 1939 SE Hawthorne Blvd. • 232-5944 • IGTA member

In Touch Travel 121 SW Morrison St. #270 • 223-1062/ (800) 568-3246 • IGTA member

Portland (503)

LESBIGAY INFO: Queer Alliance: 874-6596. Phoenix Rising: 9am-5pm 223-8299.

LESBIGAY PAPER: Just Out: 236-1252.

WHERE THE GIRLS ARE: Snacking granola while cycling (that's motorcycling) in the mountains, wearing boots and flannel. (Aw, hell, we don't know!)

LESBIGAY AA: Gays in Sobriety: 774-4060, 32 Thomas St. (Williston W. Church), 6:30pm Sun, 8pm Th.

LESBIGAY PRIDE: July, 295-9788.

ANNUAL EVENTS: June - The Gathering: 482-2026, annual pagan camp in the Oregon Woods. September - Northwest Women's Music Celebration: participatory event for musicians,

songwriters & singers, NOT performance-oriented. October 10-14 - Living in Leather: (614) 899-4406, national conference for the leather, SM and fetish communities.

CITY INFO: 222-2223. Oregon Welcome Center: 285-1631.

BEST VIEW: International Rose Test Gardens at Washington Park.

WEATHER: You'd better love your winters cold (low 30s at night), grey and WET! But all the rains give Portland its lush landscape that bursts into beautiful colors in the spring and fall. Summer brings sunnier days. (Temperatures can be in the 50s one day and the 90s the next.)

TRANSIT: Radio Cab: 227-1212.

J&M Travel 4370 NE Halsey Ste. 138 • 249-0305/ (800) 875-0305 • IGTA member

Kaz Travel 1975 SW 1st Ave. Ste. K • 223-4585/ (800) 637-3874 • IGTA member

Mikuni Travel Service 1 SW Columbia St. Ste. 1010 • 227-3639/ (800) 248-0624 • IGTA member

Oregon Tourism Division • (800) 547-7842

Travel Agents International 917 SW Washington St. • 223-1100/ (800) 357-3194 • ask for Rip • IGTA member

Travel Corner 17175 SW T.V. Hwy., Aloha • 649-9867/ (800) 327-0840 • IGTA member• women-owned

The Travel Shop 10115 SW Nimbus Ctr. Ste. 600, Tigard • 684-8533/ (800) 285-8835 • ask for Mark

SPIRITUAL GROUPS

Dignity 13th & SW Clay (St. Stephen's Church) • 295-4868 • 7:30pm Sat

MCC Portland 1644 NE 24th St. (at Broadway) • 281-8868 • 10am Sun • wheelchair access

Pagan Info Line • 650-7045 • also publishes 'Open Ways' newsletter

Reach Out! PO Box 1173, Clackamas, 97015 • support group for lesbigay Jehovah's Witnesses & Mormons

Sisterspirit PO Box 9246, 97207 • 294-0645 • celebration w/ women sharing spirituality

PUBLICATIONS

Just Out PO Box 14400, 97214-0400 • 236-1252 • bi-monthly

EROTICA

It's My Pleasure 4258 SE Hawthorne • 236-0505 • 10am-7pm, 11am-5pm Sun • sex toys & books for women

Leatherworks 2908 SE Belmont St. • 234-2697 • noon-6pm Tue-Sat

Prineview   (503

ACCOMMODATIONS

▲ **Prineview B&B** 4934 NW O'Neil Hwy. • 416-0167 • lesbians/gay men • full breakfast • hot tub • swimming • nudity • pet okay • kids okay • also outdoor bar • gay-owned/run

---

Rogue River (541)

ACCOMMODATIONS

Whispering Pines B&B/Retreat 9188 W. Evans Creek Rd. • 582-1757/ (800) 788-1757 • popular • lesbians/gay men • full breakfast • hot tub • swimming • 32 acres of pine & pasture cradled in the Cascade foothills

Roseburg (503)

INFO LINES & SERVICES

Gay/Lesbian Switchboard • 672-4126 • also publishes 'Gay Ol' Times' newsletter

BARS

Roma Cocktail Lounge & Restaurant 5096 Hwy. 99 S. • 679-7100 • 11am-2am (kitchen closes at 10pm) • live shows • Italian

Salem (503)

BARS

Sneakers Bar & Dance Club 300 Liberty St. SE • 363-0549 • 4pm-2:30am (restaurant clsd Sun-Mon) • lesbians/gay men • dancing/DJ • live shows • karaoke • country/western Tue • also a restaurant • some veggie • $10-20 • wheelchair access

RESTAURANTS & CAFES

Dahlia's 189 Liberty St. NE (Reed Opera House) • 363-5414 • lunch & dinner • some veggie • $9-16

Off Center Cafe 1741 Center St. NE • 363-9245 • popular • some veggie • popular breakfast • call for hours • wheelchair access • $7-12

BOOKSTORES & RETAIL SHOPS

Rosebud & Fish 524 State St. • 399-9960 • 10am-7pm, noon-5pm Sun • alternative bookstore

SPIRITUAL GROUPS

Dignity 1020 Columbia St. (St. Vincent's Church) • 363-0006 • 7:30pm 2nd & 4th Sat

First Unitarian Society of Salem 490 19th St. NE • 364-0932 • 9:15am & 11am Sun (10am only summers)

Sweet Spirit MCC 1410 12th St. SE • 363-6618 • 11am Sun

PUBLICATIONS

Community News PO Box 663, 97308 • 363-0006 • monthly

Sandy (503)

ACCOMMODATIONS

Cedar Grove Cottage 58180 E. Marmot Rd. • 557-8292 • gay-friendly • spa • fireplace • near Sandy River • secluded • sleeps 2-4

Sutherlin

PUBLICATIONS

The News PO Box 1720, 97470

Tillamook

INFO LINES & SERVICES

Tillamook County GALA PO Box 592, Pacific City, 97135 • lesbigay support • monthly potlucks

Tiller (503)

ACCOMMODATIONS

Kalles Family RV Ranch 233 Jackson Creek Rd. • 825-3271 • lesbians/gay men • near outdoor recreation • camping sites & RV hookups • between Medford & Roseburg

Waldport (503)

ACCOMMODATIONS

Cliff House B&B Yaquina John Point at 1450 Adahi St. • 563-2506 • gay-friendly • full breakfast • near outdoor recreation • hot tub • oceanfront

Yachats (541)

ACCOMMODATIONS

Morningstar Gallery & B&B 95668 Hwy. 101 S. • 547-4412 • gay-friendly • full breakfast • hot tub • oceanfront property w/ fabulous views

Oregon House 94288 Hwy. 101 • 547-3329 • gay-friendly • 9 suites w/ kitchen • some w/ jacuzzi • no smoking, no dogs, no TVs • wheelchair access

See Vue Motel 95590 Hwy. 101 S. • 547-3227 • gay-friendly • uniquely decorated oceanview units on a cliff where the mountains meet the sea

Pennsylvania

Allentown (610)

INFO LINES & SERVICES

Gays/Lesbians of Reading & Allentown PO Box 1952, 18105 • (610) 868-7183 • social group • also newsletter

Lehigh Valley Lesbians • (610) 439-8755 • call for times & locations

Your Turf • (610) 439-8755 • 7pm Fri • lesbigay youth group • call for locations

BARS

Candida's 247 N. 12th St. • (610) 434-3071 • 4pm-2am, from 2pm Fri-Sun • lesbians/gay men • neighborhood bar

Moose Lounge 28-30 N. 10th St. • 432-0706 • 2pm-2am • popular • mostly gay men • piano bar • food served • also Stonewall • 10pm-2am • dancing/DJ • country/western Tue • live shows Wed • karaoke Sun

SPIRITUAL GROUPS

Grace Covenant Fellowship Church 247 N. 10th St. • 740-0247 • 10:45am Sun

MCC 6th & Walnut (St. John's UCC) • 439-8755 • 6pm Sun • wheelchair access

Altoona (814)

INFO LINES & SERVICES

Gay/Lesbian/Bisexual Helpline • 942-8101 • 7pm-10pm Th-Sun

Beaver Falls

BARS

A.S.S. (Alternative Subway Stop) 1204 7th Ave. (rear entrance) • 8pm-2am, clsd Sun • mostly gay men • dancing/DJ • no phone

Bethlehem (610)

BARS

Diamonz 1913 W. Broad St. • 865-1028 • 3pm-2am, from 2pm wknds • mostly women • dancing/DJ • live shows • also a restaurant • fine dining (clsd Mon) • some veggie • wheelchair access • $7-13

Bradford

INFO LINES & SERVICES

University of Pitt-Bradford BiGALA c/o Director of Student Activities 200 Campus Dr./235 Commons, 16701

Bridgeport (610)

BARS

Lark 302 Dekalb St. (Rte. 202 N.) • 275-8136 • 8pm-2am, from 4pm Sun • mostly gay men • dancing/DJ • dinner served

East Stroudsburg (717)

ACCOMMODATIONS

▲ **Rainbow Mtn. Resort & Restaurant** RD 8, Box 8174 • 223-8484 • popular • lesbians/gay men • B&B/deluxe stes. • cabins • olympic pool • also full bar • dancing/DJ Fri-Sat • piano bar 7pm-2am • also restaurant • gourmet American • some veggie • $13-20 • woman-owned

Edinboro (814)

INFO LINES & SERVICES

Identity University Center, Edinboro University of Pennsylvania, 16444 • 732-2000

Emlenton (412)

ACCOMMODATIONS

Allegheny House 214 River Ave. (on I-80 near I-79) • 867-9636/ (800) 547-8499 • gay-friendly • full breakfast • riverfront

Ephrata (717)

TRAVEL & TOUR OPERATORS

Zeller Travel 4213 Oregon Pike • 859-4710/ (800) 331-4359 • IGTA member

Erie (814)

INFO LINES & SERVICES

Bridges PO Box 3063, 16508-3063 • 456-9833 • lesbigay resources & networking • also publishes 'Erie Gay Community Newsletter'

Lambda Group AA 7180 New Perry Hwy. (Unitarian Universalist Church) • 452-2675 • 8pm Sun • wheelchair access

Trigon: Lesbian/Gay/Bisexual Coalition Box 794 Behrend College, 16563 • 898-6164

Womynspace (at the Unitarian Universalist Church) • 454-2713 • 7:30pm 1st Sat • alcohol/smoke-free women's coffeehouse

ACCOMMODATIONS

Castle Great House 231 W. 21st St. • 454-6465 • lesbians/gay men • fireplaces

BARS

Embers 1711 State St. • 454-9171 • 8pm-2am, clsd Sun • mostly gay men • dancing/DJ • piano bar

Leeward Lounge 1022 Bridge St., Ashtabula • (216) 964-9935 • 8pm-2am • lesbians/gay men • food served

Lizzy Bordon's Part II 3412 W. 12th St. • 833-4059 • 9pm-2am, clsd Sun • popular • lesbians/gay men • dancing/DJ • wheelchair access

RESTAURANTS & CAFES

Cup-A-Ccinos Coffeehouse 18 N. Park Row • 456-1151 • 7:30am-11pm, clsd Sun • live shows • wheelchair access

La Bella Bistro 556 W. 4th • 454-3616 • lunch & dinner, clsd Sun • BYOB • $9-20

Pie in the Sky Cafe 463 W. 8th St. • 459-8638 • clsd Sun • BYOB • wheelchair access • $9-15

BOOKSTORES & RETAIL SHOPS

Perceptions 328 W. 6th • 454-7364 • 11am-7pm, til 5pm Sat, clsd Sun & Wed • metaphysical bookstore

SPIRITUAL GROUPS

Unitarian Universalist Congregation of Erie 7180 New Perry Hwy. • 864-9300

Gettysburg

INFO LINES & SERVICES

Gettysburg College Lambda Alliance Box 2256, Gettysburg College, 17325

Greensburg (412)

INFO LINES & SERVICES

Gay/Lesbian Outreach Coalition c/o Office of Student Life, University of Pittsburgh, 15601

BARS

Safari Lounge 108 W. Pittsburgh St. • 837-9948 • 9pm-2am, clsd Sun • popular • mostly gay men • dancing/DJ • patio • wheelchair access

Harrisburg (717)

INFO LINES & SERVICES

Gay/Lesbian Switchboard • 234-0328 • 6pm-10pm Mon-Fri

BARS

Neptune's Lounge 268 North St. • 233-3078 • 4pm-2am, from 2pm Sun • popular • mostly gay men • neighborhood bar • dinner menu 5pm-9pm Tue-Th

Stallions 706 N. 3rd St. (rear entrance) • 233-4681 • 4pm-2am, clsd Sun • popular • mostly gay men • dancing/DJ • also a restaurant • dinner Th-Sat, Sun brunch • wheelchair access

Strawberry Cafe 704 N. 3rd St. • 234-4228 • 2pm-2am, clsd Sun • popular • mostly gay men • neighborhood bar • videos • wheelchair access

RESTAURANTS & CAFES

Colonnade 300 N. 2nd St. • 234-8740 • 7am-8pm, clsd Sun • seafood • full bar • wheelchair access • $8-15

Paper Moon 268 North St. • 233-0581 • 6pm-11pm Fri-Sat, noon-3pm Sun • lesbians/gay men • $5-10

TRAVEL & TOUR OPERATORS

Pennsylvania Bureau of Travel • (800) 847-4872

SPIRITUAL GROUPS

Dignity PO Box 297, 17108 • 232-2027

MCC of the Spirit 6th & Herr St. (Friends Meeting House) • 236-7387 • 7pm Sun

Johnstown (814)

BARS

Lucille's 520 Washington St. • 539-4448 • 9pm-2am, clsd Sun-Mon • lesbians/gay men • dancing/DJ • live shows

Kutztown (610)

ACCOMMODATIONS

Grim's Manor B&B 10 Kern Rd. • 683-7089 • gay-friendly • full breakfast • hot tub • 200 yr. old historical stone farmhouse & outbuildings on 5 secluded acres

Lancaster (717)

INFO LINES & SERVICES

Gay/ Lesbian Helpline • 397-0691 • 7pm-10pm Sun, Wed & Th

Pink Triangle Coalition PO Box 31, 17603 • also sponsors youth group meetings

ACCOMMODATIONS

Maison Rouge 2236 Marietta Ave. • 399-3033 • gay-friendly • full breakfast

BARS

Sundown Lounge 429 N. Mulberry St. • 392-2737 • 8pm-2am, clsd Sun • mostly women • dancing/DJ

Tally Ho 201 W. Orange • 299-0661 • 6pm-2am, from 8pm Sun • popular • lesbians/gay men • dancing/DJ

RESTAURANTS & CAFES

Loft (above Tally Ho) • 299-0661 • lunch Mon-Fri, dinner Mon-Sat • French/American • $15-25

BOOKSTORES & RETAIL SHOPS

Borders Bookshop 940 Plaza Rd. • 293-8022 • open til 11pm • some lesbigay titles

SPIRITUAL GROUPS

MCC Vision of Hope 130 E. Main St., Mountville • 285-9070 • 10:30am & 7pm Sun

Lancaster County (717)

WOMEN'S ACCOMMODATIONS

DalEva Farms PO Box 6, Drumore, 17518 • 548-3163 • women only

Milford (212)

WOMEN'S ACCOMMODATIONS

K'saan • (212) 663-2963 • women only • swimming • log house on 45 wooded acres • weekend or weekly rentals only • sleeps 2-6 • $200-575

New Hope (215)

INFO LINES & SERVICES

AA Gay/Lesbian • 862-0327 • contact for mtgs.

ACCOMMODATIONS

Backstreet Inn 144 Old York Inn Rd. • 862-9571 • gay-friendly • full breakfast • swimming

The Fox & Hound B&B 246 West Bridge St. • 862-5082/ (800) 862-5082 • gay-friendly • B&B • elegant 1850s stone manor located on two acres of parklike setting

Lexington House 6171 Upper York Rd. •
794-0811 • lesbians/gay men • swimming
• tranquil 1789 home offering a charming
old world country setting

The Raven 385 West Bridge St. • 862-
2081 • popular • mostly gay men •
swimming • also a restaurant • cont'l •
full bar • $15-20

Riverside B&B 58 N. Main St. • 862-0216
• mostly gay men • New Hope's most
exclusive guest house

BARS

Cartwheel 427 York Rd. (US 202) • 862-
0880 • 5pm-2am •
lesbians/gay men • dancing/DJ • live
shows • piano bar • also a restaurant •
dinner • wheelchair access

Ladies for the 80s • (609) 784-8341 •
scheduled parties for women by women
• call for times & locations

RESTAURANTS & CAFES

Country Host 463 Old York Rd. (Rte. 202)
• 862-5575 • 7am-10pm • American •
full bar • wheelchair access • $7-12

Havana 105 S. Main St. • 862-9897 •
11am-midnight, bar til 2am • live shows
• some veggie • $9-16

Karla's 5 W. Mechanic St. • 862-2612 •
lunch, dinner & late night breakfast Fri-
Sat • live shows • Italian • some veggie
• full bar • $15-25

Mother's 34 N. Main St. • 862-5270 •
9am-10pm • American • some veggie •
$10-20

Odette's South River Rd. • 862-3000 •
11am-10pm (piano bar & cabaret til 1am)
• cont'l • some veggie • wheelchair
access • $15-25

Wildflowers 8 W. Mechanic St. • 862-
2241 • noon-10pm (seasonal) • BYOB •
outdoor dining • some veggie • $8-15

BOOKSTORES & RETAIL SHOPS

▲ **Book Gallery** 19 W. Mechanic St. • 862-
5110 • 11am-7pm (call for Feb-May
hours) • feminist/lesbian

Ember'glo Gifts 27 W. Mechanic St. •
862-2929 • 11am-6pm (clsd Tue winters)

TRAVEL & TOUR OPERATORS

Flight of Fancy, Inc. PO Box 234, 408
York Rd., 18938 • 862-9665/ (800) 691-
1980

EROTICA

Grown Ups 2 E. Mechanic St. • 862-9304
• opens 11am

New Milford (717)

ACCOMMODATIONS

Oneida Camp & Lodge PO Box 537, 18834 • 465-7011 • mostly gay men • swimming • nudity • oldest gay-owned & operated campground dedicated to the gay & lesbian community

Norristown (610)

BARS

Doubleheader 354 W. Elm St. • 277-1070 • 8pm-2am, clsd Sun-Mon • lesbians/gay men • dancing/DJ • leather • videos

Philadelphia (215)

INFO LINES & SERVICES

AA Gay/Lesbian • 574-6900

BiUnity • 724-3663 • bisexual social/support group

Dyke TV Channel 54 • 9pm & midnight Th • 'weekly, half-hour TV show produced by lesbians, for lesbians'

Female Trouble • 386-1120 • bi-monthly • social/educational woman-woman S/M group • 18+ • newsletter

Gay/Lesbian Radio WXPN-FM 88.5 • 'Gaydreams' 9pm Sun

Gay/Lesbian Switchboard • 546-7100 • 7pm-10pm

Gay/Lesbian/Bisexual/Transgendered Community Center 201 S. Camac St. (Penguin Place) • 732-2220 • also houses Lesbigay Archives/Library of Philadelphia

GROWP (Greater Roundtable of Women Professionals) PO Box 35010, 19128-0510 • (610) 789-4938 • lesbian social group

Open Home Lesbian Center • 247-5545 • healing & services center for women

Penn Women's Center 119 Houston Hall, 3417 Spruce St. • 878-8611

Sisterspace of Phildelphia 351 S. 47th St. # B-101, 19143 • 476-8856 • sponsors 'Sisterspace Pocono Weekend', dances, events, workshops • also publishes newsletter

Tell-A-Woman Switchboard • 564-5810

Unity Inc. 1207 Chestnut St. • 851-1912 • 9am-5pm Mon-Fri, clsd wknds • lesbigay support/social services

ACCOMMODATIONS

Antique Row B&B 341 S. 12th St. • 592-7802 • gay-friendly • full breakfast • small, European-style B&B located in historic (circa 1820) townhouse in heart of gay community

Bag & Baggage B&B 338 S. 19th St. • 546-3807 • gay-friendly

Gaskill House 312 Gaskill St. • 413-2887 • gay-friendly • fireplaces • patio

Glen Isle Farm 30 mi. out-of-town in Downingtown • (610) 269-9100/ (800) 269-1730 • gay-friendly • full breakfast • near outdoor recreation • IGTA member

Sarah P. Wilson House 155 Main St., Phoenixville • (610) 933-0327 • gay-friendly • full breakfast

Travelodge-Stadium 2015 Penrose Ave. • 755-6500 • gay-friendly • swimming • also a restaurant • full bar • wheelchair access

BARS

2-4 Club 1221 St. James St. • 735-5772 • 11pm-3am, from midnight Mon-Th • mostly gay men • dancing/DJ • private club

Bike Stop 204 S. Quince • 627-1662 • 1pm-2am • popular • mostly gay men • dancing/DJ • live shows • leather crowd (very leather-women-friendly) • home bar of female Trouble • 4 flrs. • also Cafe on Quince • eclectic American • some veggie • $6-16

Black Banana 205 N. 3rd • 925-4433 • 10pm-3am, clsd Mon • gay-friendly • dancing/DJ • alternative

Club Revival 24 S. 3rd St. • 627-4825 • 10pm-? • gay-friendly • dancing/DJ • private club

Harmony Zone 254 S. 12th St. • 545-8088 • 4pm-2am, from 1pm Sun • lesbians/gay men • dancing/DJ • live shows • food served • women's night Th

Key West 207 S. Juniper • 545-1578 • 4pm-2am, from 11am Sun • lesbians/gay men • dancing/DJ • live shows • also a restaurant • American • dinner Wed-Sat, Sun brunch • wheelchair access • $8-15

Ladies for the 80's • 784-8341 • call for events • mostly women

Paragon 1415 Locust St. • 545-8419 • 4pm-2am, clsd Mon • mostly gay men • dancing/DJ • 18+ • live shows • women's night Wed

Penny's Playhouse 5300-02 Market St. • 471-1958 • 11am-2am, clsd Sun • gay-friendly • mostly African-American • live shows

Raffles 243 S. Camac St. • 545-6969 • 4pm-2am • popular • lesbians/gay men • dancing/DJ • 3 bars including piano bar • country/western Wed-Sun • also a restaurant • cont'l • $7-12

Rodz 1418 Rodman St. • 546-1900 • 5pm-2am, from noon Sun • lesbians/gay men • piano bar • also Tyz • lesbians/gay men • dancing/DJ • also a restaurant • cont'l • some veggie • $10-20

Westbury 261 S. 13th & Spruce • 546-5170 • 10am-2am • mostly gay men • neighborhood bar • also a restaurant • gourmet homecooking • some veggie • wheelchair access • $9-14

Woody's 202 S. 13th St. • 545-1893 • 11am-2am • popular • mostly gay men • dancing/DJ • food served • wheelchair access

RESTAURANTS & CAFES

16th Street Bar & Grill 264 S. 16th St. • 735-3316 • opens 11:30am • Mediterranean • some veggie • full bar • $10-20

Adobe Cafe 4550 Mitchell St., Roxborough • 483-3947 • some veggie • full bar • patio • $9-12

Alouette 334 Bainbridge St. • 629-1126 • call for hours • French/Asian • $20-30

Astral Plane 1708 Lombard St. • 546-6230 • 5pm-11pm • American • some veggie • full bar • $10-20

Backstage Bar & Restaurant 614 S. 4th St. • 627-9887 • 4pm-2am, dinner from 6pm-10pm, Sun brunch • cont'l • $10-20

Cafe on Quince 202 S. Quince St. • 592-1750 • clsd Mon • lunch, dinner & Sun brunch • women-owned/run

Cheap Art Cafe 260 S. 12th St. • 735-6650 • 24hrs • some veggie

Circa 1518 Walnut St. • 545-6800 • 11am-midnight, til 2am Th-Sat, clsd Sun • also full bar • dancing/DJ seasonally • live shows • wheelchair access

Diner on the Square 1839 Spruce St. • 735-5787 • 24hrs • $7-10

Inn Philadelphia 251 S. Camac St. • 732-2339 • 4:30pm-2am • cont'l • some veggie • full bar • Sun brunch • $12-26

Philadelphia (215)

LESBIGAY INFO: Gay/Lesbian Switchboard: 546-7100, Wed.-Fri. 6pm-11pm, Sat.-Tues. 7pm-10pm. Tell-A-Woman Switchboard: 564-5810.

LESBIGAY PAPER: Philidelphia Gay News: 625-8501.

WHERE THE GIRLS ARE: Partying downtown near 12th St., south of Market.

LESBIGAY AA: 574-6900.

LESBIGAY PRIDE: June: 564-3332.

ANNUAL EVENTS: January 26-28 - Blue Ball: 575-1110, AIDS benefit weekend highlighted by Saturday night dance. May 3-5 - Pridefest Philadelphia: 790-7820, weekend of gay/lesbian film, performances, literature, sports, seminars, parties & more. June 13-16 - Womongath-ering: (609) 694-2037, women's spirituality fest. December 31 - Mummer's Strut: 732-3378, New year's Eve party benefitting Pridefest.

CITY INFO: 636-1666.

BEST VIEW: Top of Center Square, 16th & Market.

WEATHER: Winter temperatures hover in the 20ºs. Summers are humid with temperatures in the 80ºs and 90ºs.

TRANSIT: Yellow Cab: 922-8400.

Liberties 705 N. 2nd St. • 238-0660 • lunch & dinner, clsd Sun • full bar • live jazz wknds • $10-16

Makam's Kitchen 2401 Lombard • 546-8832 • cafe food (some macrobiotic)

Mont Serrat 623 South St. • 627-4224 • noon-midnight • healthy American • some veggie • full bar • $6-15

My Thai 2200 South St. • 985-1878 • 5pm-10pm, til 11pm Fri-Sat • $10-20

Palladium 3601 Locust Walk • 387-3463 • cont'l • some veggie • wheelchair access • $10-25

Roosevelt's Pub 2222 Walnut • 636-9722 • lunch & dinner • some veggie • full bar • $5-12

Savoy Restaurant 232 S. 11th St. • 923-2348 • 24hrs • popular • American • popular afterhours • $5-7

Seville Diner 1701 Spruce St. • 735-4611 • noon-10pm • lesbians/gay men • live shows • also Galileo's Observatory on the 2nd flr. • open 4pm-2am

Shing Kee 52 N. 9th St. • 829-8983 • BYOB • gay-owned/run

Waldorf Cafe 20th & Lombard Sts. • 985-1836 • dinner • cont'l • some veggie • full bar • wheelchair access • $12-18

GYMS & HEALTH CLUBS

12th St. Gym 204 S. 12th St. • 985-4092 • 6am-11pm • gay-friendly

BOOKSTORES & RETAIL SHOPS

Afterwords 218 S. 12th St. • 735-2393 • 10am-midnight

Giovanni's Room 345 S. 12th St. • 923-2960 • call for hours, open 7 days a week • popular • lesbian/gay/feminist bookstore

Step-by-Step Books 126 West Chester Pike, Havertown • (610) 789-4870 • call for hours • recovery • women's issues • lesbian titles

Thrift for AIDS 629 South St. • 592-9014 • noon-9pm

Urban Necessities 1506 Spruce St. • 546-6768 • 'housewares fit for a queen'

TRAVEL & TOUR OPERATORS

Lambda Travel 21 S. 5th St. #545 • 925-3011/ (800) 551-2240 • ask for Scott • IGTA member

Philadelphia

*T*hough it's packed with sites of rich historical value, don't miss out on Philadelphia's multi-cultural present. To get a feel for it, browse the **Reading Terminal Market**, an ancient (for the US) and quaint farmer's market preserved within the new Convention Center. Here, smalltime grocers and farmers of many cultures sell their fresh food the Philadelphian way: old-fashioned.

A vital element in many of these cultures is the growing lesbian community, which seems to be growing in many directions. You'll find many bars with a mixed lesbigay clientele and several with women's nights such as the **Harmony Zone**.

Giovanni's Room is the lesbian/gay bookstore – always a good place to start for information on local goings-on of note; you can find the **Philadelphia Gay News** and **Au Courant** there, as well as **Labyrinth**, the women's monthly. For those of us in "the program," **Step-by-Step** is a bookstore just for you, with plenty of women's and lesbian titles as well.

Sigmund Travel 262 S. 12th St. • 735-0090 • IGTA member

Will Travel 118 S. Bellevue Ave., Longhorn • 941-4492/ (800) 443-7460 • IGTA member

SPIRITUAL GROUPS

Beth Ahavah 8 Letitia St. • 923-2003 • 8pm 1st, 3rd & 5th Fri

Dignity 330 S. 13th St. (Church of St. Luke) • 546-2093 • 7pm Sun

Integrity 1904 Walnut St. (Holy Trinity Church) • 382-0794 • 7pm 1st & 3rd Wed

MCC PO Box 8174, 19101 • 563-6601 • 10:30am Sun at 425 S. Broad St. & 7pm Sun at 2125 Chestnut St.

PUBLICATIONS

Au Courant News Magazine 2124 South St. • 790-1179 • weekly

BiFocus PO Box 30372, 19103 • bisexual newsletter

Labyrinth PO Box 58489, 19102 • 546-6686 • monthly • women's newspaper

PGN (Philadelphia Gay News) 505 S. 4th St. • 625-8501 • weekly

EROTICA

Both Ways 201 S. 13th St. • 985-2344 • piercings • leather

Pleasure Chest 2039 Walnut • 561-7480 • clsd Sun-Mon

Pittsburgh   (412)

INFO LINES & SERVICES

AA Gay/Lesbian • 471-7472

Asian-Pacifica Lesbians of Pittsburgh PO Box 81531, 15217

Gay/Lesbian Community Center Phoneline • 422-0114 • 6:30pm-9:30pm, 3pm-6pm Sat, clsd Sun • info & referrals for all sexual minorities

ISMIR (International Sexual Minorities Information Resource) PO Box 81869, 15217-0869 • 422-3060 • monthly calendar of regional, national, international lesbigay events • e-mail: ismir@aol.com

ACCOMMODATIONS

Brewers Hotel 3315 Liberty Ave. • 681-7991 • gay-friendly • food served • nightly, weekly, monthly rates

Camp Davis 311 Red Brush Rd., Boyers, 16020 • 637-2402 • May-2nd wknd Oct • lesbians/gay men • variety of events • 1 hour from Pittsburgh

Inn on the Mexican War Streets 1606 Buena Vista St. • 231-6544 • lesbians/gay men

Priory 614 Pressley • 231-3338 • gay-friendly • 24 room Victorian • wheelchair access

BARS

Auntie Mame's 965 Liberty Ave. • 391-9990 • 5pm-2am, clsd Sun • mostly gay men • karaoke • videos

Brewery Tavern (at Brewers Hotel) • 681-7991 • 10am-2am, from noon Sun • gay-friendly

C.J. Deighan's 2506 W. Liberty Ave., Brookline • 561-4044 • 9pm-2am, clsd Sun-Mon • lesbians/gay men • dancing/DJ • live shows • food served • more men Wed • more women Th • wheelchair access

Donny's Place 1226 Herron Ave. • 682-9869 • 5pm-2am, from 3pm Sun • popular • lesbians/gay men • dancing/DJ • country/western • live shows • food served

House of Tilden 941 Liberty Ave. (2nd flr.) • 391-0804 • 10pm-3am • lesbians/gay men • dancing/DJ • private club

Huggs Restaurant & Lounge 704 Thompson Ave., McKees Rocks • 331-9011 • 4pm-2am, clsd Sun • lesbians/gay men • country/western • karaoke • food served

Metropol 1600 Smallman St. • 261-4512 • 8pm-2am, clsd Mon-Tue • popular • gay-friendly • dancing/DJ • live shows • more gay Th • wheelchair access

New York, New York 5801 Ellsworth Ave. • 661-5600 • 4pm-2am, from 11am Sun • popular • mostly gay men • piano bar Wed & Fri • karaoke Sun • also a restaurant • American • some veggie • $9-15 • patio • wheelchair access

Real Luck Cafe 1519 Penn Ave. • 566-8988 • 3pm-2am • lesbians/gay men • neighborhood bar • food served • cafe menu • some veggie • wheelchair access • $5

RESTAURANTS & CAFES

Common Grounds Coffeehouse 5888 Ellsworth Ave. • 362-1190 • 10am-midnight, til 2am Fri-Sat, 10am-10pm Sun • patio • wheelchair access • lesbian-owned/run

Rosebud 1650 Smallman St. • 261-2221 • 5pm-2am, from 9pm Sun, clsd Mon • live shows • American • wheelchair access • $8-15

Sips 238 Shaddy Ave. • 361-4478 • 8am-midnight, from 10am wknds • live shows • Middle Eastern • patio • $3-6

Strip Bar Cafe 1814 Penn Ave. • 471-1043 • 8am-11pm, til 4am Fri-Sat • Mediterranean

BOOKSTORES & RETAIL SHOPS

Bookstall 3604 5th Ave. • 683-2644 • 9:30am-5:30pm, clsd Sun • general

Getrude Stein Memorial Bookstore 1003 E. Carson St. • 481-9666 • 5:30pm-8pm Th-Fri, noon-6pm Sat, til 3pm Sun • women's

Slacker 1321 E. Carson St. • 381-3911 • noon-10pm, til 7pm Sun • magazines • clothing • leather • piercings • wheelchair access

St. Elmo's Books & Music 2214 E. Carson St. • 431-9100 • 10am-9pm, til 5pm Sun • progressive

True Colors PO Box 495, Carnegie, 15106 • 734-6650 • mail order catalog

TRAVEL & TOUR OPERATORS

Alternative Travels 900 Penn Ave. • 279-8595

Bon Ami Travel Service 309 1st St., Apollo • 478-2000 • IGTA member

Holiday Travel 5832 Library Rd., Bethel Park • 835-8747

Turkaly & Associates/Classic Travel 1319 Boyle St. • 322-1696 • IGTA member

SPIRITUAL GROUPS

1st Unitarian Church Moorewood Ave. at Ellsworth • 621-8008 • 11am Sun (10am summers) • also Three Rivers Unitarian Universalists for Lesbian/Gay Concerns • 343-2523 • potluck last Fri

MCC 4836 Ellsworth Ave. (Friends Meeting House) • 683-2994 • 7:30pm Sun

PUBLICATIONS

Out 747 South Ave. • 243-3350 • monthly

Poconos   (717)

WOMEN'S ACCOMMODATIONS

▲ **Blueberry Ridge** RR1 Box 67, Scotrun, 18355 • 629-5036 • women only • full breakfast • hot tub • B&B in the woods • all meals on holidays • $55-70

Stoney Ridge RD 1, Box 67, Scotrun, 18355 • 629-5036 • women only • near outdoor recreation • kitchens • fireplaces • secluded log home • $250 wknd/$450 week

ACCOMMODATIONS

▲ **Rainbow Mtn. Resort & Restaurant** RD 8, Box 8174, East Stroudsburg, 18301 • 223-8484 • popular • lesbians/gay men • nestled high atop a Pocono mtn. on 85 private wooded acres w/ spectacular view of surrounding mtns. (see ad under East Stroudsburg)

Reading   (610)

INFO LINES & SERVICES

Berks Gay/ Lesbian Alliance PO Box 417, 19603 • 373-0674

Gays/Lesbians of Reading & Allentown PO Box 1952, Allentown, 18105 • 868-7183 • social group • also newsletter

BARS

Nostalgia 1101 N. 9th St. • 372-5557 • 9am-11pm, til 2am Fri-Sat • mostly women • neighborhood bar • live shows

Rainbows 935 South St. (below Adams Apple) • 373-7929 • 8pm-2am Fri-Sat only • mostly women • dancing/DJ

Scarab 724 Franklin • 375-7878 • 8pm-2am, clsd Sun • popular • lesbians/gay men • dancing/DJ

Scranton   (717)

BARS

Club 707 707 Pittston Ave. • 341-3411 • 9pm-2am, clsd Sun • lesbians/gay men • dancing/DJ

Paragons 222 Wyoming Ave. • 8pm-2am, clsd Sun • lesbians/gay men • dancing/DJ • inquire locally

Silhouette Lounge 523 Linden St. • 344-4259 • 10am-2am, clsd Sun • mostly gay men • neighborhood bar • leather

State College   (814)

INFO LINES & SERVICES

Gay/Lesbian Switchboard • 237-1950 • 6pm-9pm

Women's Resource Center 140 W. Nittany Ave. • 234-5222 • 9am-7pm Mon-Fri • info • referrals • groups • wheelchair access

Bars

Chumley's 108 W. College • 238-4446 • 4pm-2am, from 6pm Sun • popular • lesbians/gay men • wheelchair access

Players 112 W. College Ave. • 234-1031 • 9pm-2am • gay-friendly • dancing/DJ

West Grove (610)

Bars

Trib's Waystation 627 W. Baltimore Pike • 869-9067 • 11am-1am, til 2am Fri-Sat • gay-friendly • also a restaurant • American • patio • wheelchair access • $8-13

Wilkes-Barre (717)

Bars

Rumors Lounge 315 Fox Ridge Plaza • 825-7300 • 5pm-2am, from 8pm Mon-Tue • popular • lesbians/gay men • dancing/DJ • also a restaurant • wheelchair access

Selections 45 Public Square, Wilkes-Barre Center • 829-4444 • 7pm-2am, clsd Sun • popular • lesbians/gay men • dancing/DJ • live shows • also a restaurant • American • wheelchair access • $5-15

The Vaudvilla (The Vaude) 465 Main St., Kingston • 287-9250 • 9pm-2am, clsd Sun • popular • lesbians/gay men • dancing/DJ • live shows

Williamsport (717)

Info Lines & Services

Gay/Lesbian Switchboard of North Central PA PO Box 2510, 17703 • 327-1411 • 6pm-9pm, clsd Sun

Bars

Peachie's Court 320 Court St. • 326-3611 • 9am-2am, from 11am Sun • lesbians/gay men • dancing/DJ • wheelchair access

Rainbow Room 761 W. 4th St. • 320-0230 • 4pm-2am, clsd Sun • popular • lesbians/gay men • dancing/DJ • videos • food served

York (717)

INFO LINES & SERVICES

York Area Lambda PO Box 2425, 17405
• 848-9142/ 292-1665 • lesbigay
social/educational group • also publishes
newsletter

BARS

Atland's Ranch Rd. 4, Spring Grove •
777-4479 • 8pm-2am Fri-Sat only • popular • lesbians/gay men • dancing/DJ

Fourteen Karat 659 W. Market St. • 843-
9159 • 7pm-2am, clsd Sun • mostly gay
men • neighborhood bar • dancing/DJ Fri
& alternate Sat

BOOKSTORES & RETAIL SHOPS

Her Story Bookstore 2 W. Market St.,
Hallam • 757-4270 • 11am-7pm, 9am-
5pm Sat, noon-5pm Sun • women's
books • gifts • gourmet coffee • women-
owned/run

Rhode Island

Newport (401)

ACCOMMODATIONS

Brinley Victorian Inn 23 Brinley St. • 849-7645 • gay-friendly • charming New England Victorian B&B • lesbian following

Hydrangea House Inn 16 Bellevue Ave. • 846-4435/ (800) 945-4667 • popular • lesbians/gay men • B&B • full breakfast • near beach

Melville House Inn 39 Clark St. • 847-0640 • lesbians/gay men • full breakfast

BARS

David's 28 Prospect Hill St. • 847-9698 • 2pm-1am (from 5pm winters Mon-Fri) • popular • lesbians/gay men • dancing/DJ • Sun T-dance • patio

Pawtucket (401)

INFO LINES & SERVICES

Women's Growth Center 97 Knowles St. • 728-6023 • 9am-9pm Mon-Fri • counseling • referrals

TRAVEL & TOUR OPERATORS

4 Seasons Travel 47 John St. • 722-5888

Providence (401)

INFO LINES & SERVICES

AA Gay/Lesbian • 438-8860 • call for various mtgs.

Gay/Lesbian Helpline of Rhode Island • 751-3322 • 7pm-11pm

Lesbian/Gay/Bisexual Alliance PO Box 1930, SAO, Brown University, 02912 • 863-3062

Sarah Doyle Women's Center 185 Meeting St. (Brown University) • 863-2189 • referral service • resource center • also lesbian collective group

BARS

Blinky's 125 Washington • 272-6950 • noon-1am, til 2am Fri-Sat • lesbians/gay men • live shows • videos • wheelchair access

Club Cabana 681 Valley St. • 331-8355 • 7:30pm-2am, clsd Mon-Tue • mostly women • dancing/DJ • live shows

Club In Town 95 Eddy St. • 751-0020 • noon-1am, til 2am Fri-Sat • popular • mostly gay men • piano bar • videos

Devilles 10 Davol Square (Simmons Bldg.) • 751-7166 • opens 4pm, from 6pm wknds, clsd Mon • mostly women • neighborhood bar • dancing/DJ Wed-Sat • wheelchair access

Galaxy 123 Empire St. • 831-9206 • noon-1am • popular • mostly gay men • dancing/DJ • live shows • karaoke • videos • wheelchair access

Generation X 235 Promenade St. • 521-7110 • 9pm-2am, clsd Mon-Tue • popular • mostly gay men • dancing/DJ • alternative

Gerardo's 1 Franklin Square • 274-5560 • 4pm-1am, til 2am Fri-Sat • lesbians/gay men • dancing/DJ • live shows • wheelchair access

Mirabar 35 Richmond St. • 331-6761 • 3pm-1am • mostly gay men • dancing/DJ • piano bar • wheelchair access

Skippers 70 Washington (at Union) • 751-4241 • noon-? • mostly gay men • piano bar • patio

Union Street Station 69 Union St. • 331-2291 • noon-1am, til 2am Fri-Sat • mostly gay men • dancing/DJ • wheelchair access

RESTAURANTS & CAFES

Al Forno 577 South Main St. • 273-9760 • popular • Little Rhody's best dining experience • $13-24

Down City Diner 151 Weybossett St. • 331-9217 • full bar • popular Sun brunch (very gay)

Rue de L'Espoir 99 Hope St. • 751-8890 • 11:30am-2:30am lunch, 5pm dinner, clsd Mon • popular • full bar• women-owned • $12-20

Troye's Southwestern Grill 404 Wickenden St. • 861-1430 • 6pm-10pm dinner, clsd Sun-Mon • BYOB

BOOKSTORES & RETAIL SHOPS

Books on the Square 471 Angell St. • 331-9097 • opens 9am, from 10am Sun • general • some lesbigay titles

TRAVEL & TOUR OPERATORS

Travel Concepts 60 Broadway #906 • 453-6000/ (800) 983-6900 • IGTA member

SPIRITUAL GROUPS

Dignity PO Box 2231, Pawtucket, 02861 • 727-2657

Smithfield   (401)

BARS

Loft 325 Farnum Pike • 231-3320 • 2pm-1am, from 11am wknds & summer • lesbians/gay men • swimming • dancing/DJ • food served • also Sun brunch • wheelchair access

Warwick   (401)

BOOKSTORES & RETAIL SHOPS

Barnes & Noble 1441 Bald Hill Rd. • 828-7900

Westerly   (401)

ACCOMMODATIONS

Villa 190 Shore Rd. • 596-1054/ (800) 722-9240 • gay-friendly • B&B • hot tub • swimming • fireplaces • close to beaches

Woonsocket   (401)

BARS

Kings & Queens 285 Front St. • 762-9538 • 7pm-1am, til 2am Fri-Sat • lesbians/gay men • neighborhood bar • dancing/DJ

South Carolina

Aiken

INFO LINES & SERVICES

Last Sunday PO Box 284, 29802 • women's social group • newsletter

Charleston (803)

INFO LINES & SERVICES

Acceptance Group (Gay AA) St. Stephen's Episcopal (Anson St.) • 762-2433 • 8pm Tue & 6:30pm Sat • also meets at MCC 8pm Th

LGLA (Lowcountry Gay/Lesbian Alliance) PO Box 98, 29402 • 720-8088 • info • referrals

ACCOMMODATIONS

1854 B&B 34 Montagu St. • 723-4789 • lesbians/gay men • distinctive antebellum dwelling of Italianate design in the heart of historic Charleston

Charleston Beach B&B PO Box 41, Folly Beach, 29439 • 588-9443 • lesbians/gay men • full breakfast • swimming • nudity • located across from the Atlantic Ocean w/ unobstructed views • 8-person spa • Sun BBQ

▲ **Charleston Columns** 8 Vanderhorst St. • 722-7341 • lesbians/gay men • intimate & hospitable antebellum lodging in the city's historic district • off-street parking

Happy Landing Folly Beach • 722-5990 • popular • gay-friendly • swimming • rustic log cabin • sleeps 6 • close to beach

BARS

Arcade 5 Liberty St. • 722-5656 • 9:30pm-?, clsd Mon-Wed • popular • mostly gay men • dancing/DJ • live shows

Deja Vu II 445 Savannah Hwy. • 556-5588 • 5pm-2am • mostly women • dancing/DJ • live shows • food served • wheelchair access

Dudley's Inc. 346 King St. • 723-2784 • 4pm-2am, from 2pm Sun • popular • mostly gay men • neighborhood bar • private club • karaoke Wed • live shows Th

RESTAURANTS & CAFES

Bear E. Patch 801 Folly Rd. • 762-6555 • 7am-8pm • sandwiches • cafe • patio

Cafe Suzanne 4 Center St. • 588-2101 • 5:30pm-9:30pm, clsd Tue • live jazz • $10-15

Johns Island Cafe 3406 Maybank Hwy., Johns Island • 559-9090 • breakfast, lunch Mon-Sat, dinner Wed-Sat • popular • Southern homecooking • $6-11

SPIRITUAL GROUPS

MCC Charleston 2010 Hawthorne Dr. Ste. 4 • 747-6736 • 9am & 11am Sun, 7:30pm Wed

PUBLICATIONS

Front Page PO Box 27928, Raleigh, NC 27611 • (919) 829-0181

In Unison PO Box 8024, Columbia, 29202 • 771-0804

Q Notes PO Box 221841, Charlotte, NC 28222 • (704) 531-9988

Columbia   (803)

INFO LINES & SERVICES

AA Gay/Lesbian • 254-5301 • call for times & locations

South Carolina Gay/Lesbian Community Center/Info Line 1108 Woodrow St. • 771-7713 • 24hr message, center hours vary

BARS

Affairs 712 Huger St. • 779-4321 • 4pm-2am • mostly gay men • neighborhood bar • patio

Candy Shop 1903 Two Notch Rd. • mostly gay men • dancing/DJ • mostly African-American • private club

Capital Club 1002 Gervais St. • 256-6464 • 5pm-2am • mostly gay men • neighborhood bar • professional • private club • wheelchair access

Metropolis 1801 Landing • 799-8727 • 10pm-?, from 9pm Fri-Sun, clsd Mon-Wed • lesbians/gay men • dancing/DJ • live shows • private club

Pipeline 1109 Assembly • 771-0121 • 9pm-6am, clsd Sun-Tue • lesbians/gay men • neighborhood bar • live shows • private club

Shandon Club 2406 Divine St. • 771-0339 • 5pm-2am • lesbians/gay men • professional • piano bar • private club • wheelchair access

▲ **Traxx** 416 Lincoln St. • 256-1084 • 4pm-? • mostly women • dancing/DJ • live shows • private club • wheelchair access

BOOKSTORES & RETAIL SHOPS

Intermezzo 2015 Devine St. • 799-2276 • 10am-midnight • general bookstore

Stardust Books 2805 Devine St. • 771-0633 • spiritual

TRAVEL & TOUR OPERATORS

B&A Travel Service 2728 Devine St. • 256-0547/ (800) 968-7658 • ask for John • IGTA member

South Carolina Division of Tourism • 734-0235

Travel Unlimited 612 St. Andrews Rd. #9 • 798-8122/ (800) 849-2244 • IGTA member

SPIRITUAL GROUPS

MCC Columbia 1111 Belleview • 256-2154 • 11am Sun

PUBLICATIONS

In Unison PO Box 8024, 29202 • 771-0804

Virago PO Box 11193, 29211 • 256-9090 • publishes lesbian newsletter

Florence

BARS

Zippers 3027 E. Palmetto St. • lesbians/gay men • dancing/DJ • live shows • temporarily closed • please inquire locally

Greenville   (803)

WOMEN'S ACCOMMODATIONS

Ladyslipper Dell B&B • 834-0888 • wknds only • women only • full breakfast • $50

BARS

Castle 8 Le Grand Blvd. • 235-9949 • 10pm-4am, clsd Mon-Wed • popular • lesbians/gay men • dancing/DJ • live shows • private club • wheelchair access

New Attitude 706 W. Washington St. • 233-1387 • 10pm-? wknds • popular • lesbians/gay men • dancing/DJ • mostly African-American

SPIRITUAL GROUPS

MCC 37 E. Hillcrest Dr. (Unitarian Fellowship) • 233-0919 • 7pm Sun • also Th discussion group • wheelchair access

PUBLICATIONS

In Unison PO Box 8024, Columbia, 29202 • 771-0804

Hilton Head (803)

BARS

Moon Jammers 11 Heritage Plaza, Pope Ave. • 842-9195 • 8pm-2am • mostly gay men • neighborhood bar • dancing/DJ • alternative • private club • wheelchair access

Myrtle Beach (803)

BARS

Illusions 1012 S. Kings Hwy. • 448-0421 • 9pm-? • lesbians/gay men • dancing/DJ • live shows • women's night Th

Time Out 520 8th Ave. N. • 448-1180 • 6pm-?, til 2am Sat • popular • mostly gay men • neighborhood bar • dancing/DJ • private club

Rock Hill (803)

BARS

Hideaway 405 Baskins Rd. • 328-6630 • 8pm-?, clsd Mon-Wed • lesbians/gay men • neighborhood bar • dancing/DJ • live shows • private club

Santee (803)

TRAVEL & TOUR OPERATORS

All Around Travel Network 1568 Village Square Blvd. • 854-2475 • IGTA member

Spartanburg (803)

BARS

Cheyenne Cattlemens Club 995 Asheville Hwy. • 573-7304/ (800) 428-9808 • 8pm-2am, til 4am Fri, from 3pm Sun • mostly gay men • dancing/DJ • live shows • private club

TRAXX

A PRIVATE ESTABLISHMENT

416 LINCOLN STREET
COLUMBIA, SC 29201
(803) 256 - 1084

South Dakota

Hill City (605)

BOOKSTORES & RETAIL SHOPS

Oriana's Bookcafe 349 Main St. • 574-4878 • 7am-10pm • also a restaurant • cafe menu • plenty veggie • also espresso bar • $5-10

Pierre

TRAVEL & TOUR OPERATORS

South Dakota Dept. of Tourism 711 Wells Ave., 57501-3335 • (800) 732-5682

Rapid City (605)

ACCOMMODATIONS

Camp Michael 13051 Bogus Jim Rd. • 342-5590 • lesbians/gay men • B&B • full breakfast • peaceful getaway nestled in the woods of the Black Hills

Sioux Falls (605)

INFO LINES & SERVICES

Coalition PO Box 89803, 57105-9803 • 333-0603 • 24hrs • info • referrals

RESTAURANTS & CAFES

Touchés 323 S. Phillips Ave. • 335-9874 • 8pm-2am • popular • lesbians/gay men • dancing/DJ • live shows • wheelchair access

SPIRITUAL GROUPS

St. Francis & St. Clare MCC 1129 E. 9th St. • 332-3966 • 5:30pm Sun (7pm summers)

PUBLICATIONS

Progress Tribune PO Box 88812, 57105 • monthly • covers southeast SD

Tennessee

Chattanooga (615)

INFO LINES & SERVICES

Gay AA at MCC • 629-2737 • 8pm Fri

BARS

Alan Gold's 1100 McCallie Ave. • 629-8080 • 4:30pm-3am • popular • lesbians/gay men • dancing/DJ • food served • wheelchair access

Chuck's II 27-1/2 W. Main • 265-5405 • 6pm-1am, til 3am Fri-Sat • lesbians/gay men • neighborhood bar • dancing/DJ • country/western • patio

SPIRITUAL GROUPS

MCC Chattanooga 1601 Foust St. • 629-2737 • 6pm Sun • also women's meetings • monthly

Gatlinburg (615)

ACCOMMODATIONS

Laughing Otter c/o 1321 Nobel St., Unit G, Alcoa, 37701 • 983-9150 • secluded cabin w/ fireplace • sleeps up to 10

BOOKSTORES & RETAIL SHOPS

Blue Moon Signs 813 Glades Rd. • 436-8733 • unique gifts designed & hand-crafted by women • custom redwood signs • wood turnings

Haley (615)

RESTAURANTS & CAFES

Our House • 389-6616/ (800) 876-6616 • clsd Mon • popular • fine dining • some veggie • reservations only • wheelchair access • $10-20

Jamestown (615)

ACCOMMODATIONS

Laurel Creek Campground Rock Creek Rte. Box 150, 38556 • 879-7696 • clsd Dec-April • gay-friendly • swimming • camping • rentals • RV hookups • horses • hiking • gay-owned

Johnson City (615)

BARS

New Beginnings 2910 N. Bristol Hwy. • 282-4446 • 9pm-2am, 8pm-3am Fri-Sat, clsd Mon • popular • lesbians/gay men • dancing/DJ • also a restaurant • patio

SPIRITUAL GROUPS

MCC of the Tri-Cities Coast Valley Unitarian Church • 926-4393 • 7pm Sun

Knoxville (615)

INFO LINES & SERVICES

AA Gay/Lesbian 3219 Kingston Pike (Tenn. Valley Unitarian Church) • 522-9667 • 7pm Mon & Fri

Gay/Lesbian Helpline • 521-6546 • 7pm-11pm

Lambda Student Union PO Box 8529, 37996 • 525-2335 • meetings

Random Productions • 688-3428 • women-owned production company

BARS

Carousel II 1501 White Ave. • 522-6966 • 9pm-3am • popular • lesbians/gay men • dancing/DJ • live shows

Old Plantations 837 N. 5th Ave. • 637-7132 • 8pm-3am, 10pm-6am Fri-Sun • lesbians/gay men • neighborhood bar • live shows • beer/wine & set-ups only • patio • wheelchair access

Trumps 4541 Kingston Pike • 584-4884 • 5pm-3am, from 9pm wknds • lesbians/gay men • dancing/DJ • live shows

BOOKSTORES & RETAIL SHOPS

Chelsea Station News 103 W. Jackson Ave. • 522-6390 • 9am-10pm, til 1am Fri-Sat • alternative magazines & newspapers

Davis Kidd Bookstore The Commons, 113 N. Peters Rd. • 690-0136 • 9:30am-10pm, 10am-6pm Sun • general • wheelchair access

Pandora's Books 30-A Market Square • 524-1259 • 11am-6pm, til 8pm Fri-Sat, 1pm-4pm Sun • women's • wheelchair access

TRAVEL & TOUR OPERATORS

Bryan Travel, Inc. 5614 Kingston Pike, Melrose Place • 588-8166/ (800) 234-8166 • IGTA member

SPIRITUAL GROUPS

MCC Knoxville 934 N. Weisgarber Rd. (United Church of Christ) • 521-6546 • 6pm Sun

Memphis (901)

INFO LINES & SERVICES

Gay Alternative WEVL 90.0 FM • 6pm Mon • gay radio show

Gay/Lesbian Switchboard • 728-4297 • 7:30pm-11pm

Memphis Center for Reproductive Health 1462 Poplar • 274-3550 • non-profit feminist health clinic

Memphis Gay/Lesbian Community Center 1486 Madison Ave. • 726-5790 • call for events

Memphis Lambda Center (AA) 1488 Madison • 276-7379 • 8pm nightly • meeting place for 12-Step groups

BARS

501 Club 111 N. Claybrook • 274-8655 • noon-3am • mostly gay men • dancing/DJ • also sports bar • patio • wheelchair access

Amnesia 2866 Poplar • 454-1366 • lesbians/gay men • swimming • dancing/DJ • alternative • dinner nightly • hours vary • patio • wheelchair access

Apartment 343 Madison Ave. • 525-9491 • 9pm-3am, clsd Mon-Tue • lesbians/gay men • dancing/DJ • mostly African-American

Autumn Street Pub 1349 Autumn St. • 274-8010 • 1pm-3am, clsd Mon-Tue • lesbians/gay men • neighborhood bar • dancing/DJ • food served • patio • wheelchair access

Backstreet 2018 Court Ave. • 276-5522 • 8pm-?, til 6am wknds, from 3pm Sun • lesbians/gay men • dancing/DJ • more women Sun afternoon & Tue • patio • wheelchair access

Crossroads 102 N. Cleveland • 725-8156 • 11am-3am • lesbians/gay men • neighborhood bar • beer & set-ups only

David's 1474 Madison • 278-4313 • 3pm-3am, from noon Sat • mostly gay men • beer & set-ups only • patio

Nikita's Bar & Grill 2117 Peabody Ave. • 272-1700 • 7:30am-3am, from noon Sun • gay-friendly • neighborhood bar • multi-racial

Sunshine Lounge 1379 Lamar • 272-9843 • 7am-midnight, til 3am Fri-Sat • gay-friendly • neighborhood bar • beer & set-ups only • wheelchair access

WKRB in Memphis 1528 Madison • 278-9321 • 5pm-3am • mostly women • dancing/DJ • live shows • beer & set-ups only • wheelchair access

X-scape 227 Monroe • 528-8344 • 10pm-3am, clsd Mon-Wed • mostly gay men • dancing/DJ • alternative • live shows

RESTAURANTS & CAFES

Alternative Restaurant 553 S. Cooper • 725-7922 • 11am-8pm, til midnight Fri-Sat, clsd Sun • BYOB • homecooking • gay-owned • $4-9

Coffee Cellar 3573 Southern • 320-7853 • 7am-midnight, 8am-8pm Sat • patio • wheelchair access

P&H Cafe 1532 Madison • 726-0906 • 11am-3am, from 5pm Sat, clsd Sun • beer/wine • wheelchair access

BOOKSTORES & RETAIL SHOPS

Davis Kidd Booksellers 397 Perkins Rd. Extended • 683-9801 • 9:30am-10pm, 10am-6pm Sun • general • lesbigay titles

Meristem Women's Bookstore 930 S. Cooper • 276-0282 • 10am-8pm, til 6pm Th & Sat, 1pm Sun, clsd Mon-Tue • some gay men's titles • wheelchair access

SPIRITUAL GROUPS

First Congregational Church 234 S. Watkins • 278-6786 • 11am Sun

Holy Trinity Community Church 1559 Madison • 726-9443 • 11am & 7pm Sun, 7:30pm Wed • wheelchair access

PUBLICATIONS

Triangle Journal News PO Box 11485, 38111-0485 • 454-1411 • monthly

Nashville (615)

INFO LINES & SERVICES

AA Gay/Lesbian • 298-1050 • call for locations & times

Center for Lesbian/Gay Community Services 703 Berry Rd. • 297-0008 • 5pm-10pm

Gay Cable Network Channel 19 • 9pm Tue & 10pm Sat

Nashville Women's Alliance PO Box 120834, 37212 • call Center for times & locations

WOMEN'S ACCOMMODATIONS

Dancing Fish Lodge 627 Wisteria Ln., Waverly, 37185 • 296-3533 • women only • full breakfast • hot tub • charming country inn 70 miles from Nashville

ACCOMMODATIONS

Savage House 165 8th Ave. N. • 244-2229 • gay-friendly • full breakfast • historic Victorian townhouse circa 1840s

BARS

Chez Collette 300 Hermitage Ave. • 256-9134 • mostly women • neighborhood bar • women-owned/run

Chute Complex 2535 Franklin Rd. • 297-4571 • 5pm-3am • mostly gay men • dancing/DJ • country/western • 5 bars • also a restaurant • patio • wheelchair access

Connection Nashville 901 Cowan • 742-1166 • opens 8pm, gift shop from 10pm • mostly gay men • dancing/DJ • live shows • also a restaurant • American • patio • wheelchair access • $5-15

Conversations 923-C Main St. • 228-4447 • 1pm-2am • lesbians/gay men • live shows

Gas Lite 167-1/2 8th Ave. N. • 254-1278 • 4:30pm-1am, til 3am Fri-Sat, from 3pm wknds • lesbians/gay men

Juanita's 503 Wedgewood Ave. • 256-2955 • 11am-3am, from noon Sun • popular • mostly gay men • dancing/DJ • live shows • karaoke • also sandwiches/burgers • volleyball & basketball courts • patio

Pyramids 701 4th Ave. S. • 259-9514 • from 9pm, clsd Mon-Wed • mostly gay men • dancing/DJ • alternative • live shows • wheelchair access

Ralph's 515 2nd Ave. S. • 256-9682 • 5pm-midnight, til 3am Fri-Sat • mostly women • wheelchair access • women-owned/run

Roxy's 4726-A Nolensville Rd. • 333-9010 • 8pm-3am, clsd Mon-Tue • lesbians/gay men • dancing/DJ • live shows • wheelchair access

Underground 176 2nd Ave. N. • 742-8909 • 9pm-3am • gay-friendly • dancing/DJ • alternative

Victor Victoria's 111 8th Ave. N. • 244-7256 • 3pm-3am • mostly gay men • dancing/DJ • live shows • wheelchair access

Nashville & Memphis

*T*here's only one 'Country Music Capital of the World' and that's Nashville. And there's no place on earth where you can enjoy country and western music as much as at the **Grand Ole Opry** (889-6611). Many of the greats of country music have homes in Nashville, and there are plenty of bus tours to show you exactly where your favorite stars live. **The Country Music Hall of Fame and Museum** (255-5333) is also a favorite stop for us diehard country/western fans.

After you've sat still listening to great music so long you can't stand it, get up and dance. Nashville has two women's bars — **Chez Collette** and **Ralph's**. Keep your star-gazing eyes open while you're cloggin' away on the floor; you never know who you might see!

On the banks of the mighty Mississippi River, Memphis is the home of two musical phenomena: 'the blues' on Beale St. and 'the King', still very much alive at **Graceland** (800) 238-2000. Despite the stereotype of Southern cities as homophobic, Memphis has a strong lesbian community — check out **Meristem Women's Bookstore**.

RESTAURANTS & CAFES

Garden Allegro 1805 Church St. • 327-3834 • 8am-9pm, from 10am wknds • plenty veggie • juice bar • $4-7

Mad Platter 1239 6th Ave. N. • 242-2563 • lunch, dinner by reservation only, clsd Sun-Mon • Californian • some veggie • $20-30

Towne House Tea Room 165 8th Ave. N. • 254-1277 • lunch weekdays, dinner Fri-Sat • buffet American • $5-10

Worlds End 1713 Church St. • 329-3480 • 4pm-1am, clsd Mon • American • $8-15

BOOKSTORES & RETAIL SHOPS

Davis-Kidd Booksellers 4007 Hillsboro Rd. • 385-2645 • 9:30am-10pm • general • lesbigay section

TRAVEL & TOUR OPERATORS

Tennessee Tourist Development • 741-2158

SPIRITUAL GROUPS

MCC 1808 Woodmont Blvd. • 262-0922 • 7pm Sun

PUBLICATIONS

Etc. PO Box 8916, Atlanta, GA 30306 • (404) 525-3821 • weekly

Query PO Box 24241, 37202-4241 • 259-4135 • weekly

Rogersville   (423)

ACCOMMODATIONS

▲ **Lee Valley Farm** 142 Drinnon Ln. • 272-4068 • popular • lesbians/gay men • hot tub • swimming • guest farm w/ cabins & camping • all meals included • horseback riding

Saltillo   (901)

ACCOMMODATIONS

Parker House • 278-5844 • lesbians/gay men • full breakfast • swimming • Southern country house 2 hours outside Memphis • reservations only

Sewanee   (615)

ACCOMMODATIONS

Boxwood Cottage 333 Anderson Cemetery Rd. • 598-5012 • lesbians/gay men • hot tub • B&B & rental cottage

Texas

Abilene (915)

BARS

Just Friends 201 S. 14th St. • 672-9318 • 7pm-midnight, til 1am Fri, til 2am Sat, clsd Mon • lesbians/gay men • dancing/DJ • live shows • wheelchair access

SPIRITUAL GROUPS

Exodus MCC 904 Walnut • 672-7922 • 10:45am & 6pm Sun

Amarillo (806)

INFO LINES & SERVICES

Amarillo Lesbian/Gay Alliance Info Line • 373-5725 • 7:30pm 1st Tue • 'Queer Dinner Club' meets twice monthly

Gay AA (at MCC) • 372-4557 • 5:30pm Wed & 2:30pm Sat

BARS

Alexander's 1219 W. 10th St. • 372-7414 • noon-2am • lesbians/gay men • neighborhood bar • wheelchair access

Classifieds 519 E. 10th St. • 374-2435 • noon-2am, clsd Mon • lesbians/gay men • dancing/DJ • live shows • wheelchair access

Maggie's 1515 S. Harrison St. • 371-9312 • 2pm-2am • lesbians/gay men • dancing/DJ • live shows • patio • wheelchair access

The Ritz 323 W. 10th Ave. • 372-9382 • 2pm-2am • lesbians/gay men • dancing/DJ • country/western • live shows • wheelchair access

Sassy's 309 W. 6th St. • 374-3029 • 5pm-2am • lesbians/gay men • dancing/DJ

RESTAURANTS & CAFES

Italian Delight 2710 W. 10th • 372-5444 • lunch & dinner, Sun brunch • some veggie • wheelchair access • $5-10

Washington Square Cafe 1607 S. Washington • 373-5885 • 7am-8pm, til 10pm Th-Sat, from 11am Sat, clsd Sun • live shows • plenty veggie • patio

SPIRITUAL GROUPS

MCC 2123 S. Polk St. • 372-4557 • 10:30am Sun • wheelchair access

Arlington (817)

(see also Fort Worth)

INFO LINES & SERVICES

Tarrant County Lesbian/Gay Alliance 1219 6th Ave., Fort Worth • 763-5544 • info line • also publishes newsletter

Women's Fellowship (at Trinity MCC) • 265-5454 • monthly • women's social & support group • wheelchair access

BARS

Arlington 651 1851 W. Division • 275-9651 • 4pm-2am • popular • mostly gay men • dancing/DJ • live shows • wheelchair access

SPIRITUAL GROUPS

Trinity MCC 331 Aaron Ave. Ste. 125 • 265-5454 • 11am Sun, 7:30pm Wed • wheelchair access

Austin (512)

INFO LINES & SERVICES

Adventuring Outdoors • 445-7216 • call for newsletter

ALLGO (Austin Latino/a Lesbian/Gay Organization) PO Box 13501, 78711 • 472-2001 • 6:30pm 3rd Th

Bound by Desire • 473-7104 • 2nd Fri • women's S/M group

Dyke TV Channel 10 • 9pm Tue • 'weekly half hour TV show produced by lesbians, for lesbians'

Hotline • 472-4357 • 24hrs • general info • crisis counseling • some gay referrals

Mishpachat Am Echad PO Box 9591, 78766 • 451-7018 • social group for Jewish lesbians/gays

SapphFire 825 E. 53-1/2 St. Bldg. 'E' Ste. 103 • 450-0659 • 7pm 2nd & 4th Fri • social/support group • monthly potlucks

Word of Mouth Women's Theatre PO Box 1175, 78767 • 459-0364 • call for bookings & info

ACCOMMODATIONS

Driskill Hotel 604 Brazos St. • 474-5911/ (800) 527-2008 • gay-friendly • also a restaurant • full bar • wheelchair access

Omni Hotel 700 San Jacinto • 476-3700/ (800) 843-6664 • gay-friendly • also a restaurant • rooftop • health club • wheelchair access

Bars

5th St. Station 505 E. 5th St. • 478-6065 • 2pm-2am • lesbians/gay men • dancing/DJ • country/western • live shows • wheelchair access

Area 52 404 Colorado • 476-8297 • 10pm-?, clsd Mon-Tue • popular • lesbians/gay men • dancing/DJ • 18+ • 2 story dance flr. • call for events • patio

Auntie Mame's 912 Red River St. • 478-4511 • 2pm-2am • lesbians/gay men • neighborhood bar • live music Sun-Mon • patio

Blue Flamingo 617 Red River • 469-0014 • noon-2am • gay-friendly • neighborhood bar • live shows

'Bout Time 9601 N IH-35 • 832-5339 • 2pm-2am • lesbians/gay men • neighborhood bar • live shows • volleyball court • wheelchair access

Casino El Camino 517 E. 6th St. • 469-9330 • 4pm-2am, from 11am Sun • gay-friendly • food served • psychedelic punk jazz lounge

Hollywood 113 San Jacinto • 480-9627 • 7pm-2am • mostly women • dancing/DJ • patio • wheelchair access • women-owned/run

Mickey's 705 Red River • 476-3611 • 2am-6am • lesbians/gay men • dancing/DJ

Nexus 305 W. 5th • 472-5288 • 6pm-2am, clsd Mon • mostly women • dancing/DJ • wheelchair access • women-owned/run

O.H.M.S. 611 E. 7th • 472-7136 • 10pm-?, clsd Sun-Mon • gay-friendly • dancing/DJ • alternative • 18+ • patio

Proteus 501 6th St. • 472-8922 • clsd Sun-Tue • gay-friendly • dancing/DJ • alternative • theme nights • 2 flrs. • video lounge

Restaurants & Cafes

Castle Hill Cafe 1101 W. 5th St. • 476-0728 • lunch & dinner, clsd Sun • upscale Mediterranean • beer/wine • wheelchair access • $9-15

Common Market Cafe 1600 S. Congress Ave. • 416-1940 • 8am-10pm, 10am-3pm Sun • eclectic mix • some veggie

Eastside Cafe 2113 Manor Rd. • 476-5858 • lunch & dinner • American • some veggie • beer/wine • patio • wheelchair access • $8-15

Austin

Deep in the heart of Texas, state capital Austin has a mild climate, beautiful rolling terrain, and the most progressive political atmosphere in the state. If you saw *Slacker*, you saw Austin as the younger generation knows it: the "Live Music Capital of the World." The 'Deep Ellum' area of Austin is packed with live music bars – filled with the diverse world of college music every March (spring break) during the **South By SouthWest** (SXSW) alternative music festival.

Of course, once you get around to the lesbian community, you'll fall in love with the strong, independent-thinking women of this city. Women of many colors and ethnicities – Latinas, African-American women, Jewish women – meet in a variety of social and political groups. You can dance with Austin women at **Hollywood** or **Nexus**. See them perform as part of the **Word of Mouth Women's Theatre**, and bring your own covered dish – or whispered dish – to a **SapphFire** potluck. If you're like the slackers we know, you'll never want to leave Austin's close-knit universe.

Katz's 618 W. 6th St. • 472-2037 • 24hrs • NY-style deli • full bar • wheelchair access • $8-15

Mick's Mix 2230 Guadalupe • 476-8531 • 11am-11pm, til 2am Th-Sat • popular

Milieu 314 Congress • 472-1021 • lunch & dinner, clsd Sun • contemporary bistro • some veggie • beer/wine • $9-25

Sfuzzi 311 6th St. • 476-8100 • Italian • some veggie • beer/wine • wheelchair access • $12-17

West Lynn Cafe 1110 W. Lynn • 482-0950 • vegetarian • beer/wine • patio • $5-10

Bookstores & Retail Shops

Book Woman 918 W. 12th. St. • 472-2785 • 10am-9pm, noon-6pm Sun • cards • jewelry • music • wheelchair access • women-owned/run

Celebration! 108 W. 43rd • 453-6207 • 10am-6:30pm, 12:30pm-5pm Sun • women's earth magic store • women-owned/run

Congress Avenue Booksellers 716 Congress Ave. • 478-1157 • 7:45am-8pm, 9am-6pm Sat, til 4pm Sun • lesbigay section

Europa Books 2716 Guadalupe • 476-0423 • open 9am, from 10am Sat, from noon Sun • books & magazines • some lesbigay titles

Liberty Books 1014-B N. Lamar Blvd. • 495-9737 • noon-8pm, til 6pm Sun • lesbigay • wheelchair access

Lobo 3204-A Guadalupe • 454-5406 • 10am-10pm • lesbigay

Travel & Tour Operators

Buckingham Travel 604 Brazos St. #200 • 477-7736

Capital of Texas Travel, Inc. 814 San Jacinto Ste. 302 • 478-2468/ (800) 880-0068

Creative Travel Center 8670 Spicewood Springs Ste. 10 • 331-9560 • IGTA member

David Pearson Travel, Inc. 2737 Exposition Blvd. • 482-8197/ (800) 541-8583 • IGTA member

Texas Tourist Division PO Box 5064, 78763-5064 • 462-9191/ (800) 888-8TEX (out-of-state only)

Austin   (512)

LESBIGAY INFO: Austin Latino/a Lesbian & Gay Org.: 472-2001. Women's Resource Center: 472-3053. Austin Lesbian & Gay Political Caucus: 474-0750.

LESBIGAY PAPER: Texas Triangle: 476-0576. Fag Rag: 416-0100.

WHERE THE GIRLS ARE: Downtown along Red River St. or 4th/5th St. near Lavaca, or at the music clubs and cafes downtown and around the University.

LESBIGAY AA: Lambda AA: 824-2027.

ANNUAL EVENTS: Sept- Austin Gay & Lesbian Int'l Film Festival: 472-3240. May 4-5 & Aug. 31-Sept. 1 - Splash Days: 476-3611, weekend of parties in clothing-optional Hippie Hollow, highlighted by the beer barge on Sunday.

CITY INFO: Greater Austin Chamber of Commerce: 478-9383.

BEST VIEW: State Capitol.

WEATHER: Summers are real scorchers (high 90°s - low 100°s) and last forever. Spring, fall and winter are welcome reliefs.

TRANSIT: Yellow-Checker: 472-1111.

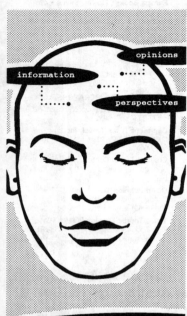

The Texas Triangle.
It's what you think.

Austin 512.476.0576
Houston 713.871.1272

THE TEXAS
T|R|I|A|N|G|L|E
the state's award-winning
gay news source

http://www.outline.com
/triangle/hp.html

SPIRITUAL GROUPS

Affirmation (Methodist) 7403 Shoal Creek Blvd. • 451-2329 • meets every other month

Dignity 27th at University (Holy Spirit Chapel) • 467-7908 • 6pm 2nd & 4th Sat

First Unitarian Church 4700 Grover Ave. • 452-6168 • 9:15am & 11:15am Sun

MCC Austin 425 Woodward St. • 416-1170 • 9am, 11am & 7pm Sun • wheelchair access

PUBLICATIONS

Fag Rag PO Box 1034, 78767 • 416-0100 • gay boy party paper w/ occasional dish on women's events

▲ **Texas Triangle** 1615 W. 6th St. • 476-0576 • statewide

Beaumont   (409)

BARS

Copa 304 Orleans St. • 832-4206 • 9pm-2am • popular • lesbians/gay men • dancing/DJ • live shows • wheelchair access

Sundowner 497 Crockett St. • 833-3989 • 4pm-2am • lesbians/gay men • dancing/DJ • live shows • beer/wine • BYOB • patio

College Station   (409)

INFO LINES & SERVICES

Gayline • 847-0321 • Texas A&M Gay/Lesbian/Bisexual Student Services

Lambda AA • 690-3030 • 8pm Wed

BARS

Club 308 S. Bryan St., Bryan • 823-6767 • 8pm-2am • popular • mostly gay men • dancing/DJ • 18+ • live shows

Dudley's Draw 311 University • 846-3030 • 11am-1am • gay-friendly • neighborhood bar • wheelchair access

Corpus Christi   (512)

INFO LINES & SERVICES

Lambda AA (at Christ's Temple MCC) • 882-8255 • call for meeting times

ACCOMMODATIONS

Anthony's By The Sea 732 S. Pearl St., Rockport • 729-6100 • gay-friendly • full breakfast • swimming • quiet retreat on 2/3 of an acre hidden by live oaks

The Sea Horse Inn 1423 11th St., PO Box 426, Port Aransas, 78373 • 749-5221 • lesbians/gay men • swimming • charming European-style inn set on the wild dunes of Mustang Island & Port Aransas

BARS

Club Unity 4125 Gollihar • 851-1178 • 3pm-2am, from noon Sun • popular • mostly women • dancing/DJ • live shows • women-owned/run

The Hidden Door 802 S. Staples St. • 882-0183 • 3pm-2am, from noon Sun • mostly gay men • leather • wheelchair access

Numbers 1214 Leopard • 887-8445 • 4pm-2am • lesbians/gay men • dancing/DJ

UBU 4701 Ayers Ste. 401 • 853-9693 • 9pm-2am Wed-Sun • gay-friendly • dancing/DJ • mostly Latino-American • live shows • wheelchair access

SPIRITUAL GROUPS

Christ's Temple MCC 1315 Craig St. • 882-8255 • 11am Sun • wheelchair access

Dallas (214)

INFO LINES & SERVICES

Asians & Friends PO Box 9142, 75209 • 480-5906 • social & support group • weekly mtgs.

Couples-Metro-Dallas PO Box 803156, 75380-3156 • 504-6775

Dallas Gay Historic Archives (at Gay/Lesbian Center)

Gay/Lesbian Community Center 2701 Reagan St. • 528-9254 • 9am-9pm, 10am-6pm Sat, from noon Sun • info • referrals • credit union • wheelchair access

Gay/Lesbian Information Line • 520-8781 • 7pm-9pm, 8pm-midnight Fri-Sat • info • referrals • crisis counseling

Lambda AA 2727 Oaklawn • 522-6259 • noon, 6pm, 8pm daily

Lesbian/Gay Welcome Wagon 2612 Bell St. • 979-0017 • community info for new arrivals

Dallas (214)

LESBIGAY INFO: Gay/Lesbian Community Center: 528-9254, 2701 Reagan, 9am-9pm, 10am-6pm Sat, from noon Sun. Gayline: 368-6283, 7pm-11pm.

LESBIGAY PAPER: Dallas Voice: 754-8710. This Week in Texas (TWT): 521-0622.

WHERE THE GIRLS ARE: Oak Lawn in central Dallas is the gay and lesbian stomping grounds, mostly on Cedar Springs Ave.

LESBIGAY AA: Lambda AA: 522-6259, 2727 Oaklawn, noon, 6pm, 8pm daily.

LESBIGAY PRIDE: September, 559-4190.

ANNUAL EVENTS: February - Black Gay/Lesbian Conference: 964-7820. June 15 - Razzle Dazzle Dallas: 407-3553, dance party & carnival benefits PWAs. September - Oak Lawn Arts Festival: 407-3553 , mid-September benefit in Lee Park for PWAs.

CITY INFO: (800)752-9222.

BEST VIEW: Hyatt Regency Tower.

WEATHER: Can be unpredictable. Hot summers (90°s -100°s) with possible severe rain storms. Winter temperatures hover in the 20°s through 40°s range.

TRANSIT: Yellow Cab: 426-6262.

LIL (Lesbian Information Line) PO Box 191443, 75219 • 521-5342 • 24hrs • recorded info • extensive listings

Littlefeather Productions PO Box 227343, 75222 • 372-2796 • produces women's concerts & other cultural events

WIL (Women In Leather) Power PO Box 796414, 75379 • 881-1467 • statewide info & referrals on leather community

ACCOMMODATIONS

▲ **The Courtyard on the Trail** 8045 Forest Trail • 553-9700 • lesbians/gay men • full breakfast • swimming

▲ **The Inn on Fairmount** 3701 Fairmount • 522-2800 • lesbians/gay men • hot tub

Melrose Hotel 3015 Oaklawn Ave. • 521-5151/ (800) 635-7673 • gay-friendly • intimate historic hotel in heart of Oaklawn district • very popular piano bar & lounge • 4-star restaurant on premises

BARS

Bamboleo's 5027 Lemmon St. • 520-1124 • 9pm-2am Fri-Sun • lesbians/gay men • dancing/DJ • mostly Latino-American • wheelchair access

Boxx Office/Las Mariposas 2515 N. Fitzhugh • 828-2665 • 6pm-2am • mostly gay men • dancing/DJ • multi-racial • live shows • women's night Sat • wheelchair access

The Brick 4117 Maple • 521-3154 • 2pm-2am, til 4am Fri-Sat • mostly gay men • dancing/DJ • leather • also leather shop • patio

Buddies 3415 Mahanna • 526-8720 • 11am-2am, from noon Sun • lesbians/gay men • dancing/DJ • live shows

Club Escape 2525 Wycliff #130 • 521-7255 • 9pm-?, from 7pm Sun • gay-friendly • live shows • ladies night Fri

The Desert Moon 5039 Willis Ave. • 828-4471 • 5pm-2am, from 3pm Fri-Sun, clsd Mon • popular • mostly women • dancing/DJ • country/western • live shows

Hideaway Club 4144 Buena Vista • 559-2966 • 8am-2am, from noon Sun • lesbians/gay men • professional • 2 bars including piano bar • patio

J.R.'s 3923 Cedar Springs Rd. • 528-1004 • 11am-2am • popular • mostly gay men • grill until 4pm

John L.'s 2525 Wycliff #120 • 520-2525 • 4pm-2am • lesbians/gay men • professional • cabaret • wheelchair access

Dallas

Dallas has grown to be one of America's most dynamic cities, though Houston is actually bigger. With its glass and steel skyline, this city announces to the world that BIG things are happening in Texas. You can 'shop until you drop' in the **Galleria** (702-7100). You can play at the popular amusement park **Six Flags Over Texas** (640-8900). You can sample Tex-Mex cooking. You can even go back in time at the **John F. Kennedy Memorial** at Houston and Elms Streets.

You might have guessed this city is also home to a BIG lesbian and gay community. First off, call the **Lesbian Information Line**, a 24-hour taped infoline. Then check the flyers at **Crossroads Market** and **Lobo**.

Next, cruise the women's bars: **Desert Moon** is a popular country/western bar, and **Sue Ellen's** is one of the five lesbian/gay bars at **The Crossroads** complex in Oak Lawn. **Jug's** wins Dallas' award for most in/appropriately named lesbian bar, while **Bamboleo's** attracts lesbian and gay Latinos. To pick up the latest lesbian/gay papers, check out Crossroads Market or Lobo After Dark.

Jug's 3810 Congress • 521-3474 • noon-2am • mostly women • dancing/DJ • live shows • wheelchair access • women-owned/run

Pub Pegasus 3326 N. Fitzhugh • 559-4663 • 10am-2am, from 8am Sat, from noon Sun • mostly gay men • neighborhood bar • more women Fri & Sun • wheelchair access

Side 2 Bar 4006 Cedar Springs Rd. • 528-2026 • 10am-2am • lesbians/gay men • neighborhood bar • wheelchair access

Sue Ellen's 3903 Cedar Springs • 559-0707 • 3pm-2am, from noon wknds • popular • mostly women • dancing/DJ • live shows Th • wheelchair access

Village Station 3911 Cedar Springs Rd. • 526-7171 • 9pm-3am, from 5pm Sun • popular • mostly gay men • dancing/DJ • 2 flrs. • Sun T-dance • also Rose Room cabaret

RESTAURANTS & CAFES

Black-Eyed Pea 3857 Cedar Springs Rd. • 521-4580 • 11am-10:30pm • Southern homecooking • some veggie • wheelchair access • $5-10

The Bronx Restaurant & Bar 3835 Cedar Springs Rd. • 521-5821 • lunch & dinner, Sun brunch, clsd Mon • American • some veggie • wheelchair access • $8-15

Hunky's 4000 Cedar Springs Rd. • 522-1212 • 11am-10pm • popular • grill menu • beer/wine • wheelchair access • $5-10

Panda's 3917 Cedar Springs Rd. • 528-3818 • til 3am • popular • Chinese • some veggie • full bar • $8-15

The Wok 4006 Cedar Springs Rd. • 528-0000 • 10am-3am • some veggie • $8-15

BOOKSTORES & RETAIL SHOPS

Babylon 4008-D Cedar Springs Rd. • 522-5887 • noon-8pm, 1pm-5pm Sun • cards • jewelry • artwork • gifts

Crossroads Market 3930 Cedar Springs Rd. • 521-8919 • 10am-10pm, noon-9pm Sun • lesbigay bookstore • wheelchair access

TapeLenders 3926 Cedar Springs Rd. • 528-6344 • 9am-midnight

TRAVEL & TOUR OPERATORS

Strong Travel 8201 Preston Rd. Ste. 160 • 361-0027/ (800) 747-5670 • IGTA member

Travel Friends 8080 N. Central Ste. 400 • 891-8833/ (800) 862-8833 • IGTA member

Travel With Us 6116 N. Central Expressway Ste. 175 • 987-2563 • IGTA member

SPIRITUAL GROUPS

Affirmation (Methodist) at North Haven United Methodist • 528-4913 • 7:30pm 4th Mon

Cathedral of Hope MCC 5910 Cedar Springs • 351-1901 • 9am, 11am & 6:30pm Sun, 6:30pm Wed • call for events • wheelchair access

Congregation Beth El Binah • 497-1591 • variety of services for lesbian/gay Jews

Dignity-Dallas 6525 Inwood Rd. (St. Thomas the Apostle) • 521-5342x832 • 5:30pm (6:30pm summers) Sun • wheelchair access

First Unitarian Church of Dallas 4015 Normandy • 528-3990 • 9am & 11am Sun (only 10am Sun summers)

Holy Trinity Community Church 4402 Roseland • 827-5088 • 11am Sun

White Rock Community Church 722 Tennison Memorial Rd. • 320-0043 • 9am, 10:30am & 7:30pm Sun, 7pm Wed

PUBLICATIONS

Dallas Voice 3000 Carlisle Ste. 200 • 754-8710 • weekly

Lesbian Visionaries PO Box 191442, 75219 • 528-2426 • sponsors LIL • produces newsletter

▲ **Texas Triangle** 1615 W. 6th St., Austin, 78703 • (512) 476-0576 • statewide • see ad under Austin

TWT (This Week in Texas) 3300 Regan Ave. • 521-0622 • weekly • statewide

EROTICA

Leather by Boots 4038 Cedar Springs Rd. • 528-3865 • noon-8pm, clsd Sun

Shades of Grey Leather 3928 Cedar Springs Rd. • 521-4739

The Inn on Fairmount

In the Heart of Gay & Lesbian Dallas

❖ Continental Breakfast
❖ Evening Wine & Cheese
❖ Close to Bars & Restaurants
❖ Direct Dial Telephones

❖ Private Baths
❖ Jacuzzi
❖ Color TV's
❖ Visa, MC Accepted

3701 Fairmount, Dallas, TX 75219
(214) 522-2800 FAX 522-2898

The ambiance of an inn, the luxury of a fine hotel.

Denison (903)

BARS

Goodtime Lounge 2520 N. Hwy. 91 N. • 463-9944 • 6pm-2am, from 2pm Sun • lesbians/gay men • live shows • more women Wed • wheelchair access

Quad Angles Hwy. 1714 • 786-9996 • mostly women

Denton (817)

BARS

Bedo's 1215 University Dr. E. • 566-9910 • 8pm-midnight, from 6pm Fri, til 1am Sat, from 5pm Sun • lesbians/gay men • dancing/DJ • live shows • private club • women-owned/run

SPIRITUAL GROUPS

Harvest MCC 5900 S. Stemmons • 321-2332 • 10:30am Sun

El Paso (915)

INFO LINES & SERVICES

Lambda AA • 833-9544 • 7:30pm Mon

Lambda Line/Lambda Services PO Box 31321, 79931 • 562-4297 • 24hrs • info • referrals

BARS

Briar Patch 204 E. Rio Grande St. • 546-9100 • noon-2am • lesbians/gay men • neighborhood bar

The Hawaiian 919 Paisano St. • 541-7009

The Old Plantation 219 S. Ochoa St. • 533-6055 • 8pm-2am, til 4am Th-Sat, clsd Mon-Wed • popular • lesbians/gay men • dancing/DJ • live shows • patio • wheelchair access

San Antonio Mining Co. 800 E. San Antonio Ave. • 533-9516 • 3pm-2am • popular • lesbians/gay men • dancing/DJ • videos • patio • wheelchair access

U-Got-It 216 S. Ochoa • 533-9510 • 8pm-2am, clsd Sun-Tue • mostly gay men • dancing/DJ • live shows • more women Fri • wheelchair access

The Whatever Lounge 701 E. Paisano St. • 533-0215 • 3pm-2am • mostly gay men • dancing/DJ • mostly Latino-American • beer/wine • BYOB • wheelchair access

SPIRITUAL GROUPS

MCC 916 E. Yandell • 591-4155 • 6pm Sun, 7pm Wed

Fort Worth (817)

INFO LINES & SERVICES

Lambda AA 3144 Ryan Ave. • 921-2871 • 8pm daily • call for other mtgs.

Second Tuesday 877-5544 • lesbian social group

Tarrant County Lesbian/Gay Alliance 1219 6th Ave. • 877-5544 • info line • also publishes newsletter

ACCOMMODATIONS

Two Pearls B&B 804 S. Alamo St., Weatherford • 596-9316 • lesbians/gay men • full breakfast • remodeled & modernized 1898 home located on an acre • women-owned/run

BARS

651 Club Fort Worth 651 S. Jennings Ave. • 332-0745 • noon-2am • mostly gay men • dancing/DJ • country/western • more women Fri-Sat • wheelchair access

Ashburns 3012 E. Rosedale • 534-6630 • 4pm-2am • lesbians/gay men • neighborhood bar • dancing/DJ • live shows • beer/wine • wheelchair access

Cowgirls Oasis 1263 W. Magnolia • 924-0224 • 5pm-2am, clsd Wed • mostly women • BYOB

D.J.'s 1308 St. Louis St. • 927-7321 • 7pm-2am, til 3am Fri-Sat, clsd Mon-Tue • popular • lesbians/gay men • dancing/DJ • live shows • also a restaurant

TRAVEL & TOUR OPERATORS

Country Day Travel 6022 Southwest Blvd. • 731-8551 • IGTA member

SPIRITUAL GROUPS

Agape MCC 4516 SE Loop 820 • 535-5002 • 9am & 11am Sun • wheelchair access

First Jefferson Unitarian Universalist 1959 Sandy Ln. • 451-1505 • 11am Sun • lesbigay group 7pm 1st Th • wheelchair access

PUBLICATIONS

Alliance News 1219 6th Ave. • 877-5544 • monthly

Galveston (409)

INFO LINES & SERVICES

Lambda AA ACCT office (23rd & Ursula) • 684-2140 • 8pm Th & 5pm Sun

Bars

Evolution 2214 Ships Mechanic Rd. •
763-4212 • 4pm-2am, til 4am Fri-Sat •
popular • lesbians/gay men • dancing/DJ
• videos

Kon Tiki Club 315 23rd St. • 763-6264 •
4pm-2am • popular • lesbians/gay men
• dancing/DJ • live shows

Robert's Lafitte 2501 'Q' Ave. • 765-9092
• 10am-2am, from noon Sun • mostly
gay men • live shows • wheelchair access

Gun Barrel City   (903)

Bars

231 Club 231 W. Main St. (Hwy. 85) •
887-2061 • 6pm-midnight, til 1am Sat •
gay-friendly • neighborhood bar • wheelchair access

Harlingen   (210)

Bars

Zippers 319 W. Harrison • 412-9708 •
8pm-2am • lesbians/gay men • live
shows • patio • wheelchair access

Houston   (713)

Info Lines & Services

Gay/Lesbian Hispanics Unidos PO Box
70153, 77270 • 225-2301 • 7pm 2nd Wed

Gay/Lesbian Radio KPFT-90.1 FM • 526-
4000 • 'After Hours' midnight-2:30am Sat
• 'Lesbian/Gay Voices' 6pm Fri

Gay/Lesbian Switchboard PO Box
66469, 77266 • 529-3211 • 3pm-midnight

Houston Area Women's Center 3101
Richmond #150 • 528-6798 • 9am-9pm,
til noon Sat, clsd Sun • wheelchair
access

Houston Outdoor Group PO Box 980893,
77098 • 526-7688 • monthly socials &
camping

Lambda AA Center 1201 W. Clay • 528-
9772 • noon-11pm, til 1am Fri-Sat •
wheelchair access

LOAFF (Lesbians Over Age Fifty) 1505
Nevada (Houston Mission Church) • 661-
1482 • 2pm 3rd Sun • call for more info

Women's Center Hotline (at Houston
Area Women's Center) • 528-2121 • 24hr
hotline • info & referrals during office
hours

Accommodations

The Lovett Inn 501 Lovett Blvd.,
Montrose • 522-5224/ (800) 779-5224 •
gay-friendly • swimming • distinctive
lodging in historic home of former
Houston mayor & Federal Court judge

Bars

Bacchus II 2715 Waughcrest • 523-3396
• 4pm-2am, from 2pm Sun • popular •
mostly women • dancing/DJ • live shows

Backyard Bar & Grill 10200 S. Main •
660-6285 • 5pm-2am, from noon wknds
• gay-friendly • food served • dinner
theater (Fri-Sun) • variety of events • volleyball courts • wheelchair access

Chances 1100 Westheimer St. • 523-7217
• 4pm-2am, from noon wknds • les-
bians/gay men • dancing/DJ • live shows
• also a restaurant • coffeeshop menu •
some veggie • patio • wheelchair access
• $4-10

Club 403 403 Westheimer • 523-0030 •
10am-2am • lesbians/gay men • danc-
ing/DJ • live shows Sat • wheelchair
access

Cousins 817 Fairview • 528-9204 • 7am-
2am • lesbians/gay men • neighborhood
bar • live shows

Ean's 112 Travis • 227-0505 • 8pm-? Sat
• mostly women • live shows

Gentry 2303 Richmond • 520-1861 •
2pm-2am, from noon wknds • popular •
mostly gay men • neighborhood bar •
live shows • wheelchair access

Heaven 810 Pacific • 521-9123 • 9pm-
2am Wed-Sat, from 7pm Sun • popular •
mostly gay men • dancing/DJ • videos •
live shows Th • 18+ Wed & Sat

The Hill 15346 Kuykendahl near
Intercont'l Airport, N. side • 587-8810 •
6pm-2am • popular • lesbians/gay men
• neighborhood bar • dancing/DJ •
wheelchair access • women-owned

Inergy 6121 Hillcroft St. • 771-9611 •
6pm-2am Wed-Sun • popular • les-
bians/gay men • dancing/DJ • live shows

J.R.'s 808 Pacific • 521-2519 • 11am-
2am • popular • mostly
gay men • live shows • videos • also
lunch grill • wheelchair access

Jo's Outpost 2818 Richmond • 520-8446
• 11am-2am • mostly gay men • neighborhood bar • wheelchair access

Missouri St. Station 1117 Missouri St. • 524-1333 • 4pm-2am, clsd Sun • lesbians/gay men • live shows • karaoke Tue • wheelchair access

Past Time 617 Fairview • 529-4669 • 7am-2am • lesbians/gay men • neighborhood bar

Plaza 9200 9200 Buffalo Speedway • 666-3464 • 4pm-2am, clsd Mon • popular • lesbians/gay men • volleyball • also 3 other bars • patio • wheelchair access • women-owned

RESTAURANTS & CAFES

A Moveable Feast 2202 W. Alabama • 528-3585 • 9am-10pm • plenty veggie • also health food store • wheelchair access • $7-12

Baba Yega's 2607 Grant • 522-0042 • 10am-10pm • popular • American • plenty veggie • full bar • patio • $5-10

Barnaby's Cafe 604 Fairview • 522-0106 • 11am-10pm, til 11pm Fri-Sat • popular • beer/wine • wheelchair access

Black-Eyed Pea 2048 W. Grey • 523-0200 • 11am-10pm • popular • Southern • full bar • wheelchair access • $5-10

Brasil 2604 Dunlavy • 528-1993 • 9am-2am • cafe

Chapultepec 813 Richmond • 522-2365 • 24hrs • live shows • Mexican • some veggie • magaritas • $8-15

Charlie's 1102 Westheimer • 522-3332 • 24hrs • lesbians/gay men • full bar • wheelchair access • $5-10

House of Pies 3112 Kirby • 528-3816 • 24hrs • popular • American • wheelchair access • $5-10

Ninfa's 2704 Navigation • 228-1175 • 11am-10pm • popular • Mexican • some veggie • $7-12

Ninos 2817 W. Dallas • 522-5120 • lunch & dinner, clsd Sun • Italian • some veggie • full bar • wheelchair access • $10-20

Pot Pie Pizzeria 1525 Westheimer • 528-4350 • 11am-11pm, clsd Mon • Italian • some veggie • beer/wine • $5-10

Q Cafe 2205 Richmond Ave. • 524-9696 • 4pm-2am • quesidillas & more • plenty veggie • full bar • wheelchair access

Spanish Flower 4701 N. Main • 869-1706 • 24hrs • Mexican • some veggie • $7-12

Houston (713)

LESBIGAY INFO: Gay/Lesbian Switchboard: 529-3211, 3pm-midnight. Women's Center Hotline: 528-2121.

LESBIGAY PAPER: Houston Voice: 529-8490. This Week in Texas (TWT): 527-9111.

WHERE THE GIRLS ARE: Strolling the Montrose district near the intersection of Montrose and Westheimer, or out on Buffalo Speedway at the Plaza.

LESBIGAY AA: Lambda AA Center: 528-9772, 1201 W. Clay, 5pm-midnight.

LESBIGAY PRIDE: 529-6979.

CITY INFO: (800)231-7799.

BEST VIEW: Spindletop, the revolving cocktail lounge on top of the Hyatt Regency.

WEATHER: Humid all year round — you're not that far from the Gulf. Mild winters, although there are a few days when the temperatures drop into the 30ºs. Winter also brings occasional rainy days. Summers are very hot.

TRANSIT: Yellow Cab: 236-1111.

GYMS & HEALTH CLUBS

Fitness Exchange 3930 Kirby Dr. Ste. 300 • 524-9932 • 6am-10pm, 10am-8pm wknds • popular • gay-friendly • hot tub • aerobics • weights • tanning

YMCA Downtown 1600 Louisiana St. • 659-8501 • 5am-10pm, 8am-6pm Sat, from 10am Sun • gay-friendly • swimming

BOOKSTORES & RETAIL SHOPS

Crossroads Market 610 W. Alabama • 942-0147 • 10am-9pm, noon-6pm Sun • lesbigay bookstore • wheelchair access

Inklings: An Alternative Bookstore 1846 Richmond Ave. • 521-3369 • 10:30am-6:30pm, noon-5pm Sun, clsd Mon • lesbigay & feminist • jewelry • music • videos

Lobo-Houston 1424-C Westheimer • 522-5156 • 10am-10pm • lesbigay bookstore • wheelchair access

TRAVEL & TOUR OPERATORS

Advance Travel 10700 NW Freewy Ste. 160 • 682-2002/ (800) 292-0500 • popular

Brown & Wilkins 3311 Richmond Ave. Ste. 230 • 942-0664/ (800) 441-2021 • IGTA member

DCA Travel 1535 W. Loop S. Ste. 115 • 629-5377/ (800) 321-9539

Woodlake Travel 1704 Post Oak Rd. • 840-8500/ (800) 245-6180 • ask for George or Alex • IGTA member

SPIRITUAL GROUPS

Dignity-Houston 1307 Yale Ste. 8 • 880-2872 • 7:30pm Sat, 5:30pm Sun

Maranatha Fellowship MCC 3400 Montrose Ste. 600 • 528-6756 • 11am Sun

MCC of the Resurrection 1919 Decatur St. • 861-9149 • 9am & 11am Sun

Mishpachat Alizim PO Box 980136, 77298-0136 • 748-7079 • worship & social/support for lesbian/gay Jews

PUBLICATIONS

Houston Voice 811 Westheimer Ste. 105 • 529-8490 • weekly

▲ **Texas Triangle** 1615 W. 6th St., Austin, 78703 • (512) 476-0576 • statewide • see ad under Austin

TWT (This Week In Texas) 811 Westheimer #111 • 527-9111 • weekly • statewide

Houston

*A*lthough outwardly Houston has the industrial appearance of a Northeastern city like Gary, Indiana or parts of New Jersey, Houston is a booming cultural center, still pulling itself up from the devastating recession.

Speaking of booming, Houston's lesbian and gay community is growing by leaps and bounds. Just take a little spin around the Montrose area and you'll see what we mean.

You'll find **Bacchus II**, the women's bar, three lesbian/gay bookstores, a women's center and many gay bars. Find out the latest scoop from the weekly **Houston Voice**. For a nourishing meal, even vegans are catered to at **A Moveable Feast** restaurant and health food store.

EROTICA

Leather By Boots 2424 Montrose • 526-2668 • noon-8pm

Leather Forever 711 Fairview • 526-6940 • noon-8pm

Katy (713)

TRAVEL & TOUR OPERATORS

In Touch Travel 1814 Powderhorn • 347-3596 • IGTA member

Laredo (210)

BARS

Discovery 2019 Farragut • 722-9032 • 6pm-2am Wed-Sun • dancing/DJ • mostly Latino-American • live shows • beer/wine

Longview (903)

BARS

Choices 446 Eastman Rd. • 753-9221 • 4pm-2am • popular • lesbians/gay men • dancing/DJ • live shows • volleyball court • patio

BOOKSTORES & RETAIL SHOPS

Newsland 301 E. Marshall • 753-4167 • 9am-6pm, clsd Sun

SPIRITUAL GROUPS

Church With A Vision MCC 420 E. Cotton St. • 753-1501 • 10am Sun

Lubbock (806)

INFO LINES & SERVICES

AA Lambda/Community Outreach AA • 828-3316 • 8pm Mon & Fri St. John's Methodist 15th & Univ. Rm. 212 • also 8pm Tue & Th at Community Outreach Center • 102 N. Ave. 'S'

LLGA (Lubbock Lesbian/Gay Alliance) PO Box 64746, 79464 • 762-1243 • 7:30pm 2nd Wed • social group & newsletter at Community Outreach Center

BARS

The Place 2401 Main St. • 744-4222 • 8pm-2am • lesbians/gay men • dancing/DJ

SPIRITUAL GROUPS

MCC 5501 34th St. • 792-5562 • 11am & 7pm Sun, 7:30pm Wed • wheelchair access

PUBLICATIONS

Dimensions PO Box 856, 79408 • 797-9647 • monthly • women's magazine covers TX, OK, NM & New Orleans, LA

McAllen (210)

BARS

Just Tery's 1500 N. 23rd • 682-2437 • 7pm-2am, clsd Mon-Tue • mostly gay men • dancing/DJ • live shows • wheelchair access

P.B.D.'s 2908 Ware Rd. (at Daffodil) • 682-8019 • 8pm-2am • mostly gay men • neighborhood bar • patio • wheelchair access

Tenth Avenue 1820 N. 10th St. • 682-7131 • 8pm-2am Wed-Sun • lesbians/gay men • dancing/DJ • mostly Latino-American • live shows • wheelchair access

Odessa/Midland (915)

INFO LINES & SERVICES

Free & Clean Lambda Group (Gay AA) 2435 E. Roper (The Basin) • 337-1436 • 7pm Fri

BARS

Mining Co. 409 N. Hancock • 580-6161 • 9pm-2am Wed-Sun • lesbians/gay men • dancing/DJ • live shows • beer/wine • BYOB • wheelchair access

Nite Spot 8401 Andrews Hwy. • 366-6799 • 8pm-2am, clsd Mon • popular • lesbians/gay men • dancing/DJ • live shows • videos • wheelchair access

SPIRITUAL GROUPS

Holy Trinity Community Church 402 E. Gist, Midland • 570-4822 • 11am Sun

Prodigal Ministries Community Church 1500 E. Murphy • 563-8880 • 10:30am Sun • wheelchair access

Port Aransas (512)

ACCOMMODATIONS

Port Aransas Inn 1500 11th St. • 749-5937 • gay-friendly • full breakfast • hot tub • swimming

San Angelo   (915)

BARS

Silent Partners 3320 Sherwood Wy. •
949-9041 • 6pm-2am, clsd Mon • lesbians/gay men • dancing/DJ • live shows
• country/western on Wed • women-owned/run

San Antonio   (210)

INFO LINES & SERVICES

Dyke TV Channel 20 • 1pm Mon •
'weekly half hour TV show produced by
lesbians, for lesbians'

The Happy Foundation 411 Bonham •
227-6451 • lesbian/gay archives

Lambda Club AA 8546 Broadway Ste.
255 • 824-2027 • 8:15pm daily

LISA (Lesbian Info San Antonio) • 828-5472 • 24hr taped info on women's
events, activities & resources

San Antonio Gay/Lesbian Switchboard
• 733-7300 • 7pm-11pm

Tuesday Night Discussion 8021
Pinebrook (Nexus) • 341-2818 • 7pm 1st
Tue: lesbian topic, 3rd Tue: lesbian/gay
topic

ACCOMMODATIONS

▲ **Adelynne Summit Haus I & II** 427 W.
Summit • 736-6272 • gay-friendly • full
breakfast

The Garden Cottage PO Box 12915,
78212 • (800) 235-7215 • private cottage

▲ **The Painted Lady B&B** 620 Broadway •
220-1092 • popular • lesbians/gay men •
private art deco stes. • some w/ kitchenettes

Park Motel 3617 Broadway • 826-3245 •
lesbians/gay men • vintage 1936 motor
court

San Antonio B&B • 222-1828 • lesbians/gay men • full breakfast • hot tub

BARS

2015 Place 2015 San Pedro • 733-3365 •
2pm-2am • mostly gay men • neighborhood bar • live shows • patio

Adelynne's Summit Haus and Summit Haus II

Outstanding 1920's B & B residences near the heart of San Antonio

* The comfort and privacy of home
* The elegance of German Biedermeier furnishings
* The convenience of easy access to San Antonio attractions
* All for less than most hotels

For rates and reservations...

800-972-7266
210-736-6272
Fax: 210-737-8244

B.B.'s Pub 5307 McCullough • 828-4222 • 2pm-? • lesbians/gay men • neighborhood bar • Irish pub known as the gay 'Cheers' • women-owned/run

The Bonham Exchange 411 Bonham St. • 271-3811 • 4pm-?, from 8pm wknds, after hours Fri-Sat • popular • gay-friendly • dancing/DJ • videos • 18+ on Wed • patio

Cowboy's 622 Roosevelt • 532-9194 • 4pm-2am, clsd Mon • lesbians/gay men • country/western

Industria 450 Soledad • 227-0484 • 4pm-2am • lesbians/gay men • dancing/DJ • alternative • videos • on the river walk • wheelchair access

Lorraine's South Presa (at Military) • 532-8911 • 4pm-2am • gay-friendly • dancing/DJ • alternative

Miriam's 115 General Krueger • 308-7354 • 2pm-2am • mostly women • dancing/DJ • live shows • women-owned/run

New Ponderosa 5007 S. Flores • 924-6322 • 6pm-2am • lesbians/gay men • dancing/DJ • mostly Latino-American • wheelchair access • women-owned/run

Nexus SA (San Antonio) 8021 Pinebrook • 341-2818 • 6pm-2am, 7pm-4am Sat, clsd Mon • mostly women • dancing/DJ • country/western • wheelchair access • women-owned/run

Nite Owl 330 San Pedro Ave. • 223-6957 • 2pm-2am, from noon Sun • mostly gay men • neighborhood bar • more women weekdays • patio • wheelchair access

Riddum's 10221 Desert Sands • 366-4206 • 8pm-2am • gay-friendly • dancing/DJ

The Saint 1430 N. Main • 225-7330 • 9pm-2am Fri, til 4am Sat only • mostly gay men • dancing/DJ • alternative • 18+ • live shows

Silver Dollar Saloon 1418 N. Main Ave. • 227-2623 • 2pm-2am • mostly gay men • dancing/DJ • country/western • videos • 2-story patio bar • 'Trash Disco' Sun • wheelchair access

Sparks 8011 Webbles St. • 653-9941 • 3pm-2am • mostly gay men • live shows • videos • karaoke Mon & Th

Wild Country 414 W. Laurel St. • 228-9378 • 2pm-2am • mostly gay men • dancing/DJ • country/western • videos • leather/cowboy store • 614-9217

San Antonio

*A*lthough its moment of glory was more than 150 years ago, The Alamo has become a mythological symbol that still greatly influences San Antonians of today. Just to remind you, The Alamo was a mission in which a handful of Texans – including Davy Crockett and Jim Bowie – kept a Mexican army of thousands at bay for almost two weeks.

San Antonians are fiercely proud of this heritage, and maintain a rough-n-ready attitude just to prove it. This is just as true of the dykes in San Antonio as anyone else. You'll find them at **Miriam's** or **Nexus** acting like cowgirls, or at **Textures Bookstore**.

There's no gay ghetto in this spread-out city, but the lesbian-friendly businesses are clustered along various streets, including S. Flores and McCullough, North Main, and elsewhere. For sightseeing, there's always **The Alamo**, and the 2.5-mile **Texas Star Trail** walking tour that starts and ends there. The architecture in old San Antonio is quaint and beautiful – stop by **The Bonham Exchange** for just a taste.

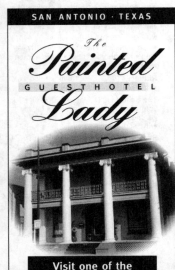

RESTAURANTS & CAFES

8th St. Bar & Grill 416 8th St. • 271-3227 • lunch & dinner • bar has lesbian following • 4:30pm-midnight, til 2am Fri-Sat • patio

Giovanni's Pizza & Italian Restaurant 1410 Guadalupe • 212-6626 • 10am-7pm, clsd Sun • some veggie • $7-12

BOOKSTORES & RETAIL SHOPS

Textures Bookstore 5309 McCullough • 805-8398 • 11am-6pm, til 5pm wknds, from 1pm Sun • women's

TRAVEL & TOUR OPERATORS

Ampersand Travel 5625 Evers Rd. • 647-4100

Odyssey Travel 11829 Perrin Beitel • 656-0083/ (800) 999-4905 • IGTA member

SPIRITUAL GROUPS

Dignity St. Anne's St. & Ashby Pl. (St. Anne's Convent) • 558-3287 • 5:15pm Sun

MCC San Antonio 1136 W. Woodlawn • 734-0048 • 10:30am & 7pm Sun • wheelchair access

Re-Formed Congregation of the Goddess PO Box 12931, 78212 • 828-4601 • monthly • Dianic Wicca group

River City Living MCC 202 Holland • 822-1121 • 11am Sun

Sherman (903)

TRAVEL & TOUR OPERATORS

About Travel 5637 Texoma Pkwy. • 893-6888/ (800) 783-6481

Temple (817)

BARS

Hard Tymes 414 S. 1st St. • 778-9604 • 9pm-2am, clsd Mon • mostly gay men • military clientele

Texarkana (501)

BARS

The Gig 201 East St. (Hwy 71 S.), Texarkana, AR • 773-6900 • 8pm-5am, clsd Mon • lesbians/gay men • dancing/DJ • live shows • private club • patio

Tyler (903)

SPIRITUAL GROUPS

St. Gabriel's Community Church 13904
Country Rd. 193 • 581-6923 • 10:30am
Sun • newsletter • wheelchair access

Waco (817)

INFO LINES & SERVICES

Gay/Lesbian Alliance of Central Texas
PO Box 9081, 76714 • 752-7727/ (800)
735-1122 (in-state only) • info & newsletter • also pride shop

BARS

David's Place 507 Jefferson (at 5th) •
753-9189 • 7pm-2am • lesbians/gay men
• dancing/DJ • live shows • wheelchair
access

SPIRITUAL GROUPS

Central Texas MCC From the Heart
1601 Clay • 752-5331 • 10:45am Sun,
7:30pm Wed

Church of the Living Christ 400 S. 1st ,
Hewitt • 666-9102 • 11am Sun

**Unitarian Universalist Fellowship of
Waco** 4209 N. 27th St. • 754-0599 •
10:45am Sun

Wichita Falls (817)

BARS

Rascals 811 Indiana • 723-1629 • 6pm-
2am, clsd Mon • lesbians/gay men •
dancing/DJ • live shows • BYOB

SPIRITUAL GROUPS

MCC 1407 26th St. • 322-4100 • 11am
Sun, 7pm Wed

Utah

Escalante (801)

ACCOMMODATIONS

Rainbow Country B&B & Tours 586 E. 300 S. • 826-4567/ (800) 252-8824 • gay-friendly • full breakfast

Ogden (801)

BARS

Brass Rail 103 27th St. • 399-1543 • 3pm-1am • popular • lesbians/gay men • dancing/DJ • private club • women's night Fri • patio

Park City (801)

BOOKSTORES & RETAIL SHOPS

A Woman's Place Bookstore 1890 Bonanza Dr. • 649-2722 • 10am-7pm, til 6pm Sat, noon-5pm Sun • women-owned/run

TRAVEL & TOUR OPERATORS

Resort Property Management PO Box 3808, 84060 • (800) 243-2932 • IGTA member

Salt Lake City (801)

INFO LINES & SERVICES

Concerning Gays & Lesbians KRCL 91 FM • 363-1818 • 12:30pm-1pm Wed

Gay Helpline • 533-0927 • info • support

Utah Stonewall Center 770 S. 300 W. • 539-8800 • 1pm-9pm, clsd Sun • info • referrals • meetings • wheelchair access

ACCOMMODATIONS

Aardvark B&B • 533-0927/ (800) 533-4357 • mostly gay men • full breakfast • call for reservations & info • wheelchair access

Anton Boxrud B&B 57 S. 600 E. • 363-8035/ (800) 524-5511 • gay-friendly • full breakfast

Peery Hotel 110 W. 300 S. • 521-4300 • gay-friendly • also a restaurant • full bar • wheelchair access

Saltair B&B/Alpine Cottages 164 S. 900 E. • 533-8184/ (800) 733-8184 • gay-friendly • full breakfast • oldest continuously operating B&B in Utah • also charming cottages from the 1870s

BARS

Bricks Club 579 W. 2nd S. • 328-0255 • 6pm-1am, from 8am Sun • popular • mostly gay men • dancing/DJ • live shows

Kings 108 S. 500 W. • 521-5464 • 10am-1am • lesbians/gay men • dancing/DJ • private club • patio • wheelchair access

Paper Moon 3424 S. State St. • 466-8517 • 4pm-1am • mostly women • dancing/DJ • private club • wheelchair access

Radio City 147 S. State St. • 532-9327 • 11am-1am • mostly gay men • beer only • wheelchair access

The Sun 702 W. 200 S. • 531-0833 • noon-1am, til 2am Fri-Sat • popular • lesbians/gay men • dancing/DJ • private club

The Trapp 102 S. 600 W. • 531-8727 • 11am-1am • lesbians/gay men • country/western • private club • patio • wheelchair access

Vortex 32 Exchange Pl. • 521-9292 • 9pm-2am, clsd Sun-Tue • gay-friendly • dancing/DJ • alternative

RESTAURANTS & CAFES

Baci Trattoria 134 W. Pierport Ave. • 328-1333 • clsd Sun • some veggie • full bar • wheelchair access • $6-25

Bill & Nadas Cafe 479 S. 600 E. • 359-6984 • 24hrs

China Star 1300 E. 240 S. • 583-3800 • lunch & dinner • some veggie • full bar • dinner only on wknds • $5-10

Coffee Garden 898 S. 900 E. • 355-3425 • 7am-10pm • wheelchair access

Market St. Grill 50 Market St. • 322-4668 • lunch, dinner, Sun brunch • seafood-steak • full bar • wheelchair access • $15-30

Rio Grande Cafe 270 S. Rio Grande • 364-3302 • lunch, dinner • Mexican • some veggie • full bar • $4-8

BOOKSTORES & RETAIL SHOPS

A Women's Place Bookstore 1400 Foothill Dr. Ste. 236 • 583-6431 • 10am-9pm • wheelchair access • women-owned/run

Cahoots 878 E. 900 S. • 538-0606 • wheelchair access

Gypsy Moon Emporium 1011 E. 900 S. • 521-9100 • 11am-6pm, clsd Sun • metaphysical

TRAVEL & TOUR OPERATORS

Olympus Tours & Travel 311 S. State St. Ste. 110 • 521-5232/ (800) 338-9661

SPIRITUAL GROUPS

Affirmation (Mormon) PO Box 1152 (at Utah Stonewall Center), 84110 • 534-8693 • 5pm Sun

Restoration Church (Mormon) • (800) 677-7252 • call for info

Sacred Light of Christ MCC 823 S. 600 E. • 595-0052 • 11am Sun

PUBLICATIONS

Labrys 2120 S. 700 E. Ste. H-233, 84106 • 486-6473

Pillar of the Gay Community PO Box 520898, 84152 • 485-2345 • monthly

EROTICA

Mischevious 559 S. 300 W. • 530-3100 • wheelchair access

Springdale (801)

ACCOMMODATIONS

Red Rock Inn 998 Zion Park Blvd. • 772-3836 • gay-friendly • full breakfast • wheelchair access

Torrey (801)

ACCOMMODATIONS

Sky Ridge B&B Inn Hwy. 24 • 425-3222 • gay-friendly • full breakfast • hot tub • near Capitol Reef National Park • women-owned/run

Vermont

Andover (802)

Accommodations

The Inn At High View East Hill Rd. • 875-2724 • gay-friendly • full breakfast • swimming • sauna • ski trails • hiking

Arlington (802)

Accommodations

Candlelight Motel Rte. 7-A, PO Box 97, 05250 • 375-6647/ (800) 348-5294 • gay-friendly • near outdoor recreation • swimming • IGTA member

Hill Farm Inn RR #2, Box 2015, 05250 • 375-2269/ (800) 882-2545 • gay-friendly • full breakfast • country inn on 50 acres of farmland • mtn. views • dinner available Th-Sat • wheelchair access

Bennington

Accommodations

Gypsy Lady RD 2 Box 56-W (N. Bennington Rd., 7mi N. of town) • (518) 686-7275 • mostly women • rual B&B • hot tub • sauna

Brattleboro (802)

Info Lines & Services

BAGL (Brattleboro Area Gays/Lesbians) PO Box 875, 05302 • 254-5947

Accommodations

Mapleton Farm B&B RD 2 Box 510 , Putney • 257-5252 • gay-friendly • full breakfast

Bars

Rainbow Cattle Company Rte. 5, Dummerston • 254-9830 • 11am-2am • lesbians/gay men • 2 bars • dancing/DJ • country/western

Restaurants & Cafes

Common Ground 25 Elliott St. • 257-0855 • lunch & dinner, clsd Tue • popular • vegetarian/local fish • plenty veggie • beer/wine • $6-13

Peter Haven's 32 Elliott St. • 257-3333 • 6pm-10pm Tue-Sat • popular • lesbians/gay men • cont'l

Bookstores & Retail Shops

Everyone's Books 23 Elliott St. • 254-8160 • 10am-6pm, 1pm-5pm Sun • wheelchair access

Burlington (802)

Info Lines & Services

AA Gay/Lesbian St. Paul's Church on Cherry St. • 658-4221 • 7pm Th

Bi-Cycle c/o Micha Wolfgang, PO Box 8456, 05402 • 862-8246 • support & pen-pal network for lesbigays & their kids • also Goddess/Pagan gatherings

Outright Vermont PO Box 5235, 05401 • 865-9677 • support/educational group for lesbigay youth • also hotline

Univ. of VT Gay/Lesbian/Bisexual Alliance B-163 Billings, UVM, 05405 • 656-0699

Vermont Gay Social Alternative PO Box 237, 05402 • 658-7630

Accommodations

Allyn House 16 Orchard Ter. • 863-0379 • gay-friendly • full breakfast • no smoking

Howden Cottage B&B 32 N. Champlain St. • 864-7198 • lesbians/gay men • no smoking • cozy lodging & warm hospitality • cont'l breakfast

Bars

135 Pearl 135 Pearl St. • 863-2343 • 8pm-2am • popular • lesbians/gay men • dancing/DJ • also smoke-free juice bar downstairs • 18+ Fri • wheelchair access

Restaurants & Cafes

Alfredo's 79 Mechanics Ln. • 864-0854 • 5pm-10pm, from 3pm Sun • Italian • some veggie • full bar • wheelchair access • $6-12

Daily Planet 15 Center St. • 862-9647 • 11:30am-10:30pm • eclectic ethnic • plenty veggie • full bar • $6-15

Silver Palace 1216 Williston Rd. • 864-0125 • noon-10pm • Chinese • some veggie • full bar • $10-15

Bookstores & Retail Shops

Chassman & Bem Booksellers 81 Church St. Market Place • 862-4332 • 9am-9pm, til 5pm Sun

Publications

Out in the Mountains PO Box 177, 05402 • monthly

East Corinth (802)

BOOKSTORES & RETAIL SHOPS

Heartland Books PO Box 1105-WT, East Cornith, 05040 • 439-5655 • catalog for lesbians

East Hardwick (802)

WOMEN'S ACCOMMODATIONS

▲ **Greenhope Farm** RFD Box 2260, 05836 • 533-7772 • women only • guesthouse • full breakfast • horse-riding • near skiing • $45-75

Hartland Four Corners (802)

ACCOMMODATIONS

Twin Gables PO Box 101, 05049 • 436-3070 • gay-friendly • near outdoor recreation

Hyde Park (802)

ACCOMMODATIONS

Arcadia House PO Box 520, 05655 • 888-9147 • lesbians/gay men • swimming

Fitch Hill Inn RFD 1, Box 1879, 05655 • 888-5941/ (800) 639-2903 • gay-friendly • full breakfast • swimming • colonial farmhouse situated at the top of maple forested hill • dinner by arrangement

Killington (802)

ACCOMMODATIONS

Cortina Inn Rte. 4 • 773-3331/ (800) 451-6108 • gay-friendly • hot tub • swimming

Manchester Center (802)

BOOKSTORES & RETAIL SHOPS

Northshire Bookstore Main St. • 362-2200 • 10am-5:30pm, til 9pm Fri

Middlebury

INFO LINES & SERVICES

MGLBA (Middlebury Gay/Lesbian/Bisexual Alliance) Drawer 8, Middlebury College, 05753

Montgomery Center (802)

ACCOMMODATIONS

Phineas Swann B&B PO Box 43, Main St., 05471 • 326-4306 • gay-friendly • full breakfast • near outdoor recreation

Montpelier (802)

INFO LINES & SERVICES

Vermont Coalition of Lesbians/Gays PO Box 1125, 05602 • 889-9413 • political group

RESTAURANTS & CAFES

Julio's 44 Main St. • 229-9348 • Mexican

Sarducci's 3 Main St. • 223-0229 • Italian • some veggie • full bar • wheelchair access • $8-15

Plainfield

INFO LINES & SERVICES

Lesbian/Gay/Bisexual Alliance Goddard College, 05667

Rutland

INFO LINES & SERVICES

Rutland Area Gay/Lesbian Connection PO Box 218, 05736

St. Johnsbury (802)

INFO LINES & SERVICES

Game Ends 23 North Ave., 05819 • 748-5849 • social activities group

Umbrella Women's Center 1 Prospect Ave. • 748-8645 • lesbian support & resources

WOMEN'S ACCOMMODATIONS

Highlands Inn PO Box 118-WT, Bethlehem, NH, 03574 • 869-3978 • a lesbian paradise • sign always reads 'No Vacancy'

Stowe (802)

ACCOMMODATIONS

Buccaneer Country Lodge 3214 Mountain Rd. • 253-4772/ (800) 543-1293 • popular • gay-friendly • full breakfast • swimming • country lodge near skiiing • full kitchen stes.

Waterbury (802)

ACCOMMODATIONS

Grünberg House B&B RR 2, Box 1595, Rte. 100 S., 05676-9621 • 244-7726/ (800) 800-7760 • gay-friendly • full breakfast • chalet on a secluded hillside in the Green Mtns. • jacuzzi • sauna

West Dover (802)

TRAVEL & TOUR OPERATORS

New England Vacation Tours Rte. 100 Mt. Snow Village • 464-2076/ (800) 742-7669 • IGTA member

Woodstock (802)

ACCOMMODATIONS

Maitland-Swan House PO Box 72, Taftsville, 05073-0072 • 457-5181/ (800) 959-1404 • gay-friendly • full breakfast • gracious accommodations in an early 19th century home

Rosewood Inn • 457-4485/ (203) 829-1499 • gay-friendly • full breakfast • women-run

South View B&B PO Box 579, Rowe Hill Rd., Brownsville, 05037 • 484-7934 • gay-friendly • classic Vermont log home • women-owned/run

Worchester (802)

INFO LINES & SERVICES

Women in the Woods RFD 1 Box 5620, 05682 • 229-0109 • lesbian social group

Virginia

Alexandria (703)

TRAVEL & TOUR OPERATORS

Just Vacations, Inc. 501 King St. • 838-0040 • IGTA member

Passport Executive Travel 105 N. Washington St. • 549-5559/ (800) 344-7794 • IGTA member

Arlington (703)

INFO LINES & SERVICES

Arlington Gay/Lesbian Alliance PO Box 324, 22210 • 522-7660 • monthly mtgs.

ACCOMMODATIONS

Highgate House B&B 1594 Colonial Terr. • 524-8431 • lesbians/gay men • full breakfast

PUBLICATIONS

Woman's Monthly 1001 N. Highland St. Ste. PH, 22201 • 527-4881

Cape Charles (804)

ACCOMMODATIONS

Sea Gate B&B 9 Tazewell Ave. • 331-2206 • gay-friendly • full breakfast • near beach on a quiet, tree-lined street • afternoon tea

Charlottesville (804)

INFO LINES & SERVICES

Gay AA (at Unitarian Church on Rugby Rd.) • 971-7720 • 7:30pm Th

Gay/Lesbian Information Service PO Box 2368, 22902 • also contact for Piedmont Triangle Society • active social group

Kindred Spirits • 971-1555 • 2nd Fri • women's social clearinghouse for region

Lesbian/Bisexual & Questioning Women • 296-3574

Women's Center 14th & University (UVA) • 982-2361 • 8:30am-5pm Mon-Fri

WOMEN'S ACCOMMODATIONS

Intouch Women's Center Rte. 2 Box 1096, 23084 • 589-6542 • women only • campground & recreational area

Thousand Acres PO Box 758, Farmville, 23901 • 574-8807 • women only • B&B • 1 hour S. of Charlottesville on a private river • women-owned/run • $50-70

ACCOMMODATIONS

The Mark Addy Rte. 1, Box 375, Nellysford, 22958 • 361-1101/ (800) 278-2154 • gay-friendly • full breakfast • swimming • wheelchair access

BARS

Club 216 216 W. Water St. (rear entrance) • 296-8783 • 9pm-2am, clsd Sun-Wed • popular • lesbians/gay men • dancing/DJ • live shows • private club

RESTAURANTS & CAFES

Eastern Standard/Escafe 102 Old Preston Ave. (W. end downtown mall) • 295-8668 • 5pm-midnight, til 2am Fri-Sat, clsd Sun-Mon • Asian/Meditarian • full bar • patio • gay-owned/run • $8-16

SPIRITUAL GROUPS

Chavurah • 982-2361 • lesbigay Jewish study group

MCC 717 Rugby Rd. (Thomas Jefferson Memorial Church) • 979-5206 • 6pm Sun

PUBLICATIONS

Lambda Letter PO Box 1754, 22902

Chesterfield (804)

ACCOMMODATIONS

Historic Bellmont Manor 6600 Belmont Rd. • 745-0106 • gay-friendly • full breakfast • wheelchair access

Colonial Beach (804)

ACCOMMODATIONS

Tucker Inn 21 Weems St. • 224-2031 • mostly women • full breakfast • beachside lodging in a small turn-of-the-century vacation spot 75 miles SE of Washington, DC

Culpepper (703)

TRAVEL & TOUR OPERATORS

Culpepper Travel 763 Madison Rd. Ste. 208-B • 825-1258/ (800) 542-4881 • IGTA member

Falls Church (703)

SPIRITUAL GROUPS

MCC of Northern Virginia (at Fairfax Unitarian Church) • 532-0992 • 6pm Sun • wheelchair access

Fredericksburg (540)

RESTAURANTS & CAFES

Merrimans 710 Caroline St. • 371-7723

BOOKSTORES & RETAIL SHOPS

The Purple Moon 810 Caroline St. • 372-9885 • 10am-5pm, from noon Sun, clsd Mon • women's • wheelchair access

Keyser (304)

WOMEN'S ACCOMMODATIONS

Doetail Womyn's Retreat Rte. 2 Box 243-B, 26726 • 788-0664 • women only • B&B • swimming • 10 mi S. of Cumberland, MD • $40-75

Luray (703)

ACCOMMODATIONS

Ruffner House Rte. 4 Box 620, 22835 • 743-7855 • lesbians/gay men • full breakfast • swimming

Lynchburg (804)

INFO LINES & SERVICES

Lesbian/Gay Helpline PO Box 10511, 24506 • 847-5242 • info • referrals

New Market (703)

ACCOMMODATIONS

A Touch of Country B&B 9329 Congress St. • 740-8030 • gay-friendly • full breakfast • women-owned/run

Newport News (804)

BOOKSTORES & RETAIL SHOPS

Out of the Dark 530 Randolph Rd. • 596-6220 • 10am-6pm, til 8pm Fri-Sat, clsd Sun-Mon • women's • wheelchair access

EROTICA

Mr. D's Leather & Novelties 9902-A Warwick Blvd. • 599-4070 • 11am-7pm, til 8pm Fri-Sat, noon-5pm Sun • wheelchair access

Norfolk (804)

INFO LINES & SERVICES

AA Gay/Lesbian 1610 Meadow Lake Dr. (Triangle Services Center) • 622-3701

Mandamus Society PO Box 1325, 23501 • 625-6220 • active social group

BARS

Charlotte's Web 6425 Tidewater Dr. (Roland Park Shopping Center) • 853-5021 • 10am-2am • mostly women • dancing/DJ • men's night Tue • country/western Th • Sun brunch

Club Rumours 4107 Colley Ave. • 440-7780 • 11am-2am • lesbians/gay men • dancing/DJ • more women Wed & Fri

The Garage 731 Granby St. • 623-0303 • 8am-2am • popular • mostly gay men • also a restaurant • American • wheelchair access • $3-9

Hershee Bar 6117 Sewells Pt. Rd. • 853-9842 • 4pm-2am, from noon wknds • mostly women • dancing/DJ • live shows • food served • some veggie • $2-7

Late Show 113 E. Princess Anne Rd. (rear entrance) • 623-3854 • 10pm til dawn • popular • lesbians/gay men • dancing/DJ • private club

Ms. P 6401 Tidewater Dr. • 853-9717 • 10am-2am • mostly women • dancing/DJ

Nutty Buddys 143 E. Little Creek Rd. • 588-6474 • 4pm-2am • popular • lesbians/gay men • neighborhood bar • dancing/DJ • also a restaurant • American • some veggie • $10-15

RESTAURANTS & CAFES

Charlie's Cafe 1800 Granby St. • 625-0824 • 7am-3pm • some veggie • beer/wine • wheelchair access • $3-7

Mal's Diner 119 W. Charlotte St. • 627-4491 • 7am-6pm, til 2pm wknds

Uncle Louie's 132 E. Little Creek Rd. • 480-1225 • 11am-11pm, bar til 2am • Jewish fine dining • wheelchair access • $5-15

White House Cafe-Private Eyes 249 W. York St. • 533-9290 • 10am-2am • American • some veggie • full bar • wheelchair access • $7-14

BOOKSTORES & RETAIL SHOPS

Outright Books & Cafe 9229 Granby St. • 480-8428 • 11am-8pm, clsd Sun • lesbigay • wheelchair access

Phoenix Rising East 808 Spotswood Ave. • 622-3701/ (800) 719-1690 • noon-7pm, til 5pm Sun • lesbigay bookstore

Two of a Kind 6123 Sewells Pt. Rd. • 857-0223 • 11am-9pm, til 11pm Wed-Th, til 2am Fri-Sat, noon-7pm Sun • lesbigay • wheelchair access • lesbian-owned/run

TRAVEL & TOUR OPERATORS

Moore Travel Inc. 7516 Granby St. • 583-2361

SPIRITUAL GROUPS

All God's Children Community Church 9229 Granby St. • 480-0911 • 10:30am Sun, 7:30pm Wed

Dignity 600 Tabbot Hall Rd. • 625-5337 • 6:30pm Sun

MCC New Life 1530 Johnston Rd. • 855-8450 • 10:30am Sun

PUBLICATIONS

Our Own Community Press 739 Yarmouth St. • 625-0700 • monthly

Out & About PO Box 120112, 23502 • 727-0037 • monthly • covers Richmond & Hampton roads area

Richmond (804)

INFO LINES & SERVICES

AA Gay/Lesbian • 355-1212

Richmond Lesbian Feminist • 379-6422 • community entertainment & educational group

Richmond Organization for Sexual Minority Youth PO Box 5542, 23220 • 353-2077 • 3pm-8pm Mon & Wed

BARS

Babe's of Carytown 3166 W. Cary St. • 355-9330 • 11am-midnight, til 2am Fri-Sat • mostly women • dancing/DJ • food served • homecooking • some veggie • wheelchair access • women-owned/run • $4-7

Chaplin's Grill/Sanctuary Dance Club 2001 E. Franklin St. • 643-7520 • lunch & dinner, club from 10pm, clsd Mon-Tue • lesbians/gay men • live shows • ladies night Th

Christopher's Restaurant & Lounge 2811 W. Cary St. • 358-6469 • 3pm-2am, from 11am Sun • popular • mostly gay men • neighborhood bar • American • some veggie • patio • wheelchair access • $4-8

Club Colors 536 N. Harrison St. • 353-9776 • 10pm-3am Fri-Sun • mostly gay men • dancing/DJ • multi-racial • ladies night Fri

Fielden's 2033 W. Broad St. • 359-1963 • popular • lesbians/gay men • dancing/DJ • private club • call for hours

Pyramyd Bar & Restaurant 1008 North Blvd. • 358-3838 • 6pm-2am, til 3am Fri-Sun, clsd Mon-Tue • popular • lesbians/gay men • dancing/DJ • also a restaurant • ladies night Th • wheelchair access

RESTAURANTS & CAFES

Broadway Cafe & Bar 1624 W. Broad St. • 355-9931 • 5pm-2am, from 7pm wknds • American • wheelchair access • $7-10

BOOKSTORES & RETAIL SHOPS

Biff's Carytown Book Store 2930 W. Cary St. • 359-4831 • 10am-7pm, til 3pm Sun

Phoenix Rising 19 N. Belmont Ave. • 355-7939/ (800) 719-1690 • 11am-7pm • lesbigay bookstore

TRAVEL & TOUR OPERATORS

Covington International Travel 4401 Dominion Blvd., Glen Allen • 747-4126/ (800) 922-9238 • ask for Roy • IGTA member

Virginia Division of Tourism • (800) 847-4882

SPIRITUAL GROUPS

Diginity-Integrity 815 E. Grace (St. Paul's Episcopal Church) • 355-0584 • 6:30pm Sun • wheelchair access

MCC Richmond 2501 Park Ave. • 353-9477 • 10:45am & 6:30pm Sun

Roanoke   (540)

BARS

Back Street Cafe 356 Salem Ave. • 345-1542 • 7pm-2am, til midnight Sun • lesbians/gay men • neighborhood bar • wheelchair access

The Park 615 Salem Ave. • 342-0946 • 9pm-2am, clsd Mon-Tue & Th • popular • lesbians/gay men • dancing/DJ • live shows • private club

The Stag 9 W. Salem Ave. • 982-1668 • 2pm-2am, from 7pm Sun-Mon • mostly gay men • neighborhood bar

BOOKSTORES & RETAIL SHOPS

Phoenix Rising West 26 Kirk Ave. SW • 985-6886/ (800) 719-1690 • noon-7pm, t 9pm Fri-Sat • lesbigay bookstore

SPIRITUAL GROUPS

MCC of the Blue Ridge 2015 Grandin Rd. SW (Unitarian Church) • 344-4444 • 3pm Sun

Unitarian Universalist Church 2015 Grandin Rd. SW • 342-8888 • 11am Sun

PUBLICATIONS

Blue Ridge Lambda Press PO Box 237, 24002 • 890-6612 • newsletter • covers western VA

Stanley   (540)

ACCOMMODATIONS

The Ruby Rose Inn Rte. 2 Box 147 • 778 4680 • gay-friendly • full breakfast • in the Shenandoah Valley • women-owned/run

Virginia Beach   (804)

ACCOMMODATIONS

Coral Sands Motel 2307 Pacific Ave. • 425-0872/ (800) 828-0872 • lesbians/gay men • motel/guesthouse • near ocean

BARS

Ambush 2838 Virginia Beach Blvd. • 498-4301 • 4pm-2am • mostly gay men • neighborhood bar

Danny's Place 2901 Baltic Ave. • 428-4016 • 5pm-2am, clsd Mon • lesbians/gay men • dancing/DJ • food served • American • wheelchair access • $4-8

TRAVEL & TOUR OPERATORS

Alternative Adventures in Travel 6529 Auburn Dr. • 424-6362 • IGTA member

Travel Merchants, Inc. 332 N. Great Neck Rd. #104 • 463-0014/ (800) 637-486 • IGTA member

PUBLICATIONS

Lambda Directory 198 S. Rosemont Rd. • 486-3546

Washington

Anacortes (360)

ACCOMMODATIONS
Blue Rose B&B 1811 9th St • 293-5175 • gay-friendly • full breakfast

Bellevue (206)

SPIRITUAL GROUPS
East Shore Unitarian Church 12700 SE 32nd St. • 747-3780 • 9:15am & 11:15am Sun

Bellingham (360)

INFO LINES & SERVICES
Lesbian/Gay/Bisexual Alliance Western Washington University • 650-6120 • social/political group

BARS
Rumors 1317 N. State St. • 671-1849 • noon-2am • lesbians/gay men • dancing/DJ • multi-racial • beer/wine

BOOKSTORES & RETAIL SHOPS
Village Books 1210 11th St. • 671-2626 • 9am-10pm, til 8pm Sun

SPIRITUAL GROUPS
Song of Messiah MCC 929 N. State St. Ste. B • 671-1172 • 6pm Sun & 7pm Wed

Bremerton (360)

INFO LINES & SERVICES
West Sound Family • 792-3960 • lesbi-gay social/support group

BARS
Brewski's 2810 Kitsap Wy. (enter off Wycuff St.) • 479-9100 • 11am-2am • gay-friendly • neighborhood bar • piano bar • wheelchair access

Chelan (509)

ACCOMMODATIONS
Whaley Mansion 415 3rd St. • 682-5735/ (800) 729-2408 • gay-friendly • full breakfast • small resort • 2 houses

Columbia River Gorge
(509)

ACCOMMODATIONS

Sojourner Inn 142 Lyons Rd., Home Valley • 427-7070 • gay-friendly • full breakfast • wheelchair access

Ellensburg
(509)

INFO LINES & SERVICES

Central Gay/Lesbian Alliance • 963-1391 • contact Sally Thelen for more info

Everett
(206)

INFO LINES & SERVICES

AA Gay/Lesbian 2324 Lombard (church basement) • 252-2525 • 7pm Mon

BARS

Everett Underground 1212 California Ave. • 339-0807 • 4pm-2am • lesbians/gay men • dancing/DJ • food served

BOOKSTORES & RETAIL SHOPS

Orion at Twilight/Highlights 2934-B Colby Ave., 98201 • 303-8624 • metaphysical store • also publishes pagan newsletter

Gig Harbor
(206)

WOMEN'S ACCOMMODATIONS

▲ **Inn the Woods** 4416 150th St. Court NW • 857-4954 • women only • B&B • hot tub • shared baths • cont'l breakfast in room • massage • $85

TRAVEL & TOUR OPERATORS

Blue Heron Sailing PO Box 173, 98335 • 851-5259 • women-owned/run

Index
(360)

ACCOMMODATIONS

Bush House Country Inn 300 5th St. • 793-2312 • gay-friendly • full breakfast • suite available • also a restaurant & cocktail lounge

Wild Lily Ranch B&B PO Box 313, 98256 • 793-2103 • lesbians/gay men • hot tub • swimming • fireplaces • nudity • riverside cabins

La Conner
(360)

ACCOMMODATIONS

The White Swan Guesthouse 1388 Moore Rd., Mt. Vernon • 445-6805 • gay-friendly • circa 1890 farmhouse B&B • also cabin available

Langley
(206)

ACCOMMODATIONS

The Gallery Suite B&B 302 First St. • 221-2978 • condo rental on the water • art gallery/B&B

The Sea Haven II 3766 S. Bells Rd. • 730-3766 • gay-friendly • cozy cottage on Whidbey Island w/ a spectacular view of Cascade Mtn. Range • women-owned/run

The Whidbey Inn 106 1st St. • 221-7115 • gay-friendly • full breakfast • located on bluff over Saratoga Passage Waterway & Mtns.

Lopez Island
(206)

ACCOMMODATIONS

The Inn at Swifts Bay Rte. 2 Box 3402, 98261 • 468-3636 • popular • gay-friendly • Tudor-style B&B on the San Juan Islands • spa • fireplace • IGTA member

Mt. Vernon
(360)

RESTAURANTS & CAFES

Deli Next Door 202 S. 1st St. • 336-3886 • 9am-7pm, til 4pm Sun • healthy American • plenty veggie • wheelchair access • $4-6

BOOKSTORES & RETAIL SHOPS

Scott's Bookstore 120 N. 1st St. • 336-6181

PUBLICATIONS

Skagit Gay Times/GLBS 1500-A E. College Wy. #458 • 428-9217

Ocean Park
(206)

WOMEN'S ACCOMMODATIONS

Iris Guesthouse Box 72 Territory Rd., Oysterville, 98640 • 665-5681 • mostly women • full kitchen privileges

ACCOMMODATIONS

Shakti Cove PO Box 385, 98640 • 665-4000 • mostly women • cottages

Olympia (206)

INFO LINES & SERVICES

Free at Last AA 20th St. & Capital Wy. (St. John's Church) • 753-9934 • 7:30pm Th & Sat

Lesbian/Gay/Bisexual Support Services • 943-4662 • 24hr info & referrals

Queer Alliance Evergreen State College • 866-6000x6544 • noon-4pm Mon-Fri • social/support group

BARS

Thekla 116 E. 5th Ave. • 352-1855 • 6pm-2am • gay-friendly • dancing/DJ • wheelchair access

RESTAURANTS & CAFES

Smithfield Cafe 212 W. 4th Ave. • 786-1725 • 7am-8pm • popular • lesbians/gay men • plenty veggie • wheelchair access • $4-7

BOOKSTORES & RETAIL SHOPS

Bulldog News 116 E. 4th Ave. • 357-6397 • 7am-9pm

SPIRITUAL GROUPS

Eternal Light MCC 219 'B' St. • 352-8157 • 7pm Sun

Port Townsend (206)

ACCOMMODATIONS

Gaia's Getaway 4343 Haines St. • 385-1194 • mostly women • large studio apartment in a small seaport village on the Olympic peninsula • women-owned/run

The James House 1238 Washington St. • 385-1238 • gay-friendly • B&B • no smoking • near tennis, golf & kayaking

Ravenscroft Inn 533 Quincy St. • 385-2784 • gay-friendly • classic seaport inn w/ views of Puget Sound • full gourmet breakfast

Seattle (206)

INFO LINES & SERVICES

Aradia Women's Health Center 112 Boylston Ave. E. • 323-9388 • 10am-6pm Mon-Fri • women's health care providers

Seattle (206)

LESBIGAY INFO: Greater Seattle Business Assoc. (lesbigay): 443-4722. Lesbian Resource Center: 322-3953.

LESBIGAY PAPER: Seattle Gay News: 324-4297.

WHERE THE GIRLS ARE: Living in the Capitol Hill District, south of Lake Union, and working in the Broadway Market, Pike Place Market, or behind the counter at Cafe Vivace on Denny.

LESBIGAY AA: Capitol Hill Alano: 587-2838, 123 E. Boylston, noon, 5:30pm, 8pm.

LESBIGAY PRIDE: 292-1035.

CITY INFO: 461-5800.

BEST VIEW: Top of the Space Needle. Or if you can stand a wait in line twice as long as the ride itself, check out the World's Fair Monorail too.

WEATHER: Winter's average temperature is 50° while summer temperatures can climb up into the 90°s. Be prepared for rain at any time during the year.

TRANSIT: Farwest: 622-1717.

Seattle

*S*eattle's lush natural beauty — breathtaking views of the sound and Cascade Mountains — is actually more incredible than most let on. In addition, Seattle has small-town friendliness, as well as an international reputation for sophisticated cafe culture and for Grunge music and fashion.

The Space Needle is located in the **Seattle Center**, a complex that includes an opera house, Arena Coliseum and the Pacific Science Center. Another landmark is the quaint/touristy **Pike Place Market** (where all those commercials that feature mounds of fish are filmed).

For the perfect day trip, ferry over to the Olympic Peninsula and enjoy the fresh wilderness, or cruise by "Dykiki" a waterfront park on Lake Washington. Or sign up for an outdoors trip with one of the women-owned tour operators: **Adventure Associates** has trips listed in our Tours & Adventures section in the back, or try **Womantrek** or **Winds of Change**.

For shopping, the **Broadway Market** in queer Capitol Hill is a multi-cultural shopping center. We're told the dyke-watching is best from the Market's espresso bar. If you've never been to a juice bar, check out the **Gravity Bar** at the Market — you can get almost any fruit or vegetable in liquid, shake or sandwich form here.

Speaking of coffee, Seattle's hazy days have nurtured a haute coffee culture here — so be careful to order your java correctly, or ask questions if you're unsure. The natives respect frank ignorance more than confused pretense. Lattés — one-third espresso, two-thirds milk — are the standard, and come iced or hot. Milk-intolerant coffee-lovers can even get Soy Lattés in some cafes!

Beyond the Closet is the local lesbigay bookstore where you can get a copy of the **Seattle Gay News**. Seattle's main women's bar, **Wildrose Tavern**, is for the 30+ crowd, while 20-somethings head for the mixed **Re-bar** or **Weathered Wall**. Big-boned gals line-dance at **Timberline**.

For sex toys, check out **Toys in Babeland** women's erotica. Pick up your safer sex supplies at the non-profit **Rubber Tree**, and those sex-inducing clothes at **Sin**.

And if you've ever dreamed of a women-only guest house on an island, you'll find it on Vashon Island — only a fifteen minute ferry ride away from Seattle.

Association of Lesbian Professionals PO Box 20424, 98102

Capitol Hill Alano 123 E. Boylston • 587-2838 • noon, 5:30pm, 8pm

Counseling Service for Sexual Minorities 200 W. Mercer Ste. 300 • 282-9307 • noon-9pm Mon-Fri

Dyke TV Channel 29 • 12:30pm Th • 'weekly half hour TV show produced by lesbians, for lesbians'

GSBA (Greater Seattle Business Association) 2033 6th Ave. #804, 98121 • 443-4722 • publishes extensive directory

Lambert House 1818 15th Ave. • 322-2735 • 4pm-10pm, til midnight Fri-Sat • drop-in center for sexual minority youth

Lesbian Resource Center 1808 Bellevue Ave. Ste. 204 • 322-3953 • 2pm-7pm Mon-Fri

Powersurge 1202 E. Pike St. #819 • 233-8429 • dyke S/M conference

Seattle Bisexual Women's Network • 783-7987 • active social/support organization

The TEN (The Eastside Network) • 450-4890 • social/support group for Seattle's East Side

ACCOMMODATIONS

Bacon Mansion/Broadway Guesthouse 959 Broadway E. • 329-1864/ (800) 240-1864 • gay-friendly • classical Edwardian-style Tudor • IGTA member

Capitol Hill Inn 1713 Belmont Ave. • 323-1955 • full breakfast • elegant Queen Anne house

Chambered Nautilus B&B 5005 22nd Ave. NE • 522-2536 • gay-friendly • full breakfast • porches • gardens

The Country Inn 685 NW Juniper St., Issaquah • 392-1010 • gay-friendly • full breakfast • hot tub • private estate

▲ **Gaslight Inn** 1727 15th Ave. • 325-3654 • popular • gay-friendly • swimming

▲ **Hill House B&B** 1113 E. John St. • 720-7161/ (800) 720-7161 • lesbians/gay men • full breakfast

The Island Within B&B PO Box 2241, Vashon Island, 98070 • 567-4177 • gay-friendly • cottages • kitchens • private cottage in a lovely wooded setting on the west side of Vashon Island

▲ **Landes House B&B** 712 11th Ave. E. • 329-8781 • lesbians/gay men • hot tub • two 1906 houses joined by deck • near Broadway

Scandia House 2028 34th Ave. S. • 722-6216 • gay-friendly

The Shafer-Baillie Mansion 907 14th Ave. E. • 322-4654 • gay-friendly

BARS

Changes 2103 N. 45th St. • 545-8363 • noon-2am • mostly gay men • neighborhood bar

Changes Too 1501 E. Olive Wy. • 322-6356 • noon-2am • mostly gay men • dancing/DJ • wheelchair access

Double Header 407 2nd Ave. • 624-8439 • 10am-1am • mostly gay men • neighborhood bar • one of the oldest gay bars in US

The Easy 916 Pike • 323-8343 • 11am-2am, from 9am wknds • mostly women • dancing/DJ • live shows • beer/wine • food served

Elite Two 1658 E. Olive Wy. • 322-7334 • noon-2am, from 10am wknds • lesbians/gay men • neighborhood bar

Encore Restaurant & Lounge 1518 11th Ave. • 324-6617 • 11am-2am, from 8am wknds • lesbians/gay men • American • some veggie • wheelchair access • $5-15

Hana Restaurant & Lounge 1914 8th Ave. • 340-1536 • noon-2am • gay-friendly • piano bar • Japanese • wheelchair access

Neighbors Restaurant & Lounge 1509 Broadway (entrance on alley) • 324-5358 • 4pm-2am, til 4am Fri-Sat, clsd Mon • popular • mostly gay men • dancing/DJ • piano bar 2pm-8pm

R Place 619 E. Pine • 322-8828 • 2pm-2am • mostly gay men • neighborhood bar • videos • 3 stories

Re-bar 1114 Howell (at Boren Ave.) • 233-9873 • 9pm-2am • gay-friendly • dancing/DJ • 'Queer Disco' Th

Romper Room 106 1st Ave. N. • 284-5003 • 4pm-2am • gay-friendly • dancing/DJ • beer/wine • more lesbians Fri-Sat

Tacky Tavern 1706 Bellevue Ave. • 322-9744 • 11am-2am • mostly gay men • neighborhood bar

Thumpers 1500 E. Madison St. • 328-3800 • 11am-2am • popular • mostly gay men • food served • more women in dining room • patio • wheelchair access • $7-15

Timberline Tavern 2015 Boren Ave. • 622-6220 • 6pm-2am • lesbians/gay men • dancing/DJ • country/western • beer/wine • dance lessons 7:30pm Tue-Fri

The Vogue 2018 1st Ave. • 443-0673 • 9pm-2am • gay-friendly • dancing/DJ • live shows • call for events

Weathered Wall 1921 5th Ave. • 448-5688 • 9pm-2am • popular • gay-friendly • dancing/DJ • alternative • live shows • call for events

Wildrose Tavern & Restaurant 1021 E. Pike St. • 324-9210 • 11am-midnight, til 2am Fri-Sat • mostly women • live shows • food served • some veggie • beer/wine • wheelchair access • $4-6

RESTAURANTS & CAFES

Addis Cafe 1224 E. Jefferson • 325-7805 • 8am-midnight • popular • Ethiopian • plenty veggie • $3-7

Black Cat Cafe 4110 Roosevelt Wy. NE • 547-3887 • 10am-10pm, til 7pm Sun, clsd Mon • vegetarian • funky atmosphere • wheelchair access • under $5

Cafe Flora 2901 E. Madison • 325-9100 • 11:30am-10pm, 9am-2pm Sun • popular • vegetarian • beer/wine • wheelchair access • $5-14

Cafe Illiterati 5327 Ballard Ave. NW • 782-0191 • 9am-5pm • American • plenty veggie • patio • wheelchair access • $4-7

Cafe Paradiso 1005 E. Pike • 322-6960 • 6am-1am, til 4am Fri-Sat • popular

Cafe Septieme 214 Broadway Ave. E • 860-8858 • popular

Cafe Vivace 901 E. Denny Wy. #100 • 860-5869 • popular

Dahlia Lounge 1904 4th Ave. • 682-4142 • lunch & dinner • New American • some veggie • full bar • $9-20

Frontier Restaurant & Bar 2203 1st Ave. • 441-3377 • 10am-2am • full bar • best cheap food in town • wheelchair access

Giorgina's Pizza 131 15th Ave. E. • 329-8118 • 11am-9pm, from 4pm Sat, clsd Sun

Landes House
BED & BREAKFAST
712 11th Ave. East   Seattle, WA 98102
(206) 329-8781

Gravity Bar 415 E. Broadway • 325-7186 • 9am-10pm • vegetarian/juice bar • also downtown location • 448-8826 • wheelchair access

Jack's Bistro 405 15th Ave. E. • 324-9625 • lunch & dinner • cont'l • some veggie • full bar • $10-12

Kokeb 9261 12th Ave. • 322-0485 • lunch & dinner • Ethiopian • some veggie • full bar • $5-10

Mae's Phinney Ridge Cafe 6410 Phinney Ridge N. (at 65th) • 782-1222 • 7am-5pm • breakfast menu • some veggie • Mud Room Cafe til 5pm

Plaza Mexico 4116 University Wy. NE • 633-4054 • full bar

Queen City Grill 2201 1st Ave. • 443-0975 • noon-11pm, from 5pm wknds • popular • seafood • wheelchair access

Sunlight Cafe 6403 Roosevelt Wy. NE • 522-9060 • 8am-3pm • vegetarian • beer/wine • wheelchair access • $3-9

GYMS & HEALTH CLUBS

BQ Workout (in the Broadway Market) • 860-3070 • 6am-11pm, 9am-7pm Sun • gay-friendly

BOOKSTORES & RETAIL SHOPS

Bailey/Coy Books 414 Broadway Ave. E. • 323-8842 • 10am-10pm, til 11pm Fri-Sat, 11am-8pm Sun • wheelchair access

Beyond the Closet Bookstore 1501 Belmont Ave. • 322-4609 • 10am-10pm, til 11pm Fri-Sat • lesbigay bookstore

Broadway Market 401 E. Broadway • popular • mall full of funky, queer & hip stores

Edge of the Circle 701 E. Pike • 726-1999 • 10am-8pm • alternative spirituality store

Fremont Place Book Company 621 N. 35th • 547-5970 • 11am-6pm, til 8pm Fri-Sat • progressive bookstore

Metropolis 7220 Greenwood Ave. N. • 782-7002 • cards & gifts

Pistil Books & News 1013 E. Pike St. • 325-5401

Red & Black Books 432 15th Ave. E. • 322-7323 • 10am-8pm

The Rubber Tree 4426 Burke Ave. N. • 633-4750 • 10am-7pm, clsd Sun • non-profit safer sex supplies & referrals

Seattle Leather Merchantile 1204 E. Pike • 860-5847 • great boot selection

Sin 616 E. Pine • 329-0324 • noon-8pm • leather • piercings • wheelchair access

Sunshine Thrift Shops 1605 12th Ave. #25 • 324-9774 • noon-6pm, 10am-7pm Sat • non-profit for AIDS organizations • call for details • wheelchair access

TRAVEL & TOUR OPERATORS

Adventure Associates PO Box 16304, 98116 • 932-8352 • trips for women • see ad under Tour Operators

Fodor's Cruises & Tours 600 1st Ave. Ste. 203 • 328-5385 • IGTA member

It's Your World Travel 1411 E. Olive Wy. • 328-0616/ (800) 955-6077 • IGTA member

Progressive Travels 224 W. Galer Ste. C • 285-1987/ (800) 245-2229 • IGTA member

Sunshine Travel 519 N. 85th St. • 784-8141 • IGTA member

Travel Solutions 4009 Gilman W. • 281-7202/ (800) 727-1616 • IGTA member

SPIRITUAL GROUPS

Affirmation (Mormon) PO Box 23223, 98102 • 820-5729

Congregation Tikvah Chadashah (Jewish) 20th Ave. E. & E. Prospect (Prospect Cong. Church) • 329-2590 • 2nd Fri

Dignity Seatle 723 18th Ave E. (St. Joseph's Church) • 325-7314 • 7:30pm Sun

Grace Gospel Chapel 2052 NW 64th St., Ballard • 784-8495 • 11am Sun

Integrity 1245 10th Ave. E. (Chapel of St. Mark's) • 525-4668 • 7pm Sun

MCC 2101 14th Ave. S. • 325-2421 • 11am Sun • wheelchair access

PUBLICATIONS

SGN (Seattle Gay News) 1605 12th Ave. Ste. 31 • 324-4297 • weekly

The Stranger 1202 E. Pike • 323-7203 • weekly alternative

EROTICA

Onyx Leather • 328-1965 • by appt. only

Toys in Babeland 711 E. Pike • 328-2914 • noon-8pm, clsd Mon

Seaview (360)

ACCOMMODATIONS

Sou'wester Lodge Beach Access Rd. (38th Place) • 642-2542 • gay-friendly • inexpensive suites & cabins w/ kitchens

Spokane (509)

INFO LINES & SERVICES

AA Gay/Lesbian • 624-1442 • call for locations & times

Lesbian/Gay Community Services Hotline • 489-2266 • 24hrs

BARS

Dempsey's Brass Rail 909 W. 1st St. • 747-5362 • 3pm-2am, til 3:30am Fri-Sat • popular • lesbians/gay men • dancing/DJ • food served • American • $5-12

Hour Place 415 W. Sprague • 838-6947 • 11am-2am • lesbians/gay men • dancing/DJ • food served • American • some veggie • wheelchair access • $5-8

Pumps II W. 4 Main St. • 747-8940 • 11am-2am • lesbians/gay men • dancing/DJ • live shows

BOOKSTORES & RETAIL SHOPS

Auntie's Bookstore & Cafe W. 402 Main St. • 838-0206 • 9am-9pm, 11am-5pm Sun • wheelchair access

TRAVEL & TOUR OPERATORS

Edwards LaLone Travel S. 5 Washington • 747-3000/ (800) 288-3788

The Travel Place W. 505 Parkade Plaza • 624-7434/ (800) 727-9114 • women-owned/run

SPIRITUAL GROUPS

Emmanuel MCC 412 S. Bernard • 838-0085 • 10:30am & 7pm Sun

PUBLICATIONS

Stonewall News Spokane PO Box 3994, 99220-3994 • 456-8011

Tacoma (206)

INFO LINES & SERVICES

AA Gay/Lesbian • 474-8897

Oasis • 596-2860 • lesbigay youth group run by Health Dept.

South Sound Alliance • 924-1459 • info • referrals

Tacoma Lesbian Concern PO Box 947, 98401 • 472-0422 • social events • resource list

BARS

24th Street Tavern 2409 Pacific Ave. • 572-3748 • noon-2am • lesbians/gay men • dancing/DJ • live shows • beer/wine

733 Restaurant & Lounge 733 Commerce St. • 6pm-2am, clsd Sun-Mon • lesbians/gay men • dancing/DJ • live shows

The Gold Ball Tavern 2708 6th Ave. • 572-4820 • 8am-2am • lesbians/gay men • neighborhood bar • dancing/DJ • food served • beer garden • gambling

Goodfellows 5811 N. 51st. • 761-9802 • 4pm-2am • mostly gay men • neighborhood bar • karaoke

SPIRITUAL GROUPS

New Heart MCC 2150 S. Cushman • 272-2382 • 11am Sun, 7:30pm Wed

PUBLICATIONS

Tacoma Sounds PO Box 110816, 98411-0816 • 535-4213 • monthly

Tri-Cities (509)

BARS

Luca's 3408 W. Court St., Pasco • 545-1989 • 10am-2am • lesbians/gay men • dancing/DJ • food served

The Steak Out Lounge 213 W. Kennewick, Kennewick • 582-5048 • bar 7pm-2am, restaurant 11am-9pm, clsd Sun • gay-friendly • dancing/DJ • live shows

SPIRITUAL GROUPS

River of Life MCC 619 W. Albany (Unitarian Church), Kennewick • 946-5250 • 6:30pm Sun

Vancouver (360)

BARS

North Bank Tavern 106 W. 6th St. • 695-3862 • noon-2am • lesbians/gay men • beer/wine • wheelchair access

TRAVEL & TOUR OPERATORS

First Discount Travel 11700 NE 95th St. Ste. 110 • 896-6200/ (800) 848-1926 • ask for Carl • IGTA member

Wenatchee

INFO LINES & SERVICES

North Central Washington Lesbian/Gay Alliance PO Box 234, 98807

Yakima   (509)

INFO LINES & SERVICES

TALL (Together at Last Lesbians) PO Box 976, 98907 • 454-4989

West Virginia

Charleston (304)

INFO LINES & SERVICES

West Virginia Lesbian/Gay Coalition PO Box 11033, 25339 • 343-7305

BARS

Broadway 210 Broad St. • 343-2162 • 4pm-3am, from 1pm wknds • lesbians/gay men • dancing/DJ • private club • wheelchair access

Grand Palace 617 Brooks St. • 342-9532 • 10am-?, from 1pm Sun • mostly gay men • dancing/DJ • private club • wheelchair access

Tap Room 1022 Quarrier St. (rear entrance) • 342-9563 • 5pm-2am, clsd Sun-Mon • mostly gay men • neighborhood bar • dancing/DJ • private club

TRAVEL & TOUR OPERATORS

West Virginia Tourism Division • (800) 225-5982

Wild Wonderful Travel 1517 Jackson St. • 345-0491 • IGTA member

Elkins (304)

ACCOMMODATIONS

Retreat at Buffalo Run B&B 214 Harpertown Rd. • 636-2960 • gay-friendly

Huntington (304)

BARS

Driftwood Lounge 1121 7th Ave. • 696-9858 • 3:30pm-3am • lesbians/gay men • dancing/DJ • private club • also Beehive upstairs • open Wed & wknds • mostly gay men • live shows • wheelchair access

Polo Club 733 7th Ave. (rear) • 522-3146 • 3pm-3:30am • lesbians/gay men • dancing/DJ • live shows • more women Tue • wheelchair access

The Stonewall 820 7th Ave. (rear) • 528-9317 • 8pm-3:30am • popular • lesbians/gay men • dancing/DJ • more women Wed-Th • wheelchair access

RESTAURANTS & CAFES

Calamity Cafe 1555 3rd Ave. • 525-4171 • 11am-midnight, 3pm-10pm Sun • live shows • Southern/Western • plenty veggie • full bar • wheelchair access • $10-15

Lost River (304)

ACCOMMODATIONS

The Guesthouse Settlers Valley Wy. • 897-5707 • lesbians/gay men • full breakfast • swimming • steam & spa

Martinsburg (304)

EROTICA

Variety Books & Video 255 N. Queen St. • 263-4334 • 24hrs • lesbigay

Morgantown (304)

INFO LINES & SERVICES

Gay/Lesbian Alliance of WVU/Helpline PO Box 576, 26505 • 292-4292

BARS

Class Act 335 High St. (rear entrance) • 292-2010 • 9pm-3am, from 8pm Th-Sat, clsd Mon • lesbians/gay men • dancing/DJ • private club

Parkersburg (304)

BARS

Different Strokes 604 Markest St. • 485-5113 • 8pm-3am, clsd Sun • lesbians/gay men • dancing/DJ • live shows • wheelchair access

Stonewall Jackson Lake (304)

ACCOMMODATIONS

FriendSheep Farm Rte. 1 Box 158, Orlando, 26412 • 462-7075 • mostly women • B&B • campsites • swimming • secluded retreat w/ workshops

Wheeling (304)

ACCOMMODATIONS

Row House Guest Quarters 718 Main St. • 232-5252/ (800) 371-3020 • gay-friendly • apt w/ kitchen

BARS

The Tricks 1429 Market St. (behind Market St. News) • 232-1267 • 9pm-2am, til 3am Fri, clsd Mon-Tue • lesbians/gay men • dancing/DJ • live shows

Wisconsin

Appleton (414)

Bars

Pivot Club 4815 W. Prospect Ave. • 730-0440 • 5pm-2am, from 7pm Sat, from 2pm Sun • lesbians/gay men • dancing/DJ • live shows • wheelchair access

Rascals Bar & Grill 702 E. Wisconsin Ave. • 954-9262 • 5pm-2am, from noon Sun • mostly gay men • more women Fri • patio • wheelchair access

Aztalan (414)

Bars

Crossroads Bar W. 6642 Hwy. B., Lake Mills • 648-8457 • 1pm-2am, clsd Mon • gay-friendly

Beloit (608)

Bookstores & Retail Shops

A Different World 414 E. Grand Ave. • 365-1000 • 10am-9pm, til 5pm Mon, clsd Sun • women's & children's books • wheelchair access

Eau Claire (715)

Women's Accommodations

Back of the Moon, Augusta • 286-2409 • women only • full breakfast • hot tub • $30

Bars

Midnight Rose Saloon 505 S. Barstow • 834-6599 • 4pm-2am • lesbians/gay men • dancing/DJ • country/western • unverified for '96

Scruples 411 Galloway (behind adult bookstore) • 839-9606 • 5pm-2am, from 3pm wknds • lesbians/gay men • dancing/DJ • live shows • wheelchair access

Fort Atkinson (414)

Bars

Friends 10 E. Sherman Ave. • 563-2231 • 11am-2am • gay-friendly

Green Bay (414)

Info Lines & Services

Gay AA/Al-Anon • 494-9904 • 8pm1st Mon

Bars

Brandy's II 1126 Main St. • 432-3917/ (800) 811-3917 • 1pm-2am • lesbians/ gay men • neighborhood bar

Java's/Za's 1106 Main St. • 435-5476 • 8pm-2:30am • lesbians/gay men • dancing/DJ • live shows • 18+ Sun • wheelchair access

Napalese Lounge 515 S. Broadway • 432-9646 • 4pm-2am • mostly gay men • dancing/DJ • wheelchair access

Sass 840 S. Broadway • 437-7277 • 5pm-2am, from noon Sun (winters) • mostly women • neighborhood bar • dancing/DJ

Publications

Quest PO Box 1961, 54301

Hayward (715)

Accommodations

The Lake House 5793 Division on the Lake, Stone Lake • 865-6803 • gay-friendly • full breakfast • swimming • fireplaces • wheelchair access • lesbian-owned/run

Hazelhurst (715)

Bars

Willow Haven Resort/Supper Club 4877 Haven Dr. • 453-3807 • gay-friendly • cabin rentals • also supper club • full bar • $8-16 • wheelchair access

Hixton (715)

Women's Accommodations

Inn at Pine Ridge Rte.1 Box 28 • 984-2272 • women only • B&B • hot tub • sauna • full vegetarian brunch • $75-80

Kenosha (414)

Bars

Club 94 9001 120th Ave. • 857-9958 • 7pm-2am, from 3pm Sun, clsd Mon • popular • lesbians/gay men • dancing/DJ • live shows

Kimberly (414)

RESTAURANTS & CAFES

Grand American Restaurant & Bar 800 Eisenhower Dr. • 731-0164 • 11:30am-2pm & 4pm-9pm • some veggie • full bar • wheelchair access • $6-12

La Crosse (608)

INFO LINES & SERVICES

Gay/Lesbian AA 126 N. 17th St. • 784-7600 • 7pm Wed, 1:30pm Sat

Gay/Lesbian Support Group 126 N. 17th St. • 784-7600 • 7:30pm Sun

BARS

Cavalier 114 N. 5th • 782-9061 • 2pm-2am • gay-friendly • gay evenings only

BOOKSTORES & RETAIL SHOPS

Rainbow Revolution 122 5th Ave. S. • 796-0383 • 11am-6pm, til 5pm Sat, noon-4pm Sun • progressive • wheelchair access

Red Oaks Books 323 Pearl St. • 782-3424 • 9am-8pm, til 9pm Fri, 10am-5pm wknds

PUBLICATIONS

Leaping La Crosse PO Box 932, 54602 • 783-0069 • monthly

La Farge (608)

ACCOMMODATIONS

Trillium Rte. 2 Box 121, 54639 • 625-4492 • gay-friendly • B&B • full breakfast • also cottages (sleeps 5) • 35 mi. from La Crosse

Lake Geneva (414)

ACCOMMODATIONS

Eleven Gables Inn on the Lake 493 Wrigley Dr. • 248-8393 • gay-friendly • full breakfast • Victorian comfort in a spacious lakeside inn • wheelchair access

Laona (715)

ACCOMMODATIONS

Alexander's Guest House 5371 Beech • 674-2615 • gay-friendly • swimming • dorm-style/youth hostel rooms

Madison (608)

INFO LINES & SERVICES

AA Gay/Lesbian • 255-4297

Apple Island 849 E. Washington • 258-9777 • live shows • women's space • sponsors social events

Campus Women's Center 710 University Rm. 202 (University of Wisconsin) • 262-8093 • support programs

Dyke TV Channel 4 • 8:30pm Mon • 'weekly, half hour TV show produced by lesbians, for lesbians'

Gay Line • 255-4297 • info • referrals • counseling

Lesbian Line • 255-0743

Lesbigay Campus Center 510 Memorial Union • 265-3344

Nothing to Hide cable Ch. 4 • 241-2500 • 9pm Wed • lesbigay TV

The United 14 West Mifflin St. Ste. 103 • 255-8582 • 9am-5pm, 7pm-10pm Mon-Fri • drop-in center • library • newsletter • counseling service (call ahead)

ACCOMMODATIONS

Hotel Washington 636 W. Washington Ave. • 256-3302/ (800) 429-4685 • remodeled turn-of-the-century hotel • 5 nightclubs & 1 restaurant onsite

Prairie Garden B&B W. 13172 Hwy. 188, Lodi • 592-5187/ (800) 380-8427 • lesbians/gay men • full breakfast • 30 min. from Madison

BARS

Barbara's Closet (at Hotel Washington) • 256-3302 • 5pm-2am • gay-friendly

Cardinal 418 E. Wilson St. • 251-0080 • 8pm-2am, clsd Mon • gay-friendly • dancing/DJ

Geraldine's 3052 E. Washington Ave. • 241-9335 • 4pm-2am • lesbians/gay men • dancing/DJ

New Bar (at Hotel Washington) • 256-8765 • 9pm-2am • popular • lesbians/gay men • dancing/DJ • also Rod's • 255-0609 • mostly gay men • leather

Shamrock 117 W. Main St. • 255-5029 • 2pm-2am, from 11am Fri-Sat, from 5pm Sun • lesbians/gay men • neighborhood bar • also a grill • $2-4 • wheelchair access

RESTAURANTS & CAFES

Cafe Palms (at Hotel Washington) • 256-0166 • 11am-2:30am • American • some veggie • $6-15

Monty's Blue Plate Diner 2089 Atwood Ave. • 244-8505 • 7am-9pm • some veggie • beer/wine • $5

Wild Iris 1225 Regent St. • 257-4747 • 11am-10pm, from 9am wknds • Italian/Cajun • some veggie • beer/wine • wheelchair access • $8-12

BOOKSTORES & RETAIL SHOPS

▲ **A Room of One's Own** 317 W. Johnson St. • 257-7888 • 9:30am-8pm, til 6pm Tue, Wed & Sat, noon-5pm Sun • women's books & music • wheelchair access

Borders Book Shop 3416 University Ave. • 232-2600 • 9am-10pm, 11am-7pm Sun • also espresso bar

Going Places 2860 University Ave. • 233-1920 • travel-oriented books

Mimosa 212 N. Henry • 256-5432 • progressive

Pic-A-Book 506 State St. • 256-1125 • 9am-8pm, til 5pm Sun

TRAVEL & TOUR OPERATORS

Travel/ease, Inc. 1245 E. Washington Ave. • 257-5555/ (800) 554-8728

Wisconsin Division of Tourism • (800) 432-8747

SPIRITUAL GROUPS

Affirmation Methodist 1127 University Ave. (United Methodist Church) • 256-2353

Integrity & Dignity 1001 University Ave. (St. Francis Episcopal) • 836-8886 • 7:30pm 2nd & 4th Sun (Sept-May)

PUBLICATIONS

Of A Like Mind PO Box 6677, 53716 • 244-0072 • quarterly • women's newsletter of spirituality & paganism

Solitary PO Box 6091, 53716 • 244-0072 • quarterly • lesbigay spiritual pagan journal

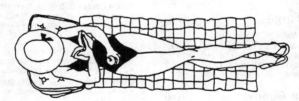

Maiden Rock (715)

ACCOMMODATIONS

Eagle Cove B&B PO Box 65, 54750 •
448-4302/ (800) 467-0279 • lesbians/gay
men • hot tub • 6 acre country retreat w/
panoramic views of Lake Pepin & the
Mississippi River Valley • wheelchair
access

Mauston (608)

WOMEN'S ACCOMMODATIONS

CK's Outback W. 5627 Clark Rd. • 847-
5247 • women only • camping • near
outdoor recreation

Milwaukee (414)

INFO LINES & SERVICES

AA Galano Club 2408 N. Farwell Ave. •
276-6936 • 12-step social group • call
after 5pm for extensive mtg. schedule

Black Gay Conciousness Raising • 933-
2136 • 7:30pm 3rd Mon • call for info

Counseling Center of Milwaukee 2038
N. Bartlett • 271-2565 • various support
groups for women

Gay Information & Services • 444-7331
• 24hr referral service

Gay People's Union Hotline • 562-7010
• 7pm-10pm

Lesbian Alliance PO Box 93323, 53203 •
264-2600

LOC (Lesbians of Color) • 351-4549 •
call for activities

ACCOMMODATIONS

Park East Hotel 916 E. State St. • 276-
8800/ (800) 328-7275 • gay-friendly • also
a restaurant • American • some veggie •
wheelchair access • $10-15

BARS

1100 Club 1100 S. 1st St. • 647-9950 •
6am-2am • mostly gay men • dancing/DJ
• food served • dinner menu • $4-15

The 3B Bar 1579 S. 2nd St. • 672-5580 •
3pm-2am, from noon wknds •
lesbians/gay men • dancing/DJ • coun-
try/western • more women wknds

Milwaukee (414)

LESBIGAY INFO: Gay Information
& Services: 444-7331, 24hr
referral service. Gay People's
Union Hotline: 562-7010, 7pm-
10pm. Greater Milwaukee Fun
Line: (800)272-0049.

LESBIGAY PAPER: Wisconsin
Light: 372-2773. In Step: 278-
7840.

WHERE THE GIRLS ARE: In East
Milwaukee south of downtown,
spread out from Lake Michigan
to S. Layton Blvd.

LESBIGAY AA: AA Galano Club:
276-6936, 2408 N. Farwell Ave.
AA Gay/Lesbian: 771-9119.

CITY INFO: 273-3950.

BEST VIEW: 41st story of First
Wisconsin Center. Call 765-
5733 to arrange a visit to the
top floor observatory.

WEATHER: Summer temperatures
can get up into 90°s. Spring
and fall are pleasantly moderate but too short. Winter
brings snows, cold temperatures and even colder wind
chills.

TRANSIT: Yellow Cab: 271-6630.

Cafe Melange 720 N. 3rd St. • 291-9889 • 11am-2am • gay-friendly • dancing/DJ • food served • American • some veggie • wheelchair access • $10 & up

Club 219 219 S. 2nd St. • 271-3732 • 4pm-2am • lesbians/gay men • dancing/DJ • multi-racial • live shows

Fannie's 200 E. Washington St. • 643-9633 • 7pm-2am, from 4pm Sun • popular • mostly women • patio • wheelchair access

Gargoyles 354 E. National • 225-9676 • 2pm-2am • mostly gay men • leather • live shows • wheelchair access

In Between 625 S. 2nd St. • 273-2693 • 5pm-2am, from 3pm wknds • mostly gay men • neighborhood bar • patio

Just Us 807 S. 5th St. • 383-2233 • 4pm-2am, from 1pm Sun • lesbians/gay men • dancing/DJ

Kathy's Nut Hut 1500 W. Scott • 647-2673 • 2pm-2am, from noon wknds • mostly women • neighborhood bar • also grill menu • caution regarding the neighborhood

La Cage (Dance, Dance, Dance) 801 S. 2nd St. • 383-8330 • 9pm-2am • popular • mostly gay men • dancing/DJ • 2 bar complex • more women wknds

Loose Ends 4322 W. Fond du Lac Ave. • 442-8469 • 4pm-2am • gay-friendly • neighborhood bar

M&M Club 124 N. Water St. • 347-1962 • 11am-2am • mostly gay men • food served • some veggie • $5-10

RESTAURANTS & CAFES

Cafe Knickerbocker 1030 E. Juneau Ave. • 272-0011 • 7am-11pm • popular • some veggie • full bar • wheelchair access • $8-15

Grubb's Pub 807 S. 2nd St. • 384-8330 • 9pm-4:30am • lesbians/gay men • grill food

Mama Roux 1875 N. Humboldt • 347-0344 • 3pm-2am • Cajun • full bar

Walkers Point Cafe 1106 S. 1st St. • 384-7999 • 11am-3am

BOOKSTORES & RETAIL SHOPS

AfterWords Bookstore & Espresso Bar 2710 N. Murray • 963-9089 • 11am-10pm, til 11pm Fri-Sat, noon-6pm Sun • lesbigay • wheelchair access

Schwartz Bookstore 209 E. Wisconsin Ave. • 274-6400 • 9am-6pm, til 8pm Th, clsd Sun

Milwaukee & Madison

*L*averne & Shirley may have been closeted, but Milwaukee's lesbian community is not! (We know what that "L" on Laverne's shirt stood for.) For you women-identified women, Milwaukee has women's groups, bars and more. The bars here are relaxed: **Fannie's** is a self-identified beer-garden with a dancefloor, while **Kathy's Nut Hut** is a more intimate bar, and **Club 219** is a mixed lesbian/gay bar with dancing. **AfterWords** is the lesbigay bookstore, and it's got an espresso bar to boot!

Just an hour-and-a-half west of Milwaukee is Madison – home of the University of Wisconsin, and a hotbed of "cultural feminism." That includes dyke separatism and feminist spirituality, as well as anti-violence and anti-porn activism. If you follow that path of feminism, call the **Lesbian Line** or **Apple Island** for current events, and stop by **A Room of One's Own** for locally published papers **Feminist Voices**, **Solitary** or **Of A Like Mind**, a pagan newsletter. For R&R, stop by the **New Bar** on women's night, Wednesday.

TRAVEL & TOUR OPERATORS

Horizon Travel N 81 W 15028 Appleton Ave., Menomonee Falls • 255-0704/ (800) 562-0219 • IGTA member

Trio Travel 2812 W. Forest Home Ave. • 384-8746/ (800) 417-4159 • IGTA member

PUBLICATIONS

In Step 225 S. 2nd St. • 278-7840

Wisconsin Light 1843 N. Palmer St. • 372-2773 • bi-monthly

Mineral Point   (608)

ACCOMMODATIONS

Chesterfield Inn/Ovens of Brittany 20 Commerce St. • 987-3682 • May-Oct • gay-friendly • full breakfast • also a restaurant • Cornish/American • some veggie • full bar • $10-16

The Cothren House 320 Tower St. • 987-2612 • full breakfast • gay-owned/run

Racine   (414)

INFO LINES & SERVICES

Gay/Lesbian Union 625 College , 54303

BARS

Jo' Dee's International 2139 Racine St. (S. Hwy. 32) • 634-9804 • 7pm-2am • lesbians/gay men • dancing/DJ • live shows

What About Me? 600 6th St. • 632-0171 • 3pm-2am • lesbians/gay men • neighborhood bar

Sheboygan   (414)

BARS

The Blue Lite 1029 N. 8th St. • 457-1636 • 2pm-2am • mostly gay men • neighborhood bar • more women wknds early

Somerset   (715)

WOMEN'S ACCOMMODATIONS

Country Guesthouse 1673 38th St. • 247-3520 • women only • rental home on 20 wooded acres in the scenic St. Croix River Valley • women-owned/run

Stevens Point   (715)

INFO LINES & SERVICES

Women's Resource Center 1209 Fremont (University of Wisconsin Nelson Hall) • 346-4242x4851 • some lesbian outreach

BARS

Platwood Club 701 Hwy. 10 W. • 341-8862 • 9pm-? Th-Sat • lesbians/gay men • dancing/DJ • wheelchair access

Sturgeon Bay   (414)

ACCOMMODATIONS

The Chanticleer 4072 Cherry Rd. • 746-0334 • gay-friendly • B&B • swimming

Superior   (715)

BARS

The Main Club 1813 N. 3rd St. • 392-1756 • 3pm-2am • popular • lesbians/gay men • dancing/DJ • patio

Molly & Oscar's 405 Tower Ave. • 394-7423 • 2pm-2am • gay-friendly • neighborhood bar

Trio 820 Tower Ave. • 392-5373 • 1pm-2am • mostly women • neighborhood bar • also a grill • wheelchair access

Wascott   (715)

WOMEN'S ACCOMMODATIONS

Wilderness Way PO Box 176, 54890 • 466-2635 • women only • resort property w/ cottages, camping & RV sites (camping $10-14, cottages $44-68) • swimming

Wausau   (715)

BARS

Mad Hatter 320 Washington • 842-3225 • 7pm-2am, from 3pm Sun • lesbians/gay men • dancing/DJ • wheelchair access

Willard   (715)

ACCOMMODATIONS

The Barn B&B N 7890 Bachelors Ave. • 267-3215 • gay-friendly • hot tub

Winter   (715)

ACCOMMODATIONS

Flambeau Forest Resort Star Rte. 67 Box 65, 54896 • 332-5236 • gay-friendly • cabins

Wyoming

Cheyenne (307)

INFO LINES & SERVICES

United Gay/Lesbians of Wyoming PO Box 2037, Laramie, 82070 • 632-5362 • info • referrals • also newsletter

Jackson (307)

INFO LINES & SERVICES

Jackson Hole GALA PO Box 7424, 83001 • 734-1234 • monthly potluck

ACCOMMODATIONS

Bar H Ranch Box 297, Driggs, ID 83422 • (208) 354-2906 • seasonal • gay-friendly

Redmond Guest House 110 Redmond St. • 733-4003 • seasonal • house rental • women-owned/run

Spring Creek Resort Box 3157, 83001 • 733-8833/ (800) 443-6139 • popular • gay-friendly • swimming • food served

RESTAURANTS & CAFES

Sweetwater 85 King St. • 733-3553 • cont'l • full bar • $7-12

BOOKSTORES & RETAIL SHOPS

Valley Books 125 N. Cache • 733-4533

Riverton (307)

RESTAURANTS & CAFES

Country Cove 301 E. Main • 856-9813 • 6am-4pm, clsd Sun • plenty veggie • wheelchair access • women-owned/run • $4-6

Thermopolis (307)

ACCOMMODATIONS

Out West B&B 1344 Broadway • 864-2700 • gay-friendly • full breakfast • hand-cast stone brick home built in 1908 w/ 18' leaded stain glass windows & beaded ceilings

International Section

CANADA

CARIBBEAN

MÉXICO

Alberta

Calgary (403)

INFO LINES & SERVICES

Front Runners AA • 265-8888 • 7:30pm Fri-Sat, 8:30pm Mon-Th

Gay Line & Center 223 12th Ave. SW #201 • 234-8973 • 7pm-10pm, call for other hours • many groups • including 'Of Color' & 'Queer Youth'

Illusions Social Club Box 2000, 6802 Ogden Rd. SE, T2C 1 B4 • 236-7072 • TV/TS Club

Lesbian Information Line • 265-9458 • info • referrals

ACCOMMODATIONS

Renawd House 605 10th Ave. NE • 277-0672 • gay-friendly

Westways Guest House 216 25th Ave. SW • 229-1758 • lesbians/gay men • full breakfast • hot tub

BARS

Boxxe Cafe 111 15th Ave. SW • 232-8433 • 11am-1am, from noon Sun • mostly women • karaoke • food served • American • patio • wheelchair access • $2-7

Detour 318 17th Ave. SW • 244-8537 • 11pm-3am, clsd Sun • lesbians/gay men • dancing/DJ

Trax 1130 10th Ave. SW • 245-8477 • 4pm-2am • mostly gay men • dancing/DJ • country/western • live shows • private club

The Warehouse 731 10th Ave. SW (alley entrance) • 264-0535 • 9pm-3am, clsd Sun & Tue • gay-friendly • dancing/DJ • private club

RESTAURANTS & CAFES

Andrews Pizza 719 Edmonton Trail NE • 230-4202 • 11am-1am • full bar • more gay weeknights • wheelchair access

Appleberry's 1219 9th Ave. SE • 265-7171 • 9am-5pm, later in summer • cafe

Cafe Beano 1613 9th St. SW • 229-1232 • 7am-11pm • some veggie • wheelchair access

Folks Like Us 110 10th St. NW • 270-2241 • 11am-10pm, til 8pm Sat, til 5pm Sun, clsd Mon • lesbians/gay men • bistro menu • plenty veggie • beer/wine • patio • lesbian-owned/run • $4-7

Grabbajabba 1610 10th St. SW • 244-7750 • 7am-11pm • lesbians/gay men • some veggie • cafe • patio • wheelchair access • $2-7

The Koop Cafe 211-B 12th Ave. SW • 269-4616 • 11am-1am

Max Beanie's Coffee Bar 1410 4th St. SW • 237-6185 • 9am-10pm, clsd Sun • wheelchair access

Pepper Specialty Foods 803 17th Ave. SW • 229-2588 • 7am-6pm • plenty veggie

Victoria's 306 17th Ave. SW • 244-9991 • lunch, dinner, wknd brunch • home-cooking • some veggie • full bar • $6-10

BOOKSTORES & RETAIL SHOPS

A Woman's Place 1412 Centre St. S. • 263-5256 • 10am-6pm, clsd Sun • many gay titles • wheelchair access

B&B Leatherworks 6802 Ogden Rd. SE • 236-7072 • 10am-6pm Tue-Sat • drag/fetish items

Books 'n Books 738-A 17th Ave. SW • 228-3337 • 10am-6pm, til 9pm Th-Fri • wheelchair access

With the Times 2212-A 4th St. SW • 244-8020 • 8:30am-11pm • wheelchair access

TRAVEL & TOUR OPERATORS

CMS Travel 1717 Kent St. NW • 289-1817 • IGTA member

Fletcher/Scott Travel 803 8th Ave. SW • 232-1180/ (800) 567-2467 (Canada only) • IGTA member

Uniglobe Swift Travel 932 17th Ave. SW #220 • 244-7887 • IGTA member

PUBLICATIONS

Outword 1412-B Centre St. • 237-5227

Perceptions PO Box 8581, Saskatoon, SK S7K 6K7 • covers western Canada

Edmonton (403)

INFO LINES & SERVICES

Gay/Lesbian Community Center 10112 124th St. • 488-3234 • 7pm-10pm • info • referrals

Gay/Lesbian Info Line • 988-4018 • 24hrs

Womonspace 9930 106th St. (basement) • 4258-0511 • meetings • social events

ACCOMMODATIONS

Northern Lights B&B 8216 151st St., T5R 1H6 • 483-1572 • lesbians/gay men • full breakfast

BARS

Rebar 10551 Whyte • 433-3600 • 8pm-3am • gay-friendly • live shows • call for events

The Roost 10345 104th St. • 426-3150 • 8pm-3am • mostly gay men • dancing/DJ • wheelchair access

RESTAURANTS & CAFES

Boystown Cafe 10116 124th St. • 488-6636 • 11am-midnight • lesbians/gay men • patio • wheelchair access

BOOKSTORES & RETAIL SHOPS

Audrey's Books 10702 Jasper Ave. • 423-3487 • 9am-9pm, til 5:30pm Sat, clsd Sun

Divine Decadence 10441 82nd Ave. • 439-2977 • 10am-9pm • hip fashions • accessories

The Front Page 10846 Jasper Ave. • 426-1206 • 8am-6pm • magazines • newspapers

Greenwood's Bookshoppe 10355 82nd Ave. • 439-2005 • 9:30am-9pm, til 5:30pm Sat, clsd Sun • wheelchair access

SPIRITUAL GROUPS

Dignity PO Box 53, T5J 2G9 • 469-4286 • 6pm Tue

MCC - Edmonton 10086 MacDonald Dr. • 429-2321 • 7:15pm Sun • also 'Wayward Daughters' group for women • 431-2128

Grand Prairie (403)

INFO LINES & SERVICES

Peace Gay/Lesbian Association Box 1492, T8V 4Z3 • 539-3325 • 7:30pm-9:30pm Tue-Sat • info • referrals • drop-in center

Lethbridge (403)

INFO LINES & SERVICES '

GALA (Gay/Lesbian Association of Lethbridge) Box 2081, T1J 4K6 • 329-4666 • 7pm-10pm Wed • info • referrals • social group

Lighthouse Social Club PO Box 24003, T1J 1T7 • 380-4257 • monthly dances & weekly events for lesbians/gays

Millet (403)

ACCOMMODATIONS

Labyrinth Lake Lodge RR1 Site 2 Box 3, T0C 1Z0 • 878-3301 • mostly women & gay men • swimming • retreat

Red Deer (403)

INFO LINES & SERVICES

Gay/Lesbian Association of Central Alberta PO Box 1078, T4W 5E9 • 340-2198

BARS

The Other Place Bay #3-4, 5579 47th St., T4N 1A1 • 342-6440 • 4pm-3am, 3pm-11pm Sun • lesbians/gay men • dancing/DJ • wheelchair access

British Columbia

Birken (604)

ACCOMMODATIONS

Birkenhead Resort Box 369, Pemberton, V0N 2L0 • 452-3255 • gay-friendly • cabins • campsites • hot tub • swimming • also a restaurant • gourmet homecooking • some veggie • full bar

Courtenay (604)

INFO LINES & SERVICES

Women's Resource Center 3205 S. Island Hwy. • 338-1133 • 10am-4am Mon-Th, til noon Fri • wheelchair access

Cranbrook (604)

INFO LINES & SERVICES

Cranbrook Women's Resource Center 20-A 12th Ave N. • 426-2912 • 9am-4pm

Duncan (604)

INFO LINES & SERVICES

Island Gay/Lesbian Society of Duncan • 748-7689

Fort Nelson (604)

INFO LINES & SERVICES

Women's Resource Center 5004 52nd Ave. W. • 774-3069 • 9am-4pm

Gokten (604)

INFO LINES & SERVICES

Golden Women's Resource Center Box 2343, V0A 1H0 • 344-5317 • 10am-3pm Mon-Th

Kelowna (604)

INFO LINES & SERVICES

Kelowna Women's Resource Center 347 Leon Ste. 107 • 762-2355 • 11am-4pm, til 8pm Wed, clsd Fri-Sun • wheelchair access

Okanagan Gay/Lesbian Organization PO Box 711 Stn. A, V1Y 7P4 • 860-8555 • taped info • sponsors dances & coffeehouse

ACCOMMODATIONS

The Flags B&B 2295 McKinley Rd., RR1 Site 10 C2, V1Y 7P9 • 868-2416 • May-Oct • lesbians/gay men • full breakfast • hot tub • swimming • nudity • mini-resort unlike most private B&Bs

Nanaimo (604)

RESTAURANTS & CAFES

Olde Firehall Coffee Roastery 34 Nichol St. Ste. 2 • 754-7733 • 9am-midnight, til 1am Fri-Sat • vegetarian • cafe • wheelchair access • $5

Nelson (604)

INFO LINES & SERVICES

Nelson Women's Center 507 Hall St. • 352-9916

West Kootaney Gay/Lesbian Line Box 725, V1C 4C7 • 354-4297 • social group

Prince George (604)

INFO LINES & SERVICES

GALA North • 562-6253 • 24hr taped message • info • social group

Teen Crisis Line • 564-8336 • 4pm-11pm

ACCOMMODATIONS

Hawthorne B&B 829 Prince George Pulp Mill Rd., V2N 2J2 • 563-8299 • gay-friendly • full breakfast

Prince Rupert (604)

INFO LINES & SERVICES

Prince Rupert Gay Info Line PO Box 881, V8J 3Y1 • 627-8900

Quesnel (604)

INFO LINES & SERVICES

Women's Resource Center 690 Mclean St. • 992-8472 • 9am-4pm Mon-Fri • wheelchair access

Revelstoke

INFO LINES & SERVICES

Lothlorien Box 8557, V0E 3G0 • info • referrals

Saltspring Island (604)

ACCOMMODATIONS

The Blue Ewe 1207 Beddis Rd. • 537-9344 • lesbians/gay men • private on 5-1/2 acres • full breakfast • hot tub w/ ocean view • nudity

Driftwood Gallery Bed & Brunch 1982 N. End Rd. • 537-4137 • gay-friendly • miniature farm for art & animal lovers

Green Rose Farm B&B 346 Robinson Rd., Ganges • 537-9927 • gay-friendly • full breakfast • heritage farm house

Summerhill Guesthouse 209 Chu-An Dr. • 537-2727 • full breakfast • on the water

Sunnyside Up B&B 120 Andrew Pl. • 653-4889 • lesbians/gay men • full breakfast • hot tub • panoramic views • deck

Tofino (604)

ACCOMMODATIONS

Raven's Haven B&B 1096 Pacific Rim Hwy. • 725-3156 • seasonal • gay-friendly • full breakfast • 5 hours E. of Vancouver • lesbian-owned

West Wind Guest House 1321 Pacific Rim Hwy. • 722-2224 • lesbians/gay men • hot tub • private hideaway retreat nestled on 2 wooded acres • 5 minutes from the beach

Vancouver (604)

INFO LINES & SERVICES

AA Gay/Lesbian • 434-3933

Vancouver Gay/Lesbian Center 1170 Bute St. • 684-6869 • switchboard 7pm-10pm

Vancouver Lesbian Center 876 Commercial Dr. • 254-8458 • 11am-6pm Th-Fri, noon-5pm Sat

Vancouver Women's Health Collective 1675 W. 8th Ave. Ste. 219 • 736-5262 • wheelchair access

Women & Sobriety 3080 Prince Edward St. • 434-3933 • 8pm Sun

WOMEN'S ACCOMMODATIONS

Stay in Touch Box 3059, V6B 3X6 • 681-2246 • women only • swimming • B&B in luxurious high rise • $75

Vancouver (604)

LESBIGAY INFO: Vancouver Gay/Lesbian Center: 684-6869.1170 Bute St., 7pm-10pm switchboard. Vancouver Lesbian Center: 254-8458, 11-6 Th-Sat listing of events & meetings.

LESBIGAY PAPER: Angles: 688-0265. Xtra West: 684-9696.

WHERE THE GIRLS ARE: In the West End, between Stanley Park and Gastown, or exploring the beautiful scenery elsewhere.

LESBIGAY AA: 434-3933.

LESBIGAY PRIDE: August, 684-2633.

CITY INFO: Vancouver Travel Info Center: 683-2000.

ATTRACTIONS: Stanley Park, Gastown, Chinatown, Capilano Suspension Bridge.

BEST VIEW: Biking in Stanley Park, or on a ferry between peninsulas and islands. Atop the surrounding mountains.

WEATHER: Cold and wet in winter (30-10c); absolutely gorgeous in summer (55-65f)!

TRANSIT: Yellow Cab: 681-1111. Vancouver Airporter: 244-9888. A Visitors' Map of all bus lines is available through the tourist office listed below. B.C. Transit: 521-0400.

"*A Country Retreat in the City*"

Selected by Best Places To Stay Guides

ALБion GUEST HOUSE

TRY OUR HOT TUB !

Enjoy our Women's Only Weekends.

(tel) **(604) 873-2287**
(fax)**(604) 879-5682**
**592 W. 19th Ave.
Vancouver, B.C.
V5Z 1W6**

ACCOMMODATIONS

▲ **Albion Guest House** 592 W. 19th Ave. • 873-2287 • lesbians/gay men • full breakfast • hot tub

Beach House 5834 Morgan Rd., Mirror Lake • 879-4547 • gay-friendly • full breakfast • private house on Lake Kootenay • weekly rental

The Buchan Hotel 1906 Haro St. • 685-5354/ (800) 668-6654 • gay-friendly • no smoking

Colibri B&B 1101 Thurlow St. • 689-5100 • gay-friendly • full breakfast • gay-owned

Columbia Cottage 205 W. 14th Ave. • 874-5327 • gay-friendly • full breakfast • 1920s Tudor • IGTA member

The French Quarter B&B 2051 W. 19th Ave. • 737-0973 • gay-friendly • cottages • full breakfast • swimming • gym

Heritage House Hotel 455 Abbott St. • 685-7777 • lesbians/gay men • live shows • 3 bars on premises

The Johnson House 2278 W. 34th Ave. • 266-4175 • gay-friendly

▲ **Mountain B&B** 258 E. Balmoral Rd. • 987-2725 • gay-friendly • full breakfast • fireplaces

Nelson House 977 Broughton St. • 684-9793 • full breakfast • jacuzzi in suite

River Run Cottages 4551 River Rd. W., Ladner • 946-7778 • gay-friendly • on the Fraser River

Rural Roots 4939 Ross Rd., Mt. Lehman • 856-2380 • lesbians/gay men • full breakfast

▲ **West End Guest House** 1362 Haro St. • 681-2889 • gay-friendly • 1906 historic Victorian inn filled w/ antiques & modern conveniences • full breakfast • some veggie

BARS

Celebrities 1022 Davie St. • 689-3180 • 9pm-2am, til midnight Sun • lesbians/gay men • dancing/DJ • women's night Sun

Chuck's Pub (at Heritage House Hotel) • 685-7777 • 11am-1:30am • lesbians/gay men • also Uncle Charlie's • mostly gay men • live shows • beer/wine

Denman Station 860 Denman • 669-3448 • 7pm-2am, til midnight Sun • mostly gay men • neighborhood bar • dancing/DJ • videos • more women Sun

Fly Girl 1545 W. 7th Ave. • 875-9907 • 9pm-2am every other Sat • popular • mostly women • dancing/DJ

Lotus Club (at Heritage House Hotel) • 685-7777 • lesbians/gay men • dancing/DJ • women's night Fri

Ms. T's 339 W. Pender St. • 682-8096 • 8pm-2am, til midnight Sun • lesbians /gay men • dancing/DJ • transgender people welcome

Muffs & Cuffs 154 W. Hastings St. (alley entrance) • 254-2543 • 10pm-2am 3rd Sat only • women only • dancing/DJ • live shows • 2 dungeons • wheelchair access

The Odyssey 1251 Howe St. • 689-5256 • 9pm-2am, til midnight Sun • popular • mostly gay men • dancing/DJ • patio

Papa's Place 1025 Granville St. (at Royal Hotel) • 685-5335 • 10am-11pm • mostly gay men • live bands Wed-Sat

Twilite Zone 7 Alexander St. • 682-8550 • gay-friendly • dancing/DJ • alternative • more gay Tue & Sat

Restaurants & Cafes

The Alabaster 1168 Hamilton St., Yaletown • 687-1758 • Italian

Cafe S'il Vous Plaît 500 Robson St. • 688-7216 • 9am-10pm, clsd Sun • homecooking • plenty veggie • wheelchair access • $3-6

Clearwater Cafe 1030 Denman • 688-6264 • noon-10pm, from 10am wknds • vegetarian • beer/wine • patio • $6-10

Coffee Boy 1240 Thurlow St. (upstairs) • 11am-4am, til 2am Sun • cafe • billiards • patio

Delilah's 1906 Haro St. • 687-3424 • 6pm-midnight • cont'l • some veggie • wheelchair access • $16-26

Doll & Penny's Cafe 1167 Davie St. • 685-5080 • 7am-3am, til 4am Fri-Sat, 9am-1am Sun • American • plenty veggie • wheelchair access • $7-10

The Edge Cafe 1148 Davie St. • 689-4742 • 7am-4am, 24hrs Fri-Sat • sandwiches/pastries • wheelchair access

Friends Cafe 1221 Thurlow St. • 685-0995 • 11am-11pm • lesbians/gay men • full bar • patio

Hamburger Mary's 1202 Davie St. • 687-1293 • 6am-4am • some veggie • full bar • $5-10

Vancouver

*J*ust three hours north of Seattle, Vancouver is literally one of the most beautiful cities in the world. Surrounded by lush Canadian forests and waterways in the saturated colors of the Northwest, the city is draped in a backdrop of snow-capped mountains.

Dykes-into-dance should check out the women's nights at the city's many mixed bars – start out at the **Lotus Club**, then try **Celebrities**, **Denman Station**, or **Fly Girl**.

Book-loving lesbians should stop by **Little Sister's** to offer support in their ongoing lawsuit against the censorious Canadian Customs. While you're at it, pick up a copy of **Xtra! West**, **Alternatives**, or the aptly named **Lezzie Smut**. Vegetarians will fare well at **La Quena** co-op, or **O-Tooz**, the only vegetarian fast food place we know of.

Latte-lovers will enjoy the many cafes. Those who love touring the potluck/support group circuit are in luck. Vancouver has a good range of lesbian-friendly services, so inquire at the **Vancouver Lesbian Center** or the **Vancouver Gay/Lesbian Community Center**.

La Di Da 1030 Davie St. • 689-3688 • 9am-midnight, til 3am wknds • fresh gourmet • some veggie • full bar • wheelchair access • $8-15

La Quena 1111 Commercial Dr. • 251-6626 • 11am-11pm • vegetarian • wheelchair access • $3-5

O-Tooz 1068 Davie St. • 689-0208 • 7am-midnight • lowfat vegetarian fastfood

Riley Cafe 1661 Granville St. • 684-3666 • noon-11pm • BBQ • some veggie • full bar • also 'Riley T' • alternative social night for lesbians/gays • 1st & 3rd Sun

The Second Cup 1184 Denman • 669-2068 • 7am-midnight • pastries • wheelchair access

BOOKSTORES & RETAIL SHOPS

Little Sister's 1221 Thurlow • 669-1753 • 10am-11pm • lesbigay bookstore

Octopus Books 1146 Commercial Dr. • 253-0913 • 10am-6pm • wheelchair access

Return to Sender 1076 Davie St. • 683-6363 • 11am-9pm, noon-6pm Sun • cards • gifts • wheelchair access

Spartacus Books 311 W. Hastings • 688-6138 • 10am-8:30pm, noon-6pm wknds • progressive bookstore

Vancouver Women's Books 315 Cambie St. • 684-0523 • 10am-6pm, clsd Sun

Women in Print 3566 W. 4th Ave. • 732-4128 • 10am-6pm, noon-5pm Sun • women's bookstore • wheelchair access

TRAVEL & TOUR OPERATORS

Partners Travel Inc. 1120 Davie St. • 687-3837 • IGTA member

PUBLICATIONS

Angles 1170 Bute St. Ste. 4-B • 688-0265

Kinesis 1720 Grant St. Ste. 301 • 255-5499 • women's newsmagazine

▲ **Lezzie Smut** 1027 Davie St. Box 364 • 252-6299 • lesbian erotica for all North America • see ad in San Francisco, CA

Xtra! West 1033 Davie St. Ste. 501 • 684-9696 • bi-weekly

Vernon (604)

INFO LINES & SERVICES
Rural Lesbian Assoc. Box 1242, V1T 6N6

ACCOMMODATIONS
Rainbows End RR 3, Site 11, Box 178, V1T 6L6 • 542-4842 • lesbians/gay men • full breakfast • wheelchair access

Victoria   (604)

INFO LINES & SERVICES

Gay/Lesbian AA • 383-7744

Hot Flashes Women's Coffeehouse 106 Superior St. • 598-4900 • 8pm 3rd Fri

Island Gay/Lesbian Association Phone Line • 598-4900 • 6pm-10:30pm • info • referrals

WOMEN'S ACCOMMODATIONS

The Back Hills 4470 Leefield RR1 • 478-9648 • women only • full breakfast • 30 min. from Victoria in the Metchosin Hills • women-owned/run • $50

ACCOMMODATIONS

Camellia House B&B 1994 Leighton Rd. • 370-2816 • lesbians/gay men • full breakfast • massage available • women-owned/run

Claddagh House B&B 1994 Leighton Rd. • 370-2816 • gay-friendly • full breakfast

Lavender Link 136 Medana St. • 380-7098 • lesbians/gay men • B&B • no smoking • 1912 tastefully renovated character home • women-owned/run

Oak Bay Guest House 1052 Newport Ave. • 598-3812 • gay-friendly • full breakfast • beaches nearby

The Weekender 10 Ebert St. • 389-1688 • June-Sept (wknds only Nov-May) • lesbians/gay men • seaside B&B

BARS

BJ's Lounge 642 Johnson (enter on Broad) • 388-0505 • noon-1am • lesbians/gay men • piano bar • lunch daily • wheelchair access

Rumors 1325 Government St. • 385-0566 • 9pm-2am, til midnight Sun • popular • lesbians/gay men • dancing/DJ

BOOKSTORES & RETAIL SHOPS

Everywoman's Books 635 Johnson St. • 388-9411 • 10:30am-5:30pm, clsd Sun • wheelchair access

Whistler   (604)

ACCOMMODATIONS

▲ **The Whistler Retreat** 8561 Drifter Wy. • 938-9245 • lesbians/gay men • B&B in spacious alpine home • outdoor hot tub • sauna • mtn. views

Manitoba

Brandon (204)

INFO LINES & SERVICES

Gays/Lesbians of Western Manitoba PO Box 22039, R7A 6Y9 • 727-4297 • 7pm-10pm Fri • info • referrals • also sponsors events

Winnipeg (204)

INFO LINES & SERVICES

Gay/Lesbian Resource Center 1-222 Osborne St. • 284-5208 • office 1pm-4:30pm, info line 7:30pm-10pm Mon-Fri • info • referrals • library

Lesbian Social Discussion Group (at Gay/Lesbian Resource Center) • 7:30pm Tue

New Freedom AA Group 300 Hugo at Mulvey (St. Michael & All Angels) • 942-0126 • 8:30pm Th, 3:30pm Sun

Women's Center 515 Portage Ave., U of Winnipeg, Graham Hall, 4th flr. • 786-9788 • drop-in resource center • wheelchair access

Women's Resource Center 1088 Pembina Hwy. • 477-1123 • wheelchair access

ACCOMMODATIONS

Winged Ox Guest House • 783-7408 • lesbians/gay men • turn-of-the-century brick home • full breakfast • some veggie

BARS

Club 200 190 Garry St. • 943-6045 • 4pm-2am, clsd Sun • lesbians/gay men • dancing/DJ • live shows • dinner served • some veggie • wheelchair access • $7-11

Gio's 272 Sherbrooke St. • 786-1236 • 9pm-2am, clsd Sun • mostly gay men • dancing/DJ • wheelchair access

Happenings 274 Sherbrooke St. (upstairs) • 774-3576 • 9pm-2am, til 3am Sat, clsd Sun • mostly gay men • dancing/DJ • private club

Ms. Purdy's Women's Club 226 Main St. • 989-2344 • 8pm-2am, clsd Sun-Mon • women only • dancing/DJ • live shows • private club • men welcome Fri • wheelchair access • women-owned/run

RESTAURANTS & CAFES

Times Change Cafe 234 Main • 957-0982 • live shows • some veggie • lunch daily, dinner Th-Sun • under $6

BOOKSTORES & RETAIL SHOPS

Dominion News 263 Portage Ave. • 942-6563 • 8am-9pm, noon-6pm Sun • some gay periodicals

McNally Robinson 100 Osborne St. S. (at River) • 453-2644 • 9:30am-9:30pm, til 6pm Sat, noon-5pm Sun • some gay titles

SPIRITUAL GROUPS

Affirm • 452-2853 • call for events

Dignity Box 1912, R3C 3R2 • 772-4322 • 7:30pm 1st & 3rd Th • call for events

MCC St. Stephen's on Broadway & Kennedy • 661-2219 • 7:30pm Sun • wheelchair access

PUBLICATIONS

Perceptions Box 8581, Saskatoon, SK S7K 6K7 • covers western Canada

EROTICA

Unique Boutique 561 Portage Ave. (may be moving) • 775-5435 • 10am-midnight, til 10pm wknds

New Brunswick

Frederickton   (506)

INFO LINES & SERVICES

Frederickton Gay Line • 457-2156 •
6pm-9pm Mon & Th

Moncton   (506)

BARS

Triangles 234 St. George/St. Alexander •
857-8775 • lesbians/gay men •
dancing/DJ

Sackville   (506)

ACCOMMODATIONS

Georgian House RR #3 • 536-1481 •
seasonal • gay-friendly • full breakfast •
1840 home appointed w/ Georgian &
Victorian antiques in quiet country setting

St. John's   (506)

ACCOMMODATIONS

Mahogany Manor 220 Germain St. •
636-8000 • gay-friendly • full breakfast •
turn-of-the-century home

BARS

Bogarts 9 Sydney St. • 652-2004 • 8pm-
2am, clsd Sun-Tue • lesbians/gay men •
dancing/DJ

Newfoundland

Corner Brook   (709)

INFO LINES & SERVICES

Women's Resource Center 2 West St.
Box 373 • 639-8522

St. John's   (709)

INFO LINES & SERVICES

Gay/Lesbian Info Line • 753-4297 •
7pm-10pm Th

Women's Centre 83 Military Rd. • 753-
0220 • 9am-5pm Mon-Fri • wheelchair
access

BARS

The Back Alley Pub 164-A Water St. •
726-6782 • 6pm-2am, from 4pm Sun •
gay-friendly • neighborhood bar

Schroders Piano Bar 10 Bates Hill •
753-0807 • 4pm-1am, til 2am Fri-Sat, til
midnight Sun • gay-friendly • live shows
• also Zapata's restaurant downstairs •
Mexican • some veggie • $9-15

Zone 216 Duckworth St. • 754-2492 •
8pm-2am, til midnight Sun • lesbians
/gay men • dancing/DJ • wheelchair
access

Stevenville   (709)

INFO LINES & SERVICES

Bay St. George Women's Center 54 St.
Clare Ave. • 643-4444 • wheelchair access

Nova Scotia

Bear River (902)

ACCOMMODATIONS

Lovett Lodge Inn 1820 Main Street • 467-3917/ (800) 565-0000 (Canada only)/(800) 341-6096 (US only) • open May to end of Oct • gay-friendly • 1892 Victorian doctor's residence • full breakfast

Halifax (902)

INFO LINES & SERVICES

Gay Line • 423-7129 • 7pm-10pm Th-Sat • call for gay AA schedule

ACCOMMODATIONS

Centretown-ville B&B 2016 Oxford St. • 422-2380 • gay-friendly • full breakfast • 1920s style bungalow w/ front veranda • located in heart of city

Fresh Start B&B 2720 Gottingen St. • 453-6616 • gay-friendly • full breakfast • small Victorian mansion near center of city

BARS

Seahorse Tavern 1665 Argyle St. • gay-friendly • neighborhood bar • true cast of characters

The Stonewall Inn 1566 Hollis St. • 425-2166 • 11:30am-2am • lesbians/gay men • neighborhood bar • food served

The Studio Lounge 1537 Barrington St. • 423-6866 • 4pm-2am, from 6pm-1am Sun • mostly gay men • dancing/DJ

RESTAURANTS & CAFES

Le Bistro 1333 South Park • 423-8428 • lunch & dinner • gay-friendly • some veggie • full bar • wheelchair access • $7-13

BOOKSTORES & RETAIL SHOPS

Entitlement Book Sellers Lord Nelson Arcade • 420-0565 • 9:30am-9pm, noon-6pm Sun • wheelchair access

Red Herring Book Store 1555 Granville St. • 422-5087 • 10am-6pm, til 9pm Th-Fri • lesbigay section • wheelchair access

Schooner Books 5378 Inglis St. • 423-8419 • 9:30pm-6pm, til 9pm Th-Fri, til 5:30pm Sun • large selection of women's titles

SPIRITUAL GROUPS

MCC 5550 Inglis St. (church) • 443-7751 • 7:30pm Sun

PUBLICATIONS

Wayves PO Box 34090 Scotia Sq., B3J 3S1

EROTICA

Atlantic News 5560 Morris St. • 429-5468

Lunenburg (902)

ACCOMMODATIONS

Brook House 3 Old Blue Rocks Rd. • 634-3826 • gay-friendly • quiet retreat in Canada's oldest German town

Shelburne (902)

ACCOMMODATIONS

The Toddle Inn 163 Water St. • 875-3229/ (800) 565-0000 • seasonal April-Dec • gay-friendly • full breakfast • restaurant & bar on premises

Sydney (902)

INFO LINES & SERVICES

Women's Unlimited Feminist Association PO Box 368, B1P 4T1 • 564-5926

Ontario

Bancroft   (613)

WOMEN'S ACCOMMODATIONS

Greenview Guesthouse Box 1192, K0L
1C0 • 332-3922 • women only • country
retreat • full breakfast & dinner • plenty
veggie • hot tub • sauna

Cambridge   (519)

BARS

Robin's Nest 26 Hobston St. (in Farmers
Bldg., Galt St. entrance) • 621-2688 •
Tue, Fri-Sat only • mostly women • coun-
try/western • call for events

Dutton   (519)

ACCOMMODATIONS

Victorian Court B&B 235 Main St. • 762-
2244 • lesbians/gay men • hot tub •
restored Victorian • patio

Fort Erie   (905)

WOMEN'S ACCOMMODATIONS

Whistle Stop Guesthouse • 871-1265 •
women only • swimming • fireplaces •
all inclusive weekends only • $125

Grand Valley   (519)

ACCOMMODATIONS

Manfred's Meadow Guest House RR #1
• 925-5306 • lesbians/gay men • swimming • sauna • spa • all meals included

Guelph   (519)

INFO LINES & SERVICES

Gay Line • 836-4550

Guelph Gay/Lesbian Equality Box 773,
N1H 6L8 • 824-4120x8575 • info • social
group

BOOKSTORES & RETAIL SHOPS

Bookshelf Cafe 41 Quebec St. • 821-
3311 • 9am-9pm (bar noon-1am) • popular • gay-friendly • also cimema &
restaurant • some veggie • $5-10

Hamilton   (905)

ACCOMMODATIONS

The Cedars Tent & Trailer Park 1039
5th Concession Rd. RR2, Waterdown •
659-3655 • lesbians/gay men •
dancing/DJ • karaoke • private campground • swimming • also social club •
dancing/DJ • karaoke • wknd restaurant •
some veggie

BARS

Cafe 121 121 Hughson St. N. • 546-5258
• noon-1am • lesbians/gay men • danc-
ing/DJ • 3 bars • also a restaurant • some
veggie • $3-10

The Embassy Club 54 King St. E. • 522-
7783 • 8pm-1am Wed-Sun • mostly gay
men • dancing/DJ

Windsor Hotel 31 John St. N. • 522-5990
• 11am-1am • gay-friendly • karaoke •
lunch daily • some veggie

BOOKSTORES & RETAIL SHOPS

The Women's Bookstop 333 Main St. W.
• 525-2970 • 10:30am-7pm, til 8pm Fri,
til 5pm Sat, clsd Sun • wheelchair access

Jasper   (613)

ACCOMMODATIONS

Starr Easton Hall Kilmarnock Rd. &
Country Rd. #6 • 283-7497 • gay-friendly
• full breakfast • also a restaurant •
internat'l fine dining • some veggie • full
bar • live shows • wheelchair access

Kingston   (613)

INFO LINES & SERVICES

Lesbian/Gay Community Directory •
531-8981 • 7pm-9pm Mon-Fri • info line

BARS

Robert's Club Vogue 477 Princess St. •
547-2923 • 4pm-1am, til 3am Fri-Sat •
popular • lesbians/gay men • dancing/DJ

RESTAURANTS & CAFES

Chinese Laundry Cafe 291 Princess St. •
542-2282 • 9am-midnight, til 2am Fri-Sat
• popular • cafe food & desserts • some
veggie • $4-8

Kitchener   (519)

BARS

Club Renaissance 24 Charles St. W. •
570-2406 • lesbians/gay men •
dancing/DJ • wheelchair access

Club XTC 1 Queen St. N • 743-3016 • 9pm-2am • lesbians/gay men • dancing/DJ • wheelchair access

TRAVEL & TOUR OPERATORS

TCB Travel 600 Doon Village Rd. • 748-0850 • ask for Linda • IGTA member

London (519)

INFO LINES & SERVICES

AA Gay/Lesbian 649 Colborne (at Halo Club) • 453-1308 • 7pm Mon & Wed

Gay Line • 433-3551 • live 7pm-10pm Mon & Th • taped info

UW Out • 432-3078 • 7:30pm-10pm Mon • lesbigay student group

BARS

52nd Street 347 Clarence St. • 679-4015 • 2pm-2am • lesbians/gay men • dancing/DJ • patio in summer • wheelchair access

Halo Club (Gay/Lesbian Community Center) 649 Colborne • 433-3762 • lesbians/gay men • dancing/DJ • live shows • private club • last Fri women only • wheelchair access • call for community center events • also monthly newsletter

Lacy's 355 Talbot St. • 645-3197 • 2pm-1am • mostly gay men • dancing/DJ • more women Fri

RESTAURANTS & CAFES

Blackfriars Cafe 46 Blackfriars • 667-4930 • 10am-10pm • popular • lesbians/gay men • plenty veggie • full bar • $4-10

BOOKSTORES & RETAIL SHOPS

Mystic Book Shop 616 Dundas St. • 673-5440 • 10am-6pm • wheelchair access

Womansline Books 711 Richmond St. • 679-3416 • 10am-5:30pm, til 6pm Fri, clsd Sun • lesbian/feminist

SPIRITUAL GROUPS

MCC 442 Williams St. • 645-0744 • 7:20pm Sun

Maynooth (613)

ACCOMMODATIONS

Wildewood Box 121, K0L 2S0 • 338-3134 • lesbians/gay men • hot tub • swimming • located on 20 acres • all meals included • wheelchair access

North Bay (705)

INFO LINES & SERVICES

Gay Nipissing Box 1362, P1B 8K5 • 495-4545 • social & support group • newsletter • wheelchair access

Oshawa (905)

BARS

Club 717 7-717 Wilson Rd. S. • 434-4297 • 2pm-2am Sat only • lesbians/gay men • also referral service • wheelchair access

Ottawa (613)

INFO LINES & SERVICES

237-XTRA • 237-9872 • touch-tone lesbian/gay visitor's info

ALGO Center 318 Lisger • 233-0152 • coffeehouse Fri • women's bar Sat • call for hours

Gayline Télégai • 238-1717 • 7:30pm-10:30pm, 6pm-9pm Fri-Sun

Lambda Line • 233-8212 • business/professional group

Pink Triangle Services 71 Back St. (above McDonald's) • 563-4818 • 1pm-5pm Mon & Wed • many groups & services

Women's Place 241 Bruyere St. • 789-2155 • 9am-4pm Mon-Th • info • referrals • drop-in center

ACCOMMODATIONS

Rideau View Inn 177 Frank St. • 236-9309/ (800) 268-2082 • gay-friendly • full breakfast

The Stonehouse B&B 2605 Yorks Corners • 821-3822 • lesbians/gay men • full breakfast

BARS

Centretown Pub 340 Somerset St. W. • 594-0233 • 2pm-1am • lesbians/gay men • dancing/DJ • live shows • leather bar upstairs • also piano bar downstairs • Th-Sat

Coral Reef Club 30 Nicholas • 234-5118 • Fri-Sat only • lesbians/gay men • dancing/DJ • more women Fri

Grrrlz on Top 123 Queen St. (upstairs) • 8pm-1am Sat only

Le Club 77 Wellington, Hull • (819) 777-1411 • 10pm-3am • popular • lesbians/gay men • dancing/DJ

Market Station 15 George St. (downstairs) • 562-3540 • noon-1am, 11am Sun (brunch) • lesbians/gay men • neighborhood bar

RESTAURANTS & CAFES

Alfonsetti's 5830 Hazeldern, Stittsville • 831-3008 • noon-11pm, from 5pm Sat, clsd Sun • Italian • plenty veggie • $12-22

Blue Moon Cafe 311 Bank • 230-1239 • 10am-midnight • lesbians/gay men • French • veggie on request • $5-15

Cafe Deluxe 283 Dalhousie St. • 241-4646 • 4pm-1am, from noon wknds • $10-13

Manfred's 2280 Carling Ave. • 829-5715 • European • some veggie • full bar • $10-16

The News 284 Elgin • 567-6397 • noon-midnight • cont'l • some veggie • $6-18

BOOKSTORES & RETAIL SHOPS

After Stonewall 105 4th Ave., 2nd flr. • 567-2221 • 10am-6pm, til 7pm Fri, noon-4pm Sun • lesbigay bookstore

Food for Thought Books 103 Clarence St. • 562-4599 • 10am-9pm

Octopus Books 798 Bank St. • 235-2589 • 10am-6pm, til 9pm Th-Fri, clsd Sun • progressive bookstore

Ottawa Women's Bookstore 272 Elgin St. • 230-1156 • 10am-6pm, til 9pm Th-Fri, 11am-4pm Sun • wheelchair access

PUBLICATIONS

Capital Xtra! 303-177 Nepean St. • 237-7133

Labrys PO Box 81104, K1P 1A5 • 237-6150

Port Sydney   (705)

ACCOMMODATIONS

Divine Lake Resort • 385-1212/ (800) 263-6600 • lesbians/gay men • resort • also cottages • breakfast & dinner included • swimming • nudity • also restaurant • some veggie • full bar • dancing/DJ • live shows

Stratford   (519)

ACCOMMODATIONS

Anything Goes B&B 107 Huron St. • 273-6557 • gay-friendly • full breakfast

Burnside Guest Home 139 William St. • 271-7076 • gay-friendly • full breakfast • hot tub • on Lake Victoria

Crackers & Antiques B&B 433 Erie St. • 273-1201 • gay-friendly • open May-Nov

The Maples of Stratford 220 Church St. • 273-0810 • gay-friendly • B&B • women-owned/run

BARS

Old English Parlour 101 Wellington St. • 271-2772 • noon-1am • gay-friendly • also a restaurant • some veggie • wheelchair access • $10-16

RESTAURANTS & CAFES

Down the Street 30 Ontario St. • 273-5886 • noon-11pm • Mediterranean/Mexican • full bar • live shows • $10-12

Sudbury   (705)

BARS

D-Bar 83 Cedar St. • 670-1189 • 8pm-1am • lesbians/gay men • dancing/DJ • live shows

Spinner's 63 Cedar St. • 670-0904 • 8pm-1am, til 3am Th-Sat • lesbians/gay men • neighborhood bar • dancing/DJ • food served • deli • wheelchair access

Thunder Bay   (807)

INFO LINES & SERVICES

Northern Women's Center 184 Camelot St. • 345-7802 • 9am-5pm Mon-Fri • wheelchair access

Toronto   (416)

INFO LINES & SERVICES

2 Spirited People of the 1st Nations 2 Carlton St. Ste. 1006 • 944-9300 • lesbigay native group

519 Church St. Community Center 519 Church St. • 392-6874 • 9:30am-10:30pm, noon-5pm wknds • info • referrals • location for numerous events • wheelchair access

925-XTRA 925-9872 • touch-tone lesbian/gay visitors info

AA Gay/Lesbian • 487-5591 • extensive schedule

Canadian Lesbian/Gay Archives 86 Temperance St. • 777-2755 • 7pm-9pm Tue-Th, 1pm-5pm Fri

Durham Alliance Association PO Box 914 , Oshawa, L1H 7H1 • 434-4297 • info & social group

Flashline • 462-7540 • DJ Denise Benson's women's event line

Toronto Area Gay/Lesbian Phone Line • 964-6600 • 7pm-10pm Mon-Fri

Women's Center 49 St. George St. (Univ. of Toronto) • 978-8201 • pro-lesbian center • call for times

Women's Counseling Referral Center 525 Bloor St. W. • 534-7501

ACCOMMODATIONS

Acorn House B&B 255 Donlands Ave. • 463-8274 • mostly gay men

Allenby B&B 223 Strathmore Blvd. • 461-7095 • gay-friendly

Amblecote B&B 109 Walmer Rd. • 927-1713 • lesbians/gay men • full breakfast • IGTA member

Burken Guest House 322 Palmerston Blvd. • 920-7842 • popular • gay-friendly • IGTA member

Catnaps Guesthouse 246 Sherbourne St. • 968-2323/ (800) 205-3694 • lesbians/gay men

Hotel Selby 592 Sherbourne St. • 921-3142/ (800) 387-4788 • popular • gay-friendly • Victorian tourist class hotel • 67 rooms & suites (some w/ fireplace) • swimming • IGTA member

Mike's on Mutual 333 Mutual St. • 944-2611 • mostly gay men • full breakfast • no smoking

Seaton Pretty 327 Seaton St. • 972-1485 • gay-friendly • full breakfast

Toronto Bed & Breakfast • 588-8800 • gay-friendly • contact for various B&Bs

Winchester Guesthouse 35 Winchester St. • 929-7949 • lesbians/gay men • hot tub

BARS

Aztec/Tango 2 Gloucester St. • 975-8612 • lesbians/gay men • dancing/DJ • Aztec dance club Th-Sun • Tango women's bar open from 4pm

Bar 501 501 Church • 944-3272 • 11am-1am • lesbians/gay men • neighborhood bar • more women Sun & Tue

Toronto (416)

LESBIGAY INFO: 519 Church St. Community Center: 392-6874, 519 Church St. Toronto Area Gay/Lesbian Phone Line: 964-6600, 7pm-10pm Mon-Fri. Xtra! Gay/Lesbian Info Line: 925-9872 (touchtone info).

LESBIGAY PAPER: Xtra!: 925-6665.

WHERE THE GIRLS ARE: On Parliament St. or elsewhere in "The Ghetto," south of Bloor St. W., between University Ave. and Parliament St.

LESBIGAY AA: 487-5591.

LESBIGAY PRIDE: July, 214-0232.

CITY INFO: 203-2500.

BEST VIEW: Sightseeing air tour or a three-masted sailing ship tour.

WEATHER: Summers are hot (upper 80°s - 90°s) and humid. Spring is gorgeous. Fall brings cool, crisp days. And winters are cold and snowy just like you imagined winters would be in Canada!

TRANSIT: Metro Cab: 364-8161. Grey Coach: 393-7911. Transit Information: 393-4636.

Boots & Bud's/Backbar (at Hotel Selby) • 921-0665 • noon-1am • popular • mostly gay men • dancing/DJ • leather • live shows • videos • 2 bars • patio • wheelchair access

Bulldog Cafe 457 Church St. • 923-3469 • noon-2am • lesbians/gay men • neighborhood bar • also a restaurant • homecooking • $8-12

Catch 22 379 Adelgide St. W. • 703-1583 • 9pm-2am, clsd Sun-Tue • gay-friendly • dancing/DJ

El Convento Rico 750 College St. • 588-7800 • 8pm-3am Wed-Sun • mostly gay men • dancing/DJ • mostly Latino-American • live shows • Latin/salsa music

Keith's Sports Bar & Grill 619 Yonge St., 2nd flr. • 922-3068 • 11am-1am • mostly gay men • neighborhood bar

Oz 15 Mercer St. • 506-8686 • clsd Tue • lesbians/gay men • dancing/DJ • women's night Fri • call for events

The Playground 11-A St. Joseph St. • 923-2595 • 12:30am-4am, from 11pm Fri-Sat, clsd Mon • lesbians/gay men • dancing/DJ

Rose Cafe 547 Parliament • 928-1495 • 5pm-1am • mostly women • dancing/DJ • food served • some veggie • women-owned/run • $5-10

Trax V 529 Yonge St. • 963-5196 • 11am-1am • popular • mostly gay men • piano bar • wheelchair access

Whiskey Saigon 250 Richmond • 593-4646 • 10pm-2am Th-Sun • lesbians/gay men • dancing/DJ

RESTAURANTS & CAFES

Archer's 796 St. Clair Ave. W. • 656-7335 • 5:30pm-10pm, clsd Mon • fixed cont'l menu • $15-up

Bemelman's Restaurant & Bar 83 Bloor St. W. • 960-0306 • 11am-1am • some veggie • $4-14

Bistro 422 422 College St. • 963-9416 • 4pm-midnight

Byzantium 499 Church St. • 922-3859 • 5:30pm-1am • lesbians/gay men • eastern Mediterranean • full bar

Cafe Diplomatico 594 College • 534-4637 • 8am-1am • popular • breakfast • in the center of Little Italy • patio

Toronto

*T*oronto, the capital city of Ontario, is the cultural and financial center of eastern Canada. Though it's not far from Buffalo, New York and Niagara Falls, Toronto has a European ambiance fostered by its eclectic architecture and peaceful diversity of cultures. Restaurants and shops from Asia, India, Europe and many other points on the globe attract natives and tourists alike to the exotic **Kensington Market** (buy your fresh groceries here). Toronto's Chinatown is just north of funky shops and artsy cafes on Queen St. West.

Toronto is also well-known for its repertory film scene, so try not to miss the two-week **Lesbian Gay Film Fest** in the spring, or the film **Festival of Festivals** in September. On Christmas Eve, get a seat at the MCC's (406-6228) annual service – the largest in the city!

Any other time of year, you'll find the women hanging out at **The Playground, Catch 22** or **OZ**. To figure out the latest women's nights, check out the weekly **Xtra!**, available at the **Toronto Women's Bookstore**, among other places.

The Courtyard (at Hotel Selby) • 921-0665 • open May-Sept • lesbians/gay men • outdoor patio • BBQ • full bar

La Hacienda 640 Queen W. • 703-3377 • lunch & dinner • Mexican • sleazy & fun

The Living Well 692 Yonge St. • 922-6770 • noon-1am, til 3am Fri-Sat • cont'l • plenty veggie • full bar • $8-12

The Mango 580 Church St. • 922-6525 • popular • lesbians/gay men • also Sun brunch • patio

Pints 518 Church St. • 921-8142 • 11:30am-1am • plenty veggie • $6-8

PJ Mellon's 489 Church St. • 966-3241 • 11am-11pm • lesbians/gay men • Thai/cont'l • some veggie • wheelchair access • $7-12

Raclette Restaurant & Wine Bar 361 Queen St. W. • 593-0934 • clsd Sun • Swiss fondue & raclette • some veggie • $10-15

Rivoli Cafe 332 Queen St. W. • 597-0794 • 11:30am-11pm, bar til 1am • international • some veggie • $8-12

The Second Cup 548 Church St. (Wellesley) • 964-2457 • 24hrs • popular • coffee/desserts

Soho Bistro 339 Queen St. W. • 977-3362 • 11am-3am, 5pm-11pm, from 5pm Sun • cont'l • some veggie • full bar • $8-12

Volo Cafe 587 Yonge St. • 928-0008 • 11am-10pm, bar til 1am • Italian • some veggie • $9-13

BOOKSTORES & RETAIL SHOPS

Ex Libris 467 Church St., 2nd flr. • 975-0580 • 11am-9pm, til 6pm Wed, Sat & Sun • new & used lesbigay bookstore

Glad Day Bookshop 598-A Yonge St. • 961-4161 • 10am-9pm, til 7pm Sat, noon-6pm Sun • lesbigay bookstore

Out in the Street 551 Church St. • 967-2759/ (800) 263-5747 • lesbigay accessories

This Ain't The Rosedale Library 483 Church St. • 929-9912 • 10am-7pm

Toronto Women's Bookstore 73 Harbord St. • 922-8744 • 10:30am-6pm, til 7pm Fri, noon-5pm Sun • wheelchair access

Urban Primitives 473 Church St. • 929-7330 • 11am-7pm • tatoos • piercing • scarification

TRAVEL & TOUR OPERATORS

La Fabula Travel & Tours Inc. 551 Church St. • 920-3229/ (800) 667-2475 • IGTA member

Talk of the Town Travel 565 Sherbourne St. • 960-1393 • IGTA member

PUBLICATIONS

The Pink Pages 392 King St. E. • 864-9132 • annual • lesbigay directory

▲ **Sorority Magazine** 1170 Bay St. Ste. 110 • 324-2225 • quarterly • lesbian publication for Canada & US • see ad in front color section

Women's Press 517 College St. Ste. 233 • 921-2425 • lesbian/feminist book publisher • catalog available

Xtra! 100 Wellesley St. E. #104 • 925-6665 • monthly • also Xtra West-Vancouver • (604) 684-9696 • also Capitol Xtra-Ottawa • (613) 237-7133

EROTICA

North Bound Leather 19 St. Nicholas St. • 972-1037 • 10am-6pm, noon-5pm Sun • toys • clothing

Priape 465 Church St. • 586-9914 • 11am-7pm

Trenton   (613)

ACCOMMODATIONS

Devonshire House B&B RR #4 (Hwy. 2) • 394-4572 • gay-friendly w/ lesbian following • full breakfast • Italianate-style red brick farmhouse circa 1875 • on 18 acres

Whitby   (905)

BARS

The Bar 110 Dundas St. W. • 666-3121 • 8pm-1am, til 3am Fri-Sat, clsd Mon-Tue • lesbians/gay men • dancing/DJ

Windsor   (519)

INFO LINES & SERVICES

Lesbian/Gay Phone Line • 973-4951 • 8pm-10pm Mon (women), Th-Fri (men)

BARS

Club Happy Tap Tavern 1056 Wyandotte St. E. • 256-8998 • 2pm-1am, from 4pm Sun • lesbians/gay men • dancing/DJ • more women Sun • wheelchair access

Silhouettes 1880 Wyandotte St. E. • 252-0887 • 4pm-1am, from 11am wknds • lesbians/gay men • neighborhood bar • also a restaurant • different meaty entres nightly & Sun brunch

Prince Edward Island

Charlottetown (902)

INFO LINES & SERVICES

Lesbian/Gay Hotline • 566-9733 • 7pm-10pm Wed (women), 7pm-10pm Th (men)

Women's Network Box 233, C1A 7K4 • 368-5040 • info & resources • also publishes feminist magazine 'Common Ground'

ACCOMMODATIONS

Blair Hall Vernon Bridge • 651-2202/ (800) 268-7005 • gay-friendly • full breakfast • home w/ old world charm situated on Orwell Bay 15 min. out of town

Charlottetown Hotel 75 Kent St. • 894-7371 • gay-friendly • swimming • also a restaurant • cont'l/seafood • lounge clsd Sun • $10-25

BARS

Baba's Lounge 81 University Ave. • 892-7377 • 5pm-2am • gay-friendly • also a restaurant • opens at 11am • Canadian/Lebanese • some veggie

Doc's Corner 185 Kent St. • 566-1069 • 11am-2am • gay-friendly • live shows • also Hillard's Dining Room • some veggie • $10-20

BOOKSTORES & RETAIL SHOPS

Book Mark 172 Queen St. (in mall) • 566-4888 • 9am-5pm, til 9pm Th-Fri • will order lesbian titles

PUBLICATIONS

Gynergy Books/Ragweed Press Box 2023, C1A 7N7 • 566-5750 • feminist press

Summerside (902)

INFO LINES & SERVICES

East Prince Women's Info Center 75 Central St. • 436-9856 • 9am-4pm Mon-Fri

Québec

Drummondville (819)

INFO LINES & SERVICES

Women's Resource (Maison des Femmes) 102 rue St-George • 477-5957 • some lesbian info

BARS

Bar le Chariot 1110 rue Montplaisir • 472-4684 • 8pm-3am, clsd Mon-Tue • gay-friendly • dancing/DJ

IDEM 1895 boul. Mercure • 477-0988 • 3pm-2am • lesbians/gay men • dancing/DJ • cafe • patio

Hull (613)

BARS

Le Club 77 rue Wellington • 777-1411 • 10pm-3am • popular • lesbians/gay men • dancing/DJ

Le Pub de Promenade 175 Promenade de Portage • 771-8810 • 11am-3am • lesbians/gay men • neighborhood bar • dancing/DJ

Joliette (514)

ACCOMMODATIONS

L'Oasis des Pins 381 boul. Brassard, St. Paul de Joliette • 754-3819 • gay-friendly • swimming • camping April-Sept. • restaurant open year-round

Lac-des-Plages (819)

ACCOMMODATIONS

L'Auvent Bleu 6 Chemin Vendee • 687-2981 • gay-friendly • full breakfast • B&B on the Maskinonge river

Magog (819)

RESTAURANTS & CAFES

Chez Jean Pierre 112 rue Principle ouest • 843-8166 • 5:30pm-9:30pm, clsd Mon • nouvelle French

Mont-Tremblant (819)

ACCOMMODATIONS

Versant Ouest B&B 110 Chemin Labelle • 425-6615/ (800) 425-6615 • lesbians/gay men • full breakfast • country home near skiing

Montréal (514)

INFO LINES & SERVICES

AA Gay/Lesbian • 376-9230

Gai Ecoute • 521-1508 • 7pm-11pm • gay info line 'en français'

Gay Line • 990-1414 • 6:30pm-10pm

Gay/Lesbian Community Center of Montréal 2035 Amherst St. • 528-8424 • 10am-10pm, til 5pm Sat, clsd Sun

Women's Center of Montréal 3585 St-Urbain • 842-4780 • 9am-5pm Mon, Wed-Fri, til 9pm Tue • wheelchair access

WOMEN'S ACCOMMODATIONS

La Douillette 7235 de Lorimier St. • 376-2183 • women only • full breakfast • cat on premises • $40-60

Le Pension Vallieres 6562 de Lorimier St. • 729-9552 • mostly women • B&B • full breakfast • $50-60

▲ **Lindsey's Bed & Breakfast** 3974 Laval Ave. • 843-4869 • women only • full breakfast • $55-75

Ronnie's B&B 781 rue Guy • 939-1443 • women only

ACCOMMODATIONS

Au Bon Vivant Guest House 1648 Amherst • 525-7744 • popular • lesbians/gay men • IGTA member

Auberge de la Fontaine 1301 Rachel St. est • 597-0166/ (800) 597-0597 • gay-friendly • full breakfast • wheelchair access

Canadian Accommodations Network Box 42-A Stn. M, H1Z 3L6 • 254-1250 • lesbians/gay men • accommodation reservation service

Chateau Cherrier 550 Cherrier St. • 844-0055/ (800) 816-0055 • April-Nov • lesbians/gay men • full gourmet breakfast

Hotel le St-Andre 1285 rue St-Andre • 849-7070 • gay-friendly

Hotel Lord Berri 1199 rue Berri • 845-9236/ (800) 363-0363 • gay-friendly • also a restaurant • Italian/cont'l • wheelchair access

Hotel Pierre 169 Sherbrooke est • 288-8519 • gay-friendly w/ lesbian following

Hotel Vogue 1425 rue de la Montagne • 285-5555/ (800) 465-6654 • popular • gay-friendly • also a restaurant • full service upscale hotel

Lindsey's
Bed & Breakfast
for women

3974 Laval Ave.
Montréal, Canada H2W 2J2
514-843-4869

1887 renovated Victorian townhouse walking distance to central downtown area, universities, conference centres, museums and galleries, Mont Royal and Old Montréal.

Close to cafés, restaurants, and teriffic shopping on Rue St. Denis & Boulevard St. Laurent.

Choose from private studio with bath & kitchenette or from one of two upstairs bedrooms that share a Victorian bathroom complete with four-poster tub.

Le Chasseur Guest House 1567 rue St-André • 521-2238 • popular • lesbians/gay men • European townhouse of the '20s • summer terrace • cont'l breakfast

Lesbian/Gay Hospitality Exchange International PO Box 612, Stn. C, H2L 4K5

Turquoise 1576 rue Alexandre de Seve • 523-9943 • gay-friendly • shared baths

BARS

Bistro 4 4040 St-Laurent (Duluth) • 844-6246 • gay-friendly • cafe

Campus 1111 Ste-Catherine est, 2nd flr. • 526-9867 • 7pm-3am • mostly gay men • live shows • women's night Sun

Citibar 1603 Ontario est • 525-4251 • 11am-3am • lesbians/gay men • neighborhood bar

City Pub 3820 St-Laurent • 499-8519 • 11am-3am • gay-friendly • beer/wine • food served

K.O.X. 1450 Ste-Catherine est • 523-0064 • 3pm-3am • popular • lesbians/gay men • dancing/DJ

L' Exit 4297 St-Denis • 2pm-2am • women only • neighborhood bar • beer only

La California 1412 Ste-Elizabeth • 843-8533 • 3pm-1am • popular • lesbians/gay men • neighborhood bar • also a restaurant • patio

Lézard 4177 St-Denis & Rachel, 2nd flr. • 289-9819 • 11pm-3am • gay-friendly • dancing/DJ • eclectic crowd • more gay Tue

NaNa Pub 1364 Ste-Catherine, 2nd flr. • 523-9325 • 2pm-3am • popular • mostly women • patio

Paco Paco 451 Rachel est • 499-0210 • lesbians/gay men • neighborhood bar

Sky 1474 Ste-Catherine est • 522-2475 • 10am-3am • popular • lesbians/gay men • dancing/DJ • alternative • more women Th

Women's Side 4075-B St-Denis • 849-7126 • 11am-2am • mostly women • neighborhood bar • also a restaurant

RESTAURANTS & CAFES

Après le Jour 901 Rachel est • 527-4141 • Italian/seafood

Montréal (514)

LESBIGAY INFO: Centre Communautaire des Gais et Lesbiennes: 528-8424. Gay Line: 931-8668, 7pm-11pm, 9am-5pm. Women's Center of Montréal: 842-4780, 9am-5pm.

LESBIGAY PAPER: Fugues: 848-1854. Gazelle: 933-5673.

WHERE THE GIRLS ARE: In the popular Plateau Mont-Royal neighborhood, or in the bohemian area on Ste-Catherine est.

LESBIGAY AA: 529-0015.

LESBIGAY PRIDE: July, 285-4011.

ANNUAL EVENTS: October 5 - Black & Blue Party: (514) 875-7026, AIDS benefit dance.

CITY INFO: Province of Québec Visitors Bureau: (800) 363-7777.

BEST VIEW: From a caleche ride (horse-drawn carriage), or from the patio of the old hunting lodge atop Mont Royal (the mountain in Parc du Mont-Royal).

WEATHER: It's north of New England so winters are for real. Beautiful spring and fall colors. Summers get hot and humid.

TRANSIT: Diamond Cab: 273-6331.

Callipyge 1493 Amherst • 522-6144 • 5pm-11pm, clsd Mon-Tue • popular • Quebecois cuisine • popular Sun brunch

Cantarelli 2181 Ste-Caterine est • 521-1817 • Italian

Chablis 1639 St-Hubert • 523-0053 • Spaninsh/French • some veggie • patio

Chez Better 1310 De Maisonneuve • 525-9832 • European sausages/great french fries • patio

Commensal 400 Sherbrooke est (St-Denis) • vegetarian

Da Salossi 3441 St-Denis • 843-8995 • Italian • some veggie

Jardin du Me-Kong 1330 Ste-Catherine • 523-6635 • Vietnamese • some veggie

L' Anecdote I 801 Rachel est • 526-7967 • lesbians/gay men • some veggie

L' Anecdote II 3751 St-Urbain & Pine • 282-0972 • mostly women • burgers/snacks

L' Express 3927 St-Denis • 845-5333 • 8am-3am • French bistro & bar • great pâté

L' Un & L' Autre 1641 rue Amherst • 597-0878 • 11am-1am, from 5pm wknds • bistro • full bar

La Campagnola 1229 rue de la Montagne • 866-3234 • popular • Italian • some veggie • great eggplant! • $12-20

La Paryse 302 Ontario est • 842-2040 • 11am-11pm • hamburgers/sandwiches • some veggie

Lux 5220 boul. St-Laurent • 271-9272 • 24hrs • mostly women

Paganini 1819 Ste-Catherine • 844-3031 • 11:30am-midnight • popular • lesbians/gay men • Italian • some veggie

Pizzédélic 1329 rue Ste-Catherine est • 526-6011 • noon-midnight • pizzerria • some veggie • also 3509 boul. St-Laurent • 282-6784 • also 370 Laurier ouest • 948-6290

Saloon Cafe 1333 Ste-Catherine est • 522-1333 • 11am-1am, til 3am Fri-Sat • popular • burgers

GYMS & HEALTH CLUBS

Physotech 1657 Amherst • 527-7587 • lesbians/gay men

BOOKSTORES & RETAIL SHOPS

L' Androgyne 3636 boul. St-Laurent • 842-4765 • 9am-6pm, til 9pm Th-Fri • lesbigay bookstore • wheelchair access

Montréal

*M*ontréal is the world's second-largest French-speaking city, and Canada's most cosmopolitan city. There is much to see and do here. You'll discover the **Place Ville-Marie**, an immense underground shopping promenade. Visit the Latin Quarter and Old Montréal, or come during the **World Film Festival** (end of August), or bike the cycling paths along the river banks.

Montréal also has a strong women's community, with four women's guesthouses, several women's bars, a lesbian/gay bookstore and a variety of women's services through the **Women's Center**. Then there's the mixed bars with women's nights.

Just remember that the people of Montréal are proud of their French heritage and language. So brush up on your high school French before you go, if you want to make friends and avoid embarrassment. If you don't speak any French, your first question to any natives should be, "Do you speak English?"

TRAVEL & TOUR OPERATORS

Gayroute CP 1036-G, Stn. C, H2L 4V3 • tours of 'Gay Canada' • send $2 + SASE for more info

SPIRITUAL GROUPS

Dignity 3484 Peel • 398-9031 • 7:30pm Mon

PUBLICATIONS

Fugues/Gazelle 1212 St-Hubert • 848-1854 • monthly

Le Guide Gai du Québec/Insiders Guide to Gay Quebec CP 5245 , H2X 3M4 • 523-9463 • annual guide book

EROTICA

Cuir Plus 1321 Ste-Catherine est • 521-7587 • 11am-6pm • leather • sex toys • wheelchair access

Priape 1311 Ste-Catherine est • 521-8451 • open 10am, from noon Sun • erotic gay material

Pointe au Pic   (418)

ACCOMMODATIONS

Auberge Mona 212 rue du Quai • 665-6793 • gay-friendly • women-owned/run

Prevost   (514)

BARS

Le Secret 3029 boul. Labelle (at Hotel Up North, Rte. 117 N.) • 224-7350 • 9pm-3am • lesbians/gay men • dancing/DJ • live shows

Québec   (418)

ACCOMMODATIONS

727 Guest House 727 rue d'Aquillon • 648-6766 • lesbians/gay men

Bed & Breakfast in Old Québec City 35 rue des Remparts • 655-7685 • gay-friendly • restored monastery w/ apts available • elegant ancestral home

Hotel la Maison Doyon 109 rue Ste-Anne • 694-1720 • gay-friendly

Le Coureur des Bois Guest House 15 rue Ste-Ursule • 692-1117 • lesbians/gay men • expanded cont'l breakfast

BARS

Bar L' Eveil 710 rue Bouvier Ste. 120 • 628-0610 • 11am-3am • lesbians/gay men • neighborhood bar

Fausse Alarme 161 rue St-Jean • 529-0277 • 4pm-3am (from 11am summers) • mostly gay men • neighborhood bar

L'Amour Sorcier 789 Côte Ste-Genevieve • 523-3395 • 11am-3am, from 9am wknds • popular • lesbians/gay men • neighborhood bar • videos • terrace

La Ballon Rouge 811 rue St-Jean • 647-9227 • 10pm-3am • popular • mostly gay men • dancing/DJ

Studio 157 157 Chemin Ste-Foy • 529-9958 • 10pm-3am Wed-Sat • popular • mostly women • dancing/DJ • live shows

Taverne Le Draque 815 rue St-Augustin • 649-7212 • 8am-3am • lesbians/gay men • neighborhood bar • wheelchair access

RESTAURANTS & CAFES

Le Commensal 860 rue St-Jean • 647-3733 • vegetarian

Le Hobbit 700 rue St-Jean • 647-2677 • opens 7:30am • some veggie

Restaurant Diana 849 rue St-Jean • 524-5794 • 8am-1am, 24hrs Fri-Sat • popular

Zorba Grec 853 St-Jean • 525-5509 • 8am-5pm • Greek • wheelchair access

Rimouski   (418)

INFO LINES & SERVICES

Maison des Femmes de Rimouski 78 Ste-Marie #2 • 723-0333 • 9am-noon, 3pm-7pm Mon-Fri • women's resource center

Rivière Du Loupe   (418)

BARS

Disco Jet rue Lafontaine • 862-6308 • 3pm-3am, clsd Mon-Tue • gay-friendly • dancing/DJ

Sherbrooke   (819)

RESTAURANTS & CAFES

Au Pot au Vin 40 rue King est • 562-8882 • lunch & dinner

St-Donat   (819)

ACCOMMODATIONS

Havre du Parc Auberge 2788 Rte. 125 N. • 424-7686 • gay-friendly • full breakfast • quiet lakeside inn

Trois Rivières (819)

INFO LINES & SERVICES

Gay Ami CP 1152, G9A 5K1 • 373-0771 • lesbigay social contacts

BARS

La Maison Blanche #3 767 St-Maurice • 379-4233 • 9pm-3am • lesbians/gay men • dancing/DJ • live shows

Verdun (514)

INFO LINES & SERVICES

Centre des Femmes de Verdun 4255 rue Wellington • 767-0384 • 9am-noon, 1pm-4pm • general women's center • limited lesbian info

Saskatchewan

Moose Jaw (306)

INFO LINES & SERVICES

Lesbian/Gay Committee • 692-2418 • social/support group

Ravenscrag (306)

ACCOMMODATIONS

Spring Valley Guest Ranch Box 10, S0N 0T0 • 295-4124 • popular • gay-friendly • 1913 character home, cabin & tipis • also a restaurant • country-style

Regina (306)

INFO LINES & SERVICES

Gay/Lesbian Live & Let Live AA 2900 13th Ave. • 7:30pm Sat (ring buzzer)

Lavender Social Club Box 671, S4P 3A3

Pink Triangle Community Services 24031 Broad St. • 525-6046

Regina Women's Community Center 2505 11th Ave. #306 • 522-2777 • 9am-4:30pm Mon-Fri

BARS

Scarth St. Station 1422 Scarth St. • 522-7343 • 8pm-2am, 6pm-midnight Sun • lesbians/gay men • dancing/DJ • live shows

SPIRITUAL GROUPS

Dignity Regina Box 3181, S4P 3G7 • 569-3666 • 6:30pm 3rd Sun

Koinonia 3913 Hillsdale Ave. • 525-8542 • 7pm 2nd & 4th Sun • interfaith worship • wheelchair access

Saskatoon (306)

INFO LINES & SERVICES

Gay/Lesbian AA • 665-6727 • also call Gay/Lesbian Line for schedule

Gay/Lesbian Line • 665-1224 • noon-4:30pm & 7:30pm-10:30pm, clsd Sun

ACCOMMODATIONS

Brighton House 1308 5th Ave. N. • 664-3278 • gay-friendly • wheelchair access • lesbian-owned/run

Bars

Diva's 220 3rd Ave. S. Ste. 110 (alley entrance) • 665-0100 • 8pm-2am, clsd Mon • lesbians/gay men • dancing/DJ • private club

Bookstores & Retail Shops

Cafe Browse 269-B 3rd Ave. S. • 664-2665 • 10am-11pm, from 1pm Sun

Out of the Closet 241 2nd Ave S., 3rd flr. • 665-1224 • lesbigay materials

Whole Earth Store 1984 Ltd. 133 3rd Ave. N. • 652-0977 • 9:30am-5:30pm, til 9pm Th • cards • gifts • imports

Spiritual Groups

Dignity Saskatoon PO Box 7283, S7K 4S2

Publications

Perceptions Box 8581, S7K 6K7 • covers western Canada

Yukon

Whitehorse   (403)

Info Lines & Services

Gay/Lesbian Alliance of the Yukon Territory PO Box 5604, Y1A 5H4 • 667-7857

Victoria Faulkner Women's Center 404-A Ogilvie • 667-2693 • 11am-6pm Mon-Fri • wheelchair access

Costa Rica

Playas Manuel Antonio
(506)

ACCOMMODATIONS

El Colibri • 77-04-32 • gay-friendly

The Vela Bar • 77-04-13 • gay-friendly

BARS

Mar y Sombra 1st Beach • popular • lesbians/gay men • dancing/DJ • roaming 'Discomovil' • inquire locally

Puntarenas

BARS

La Deriva • gay-friendly

Quepos
(506)

ACCOMMODATIONS

Casa Blanca apdo. 194, Entrada la Mariposas • 777-0253 • popular • mostly gay men • swimming

The Hotel Casa Blanca apdo. 194 Entrada La Mariposas, 6350 • 777-0253 • lesbians/gay men • swimming • walking distance to gay beach

San Jose
(506)

INFO LINES & SERVICES

Centro Feminista de Intercambio Cultural (at Casa Yemaya) • 223-3652

WOMEN'S ACCOMMODATIONS

Casa Yemaya • 223-3652 • women only • 3-story lodge • private & dorm-style rooms • conference space • Spanish classes • internships available • call or fax for directions

ACCOMMODATIONS

Colours - The Guest Residence El Triangulo, Blvd. Rohrmoser • 32-35-04/ (800) 934-5622/(305) 532-9341 (US & Canada) • popular • lesbians/gay men • swimming • premier full-service accommodations w/ tours & reservation services throughout Costa Rica

Hotel L'Ambiance 949 Calle 27 • 23-15-98 • gay-friendly • no visitors allowed in rooms • courtyard • also restaurant & bar

Joluva Guesthouse Calle 3 B, Aves. 9 & 11 #936 • 223-7961/ (800) 298-2418 • lesbians/gay men

Plaza Avenida Central between Calles 2 & 4 • 22-55-33 • gay-friendly

Scotland Apartments Ave. 1 Calle 27 • 23-08-33 • gay-friendly • rental apts

BARS

Antros Ave. 14 between Calle 7 & 9 • gay-friendly

Cuartel de la Boca del Monte Ave. 1 between Calles 19 & 21 • gay-friendly

De Ja Vu Calle 2 between Ave. 14 & 16 • 8pm-?, from 9pm Fri-Sat, clsd Mon • popular • gay-friendly

El Churro Español Calle 11 between 8 & 10 (knock on the door) • gay-friendly

La Avispa Calle 1 between Ave. 8 & 10, #834 (no name outside, knock on door) • clsd Mon • mostly women • Wed women's night

La Esmeralda Ave. Segunda between Calles 5 & 7 • lesbians/gay men • live shows • food served

La Taberna Ave. 7 between Calles Central & 1 • 6pm-midnight • mostly gay men • quiet bar for friends

Los Cucharones Ave. 6 between Calles Central & 1st (no name outside, listen for music) • opens 8pm, clsd Mon-Tue • lesbians/gay men

Monte Carlo Ave. 4 & Calle 2 (on corner) • gay-friendly

Unicoronio Ave. 8 between Calles 1 & 3 • 7pm-midnight • mostly women

RESTAURANTS & CAFES

El Balcon de Europa Calle 9 between Ave. Central & 1st • gay-friendly • Italian

La Perla Calle Central Ave. 2 (on corner)

La Piazetta Paseo Colon • Italian • $18

Manchu Pichu off Paseo Colon • Peruvian seafood • just out of downtown • $18

TRAVEL & TOUR OPERATORS

Amatirasu Tours • 223-3652/ 257-8529 • women only & gay men • tours & reservations service

PUBLICATIONS

Confidencial c/o Publicaciones Unicornio, Apartado, Curridabat • 601-2300 • monthly

Dominican Republic

Santo Domingo   (809)

ACCOMMODATIONS

Hotel David Arzobispo Novel 308, Zona Colonial • 688-8538 • gay-friendly

BARS

Pariguayso Calle Padre Billini #412 • 682-2735 • lesbians/gay men

The Penthouse Calle Saibo & 20th St. (difficult to find) • Th-Sat • popular • lesbians/gay men • dancing/DJ

RESTAURANTS & CAFES

Cafe Coco Calle Sanchez 153 • 687-9624 • noon-10pm • small English restaurant • full bar

Le Pousse Cafe 107 19 de Marzo • popular • lesbians/gay men • dancing/DJ

French West Indies

St. Barthelemy   (590)

ACCOMMODATIONS

Hostellerie Des 3 Forces • 27-61-25/ (800) 932-3222 • popular • gay-friendly • swimming • food served • mountaintop new age/metaphysical retreat/inn • IGTA member

Hotel Normandie • 27-62-37 • gay-friendly

St. Bart's Beach Hotel Grand Cul de Sac • 27-60-70 • gay-friendly

BARS

American Bar Gustavia • gay-friendly • food served

Le Sélect Gustavia • 27-86-87 • more gay after 11pm • gay-friendly

RESTAURANTS & CAFES

Eddie's Ghetto Gustavia • Creole

Newborn Restaurant Anse de Caye • 27-67-07 • French Creole

St. Martin   (590)

BARS

Pink Mango at Laguna Beach Hotel, Nettle Bay • 87-59-99 • 6pm-3am • popular • lesbians/gay men • dancing/DJ

Puerto Rico

Aguada   (809)

ACCOMMODATIONS

San Max PO Box 1294, 00602 • 868-2931 • lesbians/gay men • guesthouse & studio apt on beach • weekly rentals

BARS

Johnny's Bar Carretera 115 • lesbians/gay men • inquire at San Max accommodations for directions

Aguadilla   (809)

BARS

Carl's by the Sea Carretera Parque Colon • 882-2888 • opens 7pm, clsd Mon • mostly gay men • dancing/DJ • wheelchair access

Cabrojo

BARS

Rico's Hacienda La Esperanza Rd. 312 km. 3.5, Carbrojo • 2pm-midnight, til 1am Fri-Sat • mostly gay men • drag shows & dancing/DJ Sat

Caguas

BARS

Villa Camito Country Club off old Hwy. 3 (turn right at Cafe de los Pisos) • opens 6pm Fri-Sat, from 4pm Sun • popular • lesbians/gay men • live shows • food served

Isabela

BARS

Villa Ricomar 8 Calle Paz, Carretera 459, Barrio Jobos • opens 9pm Fri-Sat, from 6pm Sun • lesbians/gay men • dancing/DJ • live shows

Loiza

BARS

El Grillo (Cuquito's Place) Rio Grand Rd. • lesbians/gay men

Privacy
Café - Bar
Gay Beach
Redesigned Spaces
Continental Breakfast
Special Weekly Rates

Tropical Gardens
By The Ocean

OCEAN PARK BEACH INN
Calle Elena #3
San Juan • P. R. 00911
809 • 728 • 7418
(Phone & Fax)

1 • 800 • 292 • 9208

San German

BARS

Norman's Bar Carretera 318, Barrio Maresúa • lesbians/gay men • dancing/DJ • salsa & merengue

The World Upside Down Road 360 km. 1 • 892-7067 • 10pm-7am Wed, Fri-Sat • gay-friendly • dancing/DJ

San Juan　　　(809)

INFO LINES & SERVICES

CONCRA 112 Ave. Universidad, Santa Rita, Rio Piedras • 753-9443 • STD/HIV clinic • health care & referrals

ACCOMMODATIONS

Atlantic Beach Hotel 1 Calle Vendig, Condado • 721-6900 • popular • lesbians/gay men • also a restaurant • full bar • IGTA member

Casablanca Guest House 57 Caribe St., Condado • 722-7139 • popular • gay-friendly • 1 blk. to beach

Condado Inn 6 Condado Ave., Condado • 724-7145 • lesbians/gay men • guesthouse w/ terrace restaurant & lounge • near beach

▲ **Embassy Guest House** 1126 Seaview, Condado • 725-8284 • mostly gay men • across the street from beach

Gran Hotel El Convento 100 Christo St., Old San Juan • 723-9020/ (800) 468-2779 • popular • gay-friendly • swimming

L' Habitation Beach Guesthouse 1957 Calle Italia, Ocean Park • 727-2499 • mostly gay men • swimming • also a restaurant

La Condessa 2071 Cacique St. • 727-3698/ (800) 727-0491 • popular • gay-friendly • B&B • swimming • also a restaurant • full bar

Numero Uno on the Beach 1 Calle Santa Ana, Ocean Park • 726-5010 • popular • gay-friendly • swimming • also bar & grill • wheelchair access

▲ **Ocean Park Beach Inn** Calle Elena # 3, Ocean Park • 728-7418/ (800) 292-9208 • popular • lesbians/gay men • swimming • food served • two intimate buildings around a lush, tropical courtyard w/ views of the sea & San Juan's skyline • IGTA member • gay-owned/run

▲ **Ocean Walk** Atlantic Place # 1, Ocean Park • 728-0855/ (800) 468-0615 • lesbians/gay men • swimming • former Spanish-style home on the beach w/in walking distance of shops & casinos of Condado area • near women's bar • IGTA member

BARS

Abbey Disco Calle Cruz #251 • 725-7581 • gay-friendly • dancing/DJ • gay Sun

Barefoot Bar 2 Calle Vendig, Condado • 724-7230 • 9am-3am • popular • mostly gay men • beach bar

Cups Calle San Mateo #1708, Santurce • 268-3570 • clsd Mon • lesbians/gay men • dancing/DJ

El Danuvio Azul Calle San Juan #613, Santurce • 8pm-4am, clsd Sun

Junior's Bar 602 Calle Condado, Santurce • 6pm-2am, til 4am Fri-Sat • lesbians/gay men • neighborhood bar • dancing/DJ • salsa & merengue

Krash 1257 Ponce de Leon, Santurce • 722-1131 • 9pm-4am, clsd Mon • popular • lesbians/gay men • dancing/DJ • live shows

La Laguna Night Club 53 Calle Barranquitas, Condado • from 10pm • popular • mostly gay men • dancing/DJ • live shows

Norman's Carretera 318 Barrio Maresua, San German • 6pm-1am • lesbians/gay men • neighborhood bar • dancing/DJ

Taboo Calle Loiza #1753, Santurce • 728-5906 • 8pm-?, clsd Sun • lesbians/gay men • dancing/DJ • private club

Tia Maria's Jose de Diego, Stop 22, Ponce de Leon • popular • gay-friendly • liquor shop & bar

RESTAURANTS & CAFES

Amanda's Cafe 424 Norzagaray, Old San Juan • 722-1682 • 11am-2am, til 4am Fri-Sat

Cafe Amadeus Calle San Sebastian • 722-8635 • popular

Cafe Berlin 407 Plaza Colon, Old San Juan • 722-5205 • popular • espresso bar

Golden Unicorn 2415 Calle Laurel • 728-4066 • 11am-11pm • Chinese

Panache 1127 Calle Seaview, Condado • 725-2400 • dinner only • popular • French

Sam's Patio 102 San Sebastian, Old San Juan

TRAVEL & TOUR OPERATORS

Travel Maker International Tours San Claudio Mail Stations, Box 224, Rio Piedras, 00926 • 755-5878 • ask for Ruben • IGTA member

PUBLICATIONS

Puerto Rico Breeze Castillo del Mar #1397, Isla Verde, 00979 • 268-5101

Vieques Island   (809)

ACCOMMODATIONS

New Dawn's Caribbean Retreat PO Box 1512 , 00765 • 741-0495 • gay-friendly • guesthouse & tentsites • bar & restaurant Dec-April • wheelchair access • lesbian-owned/run

Virgin Islands

St. Croix   (809)

ACCOMMODATIONS

▲ **On The Beach Resort** 127 Smithfield Rd., Frederiksted • 772-1205/ (800) 524-2018 • gay-friendly • beachfront resort • swimming • also a restaurant • full bar

Prince Street Inn 402 Prince St., Frederiksted • 772-9550 • gay-friendly • 6 apts w/ kitchen • near beach

TRAVEL & TOUR OPERATORS

Calparrio International Travel 227 King St., Frederiksted • 772-9822/ (800) 537-6239 • IGTA member

St. John   (809)

ACCOMMODATIONS

Maho Bay & Harmony V.I. National Park • 776-6240/ (800) 392-9004 • gay-friendly • camping & an environmentally aware resort

St. Thomas   (809)

ACCOMMODATIONS

Blackbeard's Castle atop Blackbeard's Hill, PO Box 6041, 00801 • 776-1234/ (800) 344-5771 • popular • gay-friendly • small intimate hotel on a historic site overlooking town & harbor • swimming • also a restaurant • American/Caribbean

Danish Chalet Guest House Solberg Rd. • 774-5764/ (800) 635-1531 • gay-friendly • overlooking harbor • spa • deck

Harbour Lites Nisky Mail Service 442, 00802 • 775-2476 • lesbians/gay men • swimming • nudity • intimate B&B overlooking brilliant Charlotte Amalie Harbour • patio

Hotel 1829 Government Hill • 776-1829/ (800) 524-2002 • gay-friendly • swimming • also a restaurant • full bar

Pavilions & Pools Hotel 6400 Estate Smith Bay • 775-6110/ (800) 524-2001 • gay-friendly • one-bdrm villas each w/ its own private swimming pool

RESTAURANTS & CAFES

Lemon Grass Cafe Balcony Square • 777-1877 • noon-2am, til 4am Th-Sat, clsd Sun • popular • lesbians/gay men • dancing/DJ • American eclectic • plenty veggie • patio • $7-15

TRAVEL & TOUR OPERATORS

Journeys by the Sea, Inc. 6501 Redhook Plaza, Ste. 201 • 775-3660/ (800) 825-3632 • yacht vacations • day sails

Casa Camelinas

❦

**A Unique Bed & Breakfast
in Historic Morelia
Catering to Women**

You will love this colonial city only 2½ hours from Mexico City. Our women-owned B&B is also a great jumping-off point for sightseeing in other quaint towns specializing in wonderful arts and crafts. For the authentic Mexico, clean, safe, lovely surroundings, two light meals and (if you wish) Spanish tuition from a tenured teacher right on our premises, we encourage you to contact us for a brochure at 415-661-5745.

❧

Also see our web page at
http://www.frsa.com/camelinas

Telephone: +52-43-140963
Facsimile: +52-43-143864
E-Mail: Camelinas@aol.com

México

Acapulco, Gro.   (74)

ACCOMMODATIONS

Royale De Acapulco & Beach Club Calle Caracol 70, Fraccion Amiento Farallón • 84-37-07 • gay-friendly • swimming • food served

Villa Costa Azul 555 Fdo. Magallanes • 84-54-62 • lesbians/gay men • swimming • IGTA member

BARS

Demas Privada Piedra Picuda #17 (behind Carlos & Charlie's) • opens 10pm • popular • lesbians/gay men • dancing/DJ

Queens Club Calle Adolfo López Mateos 8 • 10pm-5am Th-Sun • mostly women • dancing/DJ • live shows

RESTAURANTS & CAFES

Beto's Beach Restaurant Condessa Beach • popular • lesbians/gay men

Chicken Choza Benito Juárez St. (1/2 blk off Zócalo) • popular • lesbians/gay men • full bar • gay-owned/run

Denny's 129 Costera Miguel Aleman • open late • W. side of Zócalo/Plaza Alvarez

La Guera de Condesa Condesa Beach • popular

Le Bistrquet Andrea Doria #5, Fracc. Costa Azul • 84-68-60 • popular • turn off the costera at the Oceanic Park • patio

Camelinas, Mor.   (43)

ACCOMMODATIONS

▲ **Casa Camelinas** 2-1/2 hours from Mexico City • 140963/ (415) 661-5745 • women only • food served

Cancún, Q.R.

ACCOMMODATIONS

Caribbean Reef Club 20 mi. S. in Puerto Morelos • (800) 322-6286 • popular • gay-friendly • swimming • food served

BARS

Karamba Tulum Ave. • popular • mostly gay men • dancing/DJ • live shows

Picante Bar Avenida Tulum, east of Ave. Uxmal • 9:30pm-4am • popular • mostly gay men

GYMS & HEALTH CLUBS

Shape Calle Conoco, 1 blk from San Yaxchen • gay-friendly

Ensenada, B.C.N.

BARS

Coyote Club 1000 Blvd. Costero #4 & 5 at Diamante • 9pm-3am, from 6pm Sun, clsd Mon • lesbians/gay men • dancing/DJ • gay-owned/run

Guadalajara, Jal.   (36)

BARS

La Malinche 1230 Alvaro Obregón St. at Calle 50, Libertad District • 9pm-3am • mostly gay men • dancing/DJ • live shows • food served • popular late night

Monica's Disco Bar 1713 Alvaro Obregón St., Libertad District • 643-9544 • 9pm-3am, clsd Mon • popular • dancing/DJ • live shows

SOS Club 1413 Ave. La Paz • 11pm-3am, clsd Mon • popular • lesbians/gay men • dancing/DJ • live shows

RESTAURANTS & CAFES

Brasserie 1171 Prisciliano Sanchez St., downtown Juárez District

Copa de Leche 414 Juárez Ave., Juárez District • 14-5347 • 7am-10pm • live shows

Sanborn's Juárez Ave. at 16 de Septiembre St.

Sanborn's Vallarta 1600 Vallarta Ave., downtown Juárez District • 14-53-47

La Paz, B.C.S.   (682)

ACCOMMODATIONS

Casa La Paceña Calle Bravo 106 • 25-27-48/ (800) 638-4552 • gay-friendly

Gran Baja near harbor Mariano Abasolo • gay-friendly

Hotel Perla 1570 Ave., Alvaro Obregón • 2-07-77x131 • gay-friendly

BARS

Bar Intimo Calle 16 de Septiembre • lesbians/gay men

Manzanillo, Col.   (333)

ACCOMMODATIONS

Pepe's c/o 2698 Pacific Ave., San Francisco, CA 94115 • 3-06-16/ (415) 346-4734 • gay-friendly • food served

Matamoros, Tamps.

BARS

Moutezuma Lounge St. 6 Gonzalez • gay-friendly

Mazatlan, Sin.   (67)

BARS

Pepe Toro Ave. de las Garzas 18, Zona Dorado • 8pm-4am • lesbians/gay men • dancing/DJ • not busy til midnight

Valentino's Ave. Camarón Sabalo • gay-friendly • dancing/DJ

RESTAURANTS & CAFES

Restaurante Rocamar Ave. del Mar, Zona Costera • 81-6008

Merida, Yuc.   (992)

ACCOMMODATIONS

Casa Exilio Calle 68, N. 495 between. 57 & 59, Yucatan • 28-25-05 • popular • lesbians/gay men • guesthouse • full breakfast • swimming • IGTA member

BARS

Disco Charros Calle 60 & 53 • lesbians/gay men • dancing/DJ

Los Tulipanes Domicilo Conocido • lesbians/gay men

Romanticos Piano Bar Calle 60 #461 • 9pm-3am • lesbians/gay men • live shows • patio

RESTAURANTS & CAFES

Cafe Express Calle 60 across from Hidalgo Park

Mexicali, B.C.N.

BARS

Copacabana Ave. Tuxtla Gutierrez at Baja California St. • mostly women • neighborhood bar

El Taurino Calle Zuazua at Ave. José Maria Morelos • popular • lesbians/gay men

Los Panchos Ave. Juárez 33 • lesbians/gay men • oldest gay bar in Mexicali

Manolo Bar 265 Prolongación Reforma, downtown • popular • lesbians/gay men • live shows

Tare Calle Uxmal & Ave. Jalisco • lesbians/gay men

México City, D.F. (905)

Info Lines & Services

Casa de la Sal A.C. Córdoba 76, Roma Sur, México, D.F., 067000 • 207-8042

Gay/Lesbian AA 123 Culiacán Atlas, Colonia Hipodromo Condessa • 8pm Mon-Sat, 6pm Sun

Bars

Anyway Calle Monterrey 47 • 10pm-3am • lesbians/gay men • dancing/DJ • live shows • videos

Butterfly Disco Calle Izazaga 9 at Ave. Lazaro Cárdenas Sur • 9pm-4am, clsd Mon • popular • lesbians/gay men • live shows

El Don II 79 Tonalá St. • 9pm-4am • lesbians/gay men • dancing/DJ

Fancy Calle Artículo 123 #66-D • gay-friendly • dancing/DJ • live shows

Trastevere Calle Carlos Arellano 4, Ciudad Satélite • lesbians/gay men • dancing/DJ

Restaurants & Cafes

El Hábito 13 Madrid St., Coyoacan District • live shows • avante-garde theater

La Fonda San Francisco Calle Velázquez de Leon 126 • 546-4060 • noon-1am • lesbians/gay men • live shows

La Opera Calle 5 de Mayo 10 • 1pm-midnight, clsd Sun

Bookstores & Retail Shops

El Angel Azul 64 Londres A&B • periodicals • clothing

Travel & Tour Operators

The Gay Travel Club Ave. Mexico 99-PB Col. Hipodromo, Condesa, D.F. C., 06170 • 264-0564

Stag Travel & Tours Hamburgo 214-31 Col. Juárez, 06600 • 525-4658 • IGTA member

Monterey, N.L.

Accommodations

Hotel Royalti 260 Ave. Hidalgo • gay-friendly

Bars

Arcano Calle Ruperto Martinez Oriente • clsd Sun-Tue • lesbians/gay men • dancing/DJ

Fridas Calle Padre Mier Poniente • lesbians/gay men • live shows

Oskar Calle Arteaga Poniente 424 • gay-friendly • videos

Scorpios Calle Padre Mier Oriente 860 • popular • lesbians/gay men • dancing/DJ • live shows

Bookstores & Retail Shops

Revisteria Johnny Calle Aramberri 807 Poniente

Puerto Vallarta, Jal. (322)

Accommodations

Casa de los Arcos • 2-59-90 • gay-friendly • vacation rental near beach

Casa Dos Comales Calle Aldama 274 • 3-20-42 • gay-friendly • apts

Casa Panoramica Carretera a Mismaloya • 745-7805 • gay-friendly • full breakfast • IGTA member

Jungle Nancy Villa (800) 936-3646 • lesbian-owned

Villa Felíz PO Box 553, Jalisco, 48300 • 2-07-98/ (714) 752-5456x277 (U.S. only) • (416) 925-9621 (Canada only) • lesbians/gay men • full breakfast

Bars

Blue Chairs (Tito's) Southern Los Muertos Beach • popular • lesbians/gay men • food served

Club Paco Paco Ignacio L. Vallarta 278 • 3pm-6am • popular • lesbians/gay men • dancing/DJ

Los Balcones Avenida Juárez at Libertad • 10pm-3am • lesbians/gay men • dancing/DJ

Studio 33 Avenida Juárez 728 • gay-friendly • dancing/DJ

Zotano Morelos 101, Plaza Rio (north at bridge) • gay-friendly • dancing/DJ • coffeehouse upstairs

Restaurants & Cafes

Adobe Cafe 252 Basilio Badillo • southwestern

Bombo's 327 Corona • popular • gourmet international

Cafe Sierra Insurgentes 109 • 2 -27-48 • 9am-11pm • popular • lesbians/gay men • full bar

Cuiza Isla Rio Cuale, West Bridge • 2-56-46 • lesbians/gay men

De Claire's 269 Basilio Badillo

Le Bistro Jazz Cafe Isla Ria Cuale #16-A • popular • professional

Memo's Casa de los Hotcakes 289 Basilio Badillo • popular

Papaya 3 169 Abasalo • natural food/sandwiches

Santos Francisca Rodriquez 136 • 2-56-70 • clsd Mon • lesbians/gay men • full bar

Sego's 625 Aguiles Serdán • popular • steaks/Mexican

Bookstores & Retail Shops

Safari Accents 244 Olas Atlas

Studio Rustiko Basilo Badillo 300 • gay-owned & operated

Travel & Tour Operators

Doin' It Right Tours & Travel (800) 936-3646 / (415) 621-3576 • IGTA member

Tijuana, B.C.N. (66)

Info Lines & Services

Gay/Lesbian Info Line • 88-0267

Accommodations

Fiesta Americana Hotel 4500 Blvd. Agua Caliente • 81-70-00 • popular • gay-friendly • expensive rates

La Villa De Zaragoza 1120 Ave. Madero • 85-18-32 • lesbians/gay men

Palacio Azteca Hotel 213 Cuauhtémoc Sur Blvd. (16 de Septiembre Ave.) • lesbians/gay men

Plaza De Oro Hotel 2nd St. at Ave. 'D' • 85-14-37 • lesbians/gay men

Bars

El Taurino Bar 198 Niños Héroes Ave. between 1st St. & Coahuila • 85-24-78 • 10am-3am, til 6am wknds • popular • lesbians/gay men • live shows

Emilio's Cafe Musical 1810-11 Calle Tercera (3rd St.), downtown • 88-02-67 • from dusk til 3am • popular • gay-friendly • live shows • beer/wine • food served • also coffeehouse

Los Equipales 2024 7th St. (opposite Jai Alai Palace) • 88-30-06 • opens 9pm, clsd Mon-Tue • popular • lesbians/gay men • dancing/DJ • live shows

Mike's 1220 Revolución Ave. & 6th St. • 85-35-34 • 9pm-6am Mon-Tue • popular • lesbians/gay men • dancing/DJ • live shows

Noa Noa Calle Primera & 154 'D' Miguel F. Martinez Ave. • clsd Mon, opens 9pm • lesbians/gay men • dancing/DJ • live shows

Terraza 9 1928 Sixth St. at Ave. Revolución • 88-17-36 • 8pm-2am • popular • lesbians/gay men

Veracruz, Ver.

Accommodations

Hotel Diligencias Independencia, frente al Zócalo, Centro • gay-friendly • food served

Bars

Acuario's Boca del Rio, Ver. Boulevard • lesbians/gay men • (at Canales & Revolución)

Cocoteros at end of Boulevard • lesbians/gay men • dancing/DJ

Hippopotamos Fracc. Costa Verde • gay-friendly • dancing/DJ • live shows

Your

ADMIT ONE
985003 985003
W.I. Rogers Company

to the latest Lesbian Travel Info:

> latest updates

> links to gay travel info

> current calendar of
  queer events & festivals

> Top Websites for
  Lesbian/Gay Travellers

http://www.damron.com/

> interactive forms

> constantly expanding

> Netscape enhanced

Any questions?
WT@damron.com

Damron
Cyber
Suitcase

FLEX YOUR FINGERS

Hey Writers! Throw together 150-500 words about the scene in your city. Sign it over to Damron. **Win CASH!** Show your friends Your Name and Essay in the next edition of the Women's Traveller. Maybe even win a plush hotel room in San Francisco!

Check out the details in the front color section.

HOT TIPS:

Keep it short! A few well-placed adjectives are preferable to long sentences describing the ambiance of each cafe or bar.

Emphasize the diversity your city offers. Include events and places for women of color, differently abled women, older women, young women, large women and women of different backgrounds (such as transgendered, bisexual, butch, femme, leather, separatist, etc).

Tell us about it! Don't just list places and events. Compose a witty, entertaining short essay that highlights popular lesbian gathering places as well as those that are unique-but-not-well-known.

Pretend you're just visiting. Think about your city in terms of a woman just coming through town for a few days - what would be most interesting or valuable? Where do you take friends who stay with you for a few days?

Dear Reader,

We depend on you.

Because **You** *are the real travel experts!*

So here's a little incentive:

If you're the first reader to tell us about something
we oughta list – *and we don't already know about it, of course* –
we'll send you a **FREE copy** *of next year's book!*

• • • • ✂ •

Here's a New Listing!

Business Name _____

Phone# _____

Address _____

City _____

State _____ **Zip** _____ **Country** _____

Category (check one)
- ❏ Info Line/Service
- ❏ Women's Accommodation
- ❏ Accommodation
- ❏ Bar
- ❏ Restaurant/Cafe
- ❏ Gym
- ❏ Bookstore/Retail
- ❏ Travel Agency
- ❏ Tour Operator
- ❏ Publication
- ❏ Spiritual Group
- ❏ Erotica
- ❏ Other: _____

Clientele (check one)
- ❏ Lesbians/Gay Men
- ❏ Mostly Women
- ❏ Women Only
- ❏ Mostly Men
- ❏ Straight/Gay

Comments:

Clip-and-Send This Coupon

To: Women's Traveller/Editor
PO Box 422458
San Francisco, CA 94142

Or Fax: [415] 703-9049
Or Email: Update@Damron.com

How was your summer vacation?

Did yoy go to a neat-o women's festival?
Know of one happening next year?
Help us update our Calendar Sections!

Tell us about an event or festival of interest to lesbians or gay men

Just keep in mind:
- *The event should appeal to people from across state lines.*
- *It should be open to the public (not members only).*

• • • • • ✂ •

Add this to your Calendar!

Event _____

Phone# (IMPORTANT!) _____

1997 Event Dates _____

In what city will Event be held in 1997? _____

Cost_____ How many attend? _____

Description of Event _____

_____

_____

_____

Producer/Organization _____

Address _____

City_____

State _____ Zip _____ Country _____

Clip-and-Send This Coupon

To: Women's Traveller/Calendar
PO Box 422458
San Francisco, CA 94142

OR FAX: [415] 703-9049

OR EMAIL: Calendar@Damron.com

Clientele (check one)
- ❏ Lesbians/Gay Men
- ❏ Mostly Women
- ❏ Women Only
- ❏ Mostly Men
- ❏ Straight/Gay

Travel & Tours Section

CAMPING & RV

TOUR OPERATORS

TOURS & ADVENTURES

EVENTS & FESTIVALS

CAMPING & RV

NOTE: Sites primarily for women are highlighted in green.

United States

Alaska

FAIRBANKS

Billies B&B & Hostel 2895 Mack Rd., Fairbanks, AK 99709 • (907) 479-2034 • B&B & 6 campsites • also hostel

Arizona

APACHE JUNCTION

RVing Women 201 E. Southern, Apache Junction, 85219 • (800) 333-9992 / (602) 983-4678 • women only • members-only women's RV club • newsletter • campsites

COTTONWOOD

Mustang B&B 4257 Mustang Dr., Cottonwood, AZ 86326 • (520) 646-5929 • lesbians/gay men • also 1 RV hookup • B&B

Arkansas

EUREKA SPRINGS

Greenwood Hollow Ridge Rte 4, Box 155, Eureka Springs, AR 72632 • (501) 253-5283 • lesbians/gay men • exclusively gay • on 5 quiet acres • B&B • RV • full breakfast • near outdoor recreation • shared baths • private baths • kitchens

California

ALLEGHANY

Kenton Mine Lodge PO Box 942, Alleghany, CA 95910 • (916) 287-3212 • gay-friendly • in the Sierras • cabins • campsites

CLEARLAKE

SeaBreeze Resort 9595 Harbor Dr., Glenhaven, CA 95443 • (707) 998-3327 • gay-friendly • RV • cottages • swimming

GARBERVILLE

Giant Redwoods RV & Camp PO Box 222, Myers Flat, CA 95554 • (707) 943-3198 • gay-friendly • located off the Avenue of the Giants on the Eel River

PLACERVILLE

Rancho Cicada Retreat PO Box 225, Plymouth, CA 95669 • (209) 245-4841 • lesbians/gay men • secluded riverside retreat in the Sierra foothills w/ two-person tents & cabin • swimming • nudity

RUSSIAN RIVER

Faerie Ring Campground 16747 Armstrong Woods Rd., Guerneville, CA 95446 • (707) 869-4122 / (707) 869-2746 • gay-friendly • on 14 acres • campsites • RV • near outdoor recreation

Fife's Resort PO Box 45, Guerneville, CA 95446 • (800) 734-3371 / (707) 869-0656 • lesbians/gay men • cabins • campsites • swimming • IGTA member

Redwood Grove RV Park & Campground 16140 Neely Rd., Guerneville, CA 95446 • (707) 869-3670 • gay-friendly

Riverbend Campground & RV Park 11820 River Rd., Forestville, CA 95436 • (707) 887-7662 • gay-friendly

Schoolhouse Canyon Park 12600 River Rd., Guerneville, CA 95446 • (707) 869-2311 • gay-friendly • private beach • campsites • RV

Willows 15905 River Rd., Guerneville, CA 95446 • (800) 953-2828 / (707) 869-2824 • lesbians/gay men • old-fashioned country lodge & campground

WHITTIER

Whittier House 12133 S. Colima Rd., Whittier, CA 90604-9213 • (310) 941-7222 • mostly women • near Disneyland • B&B • cottages • RV • full breakfast • hot tub • IGTA member

Colorado

MOFFAT

Harmony Ranch Women's Retreat Center PO Box 398, Moffat, CO 81143 • (719) 256-4107 • women only • B&B • cottages • campsites

Florida

CRESCENT CITY

Crescent City Campground Rte. 2 Box 25, Crescent City, FL 32112 • (800) 634-3968 / (904) 698-2020 • gay-friendly • tenting sites & RV hook-ups • laundry & showers

LAKELAND

Sunset Motel & RV Resort 2301 New Tampa Hwy., Lakeland, FL 33801 • (813) 683-6464 • gay-friendly • motel, apts, RV hookups & private home all sharing 3 acres • swimming

MIAMI

Something Special 7762 NW 14th Ct. (private home), Miami, FL • (305) 696-8826 • women only • also tent space

OCALA

Phil's Place 5501 Hwy. 316, Reddick, FL 32686 • (904) 591-9924 • lesbians/gay men • camping available

WEST PALM BEACH

Whimsey (407) 686-1354 • also camping/RV space • resources & archives

Georgia

ATLANTA

Swiftwaters Rte. 3 Box 379, Dahlonega, GA 30533 • (706) 864-3229 • women only • deck • on scenic river • B&B • cabins • campsites • hot tub

Hawaii

HAWAII (BIG ISLAND)

Kalani Honua Retreat RR2 Box 4500, Beach Rd., Hawaii (Big Island), HI 96778 • (800) 800-6886 / (808) 965-7828 • gay-friendly • coastal retreat • conference center & campground w/in Hawaii's largest conservation area • swimming • IGTA member

Wood Valley B&B Inn PO Box 37, Hawaii (Big Island), HI 96777 • (808) 928-8212 • mostly women • plantation B&B • veggie breakfast • tent sites • sauna • nudity

MAUI

Camp Kula - Maui B&B PO Box 111, Maui, HI 96790 • (808) 878-2528 • lesbians/gay men • centrally located hideaway on the lush, rolling green slopes of Mt. Haleakala • HIV+ welcome • B&B • campsites • swimming

Maine

CAMDEN

Old Massachusetts Homestead Campground PO Box 5 Rte. 1, Lincolnville Beach, ME 04849 • (207) 789-5135 • 5 cabins • 68 campsites • 38 RV hookups (separate campground for tenters) • swimming

N. WATERFORD

Bear Mountain Village (207) 782-2275 (winter) / (207) 583-2541 • gay-friendly • on the lake • hosts womyn's festivals in June & August • cabins • campsites

SEBAGO LAKE

Maine-ly For You RR 2 Box 745, Harrison, ME 04040 • (207) 583-6980 • gay-friendly • cottages • campsites

Massachusetts

MARTHA'S VINEYARD

Webb's Camping Area RFD 3, Box 100, Martha's Vineyard, MA 02568 • (508) 693-0233 • lesbians/gays

PROVINCETOWN

Coastal Acres Campground PO Box 593, Provincetown, 02657 • (508) 487-1700 • gay-friendly • walking distance to downtown • campsites

Michigan

OWENDALE

Windover Resort 3596 Blakely Rd., Owendale, MI 48754 • (517) 375-2586 • women only • campsites • swimming

SAUGATUCK

Camp It Rte. 6635 118th Ave. , Fennville, MI 49408 • (616) 543-4335 • lesbians/gay men • campsites

Minnesota

KENYON

Dancing Winds Farm 6863 Country 12 Blvd., Kenyon, MN 55946-4125 • (507) 789-6606 • mostly women • B&B & working dairy farm • tentsites • work exchange • full breakfast

Mississippi

OVETT

Camp Sister Spirit PO Box 12, Ovett, MS 39462 • (601) 344-2005 • women only

Montana

BOULDER

Boulder Hot Springs Hotel & Retreat PO Box 930, Boulder, MT 59632 • (406) 225-4339 • gay-friendly • spirituality/recovery retreat • hot springs • camping available • irregular hours • call for info

RONAN

North Crow Vacation Ranch 2360 N. Crow Rd., Missoula, MT 59864 • (406) 676-5169 • lesbians/gay men • 35-acre campground w/ cabins • tipis • 80 mi. S. of Glacier Park • hot tub • nudity

New Jersey

PLAINFIELD

▲ **Pillars** 922 Central Ave., Plainfield, NJ 07060-2311 • (800) 372-7378 / (908) 753-0922 • gay-friendly • Georgian/Victorian mansion on an acre of trees & wildflowers • B&B • RV • campsites

CAMPING & RV

New Mexico

THOREAU

Zuni Mountain Lodge at Blue Water Lake HC62 Box 5114, Thoreau, NM 87323-9515 • (505) 862-7769 • gay-friendly • full breakfast & dinner • campsites

North Carolina

HOT SPRINGS

Duckett House Inn Hwy. 209 S., Hot Springs, NC 28743 • (800) 306-5038 / (704) 622-7621 • lesbians/gay men • Victorian farmhouse B&B w/ camping on Appalachian Trail • also a restaurant • vegetarian (reservations required)

Ohio

ATHENS

Susan B. Anthony Memorial Unrest Home Community PO Box 5853, Athens, 45701 • women only • by reservation only • outdoor kitchens • no electricity • swimming

COLUMBUS

Summit Lodge Resort & Guesthouse PO Box 951-D, Logan, OH 43138 • (614) 385-6822 • mostly gay men • camping available, hot tub & sauna • swimming • nudity

GUYSVILLE

Moon Ridge Rte. 1 Box 240, Guysville, OH 45735 • mostly women • campground

Oklahoma

EL RENO

Good Life RV Resort Exit 108 I-40 1/4 mile S., El Reno, OK 73036 • (405) 884-2994 • gay-friendly • 31 acres of wooded countryside w/ 100 campsites & 100 RV hookups • swimming

Oregon

DAYS CREEK

Owl Farm PO Box 133, Days Creek, 97429 • (503) 679-4655 • women only • open women's land for retreat or residence • camping sites available • write for info • call for directions

GRANTS PASS

Womanshare PO Box 681, Grants Pass, OR 97526 • (503) 862-2807 • women only • cabin & campground • meals included • hot tub

O'BRIEN

Mountain River Inn PO Box 34, O'Brien, OR 97534 • (503) 596-2392 • women only • also camping & RV sites • unconfirmed fall '95 • full breakfast

ROGUE RIVER

Whispering Pines B&B/Retreat 9188 W. Evans Creek Rd., Rogue River, OR 97537 • (800) 788-1757 / (541) 582-1757 • lesbians/gay men • 32 acres of pine & pasture cradled in the Cascade foothills • campsites • full breakfast • hot tub • swimming

TILLER

Kalles Family RV Ranch 233 Jackson Creek Rd., Tiller, OR 97484 • (503) 825-3271 • lesbians/gay men • camping sites & RV hookups • between Medford & Roseburg • near outdoor recreation

Pennsylvania

NEW MILFORD

Oneida Camp & Lodge PO Box 537, New Milford, PA 18834 • (717) 465-7011 • mostly gay men • oldest gay-owned & operated campground dedicated to the gay & lesbian community • swimming • nudity

PITTSBURGH

Camp Davis 311 Red Brush Rd., Boyers, PA 16020 • (412) 637-2402 • lesbians/gay men • variety of events • 1 hour from Pittsburgh

Tennessee

JAMESTOWN

Laurel Creek Campground Rock Creek Rte. Box 150, Jamestown, TN 38556 • (615) 879-7696 • gay-friendly • camping • rentals • RV hookups • horses • hiking • swimming

ROGERSVILLE

▲ **Lee Valley Farm** 142 Drinnon Ln., Rogersville, TN 37857 • (423) 272-4068 • lesbians/gay men • guest farm w/ cabins & camping • all meals included • horseback riding • hot tub • swimming

Virginia

CHARLOTTESVILLE

Intouch Women's Center Rte. 2 Box 1096, Charlottesville, VA 23084 • (804) 589-6542 • women only • campground & recreational area

Washington

INDEX

Wild Lily Ranch B&B PO Box 313, Index, WA 98256 • (206) 793-2103 • peaceful B&B nestled among towering firs & cedars on the Skykomish River • campsites • cabins • swimming • hot tub • fireplaces

OCEAN PARK

Iris Guesthouse Box 72 Territory Rd., Oysterville, WA 98640 • (206) 665-5681 • mostly women • full kitchen privileges • campsites

West Virginia

STONEWALL JACKSON LAKE

FriendSheep Farm Rte. 1 Box 158, Orlando, WV 26412 • (304) 462-7075 • mostly women • secluded retreat w/ workshops • B&B • campsites • swimming

Wisconsin

MAUSTON

CK's Outback W. 5627 Clark Rd., Mauston, WI • (608) 847-5247 • women only • camping • near outdoor recreation

WASCOTT

Wilderness Way PO Box 176, Wascott, WI 54890 • (715) 466-2635 • women only • resort property w/ cottages, camping & RV sites (camping $10-14, cottages $44-68) • swimming

WINTER

Flambeau Forest Resort Star Rte. 67 Box 65, Winter, WI 54896 • (715) 332-5236 • gay-friendly • cabins • campsites

Canada

British Columbia

BIRKEN

Birkenhead Resort Box 369, Pemberton, BC V0N 2L0 • (604) 452-3255 • gay-friendly • also a restaurant • gourmet homecooking • some veggie • full bar • cabins • campsites • hot tub • swimming

Ontario

HAMILTON

Cedars Tent & Trailer Park 1039 5th Concession Rd. RR2, Waterdown, OT L0R 2H0 • (905) 659-7342 / (905) 659-3655 • lesbians/gay men • private campground • swimming • also social club • dancing/DJ • karaoke • wknd restaurant • some veggie

Saskatchewan

RAVENSCRAG

Spring Valley Guest Ranch Box 10, Ravenscrag, SK S0N 0T0 • (306) 295-4124 • gay-friendly • 1913 character home, cabin & tipis • also a restaurant • country-style • B&B • campsites • cabins

Québec

JOLIETTE

L'Oasis des Pins 381 boul. Brassard, St. Paul de Joliette, PQ J0K 3E0 • (514) 754-3819 • gay-friendly • camping April-Sept. • restaurant open year-round • swimming

Caribbean

Puerto Rico

VIEQUES ISLAND

New Dawn's Caribbean Retreat PO Box 1512, Vieques Island, PR 00765 • (809) 741-0495 • gay-friendly • guesthouse & tentsites • bar & restaurant Dec-April

Virgin Islands

ST. JOHN

Maho Bay & Harmony V.I. National Park, St. John, VI • (800) 392-9004 / (809) 776-6240 • gay-friendly • camping & an environmentally aware resort

TOUR OPERATOR

NOTE: Tour Operators offering trips for **"women only"** or **"mostly women"** are highlighted in green.

Above All Travel (602) 946-9968 • gay/lesbian • worldwide cruises & tours

▲ **Adventure Associates** PO Box 16304, Seattle, WA 98116 • (206) 932-8352 • mostly women • co-ed & women-only outdoor adventures • IGTA member

Adventures for Women PO Box 515, Montvale, NJ 07645 • (201) 930-0557 • women only • hiking, canoeing & cross-country skiing in the Adirondacks

African Pride Safaris 673 NE 73rd St., Miami, FL 33138 • (800) 237-4225 / (305) 756-7567 • gay/lesbian • IGTA member

Ahwahnee Whitewater Expeditions PO Box 1161, Columbia, CA 95310 • (209) 533-1401 • straight/gay • women-only, co-ed & charter rafting • IGTA member

Alaska Women of the Wilderness PO Box 773556, Eagle River, AK 99577 • (907) 688-2226 / (800) 770-2226 (AK only) • women only • trips, courses & seminars designed to promote self-reliance in the outdoors

All About Destinations Gallery 3 Plaza, 3819 N. 3rd St., Phoenix, AZ 85012-2074 • (800) 375-2703 / (602) 277-2703 • gay/lesbian • group cruises • IGTA member

Allegro Travel 900 West End Ave. #12C, New York, NY 10025 • (800) 666-3553 / (212) 666-6700 • gay/lesbian • 22 departures yearly to Russia, Italy, Egypt & Scandinavia

Alyson Adventures PO Box 181223, Boston, MA 02118 • (800) 825-9766 / (617) 247-8170 • gay/lesbian • IGTA member

Amatirasu Tours Apartado 372-2050, San Pedro, Montes de Oca, San Jose, Costa Rica • (506) 223-3652 • gay/lesbian • Amatirasu is the African goddess of travel • tours • reservations

Amazon Tours & Cruises 8700 W. Flagler #190, Miami, FL 33174 • (800) 423-2791 • gay/lesbian • weekly cruises in upper Amazon • IGTA member

Another Way RFD5 Box 290-B1, Webster, NH 03303 • (603) 648-2751 • women only • comfortable camping tours in New England, Canada & Florida • IGTA member

Arizona Adventure (602) 204-2422 • straight/gay • 3-day hikes, horse rides & tours

Artemis Sailing Charters PO Box 931, Driggs, ID 83422 • (800) 838-7783 / (208) 354-8804 • women only • sailing adventures worldwide

Artemis Wilderness Tours PO Box 1574, El Prado, NM 87529 • (505) 758-2203 • mostly women • whitewater boating & rafting in New Mexico & Colorado

Atlas Travel Service 8923 S. Sepulveda Blvd., Los Angeles, CA 90045 • (800) 952-0120 / (310) 670-3574 • straight/gay • IGTA member

Bar H Ranch PO Box 297, Driggs, ID 83422 • (208) 354-2906 • mostly women • guesthouse • summer horseback trips in Wyoming's Tetons near Jackson Hole, WY

Blue Moon Explorations PO Box 2568, Bellingham, WA 98227 • (800) 966-8806 / (206) 966-8805 • women only • sea kayaking, rafting, ski trips in Pacific Northwest & Hawaii

Cloud Canyon Backpacking 411 Lemon Grove Lane, Santa Barbara, CA 93108 • (805) 969-0982 • women only • seasonal wilderness backpacking in Southern California, Utah & the Sierra Nevadas

▲ **Club Le Bon** PO Box 444, Woodbridge, NJ 07095 • (800) 836-8687 / (908) 826-1577 • mostly women • tours for gay/lesbian parents & kids

▲ **Common Earth Wilderness Trips** 660 Amaranth Blvd., Mill Valley, CA 94941 • (415) 383-1239 • women only • non-profit women-owned • sliding scale • multicultural • backpacking & kayaking in California, the Southwest & Alaska

Crossing Worlds Mystical Earth Journeys Box 314, Sedona, AZ 86336 • (602) 204-1946 • women only • year-round spirituality retreats

Cruise Express 1904 3rd Ave., Ste. 900, Seattle, WA 98101 • (800) 682-1988 / (206) 467-0467 • gay/lesbian • cruises & tours • IGTA member

Cruisin' the Castro 375 Lexington St., San Francisco, CA • (415) 550-8110 • gay/lesbian • guided walking tour of the Castro • IGTA member

Custom Cruises International 482 Great House Dr., Milpitas, CA 95035 • (408) 945-8286 • gay/lesbian

Different Strokes Tours 1841 Broadway Ste. 607, New York, NY 10023 • (800) 688-3301 / (212) 262-3860 • gay/lesbian • cultural safaris worldwide • IGTA member

Doin' It Right Tours & Travel 1 St. Francis Pl. Ste. 2106, San Francisco, CA 94107 • (415) 621-3576 • gay/lesbian • gay cultural exchange tours • SF accommodations • IGTA member

Earth Walks (505) 988-4157 • straight/gay • guided tour of American Southwest & Mexico

Eco-Explorations (408) 335-7199 • gay/lesbian • scuba & kayak adventures in Monetery Bay, CA & worldwide

Executive Tour Associates PO Box 42151, Mesa, AZ 85274 • (800) 382-1113 / (602) 898-8853 • gay/lesbian • IGTA member

Fiesta Travel 323 Geary St. #619, San Francisco, CA 94102 • (800) 200-0582 / (415) 986-1134 • gay/lesbian • tours to Latin America for New Year's & Carnival in Rio

Florida Adventures PO Box 677893, Orlando, FL 32867 • (407) 677-0655 • gay/lesbian

Full Moon Adventures General Delivery , Costa Rica • (800) 296-6292 / (804) 357-6860 • gay/lesbian • culturally-sensitive custom trips to Guatemala & Belize

GAYVentures 2009 SW 9th St., Miami, FL 33135 • (800) 940-7757 / (305) 541-6141 • gay/lesbian • Costa Rica tours • IGTA member

Great Canadian Ecoventures PO Box 155, 1896 W. Broadway, Vancouver, BC V6J-1Y9 • (800) 667-9453 / (604) 730-0704 • straight/gay • wildlife photography tours

Hawk, I'm Your Sister PO Box 9109-WT, Santa Fe, NM 87504 • (505) 984-2268 • mostly women • wilderness canoe trips & writing retreats in the Americas & Russia

Her Wild Song PO Box 515, Brunswick, ME 04011 • (207) 721-9005 • women only • spiritually aware wilderness journeys

Holbrook Travel 3540 NW 13th St., Gainesville, FL 32609 • (904) 377-7111 • straight/gay • natural history tours in Central America

458

OPERATOR TOUR

Holidays on Skis 810 Belmar Plaza, Belmar, NJ 07719 • (800) 526-2827 / (908) 280-1120 • gay/lesbian • ski trip to International Gay Ski Week • IGTA member

International Gay Rodeo Association (303) 832-4418 • gay/lesbian • rodeo competitions & shows nation-wide

International Tours & Cruises 1235 N. Main St., Madisonville, KY 42431 • (800) 844-2072 / (502) 821-0025 • gay/lesbian • worldwide tours • ask for Art Nance

Kenai Peninsula Guided Hikes HCR 64 Box 468, Seward, AK 99664 • (907) 288-3141 • gay/lesbian • guided day hikes in Alaska

Lost Coast Llama Caravans 77321 Usal Rd., Whitehorn, CA 95489 • mostly women • women-led pack trips

▲ **Mariah Wilderness Expeditions** PO Box 248, Port Richmond, CA 94807 • (800) 462-7424 / (510) 233-2303 • mostly women • woman-owned whitewater rafting in California & Central America

McNamara Ranch 4620 County Rd. 100, Florissant, CO 80816 • (719) 748-3466 • straight/gay • horseback tours for 2-3

Merlyn's Journeys for Women Star Route 3, Box 145, Angel's Camp, CA 95222 • (209) 736-4651 • women only • private villa getaways for 10-12 women • van tours • West Coast

Multi-Travel & Tours 855 Washington Ave., Miami Beach, FL 33139 • (800) 762-3688 / (305) 672-4600 • gay/lesbian • ski tours & more

New Dawn Adventures PO Box 1512, Vieques, PR 00765 • (809) 741-0495 • gay/lesbian • Caribbean retreat, bunkhouse & campground

New England Vacation Tours PO Box 571 - Rte. 100, West Dover, VT 05356 • (800) 742-7669 / (802) 464-2076 • gay/lesbian • fall foliage & party weekend tours conducted by a mainstream tour operator

▲ **Northern Alternative** 202 W. Sheridan St., Ely, MN 55731 • (800) 774-7520 / (218) 365-2894 • women only • wilderness adventures including skiing, snow shoeing, dog sledding & ice fishing

Ocean Voyager (800) 435-2531 / (718) 624-3063 • gay/lesbian • cruise consultants

OceanWomyn Kayaking (206) 325-3970 • women only • guided sea kayaking adventures

Women Owned And Operated

Fully Guided And Outfitted Canoe Trips In The Boundary Waters Of Northern Minnesota.
Relax And Enjoy this Unique Wilderness Experience, We'll Take Care Of The Rest!

Call For A Free Brochure Detailing Our 1995 Adventures
1-800-774-7520

Odyssey Travel 11829 Perrin Beitel, San Antonio, TX 78217 • (800) 999-4905 / (210) 656-0083 • gay/lesbian • reservations, tours of San Antonio • IGTA member

▲ **Olivia Cruises** 4400 Market St., Oakland, CA 94608 • (800) 631-6277 / (510) 655-0364 • women only • huge cruises to Alaska, Caribbean, Mediterranean & Club Med Ixtapa (see ad in front color section)

Our Family Abroad 40 W. 57th St., New York, NY 10019 • (800) 999-5500 / (212) 459-1800 • gay/lesbian • guided motor-coach tours to Europe, Asia, Africa & South America

Out 'n Arizona / Cowgirls N' Ghost Towns Dept. 215, PO Box 22333, Tempe, AZ 85285 • (800) 897-0304 / (602) 234-1168 • gay/lesbian • fall & winter van tours

Outdoor Vacations for Women Over 40 PO Box 200, Groton, MA 01450 • (508) 448-3331 • women only

Outland Adventures PO Box 16343, Seattle, WA 98116 • (206) 932-7012 • straight/gay • ecologically sensitive cultural tours, snorkeling & biking adventures in Central America, Canada, Alaska & Washington State

Paddling South & Saddling South 4510 Silverado Trail, Calistoga, CA 94515 • (707) 942-4550 • women only • horseback & sea kayak trips in Mexico

Pangaea Expeditions PO Box 5753, Missoula, MT 59806 • (406) 721-7719 • women only • river rafting in Montana

Parkside Travel 3310 Kent Rd. Ste. 6, Stowe, OH 44224 • (800) 552-1647 / (216) 688-3334 • gay/lesbian • also Gay Travel Club membership & discounts

Passport Travel & Tours 415 E. Golf Rd. #111, Arlington Heights, IL 60005 • (800) 549-8687 / (708) 364-0634 • gay/lesbian • upscale tours to Europe incorporating local gay history & culture

Peppermint Tours (800) 589-6885 / (904) 625-8886 • mostly gay/lesbian • gay-owned motorcoach tours

Pink Pyramid Tours 2 W. 45th Ste. 1101, New York, NY 10036 • (800) 874-1811 / (212) 869-3890 • gay/lesbian • tours to eastern Mediterranean & South America

Pink Triangle PO Box 14298, Berkeley, CA 94712 • (510) 843-0181 • gay/lesbian • yearly worldwide country/western & square-dancing tours

1998 AUG 1-8
GAY GAMES 5
AMSTERDAM

To subscribe to the 1998 Amsterdam Gay
Games Quarterly Newsletter please send
a postcard with your name and address in
clear writing to:
Stichting Gay and Lesbian Games
Amsterdam 1998, P.O.box 2837, 1000 CV
Amsterdam, the Netherlands

Friendship through Culture and Sport

Portuguese Princess Whale Watch (508) 487-2400 • gay/lesbian • whale-watching cruises booked through Provincetown Reservations

Progressive Travels 224 W. Galer Ste. C, Seattle, WA 98119 • (800) 245-2229 / (206) 285-1987 • gay/lesbian • luxury walking and biking tours of Europe and the Pacific Northwest • IGTA member

Rainbow Adventures (800) 881-4814 • gay/lesbian • sailing charters

Robin Tyler Tours 15842 Chase St., North Hills, CA 91343 • (818) 893-4075 • women only • produces West Coast Women's Music & Comedy Festival • cruises

▲ **Rock Woman Journeys Home** PO Box 6548, Denver, CO 80206 • (800) 676-5404 • women only

Royal Tours & Travel 1742 E. Broadway, Long Beach, CA 90802 • (800) 828-6759 / (310) 938-7370 • straight/gay

Sea Safaris Sailing 12060 Carver Ave., New Port Richey, FL 34654 • (800) 497-2508 / (813) 626-7613 • straight/gay • some women-only charter sail trips & cruises to the Caribbean

Sea Sense 25 Thames St., New London, CT 06320 • (800) 332-1404 / (203) 444-1404 • women only • custom sailing courses in Florida, Lake Michigan, New England & the Virgin Islands

Skylink 2953 Lincoln Blvd., Santa Monica, CA 90405 • (800) 225-5759 / (310) 452-0506 • gay/lesbian • low-cost, air-included tours worldwide for women in couples or single

Spirit International Travel Club (800) 823-4784 • gay/lesbian

Underseas Expeditions PO Box 9455, Pacific Beach, CA 92169 • (800) 669-0310/ (619) 270-2900 • gay/lesbian • warm water diving • scuba trips worldwide • IGTA member

Venus Adventures PO Box 39, Peaks Island, ME 04108 • (207) 766-5655 • women only • goddess-oriented international tours for women to sacred sites

Voyages & Expeditions 8323 Southwest Freeway #800, Houston, TX 77074 • (800) 818-2877 / (713) 776-3438 • gay/lesbian • group & individual deluxe cruises

Walk In Beauty Womyn's Wilderness Trips HC 70 Box 17, Ponca, AR 72670-9620 • (501) 861-5506 • women only • eco-tours, accommodations available

Water Sport People (305) 296-4546 • straight/gay • scuba-diving instruction, group charters

Whelk Women PO Box 1006WT, Boca Grande, FL 33921 • (813) 964-2027 • women only • custom boat tours for women, outfitted camping • accommodations

Wild Women Expeditions PO Box 145, Stn. B, Sudbury, OT P3E 4N5 • (705) 866-1260 • women only • Canada's only women-run canoe excursions • all equipment supplied • riverside basecamp on the Spanish River • sauna

Women in the Wilderness 566 Ottawa Ave., St. Paul, MN 55107 • (612) 227-2284 • women only • teaches outdoor skills & nature study

Women on the Water PO Box 502, Key West, FL 33041 • (305) 294-0662 • women only • sunset sails • day sails • snorkeling

Women's EcoScapes PO Box 1408, Santa Cruz, CA 95061 • (408) 479-0473 • women only • coral reef ecology • snorkeling, kayaking & sailing in Key West, California, Hawaii & Bahamas • dolphin-friendly whale encounters

Woodswomen 25 W. Diamond Lake Rd., Minneopolis, MN 55419 • (800) 279-0555/ (612) 822-3809 • women only • non-profit tour operator • outdoor adventures: 1 day to 3 weeks, domestic & international

January

5-8: Cross Country Skiing in Minnesota (800) 774-7520 • women only • snow shoeing • see Northern Alternative

6-21: Costa Rica Adventure (206) 932-8352 • gay/lesbian • see Adventure Associates

6-14: Sea Kayaking in Baja (907) 688-2226 • women only • see Alaska Women of the Wilderness

12-15: Cross-Country Ski Cascades (206) 932-8352 • women only • see Adventure Associates

13-Feb 3: Safari East Africa (206) 932-8352 • gay/lesbian • see Adventure Associates

13-20: Amazon Rainforest Canoe Trek (800) 836-8687 • mostly women • see Club Le Bon

16-20: Horsepacking in Baja (907) 688-2226 • women only • see Alaska Women of the Wilderness

February

4-11: Whistler Gay Ski Week (800) 695-0880 • gay/lesbian • see Advance Damron Vacations

9-12: Cross Country Skiing and Dogsledding in Minnesota (800) 774-7520 • women only • see Northern Alternative

10-17: Sea of Cortez Learn to Sail (800) 462-7424 • women only • see Mariah Wilderness Expeditions

10-17: Dive Roatan, Bay Islands, Honduras (800) 669-0310 • gay/lesbian • see Underseas Expeditions

11-17: Cross Country Ski Yellowstone Park (206) 932-8352 • women only • see Adventure Associates

14-17: Sea Kayaking in the Everglades (207) 721-9005 • women only • see Her Wild Song

16-19: Cross Country Ski British Columbia (206) 932-8352 • women only • see Adventure Associates

16-19: Cross Country Skiing in Minnesota (800) 774-7520 • women only • snow shoeing • see Northern Alternative

16-19: Winter Wonderland Adventure (800) 279-0555 • women only • dogsledding • skiing • snowshoeing • see Woodswomen

17-Mar 3: An Island Look at New Zealand (800) 279-0555 • women only • bicycling • see Woodswomen

19-24: Canoeing in the Everglades (207) 721-9005 • women only • see Her Wild Song

21-Mar 6: Country/Western Journey to Australia (510) 843-0181 • gay/lesbian • see Pink Triangle Adventures

23-25: Healing Our Hearts: Drum Making (907) 688-2226 • women only • see Alaska Women of the Wilderness

23-Mar 4: Mardi Gras, Sydney, Australia (800) 225-5759 • gay/lesbian • see Skylink

24-Mar 2: Acapulco, Mexico Getaway (800) 836-8687 • mostly women • see Club Le Bon

25-Mar 8: Trek Copper Canyon (206) 932-8352 • gay/lesbian • see Adventure Associates

27-Mar 9: Dive the Great Barrier Reef & Gay Mardi Gras (800) 669-0310 • gay/lesbian • see Underseas Expeditions

29-Mar 4: Dogsledding Adventure (800) 774-7520 • women only • see Northern Alternative

March

2-8: Yellowstone Ski Extravaganza (800) 279-0555 • women only • see Woodswomen

4-8: Young Women, Growing Stronger: Girls Camp (907) 688-2226 • women only • see Alaska Women of the Wilderness

8-11: Cross Country Skiing and Snow Shoeing in Minnesota (800) 774-7520 • women only • see Northern Alternative

9-16: Sea Kayak Baja (206) 932-8352 • mostly women • see Adventure Associates

13-16: Women Who Run With the Dogs: Mushing Course (907) 688-2226 • women only • see Alaska Women of the Wilderness

15-17: Wine Country (209) 736-4651 • women only • see Merlyn's Journeys for Women

15-25: Ancient Egyptian Splendor (800) 999-5500 • gay/lesbian • see Our Family Abroad

16-April 5: Trek Nepal, Himalayas (206) 932-8352 • gay/lesbian • see Adventure Associates

TOURS & ADVENTURES

16-23: **Monte Carlo, French Riviera Sightseeing** (800) 836-8687 • mostly women • see *Club Le Bon*

16-22: **Vacation in Cozumel** (800) 279-0555 • women only • snorkeling, bicycling • see *Woodswomen*

17-23: **Alaska Women Pioneers: Elderhostel** (907) 688-2226 • women only • see *Alaska Women of the Wilderness*

21-24: **Dinah Shore Women's Week in Palm Springs** (800) 225-5759 • mostly women • see *Skylink*

23-30: **Sea Kayak Baja** (206) 932-8352 • mostly women • see *Adventure Associates*

23-30: **Joshua Tree Rock Climbing** (800) 279-0555 • women only • see *Woodswomen*

23-30: **Leading on the Rock** (800) 279-0555 • women only • leadership training • rock climbing • see *Woodswomen*

24-30: **Belize Eco-Voyage** (800) 462-7424 • women only • see *Mariah Wilderness Expeditions*

30-April 7: **Sea of Cortez Wilderness Kayaking** (800) 462-7424 • women only • see *Mariah Wilderness Expeditions*

April

1-9: **Sea Kayaking the Big Island** (907) 688-2226 • women only • see *Alaska Women of the Wilderness*

4-14: **Sail to the Island Kingdom of Tonga** (800) 838-7783 • women only • see *Artemis Sailing Charters*

8-15: **Grand Caribbean Cruise** (800) 631-6277 • women only • see *Olivia Cruises*

9-14: **Backpacking Arizona: Landscape of the Sacred** (207) 721-9005 • women only • see *Her Wild Song*

14-21: **Sea Kayak Baja** (206) 932-8352 • mostly women • see *Adventure Associates*

14-20: **Mexican Riviera Cruise** (800) 375-2703 • gay/lesbian • on the Song of Norway • see *All About Destinations*

20-27: **Sea Kayak Baja** (206) 932-8352 • mostly women • see *Adventure Associates*

20-27: **Canoeing the Green River: Desert River Retreat** (207) 721-9005 • see *Her Wild Song*

20-21: **Integrated Leadership Training** (800) 279-0555 • women only • see *Woodswomen*

27-May 4: **Roatan Beach, Honduras on the Beach** (800) 836-8687 • mostly women • see *Club Le Bon*

TBA: **The Best of Costa Rica** (506) 223-3652 • mostly women • see *Amatirasu Tours*

May

3-5: **Healing Our Hearts** (907) 688-2226 • women only • see *Alaska Women of the Wilderness*

3-5: **St. Croix Spring Hike** (800) 279-0555 • women only • see *Woodswomen*

8-19: **Dive Galapagos Islands** (800) 669-0310 • gay/lesbian • see *Underseas Expeditions*

10-13: **Celebrate Mothers Sea Kayak Retreat, San Juan Islands** (206) 932-8352 • women only • see *Adventure Associates*

10-12: **Namekagon River Canoeing Odyssey** (800) 279-0555 • women only • see *Woodswomen*

12-18: **Desert Slickrock Backpack** (800) 279-0555 • women only • see *Woodswomen*

17-19: **Whitewater Canoeing School** (800) 279-0555 • women only • see *Woodswomen*

18-19: **Journey's on the Ice Glacier** (907) 688-2226 • women only • see *Alaska Women of the Wilderness*

18-25: **Canoeing St. John River, Maine** (207) 721-9005 • women only • see *Her Wild Song*

24-26: **Bahamas Cruise** (800) 375-2703 • gay/lesbian • on the Nordic Empress • see *All About Destinations*

24: **Raft the Merced River** (800) 462-7424 • women only • for experienced rafters • see *Mariah Wilderness Expeditions*

29-June 2: **Canoeing Allagash River** (207) 721-9005 • women only • see *Her Wild Song*

31-June 2: **Learn to Bicycle Tour** (800) 279-0555 • women only • see *Woodswomen*

TBA: **Biking in Provence** (800) 825-9766 • mostly gay/lesbian • see *Alyson Adventures*

TBA: **Biking in Provence for Solo Lesbians** (800) 825-9766 • women only • see *Alyson Adventures*

June

1: **East Fork Carson** (209) 533-1401 • women only • class II • see *Ahwahnee Whitewater Expeditions*

1-8: **Creative Dynamics** (800) 279-0555 • women only • canoeing • rock climbing • leadership training • see *Woodswomen*

2-8: **Ancient Voices of the Land** (907) 688-2226 • women only • see *Alaska Women of the Wilderness*

2-16: **Italian Holiday** (800) 999-5500 • gay/lesbian • see *Our Family Abroad*

4-16: **Classical Greece & Turkey** (800) 999-5500 • gay/lesbian • see *Our Family Abroad*

6-12: **Sea Kayaking Aialik Bay** (907) 688-2226 • women only • see *Alaska Women of the Wilderness*

6-7: **Raft Kings River** (800) 462-7424 • women only • see *Mariah Wilderness Expeditions*

7-9: **Whale Watch Sea Kayak Weekend** (206) 932-8352 • mostly women • see *Adventure Associates*

8-9: **Raft South Fork American River** (800) 462-7424 • women only • see *Mariah Wilderness Expeditions*

8-15: **Cataract Canyon Rafting** (800) 279-0555 • women only • see *Woodswomen*

10-12: **Beginning Fly Fishing** (907) 688-2226 • women only • see *Alaska Women of the Wilderness*

11-15: **The Feminine Voice of Leadership** (907) 688-2226 • women only • see *Alaska Women of the Wilderness*

14-16: **Whale Watch Sea Kayak Weekend** (206) 932-8352 • mostly women • see *Adventure Associates*

14-16: **Sea Kayak and Hike Resurrection Bay** (907) 688-2226 • women only • see *Alaska Women of the Wilderness*

14-20: **Young Women, Strong Women: Girls Camp** (907) 688-2226 • women only • see *Alaska Women of the Wilderness*

14-17: **Horsepacking in Wisconsin** (800) 279-0555 • women only • see *Woodswomen*

15: **Merced** (209) 533-1401 • women only • class III-IV • see *Ahwahnee Whitewater Expeditions*

16-22: **Young Women, Strong Women: Girls Camp** (907) 688-2226 • women only • see *Alaska Women of the Wilderness*

16-22: **Alaska Cruise** (800) 375-2703 • gay/lesbian • on the Legend of the Seas • see *All About Destinations*

17-22: **Raft Cataract Canyon, Utah** (800) 462-7424 • women only • see *Mariah Wilderness Expeditions*

20-29: **Biking in Holland** (800) 825-9766 • mostly gay/lesbian • see *Alyson Adventures*

21-23: **Celebrate the Solstice Ocean Retreat** (206) 932-8352 • women only • see *Adventure Associates*

21-23: **Whale Watch Sea Kayak Weekend** (206) 932-8352 • mostly women • see *Adventure Associates*

21-26: **Exploring Alaska's Glaciers** (907) 688-2226 • women only • see *Alaska Women of the Wilderness*

21-28: **Alaska Cruise** (800) 631-6277 • women only • see *Olivia Cruises*

21-23: **Red Cedar Trail Festival** (800) 279-0555 • women only • bicycling • canoeing • see *Woodswomen*

22-July 2: **England, Scotland & Wales** (800) 999-5500 • gay/lesbian • see *Our Family Abroad*

22-July 8: **European Panorama** (800) 999-5500 • gay/lesbian • see *Our Family Abroad*

22-July 7: **Scenic Germany** (800) 999-5500 • gay/lesbian • see *Our Family Abroad*

23-July 6: **Imperial Capitals of Europe** (800) 999-5500 • gay/lesbian • see *Our Family Abroad*

26-July 5: **Bicycling and Hiking Denali Park** (907) 688-2226 • women only • see *Alaska Women of the Wilderness*

26-July 3: **Alaska Cruise** (800) 631-6277 • women only • see *Olivia Cruises*

27-July 8: **Galapagos Island Cruise** (800) 279-0555 • women only • snorkeling • see *Woodswomen*

30-July 8: **Normandy, Brittany & Chateaux Country** (800) 999-5500 • gay/lesbian • see *Our Family Abroad*

30-July 4: **Fourth of July Canoe Festival** (800) 279-0555 • mostly women • kids welcome • see *Woodswomen*

TBA: **East Africa Safari** (206) 932-8352 • gay/lesbian • 16 days • see *Adventure Associates*

TBA: **Biking in Loire Valley** (800) 825-9766 • mostly gay/lesbian • see *Alyson Adventures*

TBA: **Hiking in Swiss Alps** (800) 825-9766 • mostly gay/lesbian • see *Alyson Adventures*

TBA: **Moscow & St. Petersburg** (800) 999-5500 • gay/lesbian • 9 days • see *Our Family Abroad*

July

3-Aug 4: **Hike & Kayak Northwestern Fjord** (907) 688-2226 • women only • see *Alaska Women of the Wilderness*

3-7: **Raft the Salmon River in Idaho** (800) 462-7424 • women only • see *Mariah Wilderness Expeditions*

6-12: **Mountaineer & Glacier Travel** (800) 279-0555 • women only • see *Woodswomen*

9-16: **Bastille Day in Paris** (800) 999-5500 • gay/lesbian • see *Our Family Abroad*

10-20: **Luxury Yacht Cruise to Mykonos** (800) 225-5759 • women only • see *Skylink*

12-27: **Bhutan, Himalaya Shangri-La** (800) 836-8687 • mostly women • see *Club Le Bon*

14-20: **Cracks, Crevasses & Big Trees: Leadership Training** (800) 279-0555 • women only • see *Woodswomen*

14-20: **Pictographs and Canoeing Lakes & Rivers** (800) 279-0555 • women only • see *Woodswomen*

16-18: **Rafting Adventure** (800) 279-0555 • women only • kids welcome • see *Woodswomen*

20-25: **Climb the Grand Teton, Wyoming** (800) 825-9766 • mostly gay/lesbian • see *Alyson Adventures*

20-21: **Let the Kayak Rock You, Mother** (207) 721-9005 • women only • canoeing & kayaking in Maine for moms • see *Her Wild Song*

20-23: **Raft the Rogue River in Oregon** (800) 462-7424 • women only • see *Mariah Wilderness Expeditions*

21-27: **Mt. Olympus Backpack** (800) 279-0555 • women only • see *Woodswomen*

21-27: **Rainbow Island Canoeing Retreat** (800) 279-0555 • women only • see *Woodswomen*

23-27: **Canoeing Thoreau's Maine** (207) 721-9005 • women only • see *Her Wild Song*

23-Aug 2: **Swiss Alps** (800) 279-0555 • women only • see *Woodswomen*

26-27: **Raft the Tuolumne River** (800) 462-7424 • women only • for experienced rafters • see *Mariah Wilderness Expeditions*

26-27: **Camping Adventure** (800) 279-0555 • women only • kids welcome • see *Woodswomen*

27-Aug 12: **Portugal, Spain & Morocco** (800) 999-5500 • gay/lesbian • see *Our Family Abroad*

27-Aug 1: **Kenai Fjords Sea Kayak** (800) 279-0555 • women only • see *Woodswomen*

28-Aug 4: **Mediterranean Cruise: France, Spain & Italy** (800) 631-6277 • women only • see *Olivia Cruises*

28-Aug 9: **Alaska & Inside Passage Cruise** (800) 999-5500 • gay/lesbian • see *Our Family Abroad*

28-Aug 3: **Canoeing Northern Lakes Loop** (800) 279-0555 • women only • see *Woodswomen*

29-Aug 2: **Jewel Islands in a Bay: Sea Kayaking Maine** (207) 721-9005 • women only • see *Her Wild Song*

TBA: **Backpack Wilderness Coast, Washington** (206) 932-8352 • women only • 6 days • see *Adventure Associates*

TBA: **Fly Fish the Tetons, Idaho** (206) 932-8352 • women only • 6 days • see *Adventure Associates*

TBA: **Llama Trek Olympic Mountains, Washington** (206) 932-8352 • women only • 8 days • see *Adventure Associates*

TBA: **Lodge-based Hiking North Cascades, Washington** (206) 932-8352 • women only • 6 days • see *Adventure Associates*

TBA: **Raft Deschutes River, Oregon** (206) 932-8352 • women only • 5 days • see *Adventure Associates*

TBA: **Sea Kayak San Juan Islands** (206) 932-8352 • women only • 6 days • see *Adventure Associates*

TBA: **Corcovado – Backcountry Costa Rica** (506) 223-3652 • mostly women • see *Amatirasu Tours*

August

1-15: **Italian Holiday** (800) 999-5500 • gay/lesbian • see *Our Family Abroad*

2-18: **Luxury Safari to Kenya & Tanzania** (800) 225-5759 • gay/lesbian • see *Skylink*

3-14: **Kenya Kaleidoscope** (800) 237-4225 • women only • see *African Pride Safaris*

3-9: **Hiking in Denali Park** (800) 279-0555 • women only • see *Woodswomen*

4-17: **Canoeing Canadian Wilds** (800) 279-0555 • women only • see *Woodswomen*

4-18: **Magic & Mythology of Ireland** (800) 279-0555 • women only • bicycling • see *Woodswomen*

4-10: **Mt. Rainier Backpack** (800) 279-0555 • women only • see *Woodswomen*

6-18: **Classical Greece & Turkey** (800) 999-5500 • gay/lesbian • see *Our Family Abroad*

7-13: **Hiking Denali Park** (907) 688-2226 • women only • see *Alaska Women of the Wilderness*

10-11: **Glacier Journeys** (907) 688-2226 • women only • see *Alaska Women of the Wilderness*

10-26: **European Panorama** (800) 999-5500 • gay/lesbian • see *Our Family Abroad*

11-17: **Young Women, Strong Women: Girls Camp** (907) 688-2226 • women only • see *Alaska Women of the Wilderness*

11-22: **Luxury Burgundy Barge Cruise** (800) 999-5500 • gay/lesbian • see *Our Family Abroad*

11-17: **Hiking in Denali Park** (800) 279-0555 • women only • see *Woodswomen*

14-17: **Canoe Expedition** (800) 279-0555 • women only • kids welcome • see *Woodswomen*

15-21: **Sea Kayaking Nova Scotia** (207) 721-9005 • women only • see *Her Wild Song*

17-27: **England, Scotland & Wales** (800) 999-5500 • gay/lesbian • see *Our Family Abroad*

17-Sept 1: **Scenic Germany** (800) 999-5500 • gay/lesbian • see *Our Family Abroad*

18-31: **Imperial Capitals of Europe** (800) 999-5500 • gay/lesbian • see *Our Family Abroad*

18-24: **Backpacking Isle Royale** (800) 279-0555 • women only • see *Woodswomen*

23-25: **Sea Kayak & Hike Resurrection Bay** (907) 688-2226 • women only • see *Alaska Women of the Wilderness*

23-26: **Horsepacking in Wisconsin** (800) 279-0555 • women only • see *Woodswomen*

25-Sept 2: **Normandy, Brittany & Chateaux Country** (800) 999-5500 • gay/lesbian • see *Our Family Abroad*

25-29: **San Juan Sea Kayak** (800) 279-0555 • women only • see *Woodswomen*

26-27: **Tuolumne** (209) 533-1401 • gay/lesbian • class IV+ • see *Ahwahnee Whitewater Expeditions*

30-Sept 1: **Labor Day in Baja Cruise** (800) 375-2703 • gay/lesbian • on the Viking Serenade • see *All About Destinations*

31-Sept 1: **Raft Middle Fork American River** (800) 462-7424 • women only • for experienced rafters • see *Mariah Wilderness Expeditions*

TBA: **Backpack Mt. Rainier** (206) 932-8352 • women only • 6 days • see *Adventure Associates*

TBA: **Climb Mt. Olympus** (206) 932-8352 • women only • 8 days • see *Adventure Associates*

TBA: **Sail the Northern Aegean, Greece** (206) 932-8352 • women only • 16 days • see *Adventure Associates*

TBA: **Sea Kayak San Juan Islands** (206) 932-8352 • mostly women • 6 days • see *Adventure Associates*

TBA: **Wilderness Gourmet & Hiking Cascades** (206) 932-8352 • women only • 6 days • see *Adventure Associates*

September

1-7: **Annual Autumn Canoe Trip** (800) 279-0555 • women only • see *Woodswomen*

5-8: **Canoeing the St. Croix River** (207) 721-9005 • women only • see *Her Wild Song*

12-15: **Northshore Hiking** (800) 279-0555 • women only • see *Woodswomen*

13-21: **Mountain Dharma: Backpacking the Appalachian Trail** (207) 721-9005 • women only • see *Her Wild Song*

15-21: **Ancient Voices: Glacier Elderhostel** (907) 688-2226 • women only • see *Alaska Women of the Wilderness*

21-27: **2 Billion Years of Geology: Leadership Training** (800) 279-0555 • women only • see *Woodswomen*

27-Oct 11: **Italian Holiday** (800) 999-5500 • gay/lesbian • see *Our Family Abroad*

28-Oct 14: **European Panorama** (800) 999-5500 • gay/lesbian • see *Our Family Abroad*

28-Oct 12: **Golden Cities of China** (800) 999-5500 • gay/lesbian • see *Our Family Abroad*

29-Oct 5: **Grand Canyon Backpack** (800) 279-0555 • women only • see *Woodswomen*

30-Oct 5: **Napa Valley Bicycle Tour** (800) 279-0555 • women only • see *Woodswomen*

TBA: **Biking in Provence** (800) 825-9766 • mostly gay/lesbian • see *Alyson Adventures*

TBA: **Moscow & St. Petersburg** (800) 999-5500 • gay/lesbian • 9 days • see *Our Family Abroad*

October

1-13: **Classical Greece & Turkey** (800) 999-5500 • gay/lesbian • see *Our Family Abroad*

2-6: **Feminine Voices of Leadership** (907) 688-2226 • women only • see *Alaska Women of the Wilderness*

4-10: **Autumn in Provincetown** (800) 279-0555 • women only • see *Woodswomen*

5-12: **Sonora Bay Resort** (800) 631-6277 • women only • see *Olivia Cruises*

7-17: **Dive Papua New Guinea** (800) 669-0310 • gay/lesbian • see *Underseas Expeditions*

12-27: **Spectacular Far East** (800) 999-5500 • gay/lesbian • see *Our Family Abroad*

14-Nov 3: **Trekking in Nepal** (907) 688-2226 • women only • see *Alaska Women of the Wilderness*

16-Nov 3: **Nepal: A Journey Through Time** (800) 279-0555 • women only • see *Woodswomen*

18-28: **Ancient Egypt** (800) 999-5500 • gay/lesbian • see *Our Family Abroad*

18-Nov 4: **Portugal, Spain & Morocco** (800) 999-5500 • gay/lesbian • see *Our Family Abroad*

21-Nov 10: **Kilimanjaro and the Serengeti** (800) 279-0555 • women only • mountain trek & safari • see *Woodswomen*

TBA: **Biking in Loire Valley** (800) 825-9766 • mostly gay/lesbian • see *Alyson Adventures*

November

1-3: **Hiking Maine's Autumn Woods** (207) 721-9005 • women only • see *Her Wild Song*

2-12: **Costa Rica Tropical Whitewater Adventure** (800) 462-7424 • women only • see *Mariah Wilderness Expeditions*

4-11: **Ixtapa, Mexico Resort** (800) 631-6277 • women only • see *Olivia Cruises*

9-10: **Integrated Leadership Training** (800) 279-0555 • women only • see *Woodswomen*

20-24: **Women Who Run With Dogs: Mushing Course** (907) 688-2226 • women only • see *Alaska Women of the Wilderness*

22-Dec 1: **Ancient Egypt** (800) 999-5500 • gay/lesbian • see *Our Family Abroad*

23-30: **Thanksgiving in Barbados** (800) 836-8687 • mostly women • see *Club Le Bon*

23-30: **Wave Dancer Diving Cruise in Belize** (800) 669-0310 • gay/lesbian • see *Underseas Expeditions*

TBA: **Cruise Galapagos & Explore Ecuador** (206) 932-8352 • mostly women • see *Adventure Associates*

TBA: **Explore New Zealand** (206) 932-8352 • women only • 16 days • see *Adventure Associates*

December

26-Jan 6: **Sea of Cortez Wilderness Kayaking** (800) 462-7424 • women only • see *Mariah Wilderness Expeditions*

27-Jan 5: **Sea of Cortez Wilderness Kayaking** (800) 462-7424 • women only • see *Mariah Wilderness Expeditions*

TBA: **Cross Country Ski Cascades, New Year's** (206) 932-8352 • women only • 7 days • see *Adventure Associates*

TBA: **Alaska Women Pioneers: Elderhostel** (907) 688-2226 • women only • 7 days • see *Alaska Women of the Wilderness*

Calendar of
EVENTS &
FESTIVALS

NOTE:

- Events for **"mostly women"** or **"women only"** are highlighted in green.
- **"TBA"** means that the actual event dates have yet **"to be announced."**
- Events which occur on the first weekend of a month – but which start in the previous month – are listed under the second month. For example, "Rhythm Fest" begins August 30th, but is listed under "September."

January

12-15: **Gay Ski East '96**   Lake Placid, NY
c/o *Eclectic Excursions*, 3766 Mariner, Waterford, MI 48329 • (810) 673-3733 • 200+ attend • gay/lesbian

26-28: **Blue Ball**   Philadelphia, PA
c/o *AIDS Information Network*, 1211 Chesnut St., 7th flr, Philadelphia, PA 19107 • (215) 575-1110 • AIDS benefit weekend highlighted by Saturday night dance • $35-100 fee • mostly men

27-Feb 3: **Aspen Gay Ski Week**   Aspen, CO
c/o *Aspen Gay/Lesbian Community*, Box 3143, Aspen, CO 81612 • (303) 925-9249 • 2000+ attend • gay/lesbian

February

1-Mar 2: **Sydney Gay Mardi Gras**   Sydney, Australia
c/o *Sydney Gay/Lesbian Mardi Gras Committee*, (011-61-2) 557-4332 • huge international month-long festival in February, including the Int'l Lesbian/Gay Comedy Festival, culminates in the Mardi Gras parade

4-11: **Altitude '96: Whistler Gay Ski Week**   Whistler, BC
c/o *Out On The Slopes Productions*, PO Box 1370, Whistler, BC Canada V0N 1B0 • (604) 938-0772 / (800) 695-0880 (Advance Damron) • popular ski destination 75 mi. north of Vancouver • gay/lesbian

9-11: **Pantheon of Leather**   New Orleans, LA
c/o *The Leather Journal*, 7985 Santa Monica Blvd. 109-368, W. Hollywood, CA 90046 • (213) 656-5073 • annual SM community service awards, at the Radisson Hotel (800) 824-3359 • mixed gay/straight

10-20: **Mardi Gras**   New Orleans, LA
c/o *New Orleans Convention & Visitors Bureau*, 1520 Sugarbowl Dr., New Orleans, LA 70112 • (504) 566-5011 • North America's rowdiest block party • mixed gay/straight

15-19: **Black Gay/Lesbian Conference**   Dallas, TX
c/o *Black Gay/Lesbian Leadership Forum*, 1219 S. La Brea Ave., Los Angeles, CA 90019 • (213) 964-7820 • gay/lesbian

16-19: **Pantheocon**   San Jose, CA
c/o *Ancient Ways*, 4075 Telegraph Ave, Oakland, CA 94609 • (510) 653-3244 • pagan convention at the Red Lion Hotel, Starhawk ritual, Reclaiming collective • mixed gay/straight

23-25: **Outwrite**   Boston, MA
c/o *Bromfield St. Educational Foundation*, 25 West St., Boston, MA 02111 • (617) 426-4469 • annual national lesbian/gay writers & publishers conference at the Boston Park Plaza Hotel • 1500+ attend • $55-65 fee • gay/lesbian

25-1: **Cruise with Pride**   San Juan, PR
c/o *Cruiseworld*, 901 Fairview Ave. N. #A150, Seattle, WA 98126 • (800) 340-0221 • Pride Foundation fundraiser in the Caribbean, 6 days • 50+ cabins • gay/lesbian

Calendar of EVENTS & FESTIVALS

March

1-31: Gay Spring Break — Key West, FL
c/o *Key West Business Guild*, PO Box 1208, Key West, FL 33040 • (800) 535-7797 / (305) 294-5197 • parties, shows, outdoor activities and more for students, faculty and anyone who needs a spring break! • gay/lesbian

3: Winter Party — Miami Beach, FL
c/o *Dade Human Rights Foundation*, c/o SS, 1541 Brickell Ave. #1105, Miami, FL 33129 • (305) 593-6666 • AIDS benefit dance on the beach • 3500+ attend • $50 fee

9: AIDS Dance-a-thon San Francisco — San Francisco, CA
c/o *Miller Zeitchik Publicity*, PO Box 193920, San Francisco, CA 94119 • (415) 392-9255 • AIDS benefit dance at the Moscone Center • 7000+ attend • $75+ fee • mixed gay/straight

16-23: Winterfest — Lake Tahoe, NV
c/o *Ski Connections*, 10356 Airport Rd. Hangar 1, Truckee, CA 96161 • (800) 754-1888 • AIDS benefit ski weekend • $75 fee

25-31: Nabisco Dinah Shore Golf Tournament — Palm Springs, CA
(619) 324-4546 • huge gathering of lesbians for pool parties, dancing and yes, some golf-watching • mostly women

April

4-7: Gulf Coast Womyn's Festival at Camp SisterSpirit — New Orleans, LA
c/o *Camp SisterSpirit*, PO Box 12, Ovett, MS 39464 • (601) 344-1411 • They won their lawsuit – so go support a celebration of womyn's land in the South! • just north of New Orleans, LA • entertainment & politics • mostly women

15-18: Elderflower Womenspirit Festival — Mendocino, CA
PO Box 7153, Redwood City, CA 94063 • (510) 540-8463 / (916) 658-0697 • in the Mendocino Woodlands • earth-centered spirituality retreat • reasonably priced, volunteer-run • women only

19-21: Readers/Writers Conference — San Francisco, CA
c/o *A Different Light*, (415) 431-0891 • 3rd annual weekend of workshops & round-tables with queer writer & readers, at the Women's Building

TBA: AIDS Dance-a-thon L.A. — Los Angeles, CA
c/o AIDS Walk LA, PO Box 933005, Los Angeles, CA 90093 • (213) 466-9255 • AIDS benefit • $75+ fee • mixed gay/straight

TBA: Windows to the Soul — Santa Cruz, CA
PO Box 1408, Santa Cruz, CA 95061 • (408) 479-0473 • gentle camping retreat to the Pinnacles • $125-150 fee • women only

May

3-5: Geared for Life — Detroit, MI
PO Box 25138, Harper Woods, MI 48225 • (810) 358-9849 / (800) 359-6697 (OurWorld Travel) • 3rd annual AIDS fundraising art auction & parties in Motor City, topped off by Gear Party Saturday • 2000+ attend

3-5: Pridefest '96 — Philadelphia, PA
c/o *Pridefest*, 200 S. Broad St., Philadelphia, PA 19102 • (215) 732-3378 • 70 events capped by Saturday night party • gay/lesbian

4-5: Splash Days — Austin, TX
c/o *Tavern Guild*, 611 Red River, Austin, TX 78701 • (512) 476-3611 • weekend of parties in clothing-optional Hippie Hollow, highlighted by the beer barge on Sunday

6-12: LesBiGay Gathering Pahoa, HI
c/o *Pacific Men*, RR2 Box 4500, Pahoa, HI 96778 • (800) 800-6886 / (808) 965-7838 • healing & celebration of lesbian/gay natures & creativity • $490-990 fee

10-12: Virginia Women's Music Festival VA
c/o *Intouch*, Rte. 2, Box 1096, Kent's Store, VA 23084 • (804) 589-6542 • 600 attend • $85 fee • women only

17-19: Priestess Conference Wisconsin
c/o *Of a Like Mind*, Box 6021, Madison, WI 53716 • (608) 244-0072 • spirituality conference • also ongoing classes • $90-120 fee • women only

18: Wigswood Atlanta, GA
c/o *Act Up Atlanta*, 828 W. Peachtree St. NW, Ste. 206-A, Atlanta, GA 30308-1146 • (404) 874-6782 • 5th annual festival of peace, love and wigs, street party fundraiser, wig watchers welcome • 1000+ attend • $5+ fee

22-27: Campfest Memorial Day Wknd Oxford, PA
PO Box 559, Franklinville, NJ 08322 • (609) 694-2037 / (301) 598-9035 (TTY) • 'The Comfortable Womyn's Festival' • 1400+ attend • $200 fee • women only

24-26: Wimminfest Albuquerque, NM
c/o *Women in Movement in New Mexico* (WIMINM), PO Box 80204, Albuquerque, NM 87198 • (505) 255-7274 • music, comedy, art, recreation & dances • mostly women

24-27: Armory Sports Classic Atlanta, GA
1874 Piedmont Rd. Ste. 340-C, Atlanta, GA 30324 • (404) 874-2710 • softball & many other sports competitions • mostly men

24-29: Pensacola Memorial Day Weekend Pensacola, FL
c/o *Christopher St. South*, PO Box 2752, Pensacola, FL 32513-2752 • (904) 433-0353/ (904) 432-5777 • many parties on beaches & bars • 35,000+ attend

25: Beach Maneuvers Pensacola, FL
c/o *Jeffrey Sanker Enterprises*, PO Box 691745, W. Hollywood, CA 90069 • (310) 659-3555 / (213) 874-4007 • also Girl Party • 5000 attend • $30-35 fee • mostly men

25-29: Southern Women's Music & Comedy Festival Atlanta, GA
(818) 893-4075 • see Robin Tyler Tours • mostly women

TBA: International Gaia's Festival Santa Cruz, CA
c/o *Women's Spirituality Forum*, PO Box 11363, Oakland, CA 94611 • (510) 444-7724 • celebration of goddess culture & Beltane • workshops, rituals, dances, music • mostly women

TBA: Herland Spring Retreat Oklahoma City, OK
c/o *Herland*, 2312 NW 39th, Oklahoma City, OK 73112 • (405) 521-9696 • music, workshops, campfire events & potluck • boys under 10 only • $15-60 sliding scale registration • mostly women

TBA: Spoleto Festival Charleston, SC
PO Box 157, Charleston, SC 29402-0157 • (803) 722-2764 • one of the continent's premier avant-garde culture festivals, in late May • straight/gay

June

May 30-June 2: Springfest Maine® Lincolnville, ME
c/o *CPJ Productions*, PO Box 5682, Augusta, ME 04332 • (207) 993-2177 • 'gentle, apolitical' festival on Maine coast (between Belfast & Camden) with sports, concerts & self-help workshops • featuring Suede and Alix Dobkin • wheelchair access • ASL interpreter on request • 550+ attend • $40 fee • women only

1-4: National Women's Music Festival Bloomington, IN
PO Box 1427-WT, Indianapolis, IN 46206 • (317) 927-9355 / (317) 253-9966 (Dreams & Swords Bookstore #) • mostly women

2-8: California AIDS Ride
San Francisco, CA
c/o *Pallotta & Associates*, 9171 Wilshire Blvd. Penthouse Ste., Beverly Hills , CA 90210 • (310) 274-7800 • AIDS benefit bike ride from San Francisco to L.A. benefits Jeffrey Goodman Special Care Clinic • mixed gay/straight

5-9: Ancient Ways Festival — Harbin Hot Springs, CA
c/o *Ancient Ways*, 4075 Telegraph Ave., Oakland, CA 94609 • (510) 653-3244 • annual 4-day mixed gender/orientation spring festival in May or June of pan-pagan rituals, workshops and music w/ lesbian/gay campsite • mixed gay/straight

8: Guys & Gals — Kent's Store, VA
c/o *Intouch*, Rte. 2, Box 1096, Kent's Store, VA 23084 • (804) 589-6542 • live country/western music & dancing • 80 attend • $40 fee • gay/lesbian

13-16: Womongathering — Pocono Mtns, PA
PO Box 559, Franklinville, NJ 08322 • (609) 694-2037 / (301) 598-9035 (TTY) • women's spirituality fest • 300+ attend • $200 fee • women only

14: Lambda Literary Awards — Chicago, IL
c/o *Lambda Book Report*, 1625 Connecticut Ave. NW, Washington, DC 20009 • (202) 462-7924 • the 'Lammies' are the Oscars of lesbigay writing & publishing

15: Razzle Dazzle Dallas — Dallas, Texas
PO Box 224562, Dallas, TX 75222-4562 • (214) 407-3553 / (214) 528-4852 • dance party & carnival benefits PWAs • 10,000+ attend • $8-12 fee

21-30: San Francisco Int'l Lesbian/Gay Film Festival — San Francisco, CA
c/o *Frameline*, 346 9th St., San Francisco, CA 94103 • (415) 703-8650 • get your tickets early for a slew of films about us • 53,000+ attend

22: Physique '96 — San Francisco, CA
c/o *Arcadia Bodybuilding Society*, 1230 Market St., Ste. 211, San Francisco, CA 94102 • (415) 978-9495 • national gay/lesbian bodybuilding championships in mid-June • $15-25 fee • gay/lesbian

TBA: Lesbian/Gay Pride — Everywhere, USA
• Parades, parties and rainbow flags across the country. If you love a spectacle with a cast of thousands, go to one or all of the events in New York, Los Angeles and San Francisco or other metropolitan cities. Usually held the last or next-to-last Sunday in June

TBA: International Lesbian/Gay Conference — Rio de Janeiro, Brazil
c/o *International Lesbian/Gay Conference*, Rue Marché-au-Charbon 81, 1000 Brussels, Belgium • (011-32-2) 502-24-71 • int'l umbrella group for lesbian/gay organizations

TBA: International Gay Arts Fest — Key West, FL
c/o *Key West Business Guild*, PO Box 1208, Key West, FL 33041 • (800) 535-7797 / (305) 294-4603 • cultural festival of film, theatre, art, concerts, seminars, parties and a parade

TBA: Golden Threads — Provincetown, MA
c/o *Provincetown Inn*, PO Box 60475, Northampton, MA 01060-0475 • gathering for lesbians over 50 and their admirers • mostly women

TBA: New York Int'l Gay/Lesbian Film Festival — New York, NY
c/o *The New Festival*, 462 Broadway Ste. 510, New York, NY 10013 • (212) 343-2707 • week-long fest in early June

TBA: Lesbian/Gay Health Conference — Seattle, WA
c/o *Nat'l L/G Health Assoc.*, 2300 'K' St. NW, Ste 102, Washington, DC 20037 • (202) 994-4285 • health and AIDS/HIV issues facing our communities

TBA: Pagan Spirit Gathering — Mt. Horeb, WI
c/o *Circle Sanctuary*, PO Box 219, Mt. Horeb, WI 53572 • (608) 924-2216 • summer solstice celebration in Wisconsin, primitive camping, workshops, rituals • mixed gay/straight

Calendar of
EVENTS &
FESTIVALS

July

4-7: Fat Women's Gathering NJ
c/o NAAFA *Feminist Caucus*, PO Box 1154, New York, NY 10023 • (212) 721-8259 •
in Northwestern New Jersey • call about mid-Western or Western state gatherings • women only

5-7: July 4th Kickback Kent's Store, VA
c/o *Intouch*, Rte. 2, Box 1096, Kent's Store, VA 23084 • (804) 589-6542 •
watergames • 80 attend • $75 fee • women only

6-16: Los Angeles Int'l Gay/Lesbian Film Festival Los Angeles, CA
c/o *Gay/Lesbian Media Coalition*, 8455 Beverly Blvd. Ste. 309, Los Angeles, CA 90048
• (213) 951-1247

19-21: International Ms. Leather Contest Philadelphia, PA
c/o *Bare Images Productions*, 4332 Browne St., Omaha, NB 68111-1829 • (402) 451-
7987 / (800) 639-4675 • annual dyke S/M contest & celebration • mostly women

TBA: **Northampton Lesbian Festival** Northampton, MA
c/o WOW *Productions*, 160 Main St., Northampton, MA 01060 • (413) 584-8952 •
2nd-largest women's music festival • held in mid-July • mostly women

TBA: **Outfest** Los Angeles, CA
c/o *Out on the Screen*, 8455 Beverly Blvd. Ste. 309, Los Angeles, CA • (213)
951-1247 • Los Angeles' lesbian & gay film and video festival in mid-July

TBA: **Up Your Alley Fair** San Francisco, CA
c/o SMMILE, 1072 Folsom St. #272, San Francisco, CA 94103 • (415) 861-3247 •
local SM/leather street fair held in Dore Alley, South-of-Market • 8,000+ attend •
gay/lesbian

August

13-18: Michigan Womyn's Music Festival Walhalla, MI
c/o WWTMC, PO Box 22, Walhalla, MI 49458 • (616) 757-4766 / (510) 652-5441 •
music, performances, videos, movies and more • self-help, creative, spiritual,
political and other workshops • childcare • ASL interpreting • differently-abled
resources • women only

14-21: Provincetown Carnival Provincetown, MA
c/o *Provincetown Business Guild*, PO Box 421, Provincetown, MA 02657 • (800) 637-
8696 / (508) 255-7979

24-25: Sunset Junction Fair Los Angeles, CA
PO Box 26565, Los Angeles, CA 90026 • (213) 661-7771 • carnival, arts & information fair on Sunset Blvd. in Silverlake benefits Sunset Junction Youth Center •
7500+ attend • $2+ fee

TBA: **Hamburg Leather Party** Hamburg, Germany
c/o MSC *Hamburg*, Postfach 303683, D-20312, Hamburg, Germany • huge
European leather gathering & party • 3000+ attend • mostly men

TBA: **National Gay Softball World Series** Minneapolis, MN
c/o NAGAAA, 1014 King Ave., Pittsburgh, PA 15206 • (412) 362-1247 • gay/lesbian

TBA: **GMHC Morning Party** Fire Island, NY
c/o *Gay Men's Health Crisis*, 129 W. 20th St., New York, NY 10011 • (212) 337-1913 •
AIDS fundraiser

Calendar of EVENTS & FESTIVALS

September

Aug 29-Sept 1: Powersurge   Seattle, WA
c/o *Seattle Madness*, Broadway Station, PO Box 23352, Seattle, CA 98102 • (206) 233-8429 • bi-annual int'l leatherwomen's SM conference • women only

Aug 29-Sept 2: Rhythm Fest
957 N. Highland Ave., Atlanta, GA 30306 • (404) 873-1551 • atop Lookout Mountain where AL, TN and GA meet • mostly women

Aug 30-Sept 2: Festival of Babes   San Francisco, CA
c/o *Girljock*, PO Box 882723, San Francisco, CA 94188 • (510) 452-6252 • annual women's soccer tournament and celebration • mostly women

Aug 31-Sept 1: Splash Days   Austin, TX
c/o *Tavern Guild*, 611 Red River, Austin, TX 78701 • (512) 476-3611 • weekend of parties in clothing-optional Hippie Hollow, highlighted by the beer barge on Sunday

1: Southern Decadence   New Orleans, LA
c/o *Golden Lantern Bar*, 1239 Royal St., New Orleans, LA 70116 • (504) 529-2860 • gay mini-Mardi Gras • mostly men

1: Wigstock   New York, NY
c/o *Lesbian/Gay Community Services Center*, (212) 620-7310 • outrageous wig/drag/performance festival in Tompkins Square Park in the East Village • gay/lesbian

5-8: Fall Fest Maine®   ME
c/o *CPJ Productions*, PO Box 5682, Augusta, ME 04332 • (207) 377-3992 / (207) 993-2177 • 'gentle, apolitical' festival with sports, concerts & self-help workshops, wheelchair access, ASL interpreter on request • 350+ attend • $40 fee • women only

9: Northern Lights Womyn's Music Festival   MN
c/o *Aurora Northland Lesbian Center*, 8 N. 2nd Ave. E. #210, Duluth, MN 55802 • (218) 722-4903 • day-long festival in Minnesota wilderness • mostly women

13-15: Wild Western Women's Weekend   Kent's Store, VA
c/o *Intouch*, Rte. 2, Box 1096, Kent's Store, VA 23084 • (804) 589-6542 • live country/western music & dancing • 200 attend • $85 fee • women only

28: Sleaze Ball   Sydney, Australia
c/o *Sydney Gay/Lesbian Mardi Gras Committee*, (011-61-2) 557-4332 • 15,000+ attend

29: Folsom St. Fair   San Francisco, CA
c/o *SMMILE*, 1072 Folsom St. #272, San Francisco, CA 94103 • (415) 861-3247 • huge SM/leather street fair, topping a week of kinky events, including a Women's Play Party (436-0366) • hundreds of thousands of local & visiting kinky men & women attend • free • gay/lesbian

TBA: Queer Spirit   Bay Area, CA
c/o *Earth & Spirit*, 2215-R Market St. #264, San Francisco, CA 94114 • (510) 653-3244 • pagan gathering • $90-150 fee • gay/lesbian

TBA: Malibu Women's Fun Festival   Malibu, CA
c/o *MWFF*, 7985 Santa Monica Blvd. #231, W. Hollywood, CA 90046 • (213) 848-4489 • entertainment, vendors, activities and fun galore • camping, cabins & RV hookups • women only

TBA: Festival of the Goddess   Monterey, CA
c/o *In the Grove of the Goddess*, (408) 424-5525 • speakers, workshops, rituals, performance, arts and more • mostly women

TBA: West Coast Women's Music & Comedy Festival   Yosemite, CA
c/o *Robin Tyler Tours*, (818) 893-4075 • mostly women

TBA: **Women Fest** Key West, FL
201 Coppitt Rd. #106A, Key West, FL 33040 • (305) 296-4238 • concerts, dances, theater, fair, film festival, seminars and more • mostly women

TBA: **Iowa Women's Music Festival** IA
c/o *Prairie Voices Collective*, 130 N. Madison, Iowa City, IA 52242 • (319) 335-1486 • mostly women

TBA: **The Gathering** Ashland, OR
PO Box 335, Ashland, OR 97520 • (503) 482-2026 • annual women's pagan camp in the Oregon woods • 150+ attend • women only

TBA: **Northwest Women's Music Celebration** Portland, OR
PO Box 66842, Portland, OR 97290 • participatory event for musicians, songwriters & singers, NOT performance-oriented • mostly women

TBA: **Sisterspace Pocono Wknd** PA
c/o *Sisterspace of the Green Valley*, 351 S. 47th St. #B101, Philadelphia, PA 19143 • (215) 476-8856 • mostly women

TBA: **Oak Lawn Arts Festival** Dallas, Texas
PO Box 224562, Dallas, TX 75222-4562 • (214) 407-3553 / (214) 528-4852 • mid-September benefit in Lee Park for PWAs

October

5: **Black & Blue Party** Montreal, Quebec
c/o *Bad Boy Club Montreal*, 800 Rene-Levesque W. Ste. 450, Montreal, Quebec CAN H3B 1X9 • (514) 875-7026 • AIDS benefit dance • 5000+ attend • $25-35+ fee • mostly men

6: **Castro St. Fair** San Francisco, CA
(415) 467-3354 • arts & community groups street fair, co-founded by Harvey Milk

9: **Native Peoples' Day** USA
• formerly Columbus Day • celebrate the many cultures of native people displaced by invasions, pillaging of natural resources, slavery, wars, and territorial conflicts • mixed gay/straight

10-14: **Living in Leather** Portland, OR
c/o *National Leather Association*, 584 Castro St., Ste. 444, San Francisco, CA 94114-2500 • (614) 899-4406 • national conference for the leather, SM and fetish communities • 600+ attend • $115-175 fee • gay/lesbian

11: **National Coming Out Day** USA
c/o *National Coming Out Day*, PO Box 34640, Washington, DC 20043-4640 • (800) 866-6263 • come out, come out, wherever you are! • gay/lesbian

11-14: **PFLAG Convention** Washington, DC
c/o PFLAG, 1101 14th St. NW, Ste. 1030, Washington, DC 20005 • (415) 328-0852/ (202) 638-4200 • annual convention of Parents, Friends and Family of Lesbians and Gays • 1000+ attend

12: **Love Ball** Vancouver, BC
c/o *Jeffrey Sanker Enterprises*, PO Box 691745, W. Hollywood, CA 90069 • (310) 659-3555 / (213) 874-4007 • benefits Vancouver Gay/Lesbian Center • 5000 attend • $25-30 fee • mostly men

18-27: **Fantasy Fest** Key West, FL
c/o *Key West Business Guild*, PO Box 1208, Key West, FL 33041 • (800) 535-7797 / (305) 294-4603 • week-long Halloween celebration with parties, masquerade balls & parades • 55,000+ attend

31: **Halloween Spiral Dance** East Bay, CA
c/o *Women's Spirituality Forum*, PO Box 11363, Oakland, CA 94611 • (510) 893-3097 • mostly women

31: **Halloween**
New York, San Francisco, Los Angeles, New Orleans
• huge neighborhood-wide block parties raise funds to fight AIDS in cities where every day can be Halloween • mixed gay/straight

TBA: **Reel Affirmations Film Festival D.C.** Washington, DC
c/o One In Ten, (202) 986-1119 • gay/lesbian

TBA: **Provincetown Women's Week** Provincetown, MA
c/o Provincetown Business Guild, PO Box 421, Provincetown, MA 02657 • (800) 637-8696 / (508) 487-2313 • very popular – make your reservations early! • mostly women

TBA: **International Gay Rodeo Finals** Albuquerque, NM
900 E. Colfax, Denver, CO 80218 • (303) 832-4472

TBA: **Hallow's Gathering** Wisconsin
c/o Of a Like Mind, Box 6021, Madison, WI 53716 • (608) 244-0072 • 3-day pagan celebration • also Stonehaven Goddess Program throughout the year, with workshops at Stonehaven Ranch outside • $90-120 fee • women only

November

6-10: **Creating Change Conference** Alexandria, VA
c/o National Gay/Lesbian Task Force, 1734 14th St. NW, Washington, DC 20009 • (202) 332-6483 x3329 • for lesbians, gays, bisexuals, transgendered people & queers into social activism • 1500+ attend

26: **White Party Week Vizcaya** Miami, FL
c/o Health Crisis Network, PO Box 37-0098, Miami, FL • (305) 757-4444 / (305) 751-7775 • six days of festivities capped by the 11th annual White Party Vizcaya, benefitting the Health Crisis Network • $100+ fee • mostly men

TBA: **Gay/Lesbian Film Festival** Chicago, IL
c/o Chicago Filmmakers, 1543 W. Division, Chicago, IL 60622 • (312) 384-5533 • 7-10,000 attend • $75 fee • gay/lesbian

TBA: **Mix '96: New York Lesbian/Gay Experimental Film/Video Fest** New York, NY
341 Lafayette St. #169, New York, NY 10012 • (212) 501-2309 • film, videos, installations & media performances

TBA: **AIDS Dance-a-thon New York** New York, NY
c/o Gay Men's Health Crisis, PO Box 10, Old Chelsea Stn. , New York, NY 10113-0010 • (212) 807-9255 • AIDS benefit • 6000+ attend • $75+ pledges fee • mixed gay/straight

TBA: **International Lesbian/Gay Comedy Festival** South Africa
c/o Robin Tyler Tours, 15842 Chase St., North Hills, CA 91343 • (818) 893-4075 • in South Africa • see Robin Tyler Tours • gay/lesbian

December

31: **Saint-at-Large New Year's Party** New York, NY
c/o Saint-at-Large, 8 St. Mark's Place, Ste. 1A, New York, NY 10003 • (212) 674-8541 • $30-50 fee • mostly men

31: **Mummer's Strut** Philadelphia, PA
c/o Pridefest, 200 S. Broad St., Philadelphia, PA 19102 • (215) 732-3378 • New Year's Eve party benefitting Pridefest • $40-50 fee • gay/lesbian

TBA: **Gay Day at Disneyland** Anaheim, CA
c/o Odyssey Adventures, PO Box 923094, Sylmar, CA 91392 • (818) 893-2777 • $32-37 fee • gay/lesbian

February 1997

7-8: **Hearts Party**   Chicago, IL
  c/o *Test Positive Aware* (TPA), 1258 W. Belmont Ave., Chicago, IL 60657-3292 • (312)
  404-8726 • AIDS benefit • mostly men

August 1998

1-8: **Gay Games 1998**   Amsterdam, The Netherlands
  c/o *Stichting Gay/Lesbian Games*, PO Box 2837, 1000 CV Amsterdam, The
  Netherlands • gay/lesbian

A Different Light Bookstores • (800) 343-4002 • books • cards • calendars • videos • catalog

After Midnight Collection PO Box 13176, Scottsdale AZ 85267 • sexual supplies for women • send $5 for catalog

Avalon Herbaly PO Box 69, Euless TX 76039 • handmade herbal soaps & natural bath products

Avena Botanicals 219 Mill St., Rockport ME 04856 • (207) 594-0694 • organically grown herbal products for women • catalog

Bande Designs 7102 Castor Ave., Philadelphia PA 19149 • (215) 742-9823 • womyn's jewelry • send $1 for catalog

Bookwoman Books PO Box 67, Media PA 19063 • (610) 566-2990 • books • videos • posters • free catalog

Brigit Books (813) 522-5775 • lesbian & feminist titles • catalog

Brookside Soap Company PO Box 55638, Seattle WA 98155 • (206) 363-3701 • all-natural handmade soaps by women

Different Voices • (800) 824-3915 • gifts • T-shirts • pridewear • free catalog

Dreams & Swords 6503 Ferguson St., Indianapolis IN 46220 • (800) 937-2706 • women's books • music • videos • T-shirts • pride accessories • catalog

Eve's Garden 119 W. 57th St. Ste. 420, New York NY 10019-2383 • sex toys • books • videos • all from the first sexuality boutique created by women for women • send $3 for catalog

Good Vibrations 1210 Valencia, San Francisco CA 94110 • (415) 550-7399 / 974-8980 • lesbian-made erotica • sex toys • books • videos • send $2 for catalog

Heartland Books PO Box 1105N, East Corinth VT 05040 • (800) 535-3755 • lesbian & feminist titles carefully selected by lesbians who love reading • free catalog

Hide 'n Chic Box 218, Daly City CA 94016 • (800) 724-6765 • pride jewelry • leather accessories • free catalog

Lady Slipper, Inc. 3205 Hillsboro Rd., Durham NC 27705 • (919) 683-1570 • women's music • videos

Lamma's • (800) 955-2662 • women's books • music • jewelry • much more

MAIL ORDER

Lesbian Book Club • (800) 798-5828 • buy 3 & get 1 free • no membership or additional purchases • free catalog

Lielin West Jewelers PO Box 733, Benicia CA 94510 • (707) 745-9000 • women's imagery in precious metals

Lizzie Brown PO Box 389, Brimfield MA 01010 • (413) 245-9484 • woman-identified jewelry

Music for the Masses PO Box 90272, San Jose CA 95109 • T-shirts • photos • posters • videos • songbooks • all of your favorite women recording artists • send two 32¢ stamps for catalog

The Naiad Press, Inc. PO Box 10543, Tallahassee FL 32302 • (904) 539-5965 / (800) 533-1973 • lesbian books & videos

New Herizons PO Box 405, Lancaster MA 01523 • (508) 365-4340 • books • videos • jewelry • free catalog

OUT!wear Lesbian Mail Order Catalog • (708) 826-5964 • T-shirts • sweatshirts • accessories • free catalog

OUT-er Wear c/o Dragonfly Graphics 19 SW 2nd St., Gainesville FL 32601 • (800) TEES-GAY • lesbian & gay designs on T-shirts & tanks • free catalog

The Pleasure Chest • (800) 753-4536 • for all your erotic needs • catalog

Pleasure Place • (800) 386-2386 • erotic gifts • toys • catalog

Socket Science 4104 24th St. #187-1194, San Francisco CA 94114 • (415) 587-7459 • sex toys designed by and for women

Sumiche PO Box 428, Waterville OR 97489 • (503) 896-9841 • custom jewelry • commitment rings

T-shirts by Stephanie PO Box 605, Farmington NH 03835 • (603) 755-2926 • feminist T-shirts • catalog

Wimmins' Creations c/o K. Parker 1335 Taylor, Fort Wayne IN 46802 • (219) 422-9353 • crafts by several women artisans • catalog

Wolfe Video PO Box 64, New Almaden CA 95042 • (408) 268-6782 • video productions by lesbians

Womankind Books 5 Kivy St. Huntington Stn., New York NY 11746 • (800) 648-5333 • over 5,000 books & videos • free catalog

Xandria Collection PO Box 31039, San Francisco CA 94131 • sexual products from around the world • send $4 for catalog